P9-BXY-355

6th Edition

Teaching Students with Special Needs in Inclusive Settings

TOM E. C. SMITH
University of Arkansas

EDWARD A. POLLOWAY
Lynchburg College

JAMES R. PATTON
University of Texas, Austin

CAROL A. DOWDY
University of Alabama at Birmingham

Boston   Columbus   Indianapolis   New York   San Francisco   Upper Saddle River
Amsterdam   Cape Town   Dubai   London   Madrid   Milan   Munich   Paris   Montreal   Toronto
Delhi   Mexico City   São Paulo   Sydney   Hong Kong   Seoul   Singapore   Taipei   Tokyo

Vice President and Editor in Chief: Jeffery W. Johnston
Executive Editor: Ann Castel Davis
Editorial Assistant: Penny Burleson
Senior Development Editor: Hope Madden
Vice President, Director of Marketing: Margaret Waples
Marketing Manager: Joanna Sabella
Senior Managing Editor: Pamela D. Bennett
Senior Project Manager: Sheryl Glicker Langner
Senior Operations Supervisor: Matthew Ottenweller
Senior Art Director: Diane C. Lorenzo
Photo Coordinator: Carol Sykes

Permissions Administrator: Rebecca Savage
Text and Cover Designer: Candace Rowley
Cover Image: iStock
Media Producer: Rebecca Norsic
Media Project Manager: Autumn Benson
Production Coordinator: Lynn Steines, S4Carlisle Publishing Services
Composition: S4Carlisle Publishing Services
Printer/Binder: Webcrafters Inc.
Cover Printer: Lehigh-Phoenix Color
Text Font: 10/12 Garamond Book

Credits and acknowledgments for material borrowed from other sources and reproduced, with permission, in this textbook appear on appropriate page within the text.

Every effort has been made to provide accurate and current Internet information in this book. However, the Internet and information posted on it are constantly changing, so it is inevitable that some of the Internet addresses listed in this textbook will change.

Photo Credits: Katelyn Metzger/Merrill, pp. 1, 11, 12, 168; © Sally and Richard Greenhill/Alamy, p. 17; © J.R. Bale/Alamy, p. 14; Shutterstock, pp. 31, 34, 46, 47 (top), 81 (top), 206, 221, 298, 343, 402, 457, 466, 475, 477; Scott Cunningham/Merrill, pp. 41, 316, 328, 338; courtesy of Elizabeth Flippo, p. 47 (bottom); Patrick White/Merrill, pp. 67, 99, 100, 346, 365 (both); Laura Bolesta/Merrill, pp. 81 (bottom), 242 (bottom); Lori Whitley/Merrill, pp. 89, 502; David Young-Wolff/PhotoEdit Inc., p. 108; Karen Mancinelli/Pearson Learning Photo Studio, p. 114; Will Hart/Photo Edit Inc., pp. 151, 159, 189; courtesy of Brittany Nottenkamper, p. 190; Anthony Magnacca/Merrill, pp. 179, 215, 283, 301, 311, 389, 493, 498; Dennis MacDonald/PhotoEdit Inc., pp. 193, 203, 212; Michael Greenlar/The Image Works, pp. 223, 241, 242; courtesy of Andrea Gajadhar, p. 244; Vickie D. King/The Clarion-Ledger, pp. 248, 277 (top); courtesy of David Birt, p. 269; Jupiterimages/Thinkstock Royalty Free, p. 252; Getty Images, Inc.—PhotoDisc, p. 277 (bottom); Robin Nelson/PhotoEdit Inc., p. 305; James Shaffer/PhotoEdit Inc., p. 339; courtesy of Janie Eldridge, p. 348; Richard Hutchings/Photo Edit Inc., p. 351; Robin Sachs/PhotoEdit Inc., pp. 371, 392, 394; courtesy of Martha Drennan, p. 381; Photodisc/Getty Images, p. 383; courtesy of Joy Kataoka, p. 423; Getty Images—Stockbyte, Royalty Free, p. 417; Annie Pickert/Pearson, p. 434; courtesy of Sara Gillison, p. 442; © Fancy/Alamy, p. 447; courtesy of Val Sharpe, p. 482; Bill Aron/PhotoEdit Inc., p. 483; courtesy of Bill Flowers, p. 511.

Library of Congress Cataloging-in-Publication Data

Teaching students with special needs in inclusive settings / Tom E. C.
Smith ... [et al.]. – 6th ed.
    p. cm.
 ISBN-13: 978-0-13-800783-6
 ISBN-10: 0-13-800783-7
 1. Inclusive education–United States. 2. Special education–United
States. 3. Children with disabilities–Education–United States. 4.
Classroom management–United States. I. Smith, Tom E. C.
 LC1201.T43 2012
 371.9'046–dc22

                                          2011000144

10 9 8 7 6 5 4 3 2 1

www.pearsonhighered.com

ISBN 10: 0-13-800783-7
ISBN 13: 978-0-13-800783-6

ABOUT THE AUTHORS

TOM E. C. SMITH is currently Dean of the College of Education and Health Professions, and University Professor of Special Education, at the University of Arkansas. Prior to receiving his Ed.D. from Texas Tech University, he taught children with mental retardation, learning disabilities, and autism at the elementary and secondary levels. President Clinton appointed him to three terms on the President's Committee on Mental Retardation. He has served as the Executive Director of the Division on Autism and Developmental Disabilities of the Council for Exceptional Children since 1996. His current professional interests focus on legal issues and special education.

EDWARD A. POLLOWAY is the Rosel H. Schewel Professor of Education and Human Development at Lynchburg College in Virginia, where he has taught since 1976. He also serves as Vice President for Community Advancement and Dean of Graduate Studies. He received his doctoral degree from the University of Virginia and his undergraduate degree from Dickinson College in Pennsylvania. He has served twice as president of the Division on Developmental Disabilities of the Council for Exceptional Children and on the board of directors of the Council for Learning Disabilities. He also served on the committee that developed the 1992 definition of mental retardation for the American Association on Intellectual Disabilities. He is the author of 20 books and over 100 articles in the field of special education with primary interests in the areas of learning disabilities and mental retardation.

JAMES R. PATTON is an Educational Consultant and Adjunct Associate Professor at the University of Texas at Austin. He received his Ed.D. from the University of Virginia. He is a former high school biology teacher and elementary-level special education resource teacher. He has also taught students who were gifted and those who were gifted/learning disabled. His professional interests include transition, life skills instruction, adult issues related to individuals with special needs, behavioral intervention planning, and classroom accommodations. He has served on national boards of the Division on Developmental Disabilities, the Council for Learning Disabilities, and the National Joint Committee on Learning Disabilities.

CAROL A. DOWDY is Professor of Special Education at the University of Alabama at Birmingham, where she has taught since receiving her Ed.D. degree from the University of Alabama, Tuscaloosa. She has written eight books on special education and published 34 articles on learning disabilities. She has served on the national board of the Council for Learning Disabilities and the Professional Advisory Board for the Learning Disabilities Association of America, and she has worked closely with the federal department of Vocational Rehabilitation to assist in their efforts to better serve adults with learning disabilities.

130 410

PREFACE

The sixth edition of *Teaching Students with Special Needs in Inclusive Settings* reflects the major changes in how students with special needs are provided educational opportunities in today's elementary and secondary schools. Since the first edition of the book, more than 15 years ago, educators have dramatically altered the focus of educational services and interventions for this group of students. Educators currently focus on differentiating their instruction for all students to ensure appropriate educational opportertunes for the wide, diverse student populations found in America's schools. During the time since the first edition was written, when inclusion was a relatively new initiative, educating students with special needs in inclusive settings has become the norm.

This text interprets research into practical ideas for classroom teachers and other educational personnel and therefore helps our readers make the necessary, practical, and satisfying connections involved in successful inclusive teaching: connections between a conceptual understanding of the nature and characteristics of the various disabilities with which many students struggle, and the practical (and often required) procedures, collaborative practices, and instructional strategies that good educators employ to help those students learn well, be accepted within their school communities, and ultimately achieve their academic and social potential.

NEW TO THIS EDITION

There are several significant changes in the sixth edition of *Teaching Students with Special Needs in Inclusive Settings*.

- **Chapter 2: Professional Collaboration and Home–School Collaboration** takes an early look at the importance of involving families in the process of creating and maintaining an inclusive classroom.
- **Chapter 4: Managing and Differentiating Classrooms** proposes a comprehensive model for using the components of differentiation to instruct and to manage classrooms.
- **Chapter 10: Teaching Students with Sensory Impairments** focuses one complete chapter on the needs of students with vision and hearing needs.
- **Differentiating Elementary Instruction and Differentiating Secondary Instruction:** These two features propose specific ideas for designing instruction to meet individual needs in elementary and secondary classrooms.
- **Characteristics and Implications:** These chapter elements clarify the characteristics of each disability category and pinpoint instructional implications teachers need to be aware of.
- **Cross-Chapter references:** These margin notes help you make the content connections across chapters.
- **Refined Chapter Organization:** Every chapter has been reorganized and structured to better scaffold learning. Chapter objectives provide an advance organizer, and these objectives exactly match the major headings in the chapter. Chapter ending summaries are broken into sections that correspond exactly with the chapter's objectives and major headings to provide an excellent study organizer to help prepare students for quizzes on each chapter's content.
- **Categorical Chapter Organization** has been further refined so that each categorical chapter follows the same predictable format, again providing scaffolding for the reader and better preparing readers for tests and quizzes.

- *Expanded!*   Now in every chapter in the book, specific content is brought to life by visiting and revisiting one student at a time.
  - All chapters begin with a **mini case study**, with questions to consider about one student who exemplifies chapter topics.
  - For the first time, we revisit this student in every chapter in the **Selected IEP Goals and Objectives**.
  - We return to this student, re-examining his or her needs in the **Tips for Adapting a Lesson** feature, now in every chapter.

REAL STUDENTS, REAL SOLUTIONS

In every chapter a student with special needs is featured who exemplifies the topic of the chapter. The story of this student is referred to throughout the chapter and highlights this students' particular needs and the accommodations their teacher can make to assist them.

Chapter opening scenarios: Providing educational services for students with special needs in inclusive continues to evolve, and every student has unique needs. To help readers understand these differences, we begin each chapter with the story of a particular student or teacher in the context of that chapter's topic. These mini case studies offer Questions to Consider to focus the reader's attention on key issues to be covered in the chapter.

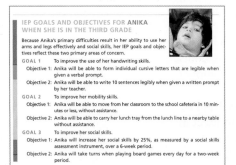

IEP Goals and Objectives: We revisit these students, presenting sample IEP goals for the students profiled in the chapter opening scenarios. This feature helps our readers look at the appropriate construction of this important document to suit the needs of this individual student.

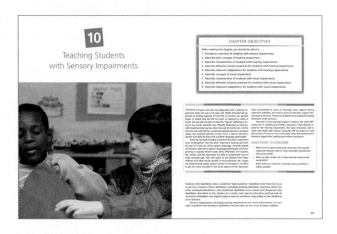

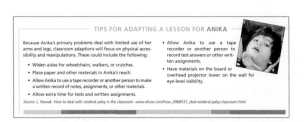

Tips for Adapting a Lesson: In this feature we return again to the chapter's opening scenario, providing practical strategies for modifying instruction to meet the particular needs of these students. This feature examines the best classroom instruction as it helps readers apply chapter concepts of differentiation.

Sample IEPs: Found in the appendices at the back of this book, these samples provide models for developing programs appropriate for three students: a girl in fourth grade and boys in the eighth and twelfth grades, respectively. They will help the reader connect the needs of his or her students with specific interventions intended to help them become more successful in school and afterwards.

DIFFERENTIATING INSTRUCTION

To draw attention to the importance of differentiating instruction, we've revised and created new special features for the sixth edition:

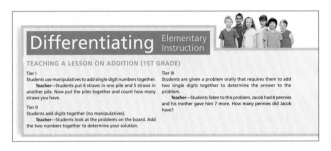

Differentiated Elementary and Secondary Instruction: These new features throughout the text offer practical, specific, research-supported strategies for working with students with special needs in inclusive classrooms. Each chapter contains a feature focusing on elementary students and secondary students.

PROMOTING INCLUSIVE PRACTICE

Understanding the roles and responsibilities of the general educator and knowing who the students are and how to plan, assess, and evaluate based on the needs of individual students will enable the reader to create inclusive classrooms. We've crafted several special features to that end:

Personal Spotlights: These features profile real teachers, parents of children with special needs, and students with special needs themselves, letting readers connect chapter content with real-life situations and providing insight into the multifaceted experiences of people most affected by the challenges of inclusion.

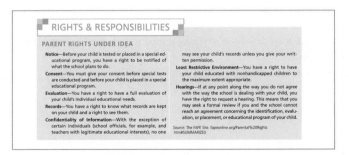

Rights & Responsibilities: These research-driven boxed readings are a critical component of the text that provide insight into the role of the general education teacher in an inclusive classroom. These boxes, found throughout the text, examine legal cases and issues that impact the instructional process for students with special needs. They have been updated to present relevant, practical information.

CHARACTERISTICS AND IMPLICATIONS: LOW-INCIDENCE DISABILITIES		
DISABILITY	**POTENTIAL DIFFICULTIES**	**EDUCATIONAL IMPLICATIONS**
Traumatic Brain Injury	Attention problems Emotional lability Aggressiveness Physical limitations Speech and language deficits Slower to respond/react	Use attention-focusing strategies. Implement behavior management planning. Provide physical access. Provide speech-language supports. Use task analysis to break down assignment. Provide extra time. Implement social skills training. Teach self-determination skills.
Orthopedic Impairments	Physical access problems Physical limitations Social skill problems	Provide physical access. Provide accommodations for physical limitations. Collaborate with related services personnel and family. Implement social skills training. Teach self-determination skills. Utilize available technology.
Other Health Impairments	Health-related issues Social skill problems	Collaborate with health professionals and family. Ensure universal precautions. Teach self-determination skills.
Severe Intellectual Disabilities	Difficulty with all academic tasks Social skills deficits	Implement functional curriculum. Focus on needed, daily living skills. Teach self-determination skills. Implement social skills Training. Utilize task analysis. Provide frequent reinforcement.

Characteristics and Implications: These new features in each of the categorical chapters clarify the characteristics of each disability category and pinpoint instructional implications that teachers need to understand to better meet the needs of their students.

SUPPLEMENTS FOR STUDENTS AND INSTRUCTORS

Online Instructor's Manual with Test Items

An expanded and improved online Instructor's Manual includes numerous recommendations for presenting and extending text content. The manual consists of chapter overviews, objectives, key terms and legislation, discussion questions, and class activities that cover the essential concepts addressed in each chapter. You'll also find a complete, chapter-by-chapter bank of test items.

Online PowerPoint Lecture Slides

The PowerPoint lecture slides are available on the Instructor Resource Center. These lecture slides highlight key concepts and summarize key content from each chapter of the text.

The electronic Instructor's Manual and online PowerPoint lecture slides are available on the Instructor Resource Center at www.pearsonhighered.com. To access these resources, go to www.pearsonhighered.com and click on the Instructor Resource Center button. Here you'll be able to log in or complete a one-time registration for a user name and password.

Pearson MyTest

Pearson MyTest is a powerful assessment generation program that helps instructors easily create and print quizzes and exams. Questions and tests are authored online, allowing ultimate flexibility and the ability to efficiently create and print assessments anytime, anywhere! Instructors can access Pearson MyTest and their test bank files by going to www.pearsonmytest.com to log in, register, or request access. Features of Pearson MyTest include:

Premium assessment content

- Draw from a rich library of assessments that complement your Pearson textbook and your course's learning objectives.
- Edit questions or tests to fit your specific teaching needs.

Instructor-friendly resources

- Easily create and store your own questions, including images, diagrams, and charts using simple drag-and-drop and Word-like controls.
- Use additional information provided by Pearson, such as the question's difficulty level or learning objective, to help you quickly build your test.

Time-saving enhancements

- Add headers or footers and easily scramble questions and answer choices—all from one simple toolbar.
- Quickly create multiple versions of your test or answer key, and when ready, simply save to MS-Word or PDF format and print!
- Export your exams for import to Blackboard 6.0, CE (WebCT), or Vista (WebCT)!

MYEDUCATIONLAB

Prepare with the Power of Classroom Practice

PEARSON
myeducationlab

Register for MyEducationLab today at www.myeducationlab.com.

MyEducationLab is an online learning tool that provides resources to help you develop the knowledge and skills you'll need to be a successful teacher. All of the activities and exercises in MyEducationLab are **built around essential learning outcomes** for teachers and **mapped to professional teaching standards**. The site provides you with opportunities both to study your course content and to practice the skills you need to become a successful classroom teacher. With MyEducationLab, you will be able to:

- Practice applying what you're learning in **interactive exercises and simulations** including the Building Teaching Skills exercises and the Classroom Management Simulations.
- Respond to **real classroom situations** as you analyze classroom video, case studies, and authentic student and teacher artifacts.
- Challenge yourself with interactive modules, case study units, and podcasts from the acclaimed IRIS Center at Vanderbilt University with the **IRIS Center Resources** section on MyEducationLab.
- Take **Practice Tests** for each chapter of your text and receive an individualized study plan that identifies your strengths and weaknesses and provides you with the resources you need to master the concepts covered in the class.
- Interact with the **IEP Tutorial** to learn how to develop appropriate IEPs and how to conduct effective IEP conferences.
- Use **Lesson Planning Software** to develop high-quality lesson plans. The software also makes it easy to integrate your state's content standards into all of your lesson plans.
- Locate your **teacher certification test** requirements, read descriptions of what the test covers, and answer sample test questions.

To start using MyEducationLab, activate the access code packaged with your book. If your instructor did not make MyEducationLab a required part of your course or if you are purchasing a used book without an access code, go to www.myeducationlab.com to purchase access to this wonderful resource!

ACKNOWLEDGMENTS

The sixth edition of *Teaching Students with Special Needs in Inclusive Settings* is the result of a great deal of effort on the part of many people. We would like to acknowledge the tremendous contribution made by numerous professionals in the field of special and general education whose daily work inspires and helps provide us with the information to share in this textbook. We also acknowledge those authors whose works we cite regularly, who have made a significant contribution to the education of children with special needs. We thank in particular Dr. Gena Barnhill for her expertise contributed as co-author of the chapter on autism spectrum disorders. We would also like to thank every member of our families who put up with our time away from them, whether it is physically or just mentally away while we ponder permissions, references, or the changes we need to make in that one last chapter. Especially we thank our spouses, Debi, Carolyn, Joy, and Jim. And, we could never have the energy to write about children without having the wonderful opportunities presented by the children in our own lives, namely Jake, Alex, Suni, Lyndsay, Kimi, Cameron, and Meredith.

As always, our extended family at Pearson deserves special thanks. We acknowledge in particular Ann Davis, our Editor; Hope Madden, our Developmental Editor; Sheryl Langner, our Production Editor; and Darcy Betts Prybella, our Marketing Manager. We also owe a great deal of thanks to individuals who were involved in the production and marketing of the text. We also wish to express our appreciation to Ray Short and Virginia Lanigan for their initial commitment to this project.

Finally, we want to thank those persons who have reviewed our text through various editions and whose ideas have informed our work in this sixth edition. These include: Glenna Billingsley, Texas State University, San Marcos; Mary Curtis, University of Texas, Brownsville; Rebecca Davis, Eastern New Mexico University; Mary Darlene Hilsenbeck, University of Louisville; and Shirley MacKinnon, Canisius College.

TECS
EAP
JRP
CD

BRIEF CONTENTS

CONTENTS

11 Teaching Students with Low-Incidence Disabilities   346

12 Teaching Students with Speech and Language Disorders   371

13 Teaching Students with Special Gifts and Talents   402

14 Teaching Students Who Are At Risk   434

SPECIAL FEATURES

1

Inclusive Education: An Introduction

After reading this chapter, you should be able to:

1. Describe the history of services available to students with special needs.
2. Define the term "students with special needs."
3. Describe current services available to students with special needs.
4. Discuss where students with disabilities should be educated and the different pros and cons of different placement options.
5. Describe the different perceptions of inclusion.
6. Discuss the critical dimensions of inclusive classrooms.

JASON is 9 years old and has Asperger's syndrome. He was diagnosed at the age of 5. Jason's parents work; his father is a truck driver for a local company and his mother works at a retail outlet store. Jason has two siblings, a sister 3 years older and a brother 2 years older. Jason's development seemed to be on target until he was about 3 years old. Prior to that time he had achieved his developmental milestones at or near expected times. He played with his cousins, enjoyed learning how to talk, and appeared to be a typical boy, frequently getting into trouble because of his high energy level and curiosity. When Jason was about 3 years old he began to withdraw from his cousins and other children his age. He seemed to prefer to play alone and often seemed to ignore other children around him. His oral language skills, while not regressing, did not develop as rapidly as they did in other children. Jason also began to exhibit behavioral outbursts and became very irritable when daily routines were changed. While his parents were concerned, they were assured by the family's pediatrician that some children's development slows down, and that Jason would catch up later.

Jason had a very significant behavioral outburst during his fifth birthday party. He screamed when his cake was being cut, saying that his mother was killing the cat that was on the cake. He withdrew totally and did not interact with his parents, siblings, or others for two days. After this episode, Jason's parents took him to the local children's hospital diagnostic center. After a two-day diagnostic work-up, Jason was diagnosed as having Asperger's syndrome.

Since his diagnosis, Jason has received special education services in his local school while being placed full-time in his regular classroom. While he has at times presented his teachers problems, for the most part he has been very successful. He typically receives one hour of resource room assistance daily, and also has a special education teacher who works with him and other students in the general classroom setting. Jason is very intelligent and does not have any difficulties with his academic work. He does have difficulties interacting with his classmates, often preferring to work or play alone rather than in groups. Occasionally he can become disruptive during group activities. While his oral language skills are sufficient to enable his success in school, he does not frequently initiate conversations with others and often becomes frustrated when pressured to do so. With continued supports, Jason should be able to succeed in school and graduate with his peers.

QUESTIONS TO CONSIDER

1. What could have resulted if Jason had been diagnosed at an earlier age?
2. What goals would be appropriate for Jason after he completes high school?
3. What should be the primary focus of Jason's interventions in school?
4. How can Jason's teachers improve his social interaction skills?

The public education system in the United States is unique. Rather than allowing only children from specific groups to access public education, the U.S. system attempts to educate all children. In some countries, students must attain a certain academic potential to be allowed to proceed through the educational system. In other countries, girls, as well as poor children, are excluded from schools. In the United States, all children are provided an opportunity to attend school for 13 or more years. This is a free, equal educational opportunity for all children, including those with parents who are not educated and those from families without financial means. Children with disabilities and those who have learning or behavior problems are also included in this educational system, as are children of all races and gender. Students do not have to pass certain tests to attend various schools, nor do their families need to pay for a comprehensive educational program. Students do not have to choose, early in their school years, the school track that they will follow. There are critics who compare the academic success of students in the United States with that of students from other countries. Although U.S. test scores often lag behind those of students in other countries, it is important to note that our educational system is universal whereas the educational systems of many of the countries we are compared with do not offer programs for all children.

The basis for our free public educational system is the U.S. Constitution, which guarantees equal opportunities for all citizens. While public schools have evolved into a system that provides educational opportunities for all students, initially that was not the case. Girls did not secure their right to equal educational opportunities until the early 1900s; racial minorities not until the 1950s and 1960s; and students with disabilities not until the 1970s and 1980s. Litigation and legislation played important roles as each group secured the right to participate in public educational programs (Murdick, Gartin, & Crabtree, 2007).

HISTORY OF EDUCATION FOR STUDENTS WITH SPECIAL NEEDS

Prior to federal legislation passed in the mid-1970s, many public schools did not provide any services for students with disabilities. Only 20% of all children with disabilities were served in public school programs in 1970 (U.S. Department of Education, 2006), and in many cases where services were provided, the services were minimal and provided in segregated settings. When Congress passed the first act mandating comprehensive services for students with disabilities in 1975 it was estimated that 3 million children with disabilities received inappropriate or inadequate services, while up to 1 million were totally excluded from the educational system (U.S. Department of Education, 2009). During this period the only option for many parents of children with disabilities was private educational programs or programs specifically designed for students with disabilities. In many cases, parents paid for these educational programs out of their own resources. Many students with disabilities, whose parents did not have adequate resources, actually stayed home and received no formal education (Katsiyannis, Yell, & Bradley, 2001).

During the beginning years of special education, some children with disabilities received services in **residential programs**, especially children with intellectual disabilities and sensory deficits (Crane, 2002). In 1965, approximately 100,000 children, from birth to 21 years of age, lived in institutions for people with intellectual disabilities in the United States (White, Lakin, Bruininks, & Li, 1991). The first school for children with deafness in the United States was established in 1817 as the American Asylum for the Education of the Deaf and Dumb (now the American School for the Deaf) (Stewart & Kluwin, 2001). The first school for children with visual problems, the New England Asylum for the Blind, was founded in 1832. In 1963, nearly 50% of children classified as legally blind in the United States lived in residential schools for the blind, which offered daily living support as well as some education and training.

Education services for students with disabilities have changed dramatically since the mid-1970s. Not only are more appropriate services provided by schools, but they are also frequently provided in general education classrooms with collaboration between special

Visit the MyEducationLab for this course to enhance your understanding of chapter concepts with a personalized Study Plan. You'll also have the opportunity to hone your teaching skills through video-based Assignments and Activities, IRIS Center Resources, and Building Teaching Skills and Disposition lessons.

education and general classroom teachers (U.S. Department of Education, 2006). Along with the increased numbers of students with disabilities served in public schools came a significant reduction in number of school-aged children residing in residential placements. Many different developments brought about these changes, including parental advocacy, enactment of new laws, and legal rulings. The federal government played a major part in the evolution of special education services, primarily through legislation, litigation, and funding.

While there have been significant changes in services for students with disabilities, these changes have occurred incrementally over a period of time. Since services for students with disabilities began there have been four distinct phases: relative isolation, integration (mainstreaming), inclusion, and empowerment (Polloway, Smith, Patton, & Smith, 1996). In the **relative isolation** phase, which included the first 60 to 70 years in the 20th century, students were either denied access to public schools or permitted to attend only in isolated settings. In the **integration** phase, which began in the 1970s, students with disabilities were mainstreamed, or integrated, into general education programs when appropriate. During the **inclusion** phase, starting in the mid-1980s, emphasis was placed on students with disabilities being included in all school programs and activities. This phase differed from the integration phase in a minor but very significant way: Although students with disabilities were in general classrooms under both integration and inclusion, in the inclusion phase it was assumed that these students belonged in general classrooms, whereas in the integration phase they were considered to be special education students who were simply placed in the general classroom part of the time, primarily for socialization. Most recently, the fourth phase of services, empowerment and self-determination, has been the focus of inclusion efforts, to better prepare students for the highest degree of independence possible (Eisenman, 2007). The idea of student-led conferences is a prime example of the focus on self-determination (Konrad, 2008). While the changes in special education since the mid-1970s have been dramatic, probably the most significant change has been acceptance of the idea that special education is a service, not a place. In other words, special education is not a classroom in a building; rather, it is the specialized instruction and services provided for students with disabilities (Causton-Theoharis & Theoharis, 2009). With more and more students with disabilities receiving all or most of their specialized instruction in general education classrooms, the reality that special education is a service and not a place is more easily acceptable.

Because universal education for all children is the model of public education in the United States, teachers in today's public schools must provide instruction and other educational services to a growingly diverse student population. In fact, the diversity of students in today's schools is far greater than in the past. Currently approximately 25% of the population comprises minority groups. The U.S. Census Bureau (2008) projects that the numbers of individuals from culturally diverse backgrounds will continue to increase over the next 40 years. Traditionally, teacher education programs have focused on teaching students who learn in similar ways and at similar levels. However, today's teachers do not have the luxury of teaching only students who learn easily and behave in a manner the teachers deem appropriate based on their own standards. They must be prepared to deal effectively with all kinds of students.

DEFINING STUDENTS WITH SPECIAL NEEDS

Fewer and fewer students fit the mold of the "typical" student. In fact, "atypical" to some degree is becoming the norm. Although this creates issues for schools, the positive result of this reality is that educators have to view each child individually and take into consideration individual strengths and weaknesses. Today's students present many differences; some of the most obvious are present in those with identified disabilities, those who are classified as gifted and talented, and those who are "at risk" for developing problems. It has been estimated that currently 13.6% of children, ages 3 to 21, or approximately 6.68 million students, are classified as disabled and are served in special education programs (National Center for Education Statistics, 2009). Another group of students experience a degree of disability that is not significant enough to result in special education eligibility. Many of these students, approximately 1 to 3% of the student population, are eligible for certain services and protections under Section 504 and the Americans with Disabilities Act (Smith & Patton, 2007; T. Smith, 2002). Still other students need special attention because of poverty, difficulties with language, or other at-risk factors (Gollnick & Chinn, 2009). Adding all of these students together, plus gifted students, who are considered to be an additional 3 to 5% of the school population, shows that 20 to 30% of all students in public schools have some special needs. Although many of these students do not meet the specific criteria to be classified as "disabled" and are therefore not eligible for special education or 504 services, school personnel cannot afford to ignore the special challenges presented by these students (Barr & Parrett, 2001).

More and more, diversity among students in public schools represents the norm rather than the exception (Gollnick & Chinn, 2009). In order for public schools to be effective with this growing diverse student population, school personnel must address the needs of all children, including children with special needs. They must be able to identify these students and help develop and implement effective programs; this requires teachers to be able to understand the types of students they need to serve.

Students with Disabilities Served in Special Education

The largest group of students with special needs in the public school system includes those formally classified as having disabilities as defined by federal legislation. This legislation, the **Individuals with Disabilities Education Improvement Act (IDEA) of 2004**, provides the legal basis for the current special education services provided in public schools; it will be discussed extensively in a later section. Under this act, students with disabilities are defined as those who exhibit one of several specific conditions that result in their need for special education and related services. Specifically, the IDEA definition of disability is:

> The term "child with a disability" means a child—"(i) with intellectual disabilities, hearing impairments (including deafness), speech or language impairments, visual impairments (including blindness), serious emotional disturbance (referred to in this title as 'emotional disturbance'), orthopedic impairments, autism, traumatic brain injury, other health impairments, or specific learning disabilities"; and "(ii) who, by reason thereof, needs special education and related services (Sec. 602)."

The number of children with disabilities served in special education programs has grown significantly since the mid-1970s (U.S. Department of Education, 2006). In 1976, a total of 3.69 million students, ages 3 to 21, or 8.3% of the school population, were served in special education programs in the 50 states, Bureau of Indian Affairs schools, and the District of Columbia. This number increased to approximately 6.68 million students, or 13.6%, in 2006 (National Center for Education Statistics, 2009). Table 1.1 shows the number of children, by disability, served during the 1976–1977, 2001–2002, and 2006–2007 school years.

IDEA includes 14 categories of disabilities that include many different types of students. For example, the broad area of **other health impairments** includes hemophilia, diabetes, epilepsy, and sickle-cell anemia. Even the category of learning disabilities comprises an extremely heterogeneous group of students. The fact that disability categories are composed of different types of students makes it impossible to draw simple conclusions about them. The following sections provide a general description of the categories of disabilities recognized in IDEA.

Intellectual Disabilities (Previously Called Mental Retardation)   Students with intellectual disabilities are usually identified through intelligence tests and measures of adaptive behavior, which indicate a person's ability to perform functional activities expected of age and cultural norms. In general, the American Association on Intellectual Disabilities (AAID) describes individuals in this classification as having significant limitations both in intellectual functioning and in adaptive behavior as expressed in conceptual, social, and practical adaptive skills. These limitations originate before age 18 (Schalock, 2010).

TABLE 1.1

Number of Children, Ages 3–21, Served in Special Education Classrooms in 1976–1977, 2001–2002, and 2006–2007 School Years

TYPE OF DISABILITY	1976–1977	2001–2002	2006–2007
All Disabilities	3,694,000	6,407,000	6,686,000
Specific Learning Disabilities	796,000	2,861,000	2,665,000
Speech or Language Impairments	1,302,000	1,391,000	1,475,000
Intellectual Disabilities	961,000	616,000	534,000
Emotional Disturbance	283,000	483,000	464,000
Hearing Impairments	88,000	78,000	80,000
Orthopedic Impairments	87,000	83,000	69,000
Other Health Impairments	141,000	350,000	611,000
Visual Impairments	38,000	28,000	29,000
Multiple Disabilities	–	136,000	142,000
Deaf-Blindness	–	2,000	2,000
Autism	–	114,000	258,000
Traumatic Brain Injury	–	22,000	25,000
Developmental Delay	–	242,000	333,000

Source: National Center for Education Statistics (2009).

Learning Disabilities   In general, students classified as having learning disabilities do not achieve at their expected levels, without any explanations. Although the cause of learning disabilities is unclear, the controversial assumption is that a neurological dysfunction causes the learning disability (Hallahan, Lloyd, Kauffman, Weiss, & Martinez, 2005). The large numbers of students classified as having learning disabilities is one of the reasons why IDEA has promoted the option of response to intervention (RTI) as a means of identifying students for this group (Reutebuch, 2008; Shapiro & Clemens, 2009).

Emotional Disturbance   Students with emotional disturbance exhibit inappropriate behaviors or emotions that result in disruptions for themselves or others in their environment. Whereas the federal government uses the term "emotional disturbance," specifically eliminating from the category children and youth who lack the skills to cope with personal relationships and common social situations (sometimes referred to as juvenile delinquents or conduct disordered), other groups prefer the terms "emotional and behavior disorders" or "behavior disorders." Mental health professionals use still other terms, such as "conduct disorder" and "depression." In addition to differing on terminology, professionals serving children with these problems also differ on definitions of the problems and the types of services they provide (Coleman & Webber, 2002).

Hearing Impairments   Students with hearing impairment include those with permanent or fluctuating impairments in hearing that adversely affect their educational performance. This category includes those classified as deaf, who have difficulties in processing linguistic information through hearing, with or without amplification (IDEA, 2004), and those classified as hard of hearing, who can process linguistic information through hearing with assistance (Stewart & Kluwin, 2001).

Visual Impairments   This category includes students who are partially sighted and those who are blind, whose educational performance may be adversely affected because of impairments in vision, even with correction (IDEA, 2004). Students who are partially sighted can generally read print, whereas those classified as blind cannot.

Orthopedic Impairments   Students who experience problems related to their physical abilities are grouped into the orthopedic impairments category. Included are students with cerebral palsy, spina bifida, amputations, or muscular dystrophy and other physical impairments. For these students, physical access to educational facilities and problems with writing and manipulation are important concerns.

Other Health Impairments   Students are classified as having other health impairments when they have limited strength, vitality, or alertness due to chronic or acute health problems. Examples of such problems include asthma, diabetes, epilepsy, hemophilia, and leukemia. Attention deficit disorder (ADD) or attention deficit hyperactivity disorder (ADHD) may be included in this category (IDEA, 2004). As with orthopedic impairment, this category includes a wide variety of disabling conditions.

Autism   Autism was not designated as a separate disability category under IDEA until the 1990 reauthorization. Autism can be described as a lifelong disability that primarily affects communication and social interactions. Children with autism typically relate to people, objects, and events in abnormal ways; they insist on structured environments and display many self-stimulating behaviors (Tryon, Mayes, Rhodes, & Waldo, 2006). The number of students served in this category is expected to increase dramatically over the next several years, as the number of children identified as having autism has increased to a prevalence of 1 in 110 children (National Centers for Disease Control, 2009).

Traumatic Brain Injury (TBI)   TBI "means an acquired injury to the brain caused by an external physical force, resulting in total or partial functional disability or psychosocial impairment, or both, that adversely affects a child's educational performance" (IDEA, 2004). TBI applies to both open and closed head injuries that affect a variety of skill areas, including cognition, memory, attention, judgment, and problem solving (Best, 2006). Open head injuries include those that result in the skull being broken or penetrated, whereas closed head injuries result from a hard blow to the head without penetrating the skull.

Speech or Language Impairments   For some children, speech difficulties are a serious problem. When the impairment results in a child's need for special education and related services, the child is considered eligible for services under IDEA. Most of these children need speech therapy (Polloway, Miller, & Smith, 2011).

Students Eligible for Section 504 and the ADA

Some students have disabilities but are not eligible under IDEA, primarily because the disability does not result in their needing special education. Many of these students are eligible for services under other federal mandates, namely Section 504 of the Rehabilitation Act and the Americans with Disabilities Act (ADA). These laws use a different definition of disability, employing a functional, not a categorical, model. Under Section 504 and the ADA, a person is considered to have a disability if that individual (1) has a physical or mental impairment that substantially limits one or more major life activities; (2) has a record of such an impairment; or (3) is regarded as having such an impairment. The acts do not provide an exhaustive list of such impairments but require the functional criterion of "substantial limitation" to be the qualifying element (Hulett, 2009; Smith & Patton, 2007).

Eligibility for Section 504 and the ADA is based on impairments that result in substantial limitations of such major life activities as breathing, walking, seeing, hearing, and learning. Schools are required to refer students who are thought to be eligible for services and protections under these laws for evaluation. If students are determined eligible, schools must provide accommodations for them in academic and nonacademic areas that enable them to receive a free, appropriate public education (Hulett, 2009; Smith & Patton, 2007).

Students Classified as Gifted and Talented

While the previous discussion focused on students who differ from their peers in a negative manner, some students differ by having above-average intelligence and learning abilities. These students, classified as gifted and talented, were traditionally defined and identified using intelligence quotient (IQ) test scores. An IQ score of 120 or higher was the primary criterion, but current criteria are much broader. Although no single definition is accepted by all groups, most focus on students who are capable of making significant contributions to society in a variety of areas, including academic endeavors and creative, mechanical, motor, or fine arts skills.

Students At Risk for School Problems

In addition to students served under IDEA, Section 504 and the ADA, and those who are classified as gifted or talented, there are other students who also present challenges for the educational system. These students, considered to be **at risk** for developing problems, manifest characteristics that could easily lead to learning and behavior problems (Morrison, 2006). Examples of these students include those who do not speak English as their primary language; those living in poverty, and students who are drug abusers. These students may present unique problems for teachers who attempt to meet their educational needs in general education classrooms. Because students in the at-risk group are not eligible for special education services, classroom teachers bear the primary responsibility for their educational programs, which may need to be modified to meet these students' needs.

CURRENT SERVICES FOR STUDENTS WITH SPECIAL NEEDS

The majority of students with special needs receive a portion of their education from classroom teachers in general education classrooms. In 2006, 96% of students with disabilities were educated in regular school buildings, and approximately 75% were served in general classrooms for 40% or more of each school day (U.S. Department of Education, 2009). Figure 1.1 provides the percentage of students, by disability category, and their school placement. Students who are gifted, at-risk, or served under Section 504 and the ADA have always been provided services in general classrooms (T. Smith, 2007), but the increase in the number of students served through IDEA in general classrooms has increased steadily since the early 1980s (National Center for Education Statistics, 2009).

As early as 1999, McLeskey, Henry, and Hedges noted that educating students with disabilities in general education settings was one of the most significant changes in public education during the previous 15 years. Since the beginning of the 21st century, the inclusion movement has only expanded, primarily because of the Individuals with Disabilities Education Improvement Act.

Individuals with Disabilities Education Improvement Act (IDEA) (PL 108-446, Dec. 3, 2004)

The purposes of the act include:

> (1)(A) to ensure that all children with disabilities have available to them a free appropriate public education that emphasizes special education and related services designed to meet their unique needs and prepare them for further education, employment, and independent living; (B) to ensure that the rights of children with disabilities and parents of such children are protected; and (C) to assist States, localities, educational service agencies, and Federal agencies to provide for the education of all children with disabilities;

| FIGURE 1.1 | Percentage of Students Ages 6 Through 21 with Disabilities Receiving Special Education and Related Services under IDEA, Part B, by Educational Environment, by Disability Category: Fall 2004 |

| | Time outside the regular class | | | |
Disabilities	<21 percent of the day (%)	21–60 percent of the day (%)	>60 percent of the day (%)	Separate environments[a] (%)
Specific learning disabilities	51.6	35.4	12.0	1.0
Speech or language impairments	88.3	6.6	4.7	0.5
Mental retardation	13.8	29.3	50.5	6.4
Emotional disturbance	32.4	22.0	28.4	17.2
Multiple disabilities	13.0	16.8	45.1	25.0
Hearing impairments	47.1	18.7	20.9	13.4
Orthopedic impairments	48.5	19.4	25.6	6.5
Other health impairments	53.9	29.2	13.6	3.3
Visual impairments	56.8	16.0	14.7	12.5
Autism	29.1	17.7	41.8	11.3
Deaf-blindness	18.8	15.1	35.3	30.8
Traumatic brain injury	37.6	28.4	25.9	8.1
Developmental delay	56.8	25.2	16.7	1.2
All disabilities	52.1	26.3	17.5	4.0

Note: The sum of the percentages may not total 100 due to rounding.

[a]The category of separate environments includes public and private *residential facilities, public and private separate schools* and *homebound/hospital environments.*

Source: U.S. Department of Education, Office of Special Education Programs, Data Analysis System (DANS), OMB #1820-0517: "Part B, *Individuals with Disabilities Education Act,* Implementation of FAPE Requirements," 2004. Data updated as of July 30, 2005. Also Tables 2-2 and 2-2a through 2-2m in vol. 2 of this report. These data are for the 50 states, District of Columbia, BIA schools, Puerto Rico and the four outlying areas.

(2) to assist States in the implementation of a statewide, comprehensive, coordinated, multidisciplinary, interagency system of early intervention services for infants and toddlers with disabilities and their families; (3) to ensure that educators and parents have the necessary tools to improve educational results for children with disabilities by supporting system improvement activities; coordinated research and personnel preparation; coordinated technical assistance, dissemination, and support; and technology development and media services; and (4) to assess, and ensure the effectiveness of, efforts to educate children with disabilities.

The passage of the original act opened the doors of public schools and general education classrooms to students with disabilities (Katsiyannis et al., 2001). It was the result of much debate that followed several federal court cases that concluded that children with disabilities were not receiving an appropriate public education. Under IDEA, schools are required to seek out and implement appropriate educational services for all students with disabilities, regardless of the severity; to provide appropriate, individualized services to students with disabilities; and to actively involve parents in the educational process. For general education teachers, the most important part of the legislation is the requirement that students with disabilities be educated with their nondisabled peers as much as possible and general classroom teachers become directly involved in their education (Hulett, 2009).

Since its original passage in 1975, IDEA has been reauthorized by Congress several times. Although each reauthorization has made changes in the original law, the basic requirements

TABLE 1.2

Key Components of the Individuals with Disabilities Education Act (IDEA) (2004)

PROVISIONS	DESCRIPTION
Least restrictive environment	Children with disabilities are educated with nondisabled children as much as possible.
Individualized education program	All children served in special education must have an individualized education program.
Due-process rights	Children and their parents must be involved in decisions about special education.
Due-process hearing	Parents and schools can request an impartial hearing if there is a conflict over special education services.
Nondiscriminatory assessment	Students must be given a comprehensive assessment that is nondiscriminatory in nature.
Related services	Schools must provide related services, such as physical therapy, counseling, and transportation, if needed.
Free appropriate public education	The primary requirement of IDEA is the provision of a free appropriate public education to all school-age children with disabilities.
Mediation/Resolution	Parents have a right, if they choose, to mediation or a resolution session to resolve differences with the school. Using mediation should not deny or delay a parent's request for a due-process hearing.
Transfer of rights	When the student reaches the age of majority, as defined by the state, the school shall notify both the parents and the student and transfer all rights of the parents to the child.
Discipline	A child with a disability cannot be expelled or suspended for 10 or more cumulative days in a school year without a manifest determination as to whether the child's disability is related to the inappropriate behavior.
State assessments	Children with disabilities must be included in districtwide and statewide assessment programs with appropriate accommodations. Alternative assessment programs must be developed for children who cannot participate in districtwide or statewide assessment programs.
RTI	Response to Intervention provides an opportunity for schools to implement interventions to determine if the student responds favorably, which would preclude referral for special education services.
Transition	Transition planning and programming must begin when students with disabilities reach age 16.

have remained relatively intact. The 1983 reauthorization provided incentives for serving preschool children whereas the 1986 reauthorization mandated services for children with disabilities ages 3 to 5. The 1990 reauthorization renamed the law to the Individuals with Disabilities Education Act (IDEA), and replaced the word *handicap* with the word *disability*. In addition, two new, separate categories of disabilities were added—autism and TBI—and schools were required to develop transition planning for students when they turned 16 years old (T. Smith, 2005).

The most recent reauthorization of the act was in 2004 as the Individuals with Disabilities Education Improvement Act. The law requires schools to do a number of important things, including identifying students who would be eligible, developing appropriate educational programs on an individual basis, educating students with their nondisabled peers when feasible, and affording due-process rights to parents and students. Table 1.2 summarizes some of the key components of the law. One of the specific changes in the 2004 reauthorization "requires that special education teachers and administrators know and understand their duties and obligations under the law" (Yell, Katsiyannis, Ryan, McDuffie, & Mattocks, 2008, p. 45). The following sections describe some of the key elements of IDEA.

Individualized Education Program (IEP)   One of the most important components of IDEA that impacts general classroom teachers is the requirement that all students with disabilities have an IEP. Gartin and Murdick (2005) go as far as to say that the IEP is "the cornerstone of the Individuals with Disabilities Education Improvement Act of 2004" (p. 327). The IEP, based on information collected during a comprehensive assessment, is developed by a group of individuals, including general classroom teachers who are knowledgeable about the student. IEPs are required to result in meaningful educational benefit for the student, which means that the IEP should be based on relevant assessments, and must include meaningful goals and appropriate educational services. The participation of parents in the development of the IEP is critical (Yell et al., 2008), although schools may proceed to develop and implement an IEP if a parent simply does not wish to meet with the team. However, parents are uniquely qualified to provide important information during the development of an appropriate program for their child (Smith, Gartin, Murdick, & Hilton, 2006). See the nearby **IEP Goals and Objectives** for Jason, along with the **Tips for Adapting a Lesson** as examples of IEP content.

Another key requirement related to the IEP is access to the general curriculum. The 2004 reauthorization of IDEA requires that students with disabilities have access to the general education curriculum. This requirement means that "educators must ensure that all students have the opportunity to participate and progress in the general curriculum, including students with significant cognitive disabilities" (Clayton, Burdge, Denham, Kleinert, & Kearns, 2006, p. 20). Browder, Trela, & Jimenez (2007) describe a means for enabling students with significant cognitive disabilities to access the general curriculum by means of matching grade-level content with alternate achievement.

Least Restrictive Environment   A second component of IDEA that directly impacts general classroom teachers is the requirement to educate students with disabilities in the **least restrictive environment (LRE)**. This means that schools must provide educational

IEP GOALS AND OBJECTIVES FOR **JASON**

Because Jason's primary difficulties are in the areas of communication and social skills (opening vignette), his IEP goals and objectives reflect these two primary concerns.

GOAL 1   To participate in group activities with peers

    Objective 1: During physical education games, Jason will remain with his group 80% of the time without disrupting the group.

    Objective 2: Given opportunity to participate in cooperative learning activities, Jason will be engaged in the activity for a minimum of 10 minutes without withdrawing or disrupting the group.

GOAL 2   To initiate more social communication with peers

    Objective 1: When given the opportunity to enter into class discussions, Jason will respond to questions 50% of the time with only one prompt.

    Objective 2: When asked to participate in a group discussion about a class activity, Jason will be involved with the discussion for at least 10 minutes without withdrawing or disrupting the group.

    Objective 3: During lunch time, Jason will engage in conversations with friends at least 10 minutes during the 30-minute lunch period.

The following adaptations focus on Jason's needs in the classroom as well as his needs in the community. Since Jason's needs primarily focus on social and communication needs, the tips for adapting a lesson target these two areas. These are examples of adaptations that could be effective with students with needs similar to Jason's.

Jason's teacher can:

- Use peer support systems, such as peer buddies and peer tutors

- Use a behavior management system that positively rewards Jason for initiating interactions with peers

- Use social stories and social autopsies

- Use direct instruction of social skills

- Use daily schedules to facilitate transition activities

- Arrange the classroom so the student has to use language

- Use what, where, who, and what happened questions

- Use speech/language pathologists for supports

---

services for students with disabilities with their nondisabled peers, in general classroom settings, unless the needs of the child cannot be met there. The law further states that special classes, separate schooling, or other issues concerning the removal of students with disabilities from general educational settings should be used only when students cannot succeed in general education classrooms, even with supplementary aids and services.

While the word *inclusion* is not part of IDEA, the LRE requirement obviously results in the inclusion of many students with disabilities in general education classrooms. The amount of time a student is placed in a general education classroom is determined by the student's IEP. Some students are able to benefit from full-time inclusion, whereas others may be able to benefit from minimal placement in general education classrooms. IDEA requires that schools provide a continuum of placement options for students, with the IEP determining the most appropriate placement. "The primary consideration when determining students' placement is their individual educational need . . ." (Yell et al., 2008, p.49). Therefore, if the IEP committee determines that the least restrictive environment for a particular child is a special classroom, then that is the LRE for that child. Schools are required, however, to justify removal of students from the general education classroom.

The majority of students served under IDEA are classified as having *mild* disabilities. For most of these students, placement in general education classrooms for at least a portion of each school day is the appropriate option. Students with more severe disabilities may be less likely to benefit from inclusion and will generally spend less time with their nondisabled peers. The implementation of the LRE concept means that all classroom teachers will become more involved with students with special needs. General education teachers and special education teachers must share in the responsibility for educating students with disabilities (Wolfe & Hall, 2003).

Due-Process Safeguards   Schools must also afford **due-process safeguards** to students with disabilities and their parents. Prior to the passage of IDEA in 1975, school personnel often made unilateral decisions about a student's education, including placement and specific components of the educational program, with limited parental input. Parents also had little recourse if they disagreed with the school. The due-process safeguards provided through IDEA prohibit this practice. Due-process safeguards make parents and schools equal partners in the special education process. Parents must be notified and give their consent before schools can take certain actions that affect their child (Smith et al., 2006).

When the school and parents do not agree on the educational program, either party can request a due-process hearing. In this administrative appeals process, parents and schools present evidence and testimony to an impartial hearing officer who decides on the appropriateness of an educational program. The process ensures that children with disabilities and their families have equal opportunities in the school (Getty & Summy, 2004). The decision of the hearing officer is final and must be implemented unless it is appealed to state or federal court. Table 1.3 provides a brief description of the due-process safeguards provided by IDEA.

TABLE 1.3

Due-Process Requirements of IDEA

REQUIREMENT	EXPLANATION	REFERENCE
Opportunity to examine records	Parents have a right to inspect and review all educational records.	300.501
Independent evaluation	Parents have a right to obtain an independent evaluation of their child at their expense or the school's expense. The school pays only if it agrees to the evaluation or if it is required by a hearing officer.	300.502
Prior notice; parental consent	Schools must provide written notice to parents before the school initiates or changes the identification, evaluation, or placement of a child.	300.503
	Consent must be obtained before conducting the evaluation and before initial placement.	300.505
Contents of notice	Parental notice must provide a description of the proposed actions in the written native language of the home. If the communication is not written, oral notification must be given. The notice must be understandable to the parents.	300.504
Impartial due-process hearing, mediation, resolution	A parent or school may initiate a due-process hearing, engage in mediation, or a resolution session to resolve a dispute.	300.507

Source: From *IDEA 2004*, Washington, DC: U.S. Government Printing Office.

Response to Intervention (RTI)   The 2004 reauthorization of IDEA allows schools to use a model of interventions to determine if students are eligible for special education services. An RTI model provides interventions at different levels that are matched to students' particular needs (Reutebuch, 2008; Shapiro & Clemens, 2009). Each intervention is more intensive. A major purpose of the RTI model is to determine if interventions will enable schools to meet the child's needs without special education services. However, as noted by Burns and VanDerHeyden (2006), RTI models should be used for more than determining eligibility. "We consider RTI to be the systematic use of data-based decision making to most efficiently allocate resources to enhance learning outcomes for all children" (p. 3). An effective RTI model should enable students with disabilities access to programs and curricula, not merely access to buildings and classrooms (Cummings, Atkins, Allison, & Cole, 2008).

CROSS-REFERENCE

Response to Intervention is addressed in more depth in Chapter 4.

Key Changes in the 2004 Reauthorization of IDEA   As with previous reauthorizations, the most recent reauthorization of IDEA leaves much of the original law intact, but it does make some changes. In general, the reauthorization "aligned IDEA with the Elementary and Secondary Education Act, as amended by the No Child Left Behind Act" (Turnbull, 2005, p. 320). In so doing, the trend to further blur the lines between special education and general education continues. "We are moving away from rather rigid, categorical approaches for serving children and toward approaches that are intended to make additional resources dependent on educational needs rather than on categorical criteria resulting in years of frustration and failure" (Prasse, 2006, p. 14). Most notable changes include the requirement that special education teachers meet the highly qualified mandate of the No Child Left Behind Act; some flexibility in the identification of children with learning disabilities; changes in the IEP; modifications in the area of discipline; and the use of evidenced-based interventions (Cook, Tankersley, Cook, & Landrum, 2008).

Section 504 and the Americans with Disabilities Act

Two additional federal laws, Section 504 of the Rehabilitation Act of 1973 and the Americans with Disabilities Act (ADA), passed in 1990, provide a strong legal base for appropriate educational services for students with disabilities. Both of these laws are civil rights laws and do not provide funding for programs; they simply require that students with disabilities are protected against discrimination because of their disability (Smith & Patton, 2007).

Section 504 and the ADA extend coverage to individuals who meet the laws' definition of disability, individuals who are "otherwise qualified." Section 504 states: "No otherwise qualified individual with a disability, shall solely by reason of her or his disability, be excluded from participation in, be denied the benefits of, or be subjected to discrimination under any program or activity receiving federal financial assistance" (29 U.S.C.A. § 794). In other words, discrimination is a factor only if the person with the disability is qualified to engage in an activity and is prevented from doing so solely on the basis of the disability (Hulett, 2009).

Section 504 applies to programs and institutions that receive federal funds. The ADA, however, applies to just about everything except churches and private clubs. As a result, virtually every public accommodation and governmental agency must comply with the ADA, regardless of whether or not it receives federal funds. Private schools that do not receive federal funds do not have to comply with Section 504, but unless they are associated with a church, they do have to comply with the ADA.

Section 504 and the ADA use a very different approach to defining disability than that used in the IDEA. Under the IDEA, individuals are considered eligible for services if they have one of the recognized disabilities and need special education. Under 504 and the ADA, a person must have a mental or physical impairment that substantially limits a major life activity. Because the definition is broadly stated, some individuals who are classified as disabled under 504 and the ADA do not meet the eligibility criteria of the IDEA. The most recent reauthorization of the ADA discounts the impact of mitigating measures, such as medication, in determining eligibility. In other words, if a student with attention deficit disorder is not experiencing a substantial limitation in a major life activity because of appropriate use of medication, the student would still be covered under Section 504 and the ADA. **Personal Spotlight** provides a description of a student who is eligible for services under Section 504 but would not be eligible under IDEA.

PERSONAL SPOTLIGHT

RYAN is 17 years old and has been classified as having Asperger's syndrome for the past 8 years. He is very bright and makes good grades in his junior classes. Ryan receives supports from inclusive special education teachers in two of his classes, geometry and chemistry. He is a very good reader and does well in classes that require a lot of reading, including American literature, history, and political science. Ryan drives himself to school and is very responsible. Ryan's parents, who both work, are very involved in his education and social life. Ryan continues to spend lots of his free time with his parents; however, since getting his own car he does more with friends. Friendships have always been an issue with Ryan, who typically has a small group of loyal friends but not a large group. In his small group, Ryan enjoys video games, watching movies, and as a 17-year-old, just hanging out. He has always had a strong interest in cars and having his own vehicle has provided him with a great deal of satisfaction.

Ryan is very aware of having Asperger's syndrome. In fact, he says he is relieved that there is an underlying reason for some of his problems. Prior to his diagnosis, Ryan just thought he wasn't liked by his peers and he did not understand why he had difficulties getting along with others. Now that he understands his disability, he is not hesitant about telling others about his problems and why he has them. Ryan says that the worst thing about his disability is social relationships. While he has some friends and does things with them socially, he feels like he would like to have a greater number of friends and be more involved with social activities.

RIGHTS & RESPONSIBILITIES

COMPARISON OF IDEA, SECTION 504, AND ADA

AREA	IDEA	504	ADA
Who is covered?	All children ages 3 to 21 who have one of the designated disability areas who need special education	All individuals who have a disability as defined; no age restrictions	Same as 504
Who must comply?	All public schools in states that participate in IDEA	An entity that receives federal funds of any kind or amount	Any business, governmental agency, or public accommodation other than churches or private clubs
What is the basic requirement?	Provide eligible children with a free appropriate public education	Do not discriminate against any individual because of a disability	Same as 504
Due-process requirements	Provide notice and gain consent before taking specific actions with a child	Provide notice	Same as 504
Specific requirements	IEP Nondiscriminatory assessment Least restrictive environment	Accommodation plan Same as IDEA Same as IDEA	Same as 504 Same as IDEA Same as IDEA
Definition of free appropriate public education (FAPE)	A student's individual program determined by an IEP	An individual program designed to meet the disabled student's educational needs as well as the needs of nondisabled students are met	Same as 504
Transition requirements	Begin transition planning at age 16	No requirement	No requirement
Assessment	Nondiscriminatory comprehensive assessment before determining eligibility and developing an IEP; required every 3 years unless determined not needed	Nondiscriminatory pre-placement assessment before determining eligibility for 504 services and protections; required before any significant change of placement	Same as 504
Complaints	Due-process hearing, mediation, and resolution session must be offered. Attorney's fees may be granted to parents or school.	Administrative appeals must be offered; parents may go straight to federal court or file complaint with the Office for Civil Rights.	Same as 504; may file complaint with Department of Justice

(continued)

COMPARISON OF IDEA, SECTION 504, AND ADA *(continued)*

AREA	IDEA	504	ADA
Designated coordinator	No requirement	At least one person in each district must be designated in writing as the district 504 coordinator	Same as 504 (ADA coordinator)
Self-study	No requirement	Each district must form a committee and do a self-study to determine any areas where physical or program discrimination occurs. A plan to correct deficiencies must be developed.	Same as 504. Only areas added since 504 self-study must be reviewed.
Monitoring agency	U.S. Department of Education— Office of Special Education	Office for Civil Rights	Department of Justice

There are many similarities and differences between IDEA and 504/ADA. The **Rights and Responsibilities** feature compares the elements of the IDEA, Section 504, and the ADA. Although school personnel must adhere to the requirements and criteria established by the U.S. Department of Education, they must also remember that many students who are ineligible for classification as disabled still need assistance if they are to succeed in educational programs.

WHERE SHOULD STUDENTS WITH DISABILITIES BE EDUCATED?

The question about where students should be educated has been discussed and debated for many years. As previously noted, students with disabilities were originally educated in segregated environments; however, with the passage of federal legislation in 1975, the emphasis shifted to educating this group of students in general classroom settings as much as possible. The topic remains one of the key issues in the field of education for children with disabilities. Simply saying the word *inclusion* "is likely to engender fervent debate" (Kavale & Forness, 2000, p. 279).

Most of the students served under IDEA are considered mildly disabled and are served in general education classrooms for at least a portion of each school day (Prater, 2003). Students with more severe disabilities—a much smaller number of students—are less likely to be included in general classrooms a significant portion of the day but may be included in general education classrooms part of the time (Wolfe & Hall, 2003). Regardless of specific placements, the trend since the 1990s has been to increase the inclusion of students with disabilities with their nondisabled peers (Norwich, 2008).

Inclusion is no longer new for schools (Hines, 2008). As previously noted, approximately 75% of all students with disabilities are included for at least 40% of each day in general education classrooms and are taught by general education classroom teachers, and almost half of all children with disabilities are educated in general education classrooms most of the day (National Center for Education Statistics, 2009). In addition to these students, some students with more severe disabilities continue to spend a significant portion of their school days outside general education settings. The debate about where to best educate students with disabilities continues, even more than 30 years after the original passage of IDEA called for serving students in the least restrictive environment. Unlike earlier debate around whether students should or should not be included with nondisabled students, the current debate centers around how much students with disabilities should be included. Students can be placed in separate classrooms most of the school day; in general education classrooms for a majority of the school day and "pulled out" periodically and provided instruction in resource settings by special education teachers; or placed full-time in general education classrooms. In this latter model, special education teachers may go into general education classrooms and work with students who are experiencing difficulties or collaborate directly with classroom teachers to develop and implement methods and materials that will meet the needs of many students. Schools use the model that best meets the individual student's needs, developed through the IEP process.

The 2004 reauthorization of IDEA requires schools to have a continuum of alternative placements available "to meet the needs of children with disabilities for special education and related services" (IDEA, 2004). This **continuum-of-services model** provides a range of placements, including instruction in regular classes, special classes, special schools, home instruction, and instruction in hospitals and institutions. Therefore, while IDEA mandates that services be provided in the least restrictive environment, it also acknowledges that schools should have placement options available to meet the needs of individual students. As previously noted, the placement decision is based on numerous factors, but should primarily hinge on the student's IEP, which is developed by a multidisciplinary team (Horrocks, White, & Roberts, 2008).

■ For most students with disabilities and other special needs, general education classroom placements are appropriate for at least part of the day.

Inclusive Education Programs

Prior to the original passage of IDEA in 1975, students with disabilities received their educational programs in specialized classrooms, typically called self-contained classrooms. Serving students with disabilities in special programs was based on the presumption that general educators did not have the skills necessary to meet the needs of all students representing different learning needs (Shanker, 1994–1995). The result was that students were removed from the general education environment and were educated by specialists. Students placed in self-contained special education classrooms rarely interacted with their nondisabled peers, often even eating lunch separately. Likewise, the special education teacher interacted very little with nondisabled students or general classroom teachers. During the late 1960s and early 1970s, parents and professionals began questioning the efficacy of the self-contained model (Smith, Price, & Marsh, 1986). With the original passage of IDEA and the requirement to serve students with disabilities in the least restrictive environment, the special class model was doomed as the preferred service model (Blackman, 1989).

The resource room model replaced the self-contained model as the predominant method of serving students with disabilities in the 1970s and remained so until the 1990s. The resource room model was a "pullout" model where students were placed in special education classes for a portion of their instruction and integrated into general education classrooms for other activities. Unfortunately, the premise with the resource room model was that students with disabilities belonged in the special education classroom and were included in general education classrooms occasionally. Serving students with this model soon gave way to a more inclusive educational model.

Since the mid-1980s there has been a call by advocates for inclusion to dismantle the dual education system (general and special) in favor of a unified system that attempts to meet the needs of all students. Rather than spend a great deal of time and effort identifying students with special problems and determining whether they are eligible for special education services, proponents of a single educational system suggest that efforts be expended on providing appropriate services to all students. This model definitely fits into the current public school scenario where diversity will continue to increase over the next foreseeable future.

Currently, the terms "inclusion" and "responsible inclusion" are used to identify the movement to provide services to students with disabilities in general education settings (Smith & Dowdy, 1998). It is acknowledged that within the context of inclusion, some services to students may be necessary outside the general education classroom. While acknowledging that some students with disabilities may need some services outside the general classroom, proponents suggest that all students with disabilities belong with their nondisabled peers. Lamar-Dukes and Dukes (2005) state that "the move toward including students with disabilities in general education is fundamentally about the delivery of services in environments where students with disabilities have sufficient and systematic opportunities to engage with students without disabilities" (p. 55). When successful, inclusive schools result in a unified educational system for all students (Burstein, Sears, Wilcoxen, Cabello, & Spagna, 2004).

Inclusive education is both a philosophy and educational practice. Philosophically, inclusive education is based on the rights of all children, regardless of ability level, to have access to a quality educational program. Causton-Theoharis and Theoharis (2008) describe inclusive schools as "places where students, regardless of ability, race, language, and income, are integral members of classrooms, feel a connection to their peers, have access to rigorous and meaningful general education curricula and receive collaborative support to succeed" (p. 26).

From the philosophical perspective, there are four assumptions underlying inclusive education (Peters, 2007):

1. All students come to school with diverse needs and abilities, so no students are fundamentally different.
2. It is the responsibility of the general education system to be responsive to all students.
3. A responsive general education system provides high expectations and standards, quality academic curriculum and instruction that are flexible and relevant, an accessible environment, and teachers who are well prepared to address the educational needs of all students.
4. Progress in general education is a process evidenced by schools and communities working together to create citizens for an inclusive society who are educated to enjoy the full benefits, rights, and experiences of societal life (p. 99).

As an educational practice, inclusive education obviously attempts to provide equal access to academic instruction and social opportunities for all students, regardless of ability levels.

There are many different advantages to inclusion, including opportunities for social interaction (Peck & Scarpati, 2004); ease in accessing the general curriculum (Abell, Bauder, & Simmons, 2005); academic improvement (Hunt, Doering, & Hirose-Hatae, 2001); and positive outcomes for students with and without disabilities (Idol, 2006). Although they may not be included as extensively as students with mild disabilities, inclusion also creates learning opportunities for students with severe disabilities (Downing & Eichinger, 2003).

Just as there are many supporters of inclusion and reasons for its implementation, there are also professionals and parents who are not supportive of the movement. Among the reasons they oppose inclusion are the following:

- General educators have not been involved sufficiently and are therefore not likely to support the model.
- General educators as well as special educators do not have the collaboration skills necessary to make inclusion successful.
- There are limited empirical data to support the model. Therefore, full implementation should be put on hold until sound research supports the effort.
- Full inclusion of students with disabilities into general education classrooms may take away from students without disabilities and lessen their quality of education.
- Current funding, teacher training, and teacher certification are based on separate educational systems.
- Some students with disabilities do better when served in special education classes by special education teachers.

Although some of these criticisms may have merit, others have been discounted. For example, research indicates that the education of nondisabled students is not negatively affected by inclusion (National Study on Inclusion, 1995). Therefore, although the movement has its critics, research on inclusion provides support for its continuation.

Barriers to Inclusion

As with any change, regardless of advantages and disadvantages, there are several barriers to the successful implementation of inclusion. These include organizational barriers, attitudinal barriers, and knowledge barriers. Organizational barriers include the way schools and classrooms are organized. This could include physical organization as well as how the schedules are developed and how teachers are assigned to classes. Attitudinal barriers focus on the beliefs of teachers, administrators, and other school personnel about students with disabilities and inclusion. Finally, knowledge barriers are simply the limited knowledge about students with disabilities and inclusive teaching strategies. While all of these barriers could make it difficult to have a successful inclusive education program, each one can be overcome with various strategies (Darrow, 2009). It is the school's role to overcome these barriers so that students with disabilities can receive an appropriate education with their nondisabled peers (Runswick-Cole, 2008).

Role of Classroom Teachers in the Inclusion Model   In an inclusive model, general classroom teachers are the primary provider of instruction for students with disabilities. As a result, they must develop strategies to facilitate the successful inclusion of this group of students (Prater, 2003). Neither classroom teachers nor special education teachers want students with disabilities simply "dumped" into general education classes (Banks, 1992), and the successful inclusion of students does not normally happen without assistance. Therefore, school personnel must work on effective, cooperative methods to provide appropriate programs to all students.

Two methods are generally used to facilitate successful inclusion: facilitating the acceptance of the students with disabilities and providing services to support their academic success. Students with disabilities who are included in general education classrooms are not always automatically accepted by their nondisabled peers. As a result, it is the teacher's responsibility to promote this acceptance. In addition to facilitating acceptance, teachers must also implement instructional strategies that can be used to support inclusion. Examples of these include: (1) response to intervention, (2) cooperative learning, (3) peer supports, (4) strategy instruction, and (5) self-determination strategies.

Classroom teachers possibly play the most important role in the success of inclusion (Hobbs & Westling, 1998). Thus, they must be able to perform many different functions, including:

- Acting as a team member on assessment and IEP committees
- Advocating for children with disabilities when they are in general education classrooms and in special programs
- Counseling and interacting with parents of students with disabilities
- Individualizing instruction for students with disabilities
- Understanding and abiding by due-process procedures required by federal and state regulations
- Being innovative in providing equal educational opportunities for all students, including those with disabilities

Sharing responsibility among classroom teachers, special education teachers, and other specialists, such as reading teachers, is the key to providing effective educational programs for all students (Voltz, Brazil, & Ford, 2001). In general, the classroom teacher controls the educational programs for all students in the classroom, including students with disabilities, students at risk for developing problems, and those classified as gifted and talented. The attitude of the teacher toward students and the general climate the teacher establishes in the classroom have a major impact on the success of all students, particularly those with disabilities.

Role of Special Education Personnel in the Inclusion Model   The inclusion of students in general classrooms results in major changes in the roles of all school personnel (Burstein et al., 2004). In an inclusive model, special education teachers may not be the students' primary instructor but they might serve in a more supportive role, either in the general classroom setting or in a resource room. In the inclusion model, special education personnel become much more integral to the broad educational efforts of the school; they take on a very challenging role (Lamar-Dukes & Dukes, 2005). Using an RTI model, the special education teacher serves as a "key consultant assisting with planning, implementation, and evaluation of interventions across the continuum of education" (Cummings et al., 2008, p. 30). The special education teacher works much more closely with classroom teachers and Title I teachers in the inclusion model that uses RTI, with the result being increased opportunities for all students (Cummings et al., 2008). Regardless of specific interventions, collaboration among school personnel is critical for success (Prater, 2003).

Resource Room Support   There are some students with disabilities whose needs cannot be met fully in the general education classroom. Some may need additional interventions, which they can receive in a resource room. In the resource room setting, students have an opportunity to receive intensive interventions, usually in small groups, that enable them to improve their areas of weakness.

In the resource room service, a key role of special education personnel is to collaborate with classroom teachers to deliver appropriate programs to students with disabilities. Resource room teachers cannot simply focus on their students only when they are in the special education classroom. Close collaboration between the resource room teacher and the classroom teacher must occur to ensure that students receiving instruction in the special education room and general education classroom are not becoming confused by contradictory methods, assignments, curricula, and so on. The special education teacher should take the lead in opening up lines of communication and facilitating collaborative efforts.

PERCEPTIONS OF INCLUSION

Although parental and teacher support for inclusion is not mandatory, it is very important. Teachers, for the most part, have expressed support for inclusion. Idol (2006) conducted a recent program evaluation of eight schools to determine the extent of inclusion of students with disabilities. Perceptions of staff related to inclusion were also studied. Idol's findings included: (1) teachers had a positive attitude toward inclusion; (2) administrators supported inclusion; (3) few teachers preferred that students with disabilities should be educated in special classes; and (4) educators thought that inclusion had a positive impact on other students. "Overall, there was a trend among the participating educators of moving more and more toward the inclusion of students with disabilities in the general education classes" (Idol, 2006, p. 91).

On a philosophical level, few arguments have been levied against this movement. Who, for example, would argue against the idea of educating students together and giving all students equal opportunities? However, a great deal of discussion has occurred related to the implementation of inclusion. "Ideology may be useful in discussions attempting to establish goals and objectives, but actual practice is best derived from scientific inquiry" (Kavale & Forness, 2000, p. 289). Most teachers and administrators agree that inclusion is a good thing (Idol, 2006), but making decisions about how to achieve it is often problematic. Studies focusing on attitudes toward inclusion have involved two primary groups: general education teachers and parents.

The attitudes and behaviors of teachers toward students is the most important factor related to successful inclusion (Weiner, 2003). These attitudes and behaviors serve as a model for other school staff and students and are therefore critical (Horrocks et al., 2008). In 2004, Burstein and colleagues determined that the satisfaction of general classroom teachers and special education teachers concerning inclusion increased over time. They viewed inclusion as benefiting both students with disabilities and their nondisabled peers, facts that Idol (2006) confirmed in her study. In a recent study, Cook, Cameron, and Tankersley (2007) found different attitudes among teachers. They found that general classroom teachers expressed more concern and rejection of students with disabilities than they did for nondisabled students. It was noted that this could be the result of dealing with student behaviors that were initially responsible for their referral for special education services, behaviors that continued to result in rejection. However, findings also indicated that teachers had greater concern for students with disabilities than their nondisabled peers.

The success of collaboration between general and special education teachers and their willingness to implement accommodations are also impacted by teachers' attitudes. After studying the impact of a particular strategy on collaboration, Carter, Prater, Jackson, and Marchant (2009) found that "teachers' philosophical beliefs about disability had an effect on their collaborative experience and influenced their opinions of classroom accommodations and adaptations" (p. 67). They found that if teachers believe that disabilities are student-centered problems, they are less inclined to implement instructional accommodations. Rather, they expect students to make their own adaptations to be successful.

Results of these studies have a direct impact on teacher preparation. Teacher education programs must do a better job of preparing teachers, both general and special education, to work together to effectively implement inclusion in their schools, and schools must provide professional development for their staff to better prepare them for inclusive schools and classrooms (Cook et al., 2007). As the inclusion movement continues to dim the line between general education and special education, general classroom teachers are expected to meet the needs of a growing, diverse set of students, including those with varying ability levels.

In addition to teachers, the principals' attitudes toward inclusion are critical. Principals are in a unique position to influence the attitudes and behaviors of other school staff. "As schools become more inclusive, there is a strong need for principals who are able to clearly define and articulate a mission which incorporates the values of acceptance" (Horrocks et al., 2008, p. 1,463). This attitude can have a significant impact on the acceptance of students with disabilities by school staff. In a study of 14 elementary teachers who had students with significant disabilities included in their classrooms, it was noted that schools needed to have an articulate vision for inclusion, and that teachers "looked to their building principals to articulate this vision and demonstrate public support for inclusion" (Lohrmann & Bambara, 2006, p. 163).

In addition to support of educators, the support of parents for the inclusion of their children with disabilities in general education settings has a great deal to do with the ultimate success the child experiences (Stivers, Francis-Cropper, & Straus, 2008). For parents of students with disabilities, the reaction to the inclusion movement is mixed, ranging from complete support of the idea to skepticism, especially concerning the concept of full-time inclusion (Runswick-Cole, 2008). Because parental support is very important in the success of inclusion programs, schools should provide ways to educate parents about the benefits of inclusion and the need for their support (Stivers, Francis-Cropper, & Straus, 2008).

Duhaney and Salend (2000) did a literature review of parental perceptions of inclusive educational settings. After reviewing 17 studies published since 1985, they concluded that "parents of children with disabilities have mixed but generally positive perceptions toward inclusive educational placements" (p. 125). In the study by Burstein and colleagues (2004), parents of children with and without disabilities reflected positive reactions to inclusion, stating that the process was beneficial for all students in the school.

Many parents who oppose inclusion are concerned that their children will simply not receive the amount of attention they would in a special education setting and that their child will be ostracized, or they are worried that many general education teachers need additional training (Strong & Sandoval, 1999). These results were confirmed in the literature review by Duhaney and Salend (2000). As a result of these concerns, school personnel should assess the impact on individual children with disabilities to ensure that inclusion results in positive outcomes.

Runswick-Cole (2008) noted that parents who oppose inclusion are more likely to have a medical view of disability, whereas parents supporting inclusion are more likely to think of their child's disability as a barrier to learning. Regardless of reason, schools must remember that parents are involved in decision making about where a student should receive educational services. Parents, therefore, have a voice in how extensively inclusion may be implemented. One way of securing and maintaining a level of parental support for inclusion is regular communication (Lohrmann & Bambara, 2006).

In order for inclusion to be successful, the attitudes of nondisabled peers need to be positive. In a national survey of over 6,000 middle school students, Siperstein, Parker, Bardon, and Widman (2007) found that attitudes of nondisabled students toward individuals with intellectual disabilities and the inclusion of these students varied considerably. Although the majority of students thought it would be "OK" to include students with intellectual disabilities in their classes, there were some varying opinions about the impact. Some findings include the following:

- 88% believe students with intellectual disabilities can make friends with nondisabled students.
- 57% believe students with intellectual disabilities can learn academic subjects easily.
- 88% believe students with intellectual disabilities can participate in team sports with other students with intellectual disabilities.
- 63% believe that teachers would focus more on students with intellectual disabilities than on the rest of the class.
- 59% believe that it would be harder to concentrate if students with intellectual disabilities were included.

Most of the students in the survey did not have significant experiences with students with intellectual disabilities. In fact, only 38% of the nondisabled students reported ever having a classmate with intellectual disabilities in their class, and fewer than 10% currently had a student with intellectual disabilities in their class. The fact that many students in the survey had limited contact with students with intellectual disabilities could easily be one of the reasons for some of the negative attitudes toward inclusion. One way of dealing with the impact of limited contact with students with disabilities is to ensure that they are introduced appropriately when they are first included in a general classroom (Campbell, 2006).

Attitudinal research provides a glimpse of the challenges faced by professionals who support teaching students with special needs in inclusive settings. First, accurate information about inclusion in general and about individuals who need to be included must be distributed to teachers, parents, and the general public. Yet, the greatest challenge will be changing an educational system that presents great barriers to inclusion, because teachers' perceptions, attitudes, and opportunities for collaboration are directly related to the success of inclusion (Weiner, 2003). As noted earlier, barriers to inclusion can be overcome; they simply need to be identified first and then strategies can be developed to circumvent their impact.

CRITICAL DIMENSIONS OF INCLUSIVE CLASSROOMS

The concept of inclusion purports that students with special needs can be active, valued, fully participating members of a school community in which diversity is viewed as the norm and high-quality education is provided through a combination of meaningful curriculum, effective teaching, and necessary supports (Halvorsen & Neary, 2001). Anything less is unacceptable. Unlike other special education models, inclusion assumes that all students belong in the general education classroom and should be pulled out only when appropriate services cannot be provided in the inclusive setting. Several key structural and philosophical differences distinguish the inclusive model and more traditional special education models. Figure 1.2 depicts some of these differences.

Obviously, including students with diverse learning needs creates challenges for educators. There are many different factors critical to the success of inclusion. Webber (1997)

| FIGURE 1.2 | Structure and Philosophy: Differences between Traditional and Inclusive Models |

Traditional Models

1. Some students do not "fit" in general education classes.
2. The teacher is the instructional leader.

3. Students learn from teachers and teachers solve the problems.
4. Students are purposely grouped by similar ability.

5. Instruction is geared toward middle-achieving students.
6. Grade-level placement is considered synonymous with curricular content.
7. Instruction is often passive, competitive, didactic, and/or teacher-directed.
8. Most instructional supports are provided outside the classroom.
9. Students who do not "fit in" are excluded from general classes and/or activities.
10. The classroom teacher assumes ownership for the education of general education students, and special education staff assume ownership for the education of students with special needs.
11. Students are evaluated by common standards.

12. Students' success is achieved by meeting common standards.

Inclusive Educational Models

1. All students "fit" in general education classrooms.
2. Collaborative teams share leadership responsibilities.
3. Students and teachers learn from one another and solve problems together.
4. Students are purposely grouped by differing abilities.
5. Instruction is geared to match students at all levels of achievement.
6. Grade-level placement and individual curricular content are independent of each other.
7. Instruction is active, creative, and collaborative among members of the classroom.
8. Most instructional supports are provided within the classroom.
9. Activities are designed to include students though participation levels may vary.
10. The classroom teacher, special educators, related service staff, and families assume shared ownership for educating all students.
11. Students are evaluated by individually appropriate standards.
12. The system of education is considered successful when it strives to meet each student's needs. Students' success is achieved when both individual and group goals are met.

Source: Adapted from "Problem-Solving Methods to Facilitate Inclusive Education," by M. F. Giangreco, C. J. Cloniger, R. E. Dennis, and S. W. Edelman, 1994, in *Creativity and Collaborative Learning: A Practical Guide to Empowering Students and Teachers*, edited by J. S. Thousand, R. A. Villa, and A. J. Nevin. Baltimore: Paul H. Brookes Publishing. Used by permission.

identified five essential features that characterize successful inclusion of students with special needs: (1) a sense of community and social acceptance, (2) an appreciation of student diversity, (3) attention to curricular needs, (4) effective management and instruction, and (5) personnel support and collaboration. Voltz, Brazil, and Ford (2001) list three critical elements: (1) active, meaningful participation in the inclusive setting, (2) sense of belonging, and (3) shared ownership among faculty. Finally, Mastropieri and Scruggs (2001) add administrative support to the list. The five dimensions for successful inclusion identified by Webber (1997) are discussed in the following sections.

Sense of Community and Social Acceptance

The physical placement of students with disabilities in inclusive classes is not the intent of inclusion. Students with special needs are truly included in their classroom communities only when they are appreciated by their teachers and accepted socially by their classmates. An understanding teacher more effectively meets students' instructional and curricular needs, and social acceptance among classmates contributes to students' self-perception of value. Both of these goals are equally critical to creating effective inclusive settings and responsible learning environments. It is imperative that we address the need for acceptance, belonging, and friendship as integral components of an inclusive educational model (Murray & Greenberg, 2006).

Teachers play the most important role in creating a positive classroom environment where students with disabilities can be accepted because they control several factors that are essential to establishing a successful inclusive setting (Favazza, Phillipsen, & Kumar, 2000). These include teacher attitudes, teacher expectations, teacher competence, teacher collaborative skills, and teacher support (Lohrmann & Bambara, 2006; Mastropieri & Scruggs, 2001). These factors are directly related to a positive classroom environment and are critical for the success of inclusion.

An important part of creating a positive classroom environment is teachers' attitudes about inclusion and students with disabilities. Teachers need to have a positive attitude about students with special needs being in their classrooms and also have high expectations of these students. Their attitudes and behaviors toward students are actually mirrored by students in the class (Lohrmann & Bambara, 2006). If teachers are not supportive of students with disabilities being included, then it is less likely that these students will be accepted by their nondisabled peers.

Teachers also must prepare students to interact with others whose physical characteristics, behaviors, or learning-related needs require special consideration. Physically placing students with disabilities in inclusive settings will not guarantee social involvement of these students with their nondisabled peers. Sometimes students need to be educated about diversity and disabilities to reduce the fear of differences. While teachers can serve as excellent role models for acceptance of diversity, they can also facilitate interactions and acceptance by orchestrating situations where students with and without disabilities interact. In studying the importance of social relationships in the lives of students, Murray and Greenberg (2006) concluded that school personnel must develop intervention strategies to help students with disabilities form better relations with their peers and with adults. Often, simply how a student with a disability is introduced to the class will have an impact on the student's acceptability (Campbell, 2006).

When determining if the school does promote a sense of community and social acceptance, school personnel can ask the following questions:

- Are students with disabilities disproportionately teased by other students?
- Do students with disabilities seem to enjoy being in the general education classroom?
- Do students without disabilities voluntarily include students with disabilities in various activities?
- Do students without disabilities seem to value the ideas and opinions of students with disabilities? Do students with disabilities seem to value the ideas and opinions of nondisabled students?
- Do students with disabilities consider the general education classroom to be their "real class"? Do they consider the general education teacher to be one of their "real teachers" (Voltz et al., 2001, p. 25)?

While students may develop friendships and a classroom community naturally, it is often necessary for school personnel to facilitate the development of these relationships. There are several different strategies teachers can use to facilitate friendships, including: (1) selecting the appropriate classroom for including some students, (2) scheduling students into classes with appropriate peers, (3) selecting student supports wisely, (4) preparing the classroom teacher, (5) preparing the general education students, (6) preparing students with disabilities, and (7) securing and maintaining family support (Boutot, 2007).

Appreciation of Student Diversity

The most important issue underlying the success of inclusion is the acceptance of diversity in general. Today's students bring a much more diverse set of backgrounds than ever before. This includes differences in language, race, ethnicity, socioeconomic status, gender, sexual orientation, and academic skills (Salend, 2008). And, there is no doubt that the diversity found in our schools will only increase in the future. The U.S. Census Bureau (2008) projects the following related to increases in diversity:

- In 2042, minorities will account for more than 50% of the population.
- In 2050, minorities will account for 54% of the population.
- In 2023, minorities will account for more than half of all children.
- In 2050, 62% of children will be from minority groups.
- Hispanic population will triple, from 46.7 million to 132.8 million between 2008 and 2050.
- Asian population will increase from 15.5 million to 40.6 million between 2008 and 2050.

Our increasingly diverse society is reflected in our student population. Teachers today have to deal with a wide variety of language and learning abilities (Rueda, Monzo, Shapiro, Gomez, & Blacher, 2005). Unfortunately, acceptance of diverse students is not likely to happen easily or without major changes in the way many schools operate (Polloway et al., 2011). While some teachers and administrators readily accept diverse students, others may not. Teachers and all other school personnel must develop an understanding of the relationship between a student's culture and behavior and view the student as part of his or her cultural background (Cartledge & Kourea, 2008).

Even though diversity is generally viewed as a good thing, it can create difficulties for teachers and schools. For example, students who do not speak English as their primary language can cause difficulties for classroom teachers, not to mention their own educational opportunities. Likewise, students with disabilities can also create challenges for classroom teachers. It is important to remember that one teacher can have a dramatic effect on the lives of all students, including those who are different and who have learning challenges. It should also be remembered that steps toward the successful inclusion of diverse students can be taken on a classroom-by-classroom and school-by-school basis. The "successful inclusion of students with disabilities requires fundamental change in the organizational structures of schools and in the roles and responsibilities of teachers" (Burstein, Sears, Wilcoxen, Cabello, & Spagna, 2004, p. 105).

The increasing diversity of today's classrooms makes teaching a very complex activity that will likely become more complex in the future as our culture becomes even more diverse (Maheady, Harper, & Mallette, 2001). As a result, it is imperative that all school personnel develop an understanding of the different cultures represented in schools and the relationship between a student's culture and behavior. Students must be viewed as part of a culture (Cartledge & Kourea, 2008).

In addition to recognizing and responding to each student's educational needs, teachers must be sensitive to the cultural, community, and family values that can have an impact on a student's educational experience. For instance, the nature of teacher-student interactions can be directly affected by certain cultural factors, or the type of home-school contact will be dictated by how the family wants to interact with the school.

Attention to Curricular Needs

Many discussions of inclusion lose track of an important consideration: what the student needs to learn. Too often inclusion as a movement becomes the priority when, in fact, the place where students with disabilities are educated should be dictated by their individual learning needs. Teachers must seriously look at the curriculum and ask what students are learning and how students with disabilities can access the curriculum (Pugach & Warger, 2001). If the individual curricular needs of a student are not being met, the curriculum must be modified or the educational placement must be reexamined. Good teachers vary their curricula to meet the needs of the students (Walther-Thomas, Lorinek, McLaughlin, & Williams, 2000).

Effective Management and Instruction

Effective management and instruction are two critical components for inclusion. If teachers lack skills in these areas, inclusion will not be successful. These practices include four elements: successful classroom management, effective instructional techniques, appropriate accommodative practices, and instructional flexibility.

Successful Classroom Management   Classrooms that encourage learning are characterized by sound organizational and management systems. Classroom management—including physical, procedural, instructional, and behavior management—sets the stage for the smooth delivery of instruction. Effective classroom management is required if students are to benefit from any form of instruction, especially in inclusive classrooms where students display a wide range of diversity (Jones & Jones, 2007). Without effective classroom organization and management, learning will not be optimal for any student.

Effective Instructional Techniques   Students with disabilities, especially those eligible for special education services, by definition, have learning problems and need special education. As a result, effective instructional techniques must be used if these students are to be successful. Universal design for learning (UDL) is one method of assisting students with disabilities achieve at successful levels in content classes. UDL uses three primary components: (1) representation—multiple ways of presenting content; (2) expression—alternative means of expressing what has been learned; and (3) engagement—an instructional plan that incorporates students' choices in projects and assignments (Kurtis, Matthews, & Smallwood, 2009). One of the primary purposes of using UDL is to meet the needs of all students, not just those with disabilities. As a result, this model works well in inclusive classrooms where diversity is the norm rather than the exception (Bouck, Courtad, Heutsche, Okolo, & Englert, 2009).

Appropriate Accommodative Practices   Some students require special adaptations to the physical environment, the curriculum, the way instruction is provided, or the assignments given to them. Many students with disabilities are capable of achieving academic success, but only with appropriate accommodations. These can be general accommodations that are appropriate for all students, or disability-specific interventions.

Instructional Flexibility   The ability to respond to unexpected and changing situations to support students with special needs is a key characteristic of responsible inclusive settings. In their study of 14 elementary teachers who had students with severe disabilities included in their classes, Lohrmann and Bambara (2006) noted that teachers had to be flexible in order to be successful. This flexibility was described as a willingness to listen to different ideas, try new ideas, think "outside the box," go with the flow, and keeping tuned in to what was happening in the classroom.

One method that results in instructional flexibility is differentiated instruction. Originally used as a tool for meeting the needs of gifted students, differentiated instruction is now considered an appropriate tool for meeting the needs of all students, including those with disabilities (van Garderen & Whittaker, 2006). Differentiated instruction can be described as planning and implementing curricula and instruction to address the diverse learning needs of students—in other words, instructional flexibility. Table 1.4 provides an overview and examples of differentiated instruction. See the nearby differentiated instruction features for examples of using this approach for elementary and secondary students.

Personnel Support and Collaboration

Students with special needs require more than instructional support; they also need personnel support to allow them to benefit from placement in inclusive settings. While the classroom teacher is the primary instructional provider for students included in general classrooms, additional supports may be needed to facilitate success. This support is typically provided by special education teachers, **paraeducators**, and other related service professionals—such as speech and language pathologists, occupational and physical therapists, and audiologists. A high level of collaboration is required for the necessary personnel resources to work together effectively. This can be accomplished through a variety of collaboration models, including collaboration-consultation, peer support systems, teacher assistance teams, and co-teaching.

The use of teams to provide services to students with disabilities, especially students included in general education classrooms, has grown significantly over the past several years.

TABLE 1.4

Overview and Examples of Key Concepts for Differentiated Instruction

ELEMENTS	EXAMPLES
Content: What is taught and how access to the information and IDEAs that matter is given	• Texts at varied reading levels • Provision of organizers to guide note-taking • Use of examples and illustrations based on student interest • Present in visual, auditory, and kinesthetic modes • Provide materials in the primary language of second-language learners
Process: How students come to understand and "own" the knowledge, skills, and understanding	• Vary the pacing of student work • Use cooperative grouping strategies (e.g., Think-Pair-Share, Jigsaw) • Develop activities that seek multiple perspectives on topics and issues • Highlight critical passages in a text • Tiered assignments
Product: Student demonstration of what he or she has come to know, understand, and be able to do	• Provide bookmarked Internet sites at different levels of complexity for research sources • Develop rubrics for success based on both grade-level expectations and individual student learning needs • Teach students how to use a wide range of product formats (e.g., presentation software)
Affect: Student linking of thought and feeling in the classroom	• Modeling respect • Help students examine multiple perspectives on important issues • Ensure consistently equitable participation of every student
Learning Environment: Classroom function and feeling	• Rearrange furniture to allow for individual, small-group, and whole-group work • Availability of supplies and materials (e.g., paint, paper, pencil) • Procedures for working at various places in the room and for various tasks

Source: From "Planning Differentiated Multicultural Instruction for Secondary Classrooms," by D. van Garderen and C. Whittaker, 2006, *Teaching Exceptional Children*, p. 14. Used with permission.

Differentiating Elementary Instruction

Salend (2008) summarized how teachers can differentiate instruction under the following situations.

How can I differentiate instruction for students?

- Tailor curricular goals and teaching strategies to individual strengths and challenges
- Use individualized curricular, teaching, and instructional materials accommodations
- Use universally designed materials
- Provide personal support
- Address students' learning styles, preferences, and sensory abilities
- Consider acceptability

How can I differentiate instruction for students who have difficulty reading and gaining information from print materials?

- Use a variety of teacher- and student-directed text comprehension strategies
- Make materials more readable

How can I differentiate instruction for students from diverse cultural and language backgrounds?

- Use a multicultural curriculum
- Use multicultural instructional materials
- Use culturally relevant and responsive teaching strategies
- Use reciprocal interaction
- Use effective ESL techniques
- Encourage students to respond

Source: Salend (2008).

Differentiating

Secondary Instruction

PREHISTORIC MAN RESEARCH PROJECT

Essential Question: How did early man survive, and what was each group of early man's greatest accomplishment to the development of present-day hunters?

Materials: textbook; trade books, periodicals, hand-outs, various websites

Task: Use a variety of resources to determine how early man contributed to modern man.

	GROUP 1	GROUP 2	GROUP 3
Topic	*Australopithecus* and *Habilis*	*Habilis* and *Erectus*	Neanderthal and Cro-Magnon
Required # of sources	1 book 1 website	2 books 2 web sites	Minimum 2 books 1 periodical 1 video
Research information	Dates of existence Physical characteristics Description of shelters & food Famous archeologist and site	All of Group 1 plus Description of tools/ inventions and how used Evidence of family or social structure	All of Groups 1 & 2 plus Evidence of religion Evidence of language Evidence of art or culture
Research writing	Word process an historical fiction narrative on your life as an *Australopithecus* or *Habilis*	Word process an historical fiction narrative on your life as an *Habilis* or *Erectus*	Word process an historic fiction on your life as a Neanderthal or Cro-Magnon
Project	Build a model Perform a demonstration Create a slogan Advertising main ideas	Build a model Write a poem or rap Create a poster with drawings, clip art, and google images	Write a poem, rap, or song Word process an informational brochure with clip art or images

Source: Marquis & Hughes, Memorial Middle School, Beverly, MA.

A primary reason for this growth is the realization that it takes a creative use of manpower to effectively implement an inclusion teaching model. General education teachers and special education teachers must share knowledge of teaching strategies and curricula in order to implement effective instruction. Several critical variables must be in place for these teams to be successful, ranging from knowing the purpose of the team to making sure that the team appreciates disagreement. Figure 1.3 lists variables for success for teams determined by Fleming and Monda-Amaya in a 2001 study.

FIGURE 1.3	Critical Variables for Team Efforts and Effectiveness, Ranked by Categories

Team Goals
Purpose of the team is clear.
Team goals are understood by all members.
Team goals are regularly reviewed.
Team goals are established by team members.
Team goals are clearly stated.
Team goals are modified by team members.
Team goals are supported by the family.
Team goals are attainable.
Team goals are prioritized.
Members anticipate both positive and negative outcomes.
Members are satisfied with goals that have been selected.

Team Roles and Team Membership
Team members are committed to the team process.
The team has a leader.
Members are accountable to the team.
Team roles are clearly understood.
Team roles are perceived by members as being important.
New team members are added when practical.
The team leader is unbiased.

Team Communication
Decisions are made for the good of the student.
Team members have adequate listening time.
Decisions are alterable.
Team members have equal opportunities to speak.
Decisions are reached by consensus.

Team Cohesion
Members feel safe sharing ideas.
The team has trust among members.

Members (especially parents) feel equally empowered.
The team has a unified goal.
The team has time to celebrate.
The team has support from superiors.
Members have respect for one another.
The team has recognition for efforts.
The team has autonomy for decision making.
The team has a healthy regard for disagreement.

Team Logistics
Progress is evaluated internally, by members.
Team procedures are clearly understood.

Team Outcomes
The team makes modifications to the plan as needed.
Members are clear about their responsibilities for the plan.
Members are committed to implementing the plan.
Solutions are practical.
A plan was implemented.
The team reviews the impact of the plan.
A plan was developed.
Parent satisfaction is part of the evaluation.
Outcomes are evaluated internally, by members.
The family is generally feeling better.
A plan was agreed on.
A decision was made.
Outcomes are evaluated at regularly scheduled times.
Members are satisfied with the plan.

Source: From "Process Variables Critical for Team Effectiveness," by J. L. Fleming and L. E. Monda-Amaya, 2001, *Remedial and Special Education, 22,* p. 168. Used with permission.

SUMMARY

History of Education for Students with Disabilities

- The U.S. public school system attempts to provide 13 years of equal educational opportunity to all American citizens.
- Today's student population is very diverse and includes students with a variety of disabilities.
- A sizable percentage of students are at risk for developing problems, present learning or behavior problems, or may be classified as having a disability.

Defining Students with Special Needs

- The largest group of students with special needs in the public school system consists of those formally classified as having disabilities.

- Intellectual disabilities, learning disabilities, and emotional and behavior disorders make up the majority of student disabilities.
- In addition to students with disabilities served under IDEA, students with disabilities served under Section 504 and the ADA, students classified as gifted and talented, and students who are at risk for developing problems are considered students with special needs.

Current Services for Students with Special Needs

- Services for students with disabilities have evolved significantly during the past 20 years.
- Public Law 94–142, now the IDEA, provides the framework for services to students with disabilities in school settings.
- IDEA provides extensive regulations related to how children are identified, evaluated, and served.
- All students served under IDEA must have an individualized education plan and be educated in the least restrictive environment.

Where Should Students with Disabilities Be Educated?

- About 70% of all students with disabilities spend a substantial portion of each school day in general education classrooms.
- Inclusion is the current model for educating students with disabilities.
- Inclusion requires schools to educate students with disabilities with their nondisabled peers as much as possible.
- In an inclusion model, students with disabilities belong with their nondisabled peers.

Perceptions of Inclusion

- General education teachers play a very critical role in providing services to students with disabilities.
- The attitudes of classroom teachers are extremely important in the quality of services rendered to students with disabilities.
- Most classroom teachers are supportive of an inclusion model.
- Parental support for inclusion is important for its ultimate success.

Critical Dimensions of Inclusion

- A sense of community is important for inclusion to be successful.
- Appreciation for diversity is critical for inclusion.
- Effective management, curricular adaptations, and flexible instructional techniques must be present in an inclusive classroom.

PEARSON
myeducationlab

The MyEducationLab for this course can help you solidify your comprehension of Chapter 1 concepts.

- Gauge and further develop your understanding of chapter concepts by taking the quizzes and examining the enrichment materials on the Chapter 1 Study Plan.
- Visit Topic 1, Inclusive Practices, to:
  - Connect with challenge-based interactive modules, case study units, and podcasts that provide research-validated information about working with students in inclusive settings by visiting the IRIS Center Resources
  - Explore Assignments and Activities, assignable exercises showing concepts in action through video, cases, and student and teacher artifacts
  - Practice and strengthen skills essential to quality teaching through the Building Teaching Skills and Dispositions lessons

2

Professional Collaboration and Home–School Collaboration

CHAPTER OBJECTIVES

After reading this chapter, you should be able to:

1. Describe the different models of professional collaboration.
2. Discuss the particular challenges for creating and maintaining inclusive classrooms.
3. Describe how to plan for successful inclusion, one student at a time.
4. Describe the concept of family in our society.
5. Describe the impact children with disabilities have on families.
6. Discuss how schools and parents can collaborate on the education of students with disabilities.
7. Describe some specific home-based interventions for families of children with disabilities.

BILL and MARY were on top of their world. They were in their late twenties and had been married for 5 years. Both had great professional jobs, and Mary was pregnant. They had planned on having two children before getting into their thirties so they could both focus on raising their family and their professional careers. Needless to say, when they found out Mary was pregnant they were very happy. Things were going according to plan. Mary had no difficulties during pregnancy, and she and Bill did not want to know the sex of their child. Not having any high risk factors, and a seemingly normal pregnancy, Bill and Mary were counting down the days until the child was born.

Bill and Mary's daughter was born after only 5 hours of labor, without any complications. As soon as the child was born the obstetrician noted that there were some indicators of spasticity, a form of cerebral palsy that results in uncontrollable muscle contractures. Bill and Mary were both heartbroken and concerned. On the advice of the physicians at the hospital, the child, named Anika, was referred to the local children's hospital for an evaluation. The evaluation revealed that Anika, indeed, had the spasticity form of cerebral palsy that affected her arms and legs. While she would likely be able to walk, the cerebral palsy would definitely impact her use of her arms and legs for her entire life. The news hit Bill and Mary hard. Not only did their child's condition not fit their plans, but the likelihood that she would need

extensive supports for her entire life made them realize that their lives were changed forever in a direction they had not intended.

The first thing Bill and Mary did after getting Anika home from the hospital was to try to find as much information as possible about cerebral palsy and spasticity, as well as services for children with this disorder. Faced with the myriad of information, they were still at a loss as to what to do first. Bill and Mary asked themselves many questions, including: (1) Should one of us quit our jobs to provide full-time care for Anika? (2) Should we even consider having other children? and (3) How can we pay for all the services that Anika may need?

QUESTIONS TO CONSIDER

1. Analyze Bill and Mary's potential feelings and possible reactions upon learning that Anika has a disability.
2. What advice, recommendations, and help would you provide for these parents?
3. What would you tell them about the advantages and challenges of inclusive preschool programs?
4. What influence could Anika's condition have on Bill and Mary's marriage?
5. How could other parents who have children like Anika help Bill and Mary deal with their crisis?

PROFESSIONAL COLLABORATION

Collaboration can be described as two or more individuals working together for a common purpose (Taylor et al., 2009). It occurs in many different places, including work settings, sports activities, domestic activities, yard work, and in just about any other endeavor where more than one individual can work with others. Collaboration is used in public education in many different ways; some examples include "grade-level meetings, departmental meetings, field trip organization, school site councils, consultation between colleagues or specialists, and curriculum planning" (Murawski & Hughes, 2009, p. 269). The inclusion of students with disabilities in general education classrooms presents an ideal opportunity for collaboration among educators. In an inclusive classroom, collaboration occurs when general classroom teachers work in partnership with special education teachers "to design environments that ensure the academic and social success for all students" (Meadan & Monda-Amaya, 2008, p. 165). This collaboration occurs both formally, when teams are formed around a particular child, and informally, when two or more teachers get together and discuss how to meet a child's specific needs (Friend & Cook, 2010). Formal collaboration is "a system of planned cooperative activities where general educators and special educators share roles and responsibilities for student learning" (Wiggins & Damore, 2006, p. 49). In other words, collaboration occurs when two or more professionals purposely work together to provide supports and services for this group of students.

Collaboration among general and special education professionals has become a key component of effective schools and a necessity for successful inclusion. It can occur in a variety of settings and activities, including prereferral efforts and IEP meetings, consulting and cooperative teaching arrangements, and teacher assistance teams. A relatively new practice, response to intervention, would not be possible without collaboration (Murawski & Hughes, 2009). Stuart and Rinaldi (2009) describe a collaborative planning framework for teachers using an RTI model. This approach can result in professional learning communities that are capable of designing and implementing instruction in an RTI approach (Stuart & Rinaldi, 2009). Effective collaboration enables teachers to expand interventions after dealing with target behaviors into areas such as classroom climate and environment (Meadan & Monda-Amaya, 2008). It provides general classroom teachers with the support that is necessary for them to successfully deliver appropriate educational services to students with disabilities and is imperative if inclusion is to be successful (Tannok, 2009).

While there are significant benefits resulting from collaboration, many schools implement collaborative models because "everyone else is doing it." Implementing a collaborative model for this reason may result in failure. In order for collaborative models to work effectively, collaboration should be implemented for the right reasons and introduced through professional development for general and special education personnel (Wiggins & Damore, 2006). There are many different ways schools can encourage collaboration among school staff; one particular model is no better than another. Educators need to understand the variations that are possible and implement the approach that best meets their needs and the needs of their students. The most important thing to remember is that when working together in a collaborative model to solve problems, teachers and students can both benefit (Santangelo, 2009).

Collaboration-Consultation

Collaboration-consultation emphasizes a close working relationship between general and special educators. Through collaborating with one another, general education and special education teachers can bring more ideas and experiences to help students achieve success. Communication skills are absolutely critical for collaboration-consultation to be successful. As with any process, the more individuals involved in a child's educational program, the more effective communication must be. Communication allows the sharing of information about a student, expertise, perceptions, concerns, ideas, and questions (Halvorsen & Neary, 2001). Without good communication, educators will not be able to work together as a team to develop and

Visit the MyEducationLab for this course to enhance your understanding of chapter concepts with a personalized Study Plan. You'll also have the opportunity to hone your teaching skills through video-based Assignments and Activities, IRIS Center Resources, and Building Teaching Skills and Disposition lessons.

■ Teachers often need to work together to solve some of the challenges created by inclusion.

deliver appropriate educational programs. A second critical requirement for collaboration-consultation is time. Teachers must have time to discuss and plan interventions regardless of the collaboration approach used. Unfortunately, the logistics of arranging planning time are often complicated. Teachers may not share planning periods, and in elementary schools teachers may not even have planning periods. Also, students with disabilities included in secondary schools may have six or seven general classroom teachers, making it extremely difficult to find time for all teachers to participate in the planning process (Halvorsen & Neary, 2001).

Making planning time available for school staff requires the support of school administrators. School administrators who support inclusion will generally find a way to arrange for planning opportunities for professionals and paraprofessionals. On the other hand, administrators who are not supportive of inclusion or do not see the need for planning time are less likely to make the time available for their teachers. Making time for teachers and other staff members to plan for specific students can be accomplished in several ways. Arranging for team members to have the same planning periods, having split schedules for teachers, using roving aides to cover classes, and providing financial incentives are only a few methods for finding planning time. Regardless of how it is accomplished, the fact remains that without time to plan, many attempts to provide supports for students with disabilities in general education classes will be unsuccessful. Table 2.1 provides some recommendations for enhancing collaboration.

Co-Teaching

Another model that provides support for students in general education classrooms is **cooperative teaching**, or **co-teaching**. Co-teaching is an instructional model in which a special education teacher and a general classroom teacher share instructional efforts and responsibilities for students with disabilities included in a general education classroom (Sileo & van Garderen, 2010). This model has become very popular and is used extensively (Murawski & Dieker, 2008). One of the positive outcomes of this model is that students do not have to leave the classroom to receive assistance in the resource room; rather, they have the support of two different teachers in the general classroom (Murawski & Hughes, 2009). While the resource room service is still important for some students, meeting their needs in the general classroom and not requiring them to go to another setting is less disruptive and results in a more inclusive environment.

Co-teaching is a logical outgrowth of collaborative efforts between teachers. It includes consultative arrangements, additional help given by special education teachers to children with and without disabilities, and the sharing of teaching assistants, especially to accompany students who are disabled in the general education classroom. This model combines the content expertise of the classroom teacher with the pedagogical skills of the special education teacher. Stated another way, successful co-teaching occurs when the "expertise of the masters of content—the content area teachers—are blended with and supported by the expertise of the masters of access—the specialists in differentiating instruction" (Villa, Thousand, & Nevin, 2008). Co-teaching is perhaps the best vehicle for attaining successful inclusive classrooms; it truly provides supported education, the school-based equivalent of supported work in which students are placed in general education classrooms and provided the necessary support by the special educator to be successful.

Co-teaching is not a simple solution for the many challenges of accommodating a broad range of students with disabilities. It requires both thoughtful planning and consideration. Scruggs, Mastropieri, and McDuffie (2007) reviewed 32 qualitative studies of co-teaching in inclusive classrooms to determine some of the variables associated with successful co-teaching efforts. Their analysis revealed that in order for co-teaching to be effective, several factors need to be present, including administrative support, planning time, training, and compatibility. Several teachers indicated that an effective co-teaching arrangement is similar to a good marriage.

TABLE 2.1

Recommendations for Enhancing Tangible and Intangible Collaboration

RECOMMENDATION	IMPLEMENTATION
Tangibles	
Develop written schedules for the classroom	Create a chart of interventions with a target date for completion and those responsible. Include daily opportunities for classroom teachers to reflect on the implementation of, and clarify focus on, interventions developed during group meetings.
Scheduled meetings	Choose a regular date and time to meet throughout the term or school year, such as the second Tuesday of each month at 3:30 p.m. Record meeting schedules and ensure that all members are aware of all scheduled meetings. Consider appointing one member to record meeting dates and provide all members with an e-mail reminder.
Specific questioning techniques	Eliminate general questions: ask specific questions only (e.g., Who will serve as the leader and follow up on ensuring tasks are completed?). Encourage members to forward questions to the group leader so these questions can be included on the meeting agenda for general discussion.
Reviewing student work	Set aside a portion of each scheduled meeting to review student work (identify a specific area to review, such as fine motor skills, at each meeting). Include not only the tangible accomplishments of the student, such as a worksheet, but also an understanding of the intangible process for the student, such as the student's enjoyment of or struggle with a specific task or method of instruction.
Intangibles	
Listen and hear	Seek to reflect on key points made by others and how the points can be incorporated into ongoing plans. Make certain members hear and understand your points.
Common vision	Articulate and record the vision, or goals, of the group (revisit the vision at the start of each meeting as a foundation for any meeting). Make sure that each member of the team is given an opportunity to share insights and thoughts and reflect on the expressions of others.
Mutual respect	Value ideas provided by each member of the collaborative team; trust that each member seeks to provide the best program. Demonstrate respect for the process by arriving at meetings on time and prepared to discuss the agenda topics and being accountable to the group for agreed-on actions.
Nurturing relationships	Recognize, accept, and support one another as professionals with unique bodies of knowledge and unique frameworks on which information and decisions will be interpreted. Appreciate that all members bring a unique set of experiences to the team.

Source: From M. T. Tannock (2009). "Tangible and intangible elements of collaborative teaching." *Intervention in School and Clinic, 44,* p. 175. Used with permission.

The planning component is critical for successfully implementing this model. If co-teachers do not have time to plan their instruction, the process will likely break down without achieving its optimal level of success (Sileo & van Garderen, 2010). Teachers involved in co-teaching activities have rated having scheduled planning time and administrative support as either very important or important (Austin, 2001). Figure 2.1 reflects the ratings of other areas by co-teachers.

Another critical issue regarding co-teaching is voluntary involvement. Setting up cooperative teaching arrangements without regard to input from the teachers themselves will

FIGURE 2.1

Comparison of percentages of very important and important responses of co-teachers in value versus access categories.

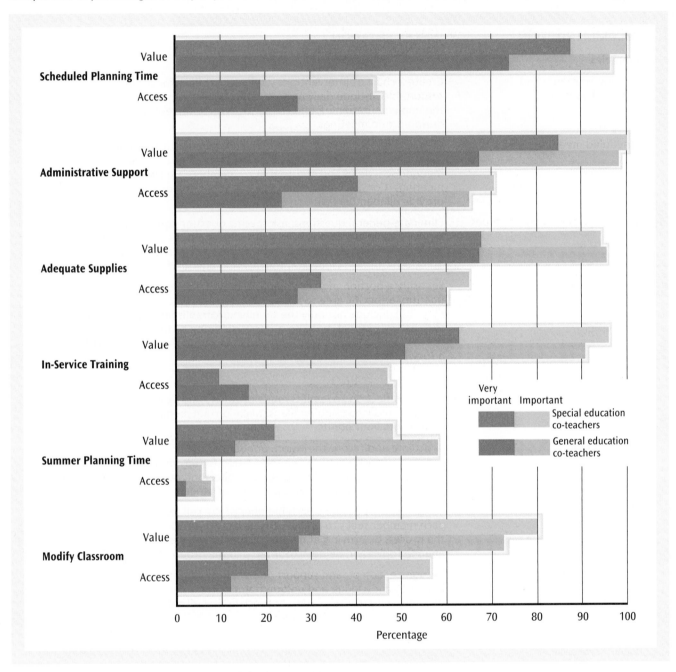

Source: From Austin, *Remedial and Special Education 4*(22). July/August 2001.

not set the stage for success for teachers or, ultimately, for students. Teachers should be given some choice and flexibility—for example, allowing general and special education teachers to select partners with whom to collaborate has worked well. Enabling teachers to select their co-teaching partners can help with compatibility; one of the obvious difficulties in implementing the co-teaching model is ensuring the compatibility of the individuals working together. Mastropieri and colleagues (2005) found that "when co-teachers are getting along and working well together, students with disabilities are more likely to be successful and have successful experiences in the inclusive environment" (p. 268).

In addition to volunteering for co-teaching assignments, having planning time and administrative support, and being compatible with each other, there are other characteristics often found among successful co-teachers. Some of these include professional enthusiasm and competence, good communication and problem-solving skills, mutual respect, flexibility, and good organizational skills (Walther-Thomas et al., 2000).

While co-teaching looks like it is a model that will continue to expand, often co-teachers burn out and may choose not to continue (Murawski & Dieker, 2008). Stivers (2008) suggested several different activities that could strengthen the relationship between co-teachers and thus prevent some of this burn-out. Examples of these suggestions include (1) set aside large blocks of time for planning, (2) try different co-teaching models, (3) re-examine the physical layout of the classroom, (4) attend professional development workshops together, and (5) address conflicts in ways that are comfortable to both parties. When conflicts do arise between co-teachers, an important element in resolving the conflict is support from the principal (Hines, 2008).

Cooperative Teaching Arrangements

Co-teaching usually occurs at set times, such as during second period every day or on certain days of each week. When students with disabilities are included in general education classrooms, the special education teacher, who becomes a co-teacher, is usually present (Friend & Bursuck, 2008). Co-teachers perform many tasks jointly, including planning and teaching, developing instructional accommodations, monitoring and evaluating students, and communicating student progress (Walther-Thomas et al., 2000).

Although co-teaching can be implemented in many ways, it essentially involves collaboration between special and general education teachers in the environment of the general education classroom, typically for several periods per day. Sileo and van Garderen (2010) discuss several different models of co-teaching, including (1) one teach, one observe; (2) team teaching; (3) alternative teaching; (4) parallel teaching; (5) station teaching; and (6) one teach, one drift. The one teach, one observe appears to be the most frequently used model (Scruggs et al., 2007). Table 2.2 summarizes each of these models.

TABLE 2.2

Characteristics of Different Co-Teaching Structures

TYPE OF CO-TEACHING STRUCTURE	CHARACTERISTICS
One Teach/One Observe	One teacher teaches the entire group, other teacher observes. Good for data collection, monitor and support student behaviors.
Team Teaching	Teachers share equally in planning and delivering instruction. Both teachers usually teach a large group of students together. Students can break into smaller groups for cooperative learning.
Alternative Teaching	One teacher teaches a small group; other teaches large group. Excellent for providing individual feedback and instruction.
Parallel Teaching	Teachers plan together and teach simultaneously to two groups. Class is typically divided into two equal or near equal groups. Provides opportunities to work with smaller numbers.
Station Teaching	Teachers divide responsibility for instructional content. Students divided into groups that work on different activities.
One Teach/One Drift	Similar to one teach/one observe. While one teacher teaches the other moves throughout classroom. Provides opportunity for checking work and giving extra support.

Source: From J. M. Sileo & D. van Garderen (2010). "Creating optimal opportunities to learn mathematics." *Teaching Exceptional Children, 42,* 14–21.

Differentiating Elementary Instruction

TEACHING A LESSON ON ADDITION (1ST GRADE)

Tier I

Students use manipulatives to add single digit numbers together.

Teacher—Students put 6 straws in one pile and 5 straws in another pile. Now put the piles together and count how many straws you have.

Tier II

Students add digits together (no manipulatives).

Teacher—Students look at the problems on the board. Add the two numbers together to determine your solution.

Tier III

Students are given a problem orally that requires them to add two single digits together to determine the answer to the problem.

Teacher—Students listen to this problem. Jacob had 8 pennies and his mother gave him 7 more. How many pennies did Jacob have?

Differentiating Secondary Instruction

The involvement of parents and other family members in intervention strategies has been described a great deal in the literature. Parents and other family members need to understand how to differentiate instruction when engaged in instructional activity. DiPipi-Hoy and Jitendra (2004) identify six general rules for parent-delivered differentiated instruction related to teaching purchasing skills to young adults with disabilities outside the home setting. These include:

1. Review the target skill prior to leaving the house.
2. Refrain from jumping in to help too quickly.
3. Do not complete the entire step when providing assistance.
4. Allow for self-correction of errors prior to intervening.
5. Direct a store clerk's attention to the student when the clerk attempts to communicate with the parent.
6. Discuss the routine, provide praise for appropriate behaviors, and address areas that need improvement with the student on the way home.

Source: From DiPipi-Hoy & Jitendra, 2004, p. 145.

Teacher Assistance Teams   Another collaborative model to provide support to students in general education classrooms is the use of **teacher assistance teams**. Teacher assistance teams can be defined as "school-based, problem-solving teams designed to enable all teachers to meet the needs of their students demonstrating difficulties" (Walther-Thomas et al., 2000, p. 140). These teams, comprised of teachers and other instructional support personnel, provide a forum where problems are raised and discussed, and solutions are developed. The use of teacher assistance teams enables educators to bring a diverse set of skills and experience to bear on specific problems. One example is for teacher assistance teams to provide suggestions for differentiating instruction. See the nearby differentiated instruction features as examples for elementary and secondary classrooms.

Westling, Cooper-Duffy, Prohn, Ray, and Herzog (2005) describe a teacher support program that incorporates different types of support. While a teacher assistance team provides useful collaborative opportunities around particular students, the teacher support program includes a wider array of supports for teachers. These include:

1. Collaborative-problem solving and mutual support sessions, where specific problems are discussed
2. Electronic networking and communication sessions, where teachers communicate via online chat rooms to discuss various issues
3. Information and materials search, where teachers request specific information about different problems they are encountering
4. On-site/in-class consultation, where a consultant actually comes to a classroom to observe and provide specific suggestions and supports

This broader range of supports is intended to help teachers deal with stress and burnout. In a study to validate the system, it was determined that the teacher support program did provide substantial supports (Westling, Herzog, Cooper-Duffy, et al., 2006).

Peer Support Systems   Educators must realize that the staffing needed to successfully support students with disabilities in inclusive settings is increasing while the resources of many schools is on the decline. One way to help address the growing staffing problem is through **peer support systems** (Kroeger & Kouche, 2006). In this model, students with disabilities in general education classrooms receive social or instructional support from their nondisabled peers (Dobbs & Block, 2004). While not the same as professional collaboration, peer support systems do result in collaborative efforts on behalf of students with disabilities. Peer support systems are some of the best means to provide assistance to this group of students in general education classrooms because students rely on the natural support of other students (Copeland et al., 2004). Peer support systems can be used for instructional support as well as social support. In the area of instruction, peer supports can be provided in any academic area. For example, peer supports have been shown to improve students' literacy skills for English language learners (McMaster, Kung, Han, & Cao, 2008). A side benefit from peer support for instruction is the improvement in the social involvement of students with disabilities (Nelson, Caldarella, Young, & Webb, 2008). And, although peer support systems are implemented to improve skills of students with disabilities, an additional benefit is that both parties benefit—students with disabilities as well as those without (Carr, 2008). Peer support for instruction can be provided in several different ways, such as peer tutoring, peer assessment, peer modeling, and cooperative learning (Ryan, Reid, & Epstein, 2004). Table 2.3 summarizes various peer support models.

When implementing any peer support system, school personnel must always remember that while these approaches may work extremely well in some situations, the peers providing the support are also students. They may provide a great deal of help, but providing the necessary support to enable students to be successful remains a professional responsibility. Prior to implementing a peer tutoring program, students involved in the program should receive some instruction in how to carry out their role as peer tutors. Primary methods for providing this training include using graphics and scripts, role-play, and video and DVD presentations (Gardner, Nobel, Hessler, Yawn, & Heron, 2007). In addition to providing instruction for peer tutors prior to implementing the program, there are other guidelines that should be considered. Figure 2.2 describes some of these guidelines.

One method of implementing peer support systems is through service learning. In this model, students with and without disabilities are engaged in community activities. This gives opportunities for students with and without disabilities to benefit from the service learning projects while providing needed supports for students with disabilities. In a study of peer buddy systems implemented through service learning, nearly 50% of all peer buddies felt that the program resulted in their providing assistance to their buddies, while enabling them to perform service activities (Hughes et al., 2001).

In addition to one-on-one peer tutoring, this model can also be implemented using a classwide approach. Classwide peer tutoring programs use a reciprocal peer support system; students serve as tutors and then reverse roles and are tutored. Research has supported this model, noting that students with and without disabilities benefit. Classwide peer tutoring

TABLE 2.3

Different Types of Peer Supports

Cooperative Learning
Cooperative learning occurs when students are involved in teaching and learning together as a team. There are numerous cooperative learning models, including teams where students rotate among groups and provide similar instruction to each group and team members provide instruction to other team members about a particular topic.

Cross-Age Tutoring
Cross-age tutoring occurs when students who are usually older provide academic support to younger students who are experiencing learning difficulties.

Peer Tutoring
Peer tutoring is either one student assisting another student or an entire class of students pair up and provide tutoring to each other. In the tutoring situations, students provide academic, instructional support to each other, either taking turns in providing support or one student serving as the primary support member of the team. Peer-assisted learning strategies (PALS) is a type of peer tutoring wherein students frequently trade teams and all students have the opportunity to serve as the tutor or tutee.

Peer Assessment
Peers are involved in evaluating academic work of peers. This model has been used extensively. A simple version is to have students trade papers and grade each other on an assignment.

Peer Modeling
Students are instructed to exhibit specific behaviors and then model those behaviors in front of their peers. Teachers make a point to discuss the students' appropriate behaviors.

Peer Reinforcement
Students, usually those without disabilities, provide reinforcement to their peers with disabilities for appropriate behaviors.

Source: From J. B. Ryan, R. Reid, and M. H. Epstein. (2004). "Peer Mediated Intervention Studies on Academic Achievement for Students with EBD." *Remedial and Special Education, 25,* 329–335.

FIGURE 2.2	Implementation Guidelines for Peer Tutoring Programs

1. Explain the purpose and rationale for the technique. Stress the idea of increased opportunities for practice and "on-task" behavior.
2. Stress collaboration and cooperation rather than competition.
3. Select the content and instructional materials for tutoring sessions.
4. Train students in the roles of tutor and tutee. Include specific procedures for (a) feedback for correct responses, (b) error correction procedures, and (c) score-keeping.
5. Model appropriate behaviors for tutor and tutee. Demonstrate acceptable ways to give and accept corrective feedback.
6. Provide sample scripts for student practice of roles. Divide the class into practice pairs and teams.
7. Let pairs practice roles of tutor as teacher circulates and provides feedback and reinforcement.
8. Conduct further discussion regarding constructive and nonconstructive pair behavior. Answer questions and problem-solve as needed.
9. Let pairs switch roles and practice new roles as teacher circulates and provides feedback and reinforcement. Repeat Step 8.

Source: From "Classwide Peer Tutoring at Work," by B. M. Fulk and K. King, 2001, *Teaching Exceptional Children, 34,* p. 49. Used with permission.

results in benefits for both teachers and students, and in instructional benefits. As with one-on-one peer tutoring, students need to receive instruction in the model prior to implementation of a classwide peer tutoring program. Teachers need to ensure that materials for tutoring and assessment criteria are available for students (Bowman-Perrott, 2009).

Using Paraprofessionals

In addition to collaborative teaching models and peer support systems, the use of paraprofessionals to provide direct support to students with learning problems is occurring more commonly. In fact it is "one of the primary mechanisms by which students with disabilities are being supported in general educational classes" (Cavkaytar & Pollard, 2009, p. 382). Paraprofessionals have been referred to as "sous-chefs," meaning they work closely with the teacher (chef) to provide instructional support and sometimes direct instruction to students with learning difficulties (Causton-Theoharis, Giangreco, Doyle, & Vadasy, 2007). The most recent IDEA amendments specifically note that "paraprofessionals who are adequately trained and supervised may assist in the delivery of special education and related services" ([Part B, Sec. 612 (a) (15)]). Therefore, IDEA provides regulatory support for using paraprofessionals in a direct support role for students with disabilities (Carroll, 2001) and indicates that paraprofessionals should have adequate training. Carroll (2001) suggests that this training should include professional interaction, communication, and conflict-management skills. The U.S. Department of Education (2003) noted that in the 2000–2001 school year, 321,657 paraprofessionals were involved in providing education services to children with disabilities.

■ Paraeducators can provide direct services to some students with special needs in general classrooms.

The mere presence of paraprofessionals in inclusive classrooms does not automatically result in their appropriate use. Having individual paraprofessionals obligated all day to one particular student can actually be detrimental because it could result in the student's separation from classmates, unnecessary dependence, and even interference with the teacher's efforts at instruction (Giangreco, Yuan, McKenzie, et. al., 2005). Paraprofessionals can have great potential at facilitating inclusion as long as proper safeguards ensure that they implement support services effectively.

One problem with using paraprofessionals is that often their role is unclear. Whereas sometimes they take a major responsibility for the education of some students with disabilities, in other settings they function primarily as clerical aides. Still, their role in providing instruction appears to be increasing. This can be accomplished through one-on-one instruction or in small groups. In addition to providing direct instruction, paraprofessionals can teach students how to use learning strategies, and then reinforce their use (Keller, Bucholz, & Brady, 2007). Quilty (2007) studied the ability of paraprofessionals to write and implement social stories for students with autism spectrum disorders. After providing paraprofessionals with appropriate training, they were able to develop and use social stories effectively with students with this group of students.

In addition to direct instructional roles, there are many other roles that paraprofessionals can play, including (1) performing clerical tasks, (2) supervising students in group settings, and (3) working with students in the areas of social skills. Regardless of the specific role played by paraprofessionals, classroom teachers must provide appropriate supervision to ensure student learning. Some elements of effective supervision of paraprofessionals include (Carnahan, Williamson, Clarke, & Sorenson, 2009):

• Establishing a shared philosophy
• Using effective communication
• Holding regularly scheduled meetings
• Evaluating paraprofessional's knowledge and experience
• Providing professional development opportunities
• Engaging in problem-solving strategies around issues

Unfortunately, some districts experience a high turnover rate among paraprofessionals. This can create problems for schools because of the difficulty in finding qualified individuals to fill this important role and the amount of time and effort required to provide training for newly employed paraprofessionals. Some of the reasons paraprofessionals have been found to leave their jobs include: (1) low wages, (2) poor benefits, (3) normal life events, such as entering college or retirement, (4) changing positions within the school, and (5) conflicts within the special education team (Ghere & York-Barr, 2007). School personnel should become proactive in order to prevent paraprofessionals from leaving their positions.

CREATING AND MAINTAINING INCLUSIVE CLASSROOMS

Responsible, inclusive classrooms do not just happen. In order for inclusive educational programs to be successful, a great deal of planning and preparation must occur. Schools cannot decide to implement an inclusive model without extensive planning and effort. The first thing schools must do is to prepare staff for inclusion.

Preparing Staff for Inclusion

A comprehensive program for preparing a school setting for inclusion must consider the involvement of all staff members. As Roach (1995) points out, "Successful planning models ensure that all teachers, paraprofessionals, and related service personnel are included in the process" (p. 298). Although many preservice training programs acquaint teachers-in-training with working with students with diverse needs, the nature of this preparation varies greatly. Moreover, many teachers who are already in the field have not been exposed to information important for implementing good inclusive practices. This conclusion is supported by the data discussed earlier in this chapter.

The primary goals of all preservice and in-service training of general education teachers include creating positive attitudes about working with students with diverse needs and allaying apprehensions and concerns teachers might have about their competence to address the needs of these students. These goals are achieved by three major training-related activities: (1) opportunities to see good examples of inclusion; (2) provision of information about inclusion, student diversity, and inclusion-related practices, together with the development of skills that a teacher needs to feel comfortable and competent when working with students with special needs; and (3) time to plan with team members.

Exposure to Good Inclusive Classrooms   Nothing is more encouraging and motivating than to see wonderful examples of what one wants to achieve. It is essential that teachers have opportunities to visit schools or classrooms that demonstrate the five critical dimensions of inclusion discussed earlier in this chapter. It is one thing to talk about these practices, and yet another to see them being implemented. A number of projects in the United States have developed model inclusion classrooms. These settings can serve as demonstration sites that teachers can observe and imitate.

Information and Skills Needed   Teachers regularly express a desire to know more about the inclusion process, the needs of students with learning-related challenges, and ways to address these needs. Teachers must find practical ways of matching individual needs with sound instructional practices. For teachers to become comfortable in making and implementing such decisions, they must have sufficient training in management techniques, instructional strategies, and curriculum adaptation tactics. Studies have shown, for example, that curriculum modifications are a very positive predictor of academic success (Lee, Wehmeyer, Soukup, & Palmer, 2010). However, the intervention may not be successful if teachers do not have the necessary skills to link appropriate accommodations with specific needs.

Teachers can also benefit from instruction in topics such as social skills, self-determination, learning strategies, and study skills. From time to time, updates and new ideas in these important areas can be offered to teaching staff to spark strategies and deepen knowledge. In turn, teachers can enhance the social acceptance of students with special needs by instructing their classes in social skills, such as how to make and keep friends.

Other skills are also needed in most inclusive arrangements. First and foremost are skills in collaboration. General education teachers will need to work collaboratively with other professionals within the school setting, especially special education staff, and with parents or other individuals who are responsible for students at home.

Preparing Students for Inclusion

The goals for preparing students for inclusion, like those for staff, focus on developing positive attitudes and allaying concerns. Ultimately, we want students to understand the needs of others who are different and to welcome them into the classroom community as valued members. Many nondisabled students have not been involved with students with special needs. As a result, the movement to inclusive schools often results in students being unprepared for dealing with such diverse classrooms. While nondisabled students are generally supportive of inclusion, they need to be prepared for the changes that accompany this educational model. Awareness programs, class discussions, simulations, guest speakers, and social interactions can pave the way for inclusion.

Awareness Programs   Over the years, an assortment of formal programs has emerged to help change the attitudes of nondisabled students toward their classmates who have special needs. Discussions and simulations are among the different ways to develop and implement these programs.

Discussions   In-class discussion is a good way to address topics related to students with special needs. Topics for discussion can be found in a variety of sources, including books and films about disabilities or famous people with special needs who have been successful in a variety of fields. Guest speakers can also be effective. Schulz and Carpenter (1995) warn, however, that "caution must be taken to ensure that the discussions are based on accurate information, avoiding the possibility that uninformed biases would form the core of the exchanges" (p. 400).

Imaginative literature offers many examples of characters with special needs. A great source of information for elementary students is children's literature. A number of books have been written about disabilities or conditions that might directly relate to students who are about to be included in a general education class. Prater and Dyches (2008) have identified the top 25 children's books that portray characters with disabilities; Table 2.4 lists these books. In addition to literature, films can also be used to stimulate discussion about people with special needs. Examples of such films include *Rainman*, about a young adult with autism; *Sybil*, mental illness; and *Forrest Gump*, intellectual disabilities. When using literature or film, teachers need to be cautious that the material included is authentic and will not be overgeneralized. It must be stressed that individuals with disabilities, like individuals without disabilities, vary significantly in their abilities and disabilities and every person is unique in specific areas.

Guest speakers with disabilities can provide positive role models for students with disabilities, give all students exposure to individuals who are different in some way, and generate meaningful class discussion. However, the choice of guest speakers must match the intended purposes of the teacher. For example, securing a guest speaker who is in a wheelchair and who has a negative attitude about his or her condition may not serve a positive purpose for the class. Advance planning and communication ensure that maximum benefit is achieved from this type of experience and also avoid inappropriate presentations. Guest speakers who are comfortable and effective when talking with students usually can be identified through local agencies and organizations.

Simulations   Simulating a specific condition, to give students the opportunity to feel what it might be like to have the condition, is a common practice. For example, visual impairment

TABLE 2.4

Top 25 Children's Books Portraying Characters with Disabilities

TITLE, AUTHOR (ILLUSTRATOR OR PHOTOGRAPHER, IF ANY), PUBLISHER, AND YEAR	DISABILITY	AWARDS	TYPE OF BOOK	GRADE LEVEL
The ADDed Touch, Robyn Watson (Susanne Nuccio), Silver Star, 2000	ADHD		Picture	K+
Al Capone Does My Shirts, Gennifer Choldenko, Putnam, 2004	Autism	Newbery Honor	Chapter	5+
The Alphabet War, Diane Burton Robb (Gail Piazza), Whitman, 2004	Learning disabilities		Picture	K+
The Bus People, Rachel Anderson, Holt, 1989	Various disabilities		Chapter	5+
Crow Boy, Taro Yashima, Viking, 1955	Autism	Caldecott Honor	Picture	K+
The Curious Incident of the Dog in the Night-Time, Mark Haddon, Random House, 2003	Autism	Dolly Gray	Chapter	9+
Dad and Me in the Morning, Patricia Lakin (Robert G. Steele), Whitman, 1994	Deafness	Schneider Family	Picture	K+
Flying Solo, Ralph Fletcher, Clarion, 1998	Communication disorders		Picture	K+
Freak the Mighty, Rodman Philbrick, Scholastic, 1993	Learning disabilities; orthopedic and other health impairments		Chapter	6+
The Handmade Alphabet, Laura Rankin (Laura Rankin), Dial, 1991	Deafness		Picture	K+
Hank Zipzer Series, Henry Winkler, Penguin Group, 2006	Learning disabilities		Chapter	4+
Hooway for Wodney Wat, Helen Lester (Lynn Munsinger), Houghton Mifflin, 1999	Communication disorders		Picture	K+
Kissing Doorknobs, Terry Spencer Hesser, Delacorte, 1998	Emotional/ behavioral disorders		Chapter	7+
Knots on a Counting Rope, Bill Martin Jr. and John Archambault (Ted Rand), Holt, 1987	Visual impairment		Picture	K+
Life Magic, Melrose Cooper, Holt, 1996	Other health impairment; learning disabilities		Chapter	4+
Lois Lowry Trilogy, *The Giver* (2000), *Gathering Blue* (2002), and *Messenger*, Delacorte Books for Young Readers, 2005	Various disabilities	Newbery Medal for *The Giver*	Chapter	6+
My Brother Sammy, Becky Edwards and David Armitage, Millbrook, 1999	Autism	Dolly Gray	Picture	K+
Rules, Cynthia Lord, Scholastic, 2006	Autism; orthopedic impairment; communication disorders	Newbery Honor	Chapter	4+
See the Ocean, Estelle Condra (Linda Crockett-Blassingame), Ideals Children's Books, 1994	Visual impairment		Picture	K+

TABLE 2.4 (continued)

TITLE, AUTHOR (ILLUSTRATOR OR PHOTOGRAPHER, IF ANY), PUBLISHER, AND YEAR	DISABILITY	AWARDS	TYPE OF BOOK	GRADE LEVEL
So B. It, Sarah Weeks, HarperCollins, 2004	Intellectual disabilities	Dolly Gray	Chapter	6+
Thank You, Mr. Falker, Patricia Polacco (Patricia Polacco), Philomel, 1998	Learning disabilities		Picture	K+
The Confessions, Janet Tashjian, Holt, 1997	Intellectual disabilities	Dolly Gray	Chapter	4+
The View from Saturday, E. L. Konigsburg, Aladdin, 1996	Orthopedic impairment	Newbery Medal	Chapter	4+
The Westing Game, Ellen Raskin, Penguin, 1978	Orthopedic impairment	Newbery Medal	Chapter	4+
Yours Turly, Shirley, Ann M. Martin, Holiday House, 1988	Learning disabilities		Chapter	4+

Source: From M. A. Prater & T. T. Dyches (2008). "Books that portray characters with disabilities." *Teaching Exceptional Children, 40,* p. 34. Used with permission.

is often simulated by blindfolding sighted students and having them perform activities that they typically use their vision to perform. In another simulation, students can use a wheelchair for a period of time to experience this type of mobility.

Although simulations can be effective in engendering positive attitudes toward individuals with special needs, this technique should be used with caution. It is impossible to understand the impact of a disability during a brief simulation and, also, some simulation activities seem to be amusing, rather than meaningful, to students. Therefore, teachers must use caution when simulations are conducted to ensure that they serve their intended purpose.

Maintaining Effective Inclusive Classrooms

Setting up a responsible inclusive classroom does not guarantee that it will remain effective over time. Constant vigilance concerning the critical dimensions of inclusive settings and ongoing reevaluation of standard operating procedures can ensure continued success. Too often teachers, both special education and general education, become disenchanted with the process and often burn out (Westling et al., 2006). This may be partly due to the educational system constantly asking teachers to do more. As federal legislation focuses more on accountability systems, many teachers feel that they do not have time to teach students—the real reason they become teachers. A system needs to be in place to monitor and evaluate inclusion programs as well as provide appropriate support for teachers involved in delivering the programs.

Westling and colleagues (2006) describe a teacher support program designed to provide the necessary assistance for teachers involved in delivering services in inclusive settings. The program was founded on five principles:

1. Teachers can help each other through collaborative problem solving as well as other types of mutual support, but can also benefit from additional expertise.
2. A support program for teachers should be available to all teachers but not required of any, should offer multiple types of support, and should allow for flexible participation.
3. A support program should provide valid information and assistance to deal with practical problems, and teachers should have the opportunity to specify the type of information or assistance they need and how it should be delivered.

4. Support must be disassociated from evaluation or judgment.

5. A support program should not create additional problems or increase stress (Westling et al., 2006, p. 137).

The teacher support program provides for problem-solving meetings, electronic networking, information materials search, peer mentoring, on-site class consultation, teacher release, and staff development workshops. After an initial review of the program it was found to have a positive impact on dealing with issues (Westling et al., 2006).

Maintaining flexibility contributes to long-term success; rigid procedures cannot adequately address the unpredictable situations that arise as challenges to management and instruction. Unforeseen problems will inevitably surface as a result of including students with special needs in general education classrooms. The more flexible a school can be in dealing with new challenges, the more likely it is that responsible inclusion will continue.

PLANNING FOR SUCCESSFUL INCLUSION ONE STUDENT AT A TIME

Regardless of how much time and effort have been expended to create an environment that is conducive for students with disabilities to achieve success in general education classrooms, the fact remains that planning must be accomplished for students on an individual basis. Students with disabilities cannot simply be placed in a classroom regardless of the supports provided or teaching methods used and be expected to succeed. School personnel must develop a planning model that provides opportunities for school staff to develop supportive, individualized inclusive environments for each student. Successful inclusion does not just happen; it must be planned and the necessary instructional and administrative supports developed.

The first action that is required, when planning for successful inclusion one student at a time, is to determine the individual needs of the student. Inclusion does not mean placing

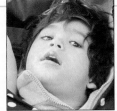

IEP GOALS AND OBJECTIVES FOR ANIKA WHEN SHE IS IN THE THIRD GRADE

Because Anika's primary difficulties result in her ability to use her arms and legs effectively and social skills, her IEP goals and objectives reflect these two primary areas of concern.

GOAL 1   To improve the use of her handwriting skills.

Objective 1: Anika will be able to form individual cursive letters that are legible when given a verbal prompt.

Objective 2: Anika will be able to write 10 sentences legibly when given a written prompt by her teacher.

GOAL 2   To improve her mobility skills.

Objective 1: Anika will be able to move from her classroom to the school cafeteria in 10 minutes or less, without assistance.

Objective 2: Anika will be able to carry her lunch tray from the lunch line to a nearby table without assistance.

GOAL 3   To improve her social skills.

Objective 1: Anika will increase her social skills by 25%, as measured by a social skills assessment instrument, over a 6-week period.

Objective 2: Anika will take turns when playing board games every day for a two-week period.

TIPS FOR ADAPTING A LESSON FOR ANIKA

Because Anika's primary problems deal with limited use of her arms and legs, classroom adaptions will focus on physical accessibility and manipulations. These could include the following:

- Widen aisles for wheelchairs, walkers, or crutches.
- Place paper and other materials in Anika's reach.
- Allow Anika to use a tape recorder or another person to make a written record of notes, assignments, or other materials.
- Allow extra time for tests and written assignments.

- Allow Anika to use a tape recorder or another person to record test answers or other written assignments.
- Have materials on the board or overhead projector lower on the wall for eye-level visibility.

Source: L. Nowak. How to deal with cerebral palsy in the classroom. www.ehow.com/how_4968531_deal-cerebral-palsy-classroom.html

PERSONAL SPOTLIGHT

ELIZABETH FLIPPO has been a special education teacher for more than 20 years. As a result, she has seen significant changes in how students with disabilities are provided educational services in our public schools. "Early in my teaching career, my classroom was always separate from the remainder of the school. We might have class in the basement, but more likely our classroom was in a portable building behind the regular school. This was simply the way it was; nobody thought anything about it. As far as we were concerned, special education should be separate." Obviously, things have changed dramatically over the past 20 years, and now more and more special education classes are in the same building as other classes. In fact, if buildings are over crowded and there are temporary buildings, it is just as likely that general education classes are in the portable buildings as special education classes.

Not only were special education students educated in separate buildings, but their curriculum was also separate. As Elizabeth notes, "my students had very little contact with their nondisabled peers. Indeed, it was rare that they were ever in the same room as other students. Some years my students even had their lunch period separate." Obviously, with the movement to include students with disabilities in general classrooms as much as possible, and the mandate that students with disabilities have access to the general curriculum, the way we educate students with disabilities has also changed dramatically. Currently, Elizabeth teaches students with severe disabilities in a middle school. "I think the way we provide services to our students now is so much better than before. Even my students with severe disabilities are included in many of the things that other students do at the school. They go to pep rallies, school assemblies, and participate in areas of the curriculum where they can achieve some level of success, such as physical education."

Elizabeth definitely thinks that the way we serve our students today is better than it was when she started teaching. "I love it," notes Elizabeth. "I think we are not only doing the right thing for these kids but it also provides an opportunity for nondisabled students to get a better understanding of their peers who are disabled. It's a win-win situation for everyone."

students in inclusive settings regardless of their needs. Rather, inclusion is assuming students belong in general education classrooms, but building programs around students' needs. When determining the least restrictive environment for an individual student during the IEP process, school personnel should be sure that each student's unique characteristics have been considered in the planning process. See the nearby IEP Goals and Objectives for Anika and the nearby box on Tips for Adapting a Lesson for Anika.

School personnel must routinely review their programs to ensure that their buildings, programs, and instructional techniques support the inclusion of students with disabilities and other special needs. Figure 2.3 includes 10 questions that can facilitate a discussion among school personnel around reviewing school programs and inclusion. Inclusion is a reality in our schools. The nearby personal spotlight shows the support for this model by a special education teacher.

FIGURE 2.3	Ten Discussion Questions Related to Inclusion

Using the scale below, rate the extent to which you agree or disagree with each statement. After rating the items independently, discuss your responses with your partner(s). Identify the area(s) that you and your partner(s) feel could be strengthened. Jointly identify strategies that could be used to strengthen these areas.

1—strongly disagree 2—disagree 3—unsure 4—agree 5—strongly agree

1. Students with disabilities are engaged in classroom learning activities along with their nondisabled peers. 1 2 3 4 5
2. Students with disabilities participate productively in classroom learning activities. 1 2 3 4 5
3. Effective instruction strategies are used to meet the educational needs of students with disabilities. 1 2 3 4 5
4. Students with and without disabilities interact frequently. 1 2 3 4 5
5. Students with disabilities seem to enjoy being in the general education classroom. 1 2 3 4 5
6. Nondisabled students voluntarily include students with disabilities in various activities. 1 2 3 4 5
7. Students with disabilities consider the general education classroom to be their "real" class. 1 2 3 4 5
8. When general and special educators are discussing students with and without disabilities words like "our" and "we" are used more often than words like "your" or "you." 1 2 3 4 5
9. Students with disabilities are included in any school accountability system that may be used. 1 2 3 4 5
10. The problems and successes involving students with and without disabilities are shared by general and special educators. 1 2 3 4 5

Comments: _____

_____

_____

_____

_____

_____

_____

Source: From "What Matters Most in Inclusive Education: A Practical Guide for Moving Forward," by D. L. Voltz, N. Brazil, and A. Ford, 2001, *Intervention in School and Clinic, 37,* p. 28. Used with permission.

Collaboration with Families of Students with Disabilities

Prior to the enactment of IDEA, schools frequently did not encourage parents of children with special needs to actively participate in the education of their children. However, given the numerous concerns that parents may have, and given the value of family input into educational programs, increasing parental involvement is a welcome trend. Federal law formally established the role of parents relative to students with special needs through IDEA (Werts, Harris, Tillery, & Roark, 2004). Regarding parental involvement, IDEA requires schools to:

- Inform parents in understandable language of impending actions regarding their child's education.
- Involve parents in decisions regarding the education of their child.
- Honor parents' decision for no special education services.
- Make available due-process rights for parents and their child.
- Enable parents to request a due-process hearing, or engage in mediation or resolution efforts in cases of disagreements with schools.

RIGHTS & RESPONSIBILITIES

PARENT RIGHTS UNDER IDEA

Notice—Before your child is tested or placed in a special educational program, you have a right to be notified of what the school plans to do.

Consent—You must give your consent before special tests are conducted and before your child is placed in a special educational program.

Evaluation—You have a right to have a full evaluation of your child's individual educational needs.

Records—You have a right to know what records are kept on your child and a right to see them.

Confidentiality of Information—With the exception of certain individuals (school officials, for example, and teachers with legitimate educational interests), no one may see your child's records unless you give your written permission.

Least Restrictive Environment—You have a right to have your child educated with nonhandicapped children to the maximum extent appropriate.

Hearings—If at any point along the way you do not agree with the way the school is dealing with your child, you have the right to request a hearing. This means that you may seek a formal review if you and the school cannot reach an agreement concerning the identification, evaluation, or placement, or educational program of your child.

Source: The FAPE Site. fapeonline.org/Parental%20Rights .htm#SUMMARIZED

Decisions about children with disabilities are so important that parents must be involved. They are the most vital members of the educational team that develops and implements programs for students with disabilities (Cavkaytar & Pollard, 2009). Such involvement has been shown to have benefits in many areas, including student achievement, improved attendance, better attitudes, improved grades and test scores, and increased motivation (Kellough & Kellough, 2008). Two IDEA principles underlie collaboration between schools and parents—parent participation and procedural due process (Lake & Billingsley, 2000). "In recognition of the important role of parents in the decision-making process, IDEA mandated that parents receive a document explaining their educational rights and responsibilities any time their child is referred for an evaluation, and at other times throughout the special education process" (Fitzgerald & Watkins, 2006, p. 497). This document should outline all of the legal rights of parents and help them understand these rights (see the nearby Rights and Responsibilities box).

Legislation and parental advocacy have established an increasingly higher degree of family involvement in the education of students with disabilities. School personnel acknowledge the merit of having parents actively participate in the educational process, including identification, referral, assessment, program planning, and implementation. Comprehensive programs of family involvement begin when children with disabilities are young and continue through the transition process out of school and into adulthood.

The challenge for educators is to consider effective ways to involve families in the education of children with disabilities. Table 2.5 describes several ways to increase family involvement. Family participation can and should occur in all areas related to the education of students with disabilities. These include involvement with the student's identification and assessment, development of the IEP, involvement with parent groups, observation of the student in the school setting, and communication with educators. Of these activities, parental participation in the IEP process typically occurs the most frequently. As with all aspects of public education, some families are very involved in their child's special education program, while others have limited involvement (Dabkowski, 2004).

Professionals can satisfy the provisions of IDEA regarding involving families by simply inviting parental participation, but school personnel should develop strategies to facilitate parental involvement or, more appropriately, family involvement. They should become proactive in getting parents to be truly involved in the educational programs of their children. Although some parents create challenges for the school because of their intense level of involvement, for the most part educational programs are greatly strengthened by parental support. A general rule is that the more involved a family, the better for the education of the child.

TABLE 2.5

Suggestions to Increase Family Involvement

Display Empathy for Families
Do not judge families.
Approach family support with understanding and compassion.

Individualize Family Participation
Encourage family participation.
Take into consideration individual family circumstances to encourage participation.

Recognize Families as Experts and Build on Family Strengths
Actively seek information from family members.
Step away from the "expert" role occasionally.

Value and Support Family Decision Making
Put your own opinions aside and listen to parents' wishes.
If not contrary to professional opinion, attempt to implement parents' wishes.

Be a Professional Ally of Families
Listen to family issues.
Express concerns related to due-process issues to administrators.

Engage Families in Open Communication
Use technology to engage in continuous dialogue with families.
Good communication provides an opportunity to enhance collaboration.

Enhance Family Access
Place children in neighborhood schools when possible.
Hold meetings when it is convenient to parents.

Offer Family Networking
Promote networking opportunities for parents.
Hold parent-to-parent programs.

Extend Support Systems
Provide supports for siblings or other caregivers.
Support sibling support groups.

Embrace and Celebrate Families' Success
Embrace and celebrate family ideas.
Celebrate even small gains made by children.

Source: B. Van Haren and C. R. Fiedler (2008). "Support and empower families of children with disabilities." *Intervention in School and Clinic, 43,* 231–235.

THE FAMILY

The viewpoint of what constitutes a family has changed dramatically in recent decades. Traditionally, a family was thought of as a group of individuals who live together, including a mother, a father, and one or more children. However, this stereotypical picture has been challenged by the reality that many, perhaps most, families do not resemble this model. As early as 1992, Allen noted, "The idealized nuclear family of yesteryear with the stay-at-home, take-care-of-the-children mother and the outside-the-home breadwinner father no longer represents the typical American family" (p. 319). Since the early 1990s, the family structure in the United States has continued to evolve. Families depicted in *The Cosby Show, Roseanne, Still Standing,* and *Everybody Loves Raymond* are no longer the norm (Smith, Gartin, Murdick, et al., 2006). The family of today, unlike the family of the early twentieth century, more simply can be described as a group of individuals who live together and care for one another's needs. Table 2.6 describes the typical family in the 1950s and the typical family today.

TABLE 2.6	
Typical Families in the 1950s and Today	
FAMILY IN THE 1950s	**FAMILY IN THE TWENTY-FIRST CENTURY**
Mother and father in the home	One parent family
Two or three siblings	Both parents work
Father works; mother stays home	Grandparents not nearby
Grandparents nearby	Children attend school in a culturally heterogeneous environment
Children attend school in a culturally homogeneous environment	

Unlike the typical family of the mid-twentieth century, today there are numerous family arrangements. For example, many families are single-parent families, most frequently with the father absent. A growing number of families are now headed by grandparents, with the children's parents unable or unwilling to accept parental responsibility. And, although not as common as they once were, some families constitute extended family units, with grandparents living with parents and children. Some children also live in foster homes, wherein foster parents fill all legal parental roles. Families are also headed by parents living in gay or lesbian relationships. School personnel must interact successfully with all types of families.

Despite undergoing major changes in its structure, the family remains the basic unit of U.S. society. It is a dynamic, evolving social force that remains the key ingredient in a child's life. Teachers must be sensitive to the background of the family to ensure that cultural differences do not interfere with school–family relationships. In addition, school personnel must remember that students' parents or guardians should be involved in educational programs regardless of the specific composition of the family. School personnel must put aside any preconceived notions they may have about various lifestyles and work with students' families to develop and implement the most effective programs for the students. Finally, professionals should adopt a family systems perspective to involve the whole family—rather than just the child—in efforts to enhance programs (Turnbull & Turnbull, 2005).

Cultural Considerations

Families today represent numerous races, cultures, socioeconomic levels, and religions. Because the diversity of students in public schools has increased dramatically over the past 25 years, the success of parent–professional partnerships often hinges on the ability of professionals to develop a level of cultural competence (Florence, 2010). This need will only increase in the future. The idea that the different cultures in this country would "melt" into a common cultural group has not happened. In fact, our culture is becoming more diverse each year. In 2008 the United States Census Bureau projected that the number of individuals from diverse cultural groups will increase significantly over the next 40 years, resulting in more than 50% of the population being comprised of minorities in 2042.

Regardless of the issues resulting from this increased diversity, professionals must be aware of their own cultural biases and attitudes and develop attitudes that enable them to appreciate and work with students and families from different cultural groups (Brown, 2007).

In order to be culturally responsive, teachers need to self reflect and ask themselves questions concerning their beliefs and feelings about cultures. Cartledge and Kourea (2008) suggested the follow questions:

1. What is the racial or gender breakdown of the students from my class that I typically send for disciplinary actions?
2. How often do I send the same students for disciplinary actions?

3. What messages am I communicating to the students who are the recipients of these actions?
4. What messages am I communicating to their classmates?
5. Is the behavior of my students getting better? How do I know? If it is not getting better, why not?
6. Do I dispense disciplinary referrals fairly on the basis of race and gender?
7. Are disciplinary actions therapeutic or simply punitive?
8. Do I distinguish culturally specific behaviors from behavioral inadequacies?
9. If students have substantial behavioral differences, have I taught them the skills that they need to know?
10. Am I punishing students for my lack of skill in effective behavior management?
11. Do I punish students because of my lack of skill in effective instruction? (p. 355)

FAMILIES AND CHILDREN WITH DISABILITIES

Any time a new child arrives in a family, whether by birth or adoption, the family structure and dynamics change dramatically. Children change the lives of the mother and father and siblings, and each child alters the dynamics of the family unit, including finances, the amount and quality of time parents can devote to individual children, the relationship between the husband and wife, and the family's future goals. When a child with a disability becomes a member of the family, whether through birth, adoption, or later onset of the disability, these changes are only exacerbated and often result in the entire family needing to make adjustments. Indeed, families with children with disabilities have unique experiences and challenges (Worcester, Nesman, Mendez, & Keller, 2008).

Some families experience another major problem—accepting and understanding the child and the disability. Parents with a limited understanding of a diagnosis will probably have difficulty in developing realistic expectations of the child, possibly creating major problems within the family. On one hand, parents might not understand the nature of a learning disability and therefore accuse the child of being lazy and not trying. On the other hand, parents may overlook the potential of students with intellectual disabilities and develop low expectations that will limit the child's success. For example, parents of adolescents might not support a school-work program for their son or daughter because they believe that adults with intellectual disabilities are not capable of holding a job.

Families who discover that their child has a disability obviously undergo a wide variety of feelings and reactions. Some of these may include grief, loss, denial, guilt, bargaining, anger, depression, acceptance, and stress (Smith et al., 2006). Other studies have found that parents of children with autism spectrum disorders experience more stress (Vermaes, 2008), have higher levels of depression (Quintero & McIntyre, 2010), and face greater problems with children's behaviors than do parents of children without disabilities (Brobst, Clopton, & Hendrick, 2009).

Some parents and other family members experience all of these different reactions while others might experience only some of them. Regardless of specific reactions, family members almost always experience some negative reactions upon learning that a child has a disability. Although it cannot be assumed that all or even most parents have particular reactions, many must deal with complicated emotions, often experienced as a "bombardment of feelings" that may recur over many years (Hilton, 1990). Sileo, Sileo, and Prater (1996) refer to the "shattering of dreams" that underlies many of these feelings. School personnel—including teachers, school social workers, counselors, and administrators—need to be aware of these dynamics and be prepared to deal with family members who are experiencing various feelings. For example, when parents say that they feel guilt after learning that their child has a disability, school personnel should listen with acceptance to the parents and help them understand the nature of the disability and the fact that they are not responsible for it. Hutton and Caron (2005) interviewed 21 families of children who had been diagnosed with autism to determine their reactions and coping. Their findings indicated that 43% felt grief and loss, 29% shock and surprise, and 10% self-blaming. Of the families in the study, 52% did say that the

FIGURE 2.4	Reactions to the Diagnosis of Autism

I went to the doctor when my son was two because he did not talk—I knew something was wrong but I was told to wait—that he will be fine. I took him to Child Development Services when he was two and a half, and I had to wait five months before seeing a psychologist, who eventually diagnosed him with autism.

When I went to my doctor and told him something was wrong, he said not to worry—that sometimes boys are just slower than girls.

I didn't challenge the diagnosis because everything fit into place. After reading about autism, I said, "This is so much like her."

Yes, I accepted the diagnosis. I knew it was autism by that time, since I had been doing a lot of my own research.

I accepted the psychologist's diagnosis. We had figured it out.

When the doctor told me, I had the same feeling as when my grandmother died.

This wasn't supposed to happen to us. I thought this was something he would grow out of.

I cried when I left the office. I felt that it was my fault, since I had been exposed to shingles early in the pregnancy.

One doctor told me, "Your son has autism and there is nothing you can do about it so just live with it." Yet I knew that wasn't the case.

The psychologist treated me like it was my fault. He said my child's behavior was because of his home environment.

I was treated with respect—in fact, one doctor said I knew more than he did!

It has been an honor to be given a child like this—to parent a child like this.

It was heartbreaking, stressful, and devastating—especially for my husband. We were quite overwhelmed with the demands and needs of our child.

Some days it is a living hell; 30 percent of the time you feel like you are in a normal family, and 70 percent of the time you feel like you are juggling so many things you don't know where you are going.

We have not taken a vacation as a family since the diagnosis.

He (my son) never gets invited anywhere and doesn't have friends over to the house.

I had a career before my child's diagnosis. Now all that doesn't seem important anymore. I work a part-time job so I can be home with my son.

Our daily life is a routine—if you throw anything different and unpredictable in, our son melts down, which affects the whole family.

When our child with autism was born, his sister was just turning two. We had the PEC System done at home, with the sister learning also; they are inseparable.

Source: From "Experiences of Families with Children with Autism in Rural New England," by A. M. Hutton and S. L. Caron, 2005, *Focus on Autism and Other Developmental Disabilities, 20,* pp. 184–187. Used with permission.

diagnosis resulted in some relief in knowing what was wrong with their child. Figure 2.4 lists some of the statements made by respondents during the interviews.

The way families deal with stress and other emotions resulting from having a child with a disability is impacted by different personality traits of parents. For example, Vermaes (2008) found that emotional stability and extraversion were associated with less stress for mothers, while agreeableness in fathers also resulted in less stress. Other external factors that have been shown to impact the way families react to children with disabilities include the family's income level, pre-existing problems within the family, spirituality, and how much support parents seek (Brobst et al., 2009).

Parents of children with disabilities experience significant difficulties. In a study of seven families raising young children with disabilities, several specific major themes emerged. These included "(a) obtaining accurate and useful information, (b) obtaining services and supports,

(c) financial stress, (d) stress among members of the family, and (e) community isolation" (Worcester et al., 2008, p. 509). The financial stress on families has been well documented—raising children with disabilities simply costs more than raising children without disabilities. Unfortunately, "poor children with disabilities and their mothers are particularly vulnerable because these families have significantly fewer resources and choices for adequately meeting their children's impairment-related needs" (Parish, Rose, & Andrews, 2010, p. 248).

School personnel need to support family members' acceptance of children with disabilities. This effort begins with assisting parents in understanding the needs of their child; at the same time, the educator should listen to the parents, to better understand the child from their perspective. Further, teachers must be sensitive to the fact that many parents do not see the school as a welcoming place for various reasons (e.g., problems the parents experienced as students themselves, negative responses communicated to them as advocates for their child). Professionals must understand that all of their actions can have a profound impact on families. For example, "the way in which diagnostic information is conveyed to the family can have a long-term influence on parents' attitudes, families' level of stress and acceptance, and coping strategies" (Hutton & Caron, 2005, p. 180).

Problems experienced by family members do not necessarily improve as the child gets older. Ankeny, Wilkins, and Spain (2009) note that families deal with a great deal of stress as their child moves through adolescent development and when their child is transitioned from public school programs to postschool environments and services. There are several things teachers can do to help families deal with this stress, including (Ankeny et al., 2009):

- Involve parents in planning for their child's future early in the transition process.
- Use a phased approach to adult service delivery.
- Take a leadership role in creating interagency linkages.
- Draw on the knowledge of different team members.
- Provide families with the names of individuals responsible for implementing and following up on various aspects of the transition plan.
- Help family members acknowledge their changing roles and responsibilities.
- Provide ongoing communication and collaboration with families.
- Communicate with parents using their preferred mode (e-mail, letter, phone, face-to-face).
- Focus on the positive characteristics and strengths of the child (p. 29).

Impact on Siblings

Like adults, siblings are important in developing and implementing appropriate educational programs. Because over 10% of the school population is identified as disabled, the number of children with siblings who are disabled is significant: A working estimate of 15 to 20% or more seems realistic. The presence of a child with a disability definitely alters the typical sibling role. Siblings often have to deal with increased parental expectations, less parent involvement in their own lives, and added responsibilities. Also, as parents and siblings age, often siblings are expected to become the primary caregiver (Quintero & McIntyre, 2010). Although not all siblings experience adjustment problems, some doubtlessly have significant difficulties responding to the disability. Hutton and Caron (2005) found that 38% of siblings in their survey reacted with resentment or jealousy, 12% with fear, and 12% with sadness. The survey found an additional 12% were accepting of their sibling, while 6% felt awkward by having a sibling with a disability. Regardless of the reactions of siblings, the presence of a child with a disability does present a unique opportunity to learn about the diversity of individual needs.

Meyer (2001) summarized the literature and noted these areas of concern expressed by siblings:

- A lifelong and ever-changing need for information about the disability or illness
- Feelings of isolation when siblings are excluded from information available to other family members, ignored by service providers, or denied access to peers who share their often ambivalent feelings about their siblings
- Feelings of guilt about having caused the illness or disability, or being spared having the condition

- Feelings of resentment when the child with special needs becomes the focus of the family's attention or when the child with special needs is indulged, overprotected, or permitted to engage in behaviors that are unacceptable if done by other family members
- A perceived pressure to achieve in academics, sports, or behavior
- Increased care-giving demands, especially for older sisters
- Concerns about their role in their sibling's future (Meyer, 2001, p. 30)

Siblings of children with disabilities need support from family members as well as from other adults. Teachers and other adults should be aware of the stress and additional impact a sibling with a disability can have on his or her brothers and sisters (Smith et al., 2006). Some considerations adults should make when dealing with children who have siblings with disabilities include:

- Express love for the sibling.
- Provide siblings with information concerning the disability.
- Keep the sibling informed concerning changes and stress on the family.
- Include the sibling in family and school meetings.
- Work for equity within the family's duties and responsibilities.
- Prevent siblings from becoming second parents in the areas of care and discipline.
- Be aware that the needs of all the children will change through the family life cycle (Smith et al., 2006, p. 61).

Parent Support

Many educators believe parents of children with disabilities benefit tremendously by attending parent support groups. One reason is that parents too frequently attribute normal and predictable misbehavior to a child's disability rather than to the age and stage of a child. Seeing that all parents face similar challenges with their children can be both comforting and empowering to parents (West, 2002). Some helpful hints parents learn through these support groups include the following (West, 2002):

1. Never compare children.
2. Notice the improvements and accomplishments of each child in the family, and always reinforce the positive.
3. Hold family meetings that allow children a weekly opportunity to voice their concerns, accept chores, and plan enjoyable family nights and outings.
4. Learn to help children become responsible by the use of logical and natural consequences rather than using punishment or becoming permissive.
5. Spend special time alone with each child in the family. Be sure that no child feels lost or left out because others require more attention.
6. Plan family events that allow children to enjoy being together.
7. Reduce criticism and increase encouragement.
8. Be sensitive to the possibility that children functioning at a higher academic level in the family may be finding their place through perfectionism and a need to excel at all costs.
9. Invest time in your marriage. A strong marriage is important to your children's sense of well-being.
10. All families experience stress. The more stress is encountered, the more time they need together to share their feelings, plan ahead, solve problems mutually, and plan time to enrich relationships.

HOME–SCHOOL COLLABORATION

In order to meet the needs of children with disabilities, educators and parents must be partners. This partnership has been a legal requirement since the first passage of IDEA as Public Law 94-142 in 1975 and has been maintained as one of the primary components of the law through all of its reauthorizations. While this mandate has opened the doors for parental involvement, it has also put a large responsibility on parents. "In fact, never before has so much been expected of parents with children with disabilities in terms of their roles as educational decision makers in partnership with professionals" (Turnbull et al., 2010, p. 43). To meet the child's needs best, classroom teachers, special education teachers, administrators, and support personnel need to be actively involved with the child's family. IDEA implies that the delivery of special education services has a foundation of schools and family members working together in a collaborative fashion (Mueller, 2009).

Unfortunately, too often partnerships between families and school personnel fall short as a result of several reasons, including (Summers et al., 2005):

- Professionals feeling unprepared to work with families
- Professionals feeling like they do not have administrative support
- Communication difficulties
- Failure to recognize and adapt to cultural differences
- Disagreement on appropriate services for the child

In working with parents of students with special needs, educators find that parents vary tremendously in knowledge and expertise about disabilities. Some parents are well-versed in special education laws and practices and have informed opinions that must be considered in effective instructional planning. Other parents are limited in their knowledge and understanding of special education law. In this case, educators are responsible to inform parents so that they can become effective advocates for their child and partners in educational programming.

Too often, families of children with disabilities feel unempowered. They feel like they have little control over what is happening with their child. Therefore, a first step in increasing family members' involvement is to empower them to become more actively involved in the special education process. Some of the ways this can happen include (1) increase family coping skills, (2) offer professional development opportunities, (3) encourage parents and students to participate in all stages of the IEP, (4) model effective problem solving for family members, and (5) help families develop a vision for their child (Van Haren & Fiedler, 2008). Professionals need to remember that parents are actually the "senior partners" in the collaborative relationship with the school (Cavkaytar & Pollard, 2009). As such, school personnel must empower families to assume this senior role.

Parents like to feel that professionals really care about their child. In a study by Nelson, Summers, and Turnbull (2004), it was determined that parents like professionals to go above and beyond their job descriptions; this shows to parents a commitment that leads them to believe that the professional is doing everything possible for the child. Parents also like professionals to be flexible in their availability (Nelson et al., 2004). Things that parents indicated as positive in establishing close partnerships with professionals included being available when parents want them, going beyond the narrow limitations of their job descriptions, and sometimes being a friend.

Another way of empowering parents in the special education process is to ensure that they have a thorough understanding about inclusive education. Stivers, Francis-Cropper, and Straus (2008) suggest a monthly guide that teachers can use to help inform parents about educating students with disabilities in inclusive settings. This guide includes:

August—Get ready for success. Mail letters to parents explaining the inclusive educational program.

September—Be partners in symbol and substance. At the annual back-to-school event, or open house, have the general classroom teacher and special education teacher present together to emphasize the collaborative relationship.

October—Recruit volunteers. Encourage parents to volunteer in the classroom.

November—Make the most of meetings. Take advantage of parent-teacher conferences to explain to parents how the inclusion program is benefitting their child.

December—Celebrate. Use school functions to demonstrate the success of inclusion.

January—Promote participation in community activities. Utilize community activities and field trips to promote inclusion outside the classroom.

February—Serve as a resource center. Enhance the classroom or school library with books that have a positive focus of individuals with disabilities.

March—Put learning on display. Share evidence of students' learning with their families.

April—Advocate for your program. Be proactive about your program's needs related to budget and other resources.

May—Have a field day. Use class picnics and other end-of-year activities to demonstrate the success of the inclusion program.

Communicating with Parents

Good communication between the school and parents is critical if a true collaborative relationship is developed. Unfortunately, many parents feel that too little communication takes place between them and the school. Perhaps this response is to be expected—approximately 50% of both general and special education teachers indicate that they have received no training in this area and consequently rate themselves as only moderately skilled (e.g., Buck et al., 1996; Epstein, Polloway, Bursuck, Jayanthi, & McConeghy, 1996). This deficiency is particularly unfortunate because many problems between parents and school personnel can be avoided with proper communication. Professionals, therefore, should make a conscious effort to begin the year with a discussion of roles and responsibilities in terms of communication (Stivers et al., 2008).

True family involvement in the education of a child cannot occur without good communication. Brandes (2005) makes the following recommendations to enhance communication between school and parents:

- Give parents your undivided attention, and be an active listener.
- Stand or sit alongside parents when communicating.
- Take notes openly while conversing with parents.
- When first meeting parents, engage them in conversation and pay close attention to what they choose to discuss.
- View parents who are challenging as an opportunity for you to grow.
- When working with angry parents, maintain a respectful demeanor and take notes rather than defend your actions at the time of the accusations.
- Allow parents to regard you as one of the experts in their child's education.
- Share the relevance of the curriculum to the student's goals.
- Share specific behavioral expectations early and regularly.
- Explain that you will try to resolve any conflict their child may have at school before you engage the parents.
- Model respect for the student by frequently acknowledging his or her efforts and achievements.
- Share some of the student's positive events that happen at school, such as successfully serving on a committee.
- Set up regular and frequent positive communication avenues such as a weekly newsletter that is sent home each Thursday.
- Be specific about when you will return phone calls, e-mails, and notes.
- Communicate often.
- Let parents know you appreciate their support and follow-through at home.
- Encourage parents to make provisions for their children who do not need to be at a meeting.
- Try to have both parents present when "major" topics are discussed.
- Start every meeting with a welcome, introductions, and review; clarification of the purpose of the current meeting and the ending time; and a recap of the meeting before everyone leaves.
- Never assume parents know how to help with homework (Brandes, 2005, pp. 52–54).

In order for communication to be effective, it must be regular and useful. Communicating with parents only once or twice per year, such as with IEP conferences, or communicating with parents regularly but with information that is not useful, will not facilitate meeting educational goals. Therefore, simply meeting the minimal requirements of IDEA, which requires communicating around specific annual meetings, does not necessarily result in effective communication.

One good way to communicate with parents is the home-to-school notebook. The home-to-school notebook is simply a notebook that the child takes daily, from school to home and back to school, containing notes from the teacher and parent about the child's activities. This particular communication device serves three functions: First, the notebook can encourage problem-solving; second, the notebook helps parents and school personnel analyze information; and finally, the notebook provides documentation of program implementation (Hall, Wolfe, & Bollig, 2003). Table 2.7 provides procedural recommendations for parents and school personnel in using a home-to-school notebook. Without both parties engaged in the day-to-day activities of the notebook, it will unlikely be a successful communication tool.

Effective communication can be informal, including telephone calls, written notes, e-mails, or newsletters. Regardless of the method used to communicate with parents, school personnel should be aware of how they convey messages. For example, they should never "talk down" to parents. They should also choose their words thoughtfully. Some words convey very negative meanings, whereas other words are just as useful in transmitting the message and are more positive. For example, a better choice than "your child is dirty" might be "your child needs to improve his grooming skills." Likewise, it would be better for a teacher to tell a parent that his or her child "has problems getting along with others" rather than "your child is mean to other children."

When communicating with parents, school personnel should also be aware of cultural and language differences. Taking these factors into consideration enhances the quality of communication with family members. School personnel must remember that the use of professional jargon can be just as much a barrier as communicating with parents whose primary language is not English (Dabkowski, 2004).

Informal Exchanges   Informal exchanges can take place without preparation. Teachers may see a parent in the community and stop to talk momentarily about the student. Teachers should always be prepared to talk briefly to parents about their children but should avoid talking about confidential information, particularly in the presence of individuals who do not need to know about it. If the conversation becomes too involved, the teacher should request that it be continued later, in a more appropriate setting.

Parent Observations   Parents should be encouraged to visit the school to observe their children in the classroom. Although the parents' presence could cause some disruption in the daily routine, school personnel need to keep in mind that parents have a critical stake in the success of the educational efforts. Therefore, they should always feel welcome. If the teacher feels that one time would be better than another, this information should be conveyed to the parent. Also, both teacher and parents should realize that children tend to behave differently when being observed by parents.

TABLE 2.7

Procedural Recommendations for Using Home-to-School Notebook

PROCEDURAL RECOMMENDATIONS FOR SCHOOL	PROCEDURAL RECOMMENDATIONS FOR PARENTS
• Entry to classroom, collect journals. • Morning routine to discuss with student what parent wrote. • Keep journals in one place during day. • Respect confidentiality. • Structure journal writing during daytime routine, versus at the end of a busy day. • Get input from specialists/teachers and others working with student (personal care aide). • If student is included in a general education setting for a substantial part of day, the journal should travel to that setting and that teacher should make an entry. • Analyze the journal; look for patterns of behavior. • Establish a routine to return journal home. • Avoid educational jargon.	• Establish routine to review journal with student. • Keep journal available. • Include information from specialists (e.g., medical personnel, occupational and physical therapists). • Obtain input from family members to include in journal entry (e.g., siblings). • Establish a consistent, quiet time to write in journal. • Review journal entries, analyze data, look for patterns of behavior. • Review journal: Are your questions being addressed?

Source: From "The Home-to-School Notebook," by T. E. Hall, P. S. Wolfe, and A. A. Bollig, 2003, *Teaching Exceptional Children, 36,* p. 72. Used with permission.

Telephone Calls   Many teachers use telephone calls effectively to communicate with parents. Parents feel that teachers are interested in their child if the teacher takes the time to call and discuss the child's progress with the parent. Teachers should remember to call when there is good news about the child as well as to report problems the child is experiencing. For example, teachers can make notes of positive behaviors and follow through with a call. Again, understanding the language and culture of the home is important when making telephone calls. Giving parents your home telephone number is an option that may reassure parents. Used appropriately, voice mail may enhance ongoing communication, especially when contact times are not mutually convenient.

Written Notes   Written communication to parents is also an effective method of communication. Teachers should consider the literacy level of the parents and use words and phrases that will be readily understandable. They should also be aware of the primary language of the home. Written communications that are not understood can be intimidating for parents. When using written communication, teachers should provide an opportunity for parents to respond, either in writing or through a telephone call.

Electronic Communication   Increasingly, e-mail offers opportunities for ongoing communication (Smith et al., 2006). As more and more families gain access to e-mail, teachers should take advantage of this form of communication. Not only is it expedient, but it also provides a record of the communication.

Home Visits   A home visit is the best way to get an understanding of the family. When possible, school personnel should consider making the extra effort required to arrange and make home visits. Parents view school personnel who make home visits as being really caring about their child (Nelson, Summers, & Turnbull, 2004). When visiting homes, school personnel need to follow certain procedures. Figure 2.5 includes a home-visit checklist that could be useful for school personnel to follow.

Although home visits are an important option, there is low teacher acceptability of this practice. General education teachers report that they consider home visits the least effective

FIGURE 2.5	Home-Visit Checklist

Before the visit:
M   Have you scheduled the home visit around the family's needs?
M   Did you send any materials home for family members to review before the home visit?
M   Did you explain to family members the purpose of the home visit?
M   Do you have good directions on how to get to the house?
M   Do you have other school staff making the home visit with you?
M   Are you familiar with the family situations (e.g., number of children, employment status, composition of family)?
M   Are you appropriately dressed for the home visit (professional but not in a way to make family members feel uncomfortable)?

During the meeting:
M   Did you arrive on time?
M   Did you make family members feel comfortable?
M   Did you provide structure to the meeting (e.g., time, topics, etc.)?
M   Did you provide a summary of the meeting at the end?
M   Did you appropriately respond to offers of food/drink?

After the meeting:
M   Did you provide some follow-up information to the family after the meeting?
M   Did you schedule another meeting, if necessary?

Source: From *Families and Children with Special Needs* (p. 96), by T. E. C. Smith, B. A. Gartin, N. Murdick, & A. Hilton, 2006. Columbus, OH: Merrill. Used with permission.

FIGURE 2.6 — Common Questions Asked by Parents and Teachers

QUESTIONS PARENTS MAY ASK TEACHERS

- What is normal for a child this age?
- What is the most important subject or area for my child to learn?
- What can I work on at home?
- How can I manage her behavior?
- Should I spank?
- When will my child be ready for community living?
- Should I plan on her learning to drive?
- Will you just listen to what my child did the other day and tell me what you think?
- What is a learning disability?
- My child has emotional problems; is it my fault?
- The doctor said my child will grow out of this. What do you think?
- Will physical therapy make a big difference in my child's control of his hands and arms?
- Have you become harder on our child? Her behavior has changed at home.
- Can I call you at home if I have a question?
- What is the difference between delayed, retarded, and learning disabled?
- What kind of after-school activities can I get my child involved in?
- Can my child live on his own?
- What should I do about sexual activity?
- What's he going to be like in five years?
- Will she have a job?
- Who takes care of him when I can no longer care for him?
- What happens if she doesn't make her IEP goals?

QUESTIONS TEACHERS SHOULD ASK PARENTS

- What activities at home could you provide as a reward?
- What particular skill areas concern you most for inclusion on the IEP?
- What behavior at home do you feel needs to improve?
- Would you be interested in coming to a parent group with other parents of my students?
- When is a good time to call you at home?
- May I call you at work? What is the best time?
- Is there someone at home who can pick up the child during the day if necessary?
- Would you be interested in volunteering in our school?
- What is the most difficult problem you face in rearing your child?
- What are your expectations for your child?
- How can I help you the most?
- What is your home routine in the evenings? Is there a quiet place for your child to study?
- Can you or your spouse do some special activity with your child if he or she earns it at school?
- Can you spend some time tutoring your child in the evening?
- Would you like to have a conference with your child participating?
- When is the best time to meet?

Source: Adapted from *The Special Educator's Handbook* (pp. 208–209), by D. L. Westling and M. A. Koorland, 1988. Boston: Allyn & Bacon. Used by permission.

(and perhaps least desirable) alternative available to them in terms of home–school collaborations (Polloway et al., 1996). Among other possible concerns, home visits for a potentially large number of children simply may be unrealistic. They tend to be more common, and perhaps more effective, at the preschool level. However, this form of communication can be essential in some instances and can take on greater significance when parents decline invitations to visit the school.

Formal Meetings   Parent-teacher meetings and conferences provide an important opportunity for collaboration. IDEA requires several formal meetings between school personnel and parents, including referral meeting, evaluation meeting, IEP meeting, and annual review meeting, and, as applicable, behavioral intervention plan (BIP) meetings. Regardless of the purpose of the meeting, school personnel should focus attention on the topics at hand. They should send advance information home (e.g., a week before the meeting) to parents and make them feel at ease about their participation. Directing parents' attention to academic, social, and transitional goals before such meetings enhances their participation.

When preparing to meet with parents to discuss children who are experiencing problems, school personnel need to anticipate the components of the discussion. Figure 2.6 provides typical questions raised at such conferences. To increase parental participation in formal conferences, school personnel may wish to consider whether parents should have an advocate present at formal conferences. The advocate could be a member of the school staff or, in some cases, will be privately contracted by the parents. An advocate can facilitate parental participation by enhancing communication, encouraging parental participation, and providing them a summary of the discussions and decisions at the end of the conference. State regulations govern this practice; teachers should consult with administrative colleagues concerning this practice.

Mediation   The legal requirements concerning the involvement of parents in their child's education provide a foundation for appropriate practices in home–school collaboration. Nevertheless, even when careful efforts at compliance are made by school personnel and when educators attempt to fulfill both the letter and spirit of the law, some conflicts are inevitable in such an emotionally charged area as the determination of an appropriate education for a student with a disability. Local education agencies are mandated by law to offer **mediation** to resolve disagreements between parents and school personnel. In mediation, the parties share their concerns and then work to develop a solution that is mutually acceptable, typically through the facilitation of a third party (Smith et al., 2006).

IDEA 2004 also provides an opportunity for parents to engage in a resolution session with school personnel in situations where there is disagreement. The resolution session is required when a due-process hearing has been requested, unless the school and parents agree not to have one. If effective, mediation or the resolution process can result in the avoidance of a hearing, the subsequent cost of attorney fees, and the potential for an adversarial relationship developing as a result of due-process hearings.

HOME-BASED INTERVENTION

In addition to participating in decision-making meetings, families can become involved with the education of a child with a disability through home-based intervention. For preschool children, home-based services are fairly common; however, parents less frequently provide instruction at home for older students. Nevertheless, such support can be very beneficial to all students with disabilities. Parents and other family members at home can get involved in the student's educational program by providing reinforcement and instructional support, as well as by facilitating homework efforts. At the same time, teachers should be sensitive to the numerous roles parents must play in addition to supporting their child with special needs. Unfortunately, some parents either feel unprepared for getting involved in home-based interventions, or they lack skills necessary to effectively engage in home-based interventions. In these situations, it is the responsibility of school personnel to provide support to families so they will develop skills and feel comfortable utilizing these skills.

Providing Reinforcement and Encouragement

Because eligibility for services under IDEA requires that students need special education, most students with disabilities experience some degree of failure and frustration because of their academic difficulties. One way that parents can assist students is to provide them with positive reinforcement and encouragement. Parents spend more time with their children than school personnel do, and are involved in all aspects of the child's life, so they can provide reinforcement in areas where a child most desires rewards, such as time with friends, money, toys, or trips. For many students, simply allowing them to have a friend over or stay up late at night on a weekend may prove reinforcing. School personnel do not have this range of reinforcers available to them; therefore, parents should take advantage of parents' repertoire of rewards to reinforce the positive efforts of students.

A special example of reinforcement is home–school contingencies, which typically involve providing reinforcement in the home that is based on the documentation of learning or behavioral reports from school. The basic mechanism for home–school contingencies is written reports that highlight a student's behavior with regard to particular targets or objectives. Two popular forms are daily report cards and passports.

Daily report cards give feedback on schoolwork, homework, and behavior. They range in complexity from forms calling for responses, to simple rating scales, to more precisely designed behavioral instruments with direct, daily behavioral measures of target behaviors. Passports typically take the form of notebooks that students bring to each class and then take home daily. Individual teachers (or all of a student's teachers) and parents can make regular notations. Reinforcement is based both on carrying the passport and on meeting the specific target behaviors that are indicated on it (Walker, Shea, & Bauer, 2006). Some overarching considerations will enhance reinforcement programs in the home. Discipline in the home involves two types of parental action: (1) imposing consequences for misbehavior, and (2) reinforcement of positive behavior. Rushed and stressed parents frequently are better in one area than another. School personnel need to let parents understand that reinforcement of positive behaviors is crucial to a child's self-esteem and growth. To see a new positive behavior or achievement and fail to reinforce it is a form of neglect that is unintentional but damaging. Parents need to train themselves to see and to reinforce positive behaviors, attitudes, and achievements.

Providing Instructional Support

Parents and other family members may become directly involved with instructional programs at home, which can be critical to student success. Unfortunately, many family members provide less direct instruction as the child gets older, assuming that the student is capable of doing the work alone. Too often, the reverse is true—students may need more assistance at home as they progress through the grades. While older children sometimes resist their parents' attempts to help, parents nevertheless should endeavor to remain involved at an appropriate level.

Parents are generally with the child more than are school personnel, so it is logical to involve them in selected instructional activities. Advocates for expanding the role of parents in educating their children adhere to the following assumptions:

- Parents are the first and most important teachers of their children.
- The home is the child's first schoolhouse.
- Children will learn more during the early years than at any other time in life.
- All parents want to be good parents and care about their child's development (Ehlers & Ruffin, 1990, p. 1).

Although the final assumption may not always be reflected in practice, it provides a positive foundation for building home programs. Because students eligible for special education under IDEA need special education, the majority of them experience some failure and related frustration in their academic work. Once established, this failure cycle can be difficult to break. In these situations it is the responsibility of school personnel to provide supports to parents that will provide them with the skills and confidence to provide home-based interventions. Turnbull and colleagues (2010) suggest the development of knowledge-to-action

(KTA) guides for parents. Using this model, parents and school personnel engage in a six-step process that funnels knowledge into an action cycle that can help parents understand how to provide home-based interventions. These steps include:

1. Identify the needs of a particular child.
2. Gather resources that are related to the identified needs of the child.
3. Identify the evidence-based resources.
4. Select those resources that are evidence-based.
5. Make resources easily understandable for end-users.
6. Format resources to match the preferences of end-users.

Following this sequence, the next step is to develop a series of knowledge-to-action guides that can be implemented by parents. Table 2.8 describes the components of a KTA guide.

Cavkaytar and Pollard (2009) describe a program in which parents and therapists worked together to deliver instruction in self-care and domestic skills to individuals with autism. Results indicated that mothers and therapists can work effectively together to provide instruction in

TABLE 2.8

Components of Knowledge-to-Action Guides

TOPIC	EXPERIENCE-BASED KNOWLEDGE	RESEARCH	POLICY
Stage 1			
Planning Transition from Early Intervention to Preschool	Video in English and Spanish Parent quotes/action steps from Community of Practice 4 family stories 4 state education department family-friendly guides	1 literature review Highlights of 2 qualitative research articles 1 audio interview/transcript with researcher and parent	3 policy advisories of IDEA and court cases with action steps PowerPoint presentation on IDEA Four R's – script for policy responses in planning meetings
Advocating for Care Coordination	3 family stories (print and audio) Audio interview with physician Family perspectives/action steps from Community of Practice (available in Chinese) Links to key national family networks Link to templates for developing care notebook	Highlights of 2 survey studies Data charts from major national survey	Policy advisory on federal and state laws Model policy from national organization Interview with parent and professional leader on policy reform
Providing Emotional Support to Families Through Parent to Parent Programs	Video of Parent to Parent support Link to Web site of national Parent to Parent network	Highlight of quantitative research synthesis and audio interview/PowerPoint of lead researcher explaining synthesis method and findings Highlight of qualitative research synthesis Highlights of one quantitative and qualitative study Link to research section of Parent to Parent Web site	1 policy advisory on parent rights to services to obtain emotional support and action steps

(continued)

TABLE 2.8 (continued)

TOPIC	EXPERIENCE-BASED KNOWLEDGE	RESEARCH	POLICY
Stage 2			
Customized Employment	Link to an online video Link to customized employment success stories Link to 2 videos for purchase	Highlight of 1 quantitative study Highlight of 2 descriptive studies	Policy Highlight of Supreme Court decision Link to identify local One-Stop Centers Link to article on employment policy
Preschool Transition for Asian American Family	Audio interview/transcript with a Korean mother Parents quotes/action steps from Community of Practice and a summary on interview with a Korean mother 1 state education department family-friendly guide in 5 Asian languages Link to Web sites on Asian American and disability resources	2 literature reviews Link to research-based book	Glossary of special education and basic legal terms in English. Chinese (simplified and traditional), and Korean Link to a Web page of special education law book Link to *English-Hmong Special Education Glossary* (Minnesota Department of Education, 2008) Link to parents' guide on preschool transition in 7 Asian languages
Cochlear Implantation: Making Decisions about Communication	Link to a national parent organization Link to cochlear implant simulations Links to 2 documentaries of families who have children with cochlear implants highlighting their decisions about communication Links to 2 blogs Link to a comprehensive guide for families considering transitioning their child from sign communciation to oral communication	Text interview with researcher PowerPoint presentation summarizing a literature review Highlight of a mixed-method research study Highlight of a qualitative research study	Policy advisory highlighting relevant portions of IDEA Policy advisory summarizing recent court decision Link to a 2-page ASHA Issues Brief on cochlear implants and IDEA
Being a Partner of Professionals for Your Child: Korean American Parents' Preparation for an IEP Meeting	Links to 2 Korean American parents' stories (in English and Korean) Korean American parents' suggestions/action steps in terms of IEP meetings Link to a special education information booklet for Korean American parents in Kansas (available in Korean)	Highlights of 2 qualitative research articles Link to Web site of Korean resources Link to a blog	Policy advisory on parent rights in English and Korean Links to resources of 2 state education departments Policy advisory highlighting 10 brief steps before an IEP meeting (in English and Korean) Policy advisory on preparation for a child's IEP meeting (including self-questions and examples of appropriate language)

Note: IDEA = Individuals with Disabilities Education Improvement Act of 2004; ASHA = American Speech-Language-Hearing Association; IEP = individualized education program.

Source: From Turnbull et al. (2010); p. 46–47. Used with permission.

these areas. Devlin and Harber (2004) describe a program in which parents and professionals collaborated with discrete trial training in the treatment of a child with autism. The program used the collaboration among family members, special education teachers, resource room teacher, and speech/language therapist to achieve various goals and objectives for the child. The end result was that after 28 weeks of intervention, significant progress was made toward the goals and objectives. The study concluded that such an intervention program, using family members as part of the intervention team, could result in significant gains by the child. In another study, Skoto, Koppebnhaver, and Erickson (2004) concluded that parental involvement with reading stories could result in positive gains by young girls with Rett syndrome.

Interventions that promote self-determination are another area where parents can be involved. Lee, Palmer, Turnbull, and Wehmeyer (2006) describe a model for parent–teacher collaboration that focuses on improving self-determination. Using the program, Self-Determined Learning Model of Support (SDLMS), parents are able to influence the self-determination of children with and without disabilities. Using such a program at home facilitates partnerships between schools and families (Lee et al., 2006).

FINAL THOUGHTS

Establishing good working relationships with parents and families enhances the school experience of their children. Thus, an important objective for the schools should be to achieve and maintain such relationships. Most professionals acknowledge the importance of the involvement of families in the schooling of their children, and this importance can be especially critical for students with disabilities. However, programs that promote home–school collaboration must aim for more than students' classroom success. Often, parental involvement has been focused on children's goals (i.e., student progress), with less attention given to parental outcomes (i.e., their particular needs). Teachers and family members all should gain from cooperative relationships that flow in both directions and are concerned with success in both home and school settings. Both general and special education teachers need to help family members understand the importance of their involvement, give them suggestions for how to get involved, and empower them with the skills and confidence they will need. Students with disabilities, and those at risk for developing problems, require assistance from all parties in order to maximize success. Family members are critical components of the educational team.

SUMMARY

Models for Professional Collaboration

- Collaboration is when two or more individuals work together for a common purpose.
- Collaboration among general and special education professionals is critical for inclusion to be successful.
- Collaboration-consultation is when the special education teacher consults with the general classroom teacher and provides advice and assistance.
- Co-teaching is the collaborative model where a special education teacher and general classroom teacher share a class.
- There are numerous co-teaching models that can be adapted by special education and general classroom teachers.
- Paraprofessionals can provide a great deal of support when they collaborate with general classroom and special education teachers.

Challenges in Creating and Maintaining Inclusive Classrooms

- Appropriately trained personnel, in adequate numbers, are a major factor in successful inclusion programs.

- Both staff and students must be prepared for inclusion.
- Once inclusion is initiated, its effectiveness must be monitored to ensure its ongoing success.

Planning for Successful Inclusion, One Student at a Time

- To be effective, planning an appropriate environment for students with disabilities must be carried out one student at a time.
- School personnel must develop supports that provide each student with the least restrictive environments possible that still meet the individual needs of each student.

Concept of Family in Our Society

- Today's family is significantly different from families of the 1950s.
- There is significantly more diversity in today's families than in those of the past.

Impact of Children with Disabilities on Families

- A major change in the past several decades in provision of educational services to students with special needs is the active involvement of families.
- Encouraging parents to participate in school decisions is essential.
- Schools need to take proactive steps to ensure the involvement of families of students with disabilities. Regardless of their own values, school personnel must involve all family members of a student with special needs, regardless of the type of family.
- Siblings of students with disabilities may experience special problems and challenges.
- Overriding attention needs to be given to cultural differences in families as a basis for collaborative programs.

How Schools and Parents Can Collaborate

- Families and schools must collaborate to ensure appropriate educational programs for students with disabilities. IDEA requires that schools involve families in educational decisions for students with disabilities.
- A critical component in any collaboration between school personnel and family members is effective communication. All types of communication, formal and informal, between school and families are important.

Specific Home-Based Intervention

- Family members should be encouraged and taught how to become involved in the educational programs implemented in the school. A variety of strategies are available to facilitate successful home intervention programs (i.e., reinforcement, instruction, homework support).

PEARSON myeducationlab

The MyEducationLab for this course can help you solidify your comprehension of Chapter 2 concepts.

- Gauge and further develop your understanding of chapter concepts by taking the quizzes and examining the enrichment materials on the Chapter 2 Study Plan.
- Visit Topic 3, Collaboration, Consultation, and Co-Teaching, as well as Topic 4, Parents and Families, to:
  - Connect with challenge-based interactive modules, case study units, and podcasts that provide research-validated information about working with students in inclusive settings by visiting the IRIS Center Resources
  - Explore Assignments and Activities, assignable exercises showing concepts in action through video, cases, and student and teacher artifacts
  - Practice and strengthen skills essential to quality teaching through the Building Teaching Skills and Dispositions lessons

3

Identifying and Programming for Student Needs

After reading this chapter, you should be able to:

1. Discuss the purpose and process for prereferral intervention strategies.
2. Describe the steps in the special education process.
3. Discuss the eligibility and planning procedures guaranteed under Section 504 of the Rehabilitation Act.

Last year was my first year to teach! I was so happy to be assigned a fourth-grade class of 25 students. My class had children from several cultures; I met with parents and planned activities to expose the class to these rich cultural differences. The special education teachers contacted me about the needs of several children who were in my class for some or all of a day. They were to collaborate on lesson plans and behavioral incentives and would be in our classroom periodically to co-teach.

My lack of experience was balanced by my eagerness and enthusiasm. I also felt that I had been well-trained by my professors to implement scientifically based interventions that would result in "universal learning" in my class. I had been given a lot of practice writing lesson plans that provided differentiated instructional techniques and used a variety of assessment measures. Each day I spent several hours planning exciting learning experiences. I was so caught up in the process of teaching that it took me a couple of months to realize that Jessica, one of my students, was floundering. Despite my efforts, she was not meeting the benchmarks identified in the general education curriculum, and there seemed to be other things troubling her.

Jessica was new to our school, so I could not consult with other teachers to gain insight. She was a puzzle. Some days were better than others. She had difficulty following directions, seldom finished her work or handed in homework; her desk and papers were a mess, and she spent too much time looking for pencils and supplies needed to complete an activity. She read slowly and laboriously and had problems decoding and predicting unknown words. I tried to talk to her, but she had little to say. She was a loner with only one or two friends with whom she seemed comfortable. I wasn't ready to refer her for a special education evaluation, but I knew she and I both needed help! The level of instruction I was providing was not working.

Fortunately, our school had a prereferral intervention team (PIT) that met weekly to discuss children like Jessica who were experiencing problems in general education classrooms. I didn't like admitting that I needed help, but I was glad that the resource was available. I let Jessica's parents know I was concerned about her progress and was seeking help within the school. I filled out the required form requesting a brief summary of the problems and attached examples of Jessica's work.

The PIT meeting, held at 7:00 A.M., gave us uninterrupted time. The team was composed of an experienced teacher from each grade, the assistant principal, the counselor, and a special education teacher. Other teachers were there to discuss children having difficulties in their classrooms. When Jessica's case was discussed, I proposed some strategies like longer periods of instruction in a smaller group for reading, peer collaboration for projects, and an individualized incentive plan. The team agreed they would be appropriate and added that I should assess progress at least every 2 weeks.

I guess I just needed the peer support to give me ideas and confidence to help Jessica. Thanks to the intervention assistance from this team, Jessica's achievement improved, and she finished fourth grade. I never had to refer her for additional testing. Both she and her parents were pleased. I think she will be successful in fifth grade. I'm glad the PIT is in place so that Jessica and others like her will have help if problems arise.

QUESTIONS TO CONSIDER

1. What suggestions can you make to help Jessica succeed in the general education classroom?
2. How would you feel about making accommodations to keep Jessica in your class if you were her teacher?
3. Do you think treating Jessica differently was fair to the other students?

RIGHTS & RESPONSIBILITIES

IDEA 2004

According to IDEA 2004 school personnel must

- Make reasonable efforts to ensure parental participation in group discussions relating to the educational placement of their child.
- Notify parents of meetings early enough to ensure they will have an opportunity to attend and use conference or individual calls if they cannot attend.
- Inform parents of the purpose, time, and location of a meeting and who will attend it.
- Notify parents that they, or school personnel, may invite individuals with special knowledge or expertise to IEP meetings.
- Notify parents of their right to refuse special education services.
- Schedule the meetings at a mutually agreed upon time and place.
- Provide written notification (in the parent or guardian's native language) before any changes are initiated or refused in the identification, evaluation, educational placement, or provision of a free, appropriate public education.
- Obtain written consent from parents before the initial evaluation, preceding initial provisions of special education and related services, or before conducting a new test as part of a reevaluation. Parents have a right to question any educational decision through due-process procedures.
- Inform parents that they have the right to an independent educational evaluation that may be provided at public expense if the evaluation provided by the education agency is determined to be inappropriate.
- Inform parents of requirements for membership on the IEP committee, including an invitation to the student to attend beginning at age 16 or younger if appropriate.
- Use interpreters or take other action to ensure that the parents understand the proceedings of the IEP meetings.
- Inform parents of requirement to consider transition services needed for students by age 16.
- Consider the student's strengths and the parental concerns in all decisions.
- Provide the parents with a copy of the IEP at no cost.
- Inform parents of their right to ask for revisions to the IEP or invoke due-process procedures if they are not satisfied.
- Notify parents of their right to mediation, resolution session, or a due-process hearing.
- Allow parents to review all records and request amendments if deemed appropriate.

Visit the MyEducationLab for this course to enhance your understanding of chapter concepts with a personalized Study Plan. You'll also have the opportunity to hone your teaching skills through video-based Assignments and Activities, IRIS Center Resources, and Building Teaching Skills and Disposition lessons.

In the preceding vignette, a concerned teacher identified Jessica's needs and reached out for resources that would help keep her successfully learning in the general education classroom. This chapter focuses on identifying the unique needs of students like Jessica and differentiating instruction to meet those needs in the inclusive classroom whenever possible. The chapter also introduces a decision-making process that could result in access to special education services or services provided to students who qualify under Section 504. This process is governed by specific guidelines outlined in the Individuals with Disabilities Education Improvement Act (2004) and Section 504 of the Rehabilitation Act, as well as by regulations developed in each state.

PREREFERRAL INTERVENTIONS

A comprehensive process of intervention should be in place in every school system to provide additional assistance to any student who continues to struggle with learning. This chapter begins with a review of two emerging advances in the general education classroom, *Universal Design for Learning* (UDL) and *Response to Intervention* (RTI). Both UDL and RTI have been shown to improve learning for all students, including those with disabilities. These practices incorporate ongoing assessment to determine the most effective, scientifically based intervention designed to keep students successfully learning in the general education classroom (Castellani, Mason, & Grossen, 2005; Edyburn, 2010). In this text, UDL and RTI will be discussed as prereferral interventions because they are literally used before a formal referral is made to consider special education eligibility. The primary focus of the chapter, however, is the delineation of the following key steps in the special education decision-making process:

- Prereferral Intervention/Response to Intervention
- Referral to consider eligibility for special education services
- Assessment/Determination of Eligibility
- Development, implementation, and review of Individualized Educational Program
- Consideration of right to services under Section 504 for any student who doesn't qualify under IDEA

CROSS-REFERENCE

Parent and student rights, as outlined by IDEA, are discussed in Chapter 1.

All educational procedures must be consistent with the due-process clause under the U.S. Constitution, which ensures no person will be deprived of legal rights or privileges without appropriate established procedures being followed. The implications of the due-process clause have resulted in regulations in IDEA (2004) that give parents and students with disabilities significant rights throughout the special education process. These rights are summarized more extensively in the Rights & Responsibilities feature. While these basic rights are guaranteed nationwide, specific procedures guiding the special education process will vary from state to state.

The process for addressing the classroom challenges presented by students with special needs is discussed throughout this chapter. The flowchart provided in Figure 3.1 shows that procedures begin with efforts to identify students having difficulty making adequate progress in the general education classroom and follow with the implementation of scientifically based interventions, accommodations, or modifications for the general education classroom designed to effectively address a student's academic or behavioral challenges. The focus is on improving learning and performance to the degree that a student can remain in the general education classroom and be successful. If these are not effective, a formal referral to evaluate eligibility for special education services results. Based on the outcome of eligibility determination, either special education and the additional services specified by IDEA are provided, or other considerations such as Section 504 eligibility are pursued.

General education personnel participate on two teams that are integral to this process. The first team, the Prereferral Intervention Team (PIT), is in place to assist the general education teacher in responding to the needs of students not making adequate progress in the classroom; this was the team described in the opening scenario. The PIT is composed primarily of general education personnel and is accessed prior to a student's referral to determine special education eligibility. The purpose of the team is to ensure the best, scientifically based practice possible is implemented to ensure success in the general education setting.

The second team, generally referred to as the Individualized Educational Plan (IEP) Team because it works to "individualize the educational program," is active throughout the remainder of the student's progress through the steps of the flowchart, beginning with the third step: formal referral for special education consideration. The composition of this team and the qualifications of the team members are specified by IDEA. Even though teamwork is required, involving several individuals should not be simply an issue of compliance. Many people should have a vested interest in the educational program for a student, and consideration of a student's needs is best accomplished by a team approach. Thus, a team, representing various disciplines and relationships with the student, makes key decisions in regard to the student. Important decisions that have to be made include whether the student should be referred for an evaluation, if the student is eligible for special education services, what the IEP should include, whether a behavior intervention plan (BIP) is needed, how progress in meeting the goals of the IEP is going to be measured, and whether reevaluation of eligibility and placement should be repeated every 3 years.

All teams, when dealing with the important issue of a student's educational program, must keep in mind certain guidelines during this process. Doing so will increase the chances that positive outcomes will be realized. Some of the most crucial guidelines are the following:

1. The best interests of the student and his or her unique needs and strengths should dictate all aspects of the decision-making process.
2. Parents are to be equal partners in the process; sensitivity to family values and cultural differences must pervade all activities.
3. Ongoing and effective home-school collaboration efforts should be established.

FIGURE 3.1

Flowchart of services for students with special needs.

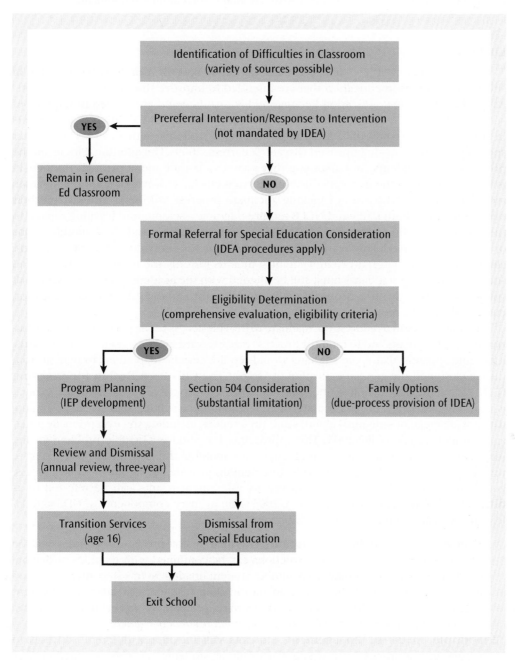

4. Parents and students have a right to and should be given information about the educational performance of the student, the special education programs and services to which the student is entitled and from which the student may receive benefits, and what will happen after formal schooling ends.

5. Each student should be taught and encouraged to participate as an active, contributing member of the team.

6. Programs and services, including the rules and regulations that apply, should be reviewed continuously, and improvements should be made whenever possible and allowable under the law.

The most recent reauthorization of IDEA (2004) maintains the basic requirements for home–school collaboration and continues to require schools to involve parents in every phase of the special education process. While future reauthorizations of IDEA will likely result in some changes, the basic intent of the law—providing a free appropriate public education to children with disabilities with parental involvement—will remain.

Universal Design for Learning

The implementation of No Child Left Behind of 2001 and IDEA of 2004 has resulted in several innovations in education that are intended to improve the outcome of students. As teachers in general education become highly qualified and are trained to implement scientifically based teaching methods to meet diverse needs and abilities of all students in their classroom, the educational experiences of students with diversity and other special needs have vastly improved (Bryant & Barrera, 2009). The additional focus on the progress of all students, and assessing that progress as they move through the benchmarks of success in the general education curriculum, have provided additional guarantees that students who are not making adequate progress will be identified and their needs addressed. Both IDEA and NCLB require ongoing assessment of learning related to the general education curricular standards for each grade level and allow modifications or accommodations during testing, if appropriate for the individual student. States are allowed to provide alternate achievement standards for only the most severely disabled students, and those standards must still be aligned with the academic standards set for all students. In this way, the progress of all students throughout the general education curriculum will be monitored.

As schools began to address the mandate to provide access to the general education curriculum to all students and to monitor progress made toward meeting grade-level standards, it became apparent that some students would require certain adaptations to benefit from their inclusion in the general education classroom. The **Universal Design for Learning (UDL)** is one flexible "whole-school" approach that contributes to progress in the general education classroom in designing assessment methods and teaching strategies to accommodate a wide range of individual abilities and preferences, including the exceptionally gifted and culturally diverse (CEC, 2005). This approach is described as a flexible, problem-solving model because the results of any intervention are monitored or assessed, and if adequate progress is not made, changes are made. Intervention provided using this flexible process, guided by data-based decisions and driven by assessment results, can be referred to as **differentiated instruction** (Tomlinson, 2005). The primary components of UDL and differentiated instruction are similar and include:

1. **Multiple Means of Representation:** The method for presenting content will be adapted—for example, verbal instructions can be combined with graphics or demonstrations or help might come from another student or adult. In this step, students are offered different methods for taking in information. Teachers can adapt for different cognitive levels, sensory or social needs, learning preferences, or technology options. This component answers the question: *What will the teacher teach?*
2. **Multiple Means of Engagement:** Students will be offered different activities to engage in the process of learning. For example, students can choose whether they would like to work alone to complete a computer search for new content or collaborate with another student to develop a power point presentation. This component takes the student's interests and motivation into account and offers different methods for students to make sense out of information. This component answers the question: *Why does the teacher use certain interventions/strategies to meet the needs of a particular student?* The questionnaire shown in the Differentiated Instruction–Elementary box is used by two collaborating teachers to assess learning preferences. Each student's responses are used to determine the type of activities he or she will engage in to complete a chapter study of ancient Rome. Students are also allowed to rank their level of interest in studying geography, architecture, music and art, religion and sports, and the roles of men, women, and children to determine their focus of new content about Rome.

3. **Multiple Means of Expression:** Students will be offered multiple methods for demonstrating their knowledge. Expression options might be auditory (oral report), visual (written report), tactile/kinesthetic (drama or puppet show), affective (group or individual), or technological (WebQuest creation, tape recording). This component results in a student-generated product and answers the question: *How will students respond to new information and how will learning be assessed?* (Rose & Meyer, 2006; Tomlinson, 2005). The Differentiated Instruction–Secondary box shows a creative list of options that students are allowed to select from to demonstrate their knowledge of new information. The traditional paper-and-pencil test can be replaced with products or activities ranging from creating a museum exhibit to designing a game where points are given for correct responses to relevant questions from the study.

The methods incorporated into these instructional plans are much more engaging and diversified. Instead of planning lessons from the beginning of the curriculum guide, the teacher begins where the students are—acknowledging the fact that learners differ in many ways that are important. Tomlinson (2005) calls this "being smart from the start!" Accommodations that may be needed to improve the learning process for individual students with and without special needs are also considered and planned for before the intervention begins.

It is important to remember that these two approaches are for the "whole class" and the teacher does not need to differentiate all elements in all the ways just identified. Tomlinson (2005), one of the biggest advocates of differentiated instruction, proposes that there are many times in a differentiated classroom that "whole-class, nondifferentiated fare is the order of the day." She notes that at any time in a lesson or unit, a teacher can adapt the content, process, or products to accommodate a student's level of readiness, learning profile, or

Differentiating Elementary Instruction

DIAGNOSING STUDENT READINESS, INTEREST, AND LEARNING PROFILE

LEARNING PROFILE QUESTIONNAIRE: HOW DO YOU LIKE TO LEARN?

	Yes	No
1. I study best when it is quiet.	☐	☐
2. I am able to ignore the noise of other people talking while I am working.	☐	☐
3. I like to work at a table or desk.	☐	☐
4. I like to work on the floor.	☐	☐
5. I work hard for myself.	☐	☐
6. I work hard for my parents or teacher.	☐	☐
7. I will work on an assignment until it is completed no matter what.	☐	☐
8. Sometimes I get frustrated with my work and do not finish it.	☐	☐
9. When my teacher gives an assignment, I like to have exact steps on how to complete it.	☐	☐
10. When my teacher gives an assignment, I like to create my own steps on how to complete it.	☐	☐
11. I like to work by myself.	☐	☐
12. I like to work in pairs or in groups.	☐	☐
13. I like to have an unlimited amount of time to work on an assignment.	☐	☐
14. I like to have a certain amount of time to work on an assignment.	☐	☐
15. I like to learn by moving and doing.	☐	☐
16. I like to learn while sitting at my desk.	☐	☐

Source: Adapted from *How to Differentiate Instruction in Mixed-Ability Classrooms* (p. 70) by C. A. Tomlinson, 2005. Upper Saddle, NJ: Pearson.

Differentiating Secondary Instruction

PRODUCT POSSIBILITIES

Design a Web page

Develop a solution to a community problem

Create a public service announcement

Write a book

Design a game

Generate & circulate a petition

Write a series of letters

Present a mime

Design & create needlework

Lead a symposium

Build a planetarium

Conduct a series of interviews

Develop a collection

Submit writings to a journal, magazine, or newspaper

Interpret through multimedia

Design a structure

Design & conduct an experiment

Collect & analyze samples

Plan a journey or an odyssey

Make an etching or a woodcut

Write letters to the editor

Design political cartoons

Formulate & defend a theory

Conduct a training session

Design & teach a class

Do a demonstration

Present a news report

Write a new law & plan for its passage

Make learning centers

Create authentic recipes

Choreograph dances

Present a mock trial

Make a plan

Compile & annotate a set of Internet resources

Design a new product

Write a series of songs

Create a subject dictionary

Make and carry out a plan

Design a simulation

Write a musical

Develop a museum exhibit

Be a mentor

Write or produce a play

Compile a newspaper

Develop an exhibit

Conduct an ethnography

Write a biography

Present a photo-essay

Hold a press conference

Develop & use a questionnaire

Conduct a debate

Make a video documentary

Create a series of illustrations

Write poems

Develop tools

Design or create musical instruments

Develop an advertising campaign

Compile a booklet or brochure

Draw a set of blueprints

Present a radio program

Do a puppet show

Create a series of wall hangings

Go on an archeological dig

Design & make costumes

Present an interior monologue

Generate charts or diagrams to explain ideas

Source: From *How to Differentiate Instruction in Mixed Ability Classrooms* (p. 89) by C. A. Tomlinson, 2005. Upper Saddle River, NJ: Pearson.

interests; however, a teacher should not be overcompensating for the students. Tomlinson's guiding principle is:

> Modify a curricular element only when (1) you see a student need and (2) you are convinced that modification increases the likelihood that the learner will understand important ideas and use important skills more thoroughly as a result. (p. 54)

Examples of ideas for developing differentiated lessons and creating differentiated classrooms at both the elementary and secondary levels are included in each of the chapters in this text.

Response to Intervention

As the highly qualified teachers implement scientifically based intervention techniques with their students with diverse needs and abilities, the assessment of each student's response to that intervention and the teacher's differentiated response to those results is critical to the learning process. This model for teaching was formalized in the IDEA amendments of 2004, as **Response to Intervention** (RTI). In this law, RTI is proposed as an alternative process recommended for identifying students who are potentially eligible for services under the category of learning disabilities. Many educators prefer this method because scientifically based intervention is provided before students have to suffer prolonged failure.

RTI procedures have also been adopted by many schools as a measure to benefit all students. Brown-Chidsey & Steege (2005) define RTI as "a systematic and data-based method for identifying, defining, and resolving students' academic and/or behavioral difficulties" (p. 144). The premise is that students fail because the intervention with the "right fit" has not been implemented. In RTI, the classroom that is designed for universal learning and is driven by differentiated instruction becomes the environment for a "test-teach-test-modify the intervention" cycle that identifies students who are not making adequate progress in the general education curriculum. Because the framework of RTI is not regulated by law, no one model has been adopted universally; more research and leadership are needed to standardize procedures and develop a model for best practice (Berkeley, Bender, Peaster, & Sanders, 2009; Werts, Lambert, & Carpenter, 2009). However, Chamberlain (2009) proposes several key tenets:

- Swift instructional response is provided to struggling students.
- Differentiated and supplemental instruction is provided as the need is indicated through assessment.
- Student progress is monitored more frequently as more intense, specialized intervention is made available.
- Practices used in the classroom are research based.

Three-Tiered Approach   The RTI model has been illustrated most often as a three-tiered approach (shown in Figure 3.2). Tier III offers the most intense, individualized intervention in the general education classroom. This model also demonstrates how RTI works for students with behavioral issues that are threatening their success in the classroom.

This first level of intervention, referred to as Tier I, reflects the work of the teacher using academic benchmarks from the general education curriculum and the school system's Code of Conduct (schoolwide expectations for behavior) as the standard or guide. Access to the general education curriculum is strengthened and the learning environment is supportive for all students. Because this model promotes "prevention," the teacher first uses the least-intrusive methods of instruction that are necessary for the student to benefit from placement in the general education classroom (Little, 2008). Classroom management is based on positive reinforcement systems, social skills are taught to all students, and behavior is closely monitored (Sprague et al., 2008).

Scientifically based intervention is implemented with flexible grouping available for all students; the configuration of groups is changed as progress is assessed formally and informally. Regrouping of students can be based on the lack of progress in meeting benchmarks, the student's interests, and other changing needs. Students can be taught individually and in both small and large groups. Learning is typically assessed at the beginning, middle, and end of the school year at a minimum. As the students' progress is measured, the teacher's methods of implementing scientifically based intervention may also be evaluated to confirm that the methods are implemented with fidelity (accuracy). These safeguards and strategies used for intervention at Tier I are expected to meet the needs of the majority of students in a whole-group setting. If a student continues to struggle to a significant degree, generally

FIGURE 3.2

Three-tiered model of behavioral and academic support systems.

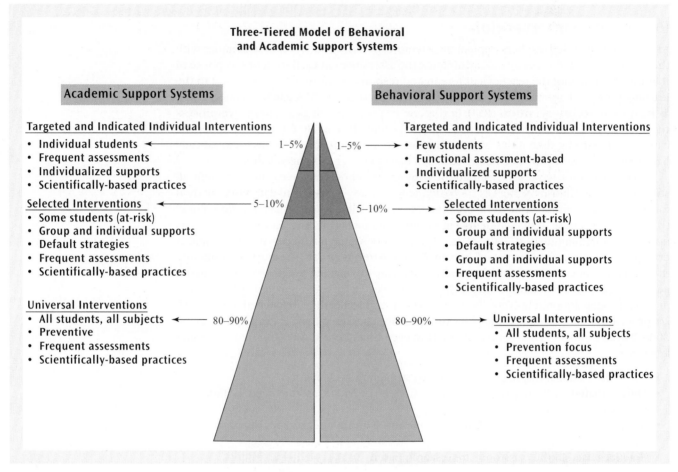

Three-Tiered Model of Behavioral
and Academic Support Systems

Academic Support Systems

Targeted and Indicated Individual Interventions
- Individual students   ←   1–5%
- Frequent assessments
- Individualized supports
- Scientifically-based practices

Selected Interventions   ←   5–10%
- Some students (at-risk)
- Group and individual supports
- Default strategies
- Frequent assessments
- Scientifically-based practices

Universal Interventions
- All students, all subjects   ←   80–90%
- Preventive
- Frequent assessments
- Scientifically-based practices

Behavioral Support Systems

1–5%   →   **Targeted and Indicated Individual Interventions**
- Few students
- Functional assessment-based
- Individualized supports
- Scientifically-based practices

5–10%   →   **Selected Interventions**
- Some students (at-risk)
- Group and individual supports
- Default strategies
- Group and individual supports
- Frequent assessments
- Scientifically-based practices

80–90%   →   **Universal Interventions**
- All students, all subjects
- Prevention focus
- Frequent assessments
- Scientifically-based practices

Source: From *RTI and Behavior: A Guide to Integrating Behavioral and Academic Supports* (p. 4) by J. Sprague, C. R. Cook, D. B. Wright, & C. Sadler, 2008. Horsham, PA: LRP Publications.

defined as falling below the 20th to 25th percentile on assessment measures, services should intensify and the student moves into the Tier II level of intervention. Only 5 to 10% of students are expected to require Tier II services (Sprague et al., 2008).

As teachers recognize the need for Tier II level of intervention for a student, often they will reach out to the school-based Prereferral Intervention Team (PIT) to brainstorm with other highly qualified and often "senior" teachers to determine the most effective strategies to enhance the educational services previously provided during the Tier I intervention plan. In Tier II academic intervention, students are generally moved into smaller groups (three to five students) determined by ability and provided supplemental instruction. Scientifically based teaching sessions are typically more frequent, last longer, and are more intense. Differentiated instruction is even more important at this level. Behavioral intervention would include increased social skills and self-management training and support. Sprague et al. (2009) also suggest identifying a school-based adult mentor and alternatives to out-of-school suspension, parent training and collaboration, and participation in community and service learning experiences.

General education teachers can be totally responsible for Tier II intervention or an intervention specialist or paraprofessional may assist the teacher. Progress is assessed more often, at least every two weeks. Again, measuring the student's response to these more intense intervention procedures is critical to the data-based decision-making component of the RTI model. Students found not to be benefitting from Tier I or Tier II intervention methods are moved into Tier III of the RTI model.

During Tier III intervention, more intensive, scientifically based academic intervention and social skills training (if relevant) is provided in smaller, homogeneous groups. The teacher-to-student ratio might be 1:1, 1:2, or 1:3. Length of academic instruction might be increased to two or three 30-minute periods a day. An individualized behavioral support plan would generally be implemented. Progress should be monitored once or twice a week, specifically measuring gains made in the target skill area. Intervention might be provided by the general education teacher, a teaching specialist, or an outside interventionist. The intervention might take place in the general education setting or outside of the classroom (Cook, 2007). Only 3 to 5% of students are expected to require Tier III intervention.

Although these prereferral procedures might seem like a way for some school systems to avoid providing costly special education services, the process has merit, as it can be a powerful way to address student needs within inclusive settings. However, the instructional strategies found in general education classrooms during the prereferral intervention period definitely will not be an answer for all students. In summary, the prereferral process involves:

1. Indication that a classroom-based problem exists that did not respond to scientifically based, differentiated instructional or behavioral interventions that were implemented during increasingly more intense and individualized interventions provided during Tiers I, II, and III of the RTI general education model.
2. Systematic measurement of the presenting problem(s) related to making adequate progress in the general education classroom. This information is monitored by highly qualified teachers and used to make data-based decisions regarding intervention.
3. Development of one or more intervention plans, in collaboration with the PIT, that contain strategies and other suggestions for addressing the student's challenges.
4. Assurances that the scientifically based interventions were implemented with fidelity.

Prereferral Process   The prereferral intervention process ordinarily begins with concerns of a classroom teacher about the performance, progress, or behavior(s) of a student. Other sources for information for the teacher and, ultimately, the intervention team could be parents, periodic reviews of student progress, or an external service provider. Hopefully, schools will establish procedures to inform parents of concerns as early as possible. Parents should be made aware of problems when information on their child's lack of progress is brought to the attention of the PIT.

Most schools provide a simple form for teachers and others to use when making a referral to this team. Information requested might include a brief description of the presenting problem, documentation of any support services the child currently receives and any interventions attempted, and the child's strengths and interests. When the form is completed, a group of school-based personnel meet to review the information provided. Throughout this text, we have referred to this team as the **Prereferral Intervention Team** (PIT); however, the teams may also be called the *intervention team, teacher assistance team, child study team,* or *building-based support team* depending on the geographical location. Frequently, the PIT will need more in-depth information on the student and will seek information in the following areas:

- Student's school history
- Previous evaluations performed: psychological, educational, speech/language, functional behavioral assessments, outside agency evaluations
- Observations (previous and new)
- Interviews (previous and new): teachers, family, student

Once the team has sufficient information to understand the nature of the presenting problem(s), members will attempt to generate suggestions to address the student's difficulties. At the outset, the team attempts to assist the teacher in targeting the most significant problems in the classroom by identifying intervention goals and the criteria by which a successful change will be measured. Then, the task is to identify effective intervention strategies such as accommodations or modifications to the environment or instructional strategies; less often, the curriculum might be modified or an alternative teaching method implemented (IDEA mandates that these be scientifically research-based). When a student's behavior is interfering with learning, strategies will be designed and implemented to help in this area. Emphasis should be placed on choosing the most positive interventions that rely on the natural support systems within a classroom and result in the least change to the general education setting and curriculum. Sometimes well-meaning educators and parents err by recommending too many accommodations or modifications, when it is actually in the child's best interest to implement the least number of changes that still result in the desired outcome.

Although some professionals and texts use the terms *accommodations* and *modifications* interchangeably, the following distinctions made by Cohen and Spenciner (2007) are helpful in seeing the range of adaptations available and the implications of each. *Accommodations* are changes made during assessment or to a child's education that do not substantially change the curriculum content, the level of instruction, or the assessment criteria. In other words, the changes do not lower the standards expected on a subject or test. Examples would be giving extra time to complete an assignment made for all students or changing a child's proximity to the teacher to increase attention or improve behavior. *Modifications* are more significant departures from the general education assessment and/or instructional program and might include substituting a text written on the same subject but using simpler wording, or requiring only half of the math problems assigned to the rest of the class. Modifications do alter the assessment criteria, curriculum content, or level of work; these changes are less likely to be made at the prereferral level of intervention and are usually documented on an IEP if the team agrees to the need. Table 3.1 provides examples of accommodations and modifications frequently used in assessment.

Typically, adaptations made for instructional programming are also available during assessment. However, some states do not allow accommodations or modifications during statewide assessment if the changes interfere with the test validity. For example, the reading comprehension portion of a test could not be read to a student because it would no longer be a valid measure of reading ability; however, the math portion of the test might be read to the student. Figure 3.3 provides a form that might be used to document the decisions and recommendations of the PIT. Note that the form also documents the person responsible for implementing the plan, support given, and timelines.

Prereferral intervention techniques are generally implemented for at least one grading period, typically 6 to 9 weeks; however, the teacher and the team can be flexible and specify a different time period, according to the needs of the individual student. When a teacher implements a new method for teaching a student, the teacher and team must carefully monitor the student's response to that intervention. The team may also recommend that more than one scientifically, research-based intervention be implemented if the first attempt fails to show improvement (Cohen & Spenciner, 2007); however, care should be taken that unnecessary delays are not made to the referral process. Contact with the classroom teachers should be an ongoing part of the PIT activities to determine whether the recommended interventions are being implemented properly and whether they are successful. However, at the end of the agreed-upon period, the team more formally evaluates the success of the prereferral intervention to determine whether the intervention goals have been met and whether a formal referral for a comprehensive special education evaluation is warranted. Note that the purpose of the prereferral team is to review concerns and design interventions, rather than to pass cases on for special education consideration. Far too often in the past, the easy action to take for a student who exhibited learning or behavioral problems was to refer him or her immediately to special education. The learning and behavioral needs of many students can, and should, be handled in the general education classroom. To do so, however, requires a system (i.e., prereferral) that offers a timely response to teachers' dilemmas and fulfills a collaborative role of providing consultation and ongoing support to benefit the student.

TABLE 3.1

Frequently Used Accommodations and Modifications

TYPE OF ACCOMMODATION OR MODIFICATION	EXAMPLE OF ACCOMMODATIONS	EXAMPLE OF MODIFICATIONS
Presentation mode	• Test is administered individually rather than administered in a group. • Examiner reads items out loud (except when student is tested in reading). • Student takes a computer-administered form of the test. • Large print forms are used. • Braille form of the test is used. • Test directions and items are signed. • A specific examiner may be chosen who is able to develop (or who already has) rapport with the student.	• Examiner uses prompts or cues.
Location of the test administration	• Test is administered in an area with reduced distractions. • Test is administered while student is using special furniture. • Test is administered in space that has special lighting.	
Response mode	• Teacher or helper marks the responses as indicated by the student. • Student indicates responses on paper that has lines or a grid. • Student uses a communication device. • Time limits for responding are extended or modified.	• Student is allowed to use a calculator for mathematics calculation. • Examiner accepts key word responses instead of complete sentences required by the test. • Student is allowed to use a spell checker, specialized software, or dictionary for writing test.
Test content	• Number of items per page is reduced but student completes all test items. • Use of bilingual glossaries and dictionaries (for English language learners).	• Fewer test items are presented.
Test format	• Test items are magnified.	• Key words in the test directions are highlighted or color-coded. • Test items are reworded. • Pictures or graphics are substituted for words.

Source: From *Assessment of Children and Youth with Special Needs* (p. 5), by L. G. Cohen and L. J. Spenciner, 2007. Boston: Allyn & Bacon.

The prereferral process appears to be both effective in helping teachers and students and efficient in forwarding referrals of only those students who need specialized services. In research settings, the PITs have also been shown to reduce unnecessary testing and placements in special education, improve student performance, and improve the attitude of teachers and their skill in handling more challenging students (Truscott, Cohen, & Sams, 2005). The Personal Spotlight provides insight from a middle school principal as he shares the impact of implementing a three-tiered intervention system in his school. Significant effects were found on the skill levels of his teachers and on the number of special education referrals.

FIGURE 3.3

Prereferral intervention plan.

Student: _____   Grade: _____   Teacher: _____

GOAL

Intervention Goal # _____

What observable, measurable changes do we want to see in the student?
_____
_____

*What criteria for success will be used?*_____
_____

INTERVENTION

| Environmental Adjustments | Instructional Adaptations |
| Curricular Modifications | Behavioral strategies motivational |

FOLLOW UP

Who is responsible for implementing the plan? _____

What supports will be available? _____
_____

How will effectiveness be evaluated? _____

Who will collect data? _____ how frequently? _____

When will the team reconvene to review intervention? _____

THE SPECIAL EDUCATION PROCESS

Unfortunately, scientifically based prereferral intervention at three levels of intensity sometimes is not able to achieve the goals that were set for a student. Moreover, in some instances in which a student displays significant learning and behavioral problems and all parties agree that a referral is appropriate, prereferral intervention is never attempted. Regardless of how a student gets to this particular stage, a referral for special education consideration marks the official beginning of the special education process.

PERSONAL SPOTLIGHT

LINDA BRADY really got excited about RTI for the first time when she attended a professional workshop in 2007 and heard Dr. John Cook from Knoxville, Tennessee share specific details about how RTI could be successfully implemented in a school system. From there, she had a vision of changing the culture in her school system, Vestavia Hills, where she is the Special Education Coordinator. One reason for her enthusiasm about RTI was the hope that she would never have to sit across from parents of a child with a suspected learning disability again and break the news that their child did not qualify for services because the assessment scores did not meet the formula used to determine a severe discrepancy. That would be a significant positive outcome, but she could also envision the payoff not only for the students with disabilities and their teachers but also for the general education students and teachers. She knew it would take a team effort, after all RTI is a "regular education initiative embedded in special education law," but she had a good relationship with her peers at the Central Office and she was up for the challenge.

The first thing Linda did was to organize a collaborative team meeting, including her colleagues in general education and administration. These individuals had collaborated before, but could they pull off a systemwide change?

The team began by looking at the RTI methods that they had in place. They were pleasantly surprised to find that they already had several pieces; for example, the school system had made a commitment to implement scientific research-based reading intervention from kindergarten through high school. Teachers had been trained to use curriculum-based assessment techniques to monitor progress. Soon the math and spelling intervention pieces were added and Tier I services were almost complete in the elementary levels. For Tier II services, the administration provided funds for the state-of-the-art Language! Program and the Shelton Multisensory Structured Language Education (MSLE), offering comprehensive, highly structured, intense intervention in reading, spelling, and writing. At Tier III, the intervention session would last for 45 minutes and would be provided daily by an instructional specialist. Teachers were invited—not mandated—to participate in the extensive RTI training that would be offered to collaborative pairs including a general and special educator.

Linda says that implementing RTI has been more difficult at the middle school and high school levels, but progress is being made. The intervention classes are being offered to students as electives and schedules are being altered to expose struggling students to the highly trained teachers. As teachers in the schools have shared their success stories and excitement over the materials, more teachers are asking for training. What started as a "top-down" culture change has progressed to a "bottom-up" effort. Linda calls their RTI program a "work in progress," but it looks like their collaborative effort has already paid off!

Figure 3.4 provides a flowchart of how the special education process works. Inherent in this process are specific timelines and actions that must be followed to be compliant with federal and state law. This figure relates closely to the major elements presented in Figure 3.1 (see page 71) and provides more detail of the formal special education process. Again, this formal referral to evaluate the student to determine eligibility for special education services follows the lack of response to treatment during the prereferral intervention phase, as determined by the PIT. It might also suggest that the difficulties are too severe to delay the special education process.

■ Members of a child study team may help develop prereferral interventions for students having problems.

Formal Referral

The format of the written referral varies across school systems; however, the form generally contains basic descriptive information (e.g., student's date of birth, grade) and evidence of the severity and duration of the problem(s) in the classroom. Individual school systems may

FIGURE 3.4

The special education process.

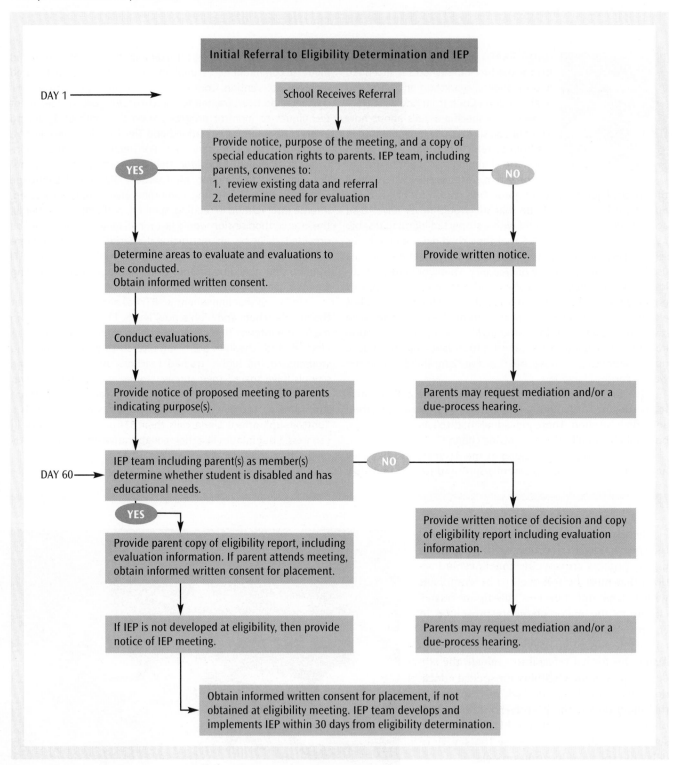

Note: The 2004 reauthorization of IDEA allows schools to pursue evaluation through due process if parents deny permission. Schools are not allowed to pursue placement for the child through due process if the parents deny consent for services.

require that documentation be written as a summary or ask that evidence be attached; the information needed usually includes:

- Work samples showing areas of weakness
- Samples of classroom tests
- Behavioral assessment/behavioral log
- Report cards
- Test information from cumulative folder
- Description and results of prereferral intervention
- Parent information, including summaries of contact documenting their concerns

At the point of referral, a new team is formulated to work together throughout the special education process. This team is referred to as the **Individualized Education Program** (IEP) team. The federal regulations of IDEA stress that every school district ensure that the IEP team assembled for each student with a suspected disability includes the following:

1. The child's parents
2. At least one regular education teacher
3. At least one special education teacher
4. A representative of the local educational agency who is:
   a. Qualified to provide, or supervise the provision of, specially designed instruction to meet the unique needs of children with disabilities
   b. Knowledgeable about the general education curriculum
   c. Knowledgeable about the availability of resources of the local education agency
5. An individual who can interpret the instructional implications of evaluation results (may be one of the team members listed above)
6. Other individuals who have knowledge or special expertise regarding the child, including related services personnel as appropriate
7. Whenever appropriate, the child with a disability (required for a transition IEP)
8. Other team members may include: an individual with expertise in instructional technology, representatives from outside agencies that may be involved in planning and/or providing transition services, and other appropriate persons deemed important by the parents or the school system (Yell, 2006).

Submitting a referral to a designated school official initiates a set of formal activities. First and foremost, a letter is sent to the parents to notify them of the referral, to inform them of their rights throughout the special education process, and to invite them and their child, if appropriate, to participate along with "other qualified professionals" in the first meeting of their child's IEP team. This meeting is usually held at the child's school and is scheduled at a mutually agreed-upon time. Some schools hold meetings in the evenings or on the weekend to accommodate working parents. Although face-to-face meetings are always desirable, computer conferencing and conference calls have been used to facilitate parental participation.

At this meeting a decision is made by the IEP team as to whether a comprehensive evaluation should be undertaken (i.e., whether the referral has merit). If the decision is yes, then the parents are asked for written consent for the evaluation. The school is allowed up to 60 days to collect the needed information and to complete the required and requested assessment. At the next meeting of the IEP team, the data are used to determine whether the child meets the eligibility criteria for a particular disability as developed within that state and whether the child needs special education and/or related services. Following is an overview of the types of assessment procedures that may be implemented after the formal referral is accepted and the roles of the general education teacher throughout that process.

Assessment Practices

Assessment applied to the educational setting is the process of observing, gathering, recording, and interpreting information to answer questions and make instructional and legal decisions about students (Cohen & Spenciner, 2007). According to the 2006 final IDEA Part B regulations, it is a dynamic, continuous process that guides and directs decisions about students with suspected or known disabilities. However, the states still vary in the types of procedures used, the specific approaches to assessment, and the criteria used to determine student eligibility.

Teachers play four major roles in regard to school-based assessment and, as a result, need to have skills in all four areas:

1. Teachers are consumers of assessment information—in this role, they must be able to understand assessment information.
2. Teachers are producers of assessment information—they must be able to generate assessment information by administering tests, conducting observations, and so on, during the prereferral RTI process as well as in the special education process.
3. Teachers are communicators of assessment information—because much of what we do in schools today is team-based, teachers must be able to share assessment information with others (professionals, parents, students).
4. Teachers are developers of assessment instruments—most teachers will find that they have to create assessment techniques to accomplish some education-related tasks. This is especially true during the time the teacher is measuring a student's response to treatment and documenting progress in meeting general education curricular benchmarks or changes in behavior.

Although assessment has always played a critical role in the special education process, the importance of assessment for all students and school personnel has increased dramatically since the passing of the No Child Left Behind Act of 2001 (NCLB). The central theme of this act is accountability for all students to have positive academic outcomes (Simpson, LaCava, & Graner, 2004). Specifically, every student, including those with special needs, is to make adequate yearly progress and ultimately meet state-identified standards measured by performance goals identifying what students should know in each academic area at each grade level. The NCLB mandates combined with the standards set forth in IDEA—that every child eligible for special education services have "access to the general education curriculum" and "make progress in that curriculum"—bring a new, increased focus on the assessment process that monitors each student's progress.

Purpose of Assessment   Assessment is critical in each of the major phases of the special education process, including the prereferral/RTI phase. During the **screening** phase, the concerns expressed by teachers and parents are the result of their informal "assessment" of the student's lack of progress. Their concern comes from their observations and interactions with the student in the natural environment. When parents and teachers get concerned, they may consult others who have worked with the child or review previous records or current work. At this point, these students are acknowledged to be at risk for failure, and the first level of assessment for special education services has begun.

If a referral is made and the IEP team accepts the referral, the **identification and eligibility** phase of assessment begins. During this phase the child is formally evaluated in all areas related to the suspected disability to determine if he or she has a disability and is eligible for special education services. This might include evaluating a student's intellectual ability, health, vision, hearing, academic achievement, social and emotional needs, level of communication, or motor skills (Bateman & Linden, 2007); the evaluations are performed individually by trained professionals. These results are studied by the IEP team along with the information gathered during the screening, prereferral/RTI, and referral phases.

If the student is determined to be eligible, assessment data are needed to identify the unique needs of the child for **program planning**. Existing data are studied further, and new data may be collected to help the IEP team select goals and objectives or benchmarks, as well as identify the most effective, research-validated methods of instruction to include in the IEP. After the IEP has been implemented, ongoing assessment is conducted to **monitor** and **evaluate** the student's progress. The IEP team predetermines the methods used for reporting and decides how often progress will be reported to parents throughout the year. The student is assessed annually to evaluate the outcome of the IEP and provide a measure of accountability. In addition, the student's eligibility or need for services is reconsidered by the IEP team every 3 years. The IEP team may agree that no changes are needed in placement and services and agree not to reevaluate, or it may decide that additional assessments are required to make that decision. The results of each phase of this assessment determine which of several approaches to assessment are used.

Approaches to Assessment   The most common methods of gathering information on students are described as formal or informal. Both of these types of assessment are used in the contemporary assessment model shown in Figure 3.5. This model provides the framework

FIGURE 3.5

Contemporary assessment model.

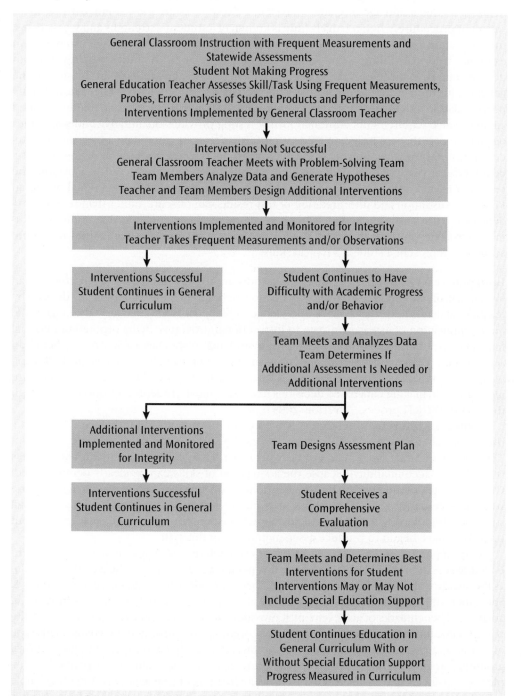

Source: From *Assessing Learners with Special Needs* (6th ed.) (p. 17) by T. Overton, 2009. Upper Saddle River, NJ: Pearson.

needed in education to meet the regulation that ongoing assessment drives the teaching-learning process. Finding a solution is the focus of this model, thus guiding the teacher or specialized team in making data-based decisions for students.

Formal Assessment   The model uses formal assessment in the beginning of the process and again later if students are referred for the comprehensive evaluation required for an eligibility decision. Formal assessment instruments are generally available commercially. Detailed guidelines for administration, scoring, and interpretation are included. They are most often **norm-referenced**; that is, the tests provide quantitative information comparing the performance of an individual student to others in his or her norm group (determined, for example, by age, grade, or gender). Test results are usually reported in the form of test quotients, percentiles, and age or grade equivalents. These tools are most useful early as an assessment procedure, when relatively little is known of a student's strengths and weaknesses; the comparative scores may help identify areas in which informal assessment can begin. An example of formal testing is the statewide assessment or **high-stakes testing** given to demonstrate that adequate yearly progress is being made and students are mastering the general education curriculum. The ability to compare the student to his or her age and grade peers is also an advantage in making eligibility and placement decisions and fulfilling related administrative requirements. Although formal testing provides quantitative and sometimes qualitative data that are based on student performance, tests can obtain a measure of a student's best performance only in a contrived situation; they cannot broadly represent a student's typical performance under natural conditions. When considered in isolation, the results of formal tests can lead to poor decisions in placement and instructional planning. Rigid administration and interpretation of test results can obscure, rather than reveal, a student's strengths and weaknesses. It has become increasingly apparent that traditional, formal approaches must be augmented with the informal assessment techniques that more accurately represent a student's typical skills.

Informal Tests   Informal assessment measures are usually more loosely structured than formal instruments and are more closely tied to teaching. Such tools are typically devised by teachers to determine what skills or knowledge a child possesses. Their key advantage is the direct application of assessment data to instructional programs. By incorporating informal tests and measurements and by monitoring students' responses each day, teachers can achieve a more accurate assessment of growth in learning or behavioral change. Following is a brief discussion of general types of informal assessment procedures. These measures are more useful in making data-based decisions needed to move students appropriately through the tiers of the RTI process (Overton, 2009).

Criterion-referenced testing (CRT) compares a student's performance with a criterion of mastery for a specific skill or task, disregarding his or her relative standing in a group. This form of informal assessment can be especially useful when documentation of progress is needed for accountability because the acquisition of skills can be clearly demonstrated. CRTs are quite helpful because they focus attention on specific skills in the curriculum, provide measures of progress toward mastery, and assist teachers in designing instructional strategies. Traditionally, teachers have developed most criterion-referenced instruments, but publishers have begun to produce assessment tools of this type.

One important and popular form of criterion-referenced assessment is **curriculum-based assessment (CBM)**, which, unlike norm-referenced tools, uses the actual curriculum as the standard and thus provides a direct link between assessment and instruction (Cohen & Spenciner, 2007). CBM involves the close monitoring of the student's progress in meeting goals set as benchmarks of achievement; it provides a method of evaluating the success of the current educational conditions and is often the stimulus for implementing change. This type of assessment can have a role in many important tasks: identification, eligibility, instructional grouping, program planning, progress monitoring, and program evaluation. A **probe** is a simple test usually created by the teacher to measure learning of a specific task. A math example would be giving a student 2 minutes to complete as many single-digit addition facts as possible and counting the number of correctly written digits. Results of these probes are often charted providing a clear view of response to intervention.

Two additional terms commonly used to describe alternative assessment methods are **authentic assessment** and **portfolio assessment**. These assessment methods use similar techniques such as requiring students to construct, produce, perform, or demonstrate a task or knowledge. These types of student responses are considered alternatives to typical testing responses, such as selecting from multiple-choice items, a technique commonly used on standardized, formal tests. An example of an authentic assessment would be setting up a mini-store in a classroom and asking the students to make purchases involving counting money and making change. Portfolio assessment is a collection of assessment results that are gathered over time to demonstrate progress (Overton, 2009). Approximately half of the 50 states use portfolio assessment to measure progress on state goals and standards for students with such severe disabilities that they cannot take the state- and districtwide assessments even with accommodations (Johnson & Arnold, 2004).

Ecological assessment is another approach used with many types of informal assessment. As educational assessment has increasingly begun to reflect a trend toward appreciating the ecology of the student, data obtained are now more frequently analyzed in relation to the child's functioning in his or her various environments. Although a full discussion of ecological assessment is beyond the scope of this chapter, the following information highlights some basic considerations, and Figure 3.6 provides a format for assessing the physical environment, the behavioral structure, instructional strategies, and student-to-student and

---

FIGURE 3.6	Assessment of Academic Environment

Name of Student: _____ Date: _____

Class: _____

Duration of observation: _____ minutes.

Check all that are observed during this observational period.

Physical Environmental Factors
_____ Seating: Individual student desks
_____ Seating: Group tables
_____ Seating: Student desks grouped in pairs or groups of four
_____ Material organized for quick student access and use
_____ Target student's materials organized

Classroom Behavioral Structure
_____ Classroom expectations (rules) posted
_____ Verbal praise for effort of students
_____ Verbal praise for target student
_____ Quiet redirection for target student when needed
_____ Inconsequential minor behaviors are ignored
_____ Transitions were smooth
_____ Time lapse to begin task less than 3 minutes (for class)
_____ Time lapse to begin task less than 3 minutes (for target student)
_____ Time lapse to begin task 5 minutes or more (for class)
_____ Time lapse to begin task 5 minutes or more (for target student)
_____ Noise level consistent with task demands
_____ Classwide behavior plan used

Classroom Teacher's Instructional Behaviors
_____ Task expectations explained verbally
_____ Task expectations explained visually (on board, etc.)
_____ Task modeled by teacher
_____ Cognitive strategies modeled by teacher first (thinking aloud)

(continued)

FIGURE
3.6   Assessment of Academic Environment   *(continued)*

Teacher-Students Interactions
_____ Academic behavior/responses shaped by teacher for all students
_____ Teacher used proximity as a monitoring technique for all students
_____ Teacher used proximity for reinforcement technique for all students
_____ Teacher used one-on-one instruction to clarify task for all students

Teacher-Target Student Interactions
_____ Academic behavior/responses shaped by teacher for target student
_____ Teacher used proximity as a monitoring technique for target student
_____ Teacher used proximity for reinforcement technique for target student
_____ Teacher used one-on-one instruction to clarify for target student
_____ Homework assignment is planned for reinforcement of skill rather than extension of work
not completed during class

Classroom Academic Structure
_____ Anticipatory set for lesson/activity
_____ Task completed by group first before individuals are expected to complete task
_____ Academic behavior/responses modeled/assisted by peers
_____ Expected response or task made by pairs, groups, or teams
_____ Expected response made by individual students
_____ Tasks, instructions were structured and clear to students
_____ Tasks, instructions were unclear to target student
_____ A variety of teaching methods (direct instruction, media, manipulatives) used
_____ Advanced organizers used; cues, prompts, presented to class

Extended Learning Experiences
_____ Homework assignment appropriate (at independent level, not emerging skill level)
_____ Homework instructions are clear
_____ Homework assignment is displayed in consistent place in room (board, etc.)
_____ Students use daily planner or other technique for homework/classwork
_____ Homework assignment is planned for reinforcement of skill rather than extension of work not completed
during class

Other concerns of academic environment:

Source: From "Promoting Academic Success Through Environmental Assessment," by T. Overton, 2006, *Intervention in School and Clinic, 39*(3),
pp. 147–153.

student-to-teacher interactions. This is an excellent source of data for teachers to use in self-reflection and to make important changes to the environment.

The focus of ecological assessment is to place the evaluation process within the context of the student's environment. Its central element is functionality—how well the student operates in the current environment or the one into which he or she will be moving. This focus shifts a program's emphasis from correcting deficits toward determining how to build on strengths, interests, and preferences. This type of assessment is particularly useful in early childhood.

Legal Requirements for Assessment   PL 94–142, the first major law dealing with special education policy, introduced many of the assessment mandates that exist today. The most recent reauthorization of IDEA in 2004 continues to address and refine the assessment process. One of the greatest challenges for special educators is accurately assessing cultur- ally and linguistically diverse students for disabilities. The majority of the requirements are regarding fair testing practices to ensure nondiscriminatory testing.

Following are the highlights of IDEA related to evaluation and assessment:

- Assessment materials must be selected and administered so as not to be racially or culturally discriminatory.
- Tests must be administered in the language and form most likely to accurately reflect what the child knows and can do developmentally, academically, and functionally.
- No single procedure or test can be the sole criterion for determining eligibility for special education.
- The student must be assessed in all areas of suspected disability. These areas might include health, vision, hearing, social and emotional status, intelligence, academic per- formance, communication status, and motor abilities.
- Information provided by parents and measures other than "tests" must also be considered.
- Any assessment measures must be validated for the specific purpose for which they are used and administered by an individual trained to give the test.
- Eligibility also cannot be determined if the deficits are found to be a reflection of a lack of instruction in reading or math.
- Finally, the assessment must address how to enable the student to participate and progress in the general education curriculum (or for a preschool student, to participate in appropriate activities). This includes participation in statewide or districtwide assess- ments given to all students. The IEP team may decide that the student with a disability should be provided accommodations or modifications such as extended time. Additional frequently used accommodations and modifications were documented in Table 3.1.

The team also may decide that participation in standardized testing is not appropriate even with adaptations. In this case, the team must identify an alternate assessment procedure that allows the student to demonstrate what he or she has learned. The decision to use an alternative means of assessment is made only for the students with the most severe disabili- ties; the assessments developed to measure their progress should also be aligned with the same curriculum standards used by all stu- dents. It is clearly the focus of NCLB and IDEA to move away from a "special education cur- riculum" and toward the use of regular assess- ment techniques measuring progress toward meeting grade-level standards in the general ed- ucation curriculum (Bateman & Linden, 2007).

In addition to racial or cultural bias in assessment, a separate concern is the accurate assessment of individuals who experience sensory or motor disabilities. For example, indi- viduals who have hearing impairments may require a nonverbal test, whereas people who have visual impairments may require enlarged print material or braille. An individual with a severe motor impairment may have limited voluntary responses and may need to respond using an eye scan or blink. They may require a paraprofessional to write for them or "bubble in" test answers. Other students may have limited receptive or expressive language capabili- ties and may require different modes for understanding the questions, making sense out of information or demonstrating what they have learned.

Students who have multiple disabilities compound the difficulties of administering the assessment task. For example, they may refuse to stay seated for an assessment session or may exhibit interfering self-stimulatory behavior (e.g., hand flapping, rocking). Such disabil- ities or behaviors may cause the test to measure problems rather than assess functioning.

■ Parental involvement in the development of the individualized education program is both a legal requirement and an important aspect in the design of appropriate school programs.

Implementation of accommodations or modifications appropriate for the needs of each student with a disability greatly reduces this type of test bias. Each of the chapters addressing the needs of students with a specific disability will include a section on effective assessment practices.

Role of the General Education Teacher in Assessment   The list that follows suggests ways in which the general education professional can take an active role in the assessment process:

- Ask questions about the assessment process. Special education teachers and school psychologists should be committed to clarifying the nature of the assessments used and the interpretation of the results.
- Encourage family participation in school activities to better understand values and differences, and let parents know that their input is valued. If communication is a problem, special education teachers may offer the support you need during a conference.
- Provide input. Formal test data should not be allowed to contradict on-going observations in the classroom about a student's ability, achievement, and learning patterns. A valid diagnostic picture should bring together multiple sources of data, including learning journals, curriculum-based measures, and portfolio assessment from the general education classroom.
- Consider issues of possible bias. Because formal assessments are often administered by an individual relatively unknown to the child (e.g., a psychologist), inadvertent bias factors between examiner and examinee may be more likely to creep into the results. Work with other staff to ensure an unbiased process.
- Avoid viewing assessment as a means of confirming a set of observations or conclusions about a student's difficulties. Assessment is exploratory and may not lead to expected results. Too often, after a student is not judged eligible for special services, various parties feel resentment toward the assessment process. However, the key commitment should be to elicit useful information to help the student, not to arrive at a foregone eligibility decision that might please the student, parent, or teacher.

Determination of Eligibility

If the decision to proceed with a **comprehensive evaluation** is affirmed, and parents consent, then the eligibility phase begins. If the parent does not consent to the initial evaluation, the school district may begin mediation or follow due-process proceedings in an attempt to have the evaluation ordered by state law.

Other eligibility criteria covered under IDEA require that the evaluation be comprehensive enough to gather functional, developmental, and academic data sufficient to determine if the student has one of the disabilities covered by IDEA, to identify his or her educational needs and present levels of performance, and to determine if the student needs special education and/or related services (Bateman & Linden, 2007). The assessment instruments and techniques used, along with the personnel who will administer them, will vary greatly within and across states. Nevertheless, the evaluation process and any assessment battery chosen must be sensitive to age, grade level, and culture, and must be comprehensive and flexible enough to address the learning and behavioral difficulties of any student referred. Because the vast majority of students who are disabled are referred during the elementary years, the process is often less visible at the secondary level. However, the demands of the middle school and high school settings are more complex, so prereferral intervention and referral procedures, including differentiated instruction and the RTI process, should be operative at these levels as well.

During the eligibility determination phase, the general education teacher will likely be called on to provide background information on the student. The teacher might be interviewed or asked to complete rating scales or checklists or participate in functional assessments. On occasion, the teacher will be asked to conduct and record direct observations of a student and provide samples of the student's academic work.

Ultimately, the IEP team, "a team of qualified professionals and the parent," is responsible for making the eligibility decision. After the pertinent assessment information is compiled on the student, the team meets again, this time to examine the data to determine whether a disability exists, whether the student meets the state eligibility guidelines for a particular disability, and whether, even if the student has a disability, the student needs special education services. At this point, a determination of whether a student qualifies for special education is made (refer to Figure 3.4). If the answer is yes, and the parents agree (providing written consent for placement), the team can proceed with the development of the **IEP**, specifying educational intervention and specific **special education services** and **related services**. Related services are those considered critical for a student to benefit from the goals of the IEP; these might include an interpreter for students who are deaf or hard of hearing, psychological services, or a paraprofessional.

The team may prefer to have a separate meeting for the IEP development and placement decision to give parents and others time to process the information presented at the eligibility determination meeting; however, this meeting must be completed within 30 days of the eligibility meeting. Special education placement should immediately follow determination of eligibility unless issues such as transportation must be addressed.

As stated previously, the IEP team can pursue an *evaluation* of a child through due process without the parents' written consent; however, the 2004 reauthorization of IDEA notes that children will not be determined eligible for services if their parents do not consent to *placement*. Parents can refuse special education and related services. If this occurs, the education agency cannot pursue special education for the child and the school would not be held in violation of providing a free, appropriate public education (Hyatt, 2007).

Placement can also be denied if the child's problems are determined to result from a lack of appropriate instruction in reading or math. The law specifically defines scientifically based reading instruction as including phonemic awareness, phonics, vocabulary development, reading fluency (including oral reading skills), and reading comprehension strategies. Another factor that must be considered is English language proficiency. Students with limited English skills cannot be determined eligible for special education or related services unless there are other causative factors documented. For example, if a student has a history of inadequate reading instruction but math instruction was appropriate, the student could be determined eligible for services for a math disability but not a reading disability. One of the most challenging tasks often faced by an IEP team is making the determination of whether the academic difficulties are the direct result of language or learning differences or lack of appropriate instruction (Salend & Salinas, 2003).

Individualized Education Program

An IEP is a requirement for every child determined eligible to receive special education services. It is a well-described legal document under IDEA and contains a summary of a child's strengths, limitations, and needs, and the corresponding special education and related services planned to address those needs. This written document is reviewed at least once annually. The overriding concept behind the IEP is that all educational programming should be driven by the unique strengths and needs of the student and the concerns of the parents for enhancing their child's education. Periodic review may involve changing methodology or delivery of instruction or adapting content to ensure the child's access to and participation in the general curriculum (Bateman & Linden, 2007). Further, the plan should be written to allow the child "reasonable educational benefit." If academic, developmental, functional, behavioral, or social needs are identified, goals need to be written to address these needs. In other words, services are determined by individual need, not by availability. Every individual on the IEP team, including the parents, should ideally come to the meeting with personal notes on the child's unique needs and related goals and services they would like to see included on the IEP. Any differences are resolved through the team process; any issues that cannot be resolved are continued under the due-process procedures previously described.

Federal Regulations for IEPs   The 2004 IDEA Reauthorization specifies the content for IEPs in general, the content for transition services for students beginning no later than age 16, and the special requirements for plans for young children from birth to age 3. The law also requires that a student be notified of the transfer of his or her rights at least one year prior to reaching the age of majority specified by law in his or her state. For example, in many states, the **age of majority** is 18; so, by this age, the student must sign the IEP verifying that this right has been explained. After this birthday, students can make decisions regarding school, independent living, and work. In extreme cases, when students are judged incapable of making their own decisions and protecting their own rights, the courts will award guardianship to parents or another advocate. One method of developing independence is to encourage and train students with disabilities to assume leadership at the IEP meeting and participate in the decision-making process (Torgesen, Miner, & Shen, 2004).

The general requirements of an IEP for students between ages 3 and 21 are as follows:

1. A statement of the child's present levels of academic achievement and functional performance, including:
   a. How the child's disability affects the child's involvement and progress in the general education curriculum
   b. For preschool children, how the disability affects the child's participation in appropriate activities
   c. For children with disabilities who take alternative assessments aligned to alternative achievement standards, a description of benchmarks or short-term objectives
2. A statement of measurable annual goals, including academic and functional goals, designed to meet the child's needs and to enable the child to be involved in and make progress in the general education curriculum
3. A description of how the child's progress toward meeting the annual goals will be measured and when periodic reports on the progress the child is making toward meeting the annual goals will be provided
4. A statement of the special education and related services and supplementary aids and services as well as a statement of the program modifications or supports that will be provided for the child [Note: The final regulations of IDEA 2004 stipulated that methods used should be backed by scientifically based research to the extent that it is practical, thus strengthening accountability and the likelihood that students will make adequate progress (Overton, 2009)]
5. An explanation of the extent, if any, to which the child will not participate with nondisabled children in the regular class and other activities
6. A statement of any individual appropriate accommodations that are necessary to measure the academic achievement and functional performance of the child on state- and districtwide assessments; and if the IEP team determines that the child should take an alternate assessment on a particular state- and districtwide assessment of student achievement, a statement of why the child cannot participate and the particular alternative assessment selected
7. The projected date for the beginning of the services and modifications, and the anticipated frequency, location, and duration of those services and modifications

The IEP offers special considerations to students with the following behaviors or conditions:

- Positive behavioral strategies, supports, and interventions, when appropriate, are provided to students whose behavior impedes their learning, or the learning of others.
- Braille instruction is provided to students who are blind or visually impaired, unless the IEP team determines that use of Braille is not appropriate.
- Opportunities for communication are provided to students with hearing impairments or language and communication needs, opportunities for communication with peers and teachers in each student's language and communication mode, including direct instruction in the mode.
- Assistive technology devices and services are provided to students with other special needs.

Key Components of an IEP Following is a brief description of the major components in an IEP. Figure 3.7 provides a format for an IEP that addresses each IEP requirement discussed. (A sample IEP using this format is also included in appendix A.)

FIGURE 3.7	Sample IEP

Unified School District
Individualized Education Program

Student: <u>Marty Glick</u>
School: <u>Hudson Elementary</u>
Placement: <u>General Education Classroom</u>
Date of IEP Meeting: <u>12/17/2008</u>
Date of Initiation of Services: <u>1/3/2009</u>
Dominant Language of Student: <u>English</u>

DOB: <u>8/5/98</u>
Grade: <u>5</u>
Disability Classification: <u>Learning Disability</u>
Notification of Family: <u>11/28/2008</u>
Review date: <u>1/3/2010</u>
Medical Alerts: <u>NONE</u>

CURRENT LEVEL OF PERFORMANCE IN THE GENERAL EDUCATION CURRICULUM
ACADEMIC/EDUCATIONAL ACHIEVEMENT
Mathematics

Marty's strongest areas, include geometry, measurement, time, and money. He has difficulty with multiplication, division, fractions, and word problems. He especially had difficulty solving problems that contained nonessential information.

Reading

Marty's reading is characterized by weaknesses in word recognition, oral reading, and comprehension. Marty had difficulty with the passages that were written at a third grade level. His oral reading of the passages revealed difficulties sounding out words and a reliance on contextual cues. He had particular problems with comprehension questions related to large amounts of information and interpreting abstractions.

Written Language

Marty's writing portfolio reveals that he has many ideas to write about in a broad range of genres. However, Marty avoids using prewriting tools such as semantic webs or outlines to organize his thoughts. Consequently, his stories don't usually follow a chronological sequence, and his reports do not fully develop the topic. He uses a variety of sentence patterns but frequently ignores the need for punctuation. Marty has difficulty editing his own work but will make mechanical changes pointed out by the teacher. He rarely revises the content or organization of his writing in a substantial manner. Marty's teacher has observed that Marty enjoys working on the computer and performs better on writing tasks when he uses a talking word processor.

SOCIAL DEVELOPMENT
Level of Social Development

Marty shows attention difficulties when attempting some academic tasks. He has a good sense of humor and seems to relate fairly well to his peers.

Interest Inventory

Marty likes working with peers and using computers. He prefers projects to tests. He likes working with his hands and fixing things.

PHYSICAL DEVELOPMENT

Marty is physically healthy and has no difficulties with his hearing and vision. He has had no major illnesses or surgeries, and he is not taking any medications.

BEHAVIORAL DEVELOPMENT

A functional assessment of Marty's classroom behavior indicates that Marty is frequently off-task and has difficulty completing his assignments. He often works on assignments for a short period of time and then works on another assignment, engages in an off-task activity such as playing with objects, leaves his work area, or seeks attention from his teacher or his peers. His behavior also appears to be affected by other activities in the classroom, the placement of his work area near certain students, and the type and difficulty of the activity.

(continued)

FIGURE 3.7   Sample IEP *(continued)*

RELATED SERVICES

Service	Frequency	Location
Group counseling	Once/week	Social worker's office

SUPPLEMENTARY AIDS AND SERVICES

Service	Frequency	Location
Collaboration teacher	2 hours/day	General education classroom
Paraprofessional	3 hours/day	General education classroom

PROGRAM MODIFICATION AND SUPPORT FOR SCHOOL PERSONNEL

Marty and his teacher will receive the services of a collaborative teacher and a paraeducator. Marty's teacher will be given time to meet with the collaboration teacher, who also will modify materials, locate resources, administer assessments, and coteach lessons. Marty's teacher also will receive training related to differentiated instruction, classroom management, and assessment alternatives and accommodations.

EXTENT OF PARTICIPATION IN GENERAL EDUCATION PROGRAMS AND WITH PEERS WITHOUT DISABILITIES

Marty will remain in his fifth-grade classroom full-time. The collaboration teacher and the paraeducator will provide direct service to Marty in the general education classroom.

RATIONALE FOR PLACEMENT

It is anticipated that Marty's educational needs can best be met in the general education classroom. He will benefit from being exposed to the general education curriculum with the additional assistance of the collaboration teacher and the paraeducator. The use of testing modifications and computers with talking word processors also should help Marty benefit from his general education program. Marty's social skills and self-concept also will be improved by exposure to his general education peers. Counseling will provide him with the prosocial skills necessary to interact with his peers and complete his work.

INSTRUCTIONAL PROGRAM

Annual Goal: Marty will read, write, listen, and speak for information and understanding. (State Learning Standard 1 for English Language Arts)

Evaluation Procedures

1. Given the choice of a narrative trade book at his instructional level, Marty will be able to retell the story, including major characters, the setting, and major events of the plot sequence.

   Teacher-made story grammar checklist

2. Given a passage from his social studies or science textbook, Marty will develop three questions that require inferential or critical thinking.

   Teacher evaluation of student response

3. Using a prewriting structure to organize his ideas, Marty will write a paragraph describing a process that shows logical development and has a minimum of five sentences.

   Writing rubric

Annual Goal: Marty will read, write, listen, and speak for literary response and expression. (State Learning Standard 2 for English Language Arts)

Evaluation Procedures

1. After choosing a favorite poem to read to his peers, Marty will memorize it and recite it with fluency and intonation.

   Peer and teacher feedback

2. Given the choice of texts with multi-syllabic words, Marty will read with 90% accuracy.

   Teacher analysis of running record

3. Given a choice of biographies, Marty will reflect upon the events and experiences which relate to his own life.

   Teacher evaluation of dialogue journal

FIGURE 3.7 Sample IEP *(continued)*

Annual Goal: Marty will understand mathematics and become mathematically confident by communicating and reasoning mathematically. (State Learning Standard 3 for Mathematics, Science, and Technology)

Evaluation Procedures

1. Given a one-step word problem with a distractor, Marty will write the relevant information and operation needed to solve it 90 percent of the time.

Teacher-made worksheet

2. Given the task of writing five one-step word problems with a distractor, Marty will write four that are clear enough for his classmates to solve.

Teacher evaluation of student response

Annual Goal: Marty will demonstrate mastery of the foundation skills and competencies essential for success in the workplace. (State Learning Standard 3a for Career Development and Occupational Studies)

Evaluation Procedures

1. When working independently on an academic task, Marty will improve his time on task by 100 percent.

Self-recording

2. When working in small groups, Marty will listen to peers and take turns speaking 80 percent of the time.

Teacher observation or group evaluation

TRANSITION PROGRAM

Marty is very interested in and skilled at working with his hands to make and fix things. In addition to using these skills as part of the educational program, Marty will participate in a career awareness program designed to explore his career interests.

This program will expose Marty to a variety of careers and allow him to experience work settings and meet professionals who are involved in careers related to Marty's interests. This program also will aid Marty in understanding his learning style, strengths and weaknesses, interests, and preferences.

Annual Goal: Marty will be knowledgeable about the world of work, explore career options, and relate personal skills, aptitudes, and abilities to future career decisions. (State Learning Standard 1 for Career Development and Occupational Studies)

Evaluation Procedures

1. Marty will identify three careers in which he may be interested and explain why he is interested in each one.

Self-report

2. Marty will research and explain the training and experiential requirements for the three careers he has identified.

Interview

3. Marty will evaluate his skills and characteristics with respect to these careers by identifying his related strengths and needs.

Self-report

4. Marty will follow and observe individuals involved in these three careers as they perform their jobs.

ASSISTIVE TECHNOLOGY AND COMMUNICATION NEEDS

Marty will be given a computer and talking word processing system with word prediction capabilities and a talking calculator to assist him with classroom activities and tests.

PARTICIPATION IN STATEWIDE, DISTRICTWIDE, AND CLASSROOM-BASED ASSESSMENTS, AS WELL AS TESTING ACCOMMODATIONS AND ALTERNATIVES

Participation in and testing accommodations during the administration of statewide and districtwide assessments: Marty will participate in all statewide and districtwide assessments and receive all statewide and districtwide approved testing accommodations. Where the district does not limit the use of testing accommodations, Marty will be provided with appropriate testing accommodations that are used during classroom-based assessments.

(continued)

FIGURE
3.7 Sample IEP *(continued)*

Participation in and testing accommodations during classroom-based assessments: Marty will participate in all classroom-based assessments. Teacher-made tests will be individually administered by the collaboration teacher in a separate location, with extended time and breaks every 30 minutes. Marty will be allowed to use a talking word processing program with word prediction capabilities. For math tests that do not assess mental computation, he will be allowed to use a talking calculator. When possible and appropriate. Marty will demonstrate his mastery of classroom content through projects and cooperative learning activities.

METHOD AND FREQUENCY OF COMMUNICATION WITH FAMILY

Marty's family will be regularly informed through IEP progress reports, curriculum-based assessments, and Marty's general education report cards. In addition, feedback on Marty's performance and progress will be shared with his family through quarterly scheduled family-teacher meetings, result of state and district assessments, and portfolio reviews.

Committee Participants	**Relationship/Role**
Ms. Rachel Tupper	5th grade teacher
Mr. Terry Feaster	Special Ed. teacher
Mr. Kris Brady	Sp. Ed. administrator
Ms. Jessica Amatura	Educational evaluator

Signature(s)

If family members were not members of the committee, please indicate:

I agree with the Individualized Education Program _____

I disagree with the Individualized Education Program _____

Harry Glick Agnes Glick _____

Parent/Guardian Signature

I participated in this meeting. I agree with the goals and services of the Individualized Educational Program

Marty Glick _____

Student's Signature

Present Level of Performance (PLOP)   The first major component in an IEP is the present level of educational performance section (PLOP). This component is the written summary of assessment data on a student's current levels of functioning. The PLOP subsequently serves as the basis for establishing annual goals. The information should include data for each priority area in which instructional support is needed. Depending on the individual student, consideration might be given to reading, math, and other academic skills, written and oral communication skills, vocational strengths and needs, social skills, behavioral patterns, study skills, self-help skills and other life skills, and motor skills. While the special education teacher may have more of a role in reporting the evaluation results, the input from parents, general education teachers, and other team members into this student profile is critical.

Performance levels can be provided in various forms, such as formal and informal assessment data, behavioral descriptions, and specific abilities delineated by checklists or skill sequences. Functional summary statements of an individual's strengths and weaknesses draw on information from a variety of sources rather than relying on a single source. Test scores in math, for example, might be combined with a description of how the child performed on a curriculum-based measure such as a computational checklist or an observation from the parents.

FIGURE 3.8	Example of a Present-Level-of-Educational-Performance Statement

Sammy is a seventh-grade student whose disability inhibits his ability to understand vocabulary associated with occupations and employment. Sammy can define orally thirty-seven out of fifty-two words correctly from a list of the most frequently used occupational vocabulary words.

Source: From *Understanding Occupational Vocabulary,* by S. Fisher, G. M. Clark, and J. R. Patton, 2003. Austin, TX: Pro-Ed.

In general, the phrasing used to define levels of performance should be positive and describe things the child can do. For example, the same information is conveyed by the two following statements, but the former demonstrates the more positive approach: "The student can identify 50% of the most frequently used occupational vocabulary words," versus "The student does not know half of the most frequently used occupational vocabulary words." Appropriately written performance levels provide a broad range of data to help generate relevant and appropriate annual goals. Federal requirements also mandate that the IEP include some sense of how the disability affects the student's involvement and progress in the general curriculum. An example of a PLOP statement that conforms to these criteria is presented in Figure 3.8. (See appendixes A and B for more examples of PLOPs and other components of an IEP.)

Measurable Annual Goals   The second, and central, IEP instructional component is annual goals. Each student's goals should be individually determined to address unique needs and abilities. It is obviously impossible to predict the precise amount of progress a student will make in a year, so goals should be reasonable projections of what the student will accomplish. To develop realistic expectations, teachers can consider a number of variables, including the chronological age of the child, the expected rate of learning, and past and current learning profiles.

Annual goals should be positive and measurable to provide a basis for evaluation. Goal statements should use terms that denote action and can be operationally defined (e.g., pronounce, write), rather than vague, general language that makes evaluation and observer agreement difficult (e.g., know, understand). Positive goals provide an appropriate direction for instruction. Avoiding negative goals creates an atmosphere conducive to good home-school relationships and makes it easier to chart student progress. Goals should also be oriented to the student. The intent is to develop a student's skills, and the only measure of effectiveness should be what is learned, rather than what is taught.

Prior to the 2004 reauthorization of IDEA, all IEPs had to include **short-term objectives**. The 2004 reauthorization requires short-term objectives in IEPs only for students with disabilities who complete alternative assessments aligned with alternative achievement standards. While the reauthorization does not require short-term objectives in IEPs, developing them is a good way to operationalize the annual goals for students. Because the requirement to monitor progress and report to parents is still required by IDEA 2004, the development of short-term objectives would facilitate this effort. As a result, short-term objectives will be provided throughout this text as examples of how goals should be broken down for instructional purposes. The four criteria applied to annual goals are also appropriate to short-term objectives. Because objectives are more narrow in focus, an objective's measurability should be enhanced with a criterion for mastery. For example, a math short-term objective might read, "Given 20 multiplication facts using numbers 1 through 5, John will give correct answers for 90%."

These benchmarks or objectives should be obtained from the general education curriculum being used by the student's nondisabled peers. Figure 3.9 contains a portion of four IEPs

FIGURE 3.9   Partial IEP Academic Examples

Unique educational needs, characteristics, and measured present levels of academic achievement and functional performance (PLOPs) (Including how the disability affects student's ability to participate and progress in the general curriculum)	Special education, related services, and supplemental aids and services (based on peer-reviewed research to the extent practicable); assistive technology and modifications or personnel support (Including anticipated starting date, frequency, duration, and location for each)	Measurable annual goals and short-term objectives (progress markers),[1] including academic and functional goals to enable students to be involved in and make progress in the general curriculum and to meet other needs resulting from the disability (Including progress measurement method for each goal)
James James is a very bright sixteen-year-old who is functionally illiterate, i.e., cannot distinguish "ladies" from "gentlemen" on doors. By shrewd guessing and a few sight words he can score from 1st to high 2nd grade on comprehension tests. His word attack skills are few, random, and ineffective.	Intensive, systematic, synthetic phonics reading instruction, 1:1 or small group (no more than four with a teacher or aide trained in the methodology used). Minimum one hour daily, plus same methodology to be used in all language arts areas consistently. Resource room and classroom.	End 1st 9 weeks: James will be able to decode all regular CVC words at 50 WPM w/ 0 errors. End 2nd 9 weeks: James will write and read the Dolch 220. End 3rd 9 weeks: James will read from 3rd-grade material at 60 WPM w/ 0–2 errors. End 4th 9 weeks: James will score above 3.5 grade equivalent on 2 standardized reading tests.
Todd Todd's reading level is between the 4th- and 5th-grade level. His oral reading fluency rate is 70 words per minute with 5–6 errors, in 4th-grade material.	Small group instruction from a reading specialist 30 minutes per day in a resource room beginning 11/24.	**Goal:** In 3 one-minute timed passages, Todd will increase his oral reading fluency to 150 WPM with 0–1 error by 11/24. STO 1: In 3 one-minute timed passages, Todd will increase his oral reading fluency to 90 WPM with 2–3 errors by 4/24. STO 2: In 3 one-minute timed passages, Todd will increase his oral reading fluency to 110 WPM with 1–2 errors by 9/24.
Tarah Tarah's expressive language skills are underdeveloped, although she scores in the average range on nonlanguage measures of intelligence. She doesn't initiate conversation and answers questions with 1- or 2-word sentences. She has a spoken vocabulary of approximately 50–100 words. Her articulation is only slightly delayed (r, l not yet perfect) at the age of 7.	One-on-one direct instruction in vocabulary provided by a speech and language pathologist (SLP) three times a week/20 min. a session. Small group, SLP-led discussions with same-age peers twice a week/20 min. a session.	**Goal:** Tarah will initiate conversation with peers at least twice a day. 1. By November, Tarah will initiate a conversation with peers or with an adult on at least one occasion per week as monitored by teacher, instructional assistants, parent volunteers, recess teachers, special ed. teacher, or SLP. 2. By March, Tarah will initiate conversation with same-age peers during speech class, or during work or play activities at least once a day.
Jeremy Jeremy lacks understanding of the processes of multiplication and division and does not know the multiplication facts beyond x2. **PLOP:** Jeremy scored 10 correct problems out of 100 on the district comprehensive test of multiplication and division.	1. 20 minutes per school day, small group (< 5) instruction with remedial math specialist in the resource room. 2. Computerized drill and practice in multiplication and division for 15 minutes each school day.	**Goal:** By the end of the school year, Jeremy will be able to complete 85 percent of multiplication and division problems correctly, on the district math test. Obj. 1: By Nov. 15 Jeremy will be able to complete a test of two-digit multiplication with at least 22 out of 25 score. Obj. 2: By Feb. 15 Jeremy will be able to complete a test of simple division with at least a 22 out of 25 score.

[1]For students who take an alternative assessment and are assessed against other than grade level standards, the IEP **must** include short-term objectives (progress markers). For other students, the IEP **may** include short-term objectives. The IEP **must** for all students clearly articulate how the student's progress will be measured, and that progress must be reported to parents at designated intervals.

Source: From *Better IEPs: How to Develop Legally Correct and Educationally Useful Programs* (4th ed., pp. 160–162), by B. D. Bateman and M. L. Linden, 2006. Verona, WI: Attainment. Adapted with permission.

IEP GOALS AND OBJECTIVES FOR JESSICA

GOAL 1   Jessica will be able to follow directions to their completion when given 50% more time than her peers.

Objective 1: Given a set of three directions, Jessica will follow each direction to its completion when given 100% more time than peers.

Objective 2: Given a set of three directions, Jessica will follow each direction to its completion when given 75% more time than peers.

Objective 3: Given a set of three directions, Jessica will follow each direction to its completion when given 50% more time than peers.

GOAL 2   Jessica will participate appropriately in group activities, including play and academic group work.

Objective 1: When working in groups, Jessica will share materials and turns appropriately, 4 out of 5 times.

Objective 2: When working in an academic group, Jessica will follow group directions appropriately, 4 out of 5 times.

Obejctive 3: When playing on the playground with a group, Jessica will wait her turn appropriately.

using the IEP format included earlier in this chapter; this figure provides examples of academic and nonacademic challenges. Throughout Chapters 6 through 11, the IEP goals and objectives feature will illustrate the goals and objectives portion of the IEP for the students featured in the chapter-opening vignettes. Remember that no IEP is perfect—it reflects the thinking of a group and reflects a team effort! See the nearby goals and objectives feature for Jessica.

Special Education and Related Services and Supplemental Aids and Services   IDEA provides a general paragraph describing commonly used related services, such as transportation, and speech, occupational, and physical therapy; the more recent regulations also provide an expanded list with definitions. However, many of our most effective education strategies and related services have been spelled out in litigation judgments. Many of the examples for these effective strategies and services cited by Bateman and Linden (2007) came from federal judges; these include:

- Small classes
- Computer access
- Texts on tape
- Highly structured environment
- Need for reteaching and repetition
- Frequent teacher feedback
- Distraction-reduced environment
- Schoolwide positive behavior support program
- Extended school year
- Intensive, effective remedial reading
- Peer tutor

No list should be considered exhaustive because the key is to identify any service, accommodation, or intervention during the prereferral/RTI phase or special education process. This enables children with a disability to benefit from their special education and assists the children in attaining their goals and objectives. Services extend to participation in extracurricular and nonacademic activities and support educational experiences with children with and without disabilities (Yell, 2006). See the nearby feature showing tips for providing instruction for Jessica.

TIPS FOR ADAPTING A LESSON FOR JESSICA

Jessica's teacher can:

- Seat Jessica in areas with the least distractions, such as away from windows and doors.
- Seat Jessica near the teacher's desk so that regular monitoring of her work is easier.
- Provide Jessica with extra time to complete her assignments.
- Orchestrate social opportunities for Jessica and other students who are shy or do not have many friends.

- Provide positive incentives for Jessica to successfully complete tasks.
- Give Jessica directions in a sequential format.
- Write assignments on the board.
- Require all students to keep their desk tops clean and orderly.
- Reinforce turn-taking and appropriate group behavior.

Parents, as well as other members of the IEP team, should come to the IEP meeting with notes on how they would like the child's educational program individualized to meet his or her unique needs. Bateman and Linden (2007) share their concern that in some locations, computer software is being used that, in effect, controls the development and the format of an IEP. Any predetermination of services, goals, or placements based on the disability, not on the individual, is totally outside of the intent of IDEA. For example, a few years ago, if you were a student with mental retardation, you were usually placed in a self-contained class where the focus was on self-care skills, and your only experience in the regular classroom was usually for music or art instruction. A student with learning disabilities was seldom given instruction in self-help or social skills, even if these skills were mentioned in the PLOP as a need.

Because the law requires that special education methods and other services be based on scientifically based research to the extent practical, old methods that are simply within a teacher's comfort level must now be reevaluated. This process should result in more effective education, especially in reading, math, and behavioral support strategies where research has validated many new techniques. The IEP must also provide documentation of the amount of service to be provided (e.g., speech therapy, three 30-minute sessions weekly), and the date the service is to begin, the duration, and the location.

Role of the General Education Teacher in the IEP Although IEPs are supposed to be developed by the whole IEP team, in practice the task has often largely fallen to special education teachers. The IEP process is not always followed as noted in the IDEA regulations and complaints have been made that some special teachers come to an IEP meeting with goals already drafted and ask parents and general education teachers to simply "sign off" on an IEP! Time is short, and this has become a common practice. However, the initial IEP is only a draft and the discussion of the child's needs by any team member should not be limited (*The Special Educator*, 2007). Clearly the intent of IDEA is to include parents and all personnel involved in providing educational intervention or support. In fact, those team members not in attendance at the IEP meeting should be given a copy of the IEP document. This is an important practice because a student with a disability will almost always require some accommodation or modification to benefit from regular classroom activities, and these should be known to all teachers (Bateman & Linden, 2007).

The role of general education teachers in the development of IEPs will vary with each child, often depending on how much time the child is in the general classroom. The 2004 reauthorization of IDEA states that a regular education teacher of the child, as a member of the IEP team, shall, to the extent appropriate, participate in the development of the IEP of the child, including the determination of appropriate positive behavioral interventions and supports, the determination of supplementary aids and services needed, the need for program modifications or content adaptations, and support for school personnel.

Ideally, the classroom teacher is very involved in the IEP meeting; this is especially true with the current emphasis on access to and progress in the general education curriculum. When the general education teacher is not in attendance, a different means of teacher input should be developed (e.g., a pre-IEP informal meeting or note); otherwise, the IEP document may not reflect the student's needs in the inclusive classroom. In particular, teachers should keep the goals and benchmarks at hand so that the IEP can influence instructional programs.

An IEP's annual goals and short-term objectives, when included, ultimately should be reflected in instructional plans in the classroom; however, they are not intended to be used as weekly plans, let alone daily plans. Teachers should refer to the document periodically to ensure that instruction is consistent with the long-term needs of the student. When significant variance is noted, it may become the basis for the IEP team to reconvene to make a change in instructional strategy or even the goals of the IEP. Bateman and Linden (2007) indicate that teachers must not lose sight of the spirit of individualization that should guide the IEP process. Teachers need to view the documents not just as a process of legal compliance but also as a tool for focusing on the unique strengths and needs of a child and meeting those needs through specially designed instruction. The IEP should be written to ensure access to the general education curriculum and to allow the student to benefit educationally. Unless guided by the rationale and spirit that infused the original development of the IEP concept, the process can degenerate into a mere bookkeeping activity. Instead, well-thought-out IEPs should form the foundation for individually designed educational programs for students with disabilities. The teacher should continue to include parents in the implementation and evaluation of the IEP. Extra effort is required, especially if the parents have limited English skills, but the effect on outcomes is significant.

Behavioral Intervention Planning   The requirement for **behavioral intervention planning** (BIP) was introduced in the 1997 amendments to IDEA and remains in the 2004 reauthorization. The process of developing a BIP begins with collecting background information to provide context for the problems and conducting a functional behavioral assessment to explore the possible triggers and the consequences of the behavior. In general, behavioral intervention plans are required for (1) students whose behaviors impede their learning or that of others, (2) students who put peers at risk because of their behaviors, and (3) students with disabilities for whom serious disciplinary action is being taken. A BIP is required on any student who is dismissed from school for more than 10 days for misbehavior. The major assumptions underlying the development of BIPs include the following:

- Behavior problems are best addressed when the causes (i.e., function) of the behaviors are known.
- Interventions that are based on positive intervention strategies are more effective than punitive ones.
- Dealing with difficult behaviors demands a team approach.

Role of the General Education Teacher in the BIP Process   The role of the general education teacher throughout the BIP process is critical to intervention outcome. General education teachers may be involved in collecting information to more fully describe the behavior under review, in assessing the functional effects of the behavior in the school setting, and in generating and implementing strategies. The teachers and support personnel involved in educating any child with a BIP should be given a copy of the plan and an explanation of their role. Last, classroom teachers should be intricately involved in monitoring the effectiveness of the interventions when students with BIPs are in their classes.

Transition Services   Services that help students with disabilities prepare for life after high school, referred to as transition services, have been mandated by law since 1990. The 2004 reauthorization of IDEA defines transition services as a coordinated set of activities designed to be a results-oriented process focusing on improving academic and functional achievement to facilitate movement from school to postschool activities. These can include postsecondary education, vocational education, employment (including supported employment for the more severely disabled), continuing and adult education, adult services, independent living, and community participation. The student and his or her family need to be actively involved in the process, and the student's strengths, interests, and preferences must be taken into account. Postsecondary goals that are appropriate and measurable and based on age-appropriate transition assessments must be included in the IEP by the time the child turns age 16. The complexity of adult life needs to be recognized and planned for. Services provided may include instruction, related services, community experiences, the development of employment, and other postschool adult living objectives, and, when appropriate, acquisition of daily living skills.

Any agency personnel, such as Vocational Rehabilitation, who might be involved in or pay for a transition service should be invited to the transition IEP meetings; however, if cooperation is not forthcoming, schools are ultimately responsible for meeting the transitional needs of the student (Bateman & Linden, 2007). Unfortunately, the nature and quality of transition services vary widely from one school district to another across the country, ranging from minimal compliance activities to what could be considered best practices in transition.

One year before the student reaches majority age, the IEP must state that the student has been informed of the rights that will transfer to him or her at the age of majority (in most states, age 18). Finally, schools are required to provide a summary of performance (SOP) to students and parents as the students exit high school. This report should include relevant information about current functional performance and academic skill levels, progress toward meeting the IEP transition goals, and recommendations to help the student meet the postsecondary goals (O'Leary, 2006).

Role of the General Education Teacher in the Transition Process. The general education teacher can contribute to the transition process in two primary ways. First, the classroom teacher, mindful of adult outcomes (i.e., the demands of everyday living), can integrate real-life topics of current or future importance into the existing curriculum, as a way to cover topics that will be relevant and meaningful to students in their classes. For example, math teachers can include budgeting and preparation of income tax forms when teaching percentages, and English teachers can have students write comparative papers on career options. Second, classroom teachers can participate by contributing information to the transition assessment phase. Here, teachers who know the academic, social, and behavioral competence of their students can provide valuable information to the transition planning process.

Assistive Technology   The need for technology-related assistance, including assistive technology devices and services, must be considered during the development of each child's IEP and made available if necessary to provide a free, appropriate public education. An **assistive technology service** includes any service that assists a child with a disability in the selection, acquisition, or use of assistive technology. For example, the IEP could include an evaluation of need and steps to procure, select, and fit a device instructions on repairing or replacing the device, and training the child or professionals to use the device.

An **assistive technology device** is broadly defined by IDEA as "any item, piece of equipment, or product system, whether acquired commercially off the shelf, modified, or customized, that is used to increase, maintain or improve the functional capabilities of a child with a disability." Assistive technology can be considered "low tech" and be as simple as using graph paper to help hold proper spacing during math problems, or "high tech," such as use of a computer to read text to a student. Examples of assistive technology used effectively for students with various disabilities are included throughout the text.

Extended School Year Services   Another service to which some students with disabilities are entitled is summer school, or, more appropriately, "the extended school year." The provision of special education and related services beyond the normal school year and at no cost to the parents emerged as a way to ensure that a natural disruption of services (i.e., summer) did not interfere with a student's continued educational progress and that there was no "regression" or loss of skills. The IEP team determines whether summer programming is necessary for the provision of a "free, appropriate public education." Decisions must be made on an individual basis and may not be offered in a standard format to any particular type of disability (Yell, 2006). Parents must be informed of their child's right to this service.

Annual Assessment of IEP and Reevaluation

Because the educational needs of children with disabilities vary over time, two critical features of the special education process are the **ongoing monitoring** of a student's progress in special education, and **reevaluation** to determine the continued need for special education and related services. By law, a student's IEP must be reviewed and revised on an annual basis. This annual review is essential for updating the student's goals and evaluating the overall results of the modifications and instructional plans implemented during the year. At the IEP meeting when this topic is discussed, the team should not only look closely at existing goals but also be open to the development of new goals in areas of need. For example, new goals may need to be written into the IEP during the transition assessment process. Further, the IEP team can identify areas needing instructional attention after examining a student's competence across a range of areas.

Reevaluation refers to testing to determine if a child is still eligible to receive special educational services. This must occur not more than once a year and at least once every 3 years, unless the parents and school agree it is not necessary. Although for many students, being admitted to special education is too frequently a one-way street, many can and should reach levels of academic competence whereby they will no longer need special education or related services. The process to dismiss students from special education can be politically charged. Some parents may not want the cessation of services for their son or daughter; some school-based professionals do not like to see services cease when they feel support may be needed to continue success in the general education curriculum. The benefits and ramifications of dismissal from special educational services should be considered carefully by the IEP team. However, it is ultimately the parents who can discontinue placement at any time.

Individualized Family Service Plan (IFSP)

This section of IDEA provides for statewide interagency programs to implement early intervention services for children from birth to age 5 who are experiencing developmental delays or who have a diagnosed mental or physical condition that puts them at risk for developing these delays. Services are intended to address a child's physical, cognitive, communication, social or emotional, and adaptive needs. A broad range of services are available including speech pathology, occupational and physical therapy, health services, home visits, and assistive technology devices. The interagency team, the student's parents, and others involved in assessment or delivery of services work together to develop a plan similar to the IEP but referred to as the Individualized Family Service Plan (IFSP).

The basic philosophy underlying the IFSP is that infants and toddlers with known or suspected disabilities, medical conditions, or other development issues are uniquely dependent on their families and can best be understood within the context of their families. Thus, the intent of the IFSP is to focus on the family unit and to support the natural caregiving role of families. Many of the components of the IFSP are the same as those of the IEP; however, there are several important differences. For example, the goals in the IFSP are called outcome statements, which reflect changes that families want to see for their child and for themselves. The outcome statements on the IFSP are family-centered rather than child-centered, as they are on the IEP. In addition, a service coordinator must be identified for each family. The coordinator is responsible for the implementation of the IFSP and coordination with other agencies and people. Each plan must be discussed and evaluated every 6 months and revised annually, if necessary (Yell, 2006). Finally, a transition plan must be included to support the child and family when moving to the next stage of services, usually special education.

SECTION 504 ELIGIBILITY AND PLANNING

Discussion of Section 504 begins in this chapter as an alternative for obtaining special services for a student when the student has been determined ineligible for special education services (refer to Figure 3.1). Section 504 is discussed more fully as a means for assisting students with ADHD; however, this civil rights statute protects and provides services for other individuals with disabilities as well. Although no funds are available through 504, any organization that receives federal money, including public and private schools, is prohibited from discriminating against any individual because of a disability.

Eligibility

Eligibility for Section 504 is based on a student having a physical or mental impairment that results in a substantial limitation in one or more major life activities (e.g., seeing, hearing, learning). A "substantial limitation" is related to two primary factors: severity of the impairment and duration (i.e., permanence of the condition). As previously suggested, Section 504 rights should be considered for any student who is referred for special education services but does not qualify under IDEA. For example, a student with a disability of a medical nature, such as epilepsy, might not require special education services and, therefore, would not be eligible for services under IDEA. However, this student does have a documented disability and might be eligible for protection under Section 504. Every public school should have a committee and process for handling 504 eligibility and planning activities. Schools should document that a logical and reasonable process for determining eligibility is used. A good plan is to have someone on staff who is knowledgeable about 504 and to develop a coherent system for addressing 504 queries. Although not required by law, a written 504 eligibility determination form is a good practice for documentation.

Reasonable Accommodations

If a student is determined to be eligible for services under 504, schools are required to provide reasonable accommodations for the student in **academic** and **nonacademic** areas. Accommodations may range from providing extended time on tests for a student with ADHD to providing dry marker boards for a student with severe allergies to chalk dust. A student with epilepsy should not be held to the same standards for attendance if frequent seizures are responsible for the absences. A reasonable accommodation provided under Section 504 might include a more liberal attendance requirement. Most accommodations are easy to implement and do not cost much money. Some accommodations that require the use of technology may be more costly.

Typically, a written accommodation plan is developed that specifies the nature and scope of the accommodations to be implemented. This document differs greatly from an IEP because it has no specifically mandated components. As a result, many accommodation plan formats have emerged, ranging from very basic to semi-elaborate. Figure 3.10 is an example of a basic 504 accommodation plan.

Role of the General Education Teacher in Section 504 Activities

General education teachers play a crucial role in identifying students who might qualify for services under Section 504. Being knowledgeable about what Section 504 provides and how one qualifies for services contributes to a classroom teacher's resourcefulness. Classroom teachers may be contacted during the eligibility determination phase to provide information to the committee to assist with the decision-making task. Teachers may also be required to monitor the effectiveness of the accommodations that are suggested.

FIGURE
3.10

Sample Section 504 Accommodation Plan

Name: __John Jones__

School: __Porter High School__   Grade: __10th__

Date: __10/6/08__   Age: __15__

Follow-up Date(s): John's plan will be reviewed and evaluated at the end of each semester.

Teachers: Mr. J. McKenzie (Social Studies), Mr. W. Dumont (English), Ms. M. Tinsley (Biology), Mr. S. Labiosa (Spanish), Ms. R. Shankar (Mathematics)

1. **General Strengths:** Individualized standardized testing indicates that John is a capable student who is performing at or near grade level. His favorite subjects in school are mathematics and science. He wants to succeed in school and is very interested in going to college.

2. **General Concerns:** John's performance in school is erratic. He completes approximately 40% of his assignments and does poorly on tests. Observation of John in his classes shows that he often calls out and frequently fidgets in his seat or leaves it without permission. His teachers also report that he rarely pays attention to directions and is often distracted by events in the classroom. They also note that John rarely interacts with his peers.

3. **Nature and Impact of Disability:** John has been diagnosed as having a Attention Deficit Disorder with Hyperactivity (ADHD) by his family physician. Behavior rating scales and observations by educators and family members suggest that John's activity level is significant and interferes with his educational and social performance in school and at home.

Goal	Accommodations	Person(s) Responsible for Accommodations
1. To increase John's work completion	A. Step-by-step written and verbal directions for assignments, including examples, will be given to John.	A. John's teachers
	B. Assignments will be broken into several shorter parts and John will receive a break of 5 minutes between assignments.	B. John's teachers
	C. A daily homework notebook system will be implemented.	C. John, John's family, and John's teachers
	D. Learning strategy instruction will be provided to John.	D. Special education teacher
2. To increase John's performance on tests	A. Study and test-taking skills instruction will be provided to John	A. Special education teacher
	B. John will receive the following testing accommodations: extended time, breaks, and testing in a separate location.	B. John's teachers
3. To increase John's on-task behavior	A. A self-monitoring system will be used by John to keep track of his on-task behavior.	A. John and John's teachers
	B. A daily behavior report card system will be implemented.	B. John, John's teachers, and John's family
	C. John's work area will be located at front of the room.	C. John's teachers
4. To increase John's socialization with peers	A. Social skills and attribution training instruction will be provided to John.	A. Special education teacher
	B. John will be taught about and encouraged to participate in extracurricular and community-based activities.	B. John, John's family, John's teachers, and John's school counselor

(continued)

FIGURE 3.10	Sample Section 504 Accommodation Plan *(continued)*

Participants:

Mr. John Jones, Student

Ms. Janice Jones, Parent

Ms. Roberta Shankar, Mathematics teacher

Mr. Jose Garcia, Special education teacher

Mr. William Dumont, English teacher

Ms. Freda Hargrove, School Counselor

Mr. Carl Rogan, District 504 Coordinator

Dr. Loren Phillips, Family physician

_____
(Parent/guardian)

I agree with the 504 accommodation plan outlined above

_____
(Parent/guardian)

I do not agree with the 504 accommodation plan outlined above.

Source: From *Creating Inclusive Classrooms* (6th ed.) (p. 30) by S. J. Salend. 2008. Upper Saddle River, NJ: Pearson.

SUMMARY

Prereferral Intervention

- Prereferral intervention is a process for assisting students struggling in the general education classroom prior to referral for a comprehensive assessment to determine eligibility for special education services.
- Three approaches used to facilitate access to the general education curriculum for all students are the Universal Design for Learning, Differentiated Instruction, and Response to Intervention.
- Response to intervention models generally function on three tiers, with each tier serving fewer students with more severe learning and behavioral difficulties. During Tier II and Tier III, scientifically based intervention is provided in smaller, more homogeneous groups and typically becomes more intense, occurs more frequently, and lasts for a longer duration.
- Prereferral intervention teams composed primarily of general educators help teachers identify alternative, scientifically based intervention strategies or generate accommodations or modifications to instruction or the classroom environment for a student continuing to experience learning difficulties.

The Special Education Process

- The formal referral process initiates a series of activities within a required timeline.
- The merit of each referral must be determined by the IEP team.
- If a referral is approved, a comprehensive assessment is initiated and may include both formal and informal tests and measurements.
- The control of bias in assessment is not only essential to accurate and fair evaluation, but is also a legal requirement.
- Eligibility, placement, and the IEP are determined by a team of individuals including the parents and students when feasible.
- Essential elements of the IEP document include present levels of educational performance, measurable annual goals, special education and related goods and services, and supplemental aids and services.
- Behavioral intervention plans are required for students when behavior is interfering with a student's ability to benefit from the general education classroom.
- Transition services must be addressed in the IEP for all students no later than age 16.
- Some students can qualify for extended school year services.

- Goals within the IEP are reviewed annually; a comprehensive reevaluation is conducted no less than every 3 years unless the IEP team decides otherwise.
- An IFSP is developed for children birth to age 5, requiring early intervention for developmental delays.
- The 2004 reauthorization of IDEA contains very specific mandates for assessment, developing the IEP or IFSP, and ensuring parental involvement throughout the special education process.

Section 504 Eligibility and Planning

- Some students who do not qualify under IDEA may qualify for services under Section 504.
- Eligibility is determined by whether a person has a physical or mental impairment that results in a substantial limitation in one or more major life activities.
- If a student qualifies under 504, an accommodation plan is typically developed to address academic and nonacademic needs.

PEARSON
myeducationlab

The MyEducationLab for this course can help you solidify your comprehension of Chapter 3 concepts.

- Gauge and further develop your understanding of chapter concepts by taking the quizzes and examining the enrichment materials on the Chapter 3 Study Plan.
- Visit Topic 8, Assessment, to:
  - Connect with challenge-based interactive modules, case study units, and podcasts that provide research-validated information about working with students in inclusive settings by visiting the IRIS Center Resources
  - Explore Assignments and Activities, assignable exercises showing concepts in action through video, cases, and student and teacher artifacts
  - Practice and strengthen skills essential to quality teaching through the Building Teaching Skills and Dispositions lessons

4

Managing and Differentiating Classrooms

After reading this chapter, you should be able to:

1. Define the basic concepts of differentiated instruction.
2. Describe a comprehensive model for differentiating classroom management.

This year has been particularly challenging for **JEANNIE CHUNG**. Jeannie has been teaching fifth grade for 10 years, but she cannot recall any year in which her students' needs were more diverse and the tasks of managing the classroom, addressing individual student needs, and motivating her students were more challenging.

Many of her students present unique needs. She has students who are reading below grade level, students who have serious difficulties paying attention, others who find it difficult to engage socially with their classmates, and many who will find the state tests, that will occur in Spring, to be daunting. However, Jeannie has one student, Sam, who poses particular challenges to her and the rest of the students in the class and is easily the most difficult student in the class.

Sam presents a number of problems. He is too frequently out of his seat and often yells out to other students across the room. He has great difficulty staying on task during instructional periods and at times spreads a contagion of misbehavior in the classroom. During large-group language arts lessons, Sam is inattentive and frequently uncooperative. Jeannie is beginning to believe that his high level of inattentive behavior may make it virtually impossible for him to progress and achieve in the general education classroom, although, at the same time, Jeannie does not see him as a candidate for a special class or other pull-out program, as he is bright and can handle the content of his classes without any problems. Nevertheless, his inattentive behavior is gradually resulting in his falling behind academically. Although it is only November, Jeannie seriously wonders whether this will be a productive year for Sam.

Sam currently receives no special education supports or services. However, Jeannie has referred Sam to the child-study team, and this group is pondering suggestions that might be effective within Jeannie's classroom as well as considering a request for a more comprehensive assessment that may elucidate instructional and/or curricular alternatives.

QUESTIONS TO CONSIDER

1. What recommendations would you give Jeannie for focusing on Sam's behavior and its consequences?
2. Which procedures can Jeannie use to significantly increase Sam's attention-to-task behaviors?
3. How can Sam's peers be involved in a comprehensive behavior management program?
4. How can cooperative teaching facilitate successful intervention in the inclusive classroom?

A general education teacher's ability to address the needs of students in his or her classroom is being tapped more now than ever before. Many school districts are implementing a response to intervention approach to working with struggling students that puts a premium on the general education teacher's versatility. In this type of setup, the teacher must be able to address individual needs by making key adjustments across a number of instructionally related areas and provide effective instruction. Responsible inclusion of students with special needs in general education classrooms is based on the premise that sound instructional design and delivery are being provided (refer to the discussion of this topic on pages 17–19).

The reality of the general education classroom setting in today's schools is captured in the following description by Sanford, Marozas, Marozas, and Patton (2011):

> As the trend toward increased inclusion of students with disabilities into general education classrooms continues, the reality has become that more students with disabilities are receiving their education in general education settings. Consequently, the instructional pressure for all teachers to teach increasingly complex curricula (special education and general education), while addressing a wide array of needs, became greater. (p. ix)

Visit the MyEducationLab for this course to enhance your understanding of chapter concepts with a personalized Study Plan. You'll also have the opportunity to hone your teaching skills through video-based Assignments and Activities, IRIS Center Resources, and Building Teaching Skills and Disposition lessons.

The ability of a general education teacher to manage his or her classroom effectively and efficiently as well as address the needs of a range of students can greatly enhance the quality of the educational experience for all students. Well-organized and well-managed classrooms allow more time for productive instruction for all students, including those with special needs. As Marzano (2003) points out: "Teachers play various roles in a typical classroom, but surely one of the most important is that of classroom manager. Effective teaching and learning cannot take place in a poorly managed classroom" (p. 13).

Teachers do indeed play various roles in their daily work in schools. Theses roles keep changing over time, and new demands are continually asked of teachers. The reason for these emerging roles is that schools are changing and the number of students with challenging needs, as underscored by Jeannie Chung, is greater than ever before.

Like Jeannie, all teachers must create a classroom setting where the needs of all students are met. This idea includes the notion of addressing the needs of not only those who are struggling but also those whose abilities are far advanced of the average student in the class. In addition to the idea that classrooms should be places where students feel valued and respected, where "care and trust have taken the place of restrictions and threats" (Kohn, 1996a, p. ix), classrooms also need to be places where learning and academic/social growth occur.

From a management perspective, the absence of heavy-handed, adult-directed management systems is characteristic of classrooms where students are valued and solid relationships between teachers and students are established (Bender, 2003). When attention is given to preventive action rather than to reactive interventions, classrooms run smoothly and without notice. Smith (2004) has referred to this notion as "invisible management" and suggests that when effective management is operant, it is virtually hard to discern, unless you know what to look for.

Sound instructional and management tactics promote learning for all students and are particularly relevant to the successful inclusion of students with special learning needs. When general and special educators working collaboratively devise these tactics, the likelihood of establishing an effective learning setting is further enhanced.

BASIC CONCEPTS ABOUT DIFFERENTIATING INSTRUCTION

The importance of sound, evidence-based techniques has been affirmed numerous times by professionals in the field of education. Although much attention is given to curricular and instructional aspects of students' educational programs, knowing how to differentiate based on needs of a range of students is more difficult to execute. Furthermore, organizational and management dimensions of the classroom are typically underemphasized in training programs, educational research, and professional conferences, despite their importance as prerequisites to instruction (Evertson & Weinstein, 2006). New teachers consistently identify this area as the most problematic area of teaching for them during the demanding first year (Jones, 2006).

The smooth functioning of the general education classroom often represents a challenge for teachers as classrooms become more diverse. Jones and Jones (2007) describe the profile of a typical first-grade class as being composed of a vast array of students with specific needs that might include any combination or all of the following: a range of disabilities, English language learners, in-school and out-of-school counseling, abusive situations and other unsafe home lives, homelessness, frequent relocation. Students with any of these features in their lives require special attention in school. Evertson, Emmer, Clements, Sanford, and Worsham (2006) accurately articulate the relationship between the diversity found in today's schools and the need for well-run classrooms:

> Students entering the nation's schools come with such widely diverse backgrounds, capabilities, interests, and skills that meeting their needs and finding appropriate learning activities requires a great deal of care and skill. Because one of the first and most basic tasks for the teacher is to develop a smoothly running classroom community where students are highly involved in worthwhile activities that support learning, establishing an effective management system is a first priority. (p. xv)

Definitions, Terminology, and Conceptual Basis

The concept of differentiating instruction, and even the term itself, have been around for a long time. Kaplan (1979) used the term "differentiated" to describe the development of curricula for students who were gifted. Without question, popularity of the concept, particularly as it applies to the general education classroom, is now omnipresent. The work of Tomlinson (1999) in the late 1990s established this concept within most discussions of the general education classroom. Historically, terms such as *adaptation, modifications*, and *accommodations* have been used to describe what is now being referred to as differentiating instruction. What we call this process is not as important as what we do as part of this process. Nevertheless, it is important to recognize and understand the definitions and terminology that are used.

Definition   For the purposes of this chapter, the following definition of *differentiated instruction* is recommended. Other definitions do exist. However, this definition developed by Hall (2002) captures, in a very clear fashion, what we mean by addressing the needs of students.

> Differentiated instruction is a process to approach teaching and learning for students of differing abilities in the same class. The intent of differentiating instruction is to maximize each student's growth and individual success by meeting each student where he or she is, and assisting the learning process. (p. 2)

This definition, or any definition of differentiating instruction, warrants some comments: (1) First, this process implies that teaching and learning should be considered from a comprehensive basis. It involves a number of dimensions that all relate to maximizing student outcomes. (2) Differentiation is needed for a range of students, including the following:

- Students already identified as having a disability.
- Students who are struggling in some fashion with the demands of school but who have not been and may never be identified as disabled.
- Students who are trying to master the English language.
- Students who are at risk for any number of issues and whose school lives and performance are impacted by outside factors.
- Students who are gifted and whose needs are as great as those with significant learning problems—however, their needs require a different type of attention.

(3) In order to address the needs of students, it is necessary to have a firm assessment of what their specific needs are. For the teacher who has a particular student in his or her class, this information is fairly obvious, or ought to be. For other school personnel who do not have direct contact with the student and who are charged with making recommendations, this information must be gathered. This process of gathering important information is detailed in the next section. (4) The bottom line in terms of differentiating instruction is that it is accomplished mostly through adjustments/accommodations to the learning environment and instructional process.

Terminology   In relation to the last point, it is very important to recognize the difference in certain terms that are used in schools to refer to the process of differentiating instruction. The terms *adaptation, modification, and accommodation* are often used interchangeably; however, these terms do, in fact, mean different things:

- **Adaptation:** refers to specific changes made to the way content is presented and the way students respond to instruction—includes all adjustments to instructional methodology and environment that enable students to engage the general education curriculum.
- **Modification:** refers to actual changes made to the content itself—in terms of content covered or content that is assessed.
- **Accommodation:** more of a general term that refers to changes that are made to support students within various educational settings.

Levels of Differentiation   Differentiating instruction should be considered as consisting of two levels. The first level is a global, or macro, level that applies to the education classroom on a general level. It incorporates the concept of universal design for learning (UDL). The practical interpretation of this level is that various features of instructional design that are essential to some students, beneficial to others, and not detrimental to anyone are implemented on a universal classroom level.

For example, one of the most common accommodations requested by students with special needs is more time to complete a test. For most students, this accommodation has to be requested through a formal process or is mandated through the IEP or 504 plan. However, in a UDL classroom, this feature is provided to anyone who needs it. As a result, it really is not an accommodation; it is merely a feature of the class. Other adjustments that can be made on a macro level that are worthy of consideration include: providing Powerpoint slides ahead of a class presentation; making available audio files of class lectures or presentations to all students; distributing notes to all students in class; allowing students to choose a project based on their interest and background for demonstrating mastery of a topic; and providing graphic organizers for all required readings.

The second level of differentiation is specific and individualized and can be considered on a micro level. Some students (e.g., students who are blind or deaf) will need very specific adjustments; other students will not need to benefit from instruction. Another way of considering this level of differentiation is that the adjustment or accommodation is often not beneficial to others in the class, as they do not need it or may actually impede their learning. These individualized adjustments will be needed as a function of a number of student factors: level of performance (skills, ability), unique presenting feature, interests/motivation, and learning styles.

Operating Procedures

When implementing tactics, strategies, conditions, or activities related to differentiating instruction, one should be guided by a process that is effective and efficient. We will describe a five-step process that should be followed when differentiating instruction.

Determine the Need for Differentiation   It is important to determine which students will need differentiation in their programs. The operative mantra is that many students will benefit from some form of differentiation. The challenge for classroom teachers is to know which students need assistance, know what exactly needs to be done, and know how to differentiate instruction. This challenge is complicated by the fact that students at both ends of the continuum of skill development and ability will need differentiation.

Identify Specific Areas of Need   As mentioned previously, many teachers will know exactly what the presenting problems of their students are. However, knowing this information in detail is essential for problem solving what adjustments need to be made within the classroom setting to address the problems. Hoover and Patton (2005) developed a simple instrument that can be used as an initial tool to isolate what areas might need attention. This screen, shown in Figure 4.1, is not a comprehensive instrument but rather an "informational device" that assists teachers in gaining a better sense of how a student functions within the general education classroom.

Implement Various Differentiation Practices—Least Intrusive First   Educators will need to incorporate many features to address the needs of a range of students into the ongoing operations of the classroom (i.e., UDL). However, the use of the more specific, individualized process will be needed often. When differentiating instruction on an individual basis, they should start with the least intrusive, yet effective, practice first. This method is recommended for a number of reasons: First, teachers simply do not have enough time to make massive, complex adjustments to their programs and instruction. Second, minor adjustments can be just as powerful and effective as more involved ones. For example, changing where a student is seated in a classroom can be done relatively easily to minimize distractions.

FIGURE 4.1	Curriculum Adaptation Quick Screen

Educator: _____ Student: _____ Subject: _____

Strategy: _____

Class setting: _____

Place a check next to each item for which the student possesses sufficient abilities to work within the classroom relative to the identified subject, strategy, and setting.

Content Needs
- Sufficient reading level
- Necessary prerequisite skills
- Necessary prior experience
- Sufficient language abilities
- Sufficient abstract thinking abilities
- Interest in subject area material
- Other:

Instructional Strategy Needs
- Motivated by strategy used
- Strategy generates active student participation
- Acquires information through strategy
- Understands strategy used
- Strategy holds student's attention to task
- Other:

Instructional Setting Needs
- Able to attend to task within type of setting used
- Able to work independently when necessary
- Possesses appropriate peer interaction skills for type of setting used
- Acquires information easily through setting used
- Participates freely in setting
- Completes assignments within setting used
- Other:

Student Behaviors
- Maintains self-control
- Completes assigned tasks on time
- Is responsible for own actions
- Uses effective self-management techniques
- Uses study and learning strategies effectively
- Exhibits appropriate behaviors for type of instructional setting used
- Other:

Source: Hoover, J., & Patton, J. R. (2005). Curriculum adaptations for students with learning and behavior problems: Differentiating instruction to meet diverse needs (3rd ed.). Austin: PRO-ED. pp. 49–50.

Monitor Student Progress   Without a doubt, much attention is being placed on the importance of monitoring the progress of students in academic, behavioral, and social areas. Similarly, it is essential that data be collected in regard to the adjustments that are made for students. Without data collection, it is impossible for teachers to know how well the accommodations are working.

Evaluate and Modify Differentiation Practices   All differentiation practices must be evaluated for their effectiveness and then decisions need to be made as to whether to continue them, terminate them, or modify them in some way.

COMPREHENSIVE MODEL
OF DIFFERENTIATING INSTRUCTION

Every classroom environment involves a number of elements that have a profound impact on the effectiveness of instruction and learning (Doyle, 1986), including the following: *multidimensionality* (a wide variety of activities occur in a classroom within the course of an instructional day); *simultaneity* (many different events occur at the same time); *immediacy* (events occur at a rapid pace); *unpredictability* (some events occur unexpectedly and cannot consistently be anticipated, but require attention nonetheless); *publicness* (classroom events are witnessed by a significant number of students who are very likely to take note of how teachers deal with these ongoing events); *history* (over the course of the school year, various events—experiences, routines, rules—will shape the evolving dynamics of classroom behavior).

Considering these elements reaffirms the complexity of teaching large numbers of students who have diverse learning needs in our schools today. To address these classroom dynamics, teachers need to be aware and competent to utilize ways to differentiate their instruction to maximize the potential opportunities for learning. Figure 4.2 depicts a comprehensive model of differentiated instruction that highlights the multifaceted nature and complexity of this concept.

This particular model is similar to models that have been developed by other professionals but differs in two major ways. First, this model emphasizes the need to look more broadly at what is meant by curriculum and content. As will be seen later in the chapter, differentiated instruction requires an understanding of the different types of curricula that exist. Second, this model stresses the importance of differentiating in the area of management and behavior.

Addressing the needs of a broad range of students is based on numerous considerations. To maximize the success of students in their classrooms, teachers must pay attention to the six key elements of differentiated instruction: setting, content, materials, intervention/instruction, management/behavior, affect.

■ The dynamics of a classroom are determined by many different student factors.

Nine overarching principles guide the development and implementation of a comprehensive model of differentiated instruction:

- All students must be valued.
- Meaningful relationships between teachers and students need to be developed and cultivated (Bender, 2003).
- Successful learning outcomes derive from a positive classroom climate.
- Teachers have control over a number of critical factors that have a major impact on student learning and behavior (Jones & Jones, 2007).
- Affording students choices contributes to effective classroom dynamics and enhances self-determination.
- Teachers and students in effective classrooms are considerate of individual differences, including cultural and familial differences.
- Proactive planning for differentiation (prevention) is preferable to reactive approaches (crisis intervention).

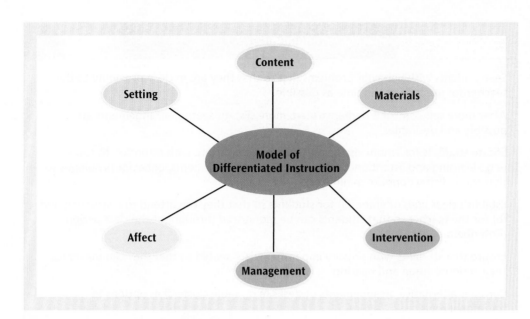

FIGURE 4.2

Model for differentiated instruction.

- Teachers should not feel that they are alone—resources such as other teachers, administrators, and parents can contribute to successful instruction.
- Effective classroom management is "invisible" (Smith, 2004).

When developing and implementing a comprehensive system of differentiating instruction, teachers must be mindful of the diverse range of students in their classrooms. One of the most overlooked areas of diversity is cultural diversity. Levin (2003) noted two very important points that teachers must acknowledge and address in regard to students who come from different cultural backgrounds: (1) schools and classrooms are not culturally neutral or culture free, and (2) because of cultural differences, many children from underrepresented groups experience cultural dissonance or lack of cultural synchronization in school (i.e., teacher and student expectations of appropriate behavior may differ).

Setting Differentiation

Setting includes the aspects of the physical environment that teachers can manipulate to enhance the "conditions" for learning. As Doyle (2006) notes, "the data on classroom design and furniture arrangements indicate that different patterns of spatial organization have little effect on achievement but some effect on attitudes and conduct" (p. 106). The physical environment of the classroom does have an impact on behavior and attitudes (McEwan, 2006). For students with certain disabilities, some features of the physical setting may need to be specially arranged to ensure that individual needs are met. Four aspects of the physical dimensions of a classroom include: preferential seating, classroom arrangements, accessibility, and specialized equipment.

Preferential Seating   Seating adjustment may be the most common one used in general education classrooms. This tactic is essential for use with students who have various hearing issues and for those students who may be having great difficulty with attention. It is certainly one of the considerations for Sam (the boy in the case study at the beginning of the chapter). The attractiveness of this tactic is that the teacher can be near the student and thus in a position to be able to assist the student in focusing.

Teachers are encouraged to consider carefully where to seat students who have problems controlling their behaviors, those who experience attention deficits, and students with sensory impairments. Figure 4.3 provides recommendations on seating arrangement. The judicious use of seating arrangements can minimize problems as well as create better learning opportunities for students.

<table>
<tr><td colspan="2">FIGURE 4.3   Seating Arrangements</td></tr>
</table>

Seat students with behavior problems first so that they are in close proximity to the teacher for as much of the time as possible.

After more self-control is demonstrated, more distant seating arrangements are possible and desirable.

Locate students for whom visual distractions can interfere with attention to tasks (e.g., learning and attentional problems, hearing impairments, behavior problems) so that these distractions are minimized.

Establish clear lines of vision (a) for students so that they can attend to instruction and (b) for the teacher so that students can be monitored throughout the class period (Rosenberg et al., 1991).

Ensure that students with sensory impairments are seated so that they can maximize their residual vision and hearing.

Consider alternative arrangements of desks (e.g., table clusters) as options to traditional rows.

Classroom Arrangements   Classroom arrangements are the physical facets of the classroom, including classroom layout (i.e., geography of the room), arrangement of desks, storage, wall use, display areas, and signs. Some suggestions for arrangements include:

- Consider establishing areas of the classroom for certain types of activities (e.g., discovery or inquiry learning, independent reading).
- Clearly establish which areas of the classroom, such as the teacher's desk, are off limits—this recommendation is also a procedural one.
- Be sure students can be seen easily by the teacher and that the teacher, or other presenters, can be seen easily by students (Evertson et al., 2006).
- Begin the year with a more-structured environment, moving to more flexibility after rules and procedures have been established.
- Notify students who are blind or partially sighted of changes made to the physical environment.
- Arrange furniture so that teachers and students can move easily around the classroom.
- Direct students' attention to the information to be learned from bulletin boards, if they are used for instructional purposes.
- Establish patterns that students can use in moving around the class and that minimize disruption—keep high-traffic areas free of congestion (Evertson et al., 2006).
- Keep frequently used teaching materials and student supplies readily accessible (Evertson et al., 2006).
- Secure materials and equipment that are potentially harmful if used without proper supervision, such as certain art supplies, chemicals, and science equipment.
- Avoid creating open spaces that have no clear purpose, as they often can become staging areas for problem behaviors (Rosenberg, O'Shea, & O'Shea, 1991).
- Provide labels and signs for areas of the room to assist younger or more delayed students in better understanding what and where things are.

Accessibility   The accessibility of the classroom warrants special attention because of legal mandates (e.g., Section 504 of the Rehabilitation Act of 1973). The concept of accessibility, of course, extends beyond physical accessibility; it touches on overall program accessibility for students with special needs. Students who are identified as disabled under IDEA, as well as students qualifying as having substantial limitations in a major life function such as walking or learning, are able to benefit from needed adjustments to the classroom. Students with disabilities must be able to use the classroom like other students and the room must be free of potential hazards or triggers (e.g., allergens). Most of the time, making a classroom physically accessible is neither difficult nor costly. Specific suggestions for creating an accessible classroom include the following:

- Ensure that the classroom is accessible to students who use wheelchairs, braces, crutches, or other forms of mobility assistance—this involves doorways, space to move within the classroom, floor coverings, learning centers, microcomputers, chalkboards or dry-erase boards, bookshelves, sinks, tables, desks, and any other areas or physical objects that students use.
- Guarantee that the classroom is free of hazards (e.g., low-hanging mobiles or plants) that could injure students who have a visual impairment.
- Label storage areas and other parts of the classroom for students with visual impairments by using raised lettering or braille.
- Pay special attention to signs identifying hazards by providing nonverbal cautions for nonreaders.

Specialized Equipment Some students with disabilities require the use of specialized equipment, such as wheelchairs, hearing aids and other types of amplification systems, communication devices, adaptive desks and trays, prone standers (i.e., stand-up desks), and medical equipment. This equipment allows programmatic accessibility and, in many instances, access to the general education curriculum. Teachers need to understand how the equipment works, how it should be used, and what classroom adaptations will need to be made to accommodate the student using it. Other students in the classroom should be introduced to the special equipment as well. Instructional lessons on specific pieces of equipment will not only be helpful in creating an inclusive environment, but may also provide a basis for curricular tie-ins in areas including health and science. Suggestions include the following:

- Identify the special equipment that will be used in the classroom prior to the arrival of the student who needs it.
- Learn how special equipment and devices work and how to identify problems or malfunctions.
- Find out how long students need to use time-specified equipment or devices.
- Structure lessons and other learning activities with the knowledge that some students will be using specialized equipment or materials.

Content Differentiation

Content is the "what" of instruction and is reflected in the curriculum that is covered in school. Curriculum can be defined as the planned and guided learning experiences under the direction of the school. It relates significantly to the content that is covered and that leads to knowledge acquisition and skills development. Differentiation in the area of content typically refers to three areas: reducing content coverage, expediting coverage (e.g., compacting), and covering additional content that is not specifically stated in the curriculum.

For some gifted students who are in general education classes, the content being introduced to students has already been mastered. Thus, differentiation requires that teachers find ways to extend the coverage (i.e., acceleration) to meet the needs of these students. Sometimes, acceleration will entail moving the student to a more advanced grade level or finding more suitable ways to meet the student's needs.

Students can be motivated by curricula that they find relevant and meaningful with regard to their daily lives. Kohn (1993) notes that a key condition for developing authentic motivation is the content of the tasks—learning that is contextualized where there is a connection to students' lives and interests. Interestingly, many of the content areas discussed in this section relate well to this notion.

Commonly, these skills are never taught directly to students, with the thinking that students learn these skills incidentally. In reality, many students who are struggling in school have not been systematically taught these key support skills. For instance, a fourth-grade teacher who is teaching math does not see social skills content as part of the math curriculum. Nevertheless, some social skills may need to be taught if certain students are going to work cooperatively in various math groups.

One way to ensure that these important skills are addressed is to include goals related to these areas in the student's IEP or 504 accommodation plan, if they have been identified. Another suggestion is to take advantage of courses and special sessions covering these skill areas that some schools provide for students. The ideal situation is the implementation of ongoing coverage of important skill areas, such as study skills, learning strategies, social skills, and life skills. Such programs introduce simple variations of the skills in the primary grades and gradually increase to more complex variations, as students progress through school. In other words, critical skills instruction becomes part of the hidden curriculum.

Study Skills   Without question, one of the most important areas in which students with special needs must achieve competence is study skills. Study skills are tools for learning and can be described as those specific skills that individuals employ to acquire, record, remember, and use information efficiently. These skills are useful not only in school but in everyday living as well.

A considerable amount of agreement exists as to which specific skills should be considered study skills; however, some disparity can be found across study skills resources. One list of the important study skills and their significance for learning is provided in Table 4.1.

Learning Strategies   Learning strategies are another set of skills that can be extremely valuable to students. Learning strategies are "task-specific techniques that students use in responding to classroom tasks" (Archer & Gleason, 1995, p. 236). Utilizing a cognitive orienta-

---

TABLE 4.1

Study Skills: Tools for Learning

STUDY SKILL	SIGNIFICANCE FOR LEARNING
Reading rate	Reading rates vary with type and length of reading assignments.
Listening	Listening skills are necessary to complete most education tasks or requirements.
Graphic aids	Graphic aids may visually depict complex or cumbersome material in a meaningful format.
Library usage	Library usage skills facilitate easy access to much information.
Reference material usage	Independent learning may be greatly improved through effective use of reference materials and dictionaries.
Test taking	Effective test-taking abilities help ensure more accurate assessment of student abilities.
Notetaking and outlining	Effective note taking and outlining skills allow students to document key points of topics for future study.
Report writing	Report writing is a widely used method for documenting information and expressing ideas.
Oral presentations	Oral presentations provide students an alternative method to express themselves and report information.
Time management	Time management assists in reducing the number of unfinished assignments and facilitates more effective use of time.
Self-management	Self-management assists students in assuming responsibility for their own behaviors.
Organization	Organizational skills help in managing learning-related activities.

Study Skills to Meet Special and Diverse Needs

Source: Hoover, J. H., & Patton, J. R. (2007). Teaching study skills to students with learning problems: A teacher's guide for meeting diverse needs (2nd ed.). Austin: PRO-ED. p. 3.

tion to learning, these types of strategies provide students with a method for using their own abilities and knowledge to acquire, organize, and integrate new information. Ultimately, successful demonstration of learning strategy competence leads to more self-regulated, independent learning, as these strategies are generalizable to other situations where a specific task is required.

Many different learning strategies exist and, accordingly, various systems for organizing learning strategies can be found as well (Archer & Gleason, 1989; Deshler, Ellis, & Lenz, 1996; Hoover & Patton, 2005). Table 4.2 shows general types of learning strategies according to the function the strategy serves, as presented in certain resource materials. A number of formalized strategies are available to assist students who are struggling with various learning-related tasks, and a select sampling of them is provided in Table 4.3.

Social Skills   Appropriate social skills are essential for success in school, on the job, and in the community. Social skills are the ability to demonstrate behaviors that are socially desirable and to refrain from displaying behaviors that elicit negative responses within the context of two or more persons interacting. Social skills should be proactive, prosocial, and reciprocal in nature so that participants of the interaction share in a mutually rewarding experience.

When social skills problems are present, they are of one of four types: (1) total skill deficit—all components of skill are absent, (2) partial skill deficit—some critical elements of the skill are absent, (3) performance deficits—the person can demonstrate skill but does not use it at all or with sufficient frequency, and (4) control deficits—undesirable social behaviors (i.e., obtrusive or excessive) are present (Sargent, 1991). Each of these situations requires a more formal approach to social skills development.

All too often, social skills development is not addressed directly within the school curriculum. For many students with special needs, social skills training should be part of the explicit curriculum. In reality, such training is part of the hidden curriculum in many schools

---

TABLE 4.2

Types of Learning Strategies as a Function of Primary Operation

ACQUIRING INFORMATION	ORGANIZING INFORMATION	DEMONSTRATING COMPETENCE
Deshler et al. (1996) • word-identification strategy • paraphrasing strategy • self-questioning strategy • visual-imagery strategy • interpreting-visuals strategy • multipass strategy	• first-letter mnemonic strategy • paired-associates strategy • listening and note-taking strategy	• sentence-writing strategy • paragraph-writing strategy • error-monitoring strategy • theme-writing strategy • assignment-completion strategy • test-taking strategy
Archer and Gleason (1989) • reading expository material • reading narrative material	• gaining information from verbal presentations (lectures, demonstrations)	• completing daily assignments • answering written questions • writing narrative and expository products • preparing for and taking tests • rehearsal
Hoover and Patton (1997) • active processing • analogy • coping • evaluation	• organization	

Source: Developed from *Teaching Students with Learning Problems to Use Study Skills: A Teacher's Guide*, by J. J. Hoover and J. R. Patton, 1997. Austin, TX: PRO-ED; *Skills for School Success*, by A. Archer and M. Gleason, 1989, North Billerica, MA: Curriculum Associates; and *Teaching Adolescents with Learning Disabilities: Strategies and Methods*, by D. D. Deshler, E. S. Ellis, and B. K. Lenz, 1996, Denver: Love Publishing.

TABLE 4.3

Selected Learning Strategies

STRATEGY	TASK AREA	PROCESS	DESCRIPTION
COPS	Writing	Capitalization correct Overall appearance Punctuation correct Spelling correct	This strategy helps students to review what they have written.
DEFENDS	Written expression	Decide on a specific position Examine own reasons for this position Form list of points explaining each reason Expose position in first sentence of written task Note each reason and associated points Drive home position in last sentence Search for and correct errors	This strategy helps learners defend a particular position in a written assignment.
PARS	Reading	Preview Ask questions Read Summarize	PARS is recommended for use with younger students and with those who have limited experiences with study strategies.
RAP	Reading comprehension	Read paragraph Ask self to identify the main idea and two supporting details Put main idea and details into own words	This strategy helps students to learn information through paraphrasing.
RDPE	Underlining	Read entire passage Decide which ideas are important Plan the underlining to include only main points Evaluate results of the underlining by reading only the underlined words	This strategy helps learners organize and remember main points and ideas in a reading selection through appropriate underlining of key words.
SCORER	Test taking	Schedule time effectively Clue words identified Omit difficult items until end Read carefully Estimate answers requiring calculations Review work and responses	This test-taking strategy provides a structure for completing various tests by helping students carefully and systematically complete test items.
SQ3R	Reading	Survey Question Read Recite Review	SQ3R provides a systematic approach to improve reading comprehension.
TOWER	Written reports	Think Order ideas Write Edit Rewrite	TOWER provides a structure for completing initial and final drafts of written reports.

Source: Adapted from *Teaching Study Skills to Students with Learning Problems: A Teacher's Guide for Meeting Diverse Needs* (pp. 132–136), by J. J. Hoover and J. R. Patton, 2007. Austin, TX: PRO-ED. Copyright 2007 by PRO-ED, Inc. Reprinted with permission.

> ## FIGURE 4.4 — Types of Social Skills
>
> **Interpersonal Behaviors:** "Friendship-making skills," such as introducing oneself, asking a favor, offering to help, giving and accepting compliments, and apologizing.
>
> **Peer-Related Social Skills:** Skills valued by classmates and associated with peer acceptance. Examples include working cooperatively and asking for and receiving information.
>
> **Teacher-Pleasing Social Skills:** School success behaviors, including following directions, doing one's best work, and listening to the teacher.
>
> **Self-Related Behaviors:** Skills that allow a child to assess a social situation, select an appropriate skill, and determine the skill's effectiveness. Other self-related behaviors include following through, dealing with stress, and understanding feelings.
>
> **Assertiveness Skills:** Behaviors that allow children to express their needs without resorting to aggression.
>
> **Communication Skills:** Listener responsiveness, turn taking, maintaining conversational attention, and giving the speaker feedback.
>
> *Source:* From "Teaching Social Skills to Students with Learning and Behavioral Problems," by L. K. Elksnin and N. Elksnin, 1998, *Intervention in School and Clinic, 33*, p. 132.

because of the ultimate importance of competence in this area. Some of the most important social skills needed in the school setting are listed in Figure 4.4.

Related Life Skills   Another curricular area that might be absent from the educational programs of many struggling students is that of life skills instruction. The inclusion of life skills topics can be extremely useful to students, both while they are in school and in the future. Life skills can be thought of as "specific competencies (i.e., knowledge, skills, and their application) of local and cultural relevance needed to perform everyday activities across a variety of settings" (Cronin, Patton, & Wood, 2007, p. 2). Without question, life skills competence is needed to deal successfully with the many challenges and demands of adulthood.

The conceptualization of life skills just provided is broad and includes skills previously discussed in areas such as study skills and social skills. A listing of other life skills would be exhaustive; however, general life skills categories include daily living, leisure and recreation, community participation and citizenship, transportation, health, self-determination, and occupational preparation.

Life skills instruction is not typically part of the curriculum for most students. Leaving the acquisition of these skills to chance rather than to a systematic program of study does not contribute to the comprehensive preparation that most students need. While coverage of these important skills is clearly appropriate for noncollege-bound students, these topics are appropriate for college-bound students as well.

The recommended tactic is to infuse real-life topics into existing content when opportunities arise to do so. Patton, Cronin, and Wood (1999) provide many examples at the elementary and secondary levels of how to infuse real-life topics into different subject area content.

Material Differentiation

Many different types of materials are used in school settings. These include a wide variety of print materials that students must be able to read and extract information from for use at a later time. Other nonprint materials such as maps, globes, models, photographs, videos, and computer-based images are also available in school settings. All of these materials can pose problems for students who are struggling in school.

The key concerns that precipitate the need to make accommodations to instructional materials, for the most part, cut across the different types of materials. Some issues relate to the student and other issues relate to the materials being used.

Certain characteristics can play a key role in limiting a student's ability to use various materials. Students may not display prerequisite skills necessary to handle the material. The conceptual complexity of the material exceeds the level at which a student understands. And finally, the students may not have sufficient background and experience to make sense of the information being presented.

Various characteristics of the materials themselves often pose major problems. The linguistic complexity of the material may be such that the student is unable to extract meaning from it. Primary sources of problem come from vocabulary and syntactic factors. In addition, the amount of information presented to students is overwhelming. Typically an emphasis has been placed on breadth of coverage rather than depth of coverage. In reference to textual materials, Deshler, Ellis, and Lenz (1996) note that "even when textbooks are written in ways that 'invite' learning, the sheer volume of information included in textbooks can be overwhelming for teachers and students alike" (p. 417). Students can be overwhelmed by the amount of information found on the Internet as well.

Far too often the design and format features of materials (e.g., advanced organizers, layout, organization, graphics, cueing, clarity, use of examples, practice opportunities) are lacking or insufficient, thus making the materials difficult to use. This is especially true for students who are encountering learning-related problems. In other words, the "considerateness" (Armbruster & Anderson, 1988) or user-friendliness of materials is frequently in question.

Textual Materials   Text-based materials, for the purpose of this chapter, are any type of material that requires reading as the primary means of obtaining information. Text-based materials typically used in classrooms include basal textbooks, workbooks, worksheets, literature, weekly periodicals, handouts, other reproduced materials, as well as text-based material read via computer. The general cautions previously mentioned hold for these types of materials.

Three general approaches can be implemented to address problems that arise with text-based materials: substitution using some type of alternative material in place of the existing textual material, comprehension enhancement of the existing material, and use of techniques that assist the student in retaining information over time. The first technique aims to avoid the problems associated with existing textual material. The next two approaches require adjustments with the use of existing material. The discussion of the various techniques for dealing with textual material, adapted from the recommendations of Schumm and Strickler (1991), offers a number of ideas for addressing problems students may have using textual material along with some concerns associated with the techniques.

Adapting Textual Material   The primary characteristic of this technique is use of an alternative method for conveying the information contained in the textual material being used with students. This approach ranges from the complete substitution of existing text to the modification of the existing text. Some of the suggestions are more likely to be implemented than others due to time, effort, and availability factors. For example:

- **Audiotape textual material:** Ideally, the material being used is already available through Recordings for the Blind and Dyslexic, and the student can qualify for this service. Otherwise, unless volunteers or other students are available to do the taping, taping may be difficult to do. Lovitt and Horton (1991) do not recommend taping on the basis that "many texts are 'inconsiderate.'" It seems apparent that if a passage is disorganized and incoherent, it will continue to be disorganized and incoherent when taped (p. 443).
- **Read the material aloud:** This suggestion has the same advantages and limitations as the taping recommendation.
- **Pair students to master textual material:** This technique has short-term and targeted usefulness and requires the availability of such supports whenever the textual material is being used.
- **Use other ways to deliver the material (e.g., direct experiences, media):** Other vehicles for delivering information are extremely useful for presenting content-laden topics. The drawback to this idea is the availability of appropriate alternatives and the time to do them.

- **Work with students individually or in small groups:** This works when students can understand the textual material to some extent and time is available on a regular basis for performing this activity.
- **Use a multilevel, multimaterial approach:** Textbooks that are written at lower readability levels are available in a number of content areas. Other supplementary reading materials that are written at a lower reading level can also be introduced. This approach allows students to remain in a specific course and gain the information they need through the use of materials they can handle. This technique is enhanced by the use of some of the other suggestions previously discussed.
- **Develop abridged versions of textual content:** The attractiveness of this suggestion is that students are able to use textual material that is suited to their reading levels. The fact that this type of material almost always needs to be developed (i.e., written) by the teacher or other personnel is a drawback due to the time and energy involved. It is for this reason that Lovitt and Horton (1991) do not recommend this technique.
- **Simplify existing textual material:** To deal with vocabulary, terminology, and expressions that are difficult for students to understand, the teacher can simplify them. In place of rewriting complete textual passages, one can place a transparency over a page of written material and, with a marker, cross out the more difficult words and substitute more understandable equivalents in the margin (Hoover & Patton, 2007).

Enhancing Comprehension   A variety of ways exist to assist students in better understanding what they read. This may be especially important for students who struggle with reading or listening comprehension. The following recommendations focus on tactics for improving comprehension of textual material, particularly grade-level material:

- **Provide students with purposes for the reading they are being asked to do:** This simply helps students appreciate what the goal of the reading assignment is.
- **Preview the reading assignment:** This very important activity, which too often is omitted, prepares students for some of the specifics of what they will encounter. This prereading activity should introduce the students to new vocabulary and concepts that they will encounter and that may pose problems. The use of a diagram or story frame may be helpful.
- **Teach students how to use format features:** An extremely useful set of skills includes the ability to use headings, boldface type, visual aids (e.g., figures, tables, exhibits, photographs), opening sections, and summaries of textual material to gain an organization and additional meaning from the textual material.
- **Engage the student prior to reading:** Stimulating thinking about what is to be read is extremely helpful. The use of an anticipation guide that asks students certain questions that will be answered during the course of their reading is one such tactic.
- **Use a study guide:** Some commercial textbooks provide these supplementary aids; other texts do not. The primary objective of using this type of aid is to guide the students through the reading material by having them respond to questions or statements related to the passages they are reading or have read. Study guides are a way of organizing and guiding the comprehension of textual material.
- **Utilize graphic organizers:** These techniques use visual formats or structures to help students organize information for better comprehension. Specific techniques include the use of a central-story-problem format, story frames or story map, and semantic mapping. An example of a story map is presented in the feature Differentiated Instruction—Elementary boxed reading.
- **Modify the nature of the reading assignment:** It might be necessary to reduce the length of the assigned reading or to slow down the pace of content being covered.
- **Highlight the textual material:** If it is possible to highlight the actual textual material prior to a student using the material, a teacher can focus the reader on important points in the passage. Highlighting can also be used prior to reading by having the student go through the text and highlight all headings, thus introducing the reader to what will be encountered.
- **Teach comprehension-monitoring strategies:** Various strategies have been developed to help students think about how well they understand what they are reading and how they can address any problems they are having.

Differentiating Elementary Instruction

SAMPLE STORY MAP TITLE: CINDERELLA (PERRAULT/JEFFERS)

Characters:

Cinderella

Stepmother, father

2 Stepsisters

Fairy Godmother, prince

Setting:

Time: Long ago

Place: Kingdom

Problem:

Father dies, Cinderella mistreated and not allowed to go to the king's ball.

Goal:

To go to the ball and meet the handsome prince.

Events to Reach Solution:

1. Fairy Godmother changes Cinderella's rags into ballgown and glass slippers and sends her to the ball in exchange for her promise to be back by midnight.
2. Cinderella dances with the prince at the ball, forgetting the time.
3. As the clocks strikes 12, she runs from the ball, losing a glass slipper.
4. Cinderella is changed back into her rags.
5. The prince searches for the girl whose foot fits the glass slipper.

Solution:

Cinderella can wear the slipper.
When she puts on the matching one, she turns back into the way she looked at the ball. She leaves with the prince to be married and live happily ever after.

Source: Adapted from "Constructing Meaning: An Integrated Approach to Teaching Reading," by K. D. Barclay, 1990, *Intervention in School and Clinic, 26,* p. 88. Copyright 1990 by PRO-ED, Inc. Reprinted with permission.

Adapt Text-Based Activities   Reorganizing and rewriting the end-of-chapter questions that are often included with the books may be needed. For students who are experiencing reading problems, these types of questions can be very frustrating.

Retaining Information Acquired Through Text   As Schumm and Strickler (1991) note, "Some students can read the words and can comprehend material during ongoing reading . . . nonetheless, some students do not perform well on tests due to difficulty with long-term memory" (p. 83). Students need to learn ways to help them retain what they have read, whether the need is test-related, which is an important reality, or for general knowledge:

- **Utilize graphic aids:** Various types of visual organizers can be used in the postreading phase.
- **Incorporate formal learning strategies:** Some specific strategies that include a retention component can be taught to students—refer back to Table 4.3 for examples of these types of strategies. Most techniques ask the student to write a short description of the main points or a summary of what they read.
- **Teach test-preparation skills:** An assortment of skills that are needed to prepare for tests work in conjunction with material that has been read. In most secondary and postsecondary settings, it is assumed that students can handle the reading material and use what has been read to respond successfully to questions that are asked on tests.
- **Teach class-discussion preparation skills:** Much like successful test performance, contributing to class discussions can require preparation, especially for students who struggle with reading the textual material on which the discussions will be based. Structured ways of organizing information may be needed.

Adapting Other Instructional Materials   In addition to text-based materials, math materials and learning aids can also present challenges to students with special needs.

Math Materials   The primary concerns addressed in this section on math materials relate to the use of the basal textbook approach that is used in most schools. If the challenges associated with using this approach to teaching math are recognized, solutions can be implemented. The key factors that teachers must consider when using math texts with students who are experiencing problems include:

- Instructor's manuals do not provide specific teaching strategies for teaching a given skill.
- Sufficient practice may not be provided.
- Movement from one skill/topic to another may be too rapid.
- Sometimes there is not enough review of previously covered topics.
- Linguistic and conceptual demands may inhibit understanding—the issues of text-based material are relevant in math as well.
- The variety of the types of activities that students do is limited.
- Activities and content are not relevant to students.
- Problem-solving applications are often too contrived (Polloway, Patton, & Serna, 2008).

Learning Aids   Brief mention needs to be given to any type of learning aid (e.g., outside readings, realistic representations, games, learning centers, in-class projects) that might be part of an instructional program. Caution must be exercised to ensure that students know how to use these materials. If textual material is part of the learning aid, some of the various suggestions offered previously may need to be included. In regard to the use of instructional games, students need to possess appropriate game-playing skills and behaviors—this is extremely critical if students play games in cooperative situations without direct teacher involvement or monitoring.

Instructional Differentiation

There are many ways to alter the teacher input/student output exchange—the specific adjustments that are needed in regard to homework, testing, and grading. No attempt is made to cover all of what is known about best and recommended practice in these areas, and many books have been written on these topics. The purpose of this section is to highlight a number of differentiation practices that can be used to optimize the learning environment for all students and that are required for students who are struggling.

Learning Considerations   Three different instructional orientations are available: teacher-directed (nature of learning is teacher led and teacher dominated), student-directed (nature of the learning is teacher facilitated but the student is the focus of the activities), and peer-directed (nature of the learning is teacher facilitated but activities are accomplished in joint manner in students groups or dyads). Most teachers use all three orientations in their classrooms. The important point is that each orientation has a set of expectations and procedures that teachers must recognize and students must understand. All three orientations are valid and should be considered in delivering sound instruction to students who are struggling.

Another learning-related issue that teachers must understand is the different types of learning. This is important because certain instructional conditions and adaptations are required for each type of learning as they are used with students with special needs. Mastropieri and Scruggs (1994) identify the different types of learning as discrimination learning, factual learning, rule learning, procedural learning, and conceptual learning. Each type of learning is used in school and home. Academic and social examples of each type of learning are presented in Table 4.4.

In working with a broad range of students, attention should also be given to the *stages of learning*. Many problems arise when these basic stages of learning are ignored or misapplied. The primary stages or levels of learning are acquisition, proficiency, maintenance, and generalization. It is crucial to recognize the aim of each stage and to apply it appropriately in instructional contexts. Table 4.5 provides a brief description of each stage and its primary aim.

TABLE 4.4

Types of Learning

LEARNING TYPE	READING	ARITHMETIC	SOCIAL
Discrimination	*p* vs. *q*	+ vs. −	cooperate vs. compete
Factual			
Associative	*l = ell*	5 + 2 = 7	Laughing at other people is rude.
Serial list	a, b, c, d, e . . .	2, 4, 6, 8, 10, 12 . . .	School song or motto.
Rule	If two vowels appear together, say the long sound of the first vowel.	To divide fractions, invert and multiply.	Do unto others as you would have others do unto you.
Concept	vowel	prime number	courtesy
Procedure	1. Read title 2. Self-question 3. Skim passage 4. Self-question 5. Read carefully 6. Answer questions	1. Count decimal places in division. 2. Move decimal point in divisor that many places to the right, insert caret. 3. Place decimal point directly above caret in quotient.	1. Walk quietly in line. 2. Take tray, utensils, and napkins. 3. Put lunch on tray. 4. Take carton of milk. 5. Walk quietly to lunch table.

Source: From *Effective Instruction for Special Education* (2nd ed., p. 42), by M. A. Mastropieri and T. E. Scruggs, 1994, Austin, TX: PRO-ED. Copyright 1994 by PRO-ED, Inc. Reprinted with permission.

Delivery of Systematic and Explicit Instruction When teaching students who are encountering challenges in school, teachers should implement the basic elements of effective teaching. Some of the more important points to review include:

- **Capitalize on location:** Having proximity to students who are experiencing learning-related problems can assist those students to attend to the important dimensions of what is occurring in the classroom, give them easier access to support, and minimize behavioral problems that might arise.
- **Utilize the demonstration-guided, practice-independent, practice-evaluation paradigm:** This method is highly effective for maximizing the probability that a skill will be learned, and includes the following sequence of stages: (1) the teacher demonstrates the behavior or skill to be taught, (2) the student is then given an opportunity to perform the behavior with guidance from the teacher (this phase may include the use of physical, verbal, visual, or gestural prompts), and (3) the student eventually practices the behavior without assistance. Ultimately, an adequate evaluation of performance is undertaken.
- **Take great care in presenting *new* information:** Mastropieri and Scruggs (1993) have identified six factors that are crucial for teaching new information to students. They refer to them as the SCREAM variables: structure, clarity, redundancy, enthusiasm, appropriate pace, and maximize engagement.
- **Use multisensory experiences:** The statements that multisensory activities can have a drastic impact on learning, as some people claim, should not deter from the fact that such activities can be instructionally useful.
- **Make needed lecture-related accommodations:** Teacher-controlled adaptations include scheduling the session so more breaks are possible, organizing the lecture so that a variety of instructional methods (e.g., discussion, media) are utilized, moving around the room, being responsive to the audience and specific students, highlighting important points, and providing advanced organizers. The use of preparatory

---

TABLE 4.5

Stages of Learning

Acquisition

The learner is in the process of acquiring but has not acquired the skill. The learner has no knowledge of how to perform the task accurately and therefore never responds correctly, no matter how many times he or she is tested. In this stage the teacher offers direct instruction, followed by practice in the skill area. Modeling may be used here.

   The aim of instruction is *accuracy* of response.

Proficiency

The learner responds accurately but with insufficient speed. The learner performs accurately, indicating acquisition of the requisite information but needs to perform the skill quickly enough to be practically automatic, so that other skills may be built upon this one and not be impeded by slow performance.

   The aim of instruction is for the teacher to reinforce the learner for faster *rates* of response.

Maintenance

The learner is expected to retain both accuracy and fluency with the skill. The learner may or may not continue to perform at a proficient level. Consequently, the teacher must periodically evaluate retention and again use direct instruction when necessary to maintain both accuracy and speed of response.

   The aim of instruction is *retention* of the skill.

Generalization

The learner is expected to transfer the skill to new situations or settings, regardless of the setting or response mode required. The teacher provides direct instruction in alternate settings and response modes when the student fails to generalize. The teacher programs for generalization in different settings and modes, varying stimulus conditions, telling students which to attend to and which to ignore, as well as training other personnel in alternative settings to maintain similar procedures.

   The aim of instruction is *expansion* of the skill across situations, behaviors, and time.

Source: Adapted from "The Resource/Consulting Teacher: An Integrated Model of Service Delivery," by L. Idol, 1989, *Remedial and Special Education, 10(6)*, p. 41. Copyright 1989 by PRO-ED, Inc. Adapted with permission.

activities like those used in enhancing comprehension of text is applicable here as well. In addition, note-taking skills and listening strategies may need to be taught. If the lecture format allows for discussion, the student may also need to develop better question-asking skills.

- **Use assistive technology:** Familiarity with the range of assistive technology (AT) options is warranted for certain students. AT ranges from low-tech applications (e.g., tape player) to high-tech (e.g., FM systems for helping students concentrate on what is being said). Teachers should know what devices are available, how to have a student evaluated, and, if such devices are used, how they work.

Instructional Planning   Three elements need to be discussed in relation to planning. First, lesson plans should include a section on accommodating students who have learning-related needs. One suggestion is to include a section on special needs as part of the lesson planning form.

The second issue is the use of different input and output modes in teaching. There are two benefits: It allows the teacher to address the needs of students and it introduces variety. Cawley, Fitzmaurice-Hays, and Shaw (1988) developed the idea of the interactive unit. This formulation was incorporated into many of the math materials that Cawley and colleagues developed. A variation of this model is illustrated in Figure 4.5. In this model, *input* refers to the way the teacher delivers information/instruction (i.e., the way a student receives information), and *output* refers to the way the student acts on this information. As can be seen, for most topical areas for which planning is needed, 24 options exist for differentiating instructional activities and experiences.

FIGURE 4.5 Student Input/Output Options

Output:	Writes	Talks	Makes	Performs	Solves	Identifies
Input: Reads						
Listens						
Views						
Does						

Source: Adapted from *Mathematics for the Mildly Handicapped: A Guide to Curriculum and Instruction,* by J. F. Cawley, A. M. Fitzmaurice-Hayes, and R. A. Shaw, 1988, Boston: Allyn & Bacon, and from *Facilitator Manual, Teacher Training Program: Mainstreaming Mildly Handicapped Students in the Regular Classroom,* by P. B. Smith and G. Bentley, 1975, Austin, TX: Education Service Center, Region XII.

The third issue related to planning is grouping. In peer-oriented learning situations such as cooperative learning arrangements, students will need to display a host of skills to be successful. When planning instruction and deciding on grouping arrangements, teachers need to consider a number of factors: purpose for the grouping, group size, physical conditions, student characteristics, and, as mentioned, the requisite academic and social (e.g., cooperative) skills. Some of the most frequently used methods for grouping are presented in Table 4.6.

In-class Activities   Three key issues relate to the way in-class activities occur. The first topic concerns how teachers present information. In addition to being explicit in the instruction that occurs, teachers need to be mindful that some students will require time devoted to the "preteaching" of vocabulary and or concepts that are new and will be introduced in the readings or lesson.

The second issue involves the reality that some students take longer to process information. As a result, it is important that these students are given a sufficient amount of time to process a question and then come up with a response. The use of "wait time" for the entire class is a good way to address this need. With this tactic, all students are told to wait to respond until signaled to do so. This allows time for those who need more processing time.

The third concern is the desire to keep students actively engaged in the ongoing instruction. One of the best ways to accomplish this goal is to have students use choral responding—that is, everyone responds to all questions. The use of clickers or some other type of system (e.g., yes/no cards) can also serve to keep students actively involved.

Assignments and Products   This component of the differentiation process involves practices that relate to the assignments that are given, the types of products that are possible, and the ways they are evaluated. Five topics are presented for which some suggestions are given. These five areas are alternative product ideas, assignment adaptations and management, homework issues, testing options, and the monitoring and evaluation of performance.

Frequently, it will become necessary to alter the assignments so that students with certain learning-related problems can handle what is assigned. Teachers can alter assignments in the following ways: shorten assignments (i.e., break them into smaller versions), change the criterion that designates successful completion of the assignment, allow more time to complete the assignment, reduce the difficulty of the content, and change the output mode. Each of these adaptations can be beneficial to certain students in the general education classroom. The important point is that none of these adaptations should be made if it is not needed; if one is needed, the least amount of change possible is desirable.

TABLE 4.6

Formats for Instruction

FORMAT	HOW FORMED	PURPOSE	ADVANTAGES	DISADVANTAGES
Whole Group	Whole group	To deliver information on new content or skill(s) to all at one time	• Cover much information in little time • Everyone hears the same information	• Does not meet needs of many students when used as the only method of instruction
Small Teacher-Led Group	Teacher formed homogeneous groups using set criteria	To provide activities to meet specific needs, either remedial or enrichment	• Able to check more accurately for student understanding	• Some students may be engaged in long periods of seatwork without being actively monitored
Small Cooperative Group	Teacher formed equivalent heterogeneous groups based on performance, gender, race, and so forth	To reinforce previously taught content and foster social skills (Note: Individual grades are a *must* to achieve these purposes.)	• More opportunity for students to "interact" with material being presented	• Sometimes only two or three of the four to five students benefit from doing the work
Small Noncompetitive Group	Random selection with teacher guidence as needed to form heterogeneous groups	To experience a process or produce a product with no individual or group academic grading involved	• Social skills fostered	• Difficult to check for individual student's understanding during activity
Student Pairs	Teacher or student selected based on reciprocal learning needs	To enhance collaborative learning through collaborative/reciprocal processes	• Can involve both students • Fosters social skills • Facilitates reciprocal learning	• One student may do all the work/thinking
Individualized Instruction	One student	To meet individual student needs, (IEPs, absentee makeup work, enrichment, remediation of content or skills)	• Teacher-student ratio a plus • Remedial/enrichment help easily given	• May be time consuming • Some students may not be actively monitored
Centers and Stations	Teacher created with equitable student access designated in a variety of ways	To enrich, extend, practice, apply new learning, and/or remediate content and/or skills	• Enriches student understanding • Students can practice skills • Students can apply new learning	• Difficult to manage time at center and problematic for nonreaders • Requires preparation time • Difficult to monitor

Source: Adapted from Evertson & Harris (2003). ©Vanderbilt University, reprinted with permission.

A good example of the need for assignment adaptation is a page from a math workbook of 16 subtraction algorithms involving money values, which has been given to students to complete. For a student who is experiencing difficulty with this type of activity but who is capable of doing the math, some type of adaptation is needed.

Another way to differentiate assignments is to use tiered assignments. In this method, assignments can be designed with varying features that can be selected based on individual student's skill levels, abilities, motivation, or interests. For example, assignments can be tiered by challenge level, complexity, reading level, product/outcome, and what is required (i.e., process).

For some time, professionals in the field of gifted education have promoted the idea of a variety of product options. Perhaps it is time that those of us who work with struggling students think along those lines as well. To give students options and some choice about those options is desirable practice. All too often teachers tend to make the same assignments to all students. For students who are struggling, and who have strengths in areas in which they are seldom allowed to show their ability, having alternative products might allow expression of those strengths.

The notion of having different outcomes for students fits with the previously discussed concept of input and output modes.

Homework Adjustments   A staple of the education diet is homework. Most of the literature supports the theory that the use of homework has a desirable effect on school learning. While homework may present special problems for students who are struggling in school and their families, certain homework-related suggestions can result in beneficial outcomes. Table 4.7 highlights 34 suggestions related to giving homework to students who might have problems in this area.

Testing Options and Adjustments   Another area that is of great interest to teachers and parents is testing. While there may be no clear solution to how to test students with special needs appropriately and with fairness to them and to their peers, some differentiating practices can be made. Polloway, Bursuck, Jayanthi, Epstein, and Nelson (1996) identified the testing adaptations that teachers thought were the most helpful to students. This ranking, presented in Table 4.8, is a useful resource for making testing adaptations.

Grading Considerations   Along with testing and homework, grading is one of the most frequently discussed topics related to students with special needs. Polloway and colleagues (1996) also identified specific adaptations teachers thought were most helpful to students with disabilities; this ranking is shown in Table 4.9.

An example of a way to blend some of the grading suggestions that teachers believe are helpful is to use an ongoing student evaluation report. This type of document, an example of which is shown in Figure 4.6, allows for regular feedback on three dimensions organized across subject areas and can be modified to address the requirements of a given school system.

Management/Behavior Differentiation

The management component of the differentiation model focuses on behavior. Establishing an effective system for managing behavior will be useful for all students in the classroom. However, for those students whose behaviors breach what is considered desirable or acceptable, certain specialized techniques will be needed.

One of the most important aspects of management involves the rules and procedures that are established to guide classroom dynamics. The guidelines discussed here provide direction to school staff and students as to what is expected of all. It is all about expectations!

The teacher must identify all general expectations, rules, procedures, and other regulations before the school year begins and should plan to teach them to students during the

TABLE 4.7

Recommended Homework Practices

Management Considerations

Assess student homework skills

Involve parents from the outset

Assign homework from the beginning of the year

Schedule time and establish a routing for assigning, collecting, and evaluating homework

Communicate the consequences for not completing assignments

Minimize the demands of teacher time

Coordinate with other teachers

Present homework instructions clearly

Verify the assignment given

Allow students to start homework in class

Use assignment books and/or folders

Implement classroom-based incentive programs

Have parents sign and date homework

Evaluate assignments

Assignment Considerations

Recognize the purpose of the homework assignment

Establish relevance

Use appropriate state-of-learning demands

Select appropriate type of activity

Keep assignments from getting too complex or novel

Ensure reasonable chance of completion and high rate of success

Adapt assignment as needed

Avoid using homework as punishment

Consider nonacademic assignments

Student Competencies

Demonstrate minimum levels of competence

Possess academic support skills

Promote interdependent learning

Develop self-management skills

Foster responsibility

Parent Involvement

Serve in a supportive role

Go through training, if available

Create a home environment that is conducive to doing homework

Encourage and reinforce student effort

Maintain ongoing involvement

Communicate views regarding homework to school personnel

Source: From "Practical Recommendations for Using Homework for Students with Learning Disabilities," by J. R. Patton, 1994, *Journal of Learning Disabilities, 27*, p. 573. Copyright 1994 by PRO-ED, Inc. Reprinted with permission.

first days of the school year. Equally important is preparation for dealing with violations of rules. Immediate and consistent consequences are needed. Various disciplinary techniques can be implemented to ensure that inappropriate behavior is handled effectively (these will be covered in a subsequent section on decreasing undesirable behaviors in this chapter).

Students with exceptional needs will benefit from being systematically taught the administrative and social rules operative in a classroom. Students who have difficulty interpreting the social and administrative rules of a classroom (e.g., students with Asperger syndrome) need this form of direct instruction.

General Expectations Most individuals respond best when they know what is expected of them. General expectations provide standards that are in place at all times in the classroom. They can be thought of as "guidelines for life at school" and include very general statements that can be invoked in many different situations. The following are representative examples of guiding principles that are adapted from Smith (2004): treat each other fairly, show respect and responsibility, school is a safe place to learn, our classroom is our community, students have the right to learn and teachers have the right to teach, be safe, kind, and productive.

Classroom Rules Rules provide a general sense of what is expected of students in a classroom setting. Rules can be specific to certain expectations; however, they apply to general

TABLE 4.8

Teachers' Ratings of Helpfulness of Testing Adaptations

RANK[a]	ADAPTATION
1	Give individual help with directions during tests.
2	Read test questions to students.
3	Simplify wording of test questions.
4	Give practice questions as a study guide.
5	Give extra help preparing for tests.
6	Give extended time to finish tests.
7	Use black-and-white copies.
8	Give feedback to individual student during test.
9	Highlight key words in questions.
10	Allow use of learning aids during tests (e.g., calculators).
11	Give frequent quizzes rather than only exams.
12	Allow students to answer fewer questions.
13	Allow oral instead of written answers (e.g., via tape recorders).
14	Give the actual test as a study guide.
15	Change question type (e.g., essay to multiple choice).
16	Teach students test-taking skills.
17	Use tests with enlarged print.
18	Test individual on less content than rest of class.
19	Provide extra space on tests for answering.
20	Give tests in small groups.
21	Give open-book/notes tests.
22	Allow word processors.
23	Allow answers in outline format.
24	Give take-home tests.

[a] Ranked from most helpful to least helpful by general education teachers.

Source: From "Treatment Acceptability: Determining Appropriate Interventions Within Inclusive Classrooms," by E. A. Polloway, W. D. Bursuck, M. Jayanthi, M. H. Epstein, and J. S Nelson, 1996, *Intervention in School and Clinic, 37*, p. 138. Copyright 1996 by PRO-ED, Inc. Reprinted with permission.

classroom situations. The rules that are chosen should be essential to classroom functioning and help create a positive learning environment (Christenson, Ysseldyke, & Thurlow, 1989; Smith & Rivera, 1995).

Reasonable classroom rules, presented appropriately, will be particularly beneficial to students with special needs who are in general education settings, as this process assists in clarifying expectations. Evertson and colleagues (2006) offer four general rules that cover many classroom behaviors: respect and be polite to all people, be prompt and prepared, listen quietly when others are speaking, and obey all school rules. Rubrics can be developed for all of these rules to assist students in recognizing the continuum of levels at which a rule can be performed along with the acceptable levels for the classroom. Some specific suggestions related to classroom rules are presented in Figure 4.7.

FIGURE 4.6 Student Evaluation Report

Student Evaluation Report

Name: _____
Date: _____

SKILL AREA	DIMENSION	EVALUATION

READING

Achievement
no competencies mastered | average | all competencies mastered
⊢————————————⊢————————————⊣

Effort
none | moderate | high
⊢————————————⊢————————————⊣

Progress
none | moderate | high
⊢————————————⊢————————————⊣

MATH

Achievement
no competencies mastered | average | all competencies mastered
⊢————————————⊢————————————⊣

Effort
none | moderate | high
⊢————————————⊢————————————⊣

Progress
none | moderate | high
⊢————————————⊢————————————⊣

| FIGURE 4.7 | Recommendations for Classroom Rules |

- Develop no more than seven rules for the classroom.
- Involve students in rule setting.
- Keep the rules brief and state them clearly.
- Explain the rules thoroughly and discuss the specific consequences if they are violated.
- State the rules in a positive way—avoid statements that are worded in a negative way, such as "not allowed."
- Post the rules in a location where all students can see.
- Discuss exceptions in advance so that students understand them.
- Teach the rules through modeling and practice and verify that all have been learned.
- Review the rules on a regular basis and when new students join the class.
- Use reminders of rules as a preventive measure for times when possible disruptions are anticipated.

Classroom Procedures   An area of classroom management that can easily be overlooked is the development of logical classroom procedures. Classroom procedures refer to the specific way in which various classroom routines and activities will be performed or the way certain situations will be handled. For example, depending on age, procedures may need to be established for using the pencil sharpener, using the rest room, and entering and leaving the classroom. Figure 4.8 provides a checklist of classroom and school-related routines that should be considered, planned for, presented to students, and practiced during the first days of school. The checklist is an adaptation of a list developed by Smith (2004).

Again, clearly defined procedures are of particular importance, especially for some students with special needs, who may have difficulty attending to details or following instructions. This is one area where adequate consideration of these classroom/school activities can prevent many behavioral-related problems from developing. Failing to address procedural issues in the classroom can cause distress for teachers if not attended to at the beginning of the school year. Teachers are often surprised by the complexity and detail associated with many seemingly trivial areas. The procedures for these areas combine to form the mosaic of one's management system. Here are some suggestions:

- Identify all situations for which a procedure will be needed.
- Develop the procedures collaboratively with the students.
- Explain (describe and demonstrate) each procedure thoroughly.
- Teach each procedure through modeling, guided practice, independent practice, and feedback, allowing every student to have an opportunity to practice the procedure and demonstrate learning on an appropriate level.
- Introduce classroom procedures during the first week of school, scheduling priority procedures for the first day and covering others on subsequent days.
- Avoid introducing too many procedures at once.
- Incorporate any school regulation of importance and relevance into classroom procedures instruction (e.g., hall passes, restroom use).

Managing Behaviors   The ability to create and maintain appropriate behaviors and to manage inappropriate behaviors that can disrupt the learning environment are important components of classroom management. As stressed previously, dealing with inappropriate behavior is only part of a comprehensive behavior management program. Management systems should also include techniques for developing new behaviors or increasing desirable behaviors within the students' repertoire. Moreover, a sound program must ensure that behaviors learned or changed will be maintained over time and generalized (e.g., demonstrated in different contexts). It must also teach self-control and self-regulatory mechanisms.

F I G U R E 4.8	Checklist of Classroom Procedures

Directions: Develop a procedure that you will teach to your students for the areas listed below that pertain to your classroom. Start by checking the procedures for which you need a specific routine. Then, in the empty column, write out how this routine will work.

Area of Focus	Specific Procedure
Room and hall use: _____ Teacher desk _____ Storage areas _____ Student desks _____ Using the pencil sharpener _____ Using the rest room _____ Using the water fountain _____ Hall pass _____ Going to lockers	
Beginning of class: _____ Students entering the classroom _____ Using cubbies/area for belongings _____ Students who are tardy _____ Absent—excused _____ Absent—unexcused _____ Absent students making up work _____ Starting the lesson _____ Turning in homework _____ Listening to P.A. announcements	
During class instruction: _____ Getting student attention _____ Passing out papers _____ Headings on papers _____ Checking out books to students _____ Passing out classroom supplies/instructional materials _____ Using classroom supplies/instructional materials _____ Collecting classroom/instructional supplies _____ Turning in class work _____ How students ask for help _____ Checking for understanding _____ Hand raising during class discussions _____ Group work _____ Watching videos _____ Sustained silent reading _____ Taking tests _____ Taking quizzes _____ Organizing notebooks _____ Using computers _____ Sharing computers _____ Student involvement in the room _____ Oral reports	

(continued)

FIGURE 4.8	Checklist of Classroom Procedures *(continued)*

Area of Focus	Specific Procedure
Ending of class session: _____ Indicating that it is time to end class _____ Students putting their materials away _____ Assigning homework _____ Putting notebooks and other materials in backpacks and backpacks on backs _____ Dismissing class at the end of the period _____ Lining up for recess, lunch, or an assembly _____ Dismissing class at the end of the day _____ Using cubbies	
Special classroom situations and events: _____ Guest speakers _____ Volunteers in the classroom _____ Visitors to the classroom _____ Interruptions or delays _____ Sending students to the office _____ Sending students to another teacher _____ Returning to the room	
Special school-related situations and events: _____ Fire drills _____ Field trips _____ Attending an assembly or other special school event _____ Taking students to a specific area of the school (e.g., library, computer lab) _____ Playground/common area _____ Lunchroom	
Behavior management considerations: _____ Incentive system for desired behavior _____ Consequences for inappropriate behavior _____ Addressing student conflicts with one another _____ Addressing student conflicts with the teacher _____ Classroom community circles	

Source: Adapted from *Conscious Classroom Management: Unlocking the Secrets of Great Teaching* (pp. 83–85), by R. Smith, 2004. San Rafael, CA: Conscious Teaching Publications.

Attention has been given to behavior that goes beyond the typical emphasis on external behavioral tactics. For instance, Bender (2003) promotes the concept of "relational discipline":

> Relational discipline focuses squarely on the relationship between the teacher and the student, and various tactics and strategies are implemented within that broader context. For it is this relationship, rather than the specific disciplinary tactics that are used, that forms the basis for appropriate classroom behavior and that eventually develops into self-discipline. (p. 3)

Related to the notion that relationship is important, Bender points out that "behavioral interventions practices" (i.e., disciplinary tactics) must be understood from a developmental perspective. Differential techniques must be considered in terms of age-related needs

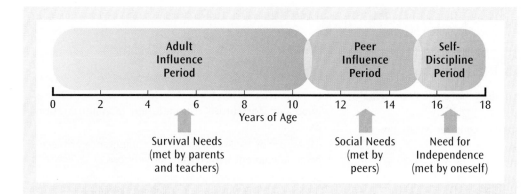

FIGURE 4.9

Relational discipline.

Source: From *Relational Discipline: Strategies for In-Your-Face Kids* (p. 35) by W. N. Bender, 2003. Boston: Allyn & Bacon. Copyright 2003 by Pearson Education. Reprinted by permission.

and predominant influences operative at a given age. Figure 4.9 illustrates these points. Bender notes that few disciplinary systems have, to any reasonable extent, built on the influence of peer groups with older students.

Behavior Management Plans   When behaviors need to be developed or when certain behaviors interfere with the learning of a student or that of his or her classmates, the development of a behavior management plan might be necessary or required, depending on the situation. Behavior management plans are much like behavior intervention plans (BIPs) that are required by IDEA for certain students. Figure 4.10 describes the basic components of a behavior management plan based on functional assessment procedures.

The BIP planning process, mandated under IDEA for any student displaying serious behavioral problems, is built on the idea of understanding the functions of behavior prior to designing ways to address it. Most behavioral plans will include intervention ideas discussed in this section. A number of sources can be consulted for more details about how to conduct a functional behavioral assessment and develop an appropriate BIP (see Fad, Patton, & Polloway, 2006; McConnell, Hilvitz, & Cox, 1998; Simpson, 1998; and Zurkowski, Kelly, & Griswold, 1998).

Positive Behavioral Supports   Because research confirms the effectiveness of behavioral techniques for promoting learning in students with special needs (see Lloyd, Forness, & Kavale, 1998), the ability to develop a behavior management plan and implement

FIGURE 4.10	Components of a Behavior Management Plan

Conduct a Functional Assessment
1. Collect information.
   - Identify and define the target behavior.
   - Identify events/circumstances associated with the problem behavior.
   - Determine potential function(s) of the problem behavior.
2. Develop hypothesis statements about the behavior.
   - Events/circumstances associated with the problem behavior.
   - Function/purpose of the behavior.

Develop an Intervention (Based on Hypothesis Statements)
1. Teach alternative behavior.
2. Modify events/circumstances associated with the problem behavior.

Source: From Using Functional Assessment to Develop Effective, Individualized Interventions for Challenging Behaviors (p. 46) by L. F. Johnson and G. Dunlap, 1993, *Teaching Exceptional Children, 25*. Used by permission.

RIGHTS & RESPONSIBILITIES

IDEA AND STUDENTS RIGHTS

- IEP team must consider whether or not a child's behavior impedes learning
- If necessary, IEP team should consider strategies to address behavior problems
- Positive behavioral supports should be considered as one strategy
- IEP includes a statement regarding behavioral intervention needs of the student
- Behavioral interventions not only support students with disabilities but also may be important for non-disabled students to support a positive learning environment
- Failure to provide behavioral supports for students who have such needs may be a violation of their FAPE
- Behavioral interventions support the inclusive placement of students

- Including behavioral interventions in student's IEP is important for future consideration of manifestation determination
- IDEA intends for states to ensure competence of teachers to implement behavioral interventions
- Special education and general education teachers should understand the following behavioral sequence:
  - Determination if behavior intervention plan is needed
  - Conduct functional behavior analysis and develop BIP
  - Implement and review BIP

Source: K. E. Hulett (2009). Legal aspects of special education. Upper Saddle River, NJ: Pearson.

interventions must be part of a teacher's repertoire. Today, professionals in the area of behavior management have been stressing the need to implement positive behavioral interventions and supports. This emphasis has been accompanied by a de-emphasis on the use of more negative and punitive tactics.

As Horner (2000) noted, "Positive behavior support involves the assessment and reengineering of environments so people with problem behaviors experience reductions in (these behaviors) and increased social [and] personal quality in their lives. . . . It is an approach that blends values about the rights of people with disabilities with the practical science about how learning and behavior change occur" (p. 181).

The essential element of positive behavior support is the emphasis on fixing environments rather than focusing just on changing the behavior of individuals. Thus, the key element is to design schools and curricula to prevent problem behaviors from occurring and thus make them "irrelevant, inefficient, and ineffective" (Horner, 2000, p. 182). The basis for effective positive behavior support programs is the use of functional behavior assessment that identifies classroom events that serve to predict the occurrence of problem behaviors and function to maintain positive behaviors (Horner, 2000).

The basis for effective positive behavior support is discussed in Chapter 7.

Creating and Increasing Desirable Behaviors   The acquisition of desired new behaviors—whether academic, personal, behavioral, social, or vocational—is a classroom goal. A new desired behavior can be affirmed with a **reinforcer**—any event that rewards, and thus strengthens, the behavior it follows. **Positive reinforcement** presents a desirable consequence for performance of an appropriate behavior. Positive reinforcers can take different forms; however, what serves as reinforcement for one individual may not hold true for another. For this reason, it is essential to determine what is reinforcing for individual students. One way to determine this information is to administer a "student interest inventory" at the beginning of the school year. Doing so should generate some ideas for creating systems to manage behavior, if needed later in the year.

Reinforcers can consist of praise, physical contact, tangible items, activities, or privileges. The use of reinforcement is the most socially acceptable and instructionally sound tactic for increasing desired behaviors. The goal of most behavioral regimens is to internalize the nature of reinforcement (i.e., self-reinforcement).

Controversy about the use of externally controlled systems that rely heavily on extrinsic rewards has brewed for years now. Some professionals (Deci, Koestner, & Ryan, 1999; Kohn, 1993) argue that the use of external rewards interferes with the development of intrinsic systems of reinforcement. Extrinsic systems of reward can be used incorrectly (e.g., rewards are provided haphazardly) and can indeed interfere with the development of more intrinsic motivation. Landrum and Kauffman's (2006) response to this controversy provides two very important points: (1) the research data do not support the idea that rewards are to be assiduously avoided, and (2) in the absence of intrinsic motivation to complete academic tasks or behave as expected in school, nothing is to be gained and much is to be lost by refusing to use extrinsic rewards to reinforce desired conduct (p. 67).

Three basic principles must be followed for positive reinforcement to be most effective: it must be meaningful to the student, contingent on the proper performance of a desired behavior, and presented immediately. In other words, for positive reinforcement to work, students must find the reinforcement desirable in some fashion, understand that it is being given as a result of the behavior demonstrated, and receive it soon after they do what was asked. Principles for the use of positive reinforcement are presented in Figure 4.11. Generally, attention to the systematic nature of the reinforcement program should parallel the severity of a student's intellectual, learning, or behavioral problem. All too often, teachers do not pay close enough attention to the principles that have been noted, and, as a result, do not implement techniques with any power. Another potential problem is that some powerful positive behavioral interventions cannot be implemented because of such factors as cost or complexity (Bender, 2003).

The first illustrative application of the principle of positive reinforcement is **contingency contracting**, a concept introduced by Homme (1969). With this method, the teacher develops contracts with students that state what behaviors (e.g., academic work, social behaviors) students are to complete or perform, and what consequences (e.g., reinforcement) the instructor will provide. These contracts are presented as binding agreements between student and teacher. To be most effective, contracts should initially reward imperfect approximations of the behavior, provide frequent reinforcement, reward accomplishment rather than obedience, and be fair, clear, and positive. The Differentiating Instruction—Secondary boxed reading shows an example of a contract for a secondary school student.

FIGURE 4.11   **Implementing Positive Reinforcement Techniques**

Determine what reinforcements will work for particular students:

- Ask the child by using direct formal or informal questioning or by administering an interest inventory or reinforcement survey.
- Ask those knowledgeable about the student (e.g., parents, friends, or past teachers).
- Observe the student in the natural environment as well as in a structured observation (e.g., arranging reinforcement alternatives from which the student may select).

Select meaningful reinforcers that are easy and practical to deliver in classroom settings (Idol, 1993).

"Catch" students behaving appropriately, and provide them with the subsequent appropriate reinforcement (referred to as the differential reinforcement of behavior incompatible with problem behavior). Begin this technique early so that students experience the effects of positive reinforcement.

Use the Premack (1959) principle ("Grandma's law": "eat your vegetables and then you can have dessert") regularly.

Use reinforcement techniques as the student makes gradual progress in developing a desired behavior that requires the mastery of numerous substeps (reinforce each successive approximation). This concept is called shaping.

Demonstrate to a student that certain behaviors will result in positive outcomes by reinforcing nearby peers.

Differentiating Secondary Instruction

CONTRACT

_____ will demonstrate the following appropriate behaviors in the classroom:

(Student's signature)

1. Come to school on time.
2. Come to school with homework completed.
3. Complete all assigned work in school without prompting.
4. Ask for help when necessary by raising hand and getting teacher's attention.

_____ will provide the following reinforcement:

(Teacher's) signature

1. Ten tokens for the completion of each of the above four objectives. Tokens for the first two objectives will be provided at the beginning of class after all homework assignments have been checked. Tokens for objectives 3 and 4 will be provided at the end of the school day.
2. Tokens may be exchanged for activities on the Classroom Reinforcement Menu at noon on Fridays.

_____

Student's signature

_____

Teacher's signature

_____

Date

Source: From _Behavior Management: Applications for Teachers and Parents_ (p. 189), by T. Zirpoli and G. Melloy, 1993. Columbus, OH: Merrill. Used by permission.

Group contingencies, which are set up for groups of students rather than for individuals, provide excellent alternatives for managing behavior and actively including students with special needs in the general education classroom. There are three types:

- **Dependent contingencies:** All group members share in the reinforcement if one individual achieves a goal (i.e., the "hero" strategy).
- **Interdependent contingencies:** All group members are reinforced if all collectively (or all individually) achieve the stated goal.
- **Independent contingencies:** Individuals within the group are reinforced for individual achievement toward a goal.

Whereas independent contingencies are used commonly, the other two forms are less widely seen in the classroom. The dependent strategy is sometimes referred to as a "hero approach" because it singles out one student's performance for attention. Although it can be abused, such an approach may be particularly attractive for a student who responds well to peer attention. A student with special needs may feel more meaningfully included in class when his or her talents are recognized in this way.

Others may feel reinforced and accepted as part of a group when interdependent contingencies are employed. The most common use of an interdependent strategy is the "good behavior game." Because it is most often used as a behavioral reduction intervention, it is discussed later in the chapter.

The benefits of group-oriented contingencies (or peer-mediated strategies, as they are often called) include the involvement of peers, the ability of teachers to enhance motivation, and increased efficiency for the teacher. In some instances, students will raise questions of fairness concerning group contingency programs. Those who typically behave appropriately may feel that they are being penalized for the actions of others if reinforcement occurs only when the whole group evidences a desired behavior. You can assure them that, ultimately, they and everyone else will benefit from group success with particular guidelines or goals.

Decreasing Undesirable Behaviors   Every teacher will face situations involving undesirable behaviors that require behavior reduction techniques. Most undesirable behavior will represent minor infractions that will require straightforward, fairly easy-to-administer interventions; some behaviors will be more disruptive, defiant, or disturbing, and will require more intrusive and complex responses. For these more severe behaviors, knowledge of the "acting-out cycle" (Colvin, 1993) and responding during the early stages will prevent the behavior from escalating or minimize the impact of the behavior on classroom dynamics. This cycle includes the following seven sequential phases: calm, triggers, agitation, acceleration, peak, de-escalation, and recovery. This section will focus more on dealing with less-severe behaviors that are typical of almost all classrooms.

Teachers can select from a range of techniques; however, it is usually best to begin with the least-intrusive interventions (Smith & Rivera, 1995) and more neutrally oriented ones. A recommended sequence of reduction strategies is depicted in Figure 4.12. As teachers consider reductive strategies, they are cautioned to keep records, develop plans of action, and follow state and local guidelines.

The use of natural and logical consequences can help children and adolescents learn to be more responsible for their behaviors (West, 1986, 1994). These principles are particularly important for students with special needs who often have difficulty seeing the link between their behavior and the resulting consequences.

With **natural consequences**, the situation itself provides the contingencies for a certain behavior. For example, if a student forgets to return a permission slip to attend an off-campus event, the natural consequence is that the student is not allowed to go and must remain at school. Thus, rather than intervening in a given situation, the teacher allows the situation to teach the student. Natural consequences are an effective way to teach common sense and responsibility (West, 1994).

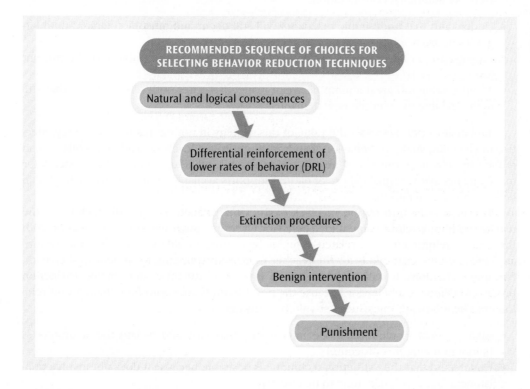

FIGURE 4.12

Recommended sequence of selected behavior reduction techniques.

In **logical consequences**, there is a logical connection between inappropriate behavior and the consequences that follow. If a student forgets lunch money, a logical consequence might be that money must be borrowed from someone else. The uncomfortable consequence is the hassle or embarrassment of requesting financial assistance. These tactics can help students recognize that their own behavior has created the discomfort and not something the teacher has done to them. When using this approach, teachers should clarify to students that they are responsible for their own behaviors. Logical consequences relate the disciplinary response directly to the inappropriate behavior.

The next option on the continuum is the use of **differential reinforcement**. A number of variations of this researched-based technique exist, such as differential reinforcement of alternative behaviors (DRA), differential reinforcement of incompatible behavior (DRI), differential reinforcement of other behavior (DRO), and differential reinforcement of lower rates of behavior (DRL). The DRL technique uses positive reinforcement strategies as a behavior reduction tool. A teacher using this procedure provides appropriate reinforcement to students for displaying lower rates of a certain behavior that has been targeted for reduction. It is important to remember that the goal should be to decrease the frequency or duration of the unwanted behavior.

An example of this technique used with groups of students is the "good behavior game" (originally developed by Barrish, Saunders, & Wolf, 1969), in which student teams receive reinforcement if the number of occurrences of inappropriate behaviors remains under a preset criterion. Tankersley (1995) provides a good overview of the use of the good behavior game:

First, teachers should define target behaviors that they would like to see improved and determine when these behaviors are most problematic in their classrooms. Criteria for winning must be set and reinforcers established; the students should be taught the rules for playing. Next, the classroom is divided into teams and team names are written on the chalkboard. If any student breaks a rule when the game is in effect, the teacher makes a mark by the name of the team of which the disruptive student is a member. At the end of the time in which the game is played, any team that has fewer marks than the preestablished criterion wins. Members of the winning team(s) receive reinforcers daily. In addition, teams that meet weekly criterion receive reinforcers at the end of the week (p. 20).

Here are additional considerations:

- Understand that undesirable behaviors will still occur and must be tolerated until target levels are reached.
- Increase the criterion level after students have demonstrated stability at the present level.
- Avoid making too great a jump between respective criterion levels to ensure that students are able to meet the new demands.

Tankersley (1995) stresses the value of this strategy in noting that it "can be very effective in changing students' behaviors, can lead to improved levels of academic skills, . . . can reduce the teacher's burden of incorporating several individual contingency systems for managing behavior, . . . [makes] use of natural supports available in the classroom, [and] can help promote generalization" (p. 26).

The next reduction option involves **extinction procedures**. In this technique, the teacher withholds reinforcement for a behavior. Over time, such action, in combination with the positive reinforcement of related desirable behaviors, should extinguish the inappropriate behavior. One example is for the teacher to cease responding to student misbehavior. For some situations, it will be necessary to involve a student's peers in the extinction process to eliminate a behavior because the peers' actions are controlling the relevant reinforcers. The following suggestions should be considered:

- Analyze what is reinforcing the undesirable behavior, and isolate the reinforcer(s) before initiating this procedure.
- Understand that the extinction technique is desirable because it does not involve punishment, but it will take time to be effective.

- Do not use this technique with behaviors that require immediate intervention (e.g., fighting).
- Recognize that the withholding of reinforcement is likely to induce an increase ("spiking" effect) in the occurrence of the undesirable behavior—as students intensify their efforts to receive the reinforcement they are used to getting—and may produce an initial aggressive response.
- Provide reinforcement to students who demonstrate appropriate incompatible behaviors (e.g., taking turns versus interrupting).

The fourth option is the use of behavior reduction techniques that border on being punishment but are so unobtrusive that they can be considered **benign tactics**. These suggestions are consistent with a concept developed by Cummings (1983), called the "law of least intervention," and that of Evertson and colleagues (2006), called "minor interventions." The main idea is to eliminate disruptive behaviors quickly with a minimum of disruption to the classroom or instructional routine. Table 4.10 includes a list of benign tactics for reducing undesirable behavior that is based on five types of prompts: physical, gestural, visual, and verbal.

The last option in this reduction hierarchy, and the one that is most intrusive and less attractive, is the use of **punishment**. It is the least preferable option because it involves the presentation of something unpleasant or the removal of something pleasant as a consequence of the performance of an undesirable behavior.

TABLE 4.10

Benign Tactics for Reducing Undesirable Behavior

TYPE OF PROMPT	SPECIFIC TACTIC
Physical	• Position yourself physically near students who are likely to create problems (proximity control). • Touch a student's shoulder gently to convey your awareness that the student is behaving in some inappropriate (albeit previously identified) way. • Place a note (e.g., post-it) on the student's desk—it does not have to have anything written on it, if the student understands the intent (Jones & Jones, 2007). • Remove seductive objects (Levin & Nolan, 2003).
Gestural	• Use subtle and not-so-subtle gestures to stop undesirable behaviors (e.g., pointing, head shaking, finger spelling). • Use hand signals to indicate any number of messages.
Visual/Auditory	• Establish eye contact and maintain it for a while with a student who is behaving inappropriately. This results in no disruption to the instructional routine. • Use sound signals—from simple devices to get student attention (Smith, 2004).
Verbal	• Redirect behavior in unobtrusive ways (i.e., not embarrassing to an individual student) that are directed to the whole class or through the use of humor. • Ask students, as a group, to look at the teacher—Note: cultural implications of this suggestion must be considered (Smith, 2004). • Stop talking for a noticeable length of time to redirect student attention. • Call on students who are not attending, but ask them questions that they can answer successfully. • Give the student a choice. • The nonpunitive time-out—ask the student if he/she would like to do something that will remove him/her from the situation for a short, defined period of time—thus, accomplishing a change of activity that might be needed (Levin & Nolan, 2003). • Use an "I-Message" (e.g., I feel concerned that. . . .; I hear you say that . . .). • Avoid sarcasm and confrontation.
Instructional	• Change the pace of the classroom activity (Levin & Nolan, 2003). • Increase interest by using humor (Jones & Jones, 2007). • Use "interest boosting" (i.e., showing interest in the student's work) (Levin & Nolan, 2003). • Provide needed re-instruction—if the student clearly is struggling (Evertson et al., 2006).

Much controversy has arisen in regard to the use of punishment. Those who espouse a positive behavioral supports attitude would argue strongly against the use of punishers. Punishment should be considered only as a last resort. However, in situations in which a more immediate cessation of undesirable behaviors is required, punishment may be necessary. Because of their potency, punishment strategies should be weighed carefully; they can interfere with the learning process if not used sparingly and appropriately. Given that all teachers are likely to use punishment at some point, the key is to ensure that it is used appropriately.

Three punishment techniques are commonly used in classrooms, and at home: reprimand, time-out, and response cost. For these forms of punishment to work, it is critical that they be applied immediately after the occurrence of the undesirable behavior and that students understand why they are being applied. A **reprimand** represents a type of punishment in which an unpleasant condition (verbal reprimand from the teacher) is presented to the student. The following are some specific ways to use this type of technique:

- Do not let this type of interchange dominate your interactions with students.
- Look at the student and talk in a composed way.
- Do not verbally reprimand a student from across the room. Get close to the student, maintain a degree of privacy, and minimize embarrassment.
- Let the student know exactly why you are concerned.
- Convey to the student that it is the behavior that is the problem and not him or her.

With **time-out**, a student is removed from a situation in which he or she typically receives positive reinforcement, thus being prevented from enjoying something pleasurable. Different ways are available to remove a student from a reinforcing setting: Students are allowed to observe the situation from which they have been removed (contingent observation), students are excluded from the ongoing proceedings entirely (exclusion time-out), and students are secluded in a separate room (seclusion time-out). The first two versions are most likely to be considered for use in general education classrooms. The following suggestions are extremely important if time-out is to be used appropriately:

- Confirm that the ongoing situation from which a student is going to be removed is indeed reinforcing; if not, this technique will not serve as a punisher and rather might be a form of positive reinforcement.
- Ensure that the time-out area is devoid of reinforcing elements. If it is not a neutral setting, this procedure will fail.
- Do not keep students in time-out for long periods of time (i.e., more than 10 minutes) or use it frequently (e.g., daily), as students will miss significant amounts of instructional time.
- As a rule of thumb with younger children, never allow time-out periods to extend beyond one minute for every year of the child's age (up to a maximum of 10 minutes).
- Use a timer to ensure accuracy in the length of time-out.
- Incorporate this procedure as one of the classroom procedures explained and taught at the beginning of the school year.
- Consider using a time-out system in which students are given one warning before being removed.
- Signal to the student when it is appropriate to return.
- Do not use this technique with certain sensitive students.
- Keep records on frequency, reason for using, and amount of time placed when using seclusion time-out procedures.

Response cost involves the loss of something the student values, such as privileges or points. It is a system in which a penalty or fine is levied for occurrences of inappropriate behavior. Some specific suggestions include:

- Explain clearly to students how the system works and how much one will be fined for a given offense.
- Make sure all penalties are presented in a nonpersonal manner.

- Confirm that privileges that are lost are indeed reinforcing to students.
- Make sure that all privileges are not lost quickly, resulting in a situation in which a student may have little or no incentive to behave appropriately.
- Tie in this procedure with positive reinforcement at all times.

Generalization and Maintenance of Behaviors   After behaviors have been established at acceptable levels, the next stages involve transferring what has been learned to new contexts and maintaining established levels of performance. Teachers often succeed in teaching students certain behaviors but fail to help them apply the skills to new situations or retain them over time. Teaching appropriate behaviors and then hoping that students will be able to use various skills at some later time is detrimental to many students with special needs because a core difficulty they experience is performing independently in the classroom.

Teachers need to program for generalization—the wider application of a behavior skill—by giving students opportunities to use new skills in different settings, with different people, and at different times. Students often need help to identify the cues that should trigger the performance of an acquired behavior, action, or skill.

To maintain their skills, students also need to practice what they have learned previously. Instructional planning should allow time for students to determine how well they have retained what they have learned. This time usually can be provided during seatwork activities or other arrangements.

Suggestions for generalization and maintenance include:

- Create opportunities for students to practice in different situations what they have learned.
- Work with other teachers to provide additional opportunities.
- Place students in situations that simulate those that they will encounter in the future, both within school and in other areas of life.
- Show students how these skills or behaviors will be useful to them in the future.
- Prompt students to use recently acquired skills in a variety of contexts.
- Maintain previously taught skills by providing ongoing practice or review.

As noted previously, the use of positive behavior supports has become more popular in working with students with special needs, particularly because of its effectiveness and its emphasis on the environment rather than on the individual. A key to behavioral generalization and maintenance, therefore, is to focus beyond the student and ensure that the learning environment is designed in such a way that students can use their newly acquired skills effectively to become accepted and active members of the classroom while enhancing their learning opportunities. In addition, key elements of generalization and maintenance relate to self-management strategies, which become essential in work with adolescents.

Self-Management   Ultimately, we want all students to be able to manage their own behaviors without external direction, as this ability is a requirement of functioning independently in life. Special attention needs to be given to those students who do not display independent behavioral control and thus must develop student-regulated strategies—interventions that, though initially taught by the teacher, are intended to be implemented independently by the student. Bender (2003) refers to this end state as the "self-discipline" phase.

An interesting contraction exists regarding the development of students' responsibility for their own behavior. While a strong research base exists for such instruction (Marzano, 2003), it does not occur very often within the K through 12 experience of most students (Shapiro & Cole, 1994). Marzano feels this occurs because providing this type of instruction "goes beyond the traditional duties of a classroom teacher" (p. 79). This situation is further exacerbated in today's schools with heightened attention to addressing the content and performance standards of the curriculum.

The concept of self-management is an outgrowth of cognitive behavior modification, a type of educational intervention for students with disabilities in use since the 1980s, which stresses active thinking about behavior. Shapiro, DuPaul, and Bradley-Klug (1998) provide a good overview of self-management:

> It is helpful to conceptualize self-management interventions as existing on a continuum. At one end, the intervention is completely controlled by the teacher ...; this individual provides feedback regarding whether the student's behavior met the desired criteria and administers the appropriate consequences for the behavior. At the other end, the student engages in evaluating his or her own behavior against the criteria for performance, without benefit of teacher ... input. The student also self-administers the appropriate consequences. In working with students with behavior problems, the objective should be to move a student as far toward the self-management side of the continuum as possible. Although some of these students may not be capable of reaching levels of independent self-management, most are certainly capable of approximating this goal. (p. 545)

Fiore, Becker, and Nerro (1993) state the rationale for such interventions: "Cognitive-behavioral [intervention] is ... intuitively appealing because it combines behavioral techniques with cognitive strategies designed to directly address core problems of impulse control, higher order problem solving, and self-regulation" (p. 166). Whereas traditional behavioral interventions most often stress the importance of teacher monitoring of student behavior, extrinsic reinforcement, and teacher-directed learning, cognitive interventions instead focus on teaching students to monitor their own behavior, to engage in self-reinforcement, and to direct their own learning in strategic fashion (Dowdy, Patton, Smith, & Polloway, 1997).

Such approaches have become particularly popular with students with learning and attention difficulties because they offer the promise of:

- Increasing focus on selective attention
- Modifying impulsive responding
- Providing verbal mediators to assist in academic and social problem-solving situations
- Teaching effective self-instructional statements to enable students to "talk through" tasks and problems
- Providing strategies that may lead to improvement in peer relations (Rooney, 1993)
- While using self-management strategies with students with special needs in inclusive settings has been far more limited than studies of using them in pull-out programs, the moderate to strong positive outcomes reported in research are encouraging (McDougall, 1998).

Student-regulated strategies form the essence of self-management. Although variations exist in how these are defined and described, the components listed in Figure 4.13 represent the central aspects of self-management.

Two components with particular utility for general education teachers are self-monitoring and self-instruction. **Self-monitoring**, a technique in which students observe and record their own behavior, has been commonly employed with students with learning problems. Lloyd, Landrum, and Hallahan (1991) note that self-monitoring was initially seen as an assessment technique, but as individuals observed their own behavior, the process also resulted in a change in behavior. Self-monitoring of behavior, such as attention, is a relatively simple technique that has been validated with children who have learning disabilities, mental retardation, multiple disabilities, attention deficits, and behavior disorders; it has also been profitable for nondisabled students (Lloyd et al., 1991; McDougall, 1998; Prater, Joy, Chilman, Temple, & Miller, 1991). Increased attention, beneficial to academic achievement, has been reported as a result.

A common mechanism for self-monitoring was developed by Hallahan, Lloyd, and Stoller (1982). It involves using a tape-recorded tone that sounds at random intervals (e.g., every 45 seconds), and a self-recording sheet. Each time the tone sounds, children ask themselves whether they are paying attention and then mark the "yes" or the "no" box on the tally sheet. Students are often not accurate in their recording, nevertheless positive changes in behavior have been observed in many research studies. While self-monitoring procedures

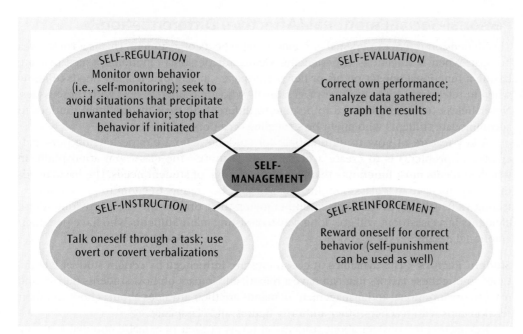

FIGURE 4.13

Components of self-management.

Source: From *Guide to Attention Deficits in the Classroom* (p. 162), by C. A. Dowdy, J. R. Patton, T. E. C. Smith, and E. A. Polloway, 1998. Austin, TX: Pro-Ed. Used by permission.

may prove problematic for one teacher to implement alone, a collaborative approach within a cooperative teaching arrangement offers much promise.

Self-instruction represents another useful intervention. Pfiffner and Barkley (1991) describe components of a self-instruction program as follows:

> Self-instructions include defining and understanding the task or problem, planning a general strategy to approach the problem, focusing attention on the task, selecting an answer or solution, and evaluating performance. In the case of successful performance, self-reinforcement (usually in the form of a positive self-statement, such as "I really did a good job") is provided. In the case of an unsuccessful performance, a coping statement is made (e.g., "Next time I'll do better if I slow down") and errors are corrected. At first, an adult trainer typically models the self-instructions while performing a task. The child then performs the same task while the trainer provides the self-instructions. Next, the child performs the task while self-instructing aloud. These overt verbalizations are then faded to covert self-instructions. (p. 525)

Clear, simple self-instruction strategies form an appropriate beginning for interventions with students with learning or attentional difficulties in the general education classroom. Such approaches are likely to enhance success. Pfiffner and Barkley (1991) recommend the STAR program, in which "children learn to Stop, Think ahead about what they have to do, Act or do the requested task while talking to themselves about the task, and Review their results" (p. 529).

Detailed and systematic procedures have been developed for implementing self-management strategies. Some basic recommendations follow:

- Allocate sufficient instructional time to teach self-management to students who need it.
- Establish a sequence of activities that move by degrees from teacher direction to student direction and self-control.
- Include objectives relevant to improved behavior and enhanced learning (e.g., increased attention yields reading achievement gains).
- Provide strategies and assistive materials (e.g., self-recording forms) for students to use.
- Model how effective self-managers operate. Point out actual applications of the elements of self-management (as highlighted in Figure 14.5), and give students opportunities to practice these techniques with your guidance.
- Provide for the maintenance of learned strategies and for generalization to other settings in and out of school.

Personal-Social-Emotional (Affective) Differentiation

This dimension refers to personal and emotional aspects of a student. This is a tricky area because when a student is experiencing significant personal/emotional issues that are having a functional impact on his or her performance in school, a teacher needs to know when to refer the student to other professionals who are trained to deal with these issues. Nevertheless, teachers will need to be able to differentiate their instructional routines to accommodate students who might be struggling on a personal level.

A key feature of how to differentiate for students who are experiencing personal/ emotional problems is to create a **classroom climate**—the classroom atmosphere in which students must function—that allows for a range of student needs. The basic needs that students have in a classroom include sense of belonging, freedom to make choices, feeling valued, being in a safe place, and enjoying their time in the class. Providing these elements in a classroom will go a long way to assisting many students who have personal/ emotional needs.

Student Factors   The dynamics of classrooms are influenced by certain student factors. Chief among these factors that can have a remarkable impact on how students behave and react to organizational and management demands are their attitudes about school and their relationships with teachers, other authority figures, and classmates.

Key factors to consider about students in terms of their personal/emotional states include (Fries and Cochran-Smith, 2006):

- Home life
- Cultural considerations
- Individual temperament
- Language abilities
- Social and interpersonal skills
- Nature of previous educational experiences
- How they feel about themselves
- Motivation—their own expectations concerning their scholastic futures (i.e., ability of being able to do the task and potential for success)
- Whether they are intrinsically or extrinsically motivated
- Perceived relevance of the instructional tasks
- Emotional factors, including levels of stress

Teacher Factors   The psychological atmosphere of any classroom depends in great part on certain teacher factors—some of which are personal and others professional. A teacher's attitudes toward students with special needs can dramatically affect the quality of education that a student will receive during the time he or she is in that teacher's classroom. The type of expectations a teacher holds for students can significantly influence learning outcomes. One's personal philosophy about education, management and discipline, and curriculum/instruction weigh heavily as well. Fries and Cochran-Smith (2006) noted that a teacher's ability "to adapt to the needs of learners" (p. 945) can also make a difference.

One particular set of skills that has bearing on the psychological aspects of the classroom is teacher communication skills. Evertson and colleagues (2006) note that the ability to communicate clearly and effectively with students influences the nature of ongoing dynamics in the classroom. They stress that to become an effective communicator, teachers need to display three related skills: constructive assertiveness (e.g., describing concerns clearly), empathic responding (e.g., listening to the student's perspective), and problem solving (e.g., ability to reach mutually satisfactory resolutions to problems).

Peer Factors   Peers are also key players in forming the psychological and social atmosphere of a classroom, especially among middle- and high-school students. Teachers must understand peer values, pressures, and needs and use this knowledge to benefit students with special needs. Valuable cooperative learning opportunities can evolve based on successful peer involvement strategies. As Kohn (1996a) notes, "Communities are built upon a foundation of cooperating throughout the day, with students continually being invited to work, play, and reflect with someone else" (p. 113).

Family-Related Factors   The final component involves a variety of family-related factors. Three major issues, all of which have cultural implications, include family attitudes toward education, level of family support and involvement in the student's education, and the amount of pressure placed on a child by the family. Extremes can be problematic—for example, a family that burdens a student (e.g., a gifted child) with overwhelming pressure to succeed can cause as many difficulties as one that takes limited interest in a child's education.

Efforts should be made to establish relationships with parents and guardians. At the very least, a letter (with correct grammar, punctuation, and spelling) should be sent to each family, describing the nature of the classroom management system. This is particularly important if no other means exists for conveying this information, such as some type of orientation. A benefit of developing a relationship with parents is that the teacher can determine a family's status on the dimensions mentioned in the previous paragraph.

The following recommendations should help create a positive, nurturing environment that contributes to positive outcomes for all students:

- Let students know that you are sensitive to their needs and concerns.
- Understand the family and cultural contexts from which students come.
- Convey enthusiasm about learning and the school experience.
- Create a supportive, safe environment in which students who are different can learn without fear of being ridiculed or threatened.
- Treat all students with fairness.
- Acknowledge all students in some personal way each day to affirm that they are valued within the room.
- Create a learning environment that provides challenge to the students, is built on success, and minimizes failure experiences common to the learning histories of students with disabilities.
- Establish that each student in the classroom has rights (e.g., not to be interrupted when working or responding to a teacher inquiry) and that you expect everyone to respect those rights.
- Instill in students the understanding that they are responsible for their own behavior.
- Convey to students that every student's thoughts and ideas are important.
- Encourage risk taking and support all students (i.e., gifted, average, and disabled) to take on scholastic challenges.
- Share philosophies, management systems, and instructional perspectives with parents or guardians.

SUMMARY

Define the Basic Concepts of Differentiated Instruction

- General education teachers are faced with classrooms that typically have many students who display a diverse range of strengths and needs.
- The concept of differentiating instruction is not new.
- The basic essence of differentiating instruction is to meet the needs of students where he or she is at and assisting the learning process.
- Different terms such as adaptation, modification, and accommodation are used to describe differentiation.
- Two levels of differentiation are possible: macro and micro levels.
- A set of operating procedures are recommended.

Describe a Comprehensive Model of Differentiating Classroom Management

- Setting differentiation involves adjustments related to seating, classroom arrangements, accessibility, and specialized equipment.
- Content differentiation involves changes made to the content of what is covered and to additional content that must be covered.
- Material differentiation primarily involves adjustments that have to be made to textual material that is used in classrooms—however, it also relates to other types of materials used for instructional purposes.
- Instructional differentiation involves adjustments related to all aspects of instruction, including how instruction is presented and how students respond to it.
- Management/Behavior differentiation relates to techniques used in a classroom setting to create a productive learning environment and to manage special behavioral issues that arise.
- Personal-Social-Emotional differentiation involves attending to specific issues of students of an individual nature that affect their academic performance and personal/social/emotional development and stability.

PEARSON myeducationlab

The MyEducationLab for this course can help you solidify your comprehension of Chapter 4 concepts.

- Gauge and further develop your understanding of chapter concepts by taking the quizzes and examining the enrichment materials on the Chapter 4 Study Plan.
- Visit Topic 4, Classroom/Behavior Management, to:
  - Connect with challenge-based interactive modules, case study units, and podcasts that provide research-validated information about working with students in inclusive settings by visiting the IRIS Center Resources
  - Explore Assignments and Activities, assignable exercises showing concepts in action through, video, cases, and student and teacher artifacts
  - Practice and strengthen skills essential to quality teaching through the Building Teaching Skills and Dispositions lessons

5

Teaching Students with Learning Disabilities

After reading this chapter, you should be able to:

1. Define learning disabilities (LD), including the basic requirements for identification.
2. Describe the characteristics of students with LD.
3. Discuss effective inclusive practices for students with LD.
4. Identify the role of teachers in making adaptations for students with LD in general education classrooms.

EMMANUEL was 6 years old when he eagerly started first grade. Problems began to emerge as the reading program expanded from picture books with lots of repetition to books containing unknown words. Emmanuel had difficulty using context clues, and he had limited phonemic awareness in decoding a new word. His first report card showed "needs improvement" in reading, listening, and following directions. The bright spot in Emmanuel's first-grade achievement was his above-average functioning in math, his ability to pay attention, and good social skills. Emmanuel was promoted to second grade.

Over the summer, his family moved to another state. Emmanuel adjusted to the new school and everything was fine during the first 9 weeks of academic review, and then he began to have trouble finishing his work. He became frustrated with written assignments and often complained of stomachaches, asking to stay home from school. Throughout this second grading period, his teachers felt that he was still adjusting to a new school so they tried to be very positive and supportive, but they were concerned that he was not meeting the general education benchmarks.

Emmanuel's school used the RTI process to respond to students not benefitting from instruction. His teacher was highly qualified and used scientifically based methods of intervention but by the end of the third grading period, Emmanuel's parents and teachers agreed that a change was needed. His story was brought to the PIT for consideration and brainstorming and, as a result, Emmanuel was provided Tier II level of intervention. Since the primary deficits were in the areas of reading and following instructions, the special education teacher put together material to develop the phonemic awareness and phonics skills that Emmanuel had not mastered. His general education teacher used these to provide additional instruction to him in a small group of students having similar challenges, and his par-

ents agreed to work on this material at home. He also worked with a fifth-grade peer helper who read with him one-on-one, three days a week. The classroom teacher agreed to restate oral instructions and confirm Emmanuel's understanding of written and oral instructions. She encouraged Emmanuel to predict unknown words based on meaning and phonemic clues and to evaluate whether the word he guessed fit with the rest of the words in the sentence. Attention was also paid to his vocabulary development. Emmanuel was assessed every two weeks to monitor progress.

When this failed to produce the desired results, Emmanuel was provided Tier III level of intervention. During this period, he was instructed by a reading specialist in a group of three students who worked together twice a day for 30 minutes. Progress was monitored once a week at least and specifically measured gains in his targeted skill areas. A motivation system was also implemented and Emmanuel could choose free time or time on the computer as a reward for reading work.

After the next 9 weeks, the PIT still felt that Emmanuel was struggling too much, so they recommended a special education referral, and his parents signed their permission for testing. His tests showed average intelligence and significant deficits in reading skills and listening despite the scientifically based interventions that had been made. The IEP team determined that Emmanuel had a learning disability and needed special education services to make adequate progress in the general education curriculum; Emmanuel's IEP was developed to allow him to benefit from his educational experience.

Although signs of learning disabilities were present, the school proceeded cautiously in identifying Emmanuel as a child with a learning disability, carefully evaluating his response to the three levels of increasingly intense intervention. When special education services were provided, they included attending a resource class for 45 minutes a day throughout third grade. Through these services, Emmanuel's reading of multisyllable words greatly improved as did his writing and listening skills. By fourth grade, he remained in the general education classroom full-time, needing only periodic support from the learning disabilities teacher.

QUESTIONS TO CONSIDER

1. What alerted Emmanuel's teacher to a possible learning disability?

2. How might his move have been a factor in his school performance?

3. Describe how Emmanuel's educational experience changed during the three tiers of RTI.

It is difficult to distinguish children like Emmanual, and all children with disabilities, from their peers by their appearance; similarly, you cannot distinguish adults with learning disabilities from other adults. You may be surprised to find that many important and famous people have made significant achievements in spite of experiencing a severe learning disability. Adults with learning disabilities can be found in all professions; they may be lawyers, doctors, blue-collar workers, politicians or artists. Read the examples that follow, and see whether you can identify the names of the individuals with learning disabilities.

1. During his childhood, this young man was an outstanding athlete, achieving great success and satisfaction from sports. Unfortunately, he struggled in the classroom. He tried very hard, but he always seemed to fail academically. His biggest fear was being asked to stand up and read in front of his classmates. He was frequently teased about his class performance, and he described his school days as sheer torture. His only feelings of success were experienced on the playing field.

   When he graduated from high school, he didn't consider going to college because he "wasn't a terrific student, and never got into books all that much." Even though he was an outstanding high-school pole vaulter, he did not get a single scholarship during his senior year. He had already gone to work with his father when he was offered a $500 football scholarship from Graceland College. He didn't accept that offer; instead he trained in track and field. Several years later, he won a gold medal in the Olympics in the grueling decathlon. This story is about Bruce Jenner.

2. This individual was still illiterate at age 12, but he could memorize anything. Spelling was always impossible for him, and as he said, he "had trouble with the A, B, and that other letter." He also was a failure at math. He finally made it through high school, but he failed his first year at West Point. He did graduate, with the help of tutors, one year late. His special talent was in military strategy, and during World War II he became one of the United States' most famous generals, George Patton.

Other famous people with LD include Charles Schwab, Tom Cruise, Cher, Nelson Rockefeller, Winston Churchill, Woodrow Wilson, F. W. Woolworth, Walt Disney, Ernest Hemingway, Albert Einstein, George Bernard Shaw, and Thomas Edison (see discussions at www.dyslexiaonline.org). These and other individuals with learning disabilities were often misunderstood and teased early in life for their inadequacies in the classroom. To be successful, they had to be creative and persistent. Adults with learning disabilities succeed by sheer determination in overcoming their limitations and focusing on their talents.

Perhaps the most difficult aspect of understanding and teaching students with learning disabilities is that the disability is hidden. When students with obviously normal intelligence fail to finish their work; interrupt inappropriately; never seem to follow directions; and turn in sloppy, poorly organized assignments, it is natural to blame poor motivation, lack of effort, and even an undesirable family life. However, the lack of accomplishment and success in the classroom does have a cause; the students are not demonstrating these behaviors to upset or irritate their teachers.

Visit the MyEducationLab for this course to enhance your understanding of chapter concepts with a personalized Study Plan. You'll also have the opportunity to hone your teaching skills through video-based Assignments and Activities, IRIS Center Resources, and Building Teaching Skills and Disposition lessons.

BASIC CONCEPTS ABOUT LEARNING DISABILITIES

A **learning disability** is a cognitive disability; it is a disorder of thinking and reasoning. Because the disability is not readily apparent and the dysfunction is presumed to be in the central nervous system, it has been difficult for professionals to reach agreement on the definition as well as the procedures for identification and eligibility determination.

The individuals with learning disabilities described earlier have experienced the frustration of living with a disability that is not easily understood or identified. Children with learning disabilities look like other students in their age group and grade. They can perform like other students in some areas, but not in others. Like Emmanuel in the chapter opening vignette, a child might have good social skills and make good grades in math, but fails in reading. Another child is able to read and write at grade level but fails in math and gets in trouble for misconduct. Students with learning disabilities also may perform inconsistently. They might know spelling words on Thursday and fail the test on Friday.

In this chapter you will study the patterns of strengths and weaknesses of children, youth, and adults who experience "unexpected underachievement" and fail to respond to scientific, research-based intervention. Professionals from many fields have joined the search for a definition and causes of these disabilities, as well as methods to identify affected children and to accommodate or remediate areas of the disability. Yet many questions remain.

Definition, Identification, and Eligibility

The history of LD began in the 1800s during an era of research on brain function. Between 1920 and 1960, the research became more focused on brain-injured adults with deficits in perception, attention, and the perceptual-motor area, and later studies broadened to include children with reading and language deficits. Since that time, more than 90 terms have been introduced into the literature to describe these individuals. The most commonly used terms included minimal brain dysfunction (MBD), brain damage, central processing dysfunction, and language delay.

To add to the confusion, several definitions were also offered to explain each term. The term "specific learning disabilities" was first adopted publicly in 1963 at a meeting of parents and professionals. Kirk (1962) developed the generic term "learning disabilities" in an effort to unite the field, which was torn between individuals promoting different theories regarding underachievement. The term was received favorably because it did not have the negative connotations of the other terms and did describe the primary characteristic of the children.

Between 1960 and 1975, professional and parent organizations were developed to promote awareness of learning disabilities. When IDEA (then called Public Law 94–142) was passed in 1975, LD was included as a disability category and a federally approved definition was in print. Special educational services could then be provided to eligible students struggling to achieve academic success in the general education classroom.

Definition

The definition included in law has been modified only slightly over the years, most recently in the 2006 *Code of Federal Regulations*, based on the 2004 IDEA reauthorization:

> Specific learning disability means a disorder in one or more of the basic psychological processes involved in understanding or in using language, spoken or written, that may manifest itself in an imperfect ability to listen, think, speak, read, write, spell, or to do mathematical calculations, including such conditions as perceptual disabilities, brain injury, minimal brain dysfunction, dyslexia, and developmental aphasia. . . . Specific learning disability does not include learning problems that are primarily the result of visual, hearing, or motor disabilities, of mental retardation, of emotional disturbance, or of environmental, cultural, or economic disadvantage. (34 C.R.F. 300.8(c)(10))

Because special education services were made available by law, dissension has existed over the definition and identification procedures, as well as the most effective methods to teach children with LD. A majority of states use the IDEA definition, but it has been criticized over the years for including concepts that are unclear or difficult to use to identify children with a learning disability. For example, you might be wondering what is meant by the concept of deficits in "psychological processes." This term is considered the most nebulous in the definition and has been interpreted in several ways, including perceptual-motor deficits, deficits in the process of taking in information, difficulty in making sense of information and expressing knowledge effectively, and deficits in cognitive processes such as attention, memory, and metacognition (the way one thinks about and controls his or her cognitive processing—e.g., self-monitoring, predicting, and planning). Although the U.S. Office of Education (USOE) did leave this term in the definition, a measure of psychological processes was omitted from the criteria for identifying students with learning disabilities. At that time the agency focused instead on identifying a discrepancy between a child's ability and his or her achievement in reading, math, written language, speaking, or listening (USOE, 1977).

Identification and Eligibility

Despite widespread criticism, the definition and criteria for identifying LD using a discrepancy model were left unchanged from 1977 to 2004. Under this model, a child could only be determined to have a learning disability when a significant discrepancy existed between cognitive ability, as measured by individually administered IQ tests, and academic achievement. Students could struggle for years until the severe discrepancy criteria could be met. "Severe discrepancy" was not federally defined, so the criteria established by individual states varied. Students could meet criteria and be provided services in one state and be denied services when moving to a different state.

The reauthorization of IDEA (2004) reflected the thinking that significant changes were needed in the policies used to identify and serve students with LD. Specifically, requiring documentation of a discrepancy between achievement and IQ was determined to be unnecessary and not sufficient for identifying individuals with specific learning disabilities (SLD). Figure 5.1 provides the most current criteria for identification mandated by Federal law.

The first component of the identification criteria that must be met requires documentation that the child is not making adequate progress in age-appropriate state standards despite being provided appropriate learning opportunities and instruction. Note that the inadequate achievement is limited to one or more of nine specific academic areas.

The second component in the identification criteria gives schools two alternatives. The recommended procedure links the deficit(s) in academic achievement to a lack of responsiveness-to-intervention (RTI). IDEA describes this approach "as a process that determines if a child responds to scientific, research-based intervention as part of the evaluation procedures." The model is based on the assumption that a student without disabilities will make satisfactory progress when given intensive, well-designed instruction (National Joint Committee on Learning Disabilities, 2005). Because the majority of students with disabilities have a learning disability, this prereferral intervention (RTI) has been widely implemented in the general education classroom; it is predicted to reduce the number of special education referrals using a problem-solving approach rather than a mathematical discrepancy formula. In support of the RTI approach, Wagner (2010) appreciates the problem-solving component, citing its flexibility in allowing various approaches to be tried, and the fact that the model brings together a team of teachers, other school personnel, as well as the parents to consider multiple factors potentially causing difficulties and to develop positive solutions for these struggling students. She notes that this problem-solving orientation correctly shifts the use of resources and effort from identification of the LD to solving the problems of the student.

Although no specific guidelines were given on implementing RTI, the National Joint Committee on Learning Disabilities (2005) summarized the key elements in the process as:

1. Research-supported instructional and behavioral supports are implemented for all general education students and progress is monitored on an ongoing basis.

FIGURE 5.1	Criteria for Identifying Students with Learning Disabilities

(1) A group of qualified professionals and the parent of the child may determine if the child has a specific learning disability if:

(a) The child does not achieve adequately for the child's age or meet the State-approved grade-level standards in one or more of the following areas, when provided with learning experiences and instruction appropriate for the child's age or State-approved grade-level standards: oral expression, listening comprehension, written expression, basic reading skill, reading fluency skills, reading comprehension, mathematics calculation, or mathematics problem solving.

(b) (i) The child does not make sufficient progress to meet age or State-approved grade-level standards in one or more of the areas identified in paragraph (a) when using a process based on the child's response to scientific, research-based intervention; or

(ii) The child exhibits a pattern of strengths and weaknesses in performance, achievement or both, relative to age, State-approved grade-level standards, or intellectual development, that is determined by the team to be relevant to the identification of a specific learning disability.

(2) The team may not identify a child as having a specific learning disability if any of the above conditions is primarily a result of:

(a) visual, hearing, or motor disability;

(b) mental retardation;

(c) emotional disturbance;

(d) cultural factors;

(e) environmental or economic disadvantage; or

(f) limited English proficiency.

Source: 34 C.F.R. 300.309 (2007).

2. Students who lag behind peers in progress receive more individualized, intensive instruction with frequent monitoring to determine the needed modifications. Parents should be notified and included in planning and monitoring at this stage.

3. Parents of students not benefiting to an acceptable degree from this level of instruction are notified of their rights, and the decision-making process regarding a referral for special education services begins. Permission is obtained to proceed with the comprehensive evaluation needed for eligibility decisions to be made.

More than one scientific research-based-intervention may be implemented, but the team must weigh continued intervention against the resulting delay in considering special education services. Schools were strongly encouraged to adopt this model, citing that it would result in earlier identification of children who may need special education services and offer more timely and effective support for all students experiencing academic difficulties, especially in the early elementary school years. Wagner (2010) also notes that RTI is more child-centered than regulation-centered. The required assessment of individual progress forces documentation that the individual child being assessed is benefitting from the intervention and doesn't assume that an intervention will work because it showed promise in research trials.

Not all professionals and parents are in full support of the RTI model. One of the criticisms is the insufficient number of scientific, research-based interventions available in all nine academic areas; at this time the majority of interventions that meet this requirement are in the area of early reading acquisition (Wagner, 2010). The National Research Center on Learning Disabilities and the six regional research centers are charged with identifying best practices in the RTI model, including identifying model programs.

The second option available to school systems more closely resembles the traditional model of identifying a discrepancy between ability and achievement. In this process, the team looks at a pattern of strengths and weaknesses that indicate a learning disability. The weak areas must still be documented in one of the eight areas of academic achievement

FIGURE 5.2

Profile of a student with learning disabilities.

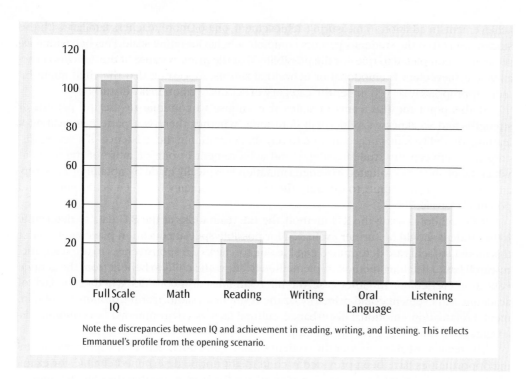

Note the discrepancies between IQ and achievement in reading, writing, and listening. This reflects Emmanuel's profile from the opening scenario.

noted: oral expression, listening comprehension, written expression, basic reading skills, reading fluency skills, reading comprehension, mathematics calculation, and mathematics problem solving. The academic achievement and/or performance can be compared to intellectual development to identify a discrepancy pattern (this was the previous practice) or achievement can be compared to age-appropriate norms for performance or state-approved grade-level standards. Figure 5.2 demonstrates a pattern of strengths and weaknesses suggesting a learning disability.

The third criterion of the identification process is also required. The team must rule out the possibility that the academic deficit(s) might be primarily caused by a condition other than a learning disability. For example, a child with a vision or hearing loss or limited English proficiency may be found to also have a learning disability but the academic deficit(s) must not be *primarily* the result of those factors.

Steps in the Identification/Eligibility Process   When a student is determined to make inadequate progress or fails to respond to Tier III level of intervention in reading, math, written expression, listening comprehension or oral expression, a referral may be made to determine the presence of a learning disability. The IEP team receives the referral, reviews the concerns stated on the referral, and develops a comprehensive evaluation plan. RTI data will be an important consideration in determining eligibility but it cannot be the sole measure in the evaluation for special education services; data should come from parents, classroom assessments and observations, and standardized and statewide assessments (Bateman & Linden, 2007).

One member of the evaluation team is assigned to observe the student in the general education classroom. This individual looks for any behaviors that might pose a limitation to success, such as inattention, impulsivity, or difficulties following directions. The student's academic deficits are noted, as well as the teacher's instructional style and the learning environment, to determine whether accommodations or modifications could be made to reduce deficits in learning. For example, comprehension of reading passages might be given in timed and untimed formats to see if extended time would increase comprehension and be an effective accommodation.

The student is also evaluated for possible vision and hearing problems to determine whether these areas could be the primary cause of the learning problems. A professional with specialized training is assigned to administer an individualized intelligence test and evaluate the student in any academic areas in which there is a suspected deficit. McNamara (2007) recommends a combination of standardized, norm-referenced, and informal tests to measure achievement. In addition to measuring achievement, one or more teachers familiar with the student and often the student's parents complete a behavior-rating scale. This behavioral assessment is completed to rule out the possibility that the primary cause of the deficit(s) in academic achievement is emotional or behavioral factors, suggesting that the child might be more appropriately served under the category of seriously emotionally disturbed.

At this point the IEP teams in states that choose to continue to use the pattern of strengths and weaknesses model will determine whether there is a pattern indicating a learning disability. States may continue to rely on determining the existence of a severe discrepancy between the student's ability and achievement in one or more of the areas in which he or she was evaluated. This determination is typically made by obtaining a discrepancy score using a formula to quantify the severe discrepancy between achievement and potential (Kavale, 2001a).

If the school is using the RTI method, the IEP team looks at the RTI data to determine if the student should be further evaluated for possible special education placement. Under this model, students are determined eligible due to a lack of responsiveness to the scientific, research-based-teaching method implemented to allow the child to benefit from the general education curriculum. In either case, the IEP team must also consider whether the lack of academic achievement could primarily be the result of a vision, hearing, or motor problem, mental retardation, emotional disturbance, cultural factors, environmental or economic disadvantage, or limited English proficiency.

The team must also consider the student's history and document that appropriate learning opportunities have been provided. A child might not be determined eligible, for example, if a student's school attendance is reviewed and the team notes that the child has moved frequently during the school years, thus causing content to be missed as a result of the differences in each school's curriculum. If, after the review, the IEP team, including the parents, determines that the student is eligible for services, the team may decide to write the individualized educational plan immediately or return to develop the plan at a separate meeting. Nearby you will find a sample of the IEP Goals and Objectives that were developed for Emmanuel to address his challenges in reading, listening, and writing.

The criteria for identifying students with learning disabilities (USOE, 2007) focus on the language, academic, and exclusion concepts and do not address the identification of deficits in areas such as attention and memory. However, it is often these characteristics and others noted in the characteristics section that create the biggest barriers to success in the general education classroom and later in the workforce. Teachers should be very familiar with the characteristics of LD and the impact they might have on functioning in a general education classroom. They should also understand that these characteristics are not manifested intentionally but occur as a result of a presumed central nervous system dysfunction.

Identifying Preschool Students   Because the federal criteria for determining a learning disability mainly involve academic and language deficits that emerge in the elementary school years, the identification of LD and the delivery of special education services for preschoolers have been difficult and often controversial. One approach described by Hallahan and colleagues (2005) has been to identify students with a generic label such as "developmental delay." In this model students are determined to be at risk for school failure and receive assistance with language, academic, or motor skills in which they are generally found to be lagging behind as compared to their peers. The advantage of this approach is that it helps a large number of students if the criterion is a small developmental delay. However, if a significant delay is required to be eligible for services, the students with potential LD may be excluded, as it is much easier to identify mental retardation using more stringent criteria and less easy to identify the more subtle indicators of a learning disability.

The alternative to the generic approach is the identification of the specific disability. Mercer and Pullen (2009) describe several issues that make this approach difficult. The greatest complication is the tremendous differences in growth and maturation that young children manifest, that are normal and may not represent a learning disability. For these reasons, school systems are cautioned against early identification of LD (Hallahan et al, 2005; Mercer & Pullen, 2009). Other concerns include the difficulty in diagnosis that results from

IEP GOALS AND OBJECTIVES
FOR EMMANUEL*

The chapter-opening vignette explains that Emmanuel is struggling primarily in the areas of reading, listening, and writing. The following sample from IEP shows his top three goals and the objectives necessary to meet them.

GOAL 1: READING   Emmanuel will read orally and demonstrate comprehension of text on the third-grade level.

Objective 1: Given a list of Dolch sight words, Emmanuel will read words through third-grade level with 80% accuracy three times in a row.

Objective 2: Given a paragraph on his reading level, Emmanuel will use context clues to predict unknown words with 70% accuracy.

Objective 3: Given a list of 10 multisyllable words in isolation and a list of 10 multisyllable words in text, Emmanuel will correctly apply phonetic patterns in decoding the words with an 80% accuracy rate.

Objective 4: Given a paragraph at his reading level, Emmanuel will read the text and respond to comprehension questions orally or in writing with an 80% accuracy rate.

GOAL 2: LISTENING   Emmanuel will increase his listening skills.

Objective 1: Given a list of words orally, Emmanuel will display his increased phonemic awareness skills by repeating them in order with 80% accuracy.

Objective 2: After listening to a story read by the teacher, Emmanuel will retell it with age-appropriate detail, with 80% accuracy.

Objective 3: Given a multistep set of oral directions, Emmanuel will follow each step with 100% accuracy.

GOAL 3: WRITING   Emmanuel will develop age-appropriate writing skills.

Objective 1: Given a list of Dolch words through third-grade level, Emmanuel will spell the words correctly with 80% accuracy.

Objective 2: Given a list of Dolch words through third-grade level, Emmanuel will apply phonetic patterns to spell multisyllable words with 80% accuracy.

Objective 3: Given the assignment to write in his daily journal, Emmanuel will write daily journal entries using age-appropriate vocabulary.

Objective 4: Given the assignment to write in his daily journal, Emmanuel will construct complete sentences, including correct capitalizations, punctuation, and grammar, with 80% accuracy.

Objective 5: Given a topic sentence, Emmanuel will generate a paragraph with at least five sentences, including a topic sentence, supporting details and a concluding sentence, with 80% accuracy.

*IDEA 2004 does not require short-term objectives except for students taking alternative assessments.

---

the inadequacy of assessment tools and procedures for this age group. Young children may have language and other skills that are lower than expected based on IQ, but it is difficult to determine whether these are the result of a learning disability, a maturational lag, or the effect of diverse educational experiences, language, and/or culture. An additional concern is the risk of diagnosing a learning disability where none exists, thus labeling and burdening the child unnecessarily. However, this argument does not address the fact that an equal risk is taken when a student who needs special educational services is not diagnosed and appropriately assisted; this student may be burdened by difficulties and failure that could have been avoided. Lyon (2010) concludes that a child must be 9 years old before discrepancy from IQ can be measured reliably. Thus, under the discrepancy model, potentially life-changing failure occurs for several years. Lyon suggests that early intervention can be so critical for disabilities in the area of reading that children with a strong family history of attention difficulties or reading failure should be labeled at-risk and placed in a preventive intervention program to strengthen their deficit areas.

Currently each state determines the proper age for identifying a child with a learning disability or one who is at risk for early school failure. Hammill (2004) identifies the following skills as effective screening items for identifying young children at risk for future reading failure: "Handling books; copying letters and numbers; writing their names; distinguishing print from nonprint markings; naming and writing letters and numbers; knowing the meaning of a few abbreviations and acronyms; discriminating among letters, numbers, and words; identifying and spelling some preprimer words" (p. 460).

Identifying Culturally and Linguistically Diverse Students   Since learning disabilities are found in almost 5% of the school-age population and the number of school-age children with cultural and language diversity is growing steadily, inevitably many children will fall into both groups. Much of the special education literature supports the idea that there is overrepresentation of culturally and linguistically diverse (CLD) learners. Chamberlain (2005) suggests that this is due to multiple variables, some of which, like poverty, are beyond the realm of education; others, like inadequate instruction and assessment practices, should be addressed. Accurately identifying a learning disability in the presence of cultural diversity is no small challenge. School personnel must carefully determine that the differences related to diversity in language or culture are not the primary cause of a student's learning difficulties. In other words, the student's learning difficulties must be significantly different when compared to peers in age, grade, and culture.

Gregory (2004) reports that too often a diagnosis of learning disability is based on intelligence and achievement tests administered in English without considering cultural and language differences (CLD). Identification is considered especially problematic when applied to students with CLD because of the problems in using standardized tests with this population. The referral itself may be made because a teacher has been ineffective in teaching a student who comes from another culture or who understands little of the language of the classroom. In this case, the child's failure to make progress may not be the result of a learning disability but the failure of the educational system to respect and adequately respond to cultural and language differences (Garcia & Guerra, 2004). Chamberlain (2005) refers to these as "cultural clashes" and suggests that teachers sometimes expect less from students from diverse cultural backgrounds and may view special education as the most viable placement option for them. As a result, a disproportionate number are referred for assessment and ultimately funneled into special education settings. However, it is certainly possible that a child with a low socioeconomic level or one who speaks English as a second language could have a central nervous system dysfunction that results in a learning disability. The IEP committee often has a big challenge in considering the diversity variable. Recommendations for anyone involved in the assessment of CLD students are found in Figure 5.3.

Prevalence and Educational Environments

In today's schools there are, by far, more students with LD than with any other disability. Critics propose that the debate over the definition and eligibility criteria is to blame for the huge rise in the prevalence of LD. A 2008 report from the U.S. Department of Education (www.ideadata.org) shows that 8.96% of the school-age population between the ages of 6 and 21 have disabilities and of that number, 3.89% or almost one-half, were identified as learning disabled. It should be noted that this prevalence figure can vary widely among states and within a state, depending on the stringency of the method used to determine eligibility as well as policies, programs, economic conditions, and changes in state populations (Mercer & Pullen, 2009). For example, Kentucky reports the lowest prevalence figure (1.55%) and Oklahoma the highest (5.6%). Gender data suggests that males are about twice as likely as females to be identified with LD (Coutinho & Oswald, 2005). Fifty-nine percent of students with LD (ages 5 to 21) spend more than 80% of their day in a general educational classroom with an additional 30% spending 40 to 80% of their day in the general educational classes (USDOE, 2008).

FIGURE 5.3	Addressing Cultural and Linguistic Diversity in the Assessment Process

Following are recommendations for anyone involved in assessment of students. These were compiled by Chamberlain (2005) from a variety of sources.

1. Understand nondiscriminatory assessment practices. Bias may occur when English tests are used for students more fluent in another language, when tests have items that are biased, and when eligibility is determined using tests covering material the student has not had an opportunity to learn.
2. Know the law. IDEA requires nondiscriminatory and valid testing instruments, tests given in the child's native language, use of more than one source of data for eligibility determination, and use of an interdisciplinary team.
3. Rely less on norm-referenced data and more on comprehensive sets of data such as curriculum-based assessment techniques that measure directly what is being taught in the classroom
4. Support well-designed prereferral intervention to lessen referrals and lead to properly identified students receiving special education services.
5. Advocate for students by using a comprehensive set of assessment procedures, being alert for the possibility of bias, and validating the results of norm-referenced tests.

Source: From "Recognizing and Responding to Cultural Differences in the Education of Culturally and Linguistically Diverse Learners," by S. P. Chamberlain, 2005, *Intervention in School and Clinic, 40*(4), p. 207.

Causation and Risk Factors

The advances in methods such as computerized imaging techniques that are reasonably reliable in detecting brain abnormalities have led to the generally accepted view that learning disabilities are the result of differences in brain function or structure (Hallahan et al., 2005). The literature suggests several causes for neurological differences or dysfunction, primarily hereditary factors and trauma experienced before birth, during birth, and after birth. Following is a summary provided by Hallahan and colleagues (2005):

1. **Genetic Factors:** Many studies have cited the large number of relatives with learning problems in children identified with learning disabilities. Chromosomal abnormalities and structural brain differences have been linked to learning disabilities.
2. **Causes Occurring before Birth:** Learning problems have been linked to injuries to the embryo or fetus caused by the mother's use of alcohol, cigarettes, or other drugs, such as cocaine and prescription and nonprescription drugs. Through the mother, the fetus is exposed to the toxins, causing malformations of the developing brain and central nervous system. Although it is known that significant amounts of overexposure to these drugs may cause serious problems, such as mental retardation, no safe levels have been identified.
3. **Causes Occurring during the Birth Process:** Traumas during birth may include prolonged labor, anoxia, prematurity, and injury from medical instruments such as forceps. Although not all children with a traumatic birth are found to have learning problems later, a significant number of children with learning problems do have a history of complications during this period.
4. **Medical and Environmental Causes Occurring after Birth:** High fever, encephalitis, meningitis, stroke, diabetes, and pediatric AIDS have been linked to LD. Malnutrition, poor postnatal health care, and lead ingestion can also lead to neurological dysfunction.

Advances in neurological research and use of computerized neurological techniques such as computerized axial tomography (CAT) scans and positron emission tomography (PET) scans have made professionals more inclined to believe in a neurological explanation of learning disabilities (Rourke, 2005). Widespread use of these tests to identify a learning disability has not been forthcoming for several reasons: such procedures are expensive and invasive, and the documented presence of a neurological dysfunction does not affect how the child is taught (Hallahan et al., 2005). However, this research is important to advance knowledge of this type of disability and in the future may help determine the effectiveness of various treatment techniques.

Through modern brain study techniques, Rourke (2005) proposed two subtypes of learning disabilities: Nonverbal LD (NLD) and Basic Phonological Processing Disabilities (BPPD). Each of these has a list of characteristics that reflect differences in academic and behavioral performance. For example, students with NLD have spelling errors that are phonetically correct; however, the students with BPPD make phonetically inaccurate misspellings. These differences may suggest differential teaching strategies. It is interesting to think about the possibility that one day brain imaging could be used to determine the best methods for teaching.

CHARACTERISTICS OF STUDENTS WITH LEARNING DISABILITIES

Learning disabilities are primarily described as deficits in academic achievement (reading, writing, and mathematics) and/or language (listening or speaking). However, children with learning disabilities may have significant problems in other areas, such as social interactions and emotional maturity, attention and hyperactivity, memory, cognition, metacognition, motor skills, and perceptual abilities. Because learning disabilities are presumed to be a central nervous system dysfunction, characteristics can be manifested throughout the life span— early childhood through adult (Bender, 2008; McNamara, 2007).

The most common characteristics of students with LD are described briefly in the following sections, concentrating on the challenges they may create in a classroom. Students with LD are a heterogeneous group. A single student will typically not have deficits in all areas. Also, any area could be a strength for a student with LD, and the student might exceed the abilities of his or her peers in that area. An understanding of the characteristics of children with learning problems is important in developing prereferral interventions, in making appropriate referrals, and in identifying effective accommodations, modifications, and intervention strategies. Figure 5.4 displays the possible strengths and weaknesses of children with learning disabilities.

Academic Deficits During the elementary school years, a learning disabled child's ability and his or her achievement across academic areas begin to vary significantly. Often puzzling to teachers and parents, these students seem to have strengths similar to those of their peers

FIGURE 5.4

Areas of possible strengths and deficits of students with learning disabilities.

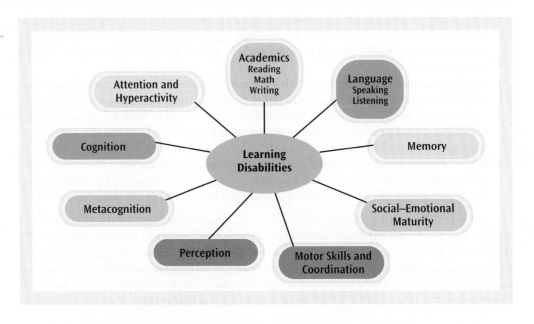

■ CHARACTERISTICS AND IMPLICATIONS: LEARNING DISABILITIES ■

AREA	POTENTIAL DIFFICULTIES	EDUCATIONAL IMPLICATIONS
Academic Development	Deficits in basic reading skills, reading fluency, reading comprehension	Teach phonemic awareness, phonics, fluency, vocabulary, and comprehension.
	Deficits in written expression	Teach handwriting, spelling, planning and revising text, integrate writing into subject areas, provide copy of notes.
	Deficits in math calculation, math reasoning	Teach math conceptual understanding, procedural fluency, strategies for real life application, adaptive reasoning, generalization, the value of math.
Language Development	Deficits in oral expression (expressive language) and listening (receptive language)	Model good language. Increase wait time for processing. Teach listening and speaking skills/strategies.
Memory	Deficits in short-term, working memory, and long-term memory	Teach memory strategies and use of memory log.
Social-Emotional Maturity	Social skill deficits, behavioral disturbances in class, less social acceptance, loneliness, anxiety, decreased motivation, learned helplessness	Teach social skills, social cues, nonverbal communication; provide more guidance and structure, and positive behavioral support.
Motor Skills and Coordination	Deficits in gross-motor activities, clumsy, limited success in group/individual sports.	Encourage use of scissors, markers in positive environment.
	Deficits in fine-motor activities such as handwriting.	Provide direct instruction in handwriting including fluency.
Perception	Deficits in auditory perception lead to misunderstandings in oral language communication and phonemic awareness.	Provide instruction in phonemic awareness, phonics. Give practice answering questions from information given orally.
	Deficits in visual perception are related to reading and writing disorders.	Provide orientation cues for confusing letters (b=bat/ball; d=drum/drumstick).
Metacognition	Difficulties in thinking, planning, reasoning to solve problems, making sense out of new information.	Teach keeping of assignment notebook. Teach goal setting and time management skills.
	Limited strategies to increase learning.	Teach self-monitoring.
Cognition	Difficulties in thinking, reasoning to solve problems, making sense out of new information.	Provide more supervision, concrete demonstrations, model thinking strategies: Think out loud! Connect new to old information.
	Limited strategies to increase learning, frequent errors.	
Attention and Hyperactivity	Difficulty focusing and sustaining attention, problems following directions, finishing work, taking notes.	Provide positive behavioral support for completing work, following directions. Teach self-regulation.
	Excess movement, interruptions	Highlight salient cues, provide study guides.

in several areas, but their rate of learning in other areas is unexpectedly slower. The term "unexpected underachievement" is frequently used to describe LD. Smith (2004) described an unexpected failure "despite adequate intelligence, schooling, and their parents' best attempts at nurturing" (p. 2). The vignette that began this chapter profiles a typical child with LD: above-average ability in math; average ability in language, attention, and social skills; and severe deficits in reading, written expression, and listening. (See the IEP goals and objectives for Emmanuel later in the chapter.)

The academic problems that identify a learning disability fall into the areas of reading, math, and written expression. The most prevalent type of academic difficulty for students with LD is reading. Lyon (2010) reports that approximately 80% of children identified as learning disabled have primary deficits in the area of reading and related language functions. Problems may be noted in basic reading skills, reading fluency, and reading comprehension. Children with LD may struggle with oral reading tasks. They may read in a strained voice with poor phrasing, ignore punctuation, and grope for words, as would a much younger child. Oral reading problems cause tremendous embarrassment to these children. Polloway, Patton, and Serna (2008) confirm that a student's self-image and feelings of confidence are greatly affected by reading experience. Deficits in reading skills can also lead to poor self-confidence, acting-out behavior, and poor motivation. More than 60% of young prisoners are illiterate (Blaunstein & Lyon, 2006).

Some children with learning disabilities may be able to say the words correctly but not remember what they have read. Comprehension problems can include one or more of the following: (1) identifying the main idea, (2) recalling basic facts and events in a sequence, and (3) making inferences or evaluating what has been read. A child with severe deficits in reading may be described as having **dyslexia**.

Another major academic problem area is mathematics. Students with LD may have problems in math calculations or math reasoning (USOE, 2006). These conceptual and skill areas include deficits in the four operations—the concept of zero, regrouping, place value, basic math concepts (e.g., one-to-one correspondence, sets)—and solving math problems. Children may have abilities in calculation but have disabilities in math reasoning; they may make many errors in calculations but be able to perform calculations to solve a math word problem. Often the rate of response interferes with success in math; for example, a child may be able to perform the skill, but is unable to complete the number of problems required during the time allowed. It is hoped that math disabilities will soon be studied as intensely as reading disabilities. A disability in math is called **dyscalculia**.

Learning disabilities in the area of **written expression** are beginning to receive more recognition as a potentially serious problem, indicating difficulties in one of the highest forms of communication (Mercer & Pullen, 2009). The three main areas of concern are handwriting, spelling, and written expression, including mechanics and creativity. The impact of written-language problems increases with a student's age because so many school assignments require a written product. A learning disability in writing is called **dysgraphia**.

Language Deficits   Language deficits are found in the areas of oral expression (expressive language) and listening comprehension (receptive language). Because these two areas control our ability to communicate with others, a deficit can have a major impact on quality of life—including life in a general education classroom. Common oral language problems include difficulty in retrieving correct words—children often use a less-appropriate word because the word they are searching for will not come to them. The response rate of children with LD may be slower than that of their nondisabled peers, and they may speak more slowly. If ample time is not allowed for a response, the student's behavior may be misinterpreted as failure to understand or refusal to participate. Children with LD tend to use simpler, less mature language and confuse sequences in retelling a story. Listening problems also can be easily misinterpreted. A child with a disability in listening demonstrates that disability in a negative way—for example, by failing to follow directions or by appearing oppositional or unmotivated. A teacher's careful observation and assessment of a student's language ability is important for ensuring the student's success. Figure 5.5 provides examples of how speech can become "twisted" for students with receptive language (e.g., listening) deficits; these deficits are referred to as **auditory processing deficits**.

A new area of concern and research for children with language-learning disabilities is the area of **pragmatics**, or use of language in social situations. Children with these dis-

| FIGURE 5.5 | Family Air Sangs (Familiar Sayings) |

These are actual "mis-heard" sayings from an individual who has a receptive language/listening learning disability.

1. ROCKER BUY BAY BEE INNER TREE HOPS
2. TURNIP OUT FIR PLAY
3. ROLAND'S TONE GADDERS NOME HOSS
4. SINKER'S HONKERS SICK SPENTZ
5. LAW TENT BRITCHES FULL IN TOWN

Source: "Recognizing and Responding to Cultural Differences in the Education of Culturally and Linguistically Diverse Learners," by S. P. Chamberlain, 2005, *Intervention in School and Clinic, 40*(4), p. 207.

abilities are often unsuccessful in fully participating in conversation. They may change the subject of a conversation or ask inappropriate questions. They may miss nonverbal language cues such as frowns. They may not understand jokes; they may laugh inappropriately or at the wrong times. Group work is often difficult, as is giving or following directions. Language disabilities can contribute significantly to difficulties in other social situations as well.

Social-Emotional Problems   Some children with LD have a real strength in the area of social skills; they are well-liked by peers and teachers. However, several characteristics of learning disabilities, like those noted in the area of language, can create difficulties in social and emotional life. Social skills deficits of children with LD include resolving conflict, managing frustrations, initiating or joining a conversation or play activities, listening, demonstrating empathy, maintaining a friendship, and working in groups.

Often positive interactions and exchange of information do not occur between children with LD and their peers or teachers. Because of behavior and language differences, children with LD need more guidance and structure. Over time, this need can create feelings of low self esteem, over-dependency, and eventually "learned helplessness" can occur. Social deficits have even been known to lead to school failure (Bryan, Burstein, & Ergul, 2004), and years of failure can create other concerns. Researchers have reported psychological problems, including feelings of anxiety, depression, inadequacy, frustration, anger, and acting out (Bender, 2008). By adolescence, a student's combined cognitive and language deficits can interfere significantly with deciding how to act in the new social situations brought about by increased independence. Social inadequacy can result in more rejection and cause serious emotional distress.

Emotional issues may mask or exacerbate a child's LD; however, positive emotional health can enhance the performance of students with LD. By being sensitive to emotional issues, teachers can take care to include students with LD in supportive situations and provide reinforcement for specific successes. General praise statements such as "Good work!" or "You are really smart!" will not have much impact because they are not believable to the students. Commenting on or rewarding specific accomplishments will be more effective. An example of a more focused positive comment for a writing sample might be, "The way you described your sister's birthday party made me feel like I was there!"

Attention Deficits and Hyperactivity   Attention is a critical skill in learning. Conte (1991) suggests that to be effective learners, children must be able to initiate attention, direct their attention appropriately, sustain their attention according to the task demands, and shift attention when appropriate. Deficits in these areas can have an impact on all aspects of success in school. When children are "not paying attention," they cannot respond appropriately to questions, follow directions, or take notes during a lecture. The excess movement of a hyperactive student can draw sharp criticism when it negatively affects the learning environment. Social problems occur when the student interrupts others and does not listen to his or her peers. Students with attention problems often have trouble finishing assignments or rush through their work with little regard for detail. Approximately 51% of students with LD are also reported to have attention problems, and it is estimated that 3.7% of school-aged children have both LD and ADHD (Smith & Adams, 2006). The comorbid occurrence of these two disabilities can be severely disabling in academic and nonacademic settings and has been found to create an increase in the need for special education services.

Memory Deficits   Students with LD have deficits in short-term memory, working memory, and long-term memory (Hallahan et al., 2005). Short-term memory problems show up when a child has difficulty repeating information heard less than 1 or 2 minutes earlier. Working memory problems occur when students are trying to take recent information and organize it for storage or link it to information previously stored in long-term memory to broaden their knowledge about a subject. These memory problems can have a negative impact on everyday tasks and situations as well as academic demands. Teachers and parents add that the memory skills are inconsistent in children with LD—for example, a student may know the multiplication facts on Thursday and fail the test on Friday. The good news is that when children with learning disabilities are taught memory strategies, they make substantial gains at all grade levels (Scruggs & Mastropieri, 2000).

Cognition Deficits   Cognition refers to the ability to reason or think (Hallahan et al., 2005). Students with problems in this area may make poor decisions or frequent errors. They may have trouble getting started on a task, have delayed verbal responses, require more supervision, or have trouble adjusting to change. They might find it difficult to understand social expectations and might require concrete demonstrations. These students also often have trouble using previously learned information in a new situation.

Metacognition Deficits   Hallahan and colleagues (2005) refer to **metacognition** as "thinking about thinking." Students with problems in this area might have difficulty focusing on listening, purposefully remembering important information, connecting that information to prior knowledge, making sense out of the new information, and using what they know to solve a problem. They often lack strategies for planning and organizing, setting priorities, and predicting and solving problems. An important component of metacognition is the ability to evaluate one's own behavior and behave differently when identifying inappropriate behavior or mistakes.

Perceptual Differences   Perceptual disorders affect the ability to recognize stimuli being received through sight, hearing, or touch, and to discriminate between and interpret the sensations appropriately. A child with a learning disability might not have any problems in these areas, or he or she might have deficits in any or all of them. Identification of deficits and training in the perceptual processes or reference to a child's "learning style" was emphasized in the early 1970s; however, it is no longer a prominent consideration in the education of children with LD.

Motor Skill and Coordination Problems   This area has also been de-emphasized in the identification of an intervention for children with learning disabilities because it is not directly related to academics. However, it is common for children with LD to display problems in gross motor areas; they often cannot throw and catch a ball or may have a clumsy gait. Common fine-motor deficits include difficulties with using scissors, buttoning clothing, and handwriting. Individuals with LD may also have a slow reaction time. Consideration of strengths or limitations in motor skills and coordination is especially important in the selection of postsecondary educational programs and, ultimately, in the identification of a career.

One emerging area of neurological research has described a specific subtype of LD referred to as a **nonverbal learning disability** (Rourke, 2005; Sousa, 2006). Students with this disability are reported to have a unique pattern of strengths; they talk early, talk a lot, and have a good vocabulary and memory for detail. Unfortunately, these strengths are coupled with a profound inability to interpret nonverbal social cues such as facial expressions, leading to difficulties in social situations and emotional stress. Motor dysfunction and visual-spatial deficits associated with math difficulties are also often present (LD Online, 2010).

EFFECTIVE INCLUSIVE PRACTICES

Intervention techniques for individuals with learning disabilities have been controversial over the years. In the 1970s, "best practice" was considered by many educators to include specialized training of auditory and visual processes. This was based on the assumption that progress in reading and other academic skills was contingent on improving skills in these areas. Class time might include having students copy increasingly more difficult visual designs or repeating a series of various "hand claps" to stimulate auditory processing. A convincing article by Hammill and Larsen (1974) analyzed research showing that perceptual training did little to improve basic academic skills. This triggered a move toward a skills approach, in which direct instruction was implemented in the areas of academic deficit. More recently, language, social-emotional, and cognitive-metacognitive areas have received positive attention. Many approaches have gained acceptance as research-based methods for improving the skills and developing the abilities of children and adults with learning disabilities. Thankfully, these have also been proven effective for all students and are available to a large degree in inclusive classrooms.

The methods of intervention have traditionally been determined by school policy or teacher preference. However, the 1999 regulations of IDEA expanded the definition of specially designed instruction to include the term "methodology," thus opening the door for the IEP team to specify the particular teaching method(s) that defines individualized instruction for a student. Ideally the IEP team decisions will be developed by parents and professionals with knowledge of methods backed by scientific research and demonstrated to benefit children with disabilities. Teachers need to be well informed on approaches so they can provide objective information to parents who seek to understand and address their child's difficulties. Both parents and educators need to closely monitor the child's "ability to benefit" from the method of instruction being used to teach new skills; this data will help the team determine when a new intervention or adaptation is needed if the child fails to make adequate progress.

Assessment data are also a critical feature in teaching all students effectively in a differentiated classroom where students with mixed abilities thrive and learn. Tomlinson (2005) encourages teachers to use assessment as a road map for thinking and planning. Initially, teachers identify key curriculum goals and learning objectives, and as they get to know their student's individual interests, needs, and abilities, they work with them to modify the content to be learned, vary the processes for learning, and/or differentiate the products that students will present to demonstrate their learning. The characteristics of students with learning disabilities described earlier will emerge in different ways to both challenge and excite the teacher and the student.

The following approaches are time-tested and research-based. They can be implemented in a general education classroom and may benefit many nondisabled students as well. The strategies are discussed according to age levels—preschool, elementary, secondary, and adult. The largest section concerns the elementary-school student; however, many elementary-level techniques are equally effective at the secondary level. An understanding of these approaches is critical, as recent federal data indicate that the majority of students with LD received at least 80% of their instruction in the general education classroom (U.S. Department of Education, 2007).

■ Most children with learning disabilities are identified during early elementary grades.

Preschool Services   In addition to the controversy surrounding assessment and identification of learning disabilities in preschool children, much has been written for and against the educational effectiveness and cost-effectiveness of early intervention programs for these children. Bender (2008) summarizes research in this area by stating that early intervention for some preschool children with learning disabilities—particularly those from low-socioeconomic minority groups—is effective. One of the expected benefits from RTI is the reduction of the overidentification of minority students (National Joint Committee on Learning Disabilities, 2005). Congress emphasized the need for early intervention services for students in kindergarten through third grade. The primary focus is on behavioral interventions and research-based literacy programs; however, services may include evaluation of educational or behavioral needs and any service or support needed (Bateman & Linden, 2007).

Mercer and Pullen (2009) provide an overview of the curriculum models primarily used in preschool programs including children with special needs: developmental, cognitive, and behavioral models. The **developmental model** stresses provision of an enriched environment. The child is provided numerous experiences and opportunities for learning. Development is stimulated through language and storytelling, field trips, and creative opportunities.

The **cognitive model** (or constructionist model) is based on Piaget's work. Stimulating the child's cognitive, or thinking, abilities is the primary focus. Activities are designed to improve memory, discrimination, language, concept formation, self-evaluation, problem solving, and comprehension. This new area of research is experiencing great success.

Concepts learned by direct instruction and the theory of reinforcement form the basis for the **behavioral model**. Measurable goals are set for each student, behaviors are observed, and desirable behavior is reinforced. Direct instruction is provided to accomplish goals, and progress is charted to provide data that determine the next instructional task. Coyne, Zipoli, and Ruby (2006) use the term "conspicuous instruction" and stress the importance of this type of intentional teaching in the five "big ideas" in literacy and beginning reading identified by the National Reading Panel (2000). These are described in detail in Table 5.1.

Figure 5.6 provides an example of beginning reading instruction designed to teach the first of the "Big Ideas": phonemic awareness and phonics skills.

Mercer and Pullen (2009) recommend a program that combines features from each approach. They suggest some structure, availability of free-choice activities, direct instruction in targeted areas, daily charting and feedback, developmental activities, and spontaneous learning experiences. These methods allow individual needs to be met in an inclusive setting without stigmatizing the children. Because preschool-age children are more likely to be falsely identified as learning disabled because of a maturational lag or lack of educational opportunities, it is particularly important to teach them in inclusive settings if at all possible and to involve families in the process.

Elementary Services   Many academic and language deficits, social-emotional problems, and cognitive and metacognitive deficits remain a problem throughout an individual's life. The intervention begun during preschool and elementary-school years can be equally important at the secondary level and for some adults.

TABLE 5.1

Big Ideas in Beginning Reading Instruction

BIG IDEA	EXAMPLE
Phonemic Awareness	
The ability to hear, identify, and manipulate the individual sounds in spoken words.	• Blending: Combining individual spoken sounds to form a word. Example: The sounds mmm . . . ooo . . . p make the word *mop*. • Segmentation: Separating a spoken word into individual sounds. Example: The word *mop* is made up of the sounds mmm . . . ooo . . . p.
Phonics	
Understanding the relationship between the letters of written language and the individual sounds of spoken language, and using these relationships to read and spell words.	• Letter–sound correspondences: Knowing the sounds that correspond to letters and the letters that correspond to sounds. Example: The letter *b* represents the sound /b/; the sound /aaa/ is represented by the letter *a*. • Regular word decoding/spelling: Reading/spelling words in which each letter represents its most common sound. Example: mat, sled, fast • Advanced phonics skills: Reading/spelling words that include more advanced spelling patterns and multiple syllables. Example: make, train, mu-sic, re-port
Fluency	
The effortless, automatic ability to read quickly and accurately in connected text.	• Accuracy: Reading grade-level text accurately. • Speed: Reading grade-level text quickly and automatically. • Prosody: Reading grade-level text with expression.
Vocabulary	
The ability to understand and use words to acquire and convey meaning.	• Vocabulary knowledge: Possessing a well-developed vocabulary acquired directly through instruction or indirectly through exposure to vocabulary in oral and/or written language. • Strategy knowledge: Applying strategies for determining the meanings of unknown words by using context or meaningful word parts (e.g., roots, affixes).
Comprehension	
The complex cognitive process involving the intentional interaction between reader and text to construct meaning.	• Priming prior knowledge/previewing/predicting. • Identifying the main idea/summarizing. • Organizing information/using text structure/using graphic organizers. • Answering and asking questions. • Self-monitoring understanding.

Source: From: "Beginning Reading Instruction for Students at Risk for Reading Disabilities: What, How, and When" (p. 163), by M. D. Coyne, R. P. Zipoli, and M. F. Ruby, 2006, *Intervention in School and Clinic, 41*(3), pp. 161–168.

FIGURE 5.6 — Beginning Reading Activities

Phoneme deletion: Children recognize the word that remains when you take away a phoneme.

Example
Teacher: What is *space* without the /s/?
Children: *Space* without the /s/ is *pace*.

Phoneme addition: Children make a new word by adding a phoneme to a word.

Example
Teacher: What word do you have if you add /p/ to the beginning of *lace*?
Children: *Place*.

Phoneme substitution: Children substitute one phoneme for another to make a new word.

Example
Teacher: The word is *rag*. Change /g/ to /n/. What's the new word?
Children: *Ran*.

Teaching phonics and word recognition:

The teacher . . .
explicitly teaches the children letter-sound relationships in a clear and useful sequence. The teacher also teaches children "irregular" words they will see and read often, but that do not follow the letter-sound relationships they are learning. These are often called **sight words**—words such *as said, is, was, are.*

The children . . .
learn to blend sounds to read words—first one-syllable words and, later, words with more than one syllable. They read easy books that include the letter-sound relationships they are learning as well as sight words that they have been taught. They recognize and figure out the meaning of compound words (words made of two words put together, such as *background*). They practice writing the letter-sound relationships in words, sentences, messages, and their own stories.

Source: From A Child Becomes a Reader (p. 33) by National Institute for Literacy.

Children with learning disabilities may have **academic and language deficits or strengths** in any or all of the following areas:

- Basic reading skills
- Reading fluency
- Reading comprehension
- Math calculation
- Math reasoning
- Written expression
- Oral expression
- Listening

These areas are usually the focus of an elementary-school curriculum, so they can most often be addressed in the general education classroom. Both general and special education teachers have been trained to provide instruction in these areas, so collaborative teaching is warranted. Because of the uneven skill development in children with LD, individualized assessment is generally required to identify areas that specifically need to be addressed. Informal methods, such as curriculum-based assessment, are usually most effective for planning instruction. This assessment, which should include an evaluation of the student's interests and strengths, may indicate the most effective method for instruction. The nearby Differentiated Instruction—Elementary boxed reading provides a clever format for teachers and students to use when collaborating to negotiate differentiated content, processes for learning, and procedures for sharing what has been learned.

One of the most critical areas of instruction for students with LD is in the area of **reading**. Many general education teachers prefer to use a reading approach based on reading various types of literature for meaning—development in areas such as phonics is assumed to occur naturally as the reader becomes more efficient. In this method, often referred to as the **whole language method**, the teacher might note difficulty with a phonetic principle during oral reading and subsequently develop a mini-lesson using text to teach the skill. Unfortunately, many children with LD do not readily acquire the alphabet code because of limitations in processing the sounds of letters and deficits in phonemic awareness.

Differentiating Elementary Instruction

I Want to Know

My question or topic is _____

_____

_____

To find out about it, I will _____

I will look of and listen to _____

I will read _____

I will draw _____

I will write _____

I will need _____

I will finish by _____.   I will share what I learned by
_____
_____
_____

Source: From *The Differentiated Classroom: Responding to the Needs of All Learners* (p. 80) by C. A. Tomlinson, 2005. Upper Saddle River, NJ: Pearson.

Research has shown a dramatic reduction in reading failure when comprehensive, explicit instructions are provided. After four decades of controversy in the meaning-versus-code emphasis debate, Carnine, Silbert, Kameenui, and Tarver (2004) strongly recommend the phonics method for beginning reading instruction. No Child Left Behind (NCLB) was specific in requiring scientific, research-based reading instruction. The five specific areas targeted are:

- Phonemic awareness
- Phonics

- Vocabulary development
- Reading fluency
- Reading comprehension (National Reading Panel, 2000)

Similarly, Hammill (2004) reviewed over 450 studies of reading and concluded that educators concerned with teaching reading should focus on direct teaching of reading skills, especially programs linking reading to writing and including the following:

- Print awareness and alphabet knowledge
- Phonics (e.g., letter-sound correspondence), word attack, and word identification
- Comprehension
- Oral and silent reading fluency, written composition, spelling, sentence punctuation, and textual composition

Teachers need to be able to assess skills of their students in each of these areas, which are considered the building blocks of reading achievement, and determine the level of intensity of instruction. As the process of teaching continues, teachers assess, determine progress and modify, and adjust teaching techniques or increase the level of intensity of instruction as the results suggest. Dr. Lyon (2010) points out that some students will need ongoing support and instruction in reading (e.g., Tier III or special education services) but by far the majority will become sufficient readers through intense, direct instruction in these basic skill areas (Tier I or Tier II).

Another way to facilitate success for students with learning disabilities in inclusive settings is teaching a **strategy** to apply during the process of learning new information or skills. A strategy is defined by Lenz, Deshler, and Kissam (2004) as an individual's approach to a task. Teaching a strategy provides a specific set of steps for thinking strategically, including how to approach difficult and new tasks, guide actions and thoughts, and finish tasks successfully and in a timely manner. Students with learning disabilities may not automatically develop strategies for learning, or the ones they develop may be inefficient. With the increased emphasis on state competency tests, it is more important than ever to retain academic content, and using strategies can be a critical factor in learning for students with special needs. However, just as students with LD have difficulty learning academic information, they often have difficulty learning and using the steps of a strategy without direct instruction. When teaching a new strategy, teachers should:

Have a clear objective and state the purpose of the strategy
Provide instruction and model the use of the strategy ("Think out loud!")
Allow guided practice with corrective feedback
Provide independent practice including opportunities to use the strategy in a variety of ways
Monitor performance and encourage questions (Mastropieri, Scruggs, & Graetz, 2003)

One very simple but effective strategy for increasing reading comprehension is a questioning strategy where students are taught how to ask and then answer these summarization strategy questions:

- Who or what is the paragraph about?
- What is happening to whom or what?
- Can you create a summary sentence in your own words using less than 10 words?

Mastropieri, Scruggs, and Graetz (2003) provide this strategy and the research to support it; however, they note that the set of instructional features recommended above are critical to successfully teach this strategy.

Students with learning disabilities in the area of **mathematics** have been described by Gersten, Jordan, and Flojo (2005) as lacking in "number sense." They propose that the traditional method of math instruction for students in special education that focuses on teaching algorithms and being drilled on number facts has led to a lack of general understanding. Their work and the research of others support the use of "responseness to intervention" for young children demonstrating math difficulties. This intervention should focus on teaching one-to-one correspondence, relative quantity (more or less than), math combinations, place value, counting strategies, and number sense (Bender, 2008; Gersten et al., 2005). Additional strategies proposed by Furner, Yahya, and Duffy (2005) include teaching vocabulary, demonstrat-

FIGURE 5.7	Effective Intervention Components

- Use clear objectives
- Follow specific sequence for teaching
  - state the purpose
  - provide instruction
  - model
  - guided practice
  - corrective feedback
  - independent practice
  - generalization practice
- Inform the students of importance of the strategy
- Monitor performance
- Encourage questions that require students to think about strategies and text
- Encourage appropriate attributions
- Teach for generalized use of the strategy

Source: From "Reading Comprehension Instruction for Secondary Students: Challenges for Struggling Students and Teachers," (p. 106), by M. A. Mastropieri, T. E. Scruggs, and J. E. Graetz, 2003, *Learning Disability Quarterly, 26*, pp. 103–116.

ing with real objects, relating vocabulary and math problems to prior knowledge and daily life experiences, using manipulatives and drawing pictures to solve math problems, using the computer and cooperative learning activities with heterogeneous student groupings, connecting math to other disciplines such as history and literature, and making cultural connections when teaching math; for example, taking "Internet field trips."

Using mnemonic strategies can also help students with LD having problems with memory in math. For example, to remember $4 \times 8 = 32$, the student might associate "door" for "4" and "gate" for "8" and a "dirty shoe" for "32," so the association to visualize would be a door on a gate by a dirty shoe (Wood & Frank, 2000). Figure 5.7 contains information on excellent websites for math activities and help with math anxiety.

Written language is often difficult to master for children and adults with LD. Unfortunately, making too many adaptations in this area can result in underdeveloped skills. For example, if a student is always allowed to use another student's notes or allowed to take tests orally in place of written exams, the short-term benefits may be helpful, but instruction and experience in taking notes and writing essay answers must be continued if growth is to occur in these areas. Graham, Harris, and MacArthur (2006) describe an impressive method for team-teaching a report-writing strategy in a general education classroom. In their method, the special education teacher takes the lead in introducing the strategy and working with the struggling writers, and the general education teacher participates in all phases of instruction. The authors point out that by explicitly teaching strategies for planning, drafting, and revising text, the struggling writers, as well as their classmates, are helped with better writing skills. Written language is another area where strategy instruction can be used to develop important skills. Figure 5.8 shows a motivating strategy to prompt a five-paragraph theme using a graphic organizer.

Improvement in **oral language** can be stimulated by promoting a better self-concept, teaching the skills of language production directly, and enriching the language environment. When students speak, teachers should listen closely to the message and respond appropriately, and save corrections for a later teaching moment. The respect that teachers show for attempts at communication will increase conversation and confidence. Providing opportunities for students to share their experiences and expertise is also a nonthreatening way to promote use of oral language. Listening and praise help reinforce talking. Bos and Vaughn (2002) reviewed the research in the area of spoken language and made the following additional recommendations:

- Increase wait time to allow sufficient time for comprehension and a response.
- Model good language.

FIGURE 5.8

Graphic organizer for five-paragraph essay.

Source: From "Effects of a Motivational Intervention for Improving the Writing of Children with Learning Disabilities" (p. 146), by J. N. García and A. M. deCaso, 2004. *Learning Disability Quarterly, 27,* pp. 141–159.

Graphic Organizer A
(one of the five organizers students can choose in this plan sheet)

- Take the student's words and briefly elaborate or expand on ideas.
- Use parallel talk and self-talk to describe what you and others are doing and thinking.
- Use a structured language program and build in activities in a variety of settings to develop generalization.

Poor **listening skills** also limit individuals with LD, influencing success both in the classroom and in social interactions. It is important for teachers to analyze the amount of listening required in their classrooms, study the barriers to good listening such as distracting noises, and teach and reinforce specific listening strategies (Swain, Friehe, & Harrington,

2004). Following is a simple strategy to cue listening behaviors that can be modified for older students (Heaton & O'Shea, 1995):

L   Look at the teacher.
I   Ignore the student next to you.
S   Stay in your place.
T   Try to visualize and understand the story.
E   Enjoy the story.
N   Nice job! You're a good listener (p. 35).

Computers and other technology can assist in teaching individuals with learning disabilities in inclusive classrooms. Olsen and Platt (1996) describe the following advantages of technology that still hold true today:

- It is self-pacing and individualized.
- It provides immediate feedback.
- It provides repetition without pressure.
- It maintains a high frequency of student response.
- It builds in repeated validation of academic success.
- It is an activity respected by peers.
- It is motivating.
- It encourages increased time on task.
- It minimizes the effects of the disability.

The computer can be used effectively for curriculum support in math, writing, language arts, social studies, science, and other areas. Various types of software provide instructional alternatives such as tutoring, drill and practice, simulation, and games. With so many choices available, teachers should carefully evaluate each program for ease of use and appropriateness for exceptional students.

Intervention related to **social interactions and emotional maturity** is critical for many students with LD. The inclusion movement provides opportunities for interactions; the question is how to best prepare both the children with disabilities and nondisabled children for positive interactions. Changing a student's self-image, social ability, and social standing is difficult. Until recently, the research and literature on LD focused primarily on the efficacy of treatments for the most obvious characteristic—academic deficits. The importance of social skills is just now being recognized and given the attention it deserves.

Intervention in the area of social standing and interaction can take two courses: changing the child or changing the environment. Optimally, both receive attention. Good teaching techniques in this area can lead to academic achievement and eventually to higher self-esteem. Teachers can create a positive learning environment and incorporate praise and encouragement for specific accomplishments, such as making positive comments about themselves and others. Teachers should also set goals and be very explicit about expectations for academic work and behavior in the class; they should monitor progress closely and provide frequent feedback (Polloway et al., 2008).

Improvement in low academic self-concept has also been made by correcting maladaptive **attributional styles**, or teaching students that their actions affect their success and to take credit for their successes. Students with higher academic self-concepts have been found to work harder to achieve (Margolis & McCabe, 2006).

Modeling prosocial skills and positive self-talk is important, as well as is providing natural opportunities for conversation and conflict resolution. A forum during group time can be used to pose potential problems and generate discussions to brainstorm possible solutions before the situations occur (Morris, 2002). Role-playing successful cooperation followed by experience in collaborative group projects can also provide positive social experiences if the teacher monitors closely. Figure 5.9 provides a lesson plan in which the goal is to provide direct instruction to teach students to interact with other individuals.

According to Bryan and colleagues (2004), research suggests that merely placing a student in an inclusive classroom does not insure social acceptance or inclusion. Direct instruction in areas of academic and social skill deficits as well as creating a positive, accepting atmosphere

FIGURE 5.9   Teaching Interaction

Following are recommendations for anyone involved in assessment of students. These were compiled by Chamberlain (2005) from a variety of sources.

1. Understand nondiscriminatory assessment practices. Bias may occur when English tests are used for students more fluent in another language, when tests have items that are biased, and when eligibility is determined using tests covering material the student

Nonverbal Behavior
1. Face the student
2. Maintain eye contact
3. Maintain a neutral or pleasant facial expression

Paraverbal Behavior
4. Maintain a neutal tone of voice
5. Speak at a moderate volume

Verbal Teaching Behavior
6. Begin with a compliment related to the student's efforts and achievements.
7. Introduce the social skill and define what the social skill means.
8. Give a rationale for learning the skill and for using the skill with others.
9. Share an experience when you used the social sill or could have used the social skill.
10. Specify each behavior (e.g., nonverbal and verbal behavior) to be considered when exhibiting the skill.
11. Demonstrate or model the use of the skill.
12. Have the student rehearse the social skill. (Observe the student's behavior.)
13. Provide positive corrective feedback.
    State what the student did correctly.
14. Practice the social skill with the student. (Make sure you do not prompt.)
15. Continue to provide corrective feedback to practice until the student masters (100 percent) the social skill in a novel situation.
16. Plan, with the student when and where to use the social skill.

Note: Make sure the student participates throughout the lesson. To do so, ask questions and let the student share ideas and thoughts. Always praise the student for participating and rehearsing the social skill.

Source: From *Strategies for Teaching Learners with Special Needs* (p. 212), by E. A. Polloway, J. R. Patton, and L. Serna, 2001. Upper Saddle River, NJ: Merrill.

in the general education classroom are needed to facilitate educational benefit. Following are simple methods to empower students and build a sense of classroom community:

- Believe in a positive classroom community and the importance of empowered students; students will follow your lead.
- Facilitate a sense of inclusion by helping students get to know and trust one another.
- Have students create a map of the people and places in the school/classroom to help them understand their place in the community.
- Have students interview one another and adults in the school.
- Highlight commonalities like characteristics and favorite activities among students.
- Play bingo, matching names with personal items (e.g., owns a pet).
- Guide students in conducting classroom meetings to facilitate a sense of power in knowing that what they say is important.
- Give students choices of activities or assignments.
- Reduce rewards for individuals and reward the group, especially for inclusive behaviors.
- Assign classroom jobs and encourage community service.
- Use a "sharing chair" technique, where students lead a group discussion of personal importance.

FIGURE 5.10	Examples of Social Skills	
Starting a conversation	Expressing your feelings	Using self-control
Asking a question	Negotiation	Keeping out of fights
Introducing yourself	Setting goals	Feeling sad
Asking for help	Working cooperatively	Responding to aggression
Learning how to listen	Dealing with frustration	Responding to failure
Apologizing	Controlling anger	Decision-making

Source: From "Social Skills Interventions for Individuals with Learning Disabilities" (p. 33), by K. A. Kavale and M. P. Mostert, 2004, *Learning Disability Quarterly, 27,* pp. 31–43.

- Teach active listening skills, where students validate others' thoughts even if they disagree.
- Display a celebration board highlighting group accomplishments and good citizenship.

An important part of promoting acceptance is having the student with the disability, family members, other teachers, and professionals understand the disability, as well as how it can be manifested and successfully addressed in home and school environments.

The overall goal of social programs is to teach socially appropriate behavior and social skills that are self-generated and self-monitored. The cognitive problems of students with LD often make this type of decision making very difficult. Often these skills, which seem to develop naturally in most children, have to be taught to LD children. Areas potentially in need of instruction are included in Figure 5.10. Although the effectiveness of social skills training has had little empirical support, it seems that this is too important a life skill to ignore, and research efforts should continue (Kavale & Mostert, 2004).

Intervention in **cognitive and metacognitive** skills has begun to receive support from LD professionals, as powerful techniques are being studied to improve learning. Some of the ideas are relatively simple and require only common sense. First, and most important, is being sure a child is paying attention to the stimulus being presented. This purpose might be achieved by dimming the lights, calling for attention, or establishing eye contact. Without attention, learning will not take place. A fun and effective strategy for gaining students' attention is presented in Figure 5.11. The strategy is introduced, modeled, and practiced with and then without teacher guidance. The chart can be posted in the room or on individual desks. New lessons can begin with the exciting prompt, "Give me five!"

Secondary Services   Academic and language deficits, social and emotional problems, and differences in cognitive and metacognitive functioning continue to plague many adolescents with LD. With the focus on content classes in middle and high school, remediation of basic skills is often minimal. This situation can be problematic for students having difficulty passing the high-school graduation exam required in many states for a regular diploma, and for those unable to read the content material at the secondary level. Students who continue to benefit from remediation should be provided these opportunities. Research-based strategies are available to teach secondary students who are struggling readers to read the all-important multisyllable words. Figure 5.12 demonstrates one strategy in which students are taught to decode unknown words by breaking them into smaller, more readable parts. This technique has the added benefit of using vocabulary more similar to that found in secondary textbooks so content or meaning can be enhanced when the actual reading or decoding challenge is at a much lower level.

With the increase in demands in secondary education programs, students with learning disabilities may need to be taught a variety of learning strategies to cope. These skills will facilitate learning but will most likely be needed in combination with adaptations or differentiated instruction techniques to make learning and performance more effective and efficient (Chamberlain, 2006). Strategies have been developed in many areas, including study skills, test taking, reading comprehension, paragraph writing, self-advocacy skills, and

FIGURE 5.11

Give Me Five strategy used to increase listening skills.

Source: From *Language Strategies for Children,* by Vicki Prouty and Michele Fagan, 1997. Eau Claire, WI: Thinking Publications (1-800-225-4769; www.ThinkingPublications.com). Copyright 1997 by Thinking Publications. Reprinted with permission.

social skills to name a few. Strategies can enable a student to handle the increased amount of content information, but it is equally important to be sure that the cognitive level of the student is sufficient to handle the strategy. Don Deshler, credited with validating the learning strategies model, warns that other elements also important to content learning include teaching critical vocabulary skills, building prior knowledge to connect to new informa-

FIGURE 5.12	Multisyllable Word Decoding Strategy

1. Circle the word parts (prefixes) at the beginning of the word.
2. Circle the word parts (suffixes) at the end of the word.
3. Underline the letters representing vowel sounds in the rest of the word.
4. Say the parts of the word.
5. Say the parts fast.
6. Make it a real word.

EXAMPLE

Source: Adapted from "Decoding and Fluency: Foundation Skills for Struggling Readers" by A. L. Archer, M. C. Gleason, and V. L. Vachon, 2003, *Learning Disability Quarterly, 26,* 89–103.

tion, and teaching an understanding of the structure of text. He also warns teachers not to overload students with too many strategies (Chamberlain, 2006).

The teacher can also make an impact on student learning and performance by accounting for individual differences when developing and implementing lesson plans. Many students fail, not because of an inability to perform but because they do not understand directions, cannot remember all the information, or cannot process verbal information fast enough. Most adults and older children automatically lower the language they use when speaking to younger children or individuals with obvious disabilities. Unfortunately they do not typically do so when speaking to school-age children and adults with LD— even though the latter may have language-based learning disabilities. To be effective, teachers need to consider the level of language used and their rate of presentation; they may need to add a demonstration to directions or check for understanding of directions and possibly repeat them individually. The recent advances in education brought about by the Universal Design for Learning philosophy have led to greater acceptance of differentiated instructional techniques that can promote learning throughout a lesson. The nearby Differentiated Instruction—Secondary boxed reading demonstrates the flow of instruction under the traditional "one size fits all" method before differentiation and then re-presents the instructional flow in a differentiated classroom where the teacher "honors and plans for individual learning needs" (Tomlinson, 2005).

Differentiation may need to extend to the body of content students are expected to learn. Wagner (2010) notes that a student struggling to write a five-page essay about the Civil War might be far more successful and feel a sense of accomplishment rather than inadequacy if writing about a familiar topic, one of personal interest, or one relevant to the real-world curriculum. Differentiating the homework load may also be needed to prevent overloading, as many students with LD will require additional time for the reading and writing requirements.

As noted earlier, a major problem for secondary students with LD is low self-concept and social and emotional problems that often stem from years of school failure. To help ameliorate unhappiness, school environments must be structured to create successful experiences. An important variable in academic success is the student's belief that he or she can manage the learning environment (Klassen, 2010). One method involves developing **self-determination skills**, or making students more active participants in designing their educational experiences and monitoring their own success; this can be done by teaching self-awareness, self-regulation, and self-advocacy skills. Students should use these skills as active participants in their IEP meetings. Such participation is particularly important when a student is exiting high school and making life-changing decisions about pursuing a postsecondary education or seeking employment.

High-school students with LD especially need to acquire transition skills (e.g., abilities that will help students be successful after high school in employment and independent living). For students in inclusive settings, teachers can find ways to integrate transition topics into the regular curriculum. For example, when an English teacher assigns letter writing or term papers, students might focus their work on exploring different career opportunities or completing college application essays. Math teachers can bring in income tax and budget forms to connect them to a variety of math skills. When planning any lesson, teachers should ask themselves, "Is there any way I can make this meaningful to their lives after high school?" See Table 5.2 for more examples.

■ Adolescents should be active participants in meetings concerning them.

Other effective cognitive and metacognitive strategies include keeping an assignment notebook (a common time management and organizational tool for many adults!) or logs. When assignments are made, students should develop projections for completing the tasks and continuously monitor their progress until the targeted assignment or goal is met. Additional activities in time management for daily living activities such as paying bills, keeping appointments, or developing a weekly schedule should also be provided (Salend, 2008). Incorporating real-life

Differentiating Secondary Instruction

Before and After: The Flow of Instruction (A Secondary Example)

BEFORE

1 The teacher introduces the unit/topic → 2 Students read assigned material → 3 Teacher gives notes → 4 Students work on an activity → 5 Students practice at home

6 Class discussion → 7 Teacher gives notes → 8 Students work on activity → 9 Students watch a video → 10 Class discussion

11 Students complete a project → 12 Students take a test → 13 Class moves to next topic

After

1 The teacher pre-assesses student knowledge, skillls, and interests → 2 Teacher introduces lesson with student knowledge and interest in mind → 3 Students read material at varied reading levels or with support, as appropriate → 4 Teacher and students debrief reading for key knowledge, concept, and principles. → 5 Teacher gives notes with a guided lecture format accompanied by a demonstration.

6 Teacher assesses student understanding with exit cards → 7 Students do an assigned tiered activity matched to current understanding → 8 Students complete one of two homework choices they feel will help them most → 9 Teacher gives notes with digest, as appropriate → 10 Students do paired journal writing with teacher-choice partner and student-choice entry

11 Students work on a jigsaw on the topic, based on their interests → 12 Teacher assigns product with common elements and student options → 13 Teacher offers review session and mini-workshop on product skills → 14 Class discussion with questions at varied levels of difficulty → 15 Students take a quiz with common and differentiated elements

Source: C.A. Tomlinson, 2005, from C.A. Tomlinson (2002) *How to differentiate instruction in mixed ability classrooms* (2nd ed.) Upper Saddle River, NJ: Pearson.

activities into high-school learning activities can have the added effect of making school more relevant and may increase the likelihood that students will persist and graduate with a diploma.

The importance of a high-school diploma is widely supported; however, research estimates that the dropout rate for students with learning disabilities is 25%, higher than that for other disabilities and far exceeding the national average (Dunn, Chambers, and Rabren, 2004). These data have negative implications for the students, their families, and our communities as well, including unemployment or underemployment, disruptions to the families, reduced income, more likely deviant behavior—even prison time, and increased dependence on social programs (Murray & Naranjo, 2008). However, the positive results for high-risk urban students identified in their research suggest that graduation outcome was affected by four primary variables: peers, family, self, and teachers. Specifically, these students who graduated against the odds were described as:

Being selective in friendship with peers to avoid negative influences

Having at least one parent who supported school effort, provided structure, and monitored progress

TABLE 5.2

Examples of Study Skill Functions in and out of the Classroom

STUDY SKILL	SCHOOL EXAMPLES	LIFE SKILLS APPLICATIONS
Reading Rate	Reviewing an assigned reading for a test	Reviewing an automobile insurance policy
	Looking for an explanation of a concept discussed in class	Reading the newspaper
Listening	Understanding instructions about a field trip	Understanding how a newly purchased appliance works
	Attending to morning announcements	Comprehending a radio traffic report
Note Taking/Outlining	Capturing information given by a teacher on how to dissect a frog	Writing directions to a party
	Framing the structure of a paper	Planning a summer vacation
Report Writing	Developing a book report	Completing the personal goals section on a job application
	Completing a science project on a specific marine organism	Writing a complaint letter
Oral Presentations	Delivering a personal opinion on a current issue for a social studies class	Describing car problems to a mechanic
	Describing the results of a lab experiment	Asking a supervisor/boss for time off from work
Graphic Aids	Setting up the equipment of a chemistry experiment based on a diagram	Utilizing the weather map in the newspaper
	Locating the most densely populated regions of the world on a map	Deciphering the store map in a mall
Test Taking	Developing tactics for retrieving information for a closed-book test	Preparing for a driver's license renewal test
	Comparing notes with textbook content	Participating in television self-tests
Library Usage	Using picture files	Obtaining travel resources (books, videos)
	Searching a computerized catalog	Viewing current periodicals
Reference Materials	Accessing CD-ROM encyclopedias	Using the yellow pages to locate a repair service
	Using a thesaurus to write a paper	Ordering from a mail-order catalog
Time Management	Allocating a set time for homework	Maintaining a daily "to do" list
	Organizing a file system for writing a paper	Keeping organized records for tax purposes
Self-Management	Ensuring that homework is signed by parents	Regulating a daily exercise program
	Rewarding oneself for controlling temper	Evaluating the quality of a home repair

Source: From *Teaching Students with Learning Problems to Use Study Skills: A Teacher's Guide* (p. 7), by J. J. Hoover and J. R. Patton, 1995. Austin, TX: Pro-Ed. Reprinted by permission.

Believing in themselves and the value of an education as well as being persistent and self-reliant but willing to ask for help

Having teachers who were involved, caring, supportive, and demanding but could "break it down" so you could understand the curriculum content (Murray & Naranjo, 2008).

A trusted source for what works in education is available through the "What Works Clearinghouse" established in 2002 by the U.S. Department of Education's Institute of Educational Sciences (Lyon, 2010). Figure 5.13 contains a link to this website and other projects

> ### FIGURE 5.13 — Websites with Information about Scientific Research-Based Practice
>
> Many websites maintain information on research based practices. In addition to searching your university library databases such as ERIC or Academic Search Premier, you may want to begin with one or more of the following:
>
> - What Works Clearinghouse (www.w-w-c.org) identifies current research studies on effective practices and intervention.
> - ERIC/OSEP Special Project (www.ericec.org/osep-sp.html#recon) disseminates federally funded special education research.
> - The Center for Innovations in Education (www.cise-missouri.edu/links/research-ep-links.html) at the University of Missouri at Columbia maintains links to research-based practices leading to effective instruction.
> - www.abledata.com provides information on assistive technlolgy and products used to assist in daily living activities.
> - www.ncddr.org provides research outcomes for over 350 projects funded by the National Institute on Disability and Rehabilitation Research.
> - www.nichd.nih.gov/crmc/.cdb/reading.html links to the National Institute of Child Health and Human Development, Reading Research Resources.
> - education.umn.edu/.NCEO is the website for the National Center on Education Outcomes.
> - ncal.literacy.lipern.edu provides information about research in literacy.

funded through a national peer review process to serve as centers of excellence and to disseminate information on scientific research-based knowledge and practice.

Adult Services   As noted earlier, the experience and instruction provided in high-school classes can have a powerful impact on the outcome for adults with LD. The relevant lessons in the life skills application of various school activities and success in the general education curriculum should be a focus as high schools acknowledge what students need to learn to be successful adults in postsecondary education, employment, and independent living environments.

The number of students with learning disabilities attending and completing college is increasing (Madaus, 2006). Many students continue to need accommodations, and those with the appropriate documentation of their disability can receive them through a college's Office of Disability Services or Student Support Services. Support given and the documentation required varies among colleges. A portion of a student's high-school transition plan should include research for the "best fit" for postsecondary services provided. Some of the more common accommodations include extra time, tutors, priority registration, E-textbooks, testing in a distraction-reduced environment, and a notetaker (Polloway, Patton, & Serna, 2008).

An important study by Raskind, Goldberg, Higgins, and Herman (2002) identified characteristics of highly successful adults with learning disabilities. One of the strongest predictors for success was the desire and willingness to persist and work extremely hard. Understanding one's strengths and limitations, identifying appropriate goals, and working proactively to meet them were also important. The successful adults developed a plan and then worked hard to accomplish their goals. They also developed and used support groups. These characteristics were more powerful predictors of success than academic achievement, IQ, life stressors, social-economic status, or race. Teachers and other individuals can encourage development of many of these factors; however, some factors, like emotional stability, seem to be innate personality traits of the individuals themselves.

The adults also were able to reframe their feelings about having a learning disability, gradually identifying and accepting their own strengths and weaknesses. Once the weaknesses were identified, they took creative action to build strategies, techniques, and adaptations to offset the impact of the disability. The study also showed that it was important to find a "goodness of fit": choosing goals that would be possible to attain. Finally, successful adults were willing to seek help from supportive people, such as a spouse or an individual at an agency. A similar observation is made by Waber (2010), who reports many adults with LD describe elementary school as their most stressful period and add that they fared better when they found a niche where their deficits were not as relevant and more emphasis could be placed on their interests, strengths, and competencies.

The level of commitment and persistence shown by these successful adults is remarkable. A study by Madaus (2006) identified the most frequently used strategies for success as:

- Setting goals and priorities
- Managing time
- Arriving to work early
- Staying at work late

One highly successful individual was told by his new boss that he was promoted to a higher level because he had a work ethic that had never been seen before. He never left until the job was done perfectly, and he was willing to do whatever was asked of him without complaining (Guyer, 2002).

Unfortunately, many adults leave high school without the skills and confidence necessary to find employment to help them realize their maximum vocational potential and to live independently. They are often deficient in choosing and carrying out the needed strategies, and they do not automatically generalize previously learned information to new challenges.

According to Madaus (2006), 72% of workers with LD reported that their learning disabilities did impact work at least occasionally. The biggest problems noted were writing skills, rate of processing information, reading comprehension, organizational skills, math computation, and time management.

These skills can be taught and should be addressed in a secondary curriculum. For adults with learning disabilities who still need support, a variety of agencies are available to address needs such as improving literacy skills, obtaining a high-school equivalency certificate (called a GED or general equivalency diploma), and meeting goals in areas such as financial aid for further education, employment, and independent living. Figure 5.14 lists examples of

FIGURE 5.14	Adult Agencies

GED Hotline (1-800-626-9433) General Education Development (GED) provides information on local GED classes and testing services, including an accommodations guide for people taking the GED test who have a learning disability.

National Literacy Hotline (1-800-228-8813) The hotline has a twenty-four-hour bilingual (Spanish/English) operator service that provides information on literacy/education classes, GED testing services, volunteer opportunities, and a learning disabilities brochure.

HEALTH Resource Center (1-800-544-3284) National clearinghouse on postsecondary education for individuals with disabilities has information specialists available 9:00 A.M.–5 P.M. ET (Monday–Friday) who provide resource papers, directories, information on national organizations, and a resource directory for people with LD.

Learning Resources Network (LERN) (1-800-678-5376) Has an operator service 8:00 A.M.–5:00 P.M. ET (Monday–Friday) that provides information to practitioners of adult continuing education. It also gives consulting information, takes orders for publications, and provides phone numbers of organizations that deal with learning disabilities.

ABLE DATA (1-800-227-0216) Provides information on more than 27,000 assistive technology products; www.abledata.com.

Association on Higher Education and Disability (AHEAD) Provides information on full participation in postsecondary education for people with disabilities; www.ahead.org.

Job Accommodation Network (JAN) (1-800-526-7234) Provides information on job accommodations and employment.

Source: From "Useful Resources on Learning Disability Issues," 2005, *LDA Newsbriefs,* January/February, pp. 12–16. Used by permission. Adapted with permission.

these important resources. The primary adult agency that offers assessment and intervention to promote employment for adults with learning disabilities is the Rehabilitation Services Administration. An office of this vocational rehabilitation agency is located in every state. Vocational evaluators are trained to identify each individual's strengths and the characteristics that will limit employment. Counselors provide a variety of employment-related services to those who are eligible, often including financial support for postsecondary training.

CLASSROOM ADAPTATIONS

One of the most important roles of inclusive educators is to identify and implement modifications (accommodations and adaptations) that address the unique learning needs of a student and at the same time maintain the integrity of the lesson, providing access to the general education curriculum (Fisher, Frey, & Thousand, 2003) or assessment process. In fact, IDEA requires that a statement of program modifications and supports be included in every child's IEP. Although there are differences in the way modifications, accommodations, and adaptations are defined, for our purposes accommodations are "changes to the delivery of instruction, method of student performance, or method of assessment that do not significantly change the content or conceptual difficulty level of the curriculum" (Miller, 2002, p. 292). For example, a teacher might allow extra time for an assignment or a test to be completed. An adaptation, frequently referred to as a modification, is a greater change or modification that does alter expectations and the level of content to be learned (Miller, 2002). Table 5.3 includes examples of modifications ranging from simple accommodations to adaptations that are more complex and difficult to implement.

One important consideration for individuals of all ages with disabilities, including learning disabilities, is the appropriate use of accommodations or modifications during testing. Use of these helps ensure that common characteristics of LD such as poor reading, distractibility, or slow work rate do not lower the results of an assessment of the child's learning. Care must be taken when implementing these accommodations or modifications because, while disallowing fair changes prevents a student from demonstrating his or her knowledge, overly permissive changes will inflate scores. Inflated scores may give students an overestimation of their abilities and may lead to unrealistic postsecondary goals. They also may reduce pressure on schools to maintain high expectations and offer students a challenging program with intense instruction (Fuchs & Fuchs, 2001). These researchers note, however, that when students can be penalized for low test scores, as is the case for "high-stakes" assessment—the gateway to promotion or graduation—a more liberal allowance of accommodations or modifications should be made. Examples of reasonable modifications and accommodations for assessment are presented in the nearby Rights & Responsibilities feature.

When teachers are developing classroom accommodations/modifications, they should remember the wide range of behaviors identified earlier that might characterize individuals with learning disabilities. The heterogeneity in this population is sometimes baffling. No child with a learning disability is going to be exactly like any other, so teachers must provide a wide range of accommodations/modifications as they differentiate to meet individual needs. In the following sections, these are discussed for each of the areas described earlier: academic and language deficits, social-emotional problems, and other differences such as attention, memory, cognition, metacognition, perception, and motor skills.

Academic and Language Deficits

Recall that students with LD may manifest deficits in the academic areas of reading skill, reading fluency, reading comprehension, math calculation, math applications, listening, speaking, and written language. While differentiation techniques in these academic areas are found throughout this text, the following are uniquely generated by a real expert—a high-

TABLE 5.3

Nine Types of Modifications

TYPE OF MODIFICATION	DESCRIPTION	EXAMPLES
Size	Change the amount or number of items the student is expected to learn or complete.	Have student complete the even-numbered problems in their math text. Have student learn 10 rather than 20 vocabulary terms.
Time	Change the amount of time allowed for learning; change amount of time for completing assignments or tests.	Give student extra week to complete science project. Give student 1½ hours instead of 1 hour to complete unit exam.
Input	Change the way instruction is presented.	Use cooperative learning. Use visual displays. Use computer-assisted instruction.
Output	Change the way students respond.	Allow student to say answers into a tape recorder rather than writing responses. Allow students to complete projects rather than take tests.
Difficulty	Change the skill level required for task completion.	Allow open-book test. Allow students to use spell-checker.
Participation	Allow for various levels of student involvement.	One student counts and distributes 20 manipulative devices to each student; other students use the devices to solve subtraction problems. One student writes report; another student draws accompanying illustrations.
Level of support	Change the amount of individual assistance.	Have paraeducator work one-to-one with student needing additional help with assignment. Arrange peer tutoring.
Alternative goals	Use same materials, but change the expected outcomes.	Given a diagram of the parts of the eye; one student labels the parts; others label the parts and their function. One student identifies the ingredients in a recipe; other students identify, measure, and mix the ingredients.
Substitute curriculum	Change the materials and instruction.	Some students read and discuss novel; some students participate in reading mastery lessons.

Source: From *Validated Practices for Teaching Students with Diverse Needs and Abilities* (p. 290), by S. P. Miller, 2002. Boston: Allyn & Bacon. Copyright © 2002 by Pearson Education. Reprinted by permission of the publisher.

school student with learning problems and ADHD and his teachers (Biddulph, Hess, & Humes, 2006):

- Provide copies of notes and overheads for students so they won't have to worry about getting all the information down, and they can pay attention and concentrate better.
- Read tests to students so they can process the information better by hearing it as they read it.

RIGHTS & RESPONSIBILITIES

EXAMPLES OF ACCOMMODATIONS AND MODIFICATIONS FOR ASSESSMENT

Timing/Scheduling
- Time of day
- Breaks during test
- Multiple test sessions
- Order of test administration
- Extend the time to complete the test
- Administer the test over several days

Setting
- Preferential seating (e.g., at the front of the room or in a study carrel)
- Small-group testing
- Individual testing (one-on-one)
- Special lighting
- Adaptive or special furniture
- Test administration in locations with minimal distractions
- Noise buffers
- Auditory trainers
- Hospital/home

Presentation
- Braille
- Large print
- Enlarging the answer sheet
- Reading directions to students
- Simplifying directions
- Interpreting/transliteration directions (e.g., sign language, cued speech)
- Written directions to accompany oral directions
- Clarifying directions
- Computer
- Increased spacing between items or (fewer?) items per page
- Reading test questions

- Interpreting/transliteration test items (e.g., sign language, cued speech)
- Audiotape version of test items
- Amplifying equipment
- Magnifying glass
- Templates
- Mask or markers to maintain place
- Highlight key word or phrases in directions
- Provide cues (e.g., arrows and stop signs) on answer form
- Secure papers to work areas with tape/magnets
- Short-segment testing booklets

Response Mode
- Student marks booklet
- Student responds verbally to scribe
- Student points to response
- Abacus
- Brailler
- Calculators
- Pencil grip
- Large diameter/special grip pencil
- Word processor/computer/typewriter
- Answer recorded on audiotape
- Augmentative or alternative communication devices
- Spell check
- Dictation to a scribe
- Use sign language
- Use template for recording

Source: From "State and Districtwide Assessments and Students With Learning Disabilities: A Guide for States and School Districts" (p. 75), by the National Joint Committee on Learning Disabilities, 2004, *Learning Disability Quarterly, 27,* pp. 67–76.

- Let a student sit close to the front of the class and not by a window. This helps the student focus on the important information and not be distracted by other students or things happening outside.
- Let a student sit with another student he or she is comfortable with and can ask for help.
- Provide a decreased amount of homework; for example, fewer math problems, or let the student have extra time to complete homework.
- Have math formulas posted for quick reference.
- Have books on tape available to help with focus and comprehension.
- Provide examples for how to complete homework.
- Make sure the student has everything needed to complete homework and understands the assignment.

- Have students use an organized binder with dividers and color-coding; have a different folder for each class.
- Let students take tests in a quiet place.
- Create study guides for tests (pp. 315–316).

For students with learning difficulties in writing, a word processor can be invaluable. It allows students to see their work in a more legible format and simplifies proofreading and revising, allowing students to focus more on developing content. The spell-checker and grammar-checker of many word-processing programs can encourage success in writing, and a talking word processor may provide valuable assistance for students who also have difficulty in reading. The following list describes recommended programs (Bryant & Bryant, 2008):

- *Write:OutLoud* has a speech-feedback component that highlights each word as it is "read" out loud to students as they write (Don Johnson, Inc.).
- *IntelliTalk II* is a talking word processor that adds a built-in scanner and has picture menus that make it easy to use (IntelliTools, Inc.).
- *Inspiration* is a tool that helps students develop visual aids such as concept maps as they brainstorm (Inspiration Software, Inc.).
- *Writing with Symbols 2000* is a symbol-supported writing and reading program that has over 8,000 pictures (Mayer-Johnson, Inc.).
- *Stanley's Sticker Stories* has a word-processing program with animated characters (Edmark, Inc.).

These and other types of technology can be critically important in facilitating success in inclusive settings for students with LD. Specific examples of technology used for students with LD are included in Table 5.4.

Individuals with LD are often deficient in choosing and carrying out the needed strategies, and they do not automatically generalize previously learned information to new challenges.

Students and adults with LD in the area of reading are also eligible to apply for services from Reading for the Blind and Dyslexic. Requests for a catalog of services and application forms can be made by calling 800-221-4792. The forms require verification of the disability by a professional in disability services. This agency will provide a cassette tape of any book requested. The tapes are available at no cost; however, there may be a one-time charge for the special equipment needed to play the tapes. Taped trade books and textbooks would be an excellent adaptation for Emmanuel, the child featured in the chapter opening vignette, as his reading skills improve to allow him to be successful with printed material on his grade level. Other adaptations appropriate for Emmanuel are identified in Tips for Adapting a Lesson.

Social-Emotional Problems

As discussed earlier, the social and emotional problems of individuals with LD can be closely tied to academic failure. Many of the academic modifications already described will encourage success in the classroom, which ultimately leads to a better self-concept, increased emotional stability, and greater confidence in approaching new academic tasks. A student who has deficits in social skills may need previously described training. However, some accommodations will still be needed even as the training begins to show results. Students may need to work in an isolated setting in the classroom during particularly challenging times. Distractions caused by peers can interfere with meeting academic challenges successfully. However, if teachers encourage the student with LD to sit in a segregated portion of the room all the time, it sends a bad message to others. Including students with disabilities in group activities, such as cooperative learning, provides them with models of appropriate interactions and authentic opportunities to practice social skills. Identify the students in the classroom who seem to work best with individuals with a learning disability, and give them more opportunities to interact. When conflicts arise, provide good modeling for the student by verbalizing the bad choices that were made and the good choices that could have been made.

TABLE 5.4

Examples of Technology for Students with Learning Disabilities

	NO-TECH	LOW-TECH	HIGH-TECH
Writing	Dictionary	Slant board	Word processor
		Keyguard	Word prediction software
		Alternate keyboard	Voice recognition software (computer software programs that recognize your voice)
		Electronic spell-checker without auditory output	
		Electronic spell-checker with auditory output	Talking word processor
		Tape recorders for note taking	Multimedia software for expression of ideas
		Pencil grip	Laptop computer
		Rubber stamp	Abbreviation expansion programs (macros)
		Adapter paper (bold line, raised line, different spacing)	Semantic organizers
Reading		Changes in text size	Optical character recognition (OCR) software/speech synthesizer (using a scanner, takes written text and turns it into spoken language via speech synthesizer)
		Changes in spacing	
		Changes in background color	
		Reading pen	
		Reading window	Electric books
			Screen readers
			Books on tape
Math	Graph paper	Modified paper (enlarged, raised line)	Software with template for math computation
	Calculation chart	Calculator	Handheld talking calculator
	Turn paper sideways	MathLine	Electronic math worksheet
		Talking watches	
		Calculator on computer	
Studying/ Organizing	Aids for organizing materials (color-coded folders, index tabs)	Appointment book	Software for organization of ideas
		Beeper/buzzer	Variable-speech-control tape recorders
	Highlight text with markers or highlight tape	Graphic organizer worksheets	Electronic organizer (e.g., Palm Pilot)
	Index cards		
Listening		Pressure-sensitive paper for user to tear off copies of notes to share with a student who has difficulty listening and taking notes	FM amplification device
			Laptop computer for note taking
			Compact word processor for note taking
			Variable-speech-control tape recorder

Source: From *Learning Disabilities: Foundations, Characteristics, and Effective Teaching* (p. 253), by D. P. Hallahan, et al., 2005. Boston: Allyn & Bacon.

TIPS FOR ADAPTING A LESSON FOR EMMANUEL

Since Emmanuel's primary deficits include reading, listening, and writing (as described in the chapter-opening vignette), the teacher's adaptations recommended here should limit the impact of these challenges during the time he is receiving intense instruction to develop new skills.

Emmanuel's teacher should

- pair him with a peer helper or provide taped material to assist in reading difficult material.

- provide many opportunities to practice reading and writing for pleasure.

- develop cooperative learning groups and use group grades for projects in content subjects.

- allow extra time or require less work when reading or writing is involved.

- read tests or find alternative methods for assessment of knowledge other than reading questions and writing responses.

- have Emmanuel repeat oral directions to ensure understanding.

- provide lecture notes or copies of overheads.

- when grading Emmanuel's written work, limit points taken off to one skill at a time (e.g., punctuation, spelling, grammar).

- when grading spelling, give credit for all correct letters in a word.

- allow Emmanuel to be a peer tutor in a lower grade to reinforce reading skills and build self-concept.

Because many of these individuals have difficulty responding appropriately to verbal and nonverbal cues, teachers should avoid sarcasm and use simple concrete language when giving directions and when teaching. If the student has difficulty accepting new tasks without complaint, consider providing a written assignment that the student can refer to for directions. When a student frequently upsets or irritates others in the classroom, teachers might agree on a contract to reduce the inappropriate behavior and reinforce positive peer interaction. Rules for the classroom should be reviewed periodically and posted for quick reference. To assist students who have difficulty making and keeping friends, teachers can subtly point out the strengths of the individual with the learning disability to encourage the other students to want to be his or her friend. Allowing the student to demonstrate his or her expertise in an area or to share a hobby may stimulate conversations that can eventually lead to friendships.

Because many of these students cannot predict the consequences of negative behavior, teachers need to explicitly explain the consequences of rule breaking and other inappropriate behavior. Although teachers can implement many behavior management techniques to reinforce positive behavior, it is important to train the student in methods of self-monitoring and self-regulation. The ultimate goal is for the student to be able to identify socially inappropriate behavior and get back on track.

Cognitive Differences

Cognitive problems include deficits in attention, perception, motor abilities, problem solving, and metacognition. To help individuals with difficulties or preferences in the area of auditory perception, it is most effective to present information visually through the overhead projector, and provide reading material, videos, and graphics to support oral information. Other individuals will respond better by hearing the information in addition to seeing it. Teachers can accommodate these individual differences by identifying the preferred style of learning and either providing instruction and directions in the preferred style or teaching in a multisensory fashion that stimulates both auditory and visual perception. Combining seeing, saying, writing, and doing provides multiple opportunities for presenting new information. It also helps children remember important information.

Difficulties in the area of motor abilities might be manifested as poor handwriting skills or difficulty with other fine-motor activities. Modifications might include overlooking the difficulties in handwriting and providing a grade based not on the appearance of the handwriting but on the content of the material. Students can also provide other evidence of their learning, such as oral reports or special projects. They can be allowed to select physical fitness activities that focus on their areas of strength rather than on their deficits.

PERSONAL SPOTLIGHT

BRITTANY NOTTENKAMPER is currently a junior at the University of Arkansas. She has been diagnosed as having dyslexia, learning disabilities, ADHD, and seizures. Brittany had a major seizure when she was two years old; however, she was not diagnosed with a seizure disorder until she was seven. Prior to her diagnosis it was thought that she had suffered a stroke. In kindergarten, Brittany began falling behind her peers. Her kindergarten teacher wanted to retain her for another year but her parents, partly on information from a physician that Brittany would likely catch up, did not agree and she was promoted to first grade. In first grade Brittany received speech therapy services. She was identified as having a learning disability in the second grade. Throughout her elementary grades Brittany received indirect special education services, speech therapy, and physical therapy for motor skill deficits. Her elementary teachers frequently modified activities for her, including reading her tests and giving her additional time.

When Brittany entered junior high school she began taking her tests in the special education classroom where she was granted extended time and tests were read to her. However, other than accommodations provided in her regular classes, Brittany did not receive any additional interventions. The same accommodations were provided for Brittany during high school.

She graduated with her peers and entered college majoring in child development. Because she did not have good ACT test scores, she was required to take remedial classes. During her sophomore year, Brittany tried out to be one of the three mascots for the University of Arkansas Razorback athletic teams. She was selected and was able to experience one of her childhood dreams—to be one of the Razorback mascots.

Brittany is on track to graduate next year with a degree in child development. She currently has a 3.4 gpa. The only accommodations she receives include extended time for tests, having her tests read orally, and having a note-taker. She attributes her success in school to hard work. Her vocational goal is to teach early childhood students with special needs. Brittany Nottenkamper is a success story. She is living proof that students with special needs can live their dreams and be very successful. A few support services, a good attitude about your disability, and hard work can lead to success.

"Being different is not always a bad thing. Everyone is unique and different in their own ways. Everyone has their own story, some are just too afraid to tell theirs."

Students with difficulties in cognitive problem-solving skills require careful direction and programming. Their deficits in reasoning skills make them especially prone to academic failures. The instructional strategies described earlier will help remedy problems in this area; also frequent practice and modeling of problem-solving strategies will strengthen developing skills.

Students with problems in the area of metacognition need to keep an assignment notebook or a monthly calendar to project the time needed to complete tasks or to prepare for tests. Students should be taught to organize their notebooks and their desks so that they can retrieve materials efficiently. If students have difficulty following or developing a plan, teachers should assist them in setting long-range goals and breaking down those goals into realistic steps. Students should be prompted with questions such as, "What do you need to be able to do this?" Students should be helped to set clear time frames in which to accomplish each step. They should be assisted in prioritizing activities and assignments, and provided with models that they can refer to often. These are the abilities linked with successful adults.

Students should be encouraged to ask for help and to use self-checking methods to evaluate their work on an ongoing basis. Teachers should reinforce all signs of appropriate self-monitoring and self-regulation in the classroom. These behaviors will facilitate success after high school.

Hallahan and colleagues (2005) provide the following general teaching guidelines to address memory, learning, and motivation problems:

- Use advance organizers to help orient students before reading or listening to new information.
- Activate the students' prior knowledge or help them build a bridge from long-term memory to new information.

- Give continuous feedback and offer practice by repeating important information at intervals to promote frequent review.
- Think out loud for students, showing them your strategies for learning new information.
- Help students develop self-efficacy by explicitly communicating expectations.
- Use active learning techniques so students can use executive functioning and memory techniques to store and retrieve new information.

After identifying an appropriate educational plan for individuals with learning disabilities and determining the accommodations or modifications that should lead to a successful educational program, the next challenge is to be sure the parents, teachers, students in the general education classroom and the student with the learning disability understand the disability and the need for differentiation and or special education. Primarily, students should be made aware that all people are different and each person has his or her own relative strengths and challenges. Literature is often one effective method available to assist with this educational process. Prater, Dyches, and Johnstun (2006) recommend 30 books that portray characters with LD across the early and upper elementary as well as secondary age levels. Each book has been chosen for the quality of writing and illustration, reflection of best practice, and the accuracy of character portrayal.

SUMMARY

Basic Concepts about Learning Disabilities

- A learning disorder is a cognitive disorder of thinking and reasoning.
- The disorder is manifested as underachievement in areas of reading, math, expressive or receptive language, or written expression.
- The recommended process of determining eligibility is based on a student's lack of response to progressively more intense, scientific research-based teaching methods provided in the general education environment.
- The process of identification also includes determination that the primary cause of the lack of achievement is not primarily due to other conditions such as vision, hearing or motor problems or limited English skills.
- Identifying a child with LD at the preschool level is difficult.
- Students with LD account for almost half of students with disabilities and most spend at least 80% of their school day in the general education classroom.
- Cultural and linguistic differences need to be taken into account when any assessment of a student's skills occurs so that the student is not mistakenly referred to a special education setting.
- LD may be caused by genetic factors or events occurring before, during, or after birth.

Characteristics of Students with Learning Disabilities

- Learning disabilities are most often identified in the academic areas of reading skills, reading fluency, reading comprehension, math calculations and/or math reasoning.
- Learning disorders in language can be found in listening or speaking.
- Other common characteristics of LD include social-emotional problems and difficulties with attention and hyperactivity, memory, cognition, metacognition, and motor skills.

Effective Inclusive Practices

- Teaching strategies for preschool children with LD include developmental, cognitive, and behavioral models.
- Interventions for elementary school children with LD address academic and language deficits, social-emotional problems, and cognitive and metacognitive problems.

- Secondary school students with LD continue to need remediation of basic skills, but they also benefit from strategies that will make them more efficient learners, and connecting the content areas to life skills.
- Successful adults with LD are goal-directed, work hard to accomplish their goals, understand and accept their strengths and limitations, are advocates for themselves, and accept appropriate support.

Classroom Adaptations

- Differentiated instruction and assessment can provide the needed modifications and/or accommodations to address the academic, language, social-emotional, and cognitive differences of students with LD.
- The role of the classroom teacher includes not only using scientific research-based teaching strategies with differentiation to address the challenges of students with LD but also helping individuals with LD and their peers, teachers and family members understand and celebrate these differences.

PEARSON
myeducationlab)

The MyEducationLab for this course can help you solidify your comprehension of Chapter 5 concepts.

- Gauge and further develop your understanding of chapter concepts by taking the quizzes and examining the enrichment materials on the Chapter 5 Study Plan.
- Visit Topic 14, Learning Disabilities/Attention Deficit Hyperactivity Disorder, to:
  - Connect with challenge-based interactive modules, case study units, and podcasts that provide research-validated information about working with students in inclusive settings by visiting the IRIS Center Resources
  - Explore Assignments and Activities, assignable exercises showing concepts in action through video, cases, and student and teacher artifacts
  - Practice and strengthen skills essential to quality teaching through the Building Teaching Skills and Dispositions lessons

6

Teaching Students with Emotional and Behavioral Disorders

After reading this chapter, you should be able to:

1. Describe the basic concepts about emotional and behavioral disorders.
2. Describe the characteristics of children and youth with emotional and behavioral disorders.
3. Identify effective inclusive practices for students with EBD.
4. Discuss the role of teachers in making classroom adaptations for students with EBD in general education classrooms.

ANTHONY is a 7-year-old first-grader who is often in trouble. On the first day of school, he stole some crayons from one of his classmates. When confronted with the fact that the crayons belonged to another student, Anthony adamantly denied stealing them. His behavior became increasingly more difficult during the first 6 months of the school year.

Ms. Chu, Anthony's teacher, uses a classroom management system that rewards students with checkmarks for appropriate behaviors. Students can redeem their checkmarks at the end of each week for various toys. Anthony has never earned enough checkmarks to get a toy. Now he openly states that he doesn't care if he ever receives any checkmarks.

Anthony's primary difficulty is his inability to leave his classmates alone. He is frequently pinching, pulling hair, or taking things from other students. Ms. Chu has separated his desk from the other students in an attempt to prevent him from bothering them. Still, Anthony manages to create disturbances regularly. Ms. Chu has sent him to the principal's office on numerous occasions. Each time he returns, his behavior improves, but only for several hours. Anthony's schoolwork suffers as a result of his behavior problems. While many of his classmates are reading and writing their names, he still has difficulties associating sounds with letters and can print his name only in a rudimentary fashion.

The teacher has had four parent conferences regarding Anthony. His mother indicates that she does not know what to do with him. Ms. Chu and Anthony's mother are both concerned that his behavior will get worse unless some solution is found. They are currently discussing whether to retain him in first grade and/or refer him for further assessments and possible special education eligibility.

QUESTIONS TO CONSIDER

1. Why did the behavior management system used by Ms. Chu not work with Anthony?
2. What positive behavior support strategies can Ms. Chu use that might result in an improvement in Anthony's behavior?
3. What other preventative strategies should be considered?
4. How would it potentially help or hurt Anthony if he were labeled as EBD?

Visit the MyEducationLab for this course to enhance your understanding of chapter concepts with a personalized Study Plan. You'll also have the opportunity to hone your teaching skills through video-based Assignments and Activities, IRIS Center Resources, and Building Teaching Skills and Disposition lessons.

BASIC CONCEPTS ABOUT EMOTIONAL AND BEHAVIORAL DISORDERS

Students with emotional and behavioral disorders (EBD) present a tremendously variant picture in terms of their characteristics and educational needs. Perhaps the only consistent finding among this group of students in educational settings is the fact that they are experiencing significant difficulties in adjusting to one or more important aspects of the school environment. Landrum, Tankersley, and Kauffman (2006) cautioned about this heterogeneity of students with EBD in general, but did conclude that the following generalizations have merit in describing this group of students: higher rates of inappropriate behavior in conjunction with lower rates of positive inappropriate behavior, academic difficulties that are related to and potentially caused by their behavioral difficulties, and social difficulties in terms of relationships with adults and peers.

Wagner and colleagues (2005) noted from their research: "Children and youth with ED are a group that has serious, multiple, and complex problems. Parents report that a wide range of disabilities affect their children, including anxiety, bi-polar disorder, depression, oppositional behavior, and psychosis. Almost two-thirds of the students were reported to have ADHD, and one-fourth were reported to have a learning disability in addition to ED" (p. 91). This chapter addresses these challenges and provides recommendations for successfully educating students with EBD. In doing so, it may unfortunately present a picture of both behavioral excesses and skill deficits. However, teachers must be committed instead to building strategies—behaviors and skills that will enable individual students to be successful in school and beyond.

Students who experience emotional and behavioral disorders receive a variety of labels. The federal government historically has identified this group as **seriously emotionally disturbed (SED)**, and later as emotionally disturbed, under IDEA. Whereas SED is the category used in most states, others classify this group of children as having behavioral disorders. The most widely accepted term by professionals in the field is **emotional and behavioral disorders (EBD)** because this term better describes the students who receive special education services. As a result, EBD is the term that is used throughout this chapter.

Definition, Identification and Eligibility

For students with EBD to be identified accurately, and appropriately served in educational programs, a critical prerequisite is an acceptable definition. The challenges of developing an acceptable definition for emotional/behavioral disorders have been discussed frequently. There are a number of difficulties with the development of an appropriate definition for emotional and behavioral disorders. Kauffman and Landrum (2009a) highlighted these difficulties by noting that the problems derived from different conceptual models for understanding the nature of emotional and behavioral disorders; different purposes of definitions based on, for example, the setting to which they are being applied (e.g., public schools, the legal system, community agencies); the difficulties related to the measurement of behavior and emotions; the range and variability of normal behavior and its relationship with deviant behavior; and the possible transient nature of some emotional and behavioral problems.

The definition used by the federal government for its category of emotionally disturbed derives from the classic work of Bower (1969). It remains only moderately changed since Bower originally developed the definition four decades ago; the only significant differences between his original and the current federal definition are highlighted in the following exerpt in italics (Kauffman & Landrum, 2009a, p. 18):

(i) The term means a condition exhibiting one or more of the following characteristics over a long period of time and to a marked extent, *which adversely affects educational performance:*

  (A) An inability to learn which cannot be explained by intellectual, sensory, or health factors;

  (B) An inability to build or maintain satisfactory relationships with peers and teachers;

  (C) Inappropriate types of behavior or feelings under normal circumstances;

  (D) A general pervasive mood of unhappiness or depression; or

  (E) A tendency to develop physical symptoms or fears associated with personal or school problems.

    (i) *The term includes children who are schizophrenic. The term does not include children who are socially maladjusted unless it is determined that they are seriously emotionally disturbed. (Federal Register,* 1999, p. 12422)

Although the Bower federal definition has been used by most states and most local educational agencies (e.g., Cullinan & Sabornie, 2004), it is vague and subjective (Shepherd,

2010), and may leave the reader wondering just what a child with emotional disturbance is like. When this definition is interpreted broadly, many more children could be served than when it is interpreted narrowly. As evidenced by the underserved nature of this disability category, most states and local school districts interpret the definition narrowly and serve far fewer children in the category than prevalence data would project as needing services.

Given the problems that are inherent in the federal definition, a number of efforts have been undertaken to develop a new definition. However, currently, no other definition has received widespread support and consequently the federal definition currently remains the applicable one for educators (Kauffman & Landrum, 2009a).

According to the Bower federal definition, there are five key eligibility characteristics: inability to learn, relationship problems, inappropriate behavior, unhappiness or depression, and physical symptoms or fears. Cullinan and Sabornie (2004) investigated these five characteristics to confirm whether students with EBD in middle- and high-school settings could be differentiated from their peers across these characteristics. Overall, their data confirmed that these adolescents who are identified as having EBD did, in fact, exceed the scores of their peers who were not disabled on measures for each of the five respective characteristics.

Most agencies, other than schools, that provide services to children and adolescents with emotional problems use the definition and classification system found in the *Diagnostic and Statistical Manual of Mental Disorders* (DSM-IV-TR) (American Psychiatric Association, 2000). With multiple definitions in use, some children may be considered disabled according to one system but not according to the other.

Students with EBD are evaluated for several purposes, including identification, assessment to determine appropriate intervention strategies, and determination of eligibility for special services. The first step is for students to be identified as potentially having emotional and behavioral problems. Teachers' awareness of the characteristics of students with these problems is critical in the identification process. Behavioral checklists can be used to identify students for possible referral for assessment.

Shepherd (2010) stressed this key role of the classroom teacher within the context of clinical judgment in identifying students with EBD:

> If a teacher suspects that a student has an emotional and behavior disorder, the teacher needs to follow the assessment process prescribed by IDEA for identifying a child with a disability. . . . This process not only provides a method for identifying students . . . , but also provides assistance for the teacher who has the student in his or her classroom. Thus, the teacher does not stand alone in his or her efforts to educate students with emotional and behavior disorders.
>
> However, the role of the teacher in identifying students with emotional and behavioral disorders cannot be underestimated. Teachers are often the first to suspect that students may have disabilities, and they are also the first ones to initiate the process that may provide needed services for their students. When they understand the nature and characteristics of (EBD) . . . , teachers can provide the intervention and strategies that allow students . . . to be successful in school. (p. 20)

Once students are identified as possibly having problems, they are referred for formal assessment to determine their eligibility for special education programs and to ascertain appropriate intervention strategies. Kaplan (1996) lists clinical interviews, observations, rating scales, personality tests, and neurological examinations as methods for obtaining relevant information. Figure 6.1 summarizes these procedures.

One approach to the assessment of students with emotional and behavioral disorders is through the use of **strength-based assessment**. Unlike widely used deficit-oriented assessment models, strength-based assessment is based on the following principles:

1. All children have strengths.
2. Assessing a child's strengths in addition to his or her deficits may result in enhanced motivation and improved performance from the child.
3. Deficits should be viewed as opportunities to learn rather than as fixed or stable.
4. Families and children are more likely to positively engage in treatment when service plans include a focus on strengths (Harniss & Epstein, 2005, p. 126).

FIGURE 6.1	Assessment Procedures for Students with Emotional and Behavioral Disorders

Clinical Interview
- The interview is the most common tool for assessment.
- Questions are directed to the child and others regarding behaviors and relevant relationships.
- Some questions are planned; some are developed as the interview progresses.
- The interview can be highly structured, using questions generated from DSM-IV-TR criteria.

Observation
- The observation can be structured with time limitations, or unstructured.
- Observations should occur in a variety of settings and at different times.

Rating Scales
- A rating scale contains a listing of behaviors to note.
- It provides for much more structure than observation.
- It ensures that certain behaviors are observed or asked about.

Personality Tests
- The two kinds of tests include self-completed inventories and projective tests.
- Both kinds can provide insightful information.
- Interpretation is subjective and needs to be done by a trained professional.

Source: Adapted from *Pathways for Exceptional Children: School, Home, and Culture,* by P. Kaplan, 1996. St. Paul, MN: West Publishing.

Given the difficulties of assessing students with emotional and behavioral problems, the use of strength-based assessments is promising in terms of their contributions to understanding the nature and needs of students with EBD. Uhing, Mooney, and Ryser (2005) reported on their studies using the Behavioral and Emotional Rating Scale, second edition (BERS-2) (Epstein, 2004). They confirmed that this scale was effective for distinguishing between students with and without emotional and behavioral disorders. They also indicated support for the use of this instrument in providing further information about students with EBD to assist in the development of educational programs.

Functional Behavioral Assessment

One important approach to assessment warrants separate consideration because of its clear implications for intervention efforts. Functional behavioral assessment (FBA) provides a consideration of specific behaviors and behavioral patterns set within an environmental context. It has been defined as "an analysis of the contingencies responsible for behavioral problems" (Malott, Whaley, & Malott, 1997, p. 433).

An FBA is a "systematic procedure . . . [to explain] why a behavior occurs by analyzing the behavior and generating hypotheses about its purpose or intended function. Ultimately, these hypotheses should assist school personnel in identifying interventions that change the student's undesirable behavior" (McConnell, Patton, & Polloway, 2006, p. viii). A sample form for analyzing behavior is presented in Figure 6.2.

When determining appropriate intervention strategies, FBA provides extensive information for teachers. A functional assessment helps teachers better understand disruptive behaviors; improved understanding can lead to an insightful intervention approach.

Classification

Children with EBD constitute a heterogeneous population. Professionals typically have subcategorized the group into smaller, more homogeneous subgroups so that these students can be better understood and served. Several different classification systems are used to group individuals with EBD.

FIGURE 6.2   Functional Behavioral Assessment: Analysis of Behavior

Student: _____

Analysis of Behavior
Prioritized Behavior #

Antecedents (Events or conditions occurring before or triggering the behavior)	Behavior (Exactly what the student does or does not do)	Consequences (Actions or events occurring after the behavior)	Function of Behavior (Hypothesized purpose of the behavior)
Setting, subject, or class:	Behavior in observable, measurable terms:	Behavior in ignored Planned Unplanned	Avoidance or escape Avoid a directive or request Avoid an assignment Escape a situation or a person
Time of day:		Peer attention	
Person(s):	Baseline measures of behavior Frequency of behavior:	Adult attention Reminder(s) Repeated directive or request	Attention Gain peer attention Gain adult attention
Interruption in routine:	per	Private meeting or conference Reprimand or warning	Self-control issue Express frustration Express anger Vengeance Power or control
Directive or request to:	Duration of behavior: per incident	Change in directive or request	Intimidation
Consequences imposed:		Loss of privilege:	Sensory or emotional reaction Fear or anxiety Sensory relief or stimulation
Lack of social attention:	intensity of behavior:	Time out in classroom	
Difficulty or frustration:		Administrative consequences:	Other(s):
Other(s):		Parent contact	
		Other(s):	

Source: From *Behavioral Intervention Planning (BIP-III)* (3rd ed.) by K. McConnell, J. R. Patton, and E. A. Polloway, 2006. Austin, TX: Pro-Ed.

One classification system that focuses on clinical elements is detailed in DSM-IV-TR (American Psychiatric Association, 2000), which is widely used by medical and psychological professionals, though less frequently by educators. The manual categorizes emotional and behavioral problems according to several subtypes, such as developmental disorders, organic mental disorders, and schizophrenia. Educators need to be aware of this classification system because of the need to interact with professionals from the mental health field. Figure 6.3 lists the major types of disorders according to this system.

FIGURE 6.3	Major Components of the DSM-IV-TR Classification System

Organic mental syndromes and disorders
Psychoactive substance-use disorders
Schizophrenia
Delusional disorders
Psychotic disorders not elsewhere classified
Mood disorders
Anxiety disorders
Somatoform disorders
Dissociative disorders
	Sexual disorders
	Sleep disorders
	Factitious disorders
	Impulse control disorders not elsewhere
	  classified
	Adjustment disorders
	Psychological factors affecting physical
	  condition
	Personality disorders

Source: Adapted from American Psychiatric Association (2000). *Diagnostic and Statistical Manual of Mental Disorders* (4th ed.). Washington, DC: American Psychiatric Publishing.

A second classification system was developed by Quay and Peterson (1987) who described six major subgroups of children with EBD as follows:

1. Individuals are classified as having a **conduct disorder** if they seek attention, are disruptive, and act out. This category includes behaving aggressively toward others.
2. Students who exhibit **socialized aggression** are likely to join a group of peers who are openly disrespectful to their peers, teachers, and parents. Delinquency and truancy are common among this group.
3. Individuals with **attention problems-immaturity** can be characterized as having attention deficits, being easily distractible, and having poor concentration. Many students in this group are impulsive and may act without thinking about the consequences.
4. Students classified in the **anxiety/withdrawal** group are self-conscious, reticent, and unsure of themselves. Their self-concepts are generally very low, causing them to retreat from immediate activities. They are also anxious and frequently depressed.
5. The subgroup of students who display **psychotic behavior** may hallucinate, deal in a fantasy world, and exhibit bizarre behavior.
6. Students with motor excess are **hyperactive**. They have difficulties sitting still, listening to other individuals, and keeping their attention focused.

Classification becomes less important when school personnel use a functional behavioral assessment and intervention model. As noted earlier, this approach primarily emphasizes determining which environmental stimuli influence inappropriate behaviors. Once these stimuli are identified and altered, the inappropriate behaviors may decrease or disappear (McConnell, Patton, & Polloway, 2006). In such instances, the process of clinically classifying a student's problem becomes less relevant to the design of educational programs.

Manifestation of the Disability

A key issue in the field of EBD is the relationship between the disability itself and the behaviors that are exhibited in school. Under IDEA guidelines, educators must determine whether the behavior in question functions as a **manifestation of the student's disability**. The key questions, as outlined in IDEA 2004, are whether the behavior was caused by, or had a direct and substantial relationship to, the child's disability; or if the behavior was the direct result of the school's failure to implement the IEP. The function of the guidelines is not to prevent educators from taking action to redirect troublesome behavior. Rather, the purpose is to prevent the misapplication of disciplinary actions that, owing to the student's particular disability, may fail to achieve the desired objective and create needless frustration for everyone involved (McConnell et al., 2006). To complete a manifestation determination for students with EBD (as well as for other disabilities), school personnel should

RIGHTS & RESPONSIBILITIES

MANIFESTATION DETERMINATION MODEL

Manifestation determination is a required element for considering the context of behaviors as related to an individual's disability. These considerations are particularly important with regard to emotional and behavioral disorders. This model provides a way to view considerations for manifestation determination.

1. Does the student possess the requisite skills to engage in an appropriate alternative behavior? The team would break the behavior down into its subcomponents using task analysis, list the subcomponents on a checklist to note their presence or absence, and select a powerful reinforcer. The reinforcer is designed to motivate the student to use the targeted skills if they exist in his repertoire. If necessary, a relevant scenario would then be generated, and the student would be asked to role-play the skills for dealing with teasing appropriately in order to earn the reinforcer. . . .

2. Is the student able to analyze the problem, generate solutions, evaluate their effectiveness, and select one? . . . The evaluator would generate a scenario in which the aggressive behavior occurred. She would then determine how well the student could answer the following questions:
   - Can the student define the problem to be solved?
   - Can the student set realistic and concrete goals to solve the problem?

   - Can the student generate a wide range of possible alternative courses of action?
   - Can the student imagine and consider how others might respond if asked to deal with a similar problem?
   - Can the student evaluate the pros and cons of each proposed solution and rank order the solutions from least to most practical and desirable?

3. Does the student interpret the situation factually or distort it to fit some existing bias? . . . A cognitive distortion exists when a student does not factually interpret aspects of the situation. . . . In addition, an evaluator can interview a student to identify any discrepancies between the event and activated thoughts.

4. Can the student monitor the behavior? This deficit area is perhaps the most difficult to evaluate because the assessment and intervention techniques for this deficit area are identical. Namely, if we want to assess a student's skill at self-monitoring, we have him self-monitor. However, the process of self-monitoring results in reactivity—obtaining a positive change in the target behavior by virtue of the student observing and recording it.

Source: Adapted from "Manifestation Determination as a Golden Fleece," by A. Katsiyannis and J. W. Maag, 2001, *Exceptional Children, 68,* pp. 93–94.

carefully consider the disability and the nature of the behavior to determine a possible relationship. Zirkel (2009) noted that a manifestation determination under federal law requires that the review include a representative of the local education agency, the parent, and also other members of the IEP team who are relevant to the collaborations. Figure 6.4 presents a flowchart for manifestation determination developed by McConnell and colleagues (2006).

Katsiyannas and Maag (2001) developed a model for conceptualizing key questions to consider. The four issues they identified are summarized in Rights & Responsibilities.

Classroom teachers should be aware of the concept of manifestation of disability within the continuing debate about disciplinary procedures for students with disabilities, including those with EBD. The debate revolves around the issues of equity, discipline, school safety, and the legal rights of students with disabilities for a free and appropriate public education with accommodations designed to be consistent with students' individual needs.

Prevalence and Educational Environments

School Prevalence   Traditionally the categories of EBD, learning disabilities (LD), and intellectual disabilities (ID) have been referred to as high-incidence disabilities (Polloway, 2005). However, as compared to children classified as having LD, in particular, the category of EBD represents a much smaller number of children. In terms of prevalence, 0.92% of the school population (ages 6 to 17) was served as EBD according to the U.S. Department of Education (USDOE, 2009).

FIGURE 6.4

Manifestation determination flowchart.

Is a placement change to an IAES, another setting, or suspension for **NOT MORE than 10 school days** being considered?

YES

If this alternative is applied to other students without disabilities for the same violation, then the student may be removed and **no Manifestation Determination is needed.**

Is a placement change to an IAES, another setting, or suspension for **MORE than 10 school days** being considered?

Is a placement change to an IEAS, another setting, or suspension that is part of a **series of removals totaling more than 10 school days and constituting a pattern** being considered?

YES

Conduct a Manifestation Determination

If the decision is made to remove the student for more than 10 school days, within 10 school days of that decision the school district, parents, and relevant IEP team members shall review all relevant information, including the following:

- The IEP
- Teacher observations
- Relevant information provided by parents

The purpose of the review is to determine if either of the following instances applies. If *either* of these two applies, the behavior is a manifestation of the disability.

1. The conduct was *caused by, or had a direct and substantial relationship to* the student's disability.
2. The conduct was a *direct result of the Local Education Agency's (school district's) failure to implement the IEP.*

Is the behavior a manifestation of the disability?

YES

NO

If the behavior is a manifestation of the disability, the student must

1. continue to receive educational services enabling progress toward IEP goals and participation in the general education curriculum; and
2. if appropriate, receive
   - a functional behavioral assessment (FBA), and
   - behavioral intervention services and modifications (BIP and modifications).

In addition, the IEP team shall

1. conduct a functional behavioral assessment, if there is not one in place;
2. implement a BIP or review a previous plan for modification; and
3. return the student to his or her previous placement, unless parents and school district agree to a change in placement as part of a modified BIP or if the violation involved weapons, drugs, or infliction of serious bodily injury.*

If the behavior is not a manifestation of the disability, you may apply the same disciplinary action applicable to students without disabilities, in the same manner, and for the same duration. This *does* include placement to an IEAS.

The student must

1. continue to receive educational services enabling progress toward IEP goals and participation in the general education curriculum; and,
2. if appropriate, receive
   - a functional behavioral assessment (FBA), and
   - behavioral intervention services and modifications (BIP and modifications).

Source: From *Behavioral Intervention Planning (BIP-III)* (3rd ed.), by K. McConnell, J. R. Patton, and E. A. Polloway, 2006. Austin, TX: Pro-Ed.

Because of the difficulty in defining and identifying emotional and behavioral disorders, the range of estimates of the prevalence of the disorder has been significant. The overall federal figure of 0.92% reflects the number of students ages 6 to 17 being served under this category. This national average masks significant state variance, ranging from 3.01% in the District of Columbia to 0.15% in Arkansas. While approximately 1% of students are identified as having emotional and behavioral disorders, it is commonly estimated that from 2 to 4% of the school population would meet eligibility criteria based on their characteristics and, further, that up to 16% of the school population exhibit behaviors that are associated with EBD. In addition, the U.S. Department of Health and Human Services estimates that over 20% of all children and adolescents between the ages of 9 and 17 have a diagnosable mental illness or a form of addictive disorder that might result in at least a minimum level of impairment (Mihalas, Morse, Allsop, & McHatton, 2009). Most relevant to our consideration here, Kauffman and Landrum (2009a) concluded that a reasonable estimate of the prevalence of emotional and behavioral disorders would be approximately 3 to 6% of the overall student population.

Prevalence can also be considered in the context of age and level of schooling. For example, data reflect a gradually increasing occurrence of EBD through the elementary grades as follows: 0.06% for kindergarten, 0.14% for first grade, 0.33% for third grade, and 0.73% for fifth grade (USDOE, 2009). On the other hand, only 10% of the students who are labeled and found eligible for EBD during elementary grades (ages 6 to 12) are subsequently declassified during high school (USDOE, 2009).

The specific prevalence figure depends on the definition used and the interpretation of the definition by individuals who classify students. However, the clear consensus is that EBD is clearly under-identified in the schools (Kauffman & Landrum, 2009b) and is the most underserved category of disability—far more students are in need of special education and supports than the currently identify "less than 1%."

It is also noteworthy to consider the occurrence of emotional behavioral disorders by placing EBD in the context of possible multiple disabilities. In instances when EBD was deemed the primary cause of disability, 37% had one additional disability (e.g., learning disabilities), while 26% had two or three additional disabilities (USDOE, 2009).

Demographic Data   Among students classified as having EBD, the clear majority are males (Reid et al., 2004). While gender variance is common in disability categories, it is most pronounced in the EBD area. Some studies have revealed that as many as 10 times more boys than girls are found in programs for students with behavioral disorders (e.g., Rosenberg, Wilson, Maheady, & Sindelar, 1992). Wagner and colleagues (2005; Newman, Wagner, Cameto, & Knokey, 2009) reported that estimates range as high as 80% male for this population; their own study confirmed this trend. Federal data indicate that 77% of students in EBD programs are male (USDOE, 2007).

A second demographic focus is the ethnicity of students who have EBD. The percentage of students with EBD who have a particular ethnic background is as follows (percentages for the overall U.S. resident population are in parentheses): Native American/Native Alaskan, 1.5% (0.98%); Asian/Pacific Islander, 1.8% (4.1%); African American, 28.4% (15.1%); Hispanic, 10.6% (17.7%); and European American, 58.3% (62.2%) (USDOE, 2009). The key area of disproportionality is African American students, who are almost twice as likely to be identified as EBD as might be predicted. Kauffman and Landrum (2009b) analyzed this pattern and posited that this disproportionality did not reflect evidence of bias, misidentification, or unreasonably high rates.

Third, several other demographic considerations are relevant in considering the population of individuals with EBD. The USDOE (2007), basing its data on parent interviews as part of the NLTS studies, noted the following data for students with EBD (general student population in parentheses): living in poverty: 30% (20%); in a two-parent household: 49% (74%); and living in a household where the head of household has a high school education or less: 60% (47%).

Educational Environment   Students with EBD are commonly included in general education classrooms, albeit to a lesser extent than students with other types of disabilities (e.g.,

IEP GOALS AND OBJECTIVES FOR ANTHONY*

The following IEP goals and objectives are consistent with the chapter-opening vignette of Anthony if he were subsequently identified as having EBD and found eligible for special education.

GOAL 1   Anthony will interact appropriately with peers in the classroom.

Objective 1: In classroom settings, Anthony will ask permission to borrow or use items from classmates 90% of the time.

Objective 2: In classroom settings, Anthony will engage in disruptions of peers no more than three times per day.

Objective 3: In classroom settings, Anthony will participate in group projects with peers without disruptions, independent of teacher monitoring of his behavior, 70 percent of the time.

GOAL 2   Anthony will complete the in-class and homework assignments successfully.

Objective 1: Given an in-class assignment, Anthony will work independently for a minimum of 15 minutes with one or no disruptions 80% of the time.

Objective 2: Given homework assignments for one week, Anthony will complete 75% of assignments on time.

Objective 3: Given in-class assignments, Anthony will complete 80% of them within the appropriate time frame.

GOAL 3   Anthony will demonstrate the ability to make sound-symbol correspondences for vowels and consonant sounds.

Objective 1: Given a series of common consonants (i.e., b, d, f, l, m, n, p, r, s, t), Anthony will correctly identify the associated sounds with 80% accuracy.

Objective 2: Given a list of vowels, Anthony will correctly identify all short vowel sounds with 90% accuracy.

Objective 3: Given a set of vowels, Anthony will correctly identify all long vowel sounds with 90% accuracy.

*IDEA 2004 does not require short-term objectives (STOs) except for students taking alternative assessments. However, they are included here both to illustrate learning benchmarks for teachers, and because many school discussions continue to use STOs.

learning disabilities). According to the USDOE (2009), 32.4% of all students (ages 6 to 21) identified as emotionally disturbed were taught in the regular class setting (i.e., general education) at least 79% of the time. An additional 22% were served in these settings between 40 and 79% of the time. Combining these figures, we can conclude that approximately 54% of students identified as EBD will spend most of their time in general education-based programs. At the same time, 28.4% of students with EBD were in regular schools but out of the general education classroom at least 60% of the time. Many students also were educated in separate environments, including separate public (7.2%) or private (5.7%) day facilities, 3.1% in public or private residential facilities, and home or hospital environments (1.2%).

Causation and Risk Factors

Many factors can cause students to display EBD or can create risks for problems. Although risk factors cannot be adjudged to be causes in the typical way that causation is conceptualized, nevertheless, a consideration of risks provides a broad view of the issues that can exacerbate the functioning of students who are identified with EBD. Table 6.1 lists common risk factors across the domains of child, family, school, and culture. This information complements the demographic data presented earlier.

Kauffman and Landrum (2009a) discussed the possible causes and correlates of emotional and behavioral disorders as including factors within the biological, family, school, and

TABLE 6.1

Examples of Possible Risk Factors for Students with Emotional and Behavioral Disorders

CHILD	FAMILY	SCHOOL	CULTURAL
Biological factors (e.g., autism)	Maternal stress/ depression	Insufficient training	Low socioeconomic status
Difficult temperament	Large families	High student–teacher ratios	High-crime neighborhoods
Substance use	Divorce	Poor instruction	Negative peer relationships
Neuropsychological deficits (e.g., language deficits)	Antisocial parent/sibling	Maladaptive working conditions	Peer rejection
Antisocial	Ineffective behavior management	Poor behavior management	Cultural expectations
Academic deficits	Abuse	Inconsistent expectations	
Low intelligence	Harsh or coercive parenting	Little academic emphasis	

Source: From "Achievement and Emotional Disturbance: Academic Status and Intervention Research," by M. H. Epstein, J. R. Nelson, A. L. Trout, and P. Mooney, 2005, in *Outcomes for Children and Youth with Emotional and Behavioral Disorders and Their Families,* p. 454, edited by M. H. Epstein, K. Kutash, and A. Duchnowski, 2005. Austin, TX: Pro-Ed.

cultural domains, further stressing that these possible factors were likely to be interactive. It is clear that determining specific causes for emotional behavioral disorders is a complex task with no easy resolution. They noted that *biological causes* can include the possibility of genetic disorders, brain dysfunction or damage (such as traumatic brain injury), health-related issues, and possibly childhood temperament considerations (e.g., newborns' inborn tendency toward certain behavioral patterns).

The *family factors* that have been explored for possible causative impact include issues related to family definition and structure (e.g., single-parent families, substitute care) and family interaction patterns (e.g., management models used by parents, possible child abuse) (Kauffman & Landrum, 2009a).

When considering *school-related factors*, it is typically difficult to analyze whether school failure is the source of emotional and behavioral problems, or if the reverse is true. Table 6.2 **presents** a graphic model for considering the directionality of these possible causes. Kauffman and Landrum (2009a) noted that school-related factors could include the fact that students identified as having emotional and behavioral disorders generally have an overall lower IQ than students in general (average in the 90s), the common pattern of academic underachievement that frequently corresponds with behavior problems in school, the failure to acquire appropriate social skills, and the overall impact of school failure on adjustment. Further, these authors also noted that schools might contribute to problems by being insensitive to the individual needs of students, by setting inappropriate expectations, and by using instructional and management strategies that may exacerbate problems (e.g., inconsistent behavioral management).

An area that is often overlooked is school instability (Rothstein, 2006). This phenomenon of changing schools is particularly a concern with students with EBD because they experience more school environmental instability than other students. Wagner and colleagues (2005) summarized this issue as follows:

> They change schools more often than students in other disability groups and nondisabled peers, with one-third of the elementary/middle school students and two-thirds of the secondary students attending at least four different schools. Furthermore, an examination of the

---

TABLE 6.2

Co-Occurrence of Emotional Disorders and Academic Underachievement

MODEL	HYPOTHESIS	DIRECTIONALITY OF INFLUENCE
1	Poor grades—aggression	Poor grades → Aggression
2	Aggression—poor grades	Aggression → Poor grades
3	Reciprocal causation	Academic failure ↔ Emotional disorders
4	Spurious relationship	Underlying factors → Emotional disorders and academic failure

Source: From "Achievement and Emotional Disturbance: Academic Status and Intervention Research," by M. H. Epstein et al., 2005, in *Outcomes for Children and Youth with Emotional and Behavioral Disorders and Their Families*, p. 452, edited by M. H. Epstein, K. Kutash, and A. Duchnowski, 2005. Austin, TX: Pro-Ed.

---

most recent move indicates that the students with [emotional disturbances] are reassigned to new schools by their school district at a rate much higher than that of both their nondisabled peers and those in other disability groups. In addition, almost half of the elementary/middle school students and three-fourths of the secondary students have been suspended or expelled. These rates are more than four times that of peers in other disability categories and of students in the general population. (p. 92)

The fourth area identified by Kauffman and Landrum (2009a) is *cultural influences.* Particular areas of concern included the absence of peers who serve as positive models for children; undesirable socialization patterns with peers; the influence of neighborhoods, such as in urban areas; and the effects of poverty on child development and, ultimately, on learning and behavior.

Many students experience EBD because of the environmental factors that affect their lives. They are far more likely to come from backgrounds that are characterized as being economically disadvantaged. While this finding is not direct evidence of causation, the correlational data in this area suggest that people from lower socioeconomic backgrounds are at increased risk for having disorders. Wagner and colleagues (2005) elaborated on this point as follows:

Youth identified as [emotionally disturbed] tend to live in households in which there are multiple risk factors for poor life outcomes. Approximately one-third live below the poverty level and in households headed by a single parent, and one-fifth live in households in which the head of the house is unemployed and not a high school graduate. Further indication of potential stress . . . is the finding that almost half (45%) of these students are reported to live in a household with another person who has a disability. All of these differences between children and youth with [emotional disturbances] and both those with other disabilities and those in the general population are statistically significant and large, indicating that the children and youth with [emotional disturbances] are more likely to have each of these risk factors that are strongly associated with the poor life outcomes. (pp. 90–91)

CHARACTERISTICS OF STUDENTS WITH EMOTIONAL AND BEHAVIORAL DISORDERS

Students with emotional and behavioral problems exhibit a wide range of characteristics that differ in type as well as intensity. They typically engage in behaviors that are rated by teachers and parents as more challenging than those of students with learning disabilities and intellectual disabilities (Sabornie et al., 2005). Their behavior is frequently disruptive, often noncompliant, and may be aggressive or verbally abusive (Reid et al., 2004). Social skills deficits are commonly observed (see Figure 6.5). This wide range of behaviors and emotions reflects the broad variety of characteristics associated with individuals with emotional and

---

FIGURE 6.5 — Types of Social Skills

Interpersonal Behaviors: "Friendship-making skills," such as introducing oneself, asking a favor, offering to help, giving and accepting compliments, and apologizing.

Peer-Related Social Skills: Skills valued by classmates and associated with peer acceptance. Examples include working cooperatively and asking for and receiving information.

Teacher-Pleasing Social Skills: School success behaviors, including following directions, doing one's best work, and listening to the teacher.

Self-Related Behaviors: Skills that allow a child to assess a social situation, select an appropriate skill, and determine the skill's effectiveness. Other self-related behaviors include following through, dealing with stress, and understanding feelings.

Assertiveness Skills: Behaviors that allow children to express their needs without resorting to aggression.

Communication Skills: Listener responsiveness, turn taking, maintaining conversational attention, and giving the speaker feedback.

Source: From "Teaching Social Skills to Students with Learning and Behavioral Problems," by L. K. Elksnin and N. Elksnin, 1998, *Intervention in School and Clinic, 33,* p. 132.

---

behavioral problems. A common way to conceptualize EBD characteristics is to categorize them as externalizing or internalizing behaviors (see Table 6.3).

Table 6.4 provides an overview of a number of characteristics that can be associated with EBD. Included within the table also are the potential difficulties associated with these characteristics and a brief summary of their educational implications, along with representative strategies. Landrum, Tankersley, and Kauffman (2006) provided an excellent analysis of the characteristics of students with EBD linked with examples of effective practices. Their work provided a foundation for a number of the educational implications summarized in Table 6.4.

Academic Achievement

While the focus of research on the characteristics of students with EBD is often on social and behavioral concerns, academic problems are a key concern as well (Sabornie et al., 2005; Wagner et al., 2005). Mihalas and colleagues (2009) noted that "students with EBD fail more courses in school, are retained more frequently, are more likely to be absent from school, have lower grade point averages, drop out of school more frequently, and are less likely to graduate high school compared to students without EBD" (p. 109) and, it might

■ Depression is a characteristic of students with emotional and behavioral disorders.

TABLE 6.3

Externalizing and Internalizing Behaviors and Emotions

EXTERNALIZING	INTERNALIZING
• Aggression	• Withdrawal
• Tantrums	• Limited activity levels
• Defiance	• Fixated on certain thoughts
• Noncompliance with rules	• Avoidance of social situations
• Disobedience	• Anxiety
• Lying and stealing	• Depression
• Destructiveness	• Inappropriate crying
• Self-control difficulties	

TABLE 6.4

Emotional and Behavioral Disorders: Characteristics and Implications

AREA	POTENTIAL DIFFICULTIES	EDUCATIONAL IMPLICATIONS
Academic Achievement	Academic responding and engagement	Provide systematic and explicit instruction of academic skills
	Below average academically in reading, writing, and mathematics	Provide structured lessons with appropriate sequencing of tasks and pacing of instruction
	Lack of academic motivation	Involve students in active learning process (practice, apply, review)
	Difficulty with strategic learning (test taking, note taking).	Stress meaningful content
		Teach strategies for decoding unknown words
		Use learning strategies to promote effective studying, reading comprehension and math problem solving
		Increase academic engagement, time on-task
		Use daily/weekly monitoring to measure task success and skills acquisition
Aggression—Acting Out Behaviors	Noncompliance with classroom, school rules	Place efforts within the context of SWPBS (see p. 215)
	Classroom disruptions (talking out, out of seat)	Focus on building positive behaviors incompatible with class disruptions
		Use differential reinforcement strategies
	Fighting at school	Relate high-probability activities (e.g., preferred activities) with low-probability activities (e.g., work completion)
	Use of profanity in inappropriate settings	
		Provide clear and direct requests to students that are associated with consequences
		Consider use of timeout and response cost procedures if/as needed (see Chapter 15)
		Teach behavioral self-control
Attention	Attention to learning tasks	Train students to be aware of the importance of attention
	Span (length of time on task) and focus (inhibition of distracting stimuli)	Teach students to actively self-monitor their attention
Inadequate Peer Relationships, Social Skill Deficits	Inappropriate or unsatisfactory interactions with peers	Select specific target behaviors to teach and reinforce
	Social isolation	Use direct instruction of skills to be acquired
	Reciprocal relations with peers	Use peer tutoring programs to promote skills and reciprocity
		Consider group contingencies (e.g., good behavior game) to involve student in initiatives with peers
		Evaluate carefully any packaged social skills programs used
		Stress generalization of learned skills across environments
Language Development	Receptive and expressive delays and disorders	Teach phonemic awareness skills
		Provide direct instruction of vocabulary words
		Encourage expression of thoughts in the classroom
		Provide appropriate language models
		Build pragmatic skills by stressing appropriate social usage

be added, these characteristics also are more common in students with EBD than for students with other disabilities as well.

Most of the research on academic achievement and behavioral disorders shows the interrelationship of these two considerations. It can be hypothesized that behavioral problems impede academic achievement but also that academic achievement deficits are predictive of subsequent behavioral problems in the classroom (see Table 6.2). Regardless of which hypothesis is more valid, it appears clear that the vast majority of students with EBD experience difficulties in academic achievement (Reid et al., 2004).

Data reported by the USDOE (2009) on achievement testing for students ages 6 to 12 confirm a pattern of underachievement. The report indicated that for passage comprehension in reading, 61% of students were below the 25th percentile, 25% were between the 25th and 60th, 9% between the 61st and 75th, and only 5% above the 75th percentile. For mathematics, the percentages of students at these levels were: 43%; 30%; 19%; and 8%, respectively.

Lane, Carter, Pierson, and Glaeser (2006) reviewed the literature on academic characteristics of adolescent students with emotional disturbance and reported that 58% of the students performed below grade level in reading and 93% in mathematics. Their own research confirmed the difficulties that these students experienced with school success in general and academic achievement in particular. They concluded that these deficits were critical as related to enabling them to "move beyond entry-level employment, obtain a diploma, and access postsecondary education opportunities" (p. 114).

The difficulty that students with EBD experience in reading also has been noted in other studies and reviews of the literature (e.g., Nelson, Benner, & Gonzalez, 2005; Wagner et al., 2005). This difficulty is compounded because, as Nelson and colleagues (2005) noted, research indicates a likely poor response by the students to otherwise generally effective interventions for prereading and reading. Given the common findings of significant problems in academic areas and lack of responsiveness to some effective practices, they stressed the vital importance of the use of appropriate interventions for young children as a way to prevent significant, subsequent problems.

A closely related concern is problems in language development (Wagner et al., 2005). Nelson, Benner, Neill, and Stage (2006) concluded that approximately 90% of students with EBD experience expressive, receptive, and/or pragmatic difficulties at the elementary level. Further, these deficits tended to be stable across age levels. Consequently, because of the relationship between language and academic skills, these problems are very likely to have a negative impact on achievement.

Reid and colleagues (2004) summarized findings in the area of achievement and, thus, key challenges for educators:

- These students typically perform one to two years below their assigned grade level.
- Their problems are identified at an early age and persist throughout elementary and secondary school.
- They achieve at lower levels in reading and math; and they consequently experience higher rates of failure and ultimately grade retention, which then biases their future in terms of lower graduation rates and a reduced likelihood of enrollment in postsecondary education programs.

Postsecondary and Adult Outcomes

A foundation for considering educational programs for students with EBD comes from a consideration of school and young adult outcomes. Data on these outcomes are provided in several key sources including the reports to Congress (USDOE, 2009) and the National Longitudinal Transition Study—2 (NLTS-2) (Newman, Wagner, Cameto, & Knokey, 2009; Wagner, Newman, Cameto, Garza, & Levine, 2005; Wagner, Kutash, Duchowski, Epstein, & Sumi, 2005).

School Exit   A challenging picture emerges from the annual federal reports on IDEA that indicates that students with EBD are the most likely, of all students with disabilities, to drop out of school. In 2003–2004, 52.3% of students with EBD exited school in this manner

(USDOE, 2009); these students were less likely to receive a high school diploma (38.3%) or certificate (8.3%). They were less likely to graduate than were students identified in the other 12 categories of disabilities (USDOE, 2009).

There is, however, a positive recent trend. The number of individuals with EBD who completed high school and received a regular diploma has increased gradually over a 10-year period from 33.7% in the 1994–1995 academic year to 38.4% in 2003–2004. Logically, there has also been a decrease in the dropout rate from 69.3% in 1985–1996 to 52.3% in 2003–2004. Nevertheless, EBD remains the disability with the highest dropout rate (USDOE, 2009).

Kortering (2009) summarized the special challenges associated with school dropout patterns in noting that while dropouts only comprised approximately 20% of the general population, they are estimated to account for over 80% of the general prison and juvenile justice population. Dropouts also often fail to access adult and community services and, consequently, their last opportunity to develop the necessary skills for successful adult adjustment, including employment, may rest with educators.

Employment   Newman and colleagues (2009) reported that only 63.4% of individuals with EBD had been employed at some point in time since high school, with just 42.3% employed at the time of interview. For those working from one to four years after high school, positions included skilled labor (10.1%), food services (17.2%), stocking and shipping (5.4%), serving as a cashier (12.9%), and clerical (7.5%). Newman and colleagues (2009) noted that students with emotional and behavioral disorders offered the following reasons for why they had left a previous or most recent job: 46.5% had quit, 31.5% had a temporary job that ended, 15.5% had been fired, and 6.6% had been laid off.

Rylance (1998) reported that the key variables that increase an individual's chances of employment include basic academic skills, high functional competence levels in school-related areas, and high-school graduation. Successful school programs for these students tended to be ones that included effective vocational education and counseling programs and that motivated students to persist in school and obtain a diploma.

Postsecondary Education   In terms of postsecondary school enrollment among EBD students, Newman and colleagues (2009) noted that 34.0% had attended any postsecondary school, inclusive of 20.6% attending community colleges; 23.2% vocational, business, or technical schools; and 5.5% in 4-year colleges. Of the students who attended postsecondary education, 62.7% did not consider themselves to have a disability, 21.2% did consider themselves to have a disability and had informed the school of this fact, and 16.2% considered that they had a disability but had not informed the school.

One encouraging finding is that students with EBD had greater success in adult education programs. Scanlon and Melland (2002) hypothesized that the context of adult programs may contribute to this success because such programs may be "less antagonizing and more accepting of any emotional or behavioral problems" (p. 253).

Other Adult Adjustment Considerations   Students with EBD often have significant challenges in adjustment within the community. Maag and Katisyannis (1998) noted that successful adjustment is affected by the high dropout rate, which makes it difficult to establish and address transition goals within the student's IEP and individual transition plan. In addition, successful transition is affected by the high rates of unemployment, the increased likelihood of incarceration, and the persistence of mental health problems in adulthood.

In terms of financial independence, young adults with EBD interviewed by Newman et al. (2009) self-reported that 49.0% had a savings account, 35.1% had a checking account, and 21.9% had a credit card. Overall, 91.5% reported an income of less than $25,000. Only 21.5% of students with emotional and behavioral disorders were living independently since leaving high school (Newman et al., 2009).

An important consideration is the possible participation in violence-related activities by individuals who were out of high school and age 18 or older. For students with EBD, 31.0% indicated they had been involved in a physical fight within the previous year and 19.8% reported carrying a weapon in the past 30 days (Newman et al., 2009). In terms of criminal justice involvement, 81.8% indicated that they had been stopped by a police officer for other than a traffic violation, 60.1% had been arrested, 39.4% had spent a night in jail, and 39.1% had been on probation or parole.

McConaughy and Wadsworth (2000) provided some guidance in predicting which individuals would fare better as adults. Based on life histories of these individuals, they concluded that young adults with good outcomes:

> tended to have more stable and quality living situations, better family relationships, more positive relationships with friends, were more goal-oriented, and experienced more successes and fewer stresses than did young adults with poor outcomes. In addition, more young adults with good outcomes held full-time jobs in the community, and fewer associated with friends who used drugs or who were in trouble with the law or violent. (pp. 213–214)

EFFECTIVE INCLUSIVE PRACTICES

Challenges for General Education Teachers

Students with emotional and behavioral disorders present significant challenges to teachers in general education settings. Their behavior may affect not only their own learning but the learning of other students as well. To place these challenges in context, Nelson and colleagues (2009) reported that schools often implement varied interventions to address the needs of these children; one study they cited indicated that schools were found to average an implementation of 14 interventions for students with EBD or at risk for EBD.

Mihalas and colleagues (2009) hypothesized that students with EBD experience difficulty for six key reasons:

1. Many are not identified early and often are not provided appropriate supports at that point in time.
2. Incongruence exists between the needs of these students and instructional practices that are used with them.
3. Many teachers are inadequately prepared to meet their needs.
4. Services provided for these students may be fragmented and not reflect the collaboration necessary with involvement of professionals from multiple disciplines.
5. The emphases on standards-based curriculum, high-stakes testing, and school accountability have combined to create more of a zero-tolerance school climate that is less conducive to addressing the broad needs of students with EBD.
6. The behaviors exhibited by these students have often been associated with interventions that resulted in students being removed from school rather than being educated in a proactive fashion within schools.

Overall, these researchers summarized the fact that the key concern is "a disconnect between what students with EBD need from schools and what they are actually provided. It is evident that the overall school milieu does not support the needs of the students. When one considers the state of outcomes of students with EBD and combines it with the truth that the educational system operates in ways contrary to the students' needs, it's apparent that lack of caring for students with EBD exists. (pp. 109–110)

Because many students with EBD are included in general education classrooms, teachers and special education teachers need to collaborate in developing and implementing intervention programs. Without this collaboration, appropriate interventions will be difficult to provide. Consistency in behavior management and other strategies among teachers and family members is critical. If students receive feedback from the special education teacher that significantly differs from the feedback received from the classroom teacher, confusion often results.

Walker, Golly, McLane, and Kimmich (2005) developed a comprehensive program to serve this purpose, as shown in the Differentiated Instruction—Elementary boxed reading. The program includes proactive and universal screening procedures for all children in kindergarten and first grade; consultants providing support for school interventions that

Differentiating Elementary Instruction

FIRST STEP TO SUCCESS: A PREVENTIVE PROGRAM FOR BEHAVIORALLY AT-RISK CHILDREN (K–2)

First Step to Success was designed as an early intervention program to address emerging patterns of antisocial behavior. The program includes three components:

1. A screening and early detection procedure that provides four different options for use by adopters.
2. A school intervention component that teaches an adaptive behavior pattern to facilitate successful adjustment to the normal demands of schooling.
3. A parent training component. . . that teaches parents how to develop their child's school success skills (e.g., cooperation, accepting limits, sharing, doing one's work). The program is set up and operated initially in the classroom by a behavioral coach (school psychologist, counselor, early interventionist, behavioral specialist) who invests approximately fifty to sixty hours of time during the approximately three-month implementation period. Coaches must be school professionals who can coordinate the roles of these participants and contribute approximately sixty hours during the implementation period. Typically, coaches are trained in the First Step screening, implementation, and parental training procedures during one- and two-day training sessions for staff members.

The coach conducts screening activities, identifies candidates who meet eligibility criteria, and secures parental consent for the child's participation as well as teacher cooperation. The coach explains to the child and classmates how the First Step program works and then he operates it during two brief daily sessions for the first five program days. On day six, the coach turns the program over to the general education classroom teacher, who operates it as part of his or her ongoing teaching routine, with supervision, assistance, and support provided by the coach. After day ten, First Step is operated independently by the classroom teacher. The behavioral coach then contacts the target child's parents to enlist their cooperation in learning how to teach the child school success skills at home. Parents meet for approximately an hour and a half weekly with the First Step coach for a six-week period. During each weekly session, parents and caregivers learn to teach one of the following school success skills: communication and sharing, cooperating, setting limits, solving problems, making friends, and developing self-confidence. The general education classroom teacher looks for, recognizes, and praises the child's display of these skills.

Source: From "The Oregon First Step to Success Replication Initiative: Statewide Results of an Evaluation of the Program's Impact," by H. Walker et al., 2005, *Journal of Emotional and Behavioral Disorders, 13,* p. 16.

---

involve the individual child, his or her peers, and teachers; and training for parents related to supporting and improving their child's adjustment in the home (Nelson et al., 2008).

Classroom teachers usually make the initial recommendation for prereferral review for child study or teacher accommodations for students with EBD. Unless the problem exhibited by the student is severe, it may have gone unrecognized until the school years. In addition to referring students for initial review, classroom teachers must be directly involved in implementing the student's IEP because the majority of students in this category receive a portion of their educational program in general education classrooms. General education classroom teachers must deal with behavior problems much of the time because there are large numbers of students who occasionally display inappropriate behaviors, although they have not been identified as having EBD.

Promoting Inclusive Practices

Because most students with emotional and behavioral disorders are generally placed in general education classrooms rather than isolated in special education settings, teachers must ensure their successful inclusion. Teachers must make a special effort to keep themselves, as well as other students, from developing a negative attitude toward students with EBD. Several tactics that teachers can adopt include:

- Using programs in which peers act as buddies or tutors
- Focusing on positive behaviors and providing appropriate reinforcements
- Using good-behavior games in which all students work together to earn rewards

---

TIPS FOR ADAPTING A LESSON FOR ANTHONY

Based on the chapter-opening vignette, the following sample classroom adaptations might be considered to enhance Anthony's learning and respond to his IEP goals and objectives.
His teacher could:

- Establish a reinforcement system based on checkmarks earned for appropriate behavior with redemption for rewards or special activities twice daily on an initial basis.
- Use peer-mediated interventions such as the "hero" technique, in which Anthony's appropriate social interactions with peers result in whole-class reinforcement (e.g., special activity).
- Use a peer tutor from an upper elementary grade to drill Anthony on vowel and consonant sounds.

- Set up a system of pictures to symbolize work assignments so Anthony can monitor his own work completion as a basis for reinforcement.
- Establish a home-school contract in which appropriate classroom behavior is linked with special opportunities provided by his mother.
- Assign homework that can be completed in 10 to 15 minutes to reinforce effective work habits and task completion.

Successful inclusive practices for students with EBD are contingent on strong teacher-student relationships that lead to a sense of caring that, in turn, results in the students being more connected to the classroom and to school, more likely to persist toward graduation, and more likely to be successful both within school and after school. Mihalas and colleagues (2009) identified a series of specific strategies that can result in stronger, caring teacher-student relationships. These include teachers assuming a role as advocate for individual students, getting to know the students and understand the lives that they live, inviting them to be partners in their educational experience, listening in active fashion to what students are communicating, asking them on a regular basis for feedback on their experiences in the classroom and in school, having students write in journals about their experiences and their reflections on those experiences, finding time to meet with individual students on a consistent basis for discussions on how to solve problems, celebrating with the students when they are successful (in order to counteract the fact that the students most often experience failure), and collaborating with other teachers and with professionals representing other disciplines (such as those involved in wraparound services) to ensure that the curricular, extracurricular, and community experiences enhance the lives and learning opportunities of these students.

Secondary School Considerations Wagner and Davis (2006) identified five key principles related to effective programming in the secondary school for students with EBD that have particular merit for considerations related to successful school inclusion. The principles include: (1) meaningful relationships as a basis for school engagement; (2) academic rigor provided through a challenging curriculum while accompanied by the academic supports necessary for success; (3) learning opportunities that are relevant to the interests of students and their future plans, particularly as they may relate to career goals; (4) attention to the multiple needs of students with emotional and behavioral disorders, such as through coursework and extracurricular activities in which the students are able to further explore their particular interests and develop skills not limited just to academic areas; and (5) active involvement of individual students and their families in transition planning so that it is person-centered and addresses key adult transition domains.

Given the high dropout rate for students with EBD, certainly a primary focus for teachers must be retention in school until graduation. Kortering and Christenson (2009) reviewed the important variables that relate to successful school completion. The key concept they identified was student engagement, which they described as "commitment to and investment in learning, identification with and belonging at school, and in terms of participation in the school environment and initiation of an activity to accomplish an outcome" (p. 7). Further, they indicated that student engagement is the "bottom line" in successful

Differentiating Secondary Instruction

School engagement: Kortering and Christenson (2009) identified a series of practical strategies that can enhance student engagement in school and promote learning. It builds on the assumption that virtually all students, when beginning high school, desire to complete school and earn a diploma. The key becomes implementing strategies that provide students success. Their recommendations are as follows (adapted from pp. 11–13):

Access to age-appropriate transition assessments: An assessment should include a background survey about family, personal interests and ambitions, likes and dislikes relative to school and career options, aptitude testing for special talents, and assessment to better understand preferences for learning and working.

Direct links between school-based learning and life: The most prominent motivation for wanting to be in school is a student's perception that it prepares him for productive adulthood. These links must be convincing so he leaves school daily with the perception of what he did enhanced the likelihood of becoming a productive adult. Those who fail to see this connection may consider other options, including the decision to drop out of school.

Opportunities to control destiny: Incorporating such opportunities for students sets the stage for perceiving competence and success.

Engagement in nonacademic aspects of school: Such participation helps develop a sense of belonging, builds positive relationships, contributes to personal development, and provides a chance to excel and become a valued member of the school environment (such as in musical groups, sports, clubs, or related activities).

Engagement in classroom learning: Learning success is the primary means to obtain the level of education necessary for suitable employment. Engagement in learning requires supportive teachers who provide interesting and relevant opportunities for learning.

Source: Adapted from Kortering, L., & Christenson, S. (2009). "Engaging students in school and learning: The real deal for school completion." *Exceptionality, 17,* pp. 10–13.

interventions that promote school completion. In order to be successful in promoting school completion, interventions therefore should "address engagement comprehensively, not only focusing on academic or behavioral skill deficits but also the social, interpersonal aspects of schooling, particularly the need for connections to other adults and peers. Thus, effective interventions must account for more than attendance and academic skills; equally important for intervention design are students' commitment to learning, perceptions of academic and social competence, achievement motivation, and sense of belonging" (p. 8). The Differentiated Instruction—Secondary boxed reading provides more information on ways to promote school engagement.

Collaboration Because students with emotional and behavioral disorders are most frequently educated in general classrooms, classroom teachers are the key to the success of these students. Too often, if these students do not achieve success, the entire classroom can be disrupted. Therefore, appropriate supports must be available to teachers. These supports may include special education personnel, psychologists and counselors, and mental health service providers.

Special educators should be available to collaborate with teachers regarding the development of behavioral as well as instructional supports. A particularly helpful way to assist classroom teachers involves modeling methods of dealing with behavior problems. Further, in many instances, students with emotional and behavioral problems will need Tier II and Tier III instruction from special educators.

School psychologists and counselors are other critical team members in providing a comprehensive program for students with EBD. They can provide intensive counseling to students; they can also consult with teachers on how to implement specific programs, such as a student's individual behavior management plan. Finally, mental health personnel can provide helpful support for teachers. Too often, mental health services are not available in schools; however, some schools are beginning to develop school-based mental health programs that are staffed jointly by school personnel and mental health staff and provide support for teachers as well as direct interventions for students. If mental health services are not available, teachers should work with school administrators to involve mental health specialists with students who display emotional and behavioral problems.

CLASSROOM ADAPTATIONS

Curricular Adaptations

Appropriate academic interventions for students with EBD often parallel those discussed for students with LD (see Chapter 5). In addition to the importance of using validated academic curricular strategies, a particular area of concern for students with EBD that requires curricular adaptations is social skills instruction. Social skills are best learned from observing others who display appropriate skills, but there are times when a more formal instructional effort must be made.

Numerous methods may be used to teach social skills and promote good social relations, including modeling, direct instruction, prompting, and positive practice. Teachers must determine the method that will work best with a particular student.

Quinn, Kavale, Mathur, Rutherford, and Forness (1999) reported a comprehensive research analysis of the use of social skills training with students with EBD. In general, they caution that it has been demonstrated that only about half of students with EBD have benefitted from social skills training, particularly when the focus was on the broader dimensions of the social domain. Greater success was obtained when the focus was on training on specific targeted social skills (e.g., social problem solving, social interaction, cooperation) than with packaged social skills curricula (Kauffman & Landrum, 2009b). Forness (1999) and Kavale (2001b) hypothesized that the reason more substantive positive effects have not been obtained from some training may be that the programs within the research studies were too limited in duration and intensity.

Another reason why social skills instruction may be problematic is that its effectiveness is challenged by the difficulty of achieving generalization across settings. Scott and Nelson (1998) cautioned teachers to realize that educational practices for achieving generalization in academic instruction are often insufficient for achieving similar outcomes in social skills instruction. They stress that any such instruction in artificial contexts will create difficulty in generalization, and therefore schoolwide instruction, modeling, and the reinforcement of appropriate social behaviors taught within the context of the classroom are likely to be most effective. This instruction may be more effective when students who are not disabled are involved in the training. While they stress the complexity of teaching social skills, Scott and Nelson (1998) also similarly stress the critical nature of learning within this area. Teachers are advised to consider social skills programs cautiously, implement them experimentally, and confirm that positive outcomes are obtained.

Instructional Adaptations

A key to effective instruction is the use of validated strategies. Research offers promising directions for effective instructional practices. As adapted from Wehby, Symons, Canale, and Go (1998), these practices should include the following:

- Providing appropriate structure and predictable routines.
- Establishing a structured and consistent classroom environment.
- Establishing a consistent schedule with set rules and consequences and clear expectations.
- Fostering positive teacher-student interaction with adequate praise and systematic responses to problem behaviors.
- Frequently implementing instructional sequences that promote high rates of academic engagement.

- Creating a classroom environment in which independent seat work is limited and sufficient time is allotted for establishing positive social interaction. (p. 52)

Landrum and colleagues (2006) concluded from their review of research on the teacher acceptability of intervention strategies that those strategies that would be most acceptable to classroom teachers and, consequently, most likely to be implemented as designed, would include strategies that are: "easy to implement, not time-intensive, positive, perceived to be effective by the teacher, and compatible with the context in which the intervention will be employed (e.g., resources available, teacher experiences, treatment philosophy, instructional environment)." As they further noted, however, "many interventions that have proven effective for addressing the behavioral and academic needs of students with EBD do not meet these criteria . . . and therefore are not likely to be implemented with integrity, if implemented at all" (p. 20). As a consequence, it is important that general education and special education teachers work together to design effective instructional strategies.

An important emphasis in effective instruction for students with EBD is to use FBA procedures (discussed earlier in the chapter) as a basis for making effective classroom adaptations. Reid and Nelson (2002) reported that FBA provides a promising approach with research validation for planning positive behavioral interventions, which can have a significant effect on improving student behavior. FBA-based approaches offer exciting opportunities to enhance instruction and influence successful inclusion practices.

■ The behavior of teachers can have great impact on effective behavior management.

Behavioral Supports

The development of **positive behavior supports (PBS)** has been a significant achievement in the education of students with special needs and has particular relevance for students with EBD. Carr, Dozier, and Patel (2002) noted:

> Positive behavior includes all those skills that increase the likelihood of success and personal satisfaction in . . . academic, work, social, recreational, community, and family settings. Support encompasses all those educational methods that can be used to teach, strengthen, and expand positive behavior and . . . increase opportunities for the display of positive behavior. The primary goal of PBS is to help an individual change his or her lifestyle in a direction that gives . . . teachers, employers, parents, friends, and the target person him- or herself the opportunity to perceive and to enjoy an improved quality of life. An important but secondary goal of PBS is to render problem behavior irrelevant, inefficient, and ineffective by helping an individual achieve his or her goals in a socially acceptable manner. (p. 5)

PBS interventions provide an alternative to an emphasis on punitive disciplinary strategies and provide guidance to students with behavioral problems to make appropriate changes in their behavioral patterns. The PBS approach emphasizes proactive, preventive strategies and early intervention with students deemed to be at risk. Further, those programs that are organized on a schoolwide basis (hence, SWPBS) have an increased likelihood of success (Nelson, Benner, & Cheney, 2005).

Sugai and Horner (2008) outlined the guiding principles behind the implementation of SWPBS programs. Table 6.5 provides a listing of these principles. They reported that over 5,600 schools throughout the United States are adopting this approach to schoolwide systemic, individualized behaviorally focused interventions that lead to the prevention of problem behaviors while promoting positive learning and social outcomes.

Lane, Wehby, Robertson, and Rogers (2007), reporting on the effectiveness of SWPBS programs for high school students, concluded that they were most effective for students with internalizing behavior patterns and less effective for students with externalizing problems or co-morbid problems (that is, a combinations of problems). As they noted, "students with externalizing behavior patterns . . . are more apt to solicit teacher retention during the

> ## TABLE 6.5
>
> ### Schoolwide Positive Behavior Supports: Guiding Principles
>
> - *Prevention* must be a priority in decreasing the (a) development, (b) future occurrences, and (c) worsening of emotional and behavioral problems.
> - Priority must be directed toward *research-based* intervention and practices.
> - A *full continuum* of effective, efficient, and relevant academic and behavior interventions and supports is needed to support all students and their families.
> - A *comprehensive system* of school-based mental health must unify and integrate education, public health, child and family welfare, juvenile justice, and mental health.
> - *Research-to-practice* must consider the careful translation and adoption of research-based interventions and practices to real living, teaching, and learning environments.
> - Self-assessment, continuous progress monitoring, and systematic *data-based decision making* must guide selection, adoption, adaptation, implementation, and evaluation of intervention decisions.
> - Research-based practices must be supported directly and formally by establishing *local behavioral capacity* for leadership, training, evaluation, and political support.
>
> *Source:* From Sugai, G., & Horner, R. H. (2008). "What we know and need to know about preventing problem behavior in schools." *Exceptionality, 16,* p. 69.

elementary years. . . . This may be even more salient at the high school level, where the consequences of externalizing behaviors (e.g., aggression, coercion) become extremely deleterious." On the other hand, "students with internalizing behaviors are even more likely to go unnoticed at the high school level where students have multiple teachers throughout the day . . . and both teachers and students are under pressure to meet increasingly challenging curricular demands. These circumstances may afford less time for personal interactions between teachers and students, making it less likely that students with internalizing behaviors will be recognized" (p.15).

A summary of evidence-based practices is included in Table 6.6. In addition, a particular focus for students with EBD should be on the development of behavioral self-control in which students are taught to use self-management strategies throughout the day (see Figure 6.6).

Behavioral Intervention Plans   According to federal guidelines, school district personnel are required to address the strategies to be employed for students with disabilities who exhibit significant behavioral problems. The required component is the development of a **behavioral intervention plan (BIP)** (see Figure 6.7).

In general, behavioral intervention plans are required for (1) students whose behaviors impede their learning or the learning of others, (2) students who put peers at risk because of their behaviors, and (3) students with disabilities for whom serious disciplinary action is being taken. A BIP is required on any student who is dismissed from school for more than 10 days for misbehavior. The major assumptions underlying the development of BIPs include the following:

- Behavior problems are best addressed when the cause (i.e., function) of the behaviors is known.
- Interventions that are based on positive intervention strategies are more effective than punitive ones.
- Dealing with difficult behaviors demands a team approach.
- Dedicating time and effort to understanding the function of a behavior and then intervening appropriately is a better way to expend effort than reacting to inappropriate behavior on an ongoing basis.

The behavioral intervention planning process typically includes the following specific steps (McConnell et al., 2006):

- Collect background information to provide context for the presenting problems.

CROSS-REFERENCE

Behavioral strategies that have merit for use with students are further discussed in Chapter 15.

TABLE 6.6

Evidence-Based Classroom Practices

1. **Maximize structure and predictability**
   - High classroom structure (e.g., the amount of teacher-directed activity)
   - Physical arrangement that minimizes distractions (e.g., walls, visual dividers), and crowding
2. **Post, teach, monitor, and reinforce expectations**
   - Post, teach, review, and provide feedback on expectations
   - Active supervision
3. **Actively engage students in observable ways**
   - Rate of opportunities to respond
   - Response cards
   - Direct instruction
   - Computer-assisted instruction
   - Classwide peer tutoring
   - Guided notes
4. **Use a continuum of strategies to acknowledge appropriate behavior**
   - Specific and/or contingent praise
   - Classwide group contingencies
   - Behavioral contracting
   - Token economies
5. **Use a continuum of strategies to respond to inappropriate behavior**
   - Error corrections
   - Performance feedback (with and without the addition of other evidence-based strategies)
   - Differential reinforcement
   - Planned ignoring plus contingent praise and/or instruction of classroom rules
   - Response cost
   - Time-out from reinforcement

Source: Kerr, M. M., & Nelson, C. M. (2010). *Strategies for addressing behavior problems in the classroom* (6th ed.). Boston: Pearson (p. 199).

- Conduct a functional behavioral assessment (FBA) to analyze the relationship of the target behavior to the environmental antecedents and consequences and explore the purpose of the behavior.
- Determine whether the behavior in question is directly related to the student's disability (i.e., whether the behavior is a manifestation of the disability).
- Determine specific goals that teach and support positive alternative behavior and decrease or eliminate negative behavior.
- Develop intervention strategies, preferably of a positive nature, that will be used and identify the person(s) who will be responsible for implementation.
- Implement the plan and evaluate its effectiveness.
- Use information from the implementation of the intervention to revisit the assessment information as a basis for further intervention efforts.

General education teachers can be involved in all aspects of the BIP process. During the first stage of collecting background information, the general education teacher plays a crucial role in supplying classroom-related information about the behaviors under review. Although the FBA is likely to be conducted by someone other than the classroom teacher, on occasion the general education teacher might be asked to be involved in generating it. Classroom teachers are quite likely to be involved in the identification of the positive interventions, strategies, and services to be used because many students requiring a BIP will receive their education in a general education classroom. Last, classroom teachers will be intricately involved in monitoring the effectiveness of the interventions when students with BIPs are in their classes.

FIGURE 6.6	Sample Behavioral Self-Control Plan to Improve Math Scores

1. Rules needed to meet goal:
   a. Every day, after school, I will go to the library.
   b. I will study math for two hours at the library.
   c. I will monitor my time so only the time spent working on math will be attributed to the two-hour period.
   d. If I have trouble with my math assignment, I will ask the proctoring teacher for help.
   e. After the two-hour period, I can spend time with my friends, talk on the phone, or have leisure time alone.
2. Goal: I will improve my math grade by at least one letter grade in a six-week period.
   a. I will complete all my daily homework assignments.
   b. I will review each lecture on a daily basis.
   c. I will develop strategies that will help me remember problem-solving procedures for math problems.
   d. I will practice and review math problems.
3. Feedback: Prior to turning in my homework, I will ask my parent or teacher to check my work. I will correct any wrong answers.
4. Measurement-monitoring of rules and subgoals:
   a. Rules: Develop a monitoring system that indicates the time spent studying at the library and asking for help when needed.
   b. Subgoals: Develop a monitoring system that indicates whether the homework, review of lecture, strategies, or practice was completed during the two-hour period.
   c. Products: Improvement on math scores should indicate progress toward goal; if progress is not seen after a two-week period, reevaluate the plan.

Source: From *Childhood Behavior Disorders: Applied Research and Practices* (2nd ed., p. 212), edited by R. Algozzine, L. Serna, and J. R. Patton, 2001. Austin, TX: Pro-Ed.

Zirkel (2009) noted that IDEA only requires a functional behavioral assessment and behavioral intervention plan when a change in placement occurs for disciplinary reasons that are related to a manifestation of the student's disability. However, this narrow legal interpretation does not invalidate the importance of these two key elements in designing and implementing effective educational programs for students with EBD.

O'Shea and Draydon (2008, pp. 107–119) further analyzed other aspects of classroom discipline that relate to the tenets of IDEA. These included the following concerns: disciplinary infractions and due-process rights, manifestation determination, student removal for 45 days placement, the appeal of decisions, functional behavioral assessments, and behavioral intervention plans. While the full analysis of these legal issues is beyond the scope of this chapter, this source can be consulted for a detailed analysis of current legal questions relating to discipline, an explanation of the particular bases within federal law, and the potential dilemmas for the schools in responding to these mandates.

Physical Adaptations

The physical arrangement of the classroom has an impact on the behaviors of students with EBD. Attention to the classroom arrangement can both facilitate learning and minimize disruptions. The following considerations can help maintain an orderly classroom:

- Arrange traffic patterns to lessen contact and disruptions.
- Arrange student desks to facilitate monitoring of all students at all times.
- Locate students with tendencies toward disruptive behaviors near the teacher's primary location.
- Locate students away from stored materials that they may find tempting.
- Create spaces where students can do quiet work, such as a quiet reading area.

FIGURE 6.7

Behavioral intervention plan.

Specific Goal(s)	Proposed Intervention(s)	Person(s) Responsible	Evaluation Methods	Evaluation Criterion	Schedule Date	Progress Codes: / = ongoing X = mastered D = discontinued Code
1. Casey will increase respectful language in class, including saying "yes, sir" or "yes, ma'am" when requested to do something.	1. Contract for • positive comments • saying "yes, ma'am" or "yes, sir" • refrain from verbal threats	1. Student Teachers Counselor	–Contract forms –Discipline referrals	1. Respectful language 90% of time	9/1/99 10/15/99 12/1/99 1/15/00 3/1/00 4/15/00 6/1/00	
2. Casey will decrease verbal threats and teasing.	2. Delay release from classroom to hallway by 5 minutes	2. Teachers		2. Contract • positive comments: 5 per day • "yes" responses: 80% of time • verbal threats: fewer than 8 per 6 weeks		
3. Casey will decrease aggressive incidents toward peers (fighting, hitting, tripping).	3. Continuum of responses to aggression: • Parent–Asst. Principal conference and suspension to AEP for 3 days • Go to antiaggression classes • Notify probation officer	3. Parents Assistant Principal Counselor		3. Aggression: No incidents in next 6 weeks		

These goals were developed with consideration of the following information:

☐ Parent concerns regarding special circumstances: _____
_____

☐ Teacher/administrator concerns regarding special circumstances: _____
_____

☑ Outside agency/professional concerns regarding special circumstances: _____
Probation officer requires notification.

Teachers should establish classroom procedures to ensure an orderly environment. These include procedures for the beginning of a period or the school day, use of classroom equipment, social interaction, the completion of work, group and individual activities, and the conclusion of instructional periods and the school day (Walker & Shea, 1995). Effective procedures undergird the concept of preventive discipline (discussed below).

Wraparound Services

The focus of this text is on the inclusion of students with disabilities in general education classrooms and the implications of this process for educators. For students with EBD, however, the school setting is only one environment that must be responsive to their needs. In addition, other needed services typically include mental health organizations, social services, and the juvenile and criminal justice systems. Kamradt, Gilbertson, and Lynn (2005) emphasized the importance of this broad-based approach to meeting students' needs. The core elements of their wraparound program are listed in Figure 6.8. For a portrait of a wraparound program, see the Personal Spotlight on "Jake."

FIGURE 6.8	Core Elements of Wraparound Approaches

- Community-based care
- Individualized services based on the needs of the client
- Adherence to culturally competent services and supports
- Family involvement in the design and delivery of services
- Team-driven planning process
- Flexible funding
- Balance of formal and informal services to support families
- Collaboration among child-serving systems
- Unconditional care (never giving up on a child)
- Presence of an ongoing evaluation process

Source: From "Wraparound Milwaukee," by B. Kamradt, S. A. Gilbertson, and N. Lynn (p. 307), in *Outcomes for Children and Youth with Emotional and Behavioral Disorders and Their Families,* edited by M. H. Epstein, K. Kutash, and A. Duchnowski, 2005. Austin, TX: Pro-Ed.

Windle and Mason (2004) validated a model for predicting emotional and behavioral problems in adolescents that illustrates the complexity of problems and, hence, programmatic needs. Based on their research, the key predictors formed a four-factor model of behavioral and emotional problems. These variables included polydrug use (alcohol, marijuana, cigarettes, drugs), delinquency (vandalism, theft, personal offenses), negative affect (depressed affect, sense of well-being, somatic complaints, interpersonal relationships), and academic orientation (school grades, educational aspirations). Based on this research, it appears reasonable to conclude that these predictors represent focal areas of concern both within and outside the school setting. While schools may be able to address some of these variables to a greater extent (i.e., academic orientation), successful programs for adolescents with behavioral and emotional problems often require a wraparound approach to services that reflects general community commitment.

Medication Considerations

Many students with emotional and behavioral problems experience difficulties in maintaining attention and controlling behavior. For students experiencing these problems, medication is frequently considered as an intervention option. Many different kinds of medication have been found to be effective with students' behavior problems, including stimulants, tranquilizers, anticonvulsants, antidepressants, and mood-altering drugs. The USDOE (2005) cites the following data on the use of medication with students with EBD (ages 6 to 12 and 13 to 17, respectively): antidepressant/antianxiety (40%, 29%), antipsychotic (24%, 29%), and other drugs (16%, 34%).

The use of medication to help manage students with emotional and behavior problems is controversial but nevertheless can be an important component of comprehensive intervention programs. Some key considerations are as follows:

1. Medication can result in increased attention of students.
2. Medication can result in reduced aggressive behaviors.
3. Various side effects can result from medical interventions.
4. The use of medication for children experiencing emotional and behavioral problems should be carefully monitored. (Smith, Finn, & Dowdy, 1993, p. 214)

Children who take medications for emotional and behavioral problems can experience numerous side effects. For example, Ritalin is commonly prescribed to help students with attention and hyperactivity problems. Several potential side effects of Ritalin include ner-

PERSONAL SPOTLIGHT

SCHOOL-BASED WRAPAROUND: JAKE'S STORY

JAKE is a 13-year-old student being raised by his maternal grandmother. By the beginning of his fifth-grade year, he had enrolled in five schools across three states. Jake's family changed schools frequently as a result of the inability to address his behavior within the school system.

Jake is beginning his second year at his current school which is participating in a special wrap around services project. Since enrolling there, he has had a total of three office referrals. In the past, he averaged three office referrals a week!

In other schools, Jake worked from the time he got home until bedtime, trying to finish his homework, but he was still failing almost all classes. He now completes his homework quickly in the evening, and he consistently receives A's and B's.

In other programs, professionals encouraged Jake's family to put him on medication, but they did not discuss the importance of other supportive services. His grandmother describes past school and mental health services as disjointed and prescriptive. Due to the coordinated supports provided to Jake and his family by school and mental health personnel, Jake's grandmother receives fewer calls from the school and can focus on supporting her family rather than leaving work to meet with school personnel. She reports feeling that she is now working in partnership with the school rather than fighting against them.

Jake's grandmother is always getting ideas about new things to try and how to modify them if they don't work. She has called it a "life-changing experience." The improvements in the family's quality of life testify to the importance of providing co-ordinated services, focusing on strengths rather than deficits, and including the family as an equal partner at all levels of decision making.

In addition to himself and his grandmother, Jake's wraparound team includes a service coordinator, intervention specialist, two teachers, and the school principal. Extended team members include his aunt, a family friend, and his coach. Initial conversations revealed that Jake is bright, is motivated, wants to succeed, and enjoys positive adult attention.

The majority of needs identified by Jake's team fell into the educational/vocational and social/recreational life domains. Due to the severity of school-related problems, the team chose to prioritize needs in the educational/vocational domain. These needs centered on classroom behavior problems and difficulty with completion of schoolwork. All core team members accepted responsibility for ensuring that the plan was implemented as written and modified as needed to meet Jake's behavioral and academic needs.

As Jake met with success at school as evidenced through a reduction in office referrals and improved grades, the team determined that the next priority was to improve his peer-interaction skills. To meet this need, Jake began participating in a highly structured after-school program with an emphasis on prosocial development. Currently, Jake is working with his intervention specialist to appropriately apply the skills he learned in the after-school program to school and classroom settings.

Source: Adapted from "Wraparound Milwaukee," B. Kamradt, S. A. Gilbertson, and N. Lynn (pp. 362–363), in *Outcomes for Children and Youth with Emotional and Behavioral Disorders and Their Families,* edited by M. H. Epstein, K. Kutash, and A. Duchnowski, 2005. Austin, TX: Pro-Ed.

vousness, insomnia, anorexia, dizziness, blood pressure and pulse changes, abdominal pain, and weight loss. Teachers can monitor side effects by keeping a daily log of student behaviors that could be attributed to the medication. Chapter 10 provides a comprehensive analysis of the use of medications for students with ASD that also has validity for students with EBD as well.

SUMMARY

Basic Concepts about Emotional and Behavioral Disorders

- Most children and youth are disruptive from time to time, but most do not require interventions. Some students' emotional or behavioral problems are severe enough to warrant interventions.

- Many problems complicate serving students with EBD, including inconsistent definitions of the disorder, the large number of agencies involved in defining and treating it, and limited ways to measure objectively the extent and precise parameters of the problem.
- The estimated prevalence of students with emotional and behavioral problems ranges from a low of less than 1% (actually found eligible for special education nationwide) to a high of over 20%.
- Students with emotional and behavioral problems are significantly underserved in schools.

Characteristics of Students with Emotional and Behavioral Disorders

- Key areas of concern include externalizing (e.g., acting out) and internalizing (e.g., social withdrawal) behaviors.
- EBD is frequently also associated with academic difficulties, such as in reading and mathematics.
- Language difficulties are also commonly noted in this population of students.

Effective Inclusive Practices for Students with EBD

- Students with EBD are commonly included in general education classes. General education teachers and special education teachers must collaborate so that there is consistency in the development and implementation of intervention methods.

Role of Teachers in Making Classroom Adaptations for Students with EBD

- A variety of curricular, instructional, and management adaptations are available to enhance the educational programs for students with EBD.
- Social skills development is important for students with EBD.
- Interventions based on FBA and PBS are important methods for reducing the impact of problems or for keeping problems from occurring.
- Special education teachers and mental health personnel need to be available to provide guidance for general education teachers who are implementing a student's behavior management plan.

PEARSON
myeducationlab

The MyEducationLab for this course can help you solidify your comprehension of Chapter 6 concepts.

- Gauge and further develop your understanding of chapter concepts by taking the quizzes and examining the enrichment materials on the Chapter 6 Study Plan.
- Visit Topic 16, Emotional and Behavioral Disorders, to:
  - Connect with challenge-based interactive modules, case study units, and podcasts that provide research-validated information about working with students in inclusive settings by visiting the IRIS Center Resources
  - Explore Assignments and Activities, assignable exercises showing concepts in action through video, cases, and student and teacher artifacts
  - Practice and strengthen skills essential to quality teaching through the Building Teaching Skills and Dispositions lessons

7

Teaching Students with Intellectual Disabilities

CHAPTER OBJECTIVES

After reading this chapter, you should be able to:

1. Discuss the basic concepts of intellectual disabilities, including definition and classification.
2. Identify common characteristics of students with intellectual disabilities and their instructional implication.
3. Describe the effective inclusive practices including transitional needs of students with intellectual disabilities.
4. Discuss classroom adaptations for students with intellectual disabilities.

JANDREW is currently a junior at Avon High School. He has been receiving special education supports throughout his school career. Prior to kindergarten, he had been identified as "at-risk" because of language delays and also in part because of the difficult home situation in which he was raised (his grandmother has been his guardian since his mother was incarcerated when Jandrew was 4 years old; his father has not been part of his life since he was an infant).

When Jandrew began elementary school, he was identified as developmentally delayed, a term that allowed the school division to provide special education services in primary school without a formal categorical label. However, when further assessments were completed when Jandrew reached the age of 6, his language, academic, and social skills were deemed consistent with the label of intellectual disabilities.

Jandrew has progressed well in part because of his continued involvement in general education classrooms through both middle and high school. With in-class support along with specialized instruction, he has developed his reading skills to the fourth-grade level with comparable achievement in mathematics and other academic areas. Currently, the focus of his program is on building his academic skills in the inclusive classroom and complementing this emphasis with a curricular focus to prepare him for success in the community.

Jandrew has become an active participant in the development of his IEP and his individual transition plan (ITP). A key current objective is to obtain his driver's license. He is currently enrolled in both an instructional program to complete the written portion of the test and the behind-the-wheel component. A longer-term focus is to prepare him for competitive employment in the community. Through a series of community-based instructional programs, he has become aware of the options available to him and an apprenticeship program at the local IGA grocery store will be available next year. Jandrew's success is a combination of his motivation to succeed, detailed planning by key individuals in his life, and ongoing support provided by teachers, his grandmother, and several significant peers who are more academically able.

QUESTIONS TO CONSIDER

1. How can the curriculum for Jandrew balance academic objectives and preparation for competitive employment and independent living?
2. What are the goals for Jandrew when he finishes high school?
3. What strategies can enhance his positive interactions with peers?
4. What available community resources will aid his transition to independent living?

BASIC CONCEPTS ABOUT INTELLECTUAL DISABILITIES

Intellectual disabilities (ID) is a powerful term used to describe a level of functioning significantly below what is considered to be "average." The term serves as a contemporary replacement for "mental retardation," a term used most commonly by professionals until this past decade. Intellectual disabilities, or mental retardation, may conjure up a variety of images, including a stereotypical photo of an adolescent with Down syndrome, a young child living in poverty and provided with limited experience and stimulation, and an adult striving to adjust to the demands of a complex society. Because *mental retardation* was used as a generic term that refers to a very diverse group of individuals, ironically, all these images and, at the same time, none of these images, may be accurate ones. Smith (2006) aptly noted this point and in the process made a strong case for a change to the term of intellectual disabilities:

> The term mental retardation has been used to describe people who are more different than they are alike. . . . It has been used as an amalgam for very diverse human conditions. The core of mental retardation as a field is the assumption that somehow there is an "essence" that eclipses all of the differences that characterize people described by the term. It is truly a box of chocolates, however. "You don't know what you're gonna get" when you reach into the category. Maybe it will be someone who needs constant care, or maybe it will be someone much like yourself but who needs help with academic skills. Maybe it will be someone with severe physical disabilities, or maybe it will be someone who you would pass on the street without notice. What is certain about the category is that it is a stigmatizing label with universally negative connotations. That may be the only "glue" that holds it together. (p. 201)

The term "mental retardation is now increasingly avoided. The almost universal negative response to the term by professionals, parents, as well as the people so labeled, gave rise to alternative terminology, just as *retardation* was an option to earlier terms such as *feebleminded* and *moron* (Polloway & Lubin, 2009). The optional term, **intellectual disabilities (ID)**, endeavors to convey a broad-based concept that places under it deficits in varied cognitive and adaptive ability areas.

In spite of the increased call for the use of ID, Polloway, Patton, Smith, Antoine, and Lubin (2009) reported that as of 2009, 27 states still used the term *mental retardation*. Bergeron, Floyd, and Shands (2008) similarly reported that this term was used by 53% of the states in 2008. The change to the term *intellectual disability* (ID) should be predominant by 2012.

The concept of **mild intellectual disabilities** requires careful consideration. It presents as an oxymoron and may unfortunately convey the fact that mild is relatively insignificant (e.g., a mild cold). Polloway (2006, p. 196) noted that "the mild concept has regularly created misconceptions within both the profession and the general population that has had implications for the eligibility of individuals for educational and other supports." Snell, Luckasson and colleagues (2009) referred instead to "people with intellectual disabilities who have higher IQs." Nevertheless, the term *mild* continues to be used in the professional literature.

An related umbrella term is **developmental disabilities**. Defined by federal guidelines, the term has become popular particularly when used to refer to programs for adults and as used by professional organizations (Stodden, 2002), although it is used far less frequently in the schools. One difficulty with the term is that a literal rendering of the definition would suggest that developmental disabilities would exclude perhaps up to 40% of those people who might otherwise have been identified as mildly intellectually disabled (Luckasson et al., 2002).

The preferred term for younger children is **developmental delay**, a federally designated term (generally consistent with the concept of developmental disabilities) that refers to children who have experienced delay, or are identified as at risk for likely experiencing delay in the future. While federal guidelines and definitions provide guidance, there is significant state

Visit the MyEducationLab for this course to enhance your understanding of chapter concepts with a personalized Study Plan. You'll also have the opportunity to hone your teaching skills through video-based Assignments and Activities, IRIS Center Resources, and Building Teaching Skills and Disposition lessons.

variance in the application of this term (Danaher, Shackelford, & Harbin, 2004). It is also very rare that the term *intellectual disabilities*, or its predecessor *mental retardation*, is applied to children who are younger than 5 years of age. This decision to eschew a label such as "intellectual disabilities" for young children is a positive one in that it delays the use of a stigmatizing term such as retardation, even though the label nevertheless may subsequently be applied once the child reaches elementary school.

We will continue to use the term "mental retardation" in this text *only* when it reflects historical considerations or, for example, certain federal reports that still use that term. Without question, being labeled retarded is stigmatizing and the label is seen as offensive by people to whom it refers. Using a more positive label, such as intellectually disabled, as well as providing opportunities to be with peers who are not disabled, must be pursued to ensure the prospect of a positive quality of life for those people who traditionally have been identified as retarded (Schalock et al., 2007).

The late 20th century witnessed momentous changes that have washed away the realities of restricted, and often abusive, settings that characterized many so-called services through the 1970s. Shifts in public attitudes and the resulting development and provision of services and supports have been phenomenal. Consequently, this is an exciting time to be participating in the changing perspectives on intellectual disabilities. The powerful and relevant message of the 21st century is that people with intellectual disabilities are capable of substantial achievements as we develop their strengths and assets.

Definition, Identification, and Eligibility

While it is challenging to formulate a definition of intellectual disabilities (ID) that can be used to govern practices such as assessment and placement, ID has been commonly characterized by two dimensions or prongs: limited intellectual ability and difficulty in coping with the social demands of the environment. In an illustrative way, Greenspan (1996) described ID as primarily a problem in "everyday intelligence," being challenged in adapting to the demands of daily life in the community.

All individuals with ID must, by definition, demonstrate some degree of impaired mental abilities, traditionally said to be reflected in an IQ significantly below average. In addition, these individuals would necessarily demonstrate less mature adaptive skills, such as social behavior or functional academic skills, when compared to their same-age peers. For some individuals, this discrepancy may not be readily apparent in a casual interaction in a nonschool setting. These individuals may be challenged most dramatically by the school setting, and thus between the ages of 6 and 21, their inability to cope may be most evident, for example, in problems with peer relationships, with difficulty in compliance with adult-initiated directions, and in meeting academic challenges.

The American Association on Intellectual and Developmental Disabilities (AAIDD) has for decades developed and revised successive definitions of mental retardation, and now ID. This organization's efforts are broadly recognized, and its definitions have often been incorporated, with modifications, into state and federal statutes. Although use of their definitions in educational regulations and practice has been uneven (see Denning, Chamberlain, & Polloway, 2000; Frankenberger & Harper, 1988; Polloway et al., 2009; Polloway, Lubin, Smith, & Patton, 2010), the AAIDD's definitions are generally considered as the basis for diagnosis in the field.

Three concepts are central to the AAIDD's definitions: intellectual functioning, adaptive behavior or skills, and the developmental period (Grossman, 1983; Luckasson et al., 1992; Luckasson et al., 2002; Schalock et al., 2010). Each is discussed below.

Intellectual Functioning   The concept of intellectual functioning was intended as a broad summation of cognitive abilities, such as the capacity to learn, solve problems, accumulate knowledge, adapt to new situations, and think abstractly. Operationally, however, it unfortunately has often been reduced to performance on a test of intelligence, typically with a flexible upper IQ range of 70 to 75. This approximate IQ range is a relatively common component of state identification practices if an IQ cut-off score is required at all (Polloway et al., 2010). The most common practice has been to recognize this ceiling level while accepting the fact that the standard error of measurement dictates the flexibility of ± 5 points. Polloway et al. (2009) reported that in terms of the intellectual assessment component of the definition, 34 states required a cut-off score or range; most commonly, the ceiling level for mental retardation was stated as either approximately IQ 70 or 2 standard deviations below the mean. Bergeron and colleagues (2008) noted that "the majority of states use an IQ cutoff of at least two SDs below the normative mean" (p. 125).

It is worth considering how an IQ score relates to this first criterion for diagnosis. An IQ of 100 is the mean score on such tests, so a person receiving a score of 100 is considered to have an average level of cognitive functioning. Based on statistical analysis, approximately 2.3% of IQs would be expected to lie below 70 and a like percentage above 130. Thus, to limit the diagnosis of ID to people with IQs of approximately 70 or below is to suggest that, hypothetically, about 2% of the tested population may have significantly subaverage general intellectual functioning. However, low IQ scores alone are not sufficient for diagnosis. Hence, we must next consider the adaptive dimension.

Adaptive Behavior   An individual's **adaptive behavior** represents the degree to which the individual meets "the standards of maturation, learning, personal independence, and/or social responsibility that are expected for his or her age level and cultural group" (Grossman, 1983, p. 11). Particularly important are the skills necessary to function independently in a range of situations and to maintain responsible social relationships. In contemporary practice, this dimension of the definition requires that an individual show significant deficits in overall adaptive behavior or in conceptual, social, or practical adaptive skills. Greenspan's (1997, 2006) model of personal competence, inclusive of his focus on a design for considering adaptive functioning, was the basis for inclusion of the focus on conceptual, practical, and social adaptive skills. Table 7.1 lists key adaptive skill areas. Each of these skills is age-relevant and represents core areas of concern for both elementary and secondary educators.

The determination of adaptive behavior requires both the administration of an adaptive behavior scale as well as the placement of data about adaptive behavior within the context of an individual's functioning in everyday life. The importance of adaptive behavior is reflected in the fact that 49 states confirmed requiring consideration of this dimension for eligibility (Polloway et al., 2009).

TABLE 7.1

Conceptual, Social, and Practical Adaptive Skills

CONCEPTUAL	SOCIAL	PRACTICAL

• Language (receptive and expressive)
 • Reading and writing
 • Money concepts
 • Self-direction
	• Interpersonal
	 • Responsibility
	 • Self-esteem
	 • Gullibility (likelihood of being tricked or manipulated)
	 • Naïveté
	 • Follows rules
	 • Obeys laws
	 • Avoids victimization
		• Activities of daily living
		   • Eating
		   • Transfer/mobility
		   • Toileting
		   • Dressing
		 • Instrumental activities of daily living
		   • Meal preparation
		   • Housekeeping
		   • Transportation
		   • Taking medication
		   • Money management
		   • Telephone use
		 • Occupational skills
		 • Maintains safe environments

Source: From *Mental retardation: Definition, classification, and systems of supports* (p. 42), by R. Luckasson et al., 2002. Washington, DC: American Association on Mental Retardation.

Developmental Period   The third definitional component is the **developmental period**. It has most often been defined as the period between conception and 18 years of age. Below-average intellectual functioning and disabilities in adaptive behavior must appear during this period for an individual to be considered to have ID.

Current Definition   The Schalock et al. (2010) definition is as follows:

> Intellectual disability is characterized by significant limitations both in intellectual functioning and in adaptive behavior as expressed in conceptual, social, and practical adaptive skills. This disability originates before age 18.
>
> The following five assumptions are essential to the application of the definition:

1. Limitations in present functioning must be considered within the context of community environments typical of the individual's age peers and culture.
2. Valid assessment considers cultural and linguistic diversity as well as differences in communication, sensory, motor, and behavioral factors.
3. Within an individual, limitations often coexist with strengths.
4. An important purpose of describing limitations is to develop a profile of needed supports.
5. With appropriate personalized supports over a sustained period, the life functioning of the person generally will improve. (p. 1)

Procedures for the identification of ID proceed directly from the specific scheme as outlined in the AAIDD definition. The key focus of the eligibility process is the application of professional judgment to data from the two key prongs of the definition, which include intellectual functioning and adaptive behavior. Schalock et al. (2010) added the following note regarding the relationship between the 2010 definition of ID and the prior 2002 definition of MR: "The term intellectual disability covers the same population of individuals who were diagnosed previously with mental retardation in number, kind, level, type, and duration of the disability, and the need of people with this disability for individualized services and supports. Furthermore, every individual who is or was eligible for a diagnosis of mental retardation is eligible for a diagnosis of intellectual disability" (p. xvi).

Although the focus in this chapter is on educational programming, it is important to note that the definition and diagnosis of ID has received significant interest in recent years in the criminal justice system. For example, for many years the courts, both state and federal, debated the wisdom of applying the death penalty to individuals with retardation. While many states historically excluded people with retardation from this penalty (if they had the death penalty at all), nevertheless, the U.S. Supreme Court previously only required that mental retardation be considered as a mitigating circumstance at sentencing (*Penry v. Lynaugh*, 1989, 1991). This changed with the *Atkins v. Virginia* (2002) decision in which the U.S. Supreme Court declared that no individual identified as mentally retarded could be executed.

As a result of the Atkins case, renewed attention has been given to precise aspects of the definition and the diagnostic process for making a determination of whether an individual is retarded. These issues have become major legal concerns and people whose functioning level puts them on the borderline have now received increased scrutiny from attorneys, judges, and juries as our society seeks to determine how to implement the Atkins decision (Patton & Keyes, 2006) (see Rights & Responsibilities).

The challenges of accurate identification, assessment, and eligibility criterion procedures have been faced by the field for many years.

Classification

The classification system still cited most often in the professional literature is the deficit system recommended by Grossman (1983). That system used the levels of mild, moderate, severe, and profound, which are summative judgments reflecting a sequence of more significant degrees of disability as based on both intelligence and adaptive behavior assessment. Among the many problems with this system was that the emphasis has primarily been on the former only, so IQ scores have frequently and unfortunately been equated with level of functioning.

Terms such as "educable" and "trainable" reflect another system that has been used in school environments. These archaic terms still remain in use today in some places; one may

RIGHTS & RESPONSIBILITIES

THE CRIMINAL JUSTICE SYSTEM: *ATKINS V. VIRGINIA* (2002)

Those of us who work in special education maintain an orientation and mindset of empowerment, capacity-building, and self-determination. The reality of the legal world, especially when it is about capital cases, however is that the total focus is on deficits. . . . The special education community attempts to downplay labels and their pejorative connotations. The legal world, however, is all about labels and their less-than-positive implications. Those of us with special education/human service backgrounds must recognize and become comfortable in this legal venue if we are going to be effective in writing reports, declarations, and affidavits, participating in depositions, or offering expert testimony in open court.

The Court's majority opinion . . . cited the Eighth Amendment, which prohibits "cruel and unusual punishment," and that there was serious concern whether either justification underpinning capital punishment, retribution and deterrence, applies to such offenders because of their perceived reduced level of culpability. "Construing and applying the Eighth Amendment in the light of our 'evolving standards of decency,' we therefore conclude that such punishment is excessive and that the Constitution places a substantive restriction on the State's power to take the life of a mentally retarded offender," wrote Justice Stevens. . . .

What is interesting is that the concept of mild mental retardation . . . has resurfaced as a primary area of professional focus. The salient issues and controversies associated with eligibility are now being raised on a level that has far more serious consequences than whether someone gets services or not. The issue is now about life or death. For those who have become involved in death penalty cases, the seriousness of these issues is professionally and personally challenging.

We must find better ways to convey to judges, juries, and attorneys on *both sides* of the bar, just what mild retardation is and how it looks to the nonprofessional. . . . People whose backgrounds include extensive experience working with individuals who have mental retardation can play a variety of critical roles in this most important work . . . a great need exists to educate the key professionals who are more and more a vital part of the criminal justice system and the public in general about mental retardation. As long as the United States continues to impose a death penalty for capital offenses, a need will remain for determining whether certain individuals meet the criteria of mental retardation in judicial proceedings.

Source: From "Death penalty issues following *Atkins,*" by J. R. Patton and D. W. Keys (2006). *Exceptionality, 14,* pp. 21–22.

---

unfortunately continue to hear students referred to as **EMR (educable mentally retarded)** and **TMR (trainable mentally retarded)**. The terms roughly correspond to **mild** and **moderate/severe**, respectively. However, by nature, these terms are inherently stereotypical and prejudicial, and consequently and appropriately have been criticized, thus gradually leading to decreased use.

An alternative is to classify ID according to only two more general levels of functioning (i.e., mild and severe/significant) and to avoid reliance on IQ scores in considerations of level of severity. With such a less-formal approach, the consideration of levels of adaptive skills serves as the yardstick for determining level of disability, resulting in a more meaningful and broad-based, though less precise, system of classification. This approach is commonly, if somewhat informally, used in the field and is consistent with the discussion in this text.

An alternative approach to classification is not derived from levels of deficit, but rather from needed **supports**. As defined by Luckasson and colleagues (2002), "supports are resources and strategies that aim to promote the development, education, interests, and personal well-being of a person and that enhance individual functioning" (p. 151). Thus, a supports model focuses on the needs rather than on the deficits of the individual. Considerations of educational needs for individuals with ID are best conceptualized within a supports model. Figure 7.1 provides a model from Thompson and colleagues (2009) to illustrate this key concept. In Table 7.2, further information concerning the concept of supports is provided by describing functions and selected representative activities.

Prevalence and Educational Environments

The 29th Annual Report to Congress (USDOE, 2009) provided a 10-year perspective on *prevalence* and confirmed limited annual variance in ID during this decade. Consistently the

FIGURE 7.1

Supports model.

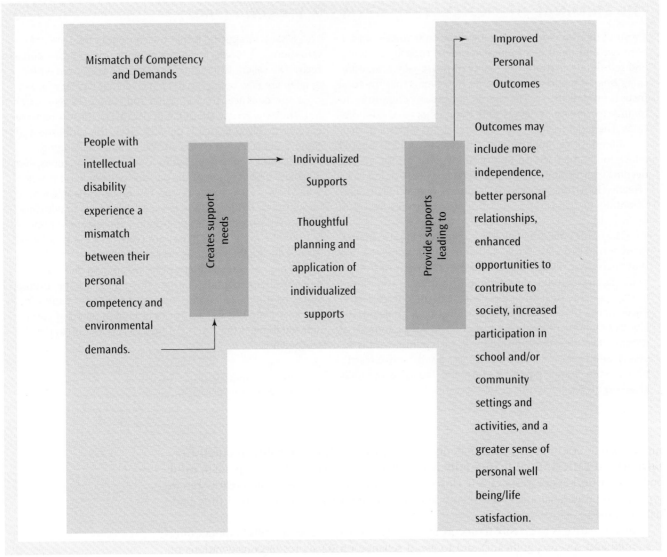

Source: Thompson, J. R., Bradley, V. J., Buntinx, W. H. E., Schalock, R. L., Shogren, K. A., Snell, M. E. et al. (2009). Conceptualization and the support needs of people with intellectual disability. *Intellectual and Developmental Disabilities, 47,* 137.

trend has been that slightly less than 1% (approximately 0.9% for 1995–2003; 0.84% in 2004) of school-age children are likely to be identified as MR or ID.

The most compelling finding related to prevalence is the significant variance across states (Polloway et al., 2010). A total of 12 states report prevalence rates in excess of 1.2%, including two states that report prevalence figures above 2% (West Virginia: 2.48% & Kansas: 2.00%). On the other hand, there are 19 states that report prevalence rates that are below 0.6%; eight states reported a prevalence figure of 0.40% or below (USDOE, 2009).

For the states with high prevalence, the population being served is likely not dissimilar to that which was commonly identified 30 or more years ago under the label mental retardation, and would likely include a sizable number of individuals with mild disabilities. On the other hand, for those states who reported serving approximately 0.4% or less of their population, this population would likely include only individuals with more significant disabilities (Polloway, Patton, & Nelson, 2011), given the fact that 0.4% is commonly cited in epidemiology studies as the most likely predictor of the number of persons with severe disabilities within a given population (e.g., Abramowicz & Richardson, 1975; MacMillan, 2007).

TABLE 7.2

Support Functions and Representative Activities

SUPPORT FUNCTION*	REPRESENTATIVE ACTIVITIES		
Teaching	Supervising	Training	Instructing
	Giving feedback	Evaluating	Collecting data
	Organizing the learning environment	Supporting inclusive classrooms	Individualizing instruction
Befriending	Advocating	Evaluating	Reciprocating
	Car pooling	Communicating	Associating and disassociating
	Supervising	Training	Socializing
	Instructing	Giving feedback	
Financial Planning	Working with SSI–Medicaid	Assisting with money management	Budgeting
	Advocating for benefits	Protection and legal assistance	Income assistance and planning/considerations
Employee Assistance	Counseling	Supervisory training	Crisis intervention/ assistance
	Procuring/using assistive technology devices	Job performance enhancement	Job/task accommodation and redesigning job/work duties
Behavioral Support	Functional analysis	Manipulation of ecological and setting events	Building environment with effective consequences
	Multicomponent instruction	Teaching adaptive behavior	
	Emphasis on antecedent manipulation		
In-Home Living Assistance	Personal maintenance/care	Communication devices	Respite care
	Transfer and mobility	Behavioral support	Attendant care
	Dressing and clothing care	Eating and food management	Home-health aides
	Architectural modifications	Housekeeping	Homemaker services
Community Access and Use	Carpooling/rides program	Recreation/leisure involvement	Community use opportunities and interacting with generic agencies
	Transportation training	Community awareness opportunities	
	Personal protection skills	Vehicle modification	Personal protection skills
Health Assistance	Medical appointments	Emergency procedures	Hazard awareness
	Medical interventions	Mobility (assistive devices)	Safety training
	Supervision	Counseling appointments	Physical therapy and related activities
	Med Alert devices	Medication taking	Counseling interventions

*The support functions and activities may need to be modified slightly to accommodate individuals of different ages.

Source: Adapted from *Mental Retardation: Definition, Classification, and Systems of Supports* (pp. 153–154), by R. Luckasson et al., 2002. Washington, DC: American Association on Mental Retardation.

The history of placement in *educational environments* for students with ID was characterized by research attention in the 1950s through the 1970s followed by a long period of philosophical, rather than empirical, focus. Throughout this period, the most common service delivery system was the self-contained class, a special class-based program in which students spent the majority of their time in a pull-out program and were integrated for certain periods throughout the school day.

Gradually, this process has changed as there has been an increased commitment to inclusion in the field of ID as there has been in education in general. Nevertheless, the placement of students into programs *outside* of general education is still predominant, with 56.9% of these students in environments removed from the general education classroom, respectively at least 60% of the day (i.e., 50.5%) or in separate environments (e.g., special schools, residential programs) (i.e., 6.4%) (Polloway et al., 2010; USDOE, 2009). Williamson, McLeskey, Hoppey, and Lentz (2006) noted that, while placement in general education-based programs increased from 27.3% to 44.7% in the 1990s, this increase essentially plateaued after 1997–1998.

As with prevalence, the data on educational environments also reflect a high degree of interstate variation. Depending upon the individual state, there is a strong commitment to educating students with intellectual disabilities in inclusive settings while other states still reflect a significant commitment to nongeneral education settings for the majority of students with ID. In any case, when evaluating placement considerations, educators should realize that setting alone does not represent an effective intervention for the students.

Causation and Risk Factors

There are hundreds of known causes of ID, and at the same time, numerous cases for which the cause is unknown. Only in about 50% of individual cases is a specific biological factor identified (Van Karnebeek et al., 2005). Those cases with an identified cause are disproportionally represented among individuals with more significant disabilities. The group of individuals with undetermined etiology includes many persons identified as having mild intellectual disability (President's Committee for People with Intellectual Disabilities [PCPID], 2007) because there simply are often no identifiable causes for mild ID (Snell et al., 2009). Polloway, Smith, and Antoine (2010) noted that causation often has been overly simplistically described as a two-group model. The first group, known and specifiable biological causes, results in intellectual disabilities at all levels. The second group is presumed to be impacted by psychosocial factors (Spinath, Harlaar, Ronald, & Plomin, 2004) coupled with other environmental influences. A combination of possible risk factors that are within the psychosocial domain include an absence of significant parental guidance and mediation, maternal education level, inadequate housing, and poor school attendance. For this hypothetical second group, possible causes can be identified but precise contributions can rarely be confirmed.

Table 7.3 outlines some representative causes to show the complexity of this area of concern. This information is limited to selected causes and brief, related information; see Polloway, Smith, and Antoine (2010) for a fuller discussion of biological causes and prevention and Beirne-Smith, Patton, and Kim (2010) for an analysis of psychosocial aspects.

CHARACTERISTICS

Given the diversity of people who may be identified as intellectually disabled, the drawing of a portrait of characteristics must be done with caution. In general, such discussion first includes attention to individuals who might be identified as having mild versus significant intellectual disabilities. That broad distinction certainly carries with it risks of simplification and error but nevertheless serves a useful function within this chapter.

Some generalizations related to mild intellectual disabilities are reasonable. Recent research on learning in students with ID has been relatively limited, and this group has been referred to as the "forgotten generation" (Fujiura, 2003). Quite simply, in considering the

TABLE 7.3

Selected Causes of Intellectual Disabilities

CAUSE	NATURE OF PROBLEM	CONSIDERATIONS
Down Syndrome	Trisomy 21 (3 chromosomes on this pair) IQ range from severe retardation to nonretarded	Wide variance in learning characteristics Classic physical signs Most common chromosomal anomaly
Environmental or Psychosocial Disadvantage	Elements of poverty environment (e.g., family constellation, resources, educational role models)	Can be related to mild disabilities Commonly associated with school failure
Fetal Alcohol Syndrome (FAS)	Caused by drinking alcohol during pregnancy Related to toxic effects of alcohol Fetal alcohol effects: less significant disorder	Associated with varying degrees of disability May be accompanied by facial and other malformations and behavioral disturbances Among the three most common biologically based causes of retardation
Fragile X Syndrome	Genetic disorder related to gene on X chromosome	Most often transmitted from mother to son Frequently associated with ID in males and LD in females (in some instances) May be accompanied by variant patterns of behavior (e.g., self-stimulation), social skills difficulties, language impairment
Hydrocephalus	Multiple causes (e.g., genetic, environmental) Disruption in appropriate flow of cerebrospinal fluid on the brain	Previously associated with enlarged head and brain damage Controlled by the implantation of a shunt
Phenylketonuria	Autosomal recessive genetic disorder	Associated with metabolic problems in processing high-protein foods Can be controlled via restrictive diets implemented at birth
Prader-Willi Syndrome	Chromosomal error: autosomal type	Associated with biological compulsion to excessive eating Obesity as a common secondary trait to ID
Tay-Sachs	Autosomal recessive genetic disorder	Highest risk for Ashkenazic Jewish people Associated with severe ID and early mortality No known cure Prevention through genetic screening

characteristics of individuals with mild ID as well as the implications for curriculum and instruction, it is important to note that the rich research literature that developed in this field has been somewhat neglected for many years. Table 7.4 presents a summary chart of possible characteristics for persons with mild ID derived from Polloway et al. (2011) based on prior reviews by Smith, Polloway, Patton, and Dowdy (2007), Patton and Keyes

TABLE 7.4

Intellectual Disabilities: Characteristics and Implications

AREA	POTENTIAL DIFFICULTIES	EDUCATIONAL IMPLICATIONS
Attention	Attention span (length of time on task)	Train students to be aware of the importance of attention.
	Focus (inhibition of distracting stimuli)	Teach students how to actively self-monitor their attention.
	Selective attention (discrimination of important stimulus characteristics)	Highlight salient cues in instruction.
Metacognition	Metacognition: thinking about thinking	Teach specific strategies (rehearsal, labeling, chunking).
	Production of strategies to assist learning	Involve students in active learning process (practice, apply, review).
	Organizing new information	Stress meaningful content.
Memory	Short-term memory—common deficit area	Strategy production is difficult; hence students need to be shown how to use strategies to proceed in an organized, well-planned manner.
	Long-term memory—usually more similar to that of people who are not disabled (once information has been learned)	Stress meaningful content.
Generalization Learning	Applying knowledge of skills to new tasks, or situations	Teach multiple contexts.
		Reinforce generalization.
	Using previous experience to formulate rules that will help solve problems of similar nature	Teach skills in relevant contexts.
		Remind students to apply what they have learned.
Motivational Considerations	External locus of control (attributing events to others' influence)	Create environment focused on success opportunities.
	Outerdirectedness (in learning style)	Emphasize self-reliance.
	Low expectations by others	Promote self-management.
	Failure set (personal expectancy of failure)	Teach learning strategies for academic tasks.
		Focus on learning to learn.
		Encourage problem-solving strategies.
Cognitive Development	Ability to engage in abstract thinking	Provide concrete examples in instruction.
	Symbolic thought, as exemplified by introspection and developing hypotheses	Provide contextual learning experiences.
		Encourage active interaction between student and the environment
Language Development	Difficulty with receptive and expressive language	Create environment that encourages verbal communication.
	Delayed acquisition of vocabulary and language rules	Encourage expression of thoughts.
	Articulation of thoughts and feelings	Provide appropriate language models.
	Possible interaction of cultural variance and language dialects	Provide opportunities for students to learn language for varied purposes and with different audiences.

TABLE 7.4 (continued)

AREA	POTENTIAL DIFFICULTIES	EDUCATIONAL IMPLICATIONS
Academic Development	Delayed acquisition of reading, writing, and mathematical skills	Use learning strategies to promote effective studying.
	Decoding of text	Teach sight words including functional applications.
	Reading comprehension	Teach strategies for decoding unknown words.
	Math computation	Provide strategies to promote reading comprehension and math problem solving.
	Problem-solving in mathematics	
	Self-directed expressive writing	Develop functional writing skills.
		Adapt curriculum to promote success.
Social-Behavorial Interactions	Classroom behavior	Promote social competence through direct instruction of skills.
	Peer acceptance	Reinforce appropriate behaviors.
	Displaying emotions appropriately	Seek self-understanding of reasons for inappropriate behavior.
		Teach self-management, self-control
Social Responding	Social perception	Involve peers as classroom role models.
	Gullibility	Provide a support system of peers for positive guidance "buddy system".
	Suggestibility	
	Acquiescence and desire to please	Teach resistance to social manipulation.
	Masking disability ("cloak of competence")	Teach Miranda rights in the legal system.

Source: Adapted from Patton & Keyes, 2006; Smith, Polloway, Patton, & Beyer, 2008; Smith, Polloway, Patton, & Dowdy, 2008; and Polloway, Patton, & Nelson, 2011.

(2006), and Smith, Polloway, Patton, and Beyer (2008). The adapted table reflects information on terminology concerning characteristics, a description of problem areas within particular domains, and the educational implications for those individuals for whom it is relevant.

Significant Disabilities

The group of individuals who are considered to have significant, or severe, disabilities is broad and includes individuals with a wide range of characteristics, as was noted earlier for individuals with mild ID. One common characteristic shared by this group is the need for extensive and ongoing supports (Snell & Brown, 2006).

Students with significant intellectual disabilities, or those in requiring extensive supports, may display a number of the same characteristics, or similar patterns of characteristics, as individuals with mild ID, but at a more pronounced level. In general, characteristics of the group include:

- Adaptive behavior difficulties
- Limited academic skills
- Significant need for social skills development
- Difficulty with generalizing knowledge and skills
- Challenges with metacognition
- Language development delays
- Possible memory problems

When students with significant disabilities as reflected in these patterns of characteristics are included in a general education classroom, it is likely that special education supports will be provided in order to facilitate successful inclusion. An important area of concern will be to individually assess the students to evaluate the specific characteristics that have implications for instruction. As noted in Chapter 2, functional assessments are most appropriate for determining intervention strategies. This will be particularly true in communication, a common area challenge for individuals with significant disabilities. Functional communication goals should be established to facilitate individuals' participation in the classroom.

One key area of concern has to do with making choices. As Stafford (2005) and others have noted, while most individuals take making choices for granted, individuals with significant disabilities are often not allowed to make choices or have not been provided guidance in learning how to make choices. As a consequence, these individuals become dependent on others to a significant degree. In the discussion on effective inclusive practices, further attention is given to the importance of empowerment, self-determination, and decision-making, which are critical to students with significant disabilities.

Perspectives on Outcomes

A critical foundation for considering educational programs for students with ID comes from a consideration of school and young adult outcomes. Data on these outcomes are provided in several key sources: the reports of Congress from the USDOE (e.g., 2009), the National Longitudinal Transition Study – 2 (NLTS-2) (Wagner, Newman, Cameto, Garza, & Levine, 2005), and a summative report of the NLTS (Newman, Wagner, Cameto, & Knokey, 2009).

The USDOE (2009) reported that dropout rates for students with ID generally have declined (from 40% in 1985 to 27.6% in 2004). Nevertheless, a substantial number of students are still not completing school as defined by federal guidelines—only 39% receive regular diplomas; those numbers have increased only 5.4% since 1995. Those students identified as ID were consistently less likely to graduate than were students identified with 11 other categories of disabilities; only students with emotional disturbance were less likely to graduate.

Snell and colleagues (2009) reported that the employment rate of individuals with ID with higher IQs was 27.6%, far below the national average of 75.1%. In addition, these data are skewed by the likelihood that the positions often held may be part-time and associated with lower wages and limited benefits. Newman and colleagues (2009) reported that 51.8% of individuals with intellectual disabilities had been employed at some point in time since high school, with 31% employed at the time of interview. Only 31.6% indicated that they found their job by themselves (the lowest percentage figure for all disability groups other than autism). The average work week was less than full-time (30.1 hours per week). The reported average hourly wage was $7.00. The majority of these positions were in unskilled labor, food services, cleaning, stocking and shipping, and serving as a cashier. On a positive note, 77.4% indicated that they liked the job either very much or fairly well. More detailed findings are provided in Table 7.5.

Special Considerations

Two key areas related to characteristics warrant special attention. The first is *educational expectations*, which serves as a foundation for understanding the characteristics and educational experiences of individuals with ID. The area owes much of its early attention to the presumption of a self-fulfilling prophecy in education. The importance of expectation in determining an individual's achievement is intuitively strong. In a comprehensive study of this area, several researchers concluded that the impact of teacher behavior on student achievement had differentiated effects based on whether students were high or low achievers (McGrew & Evans, 2004).

In the context of ID, clearly students are likely to be low achievers and are potentially thus subject to the negative impact of teachers' expectations. The result may be a diminished

---

TABLE 7.5

Summary of NLTS-2 Findings: Students with Intellectual Disabilities

AREA	FINDINGS
Transition Services	• Many students (60%) had transition planning begun by age 14 • 48.7% did not provide input in discussing their transition plans • Very few individuals (3.3%) took leadership role during transition process • General educators' involvement in transition process was minimal • Few individuals (9.8%) chose postsecondary education as transition goal • 51.4% of the students chose living independently as a transition goal • 75.8% received instruction specifically focused on transition-related topics • The program provided for most students (79.5%) was identified as "very or fairly well suited" for preparing them to achieve transition goals
Outcomes	Postsecondary School Enrollment (percentage): • any postsecondary school (15.4) • postsecondary vocational, business, or technical school (11) • 2 year/community college (5.1) Current Employment (24.8) Living Arrangements • with parents (72.2) • on own, with spouse, roommate, or in dorm (16.3) Post-school Independence: Have a . . . . • driver's license/permit (20.7) • checking account (10.1) • charge account or credit card (6.9) Leisure Time: • watching TV/videos (41) • using a computer (13.5) • listening to music (18.7) • doing hobbies, reading for pleasure (4.7) • talking on the phone with friends (9.2) • playing sports (16.3) Friendship Interactions: in past year, • saw friends outside of school or work at least weekly (46.3) • communicating by computer at least daily (21.9) Participation in Community Activities: in the past year, took part in . . . • community group (e.g., sports team, club, religious group) (23.8) • volunteer or community service activity (22.7)

Source: Wagner, M., Newman, L., Cameto, R., Garza, N., & Levine, P. (2005). *After high school: A first look at the post-school experiences of youth with disabilities: A report from the National Longitudinal Transition Study-2 (NTLS-2)*. Menlo Park, CA: SRI International.

---

level of achievement even beyond that which might be expected based on the intellectual level of the student. This hypothesis helps to explain the common finding that students with ID experience even more significant difficulties in academic learning than might have been anticipated. Key expectancy effects related to level of achievement reported by McGrew and Evans (2004) are as follows:

• Students who are high achievers are nearly invulnerable to teacher perceptions that underestimate ability. When teachers overestimate ability, these students also exhibit increased achievement.
• Students who are low achievers are differentially responsive to teachers' over- and underestimation of predicted achievement growth. When growth is underestimated, students tend to achieve less. However, when achievement growth is overestimated, students achieve more.

Differentiating Secondary Instruction

A significant concern for teaching students with intellectual disabilities is ensuring that the students are held to *high expectations*. To respond to the challenges related to teacher expectations, a number of principles are available to guide educational practice. Teacher behaviors that are associated with communicating low expectancies, and thus should be avoided, include (McGrew & Evans, 2004):

- Offering more limited opportunities to learn new material.
- Providing less "wait" time to answer questions.
- Providing answers for a student or calling on someone else.

- Using criticism for failure or offering insincere praise.
- Providing limited reinforcement and having it not be contingent on completed tasks.
- Engaging in differential treatment among students (e.g., less friendly or responsive, limited eye contact, fewer smiles).
- Providing briefer and less useful feedback to responses.
- Asking lower-level cognitive questions to the exclusion of those that challenge the students' thinking.

Therefore, low achievers experience academic growth that matches teachers' predictions for achievement. Low achievers are more susceptible to teacher self-fulfilling prophecies than are most high-achieving students (McGrew & Evans, 2004). Further information is provided in the Differentiated Instruction—Secondary boxed reading.

A second special consideration relates to a characteristic that Greenspan (2006) argued is an essential element of ID— gullibility, or vulnerability to social manipulation (see Table 7.4). If accepted as a fundamental concept in ID, it provides some explanation for the disproportionate level of behavioral problems experienced by individuals with ID as well as related disproportionately in the criminal justice system. Further, it relates directly to questions of the death penalty in the aftermath of the *Atkins v. Virginia* decision (see the Rights & Responsibilities box).

Finally, let's return to the question about weaknesses and strengths as well as deficits and supports. While the potentials and opportunities for students with intellectual disabilities are excellent, their success is most definitely determined in many instances by the supports provided by others. Therefore, it is sobering to consider that these supports can result not only in successful school and community inclusion but also in difficulties because of vulnerability, such as to a negative benefactor.

EFFECTIVE INCLUSIVE PRACTICES

Education in inclusive settings presents a unique opportunity for students with intellectual disabilities, their peers, and their teachers. Without question, educators must deliver quality programs, or else the prognosis for young adults with ID will not reflect the positive quality of life to which they, like all people, aspire.

Challenges for General Education

The data on postschool outcomes point to critical areas that educators need to address. Therefore, this section begins with this focus to provide an overall foundation for subsequent discussions. Educators should keep these concerns in mind as they develop and implement curricula and instructional plans in conjunction with special education teachers. Patton and colleagues (1996) identified four primary goals: productive employment, independence and self-sufficiency, life skills competence, and opportunity to participate successfully within the schools and the community. These four overarching goals challenge teachers to structure educational programs so that these important emphases can complement the primary focus of curriculum and instruction on state learning standards.

In relation to *employment,* teachers should build students' career awareness and help them see how academic content relates to applied situations; at the secondary level, this effort should include training in specific job skills. This concern should be the primary focus of vocational educators who work with these students.

In terms of *independence and economic self-sufficiency,* young adults need to know how to become personally responsible. As Miller (1995) stated, the educational goal "is to develop self-directed learners who can address their own wants and concerns and can advocate for their goals and aspirations" (p. 12).

The successful inclusion of students with intellectual disabilities depends on the ability of teachers and peers, and on the curriculum, to create a climate of empowerment. Empowerment involves self-efficacy, a sense of personal control, self-esteem, and a sense of belonging to a group. Empowerment is not an automatic by-product of inclusive classrooms. However, when students are members of the group and retain the right to make their own decisions, they are being prepared for the challenges and rewards of life. One essential element is self-determination (Smith, Polloway, Smith, & Patton, 2007). As Wehmeyer (1993) noted:

> Self-determination refers to the attitudes and abilities necessary to act as the primary causal agent in one's life, and to make choices and decisions regarding one's quality of life free from undue external influence or interference. (p. 16)

Zhang (2001b) noted that self-determination includes: "making choices, making decisions, solving problems, setting and attaining goals, being independent, evaluating our performance, self-studying, speaking up for self, having internal motivations, believing in one's own abilities, being aware of personal strengths and weaknesses, and applying strengths to overcome weaknesses" (p. 339).

A third key consideration is the importance *of a life skills focus* to achieving competence in everyday activities. This area includes, but is not limited to, use of community resources, home and family activities, social and interpersonal skills, health and safety skills, use of leisure time, and participation in the community as a citizen (e.g., compliance with legal and cultural standards) (see Table 7.6). With the increased commitment to inclusion, a particularly challenging consideration for both general and special educators is how to include a life skills and transitional focus within the general education curriculum beginning at the elementary-school level and continue it throughout formal schooling. A critical concern is the successful blending of a standards-based curriculum with a focus on life skills and community preparation (Hoover & Patton, 2004).

A fourth consideration, *successful school and community involvement,* requires that students experience inclusive environments. Students with ID can learn to participate in school and in the community by being included in general education classrooms. Although some might view school inclusion as an end in itself, it is better viewed as a condition that can provide instruction and training for success in subsequent inclusive community activities. Further information on the role of education in providing for successful adult adjustment is reflected in the IEP Goals and Objectives for Jandrew along with the Tips for Adapting a Lesson.

Transition Considerations   The four foci just described all point collectively to the importance of successful life transitions for students with ID. Key considerations as cited by the NLTS-2 (Wagner et al., 2005) include:

- Identifying and implementing evidence-based transition practices
- Instituting techniques for starting the transition process earlier
- Empowering students so that they are more involved in their own transition and are able to advocate for themselves
- Increasing the opportunities for further education and training
- Empowering parents by providing them with information about the transition process and what to expect when their children finish school.

General education teachers would be quite unlikely to have full responsibility for meeting the transitional needs of all of their students; nevertheless, this focus is one of the most critical

TABLE 7.6

Major Life Demands

DOMAIN	SUBDOMAIN	SAMPLE LIFE DEMANDS
Employment/Education	General job skills	Seeking and securing a job
		Learning job skills
		Maintaining one's job
	General education/training considerations	Gaining entry to postsecondary education/training settings (higher education, adult education, community education, trade/technical schools, military service)
		Finding financial support
		Utilizing academic and system survival skills (e.g., study skills, organizational skills, and time management)
	Employment setting	Recognizing job duties and responsibilities
		Exhibiting appropriate work habits/behavior
		Getting along with employer and coworkers
Home and Family	Home management	Setting up household operations (e.g., initiating utilities)
		Cleaning dwelling
		Laundering and maintaining clothes and household items
	Financial management	Creating a general financial plan (e.g., savings, investments, retirement)
		Paying bills
		Obtaining government assistance when needed (e.g., Medicare, food stamps, student loans)
	Family life	Preparing for marriage, family
		Maintaining physical/emotional health of family members
		Planning and preparing meals (menu, buying food, ordering take-out food, dining out)
Leisure Pursuits	Indoor activities	Performing individual physical activities (e.g., weight training, aerobics, dance, swimming, martial arts)
		Participating in group physical activities (e.g., racquetball, basketball)
	Outdoor activities	Engaging in general recreating activities (e.g., camping, sightseeing, picnicking)

Source: Adapted from Cronin, M. E., Patton, J. R., & Wood, S. J. (2007). Life skills instruction: A practical guide for intergrating real-life content into the curriculum at the elementary and secondary levels for students with special needs or who are placed at risk. Austin, TX: Pro-Ed (pp. 19–20).

curricular and instructional aspects of their needs. Patton and Dunn (1998) summarized the essential features of transition, highlighting the following:

- Transition efforts must start early and planning must be comprehensive.
- Decisions must balance what is ideal with what is possible.
- Active and meaningful student participation and family involvement are essential.
- Supports are beneficial and used by everyone.

SELECTED IEP GOALS AND OBJECTIVES FOR JANDREW

The importance of a focus on educational programs is reflected in this set of IEP goals and objectives for Jandrew (from the chapter-opening vignette). These goal/objective clusters each reflect the importance of applying what was learned in the academic curriculum to functional life skills:

GOAL 1   To obtain a valid driver's license.

Objective 1: Given a teacher-developed test orally, which parallels the requirements for a driver's license, Jandrew will score at 80% accuracy.

Objective 2: Given a written form of a teacher-made driver's test, Jandrew will score at 80% accuracy (with graduated, less intrusive prompts).

Objective 3: Given the state-required written test, Jandrew will successfully pass the test.

Objective 4: Given the opportunity to enroll in the behind-the-wheel educational program, Jandrew will successfully complete the program.

Objective 5: Given the opportunity to take behind-the-wheel driver's test, Jandrew will achieve at an acceptable competency level.

GOAL 2   To successfully complete apprenticeship program at IGA.

Objective 1: Given a job application for IGA, Jandrew will accurately complete the application for an apprentice position with 100% accuracy.

Objective 2: Given the opportunity to use public transportation, Jandrew will effectively use transportation to arrive on time for work on a daily basis with 100% accuracy.

Objective 3: Given this workplace setting, Jandrew will demonstrate correct application of safety rules with 100% accuracy.

Objective 4: Given necessary tools and equipment to clean the floor at work, Jandrew will demonstrate specific skills required for cleaning floor and emptying trash receptacles with 100% accuracy.

GOAL 3   To demonstrate the ability to handle personal finances in the areas of housing, food, leisure, and transportation.

Objective 1: Given a set income level, Jandrew will establish a realistic weekly budget to cover daily living expenses.

Objective 2: Given the opportunity to eat whatever he wants, Jandrew will identify elements of a nutritious diet with 80% accuracy.

Objective 3: Given the opportunity to live alone, Jandrew will be able to identify appropriate supports and be able to access assistance as needed for budget management 100% of the time.

- Community-based instructional experiences have a major impact on learning.
- The transition planning process should be viewed as a capacity-building activity.
- Transition planning is needed by all students.

Polloway and colleagues (2011) concluded their discussion of the implications of outcomes date for education as follows: "with graduation rates low for students with ID, school dropout rates relatively high, employment statistics discouraging, and social domain data suggesting limited positive, active engagement, there remains need for an increased commitment to retention in school and successful completion as well as successful transition preparation" (pp. 112–134).

Promoting Inclusive Practices

The key to including students with intellectual disabilities in the general education classroom is providing necessary and appropriate supports. These include personal supports

TIPS FOR ADAPTING A LESSON FOR JANDREW

The following selected adaptations reflect the learning and life needs as well as the classroom challenges for Jandrew. They provide an illustration of adaptations that may be effective with students with special needs.

Jandrew's teacher can:

- Use video-based training to learn the key elements in the driving manual.
- Use a software simulation of behind-the-wheel driving program.
- Use community-based instruction to illustrate application of academic concepts (e.g., consumer math) in shopping.

- Read test questions to Jandrew in social studies.
- Use weighted grades to emphasize laboratory assessments (versus solely test grades) in assigning report card grades in science.
- Develop cooperative learning groups and use group grades for literature projects in English.

(e.g., self-regulation, academic skills), natural supports (e.g., parents, friends), support services (e.g., specialized instruction), and technical supports (e.g., assistive technology). A focus on the concept of **supported education**, as a necessary complement to inclusion, assumes that individuals should be educated in inclusive classroom settings to the maximum degree possible and supported in those settings to ensure successful learning.

There has been a too-frequent tendency simply to physically place students in the general education classroom. Inclusion, as supported education, should focus on welcoming and involving people with disabilities in the general education classroom. Merely placing students with ID in general education without active classroom participation will be unlikely to result in positive gains for students. Likewise, adults with intellectual disabilities who live in the community but do not participate in community activities do not fulfill the true spirit of inclusion.

Successful inclusion, therefore, is inescapably linked to how well general education is prepared to handle students who will require differentiated strategies in terms of content, instructional materials, instruction, assignments, testing, products, setting, and management (Hoover & Patton, 2005, 2008). In a multi-tiered model of providing intervention (see Chapter 2), the need for general education teachers to be equipped to address the needs of students with intellectual disabilities is imperative.

■ Teachers need to promote an environment where social relationships can be developed.

A multi-tiered system creates a change of roles for special education personnel as well (Hoover & Patton, 2008). For example, special educators with responsibility for individuals with mild intellectual disabilities must also assume responsibility for more than just direct instruction in pull-out programs. Rather, they also must work collaboratively in preventive efforts typically associated with Tier I instruction (enhanced instructional delivery in general education programs) as well as supportive efforts often associated with Tier II instruction (ongoing collaboration in general education programs).

Beyond the curricular and instructional adaptations summarized previously, several other considerations are central to successful inclusion. The first is the creation of a sense of community in the school in general and the classroom in particular. As noted previously, successful inclusion is best achieved as a by-product of supported education—an environment where students succeed because they are welcomed, encouraged, and involved (i.e., supported) in their learning.

The challenge for teachers seeking to successfully include students with intellectual disabilities reaches beyond the students' acquisition of, for example, specific academic skills. Rather, it requires finding ways to provide a "belonging place" for them in the general education classroom. Such a place can be created through friendships, a key priority outcome for the students themselves (Fox & Emerson, 2001).

Frequently, a key individual will be the paraprofessional who is providing classroom support to these students, especially for individuals with significant disabilities who may be included in the general education classroom. Causton-Theoharis and Malmgren (2005) focused on the roles that paraprofessionals can play in terms of facilitating peer interaction. They recommended that paraprofessionals should analyze their own social relationships and focus on how those relate to the students with whom they are working. Teachers should stress the importance of peer interactions so that paraprofessionals are focused on this critical area. Attention should be given to how specific strategies can be used to facilitate this interaction. Providing information about such strategies as a way to enhance the skills of paraprofessionals will be of particular importance.

A beneficial strategy for promoting social acceptance for students (and young adults) involves "circles of support," or "circles of friends." Teachers should consider developing such systems by having students who are not disabled being part of these circles of friends not only to benefit those with disabilities but also because the individuals who are nondisabled may also benefit through enhanced attitudes, personal growth, and a sense of civic responsibility in addition to the benefits of friendship (Hughes et al., 2001).

Finally, it is of critical importance to the educators and to the lives of students with ID that families be actively involved in planning and implementation of programs. The Personal Spotlight illustrates this well.

CLASSROOM ADAPTATIONS

Curricular Adaptations

As inclusion has become the placement alternative of choice for students with disabilities in general, and individuals with intellectual disabilities in particular, the standard curriculum likewise has become the "program of choice" for more students with ID. Review of data on the preferences of general education teachers concerning modifications and adaptations for such students indicates that preferred adaptations typically revolve more around changes in instructional delivery systems and response modes (e.g., testing adaptations such as extended time) rather than in changes in the actual curriculum or the standards associated with the curricular content (e.g., Polloway, Epstein, & Bursuck, 2002; see also Chapter 15). Therefore, to the extent that these observations are verified, it is likely that a specialized curriculum may less commonly be available for students with mild ID (Patton, Polloway, & Smith, 2000). Nevertheless, given the preceding discussion, teachers need to be aware of the importance of a functional focus within the curriculum in order to enhance learning and adult outcomes.

One key focus should be on relevant and meaningful curricular content that students can master and apply to their current and future lives. Teachers should focus on the subsequent environments for which students will prepare (in terms of learning, working, residing) as a basis for curriculum design. The subsequent-environments rationale has applicability across the school levels as individuals prepare for successful transitions and life challenges. Most important is the assurance that the secondary school curriculum prepares students with ID (as well as all students) for adulthood, whether that means further education, job placement, or independent living.

Specific adaptations can enhance learning and increase relevance. Assistive technology can further enhance classroom adaptations. Although students with ID can benefit from a variety of technological applications, the key concern is that technology be used in a way that effectively enhances learning through conscious attention to the use of technology for each of the four respective stages of learning: the *acquisition* of new skills, the development of fluency and *proficiency,* the *maintenance* of skills over time, and the *generalization* of skills learned to other settings, including beyond the school and into the community.

PERSONAL SPOTLIGHT

ANDREA GAJADHAR

My child was not born with a disability; however, she became intellectually disabled as a result of illness, and because of that, my whole life was changed. It is one thing to know from the onset that you have a child with a disability, but to have a child who developed typically and then regressed is something totally different. Here you have your hopes and dreams for your first child washed away, your whole focus on life changes because this thing is so new to you. During pregnancy, the thought never crossed your mind that you could end up with a child with a disability, then it happens and it is as if you had a cup of cold water thrown on your life's fire. This whole disability thing is so new to you, and the health personnel in my country were not well-versed on this issue and did not have any answers to give to me. You are left practically on your own to deal with the issues arising from the disability.

Then you have the society to deal with, a society at that time in my country that was very ignorant when it came to disabilities, so there were no support services that you could go to. In fact everyone looked at your child in very peculiar ways. As a parent, I would be very ashamed of the way my daughter would act, some of the things she would do, or the fact that she was not speaking and I had to answer so many questions regarding her. Because of the lack of social supports, parents of children with disabilities would isolate their children from the public, not exposing them to the world. I decided on the contrary, I would not isolate my child, but would teach her to socialize. I had the support of family members and so it was not as difficult as I thought it would be. Most times I felt that it was my fault that she developed a disability, sometimes I would reflect on the times she was

sick trying to think of what it is that I did wrong, what could have been done differently to have prevented this from happening to her. People describe overprotection as a dysfunction but I do not see it this way. I live with the fear of my daughter being taken advantage of or even being the victim of abuse. Also, because of the limited knowledge of the general public on dealing with persons with disabilities, I will not allow her to go out on a date or live independently. Unless my country gets to the stage where more will be done for persons with disabilities such as employment, housing, public awareness, and laws to protect the individual rights, then I will keep her sheltered.

As a family, we have provided her with a loving atmosphere. She has a special relationship with her siblings, and what is amazing is that her sister says that anyone of her peers "who is not accepting of my sister cannot be my friend." One of my greatest fears is dying before my daughter, because inasmuch as everyone in my family and close friends are accepting and love her, I feel that no one will care for her the way I do. My fervent prayer is that she departs this life before me, in that way I will rest in peace.

It is sad that historically parents felt that they had to isolate their disabled child or place them in institutions and not even give a backward glance. I have learned that when you have gotten over the fact that your child has a disability, you begin to love them and you learn so much from them. It is a joy just having them around.

I have realized that there is now so much support for parents with children with disabilities, something I wish that I had when I was going through these emotions. Most of the issues concerning parenting and family issues, I can identify with and I can say that it has been a learning experience for me—I am still in the learning process.

Universal Design for Learning

A key consideration to help students with ID succeed in the general education curriculum is the application of the principles of the universal design for learning (UDL). The importance of a focus on UDL was underscored by the President's Committee for People with Intellectual Disabilities (PCPID, 2007). The committee noted that it can be effective by "simultaneously providing supports for learning and reducing barriers to the general education curriculum, while maintaining high achievement standards for all students [thus providing features that] facilitate the efforts of educators to better teach and support students with intellectual disabilities" (p. 13).

Wehmeyer (2006) provided a blueprint for considering effective inclusive efforts by identifying aspects consistent with a universal design for learning approach to making general education classrooms more responsive to the learning needs of this group of students. The model, presented in Figure 7.2, reflects the fact that a series of key decisions need to be made in curriculum development for students to succeed in the general education classroom. Particular emphases include the use of assistive technology, the development of curricular adaptations (see the next section), the augmentation of the curriculum (to include emphases on strategy training, self-determination), and the availability of curricular alternatives (which

FIGURE 7.2

Model for gaining access to the general curriculum.

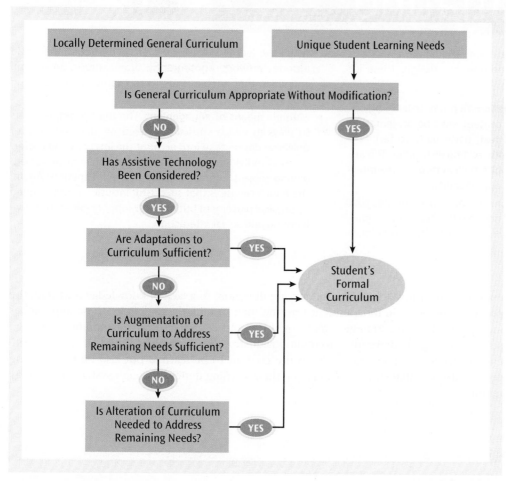

Source: From "Achieving Access to the General Curriculum for Students with Mental Retardation: A Curriculum Decision-Making Model," by M. L. Wehmeyer, D. Lattin, and M. Agran, 2001, *Education and Training in Mental Retardation and Developmental Disabilities, 36.* pp. 327–342.

stress a more functional emphasis often absent in the general curriculum). As noted earlier, one key consideration in the successful inclusion of students with intellectual disabilities is the application of universal design for learning. The Differentiated Instruction—Elementary boxed reading provides a discussion of how universal design for learning can be applied to classrooms in order to enhance the teacher's ability to educate all students.

Other Instructional Adaptations

Table 7.5 presented an outline of common characteristics along with their implications for instruction. When these characteristics are considered collectively, certain core instructional themes emerge. Teachers should focus on teaching and learning adaptations that:

- Ensure attention to relevant task demands
- Teach ways to learn content while teaching content itself
- Focus on content that is meaningful to students, to promote learning and facilitate application
- Provide training that crosses multiple learning and environmental contexts
- Offer opportunities for active involvement in the learning process

One important approach that has merit for all students is the use of cognitively oriented instructional methods (e.g., strategy training). Based on the premise that learning problems

Differentiating Elementary Instruction

Wehmeyer (2006) outlined three essential qualities associated with curricular materials based on universal design. These include the following:

- **Multiple means of representation:** To promote learning opportunities for all students, content must be presented in alternative ways to printed text, particularly to facilitate learning by those students with reading difficulties. The advent of increased use of graphics, such as through the Internet, provide particularly apt opportunities.

- **Multiple means of expression:** This principle indicates that materials based on universal design will offer students multiple ways in which to demonstrate the information that they have learned. As Wehmeyer (2010) noted, this could include "artwork, photography, drama, music, animation, and video that enable students to express their ideas and their knowledge" (p. 7).

- **Multiple means of engagement:** The third principle refers to ways in which curriculum based on the principles of universal design take into account the interests and preferences of individual students to find effective means of engaging those students in active class participation. Again, the basic premise is that successful inclusion is not defined by physical placement but rather by opportunities for active learning and social interaction.

experienced by low-achieving students are due more to a lack of knowledge regarding the processes involved in independent learning than to underlying deficits, these approaches incorporate learning strategies, metacognition, and cognitive behavior modification (e.g., self-monitoring) as alternatives to traditional instructional practices. Clearly it remains critical for teachers to focus not only on the content to be learned but also on the learning process itself so that students can lessen their learning deficits through systematic strategy training.

SUMMARY

Basic Concepts of Students with Intellectual Disabilities

- The term "intellectual disabilities" has become the preferred term to refer to students experiencing cognitive and adaptive challenges.
- The three central dimensions of the definition of ID are lower intellectual functioning, deficits or limitations in adaptive skills, and an onset prior to age 18.
- The definition also stresses the importance of assumptions related to cultural and linguistic diversity, an environmental context for adaptive skills, the strengths of individuals as well as their limitations, and the promise of improvement over time.
- Common practice in the field has been to speak of two general levels of ID, mild and significant, but contemporary classification models stress needed supports rather than levels of deficits.
- The prevalence of ID in schools has stabilized at approximately 1%.

Common Characteristics of Students with Intellectual Disabilities

- Attention difficulties can be addressed by modifying instruction to highlight relevant stimuli and by training students to monitor their own attention.
- Cognitive development for students with ID can be enhanced by emphasizing active interaction with the environment and the provision of concrete learning experiences.

- Many students with a history of failure have an external locus of control, which can be enhanced by an emphasis on success experiences and by reinforcement for independent work.
- To enhance language development, teachers should provide a facilitative environment, structure opportunities for communication, and encourage verbal language.

Effective Inclusive Practices for Students with Intellectual Disabilities

- Educational programs must be outcomes-oriented and attend to transitional concerns so that students receive the appropriate training to prepare them for subsequent environments. The curriculum should thus have a top-down orientation.
- Opportunities for inclusion are essential and should focus on social benefits such as friendship.

Classroom Adaptations for Students with Intellectual Disabilities

- Teachers should teach not only content but also strategies that facilitate learning. Examples include rehearsal, classification, and visual imagery.
- Curriculum must reflect both academic expectations and critical, functional curricular needs.

PEARSON
myeducationlab)

The MyEducationLab for this course can help you solidify your comprehension of Chapter 7 concepts.

- Gauge and further develop your understanding of chapter concepts by taking the quizzes and examining the enrichment materials on the Chapter 7 Study Plan.
- Visit Topic 15, Intellectual Disabilities, to:
  - Connect with challenge-based interactive modules, case study units, and podcasts that provide research-validated information about working with students in inclusive settings by visiting the IRIS Center Resources
  - Explore Assignments and Activities, assignable exercises showing concepts in action through video, cases, and student and teacher artifacts
  - Practice and strengthen skills essential to quality teaching through the Building Teaching Skills and Dispositions lessons

8

Teaching Students with Attention Deficit/Hyperactivity Disorder

CHAPTER OBJECTIVES

After reading this chapter, you should be able to:

1. Discuss basic concepts regarding attention deficit/hyperactivity disorder (ADHD).
2. Describe the characteristics of students with ADHD.
3. Identify effective inclusive practices for students with ADHD.

JAKE was always described as a "handful." He was the second son, so his mom was used to lots of noise and activity, but nothing prepared her for Jake. He was always into something, he climbed everything, he pulled out all the toys at once, and he was fussy and seldom slept. As he entered school, his mom hoped that the scheduled day would help, but his teachers complained and called her often to discuss how difficult Jake was to manage. He was held back in kindergarten to allow him an extra year to mature, but he didn't make the progress that was hoped for. He was still disruptive and frequently in trouble with teachers.

At the same time, everyone else seemed to love Jake. He talked all the time and could really entertain a group. From the beginning, he was an excellent athlete. Baseball, swimming, football, wrestling, and basketball kept him busy but didn't really leave enough time for homework to be completed properly. He was described as "all boy." Because he was so intelligent, he was able to make passing grades without much effort, but he never excelled in school. Teachers always called him an underachiever and told his parents frequently that he just wasn't trying. He tried medication for one year for his hyperactivity, but that was dropped over the summer and never started again.

During high school Jake was state heavyweight champion and placed fourth in the nation in wrestling. He made the re-

gional all-star football team, but his teachers still complained about his attitude and commitment to his studies; he had a short attention span and was easily distracted. Jake became frustrated as more effort was needed to pass all his subjects. He wanted to go to a good college and expected a scholarship, but he had to graduate with a grade point average that met the college standards. With this goal in mind, he agreed to begin taking medication, and he and his mom met with his teachers to develop a plan to improve his grades and behavior. Jake also met with a psychologist several times to discuss strategies that would make him more self-sufficient. The plan worked, and Jake got his scholarship. Without the adaptations, strategy training, and medication, Jake and his parents wonder how different his life would be.

QUESTIONS TO CONSIDER

1. How could Jake's early school years have been made more successful?
2. What rights did Jake have to get special accommodations from his teachers?
3. What might be Jake's most likely challenges in college? What reasonable accommodations could be made to help him be successful?

BASIC CONCEPTS ABOUT ADHD

ADHD is not hard to spot in the classroom! For some children their inattention is the clue—they don't seem to listen, their minds seem to be somewhere else, they turn in messy work with careless errors, they may not finish the work, or may finish but never turn it in. Work might be found months later crammed into a cluttered desk. These children may have trouble organizing and might start one task and shift to another before completing the first. They are not defiant or oppositional; they simply do not perform as expected based on their ability. Other children can be spotted more quickly; they are squirming, talking excessively, jumping out of their seat or interrupting the teacher at inappropriate times. They might be referred to as the "class clown."

Visit the MyEducationLab for this course to enhance your understanding of chapter concepts with a personalized Study Plan. You'll also have the opportunity to hone your teaching skills through video-based Assignments and Activities, IRIS Center Resources, and Building Teaching Skills and Disposition lessons.

Unfortunately, the disabling behaviors associated with ADHD may be misunderstood and misinterpreted as a sign of being lazy, unmotivated, and even disrespectful. ADHD is an invisible, hidden disability in that no unique physical characteristics and no definitive psychological or physiological tests can differentiate these children from others. The condition can be recognized only through specific behavioral manifestations that may occur during academic and non-academic activities such as those found in social and employment settings. In fact, the greatest limitation for someone with ADHD is difficulty in areas of self-sufficiency and what can be referred to as "street smarts" (Schuck & Crinella, 2005).

As a developmental disability, ADHD becomes apparent before the age of 7; however, as many as 75% of the children will continue to demonstrate symptoms into adolescence and about one-half of the adolescents will continue to have serious problems into adulthood (Hammerness, 2009). ADHD occurs at a fairly consistent rate in various countries throughout the world and across all cultural, racial, and socioeconomic groups. It can also affect children and adults with all levels of intelligence (Hammerness, 2009).

Attention deficit/hyperactivity disorder (ADHD) is a complex condition that has been a major concern in public education for several years. It is a complicated but intriguing condition and a real challenge for classroom teachers. This condition remains controversial because professional perspectives and personal opinions vary regarding the nature of ADHD and effective intervention techniques. In the past few years, awareness of this disability has significantly increased, along with successful intervention plans for students who struggle with it. The National Institutes of Health (NIH) released a consensus statement that, despite the controversy, there is enough scientific evidence to conclude that ADHD is a valid disorder (National Institutes of Health, 2000).

The legal basis for services and protection against discrimination for ADHD comes from IDEA and Section 504 of the Rehabilitation Act of 1973 (PL 93–112). When IDEA was reauthorized in 1990, a major debate took place as to whether to add ADHD as a separate handicapping condition. Some people were very disappointed when that change was not made. However, in 1991 the U.S. Department of Education did issue a policy memorandum indicating that students with attention deficit disorder (ADD, the department's term) who need special education or related services can qualify for those services under the category of "other health impaired" (OHI). This category includes "any chronic and acute condition that results in limited alertness and adversely affects educational performance" (U.S. Department of Education, 1991).

In 1999 the definition of OHI was actually amended to add ADD and ADHD to the list of conditions that could render a child eligible under this category. The definition provides the explanation that a child with ADD or ADHD has a heightened awareness or sensitivity to environmental stimuli, and this results in a limited alertness to the educational environment (U.S. Department of Education, 1999). In other words, the child is so busy paying attention to everything going on around him or her that attention is directed away from the important educational stimuli, and school performance is negatively affected. The OHI category continues to include ADHD (IDEA, 2004).

The number of students with ADHD requesting services under IDEA has grown dramatically, but a sizable number of students with ADHD are floundering in school and not qualifying for special education and support services that would promote academic success. In an effort to find a basis for services for this population, the U.S. Department of Education determined that Section 504 applies to these individuals and serves as a legal mandate to provide assessment and services. When students do not meet the qualifications for IDEA, Section 504 continues to be the legal basis for services to this population.

Section 504 is not a special education law but a civil rights law. It mandates special education opportunities and related aids and services to meet individual educational needs for people with disabilities as adequately as the needs of those who are not disabled. Section 504 provides protection for a larger group of individuals with disabilities and differs in some respects from IDEA. It protects any individual with a disability, defined as "any physical or mental impairment that substantially limits one or more major life ac-

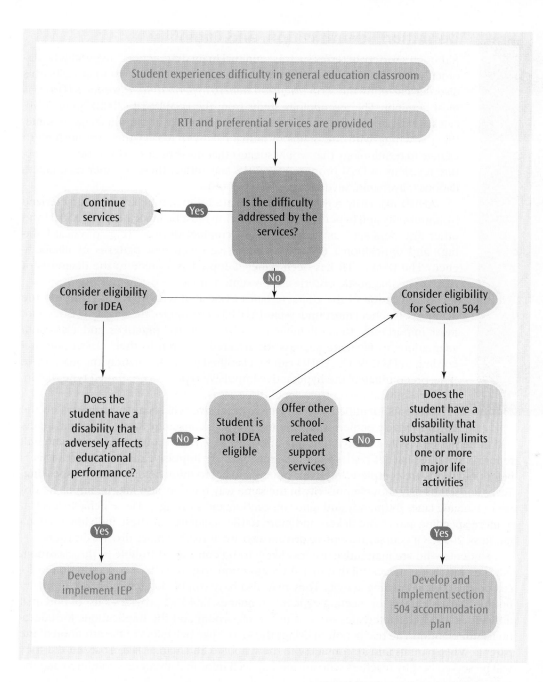

FIGURE 8.1

IDEA/504 flowchart.

Source: From *Creating Inclusive Classrooms: Effective and Reflective Practices, 6th edition* by S. J. Salend (2008), Upper Saddle River, NJ: Pearson, p. 47.

tivities." Because learning is one of the stated life activities, it was determined that this law does apply to schools, specifically those receiving federal funding. If a school has reason to believe that any student has a disability as defined under Section 504, the school must evaluate the student. If the student is determined to be disabled under the law, the school must develop and implement a plan for the delivery of services that are needed (Smith & Patton, 2007).

If a student with ADHD does not qualify for services under IDEA, services might be made available under Section 504. Although required services and procedures under Section 504 are not as specific as those found in IDEA, Section 504 does provide an avenue for accommodating the needs of students with ADHD in the schools. The intent of this law is to level the playing field for individuals with disabilities, creating an equal opportunity for success (Smith, 2002). Figure 8.1 is a flowchart demonstrating how IDEA and Section 504 work together to provide appropriate services to students with ADHD.

■ ADHD encompasses four types of disabilities: inattention, hyperactivity-impulsivity, hyperactivity, and impulsivity.

Definition, Identification, and Eligibility

Although a variety of terms such as "minimal brain dysfunction," "hyperkinetic disorder," and "attention deficit disorder" have been used in the past to describe this disorder, currently the term *attention deficit/hyperactivity disorder (ADHD)* is most common. The terminology stems from the DSM-IV-TR (2000). Some advocates are unhappy with the use of the term "disorder" because it suggests something is wrong with the brains of individuals with ADHD; they are pushing to change to terminology that would suggest that these brains work "differently." Future revisions of DSM proposed for 2012 may reflect these or other recommendations (Silverstein, Silverstein, & Nunn, 2008)

ADHD primarily refers to deficits in attention and behaviors characterized by impulsivity and hyperactivity. A distinction must be made between ADHD and other disorders such as sleep disorders, conduct disorder (e.g., physical fighting), and oppositional defiant disorder (e.g., recurrent patterns of disobedience). The DSM-IV-TR has been widely adopted as a guide to the diagnosis of ADHD. The diagnostic criteria are presented in Figure 8.2. As this figure shows, the identification of the characteristics associated with ADHD is critical in the diagnosis. Teachers must understand ADHD to recognize the characteristics and, most importantly, to implement effective inclusive practices and classroom adaptations to facilitate success for affected children in their classrooms. According to DSM-IV-TR, ADHD can be classified as predominately the inattentive type, predominately the hyperactive-impulsive type, or a combined type that includes significant symptoms in all three areas.

Students identified as hyperactive-impulsive will seem to be always on the go; they have trouble sitting still, and may talk constantly. Adolescents and adults will often not be visibly as active but they often describe their thoughts as racing and will report internal feelings of restlessness. Students who are impulsive may blurt out answers before questions are complete, interrupt others, and fail to think before acting or speaking. Teens and adults may show impulsivity in the same way, but they also may be impulsive drivers, changing lanes frequently and ignoring caution and stop signs. These behaviors result in more speeding and traffic tickets and more traffic accidents for these individuals (Hammerness, 2009). Of course, inattentive drivers also are at risk for more driving disasters.

Students who are inattentive are less likely to be considered trouble in the classroom but they may be unsuccessful due to a short attention span or lack of concentration or focus on the critical learning activity. They may also have trouble beginning a task, difficulty finishing an assignment, or meeting expected timelines. Table 8.1 provides a list of potential difficulties these characteristics present in the classroom and the implications for educational intervention. The teacher often brings the ADHD-like behaviors to the attention of the parents. When parents initiate contact with the school to find help, as Jake's parents did, they will be served best by teachers who are already well informed about this condition and the special education assessment process.

For years, the assessment and diagnosis of ADHD were considered the responsibility of psychologists, psychiatrists, and physicians, and typically these individuals are still involved in the identification process. However, the mandates of Section 504 as interpreted by the assistant secretary for civil rights (Cantu, 1993) charged public education personnel with responsibility for this assessment as needed. If a school district suspects that a child has a disability that substantially limits a major life activity such as learning, the district is required to provide an assessment. If the disability is confirmed, the school district must then develop a plan and provide services. Because teachers are often the first to suspect the presence of ADHD, they should be familiar with the specific behaviors associated with the disorder and the commonly used assessment techniques. Although specially trained school personnel must perform the formal assessment for ADHD, teachers should participate on the interdisciplinary team that reviews the assessment data to determine whether the attention problems limit learning and to plan the individualized program, if appropriate. Teachers may also be called on to complete informal assessment instruments that, with other data, will help in determining the presence of ADHD. Teachers are an important source of information in

FIGURE 8.2	Diagnostic Criteria for ADHD

A. Either (1) or (2):

1. six (or more) of the following symptoms of inattention have persisted for at least six months to a degree that is maladaptive and inconsistent with developmental level:

   Inattention:

   a. often fails to give close attention to details or makes careless mistakes in schoolwork, work, or other activities
   b. often has difficulty sustaining attention in tasks or play activities
   c. often does not seem to listen when spoken to directly
   d. often does not follow through on instructions and fails to finish schoolwork, chores, or duties in the workplace (not due to oppositional behavior or failure to understand instructions)
   e. often has difficulty organizing tasks and activities
   f. often avoids, dislikes, or is reluctant to engage in tasks that require sustained mental effort (such as schoolwork or homework)
   g. often loses things necessary for tasks and activities (e.g., toys, school assignments, pencils, books, or tools)
   h. is often easily distracted by extraneous stimuli
   i. is often forgetful in daily activities

2. six (or more) of the following symptoms of hyperactivity-impulsivity have persisted for at least 6 months to a degree that is maladaptive and inconsistent with developmental level:

   Hyperactivity:

   a. often fidgets with hands or feet or squirms in seat
   b. often leaves seat in classroom or in other situations in which remaining seated is expected
   c. often runs about or climbs excessively in situations in which it is inappropriate (in adolescents and adults, may be limited to subjective feelings of restlessness)
   d. often has difficulty playing or engaging in leisure activities quietly
   e. is often "on the go" or acts as if "driven by a motor"
   f. often talks excessively

   Impulsivity:

   g. often blurts out answers to questions before the questions have been completed
   h. often has difficulty awaiting turn
   i. often interrupts or intrudes on others (e.g., butts into conversations or games)

B. Some hyperactive-impulsive or inattentive symptoms that caused impairment were present before age seven years.

C. Some impairment from the symptoms is present in two or more settings (e.g., at school [or work] and at home).

D. There must be clear evidence of clinically significant impairment in social, academic, or occupational functioning.

E. The symptoms do not occur exclusively during the course of a Pervasive Developmental Disorder, Schizophrenia or other Psychotic Disorder, and are not better accounted for by another mental disorder (e.g., Mood Disorder, Anxiety Disorder, Dissociative Disorder, or a Personality Disorder).

Source: From *Diagnostic and Statistical Manual of Mental Disorders* (4th ed., text rev., pp. 92–93), by the American Psychiatric Association, 2000 Washington, DC: Author. Used by permission.

ADHD assessment because they spend a significant amount of time with students in a variety of academic and social situations and have a better sense of normal behaviors for the comparison group.

As soon as the school suspects that a child is experiencing attention problems, the parents should be notified and invited to meet with school personnel. It is important to respect

TABLE 8.1

Characteristics and Implications: Attention Deficit/Hyperactivity Disorder

AREA	POTENTIAL DIFFICULTIES	EDUCATIONAL IMPLICATIONS
Inattention	Easily distracted by auditory stimuli	Provide written instructions with oral instructions
	Easily distracted by visual stimuli	Provide preferential seating in most distraction reduced area
		Use private signal to cue student to stay on task
		Highlight most important material
	Sits and doesn't begin or complete assignment	Implement incentives for task initiation/completion
		Break assignments into smaller segments
		Teach student to self-pace using a timer
		Involve student in designing lesson incorporating preferred response modes
		Use peer tutoring/group work
		Vary educational activities
Hyperactivity	Doesn't sit still; has inappropriate movement	Allow student to stand while working
		Build movement into activity; provide frequent breaks
Impulsivity	Verbally or physically interrupts others	Reinforce positive behavior with praise; set up a contract for behavior change
	Rushes through work without minimal regard for detail	Teach self-monitoring; appropriate social interactions
		Provide a step-by-step checklist guiding student through self-check process

the rights that parents are guaranteed throughout this process; these are highlighted in Rights & Responsibilities boxed reading. Often the parents, the teacher, the principal, and the school counselor will attend the initial meeting. During this meeting parents should be asked to respond to the observations of the school personnel and describe their own concerns and experiences with problems in attention, impulsivity, and overactivity outside the school setting. If the team agrees that additional testing is needed, a trained individual should step in to direct the assessment process. This person must understand the impact of ADHD on the family; the bias that might occur during the assessment process because of cultural, socioeconomic, language, and ethnic factors; and other conditions that may mimic ADHD and prevent an accurate diagnosis.

Initially, a teacher who has been trained in identifying the symptoms of ADHD according to the school's criteria may begin to observe that a particular student manifests these behaviors in the classroom to a greater degree than do his or her peers. At this point, the teacher should begin to keep an anecdotal record, or log, to document the child's ADHD-like behaviors, noting the times when behaviors appear to be more intense, more frequent, or of a longer duration. Figure 8.3 provides a simple format for this observational log. For example, a teacher might document behavior typical of ADHD, such as constantly interrupting, excessive talking, not following directions, leaving a designated area, not finishing assignments, or not turning in homework. When the teacher observes that the behaviors are severe enough to have a significant impact on academic or social functioning, the counselor or individual designated to lead the formal assessment process should be contacted.

Although schools are not required to use a specific set of criteria to identify ADHD, the DSM-IV-TR criteria described earlier are the most widely accepted and are highly recommended (Zentall, 2006). A variety of methods and assessment procedures will be needed to

RIGHTS & RESPONSIBILITIES

PARENT RIGHTS UNDER SECTION 504

Section 504 of the Rehabilitation Act provides services for students identified as having a disability that substantially limits a major life activity. As parents, you have the following rights:

1. The right to be informed of your rights under Section 504 of the Rehabilitation Act.
2. The right for your child to have equal opportunities to participate in academic, nonacademic, and extracurricular activities in your school.
3. The right to be notified about referral, evaluation, and programs for your child.
4. The right for your child to be evaluated fairly.
5. The right, if eligible for services under 504, for your child to receive accommodations, modifications, and related services that will meet his/her needs as well as the needs of nondisabled students are met.
6. The right for your child to be educated with nondisabled peers as much as possible.
7. The right to an impartial hearing if you disagree with the school regarding your child's educational program.
8. The right to review and obtain copies of your child's school records.
9. The right to request attorney fees related to securing your rights under Section 504.
10. The right to request changes in the educational program of your child.

Signed: Parent(s): _____   Date: _____
School Representative: _____   Date: _____

Source: From *Section 504 and Public Schools: A Practical Guide* (p. 73), by T. E. C. Smith and J. R. Patton, 2007. Austin, TX: Pro-Ed. Adapted by permission.

provide a thorough evaluation for ADHD. The school system will most likely interview the child, parents, and teachers; obtain a developmental and medical history; review school records; review and/or evaluate intellectual and academic performance; administer rating scales to parents, teachers, and possibly peers; and document the impact of the behavior through direct observation. Figure 8.4 contains a rating form that can be used at home or at school to document activity. This form is especially helpful as it is configured to allow comparison of data for a child not suspected of having ADHD.

An interview with the child is appropriate in many cases, to determine the child's perception of teacher reports, attitudes toward school and family, and perception of relationships

FIGURE 8.3	Sample Form for Documenting Classroom Manifestations of ADHD-Like Behaviors

Teacher: _____   School: _____

Child: _____   Grade: _____   Age: _____

Class Activity	Child's Behavior	Date/Time

FIGURE 8.4

Home and classroom activity indicators.

1. Activity—off chair/up and down, talk/noisemaking
2. Inattention—changes in the focus of play or free-time activities, visual off task, verbal off task (e.g., off the subject)
3. Social impulsivity—disrupt, interrupt
4. Social negativity
   - *Verbal*—disagree/argue/command/verbal statement
   - *Physical*—negative physical contact with another or noncompliance or nonperformance of a request or an assigned task (Zentall, 1985a)

This behavior has been converted to a data collection procedure (see below)

Coding Time Intervals

Child A:	1	2	3	4	5	6	7	8	9	10	11	12	13	14	15
Up/down, noise															
Change focus															
Disrupt/interrupt															
Social negative															
Child B:	1	2	3	4	5	6	7	8	9	10	11	12	13	14	15
Up/down, noise															
Change focus															
Disrupt/interrupt															
Social negative															

		Totals	
		Child A	*Child B*
Up/down, noise/activity		Activity /15	/15
Change focus/inattention		Inattention /15	/15
Disrupt/interrupt/impulsivity		Social impulsivity /15	/15
Social negative		Social negative /15	/15
		Child A	Child B
		/60	/60

Note: The intervals are defined as 1 to 15. The observer needs to select time units of 1 to 4 minutes per interval. (If 4 minutes, then total time observed = 1 hour; if 2 minutes, then total time = 30 minutes; and if 1 minute, then total time = 15 minutes.)

Source: From *ADHD and Education Foundations, Characteristics, Methods, and Collaboration* (p. 25), by S.S. Zentall, 2006. Upper Saddle River, NJ: Pearson.

with peers. Although the child's responses will be slanted by personal feelings, the interview still is an important source of information.

The assessment of achievement and intelligence is not required in the identification of ADHD. However, the results of achievement and intelligence tests might suggest that the child can qualify for services under IDEA (2000) in categories of learning disabilities or intellectual disabilities. Also, knowing the levels of intelligence and achievement will help eventually in developing an intervention plan.

Rating scales that measure the presence of ADHD symptoms are widely used to quantify the severity of behaviors. They offer a way to measure the extent of the problem objectively. Several informants who know the child in a variety of settings should complete rating scales. The results should be compared to responses from interviews and the results of observations. Some rating scales are limited to an assessment of the primary symptoms contained in the DSM-IV-TR criteria; other assessment instruments are multidimensional and might address emotional-social status, communication, memory, reasoning and problem solving, and cognitive skills such as planning and self-evaluation.

A medical examination is not required to diagnose ADHD; however, because symptoms of certain medical conditions may mimic those of ADHD, a medical exam should be considered. No specific laboratory tests have been developed to diagnose ADHD; however, a physician might identify sleep apnea, anemia, allergies, side effects from medication, or other medical conditions as the primary cause of problem behaviors (Hammerness, 2009).

When the interdisciplinary team reconvenes to review all of the data, the following DSM-IV-TR criteria should be considered:

- Six or more of the nine characteristics of inattention and/or six or more of the nine symptoms of hyperactivity-impulsivity should be demonstrated as present for longer than 6 months.
- The behaviors observed should be considered maladaptive and developmentally inconsistent.
- The symptoms should have been observed prior to or by age 7.
- The limitations that stem from the characteristics should be observed in two or more settings (e.g., home, school, work).
- The characteristics are not considered solely the result of schizophrenia, pervasive developmental disorder, or other psychiatric disorder, and they are not better attributed to the presence of another mental disorder, such as an anxiety disorder or mood disorder.
- The symptoms must cause clinically significant impairment or distress in social, academic, or occupational functioning.

The team reviewing the data should look for consistency across reports from the assessment instruments and the informants to validate the existence of ADHD. If it is confirmed, the team must determine whether ADHD has caused an adverse effect on school performance and whether a special educational plan is needed.

After an educational plan has been developed under IDEA or 504 protection, the parents and school personnel should monitor the child's progress closely to ensure success. Adjustments may be needed occasionally to maintain progress. For example, reinforcement for good behavior may eventually lose its novelty and need to be changed. The ultimate goal is to remove accommodations and support as the child becomes capable of self-regulating his or her behavior. As the setting and school personnel change each year, reevaluating the need for special services will yield benefits. As the student becomes more efficient in learning and demonstrates better social skills under one plan, a new, less-restrictive plan must be designed to complement this growth.

Prevalence and Educational Environments

ADHD is one of the more common childhood behavioral disorders. Estimates of the prevalence of ADHD in school-age children range from a conservative figure of less than 2% to a more liberal figure of 30%; however, the United States Centers for Disease Control and Prevention (2005) report 7.8% of children between ages 4 and 17 have been diagnosed at some point in their lives with ADHD. This number reflects 11% of boys and 4.4% of girls (U.S. Department of Education, 2005). The extreme differences found in prevalence figures reflect the lack of agreement on a definition and the difficulty and variance in identification procedures. Regardless of the exact prevalence figure, a substantial number of students with this condition attend general education classrooms. The majority of children will demonstrate the combined type of ADHD, in which symptoms of inattention and hyperactivity-impulsivity are present. The second most prevalent type of ADHD in the classroom is the inattentive type, and the least common is the hyperactive-impulsive type—students with this type of ADHD have normal characteristics of focusing and listening but are abnormally active, talkative, and impulsive. Boys are more often diagnosed than girls, possibly due to higher rates of other behavioral problems like fighting, defiance, and stealing in boys that may put them under more scrutiny by school officials and doctors (Hammerness, 2009). Several individuals have noted that the prevalence of ADHD is increasing; however, it is generally felt that this perception is due to the increased media attention that alerts parents and teachers and to better training of clinicians and physicians.

Educational Environments

Under Section 504 and IDEA, a local education agency must provide a free appropriate public education to each qualified child with a disability. The U.S. Department of Education suggests that the placement of choice for children with ADHD should be the general education classroom, with appropriate adaptations and interventions.

Although students with ADHD can be found in a variety of special education settings, the majority of students classified as special education students spend more than 80% of the school day in general education classes (U.S. Department of Education, 2009). Because the general education teacher is responsible for the learning experience of students with ADHD most of the time, it is imperative that these teachers understand the condition and have strategies for dealing with it in their classrooms. Special educators must be knowledgeable in order to collaborate effectively with general educators to develop educational plans that might adapt the curriculum, instruction, and environment. Both special and general education teachers also need to be effective in providing behavioral support and skillful in teaching students to regulate their own behavior.

Causation and Risk Factors

Although the exact cause of ADHD is unknown, several theories have been proposed, and rigorous research is ongoing. Hammerness (2009) suggests that an increased risk for ADHD can result from either environmental influences or from **genes**. The influence of genes is evidenced by a higher prevalence rate in some families. Studies have shown that biological parents, siblings, and other family members of individuals with this disorder have higher rates of ADHD than expected in the general population. The fact that adopted children are less likely to have ADHD suggests that genetics is more likely a causative factor than simply living in a disorganized environment and passing that disorganization down through the family.

Barkley (2006) notes that environmental factors such as alcohol and drug consumption and smoking may influence the presence of ADHD during the prenatal period by limiting the delivery of nutrients, blood, and oxygen while the brain of the fetus is developing. Premature birth is also associated with ADHD; other possible causative events include complications during pregnancy and delivery, and exposure to toxins through contaminated foods, brain injury, and lead poisoning. It is also known that some children's brains are slow to develop and may never reach the ability for the child to function as a "healthy" child. Other research shows that the differences measured in the attention area of brains are not permanent and ADHD symptoms can improve as the brain develops. Most likely, the combination of genetic and environmental influences offers the best explanation as to cause (Hammerness, 2009).

While many factors are still being seriously considered as a potential cause of ADHD, others have little or no evidence to support them. These include exposure to aspects of the physical environment such as fluorescent lighting, soaps, and disinfectants; consumption of yeast, preservatives, food coloring, aspartame, sugar, and certain fruits and vegetables; as well as social factors and poor parental management (Weyandt, 2001).

For most ADHD students, the precise cause of the problem may never be understood. Although many parents want to understand why their children have a developmental disability such as ADHD, its cause is really not relevant to educational strategies or medical treatment. These can succeed without pinpointing the root of the problem.

CHARACTERISTICS OF STUDENTS WITH ADHD

The characteristics of ADHD manifest themselves in many different ways in the classroom. Recognizing them and identifying adaptations or strategies to lessen their impact in the classroom constitute a significant challenge for teachers. The characteristics listed in the DSM-IV-TR (2000) criteria highlight the observable behaviors. Barkley (2006) groups these characteristics into the following three most common areas of difficulty:

1. **Limited sustained attention or persistence of attention to tasks.** During tedious, long-term tasks, the students become rapidly bored and frequently shift from one uncompleted activity to another. They may lose concentration during long work periods and fail to complete routine work unless closely supervised. The problem is not due to the students' inability to comprehend the instructions, memory impairment, or defiance. The instructions simply do not regulate behavior or stimulate the desired response. One study found limitations in sustained attention characterized most of the children, while deficits in selective attention, executive attention, and orienting attention were characteristic of over half (Tsal, Shalev, & Mevorah, 2005).

2. **Reduced impulse control or limited delay of gratification.** Individuals often find it hard to wait their turn while talking to others or playing. Students may not stop to think before acting or speaking. They may have difficulty resisting distractions while concentrating and working toward long-term goals and long-term rewards, preferring to work on shorter tasks that promise immediate reinforcement.

3. **Excessive task-irrelevant activity or activity poorly regulated to match situational demands.** Individuals with ADHD are often extremely fidgety and restless. Their movement seems excessive and often not directly related to the task—for example, tapping pencils, rocking, or shifting positions frequently. They also have trouble sitting still and inhibiting their movements when the situation demands it.

Other areas of difficulty in psychological functioning include working memory or remembering to do things, sensing time or using time as efficiently as their peers, and using their internal language to talk to themselves in order to think about events and purposefully direct their own behavior. Students with ADHD have problems inhibiting their reaction to events, often appearing more emotional or hotheaded and less emotionally mature. They are easily frustrated and seem to lack willpower or self-discipline. They may have difficulty following instructions or rules, even following their own "to-do" lists. They demonstrate considerable variation in the quantity, quality, and speed with which they perform their assigned tasks. Their relatively high performance on some occasions, coupled with low levels of accuracy on other occasions, can be baffling. Low levels of performance often occur with repetitive or tedious tasks.

The symptoms are likely to change from one situation to another. More ADHD symptoms might be shown in group settings, during boring work, when students are without supervision, and when work has to be done later in the day. Individuals with ADHD behave better when there is immediate payoff for doing the right thing, when they enjoy what they are doing or find it interesting, when they are in one-on-one situations, and when they can work earlier in the day (Barkley, 2006). One researcher reported the following as the ADHD motto; it seems to summarize the challenge of ADHD in the classroom: "It's got to be fun! If it is not fun, it's got to be moving! If it's not moving and I'm not moving, maybe I can make it mad!" (Zentall, 2006).

Postsecondary and Adult Outcomes

The characteristics of ADHD may also be present in adulthood; an estimated 50–60% of children with ADHD will be impaired during their adult lives as they continue to experience severe symptoms (Barkley, 2010). For some individuals the condition continues to cause problems and limitations in the world of work, as well as in other life activities. For example, the symptoms of inattention and poor organization can lead to problems in relationships and finances (Hammerness, 2009). Table 8.2 provides a summary of common characteristics for varying age groups, including adults. Barkley (2010) reports that adults with ADHD are more likely to be fired, typically change jobs three times more often in a 10-year period than do adults without the disorder, are more likely to divorce, and typically have more traffic citations and accidents.

On the positive side, the outcome is much brighter for individuals with ADHD who receive treatment such as medication, behavior management, and social-skills training. Many adults with ADHD are very successful; for example, Albert Einstein (physicist), Terry Bradshaw (professional football player and sports analyst), Jim Carry (actor/comedian), and

---

TABLE 8.2

Characteristics of ADHD across the Lifespan

SYMPTOM	CHILDHOOD	ADOLESCENCE	ADULTHOOD
Inattention	• Making careless mistakes • Being easily distracted • Failing to listen to instructions • Failing to complete school and home tasks • Disorganization • Forgetfulness	• Being easily distracted • Difficulty concentrating • Failing to complete homework on time • Difficulty working independently • Poor follow-through on commitments • Becoming bored easily • Disorganization • Forgetfulness	• Failing to listen to instructions • Not completing paperwork • Feeling overwhelmed by large projects • Missing deadlines • Disorganization, especially related to time management • Forgetting commitments • Being late for appointments
Impulsivity	• Interrupting others • Blurting out answers • Not waiting one's turn	• Substance experimentation or abuse • Unprotected sex • More sexual partners • Temper outbursts • Driving too fast • Car crashes • Interrupting others	• Excessive use of alcohol and tobacco • Substance experimentation or abuse • Driving too fast • Car crashes • Temper outbursts • Impulsive job changes • Interrupting others • Impulsive spending • Extramarital or cohabiting affairs
Hyperactivity	• Fidgeting and squirming • Inappropriately running or jumping • Inability to play or perform activities quietly • Highly overactive behavior, as if "driven by a motor"	• Feeling "restless" and "edgy" • Appearing busy but getting little done	• Restlessness • Fidgeting • Talking excessively • Self-selecting more active jobs

Source: From *Attention Deficit Hyperactivity Disorder in Adults: The Latest Assessment and Treatment Strategies,* p. 10. (2010). By R.A. Barkley. Sudbury, MA: Jones and Bartlett Publishers.

Stephen Spielberg (filmmaker) (Silverstein, Silverstein, & Nunn, 2008). The following three reasons are also given for the success of some individuals:

- Some professions have built-in support personnel such as computer operators, administrative assistants, and accountants.
- Some jobs have built-in accommodations such as frequent travel or a stimulating work setting, such as a hospital or a high-volume sales floor.
- Some jobs require the personal qualities frequently found in individuals with ADHD, such as extroversion, spontaneity, humor, energy, risk-taking, multitasking, and entrepreneurship (Zentall, 2006).

Crawford (2002) offers this insight into the challenge of becoming successful for an individual with ADHD and LD:

> It hurts so much to try hard every day, sometimes relearning what you learned the day before because you forgot it all, and comparing yourself to others and realizing you are different! If you fail, then you don't have to push on. Others can feel sorry for you—take care of you; it's easier, at least it seems so. But what happens when we give up is that we try to find other avenues to make up for what we lost. Often, those avenues are devastatingly more painful than struggling to get what we need to be independent. Giving up our independence, giving up our dream, is like dying. The key is not to give up but to be realistic, to be optimistic, and to find the support one needs. Then, apply the hard work. Though it may take a lifetime, it is time well spent. (pp. 139–140)

A large part of a successful outcome for any person with a disability is self-determination and persistence, but so much depends on the support of others. Teachers who can identify and plan meaningful interventions to increase self-sufficiency for students with ADHD can have a powerful impact on their success during the school years as well as on their quality of life as adults.

EFFECTIVE INCLUSIVE PRACTICES FOR STUDENTS WITH ADHD

Treatment for students with ADHD is unique because professionals outside education are often involved in the process of identification and intervention. Although no magic cure has been discovered for this disorder, many practices are effective in its management. General education teachers most often hold the key responsibilities for implementation and monitoring of the success of these interventions.

Challenges for General Education Teachers

Being a member of an interdisciplinary team may be new to teachers, but general and special education teachers need to work closely with parents, physicians, and support personnel to develop, monitor, and maintain successful interventions. For many students, accommodations implemented in general education classrooms are enough to create a successful learning environment; however, other students may need special education support services and placement or at least behavioral intervention. Although controversial, research has also concluded that medical intervention is one of the most successful treatments to enhance learning for students with ADHD (Barkley, 2006; Hammerness, 2009), especially in combination with evidence-based educational and behavioral intervention (Zentall, 2006). These and other issues will be discussed in the following sections.

Cross-Reference

See more on behavioral interventions in Chapter 6.

Impact of Cultural and Linguistic Diversity   DSM-IV-TR confirms that ADHD is known to occur in various cultures with varying prevalence figures, probably due to differences in diagnostic procedures. Because the racial, cultural, and linguistic diversity of our country is continuing to enlarge, teachers will find a significant number of languages and cultures represented in their classrooms across the years. When ADHD does coexist with cultural and linguistic diversity, it presents a special set of challenges to the educator. Failure to address the special needs of these children can be detrimental to their academic and social success. Issues related to assessment and cultural diversity have been discussed previously; the same concerns exist in the identification and treatment of students with ADHD. To address the needs of multicultural students with ADHD, teachers must become familiar with their own unique values, views, customs, interests, and behaviors as well as those of their students.

Gay (2002) proposes that the frequent mismatch between the cultures of teachers and their students in regard to language, culture, and socioeconomic background causes many students to display behaviors that can be misinterpreted as ADHD. For example, students learning English will likely have difficulty concentrating and attending to large amounts of information presented in their new language (Salend & Rohena, 2003). They might be observed as fidgety, distracted, or seeming not to listen, much like students with ADHD.

Barkley (2006) raises the issue that the chaotic home environment of many minority populations existing below the poverty level exacerbates the problems of children with ADHD. DSM-IV-TR (American Psychiatric Association, 2000) requires that ADHD be distinguished from "difficulty in goal-directed behavior in children from inadequate, disorganized, or chaotic environments" (p. 91), although no guidance is given in making this differentiation. During the assessment process, individuals being interviewed should be asked to comment on how the student's behavior might be affected by his or her culture, language, or experiential background.

Accommodations can be important in both assessing and teaching children with racial, cultural, and linguistic diversity. Gestures, demonstrations, visuals, and simulations may help provide a context that promotes learning (Salend & Rohena, 2003). Teachers can also integrate personal and community experiences into teaching an academic concept to help make it relevant. The literature tells us that when teachers carefully organize and structure instruction, these students benefit. These and other strategies and accommodations appropriate for all students with ADHD, including the culturally diverse, are described later in the chapter.

Developing Educational Plans   If a local education agency decides that a child has a disability under Section 504, the school must determine the child's educational needs for regular and special education or related aids and services. Although this law does not mandate a written individualized education program, implementation of a written IEP is recommended. Most school systems have opted to develop written plans; they are generally referred to as student accommodation plans, individual accommodation plans, or 504 plans.

It is recommended that this plan be developed by a committee that includes parents, professionals, and, as often as possible, the student. The areas identified as causing significant limitations in learning should be the targets of the intervention plan. The committee should determine the least amount of adaptations needed to stimulate success in learning and social development. If medication therapy is being used, the plan should also indicate the school's role in administering the medication and special precautions or considerations regarding side effects (Austin, 2003). When a conservative intervention plan has been developed and implemented, additional goals and interventions can be added as needed.

Each local education agency must have an identified Section 504 coordinator or officer responsible for maintaining a fair and responsive evaluation process and procedures for developing effective 504 plans. This individual monitors students' needs and communicates with parents and teachers as necessary. Although it is much simpler than an IEP, a 504 plan serves to document legally the services agreed upon by the team members. Jake's 504 plan is included later in the chapter. If a student is served under IDEA under the area of "other health impaired," an IEP will be written by the team.

The Role of Medication   As many as 3% of school-age students with ADHD will be prescribed medication by their physicians to control their behavior (Connor, 2006), so teachers need to understand the types of medications commonly prescribed, the intended effects, and potential side effects. Pharmacological therapy can be defined as treatment by chemical substances that prevent or reduce inappropriate behaviors, promoting academic and social gains for children with learning and behavior problems. Studies have shown that different outcomes occur for different children. In approximately 76% of cases, children with ADHD (ages 6 and older) respond in a positive manner to stimulant medication such as methylphenidate (Ritalin or Concerta) or amphetamines (Dexedrine or Adderal) (Hammerness, 2009). The desired outcomes from this intervention include increased concentration, completion of assigned tasks, increased work productivity, better handwriting and motor skills, improved social relations with peers and teachers, increased appropriate behaviors and emotional control, and reduction of inappropriate, disruptive behaviors such as talking out loud, getting out of the seat, and breaking rules. These changes frequently lead to improved academic and social achievement as well as increased self-esteem.

For some children, the desired effects do not occur with the first medical trial or even the second. In some situations the medication has no negative effect, but simply does not lead to the hoped-for results. Parents and teachers often give up too soon, prematurely concluding that the medication did not help. It is important to contact the physician when no effect is noticed, because the dosage may need to be adjusted or a different type of medication may be needed. Barkley (2006) reports that when individuals continue to try different stimulants when one fails, the success rate rises to 90%.

Another possible response to medication is side effects, which are changes that are not desired, such as insomnia. The most common side effect, loss of appetite, occurs more than 50% of the time; however, it has not been found to affect adult stature (Barkley, 2006). When loss of appetite occurs, individuals may take the medication during or after a meal or add high-calorie snacks to their diet. Other possible side effects include anxiety or irritability, headaches, dry mouth, dizziness, or nausea (Barkley, 2010). Teachers should be asked to help the medical personnel and families monitor the effects of the medication; in some situations a lower dose may be indicated or in more severe cases, the medication should be discontinued. Teachers should be educated to understand, observe, and report this important information. Whatever medication is prescribed by the child's physician, teachers should refer to the current *Physicians' Desk Reference* or ask the physician or pharmacist for a thorough description of the possible positive and negative outcomes for that medication.

Remember, not all children diagnosed with ADHD need medication. The decision to intervene medically should come only after a great deal of thought about the possibility of a variety of interventions. Children whose impairments are minimal are certainly less likely to need medication than those whose severe impairments result in major disruptions. The following questions are recommended to be answered by an interdisciplinary team before making the final decision to use medication (Austin, 2003):

- Have other interventions been tried and, if so, why were they ineffective?
- How severe are the child's current symptoms?
- Can the family afford the costs associated with pharmacological intervention?
- Can family members adequately supervise the use of medication and prevent abuse?
- What are the attitudes and cultural perspectives of family members toward medication?
- Is there a substance-abusing family member in the home?
- Does the child have concomitant disorders such as tics or mental illness?
- Is the child overly concerned about the effects of the medication?
- Does the physician seem committed to appropriate follow-up monitoring?
- Is the child or adolescent involved in competitive sports or planning to enter the military? (The medication will be detected as a "controlled substance" in the course of urinalysis.)

Although teachers and other school personnel are important members of a therapeutic team involved in exploring, implementing, and evaluating diverse treatment methods, the decision to try medication is primarily the responsibility of the parents and the physician. Teachers are generally cautioned by their school systems not to specifically recommend medication because the school may be held responsible for the charges incurred. Educators, therefore, find themselves in a dilemma when they feel strongly that medication is needed to address the symptoms of ADHD. Because the studies are not conclusive, the use of medication to control student behavior is controversial, and individual parents may prefer not to use medication, it is best to prepare for a multimodal approach, including the cognitive and behavioral strategies addressed in the preceding sections. School personnel must respect the opinion of many that these medications are being used with far too many children (Scheffler, Hinshaw, Modrek, & Levine, 2007).

Occasionally teachers and parents will hear of alternative treatment therapies that seem to offer a "quick fix." These are often advertised in newspapers, and popular magazines, or on television, but they seldom appear in professional literature. Alternative approaches that have been used include the use of megavitamins, diet restrictions (e.g., sugar or additives), caffeine, massage therapy, chiropractic skull manipulations, biofeedback, play therapy, and herbs.

Critics caution that if an approach were that amazing, everyone would use it. Evidence supporting any treatment should be fully documented before children are submitted to the treatment and resources are invested.

Classroom Adaptations for Students with ADHD

Because no two children with ADHD are exactly alike, a wide variety of interventions and service options must be available to allow each child to benefit from his or her education in the general education classroom. Any approach addressing the needs of students with ADHD must be comprehensive. Figure 8.5 depicts a model of educational intervention built on four areas: environmental management, instructional accommodations, student-regulated strategies, and medical management. The program planned for each student is developed by a team during a collaboration process and is based on the student's individual strengths and limitations, which are identified during the assessment process. The medical management component of the model will be used frequently by physicians and families and, therefore, should be understood by teachers, who are needed to monitor the benefits of the medication and possible side effects. Following is a discussion of each strategy recommended to make school a more positive experience for students with ADHD. Reread the story of Jake, the boy described in the opening vignette, and refer to his 504 plan to identify the types of interventions that the team developed to meet his needs.

Managing the Classroom Environment

A classroom with even one or two students with ADHD can be difficult to control if the teacher is not skilled in classroom management. Rather than reacting spontaneously—and

FIGURE 8.5

Model for ADHD intervention.

Source: From *Attention-Deficit/ Hyperactivity Disorder in the Classroom: A Practical Guide for Teachers* (p. 26), by C.A. Dowdy, J. R. Patton, T. E. C. Smith, and E.A. Polloway, 1998. Austin, TX: Pro-Ed.

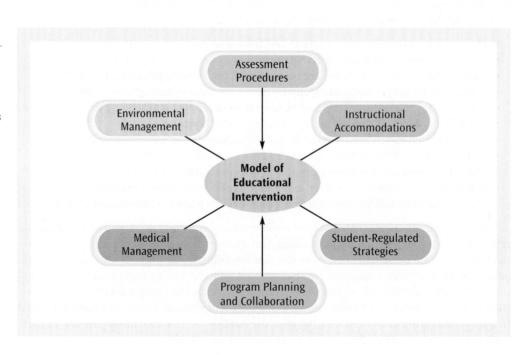

often inconsistently—to disruptive situations, teachers should have a proactive management system to help avoid crises. Good classroom management is beneficial for all students, including those with ADHD. Techniques that will be discussed include group management, management of the environment, and behavior management.

Group Management   Group management techniques benefit all members of a class, but they are critical in managing the behavior of individual students with ADHD. One of the most basic and effective techniques is to establish classroom rules and consequences for breaking those rules. Children with ADHD need to understand the classroom rules and school procedures in order to be successful. Polloway, Patton, and Serna (2008) suggest that students feel more committed to following rules when they have contributed to developing them. The rules should be displayed prominently in the room and reviewed periodically if students with ADHD are to retain and follow them. It is important for teachers to apply the rules consistently, even though students can sometimes frustrate teachers and make them want to "give in." Teachers can start the process of rule development by offering one or two rules of their own and then letting the children pick up with their own ideas. The following is a list of recommendations for developing rules:

- State rules positively and clearly. A rule should tell students what to do instead of what not to do!
- State rules in simple terms so students can easily understand them. For young students, rules can be depicted with drawings and figures.
- Limit the number of rules to no more than five or six.
- Display rules conspicuously in the room.
- Discuss and practice rules at the beginning of the year and periodically throughout the year.
- Have students with ADHD role-play how to carry out the rules is an effective technique.
- Adopt rules and consequences that you are willing to enforce, then be consistent!
- Reinforce students who abide by the rules. It is more effective to reinforce the students who abide by the rules than to punish those who break them.
- Communicate rules and consequences to parents to avoid misunderstandings. It is helpful to have parents and students sign a contract documenting their understanding of the rules.

Time Management   Time management is also important in effective classroom management. Students with ADHD thrive in an organized, structured classroom. Acting out and inappropriate behavior often occur during unscheduled, unstructured free time, when the number of choices of activities may become overwhelming. If free time is scheduled, limit the choices and provide positive reinforcement for appropriate behavior. Encourage students to investigate topics that interest them and to complete projects that bring their strengths into play. Figure 8.6 provides information regarding the types of classroom events that might trigger negative behavior for children with ADHD and other types of disabilities. Understanding these antecedent events can help teachers make adjustments that allow more children to benefit from their education in a general education classroom.

Polloway and Patton (2005) suggest that teachers begin each day with a similar routine. The particular activity is not as important as the consistency. For example, some teachers like to start the day with quiet reading or music, whereas others might begin with singing, recognizing birthdays, or talking about special events that are coming up. This routine sets the stage for a calm, orderly day, and students will know what to expect from the teacher. Secondary teachers need to advise students of scheduling changes (e.g., assembly, pep rally) and provide a brief overview of the topics and activities to be expected during the class period.

Like the beginning of the day, closure on the day's or the class period's activities is important for secondary students. Reviewing the important events of the day and describing the next day's activities help students with ADHD. This is also an excellent time for teachers to provide rewards for students who have maintained appropriate behavior during the day.

FIGURE 8.6 — Antecedents That Often Trigger Negative Behaviors for Children with Different Exceptionalities

Students with ADHD
Behavior difficulties will increase when:

- the task is effortful in its length, repetitiveness, and nonmeaningfulness;
- little opportunity exists for movement or choice;
- few opportunities exist for active involvement in learning;
- many students and only one teacher are present, and learning is large-group teacher directed;
- little supervision, feedback, or positive reinforcement takes place;
- periods of transition exist with little structure (for a review, see Zentall, 1993, 1995).

Students with ADHD Plus Aggression
Aggression occurs primarily:

- when entering new groups;
- when resources are scarce or information is needed;
- during low structure;
- during difficult tasks;
- when little flexibility exists;
- when few adults and much activity are present;
- when no apparent way to escape tasks or social demands is available;
- when a peer group values "toughness."

Students with ADHD Plus Learning Disabilities
Task avoidance behavior, such as off-task behavior, occurs primarily when:

- presented with a task that is within the student's area of specific learning disability (e.g., with reading requirements, mathematical calculations);
- presented with any kind of auditory input, such as listening tasks, group discussion, social interactions (in these contexts the child may be more likely to actively refuse, avoid, or act disruptively);
- presented with complex visual input, such as copying from the board or from dictionary to paper, art tasks using collage (with such tasks, the child may take a long time to produce work);
- asked to respond in certain ways (e.g., fine motor handwriting or talking) (with such response requirements, the child may avoid or become negative and noncompliant).

Students with ADHD and Giftedness
Off-task or disruptive behavior is observed primarily when:

- tasks are too easy;
- teachers believe that if the child can't do the easy work, he or she can't do the challenging work;
- tasks involve a lot of rote lower-level skills.

Students with ADHD and Developmental Disabilities
Disruptive behavior and poor performance occur primarily:

- during difficult, complex, higher-level tasks that require problem solving, analysis, synthesis, or reasoning abilities.

Students with ADHD and Anxiety
Avoidance, inflexible, or repetitive behavior occurs:

- when entering new groups;
- in the presence of a lot of activity and confusion;
- during difficult or unstructured (ambiguous) tasks;
- when it is noisy;
- when unpredictable activities that have not been scheduled are provided or changes in a schedule have been made.

Source: From *ADHD and Education: Foundations, Characteristics, Methods, and Collaboration* (pp. 73–74), by S. S. Zentall, 2006. Upper Saddle River, NJ: Pearson.

Section 504 Plan for Jake

Source: From *Section 504 and Public Schools (2nd ed)* (p. 51) by T.E.C. Smith & J.R. Patton, 2007, Austin, TX: Pro-Ed. Used with permission.

Name: _Jake Smith_

School/Class: _11th grade — Central High School_

Teacher: _Pratt — History, Jordan — Literature_   Date: _9/29/97_

General Strengths: _Jake is a bright student, he wants to learn and make good grades. He is very ambitious and wants to go to college and become an engineer._

General Weaknesses: _Jake has been diagnosed with ADHD. His attention span is very short and he is easily distracted. He frequently gets out of his seat and walks around the room._

Specific Accommodations:

Accommodation #1

Class: _History_   Accommodation(s): _Jake will be given extra time to complete his assignments. He will be given assignments divided into shorter objectives so that his progress can be checked sooner._

Person Responsible for Accommodation #1: _Mr. Pratt — teacher_

Accommodation #2

Class: _History_   Accommodation(s): _Jake will sit at the front of the class._

Person Responsible for Accommodation #2: _Mr. Pratt — teacher_

Accommodation #3

Class: _Literature_   Accommodation(s): _Jake will work with selected other students in cooperative learning arrangements._

Person Responsible for Accommodation #3: _Ms. Jordan — teacher_

Accommodation #4

Class: _Literature_   Accommodation(s): _An assignment notebook will be sent home each day with specific assignments noted. Parents will sign the assignment notebook daily and return it to school._

Person Responsible for Accommodation #4: _Ms. Jordan — teacher_

Accommodation #5

Class: _All classes_   Accommodation(s): _A behavior management plan will be developed and implemented for Jake for the entire day. The plan will include time for Jake to take Ritalin and will focus on positive reinforcement._

Person Responsible for Accommodation #5: _Ms. Baker — asst. prin._

General Comments:
Jake's plan will be reviewed at the end of the fall term to ensure that it is meeting his needs.

Individuals Participating in Development of Accommodation Plan:

William Pratt — teacher   _Fred Haynes — 504 Coor._

Bonita Jordan — teacher   _Hank Smith — father_

Mary Baker — asst. prin.

If parents are involved in a contract, this is the time to discuss the transmitted notes and to review homework that might have been assigned during the day.

Teachers may want to offer incentives to individual students and groups to reward outstanding work. A teacher might place a marble in a jar each time students are "caught being good." When the jar is filled, the class receives an award such as a picnic or a skating party. Another technique involves adding a piece to a puzzle whenever the teacher recognizes that the class is working especially hard. When the puzzle is complete, the class is rewarded. These group incentives can be very effective; however, some students will need an individual contract or behavior management plan to help direct their behavior. Babkie (2006) offers the following additional tips for proactive classroom management:

- Make boundaries clear for appropriate interactions with you and peers. Remember, you are not your students' friend—you are their teacher. Be sympathetic and supportive but reinforce the boundaries.
- Cue students when activities are about to change and teach transitioning skills.
- Teach cognitive strategies to facilitate success in academic and social environments.
- Pace lessons and alter the workload based on student needs and responses instead of punishing students for not "keeping up."
- Give learning a purpose by providing real-world uses for new skills.
- Use activity-based activities that are not always a paper-and-pencil task or test.
- At all times, be respectful toward students. Consider how you would want to be treated. Ensure that students are comfortable in the classroom and feel like successful, contributing members.

Physical Management   The physical environment of a classroom can also have an impact on the behavior of students with ADHD. The arrangement of the room is most important. The classroom needs to be large enough for students to have space between themselves and others, so they will be less likely to impose themselves on one another. Each student needs some personal space. The student with ADHD may need to be near the teacher in order to focus attention on the information being presented in the classroom; however, students should never be placed near the teacher as a punitive measure. A seat near the front might help the student who is distracted by someone's new hairstyle or flashy jewelry. Whenever possible, involve the student in determining the best "placement" for learning.

There should also be various places in the room where quiet activities can take place, small groups can work together, sustained attention for difficult tasks can be maintained, and a relaxed and comfortable environment can be enjoyed for a change of pace. At one time, classrooms with lots of visual stimulation were considered inappropriate for students with ADHD, leading to the creation of sterile environments with colorless walls, no bulletin boards, and teachers dressed in dull colors. This is no longer considered necessary; however, order is needed in the classroom. Assignments should be posted in the same location daily, materials and completed assignments should be placed consistently in the same place so students will be able to return them, and bulletin boards should be uncluttered. Set aside places where students who seem to be overstimulated can work in a carrel or other private space with minimal visual and auditory stimuli, and have a place for a child who seems underaroused to be able to move around and get rejuvenated (Carbone, 2001). Make sure to consider transition skills for these students. Figure 8.7 provides a strategy to help with transition.

Behavioral Support   Behavioral support techniques, especially those that reward desired behavior, can enhance the education of students with ADHD. For example, when students with ADHD are attending to their tasks, following classroom rules, or participating appropriately in a cooperative learning activity, their behaviors should be positively reinforced. Unfortunately, teachers often ignore appropriate behavior and call attention only to what is inappropriate. When students receive attention for actions that are disruptive or inconsiderate, the negative behaviors can be reinforced and may thus increase in frequency.

FIGURE 8.7	The Change Strategy to Teach Transitioning Skills

Collect my materials and put them away.
Have ready what I need for the next activity
Always watch my teacher for cues to move
Now take my seat quietly
Get my materials out and ready for the next activity
Encourage my peers to get started

Source: From "Be Proactive in Managing Classrooms" (p. 185) by A. M. Babkie, 2006, *Intervention in School and Clinic, 41*(3).

The Personal Spotlight presents a unique example of a student with ADHD who experienced behavior problems in school.

Positive reinforcement tends to increase appropriate behavior. Teachers should consider which rewards appeal most to the individuals who will receive them. Common ones include small toys, candy and other edibles, free time, time to listen to music, time in the

PERSONAL SPOTLIGHT

GROWING UP WITH ADHD

DAVE BIRT has had ADHD as long as he can remember. Now age 30, he feels that he is still working to counteract the negative experiences of his school days. Upon entering kindergarten, he could already read, and throughout elementary school he felt impatient when waiting for his peers to catch up. He qualified for the gifted program with an IQ well into the genius range, but even that program couldn't give him enough to do. He says, "The teachers would repeat things over and over. They only had to tell me once, and I learned it." As a result, Dave filled his time entertaining himself, and he soon became a behavior problem in the classroom. He was shuffled around suburban Pennsylvania school districts, but no one knew what to do for him. Soon, he simply became labeled a "troublemaker."

In the eighth grade, Dave was officially diagnosed with ADHD, but teachers still didn't know how to instruct him in the traditional classroom. The primary problem with the adaptations was the social stigma attached to them. For example, teachers had him keep assignment journals, but this special treatment made him feel like an outcast, so he didn't do it. The same applied to Ritalin—he didn't think it would help, and he wanted to avoid the stigma, so he didn't take it. Finally, a rural school district placed him in the program for students with behavior problems. Dave remembers, "They put me in the 'sped shed,' a program where the teacher had fewer students and

could keep a closer eye on them. It worked to a point, but it was based on the idea that bad kids are dumb. My misbehavior was rebellion against being treated like an idiot or an attempt to keep myself entertained." Furthermore, the program was set up only for homeroom, study halls, and lunch, so it deprived students of important socializing opportunities with the rest of the school. Dave was reluctant to socialize with the other students in the program, some of whom are now in prison. He feels that the development of his social skills suffered as a result.

Eventually, Dave tired of this routine. He signed himself out of school in eleventh grade and took the GED, scoring in the 97th percentile. He later joined the army, but the ADHD didn't allow him the patience necessary to wait for his peers to catch on to whatever they were doing.

Finally, Dave discovered something that held his interest— computers. He started his own small business building custom computers for clients, and he also took night classes and earned IT certifications. Currently he works for the wireless communications company Nextel, and he is considering attending college, perhaps to become a computer teacher. Because of his school experiences, though, he is hesitant about going back into the classroom as a full-time student. "What if I have professors who don't understand ADHD?" he worries. "I'm not going through that again." Still, he says, "I think I could be a good teacher because I understand how kids think. You have to keep them interested in order for them to learn."

Dave Birt
Boston, MA

gym, opportunities to do things for the teacher, having lunch with the teacher, praise, or hugs. Because a reward that acts as a reinforcer for one student may not work for another, teachers might generate a menu of rewards and allow students to select their own. Rewards do not have to be expensive; in fact, simply allowing students to take a break, time to get a drink of water, or time to sharpen a pencil, or giving a homework pass may be just as effective as expensive toys and games.

Another behavior-management technique is cuing or signaling students with ADHD when they are on the verge of inappropriate behavior. First, student and teacher sit down privately and discuss the inappropriate behavior that has been creating problems in the classroom. The teacher offers to provide a cue when he or she begins to notice the behavior. Teachers and students can have fun working together on the signal, which might involve flipping the light switch, tapping the desk lightly, or simple eye contact. These cuing techniques help establish a collegial relationship between the teacher and the student that says, "We are working on this together; we have a problem, but we also have a plan" (Wood, 2006).

A functional behavioral assessment may be needed to develop the most effective behavioral plan. Table 8.3 provides a guide for conducting a functional behavioral assessment. Often students need an individual contract that focuses on their particular needs. The student and teacher develop the goals to improve behavior together and then put these goals in writ-

---

TABLE 8.3

Guidelines for Conducting a Functional Behavioral Assessment

GUIDELINES	QUESTIONS
1. Identify the problematic behavior.	What does the student do that causes a problem? How does the behavior affect the student's learning? Is there a relationship between the behavior and the student's cultural and language background?
2. Define the behavior.	Have I defined the behavior in observable and measurable terms?
3. Record the behavior using an observational recording system.	What observational recording system will be used to record the behavior? (See Salend, 2008, for examples of recording systems—event recording, duration and latency recording, interval recording or time sampling, and anecdotal records.)
4. Obtain additional information about the student and the behavior.	Have I determined the student's skills, strengths, weaknesses, interests, hobbies, self-concept, attitudes, culture, language, and experiences?
5. Perform an antecedents-behavior-consequences (A-B-C) analysis.	Have I considered the events, stimuli, objects, actions, and activities that precede and trigger the behavior? Have I considered the behaviors that follow and maintain the behavior?
6. Analyze the data and develop hypotheses.	Have I examined the data to determine when, where, with whom, and under what conditions the behavior is most likely and least likely to occur? What is the purpose of the behavior? Is the behavior related to the student's disability?
7. Consider sociocultural factors.	Is the student's behavior related to her or his cultural perspectives and language background?
8. Develop a behavioral intervention plan.	Have I identified specific measurable goals that focus on the student's behavior, characteristics, and needs? Do these goals relate to the antecedents and consequences of the student's behavior?
9. Evaluate the plan.	Have I continued to collect data to determine the effectiveness of the behavior management plan? Does the plan need to be revised? Should the intervention (or interventions) be changed?

Source: Adapted from *Creating Inclusive Classrooms: Effective and Reflective Practices* (4th ed.), by S. J. Salend, 2001: Upper Saddle River, NJ: Pearson.

ing. The contract provides structure and becomes an explicit way to communicate with children with ADHD and their parents. Downing (2002) offers the following guidelines for making and using such contracts:

- Determine the most critical area(s) of concern.
- Consider when the behavior usually occurs, the events that trigger it, and why you think the behavior is occurring.
- Specify the desired behavior in measurable terms, using clear, simple words.
- Specify the reinforcers that will be used and the consequences that will follow if the contract is not fulfilled.
- See that both teacher and student sign the contract (and the parents, when appropriate).
- Keep a record of the student's behavior.
- Provide the agreed-upon consequences or reinforcements in a timely fashion.
- When the goal is reached, celebrate, and write a new contract! (A sample contract is provided in Figure 8.8.)

In severe cases, a more detailed behavioral intervention plan may be called for. Table 8.4 shows an example of a Behavioral Intervention Plan for Matthew, a student with ADHD whose characteristics are creating significant limitations to his classroom success. This plan involves a variety of interventions to address Matthew's problems with interrupting and leaving his seat inappropriately, his difficulty in completing assignments, and his ineffective social skills. To be successful, this plan must be supported, implemented, and ultimately evaluated by a team of individuals including Matthew, his family, teachers, peers, and others.

Making Instructional Adaptations

Children with ADHD most often do not have a problem with skills, they have problems with performance. However, these students are often misunderstood and labeled lazy or unmotivated, as if they are choosing not to perform at their maximum potential. Teacher comments such as "I know you can do this work, because you did it yesterday" or "You can do better; you just aren't trying" probably suggest a lack of understanding of the inconsistent performance characteristic of this disability. As one professional commented, "Students with ADHD have one good day and we hold it against them for the rest of the year!" Instead, teachers need to find ways to cope with the frustration and stress sometimes involved in working with these students, while modifying their teaching style, their curriculum, and possibly their expectations in order to engineer academic success for these students.

Modifying Teacher Behavior   Because students with ADHD, especially those with learning disabilities, are not easily stimulated, they need novelty and excitement in their learning environment. Although complete and thorough directions, structure, and consistency are extremely important, students need challenging, exciting activities to keep them focused and learning (Jakobson & Kikas, 2007). One innovative strategy that addressed learning difficulties and inattention was developed by Vesely and Gryder (2009). These educators developed and implemented a word of the day activity that teaches students an important, relevant, new vocabulary word daily and engages students in keeping a tally of the number of times that word was used by anyone throughout the day. Reading and speaking vocabularies increase while students improve in self-monitoring and selective attention. Professional journals and the Internet offer endless evidence-based ideas like this one for "jazzing up" lesson plans or developing new ones.

Incidence of inappropriate behavior increases during nonstimulating, repetitive activities. Teachers should vary activities, allow and encourage movement that is purposeful and not disruptive, and even let students stand as they listen, take notes, or perform other academic tasks. "Legal movement," such as pencil sharpening or a hall pass for walking to the restroom or getting water, might be pre-approved for a student's restless times. Here are some recommendations from Zentall (2006) for best practice in teaching strategies:

- Don't try to accomplish so much in one time period.
- Give frequent breaks or shorter assignments.

FIGURE 8.8

Example of a contingency contract.

Contract

Beginning Date: January 4

Ending Date: January 29

John agrees to:

- Finish assigned work in time allotted during social studies.

- Talk only to collaborative partner.

- Follow class rules.

Mrs. Dowdy agrees to:

- Let John select and play a computer game for 10 minutes at the end of class.

- Let John play with Lola, the class hamster, for 15 minutes on Friday if John has been successful Monday through Thursday.

Signature:_____

Signature:_____

- Increase novelty—use treasure hunts, games, group projects. For example, play the game "What's My Verb?" where one team acts out a verb for the other team to guess and use the word in a sentence.
- Use technology.
- Incorporate student interests.
- Use "real-world" projects. For example, "If we have $100 for a party, what could we afford for refreshments and entertainment?"

TABLE 8.4

Behavioral Intervention Plan for Matthew

GOALS	INTERVENTIONS	INDIVIDUALS	EVALUATION
1. To decrease Matthew's callouts and extraneous comments	1. Teach Matthew to use a self-management system that employs culturally appropriate reinforcers selected by Matthew.	1. Matthew • Teachers • Family members • School psychologist	1. Data on Matthew's callouts and extraneous comments • Teachers, student, and family interview data
2. To increase Matthew's work completion	2. Relate the content of the instructional activity to Matthew's experimental background and interests. • Use cooperative learning groups. • Promote active student responding via response cards and group physical responses. • Provide Matthew with choices in terms of the content and process of the instructional activities. • Solicit feedback from students concerning the ways to demonstrate mastery. • Use culturally relevant materials. • Personalize instruction by using students names, interests, and experiences. • Use suspense, games, technology, role-plays, and simulations. • Teach learning strategies.	2. Matthew • Teachers • Family members • Principal	2. Data on Matthew's work completion and accuracy • Teacher, student, and family interview data
3. To increase Matthew's in-seat behavior	3. Use cooperative learning groups • Use group-oriented response-cost system. • Establish a classwide peer-medication system. • Place Matthew's desk near the teacher's work area.	3. Matthew • Teachers • Peers • Family members • School Psychologist • Principal	3. Data on Matthew's in-seat behavior • Teacher, student, and family interview data
4. To increase Matthew's involvement in after-school activities	4. Teach social skills. • Pair Matthew with peers who participate in after-school activities. • Invite community groups and school-based groups to talk to the class about their after-school activities. • Share and read in class materials about community and leisure activities. • Take field trips to community facilities and after-school activities in the community. • Work with school and community groups to increase the availability of after-school activities.	4. Matthew • Teachers • Peers • Family members • Community members • Counselor • Principal	4. Data on after-school activities attended by Matthew • Teachers, student, family, counselor, and community member interview data

Source: From *Creating Inclusive Classrooms: Effective and Reflective Practices* (6th ed.) (p. 287). By S. J. Salend, 2008. Upper Saddle River, NJ: Pearson.

- Alternate high-interest and low-interest tasks.
- Increase opportunities for motor responses during or after a task. For example, use flash cards, games, and timed drills.
- Do not take away recess or other special classes. One young man said that he learned to dawdle more because he never got recess anyway.
- Assign unique topics and assignments.
- Allow students to "play" with objects (such as a "soothing" stone) during lectures or longer tasks.

During a long lecture period, teachers might also list main ideas or important questions on the chalkboard or by using the overhead projector, to help students focus on the most important information. When a student's attention does wander, a small, unobtrusive signal such as the teacher lightly tapping on the student's desk can cue the student to return to the task. To perk up tiring students, teachers can try a quick game of Simon Says or assign purposeful physical activities such as taking a note to the office, feeding the animals in the classroom, or returning books to the library.

Motivating these students can be difficult but should be a high priority. Smith, Salend, and Ryan (2001) suggest using a competency-oriented approach where students are referred to in terms of their strengths and where all students are given opportunities to assume leadership roles. They encourage teachers to offer the students choices and ask for their preferences. Establish rapport by talking to them about topics that interest them; attend after school events and cultural activities. Also important is creating a positive learning atmosphere by demonstrating your love of teaching and learning (Salend, 2010)!

Modifying the Curriculum   Although students with ADHD are typically taught in the general education classroom using the regular curriculum, they need a curriculum that focuses on "doing" and avoids long periods of sitting and listening. Such adaptations can benefit all students. For example, experience-based learning, in which students might develop their own projects, perform experiments, or take field trips, can help all students grow as active learners. Resources can be found in story problems included in traditional textbooks, curriculum-based experiments and projects, or extended activities such as writing letters to environmental groups to obtain more information than is offered in a textbook. The Differentiated Instruction—Elementary boxed reading shows a multigenre curriculum map developed by two sixth-grade language arts teachers in which students could gather information from a variety of sources to study people, places, or events from any time period of interest. They also allowed students to demonstrate what they learned using a variety of technologies and techniques based on their abilities and preferences. The Differentiated Instruction—Secondary boxed reading describes a similar process that two creative secondary teachers used to implement differentiated instruction techniques for their unit on the Vietnam War.

Just as these examples demonstrate, teachers are encouraged to vary their assessment techniques. Oral examinations, multiple-choice instead of essay or short answer, take-home tests, open-book or open-note exams, portfolio assessment, and informal measures are alternative assessment methods that provide a different perspective on measuring what students know. Students with ADHD will generally be able to take the same tests as their peers; however, testing adaptations may be needed to specifically address the ADHD characteristics. These might include extra time to take the test (usually no more than time and a half), frequent breaks, taking the exam in a distraction-reduced environment, or using a computer to record responses. See the nearby feature "Tips for Adapting a Lesson for Jake" for examples of how to meet the needs of an individual student.

Developing Student-Regulated Strategies

The previous sections on classroom environment and instructional accommodations focused on activities that the teacher directs and implements to increase the success of children with ADHD. This section describes student-regulated strategies. The following discussion provides an overview of four types of student-regulated strategies: study and organizational tactics, self-management, learning strategies, and social skills.

Differentiating Elementary Instruction

THE MULTIGENRE CURRICULUM MAP

OBJECTIVES	CONTENT/TOPIC/RESOURCES	SKILLS	PRODUCTS

Inquiry
• Gather information to answer questions
• Develop strategies for organizing, analyzing, and communicating information and integrating concepts
Reading/Writing/Oral
• Determine relevant information
• Take notes and organize information using a plan
• Engage in the writing process to compose ideas in a variety of genres
• Use technology to express ideas
• Present information effectively using eye contact, voice intonation, pace, timing and visual aids
	Content and Topics
	• Social studies related to people, places, events from any time period of interest
	Resources
	• Magazines, Internet sites, trade books from the library, electronic encyclopedias, and news articles
	• Variety of technologies:
	  • Microsoft Office (Word, Publisher, Excel, PowerPoint)
	  • Paint and Draw applications
	  • Inspiration software
	  • Digital images, clipart
		Students will demonstrate the ability to:
		• Work in partner groups to research and organize information related to a topic and make a plan to create a multigenre project that incorporates at least four different kinds of genres
		• Use technologies to create the genres and assemble the genres in such a way that ideas flow from one to another in a logical manner
		• Orally present their multigenre projects to classmates and engage others in meaningful discussions about what was learned
			Students will demonstrate what they have learned and what they are able to do using a variety of technologies:
			• Multimedia programs to create a narrative from an historical figure's point of view
			• Publishing software to create newspapers or Web pages
			• Paint/Draw programs to create political cartoons
			• Word processing to write poems, plays, obituaries, tributes, and points of view essays

Source: From "Providing Differentiated Learning Experiences Through Multigenre Projects," by D. Painter, 2009, *Intervention in School and Clinic, 44*(5), p. 289.

Study and Organizational Tactics Students with ADHD have difficulty organizing their work and developing effective, independent study skills in general education classrooms. To help them with organization, teachers may designate space for students to keep materials that are periodically cleaned out and organized. They can also establish the routine of students writing down their assignments daily in an assignment notebook, and provide notebooks or folders in different colors for each subject. Pierangelo and Giuliani (2006) suggest the following techniques to assist students with ADHD in developing study skills necessary for academic success:

- Teach children how to use Venn diagrams to organize new information in academic subjects.
- Teach children how to use a note-taking strategy such as Anita Archer's Skills for School Success (Archer & Gleason, 2002).
- Provide children with checklists that identify categories of items needed at home and school for various assignments. They can remember to check lists for themselves before departing.
- Teach children how to "unclutter" and organize their workspace for more efficient work.
- Involve children and parents in ongoing monitoring of homework.

Differentiating Secondary Instruction

USING INSTRUCTIONAL TECHNOLOGY AND ASSISTIVE DEVICES TO DIFFERENTIATE INSTRUCTION

Ms. Taravella and Ms. Camac, the school's technology specialist, were excited about developing and teaching a unit on the Vietnam War using instructional technology. They started to develop the unit by searching the Internet for content, online lesson plans, and teaching resources about Vietnam and the war. They also participated in a chat room related to teaching and technology, which also provided suggestions for the unit. Then they identified and reviewed interesting and relevant websites and resources and created their unit. They also visited the websites, which provided help in designing various web-based activities.

Since their students' experience with the Internet varied, Ms. Taravella and Ms. Camac began by teaching students about the Internet and how to use it appropriately. They modeled and provided an overview of how to access and navigate the internet and evaluate sites and web-based information. They paired experienced users with novices to perform a World Wide Web scavenger hunt that required them to conduct searches for various topics. They had students go online to www.cybersmartcurriculum.org and www.netsmartz.org to access activities that taught them how to use the Internet safely, responsibly, effectively. They brainstormed with students and framed rules for use of the internet by having students respond to such questions as "What would you do if you were asked for personal information or your password?" "What would you do if someone wanted to meet you or sell you something?" and "What would you do if you received or encountered offensive material?" They also told students not to believe everything they read or heard via the Internet. They gave students guidelines for examining and verifying sites and information, which included identifying the individuals who created the site, the dates on which it was created and updated, the location and organizational affiliation of the site, and the content of the site.

Once they were convinced that students could use the technology appropriately, Ms. Taravella and Ms. Camac assigned students to work in groups. Each group selected a variety of learning activities from a menu that included

- gathering information about the war from websites and wilds;
- viewing a DVD that portrayed actual battles and presented interviews with soldiers;
- taking a three-dimensional panoramic tour of the Vietnam Memorial through pictures that Ms. Camac had taken the previous summer with a digital camera;
- watching videos of news reports from the 1960s and 1970s and documentaries about the Vietnam War and antiwar activities throughout the United States and the world;

- exchanging e-mail messages with military experts and leaders of the antiwar movement;
- using virtual reality to attend rallies for and against the war;
- examining primary-source documents online;
- viewing and listening to podcasts that contained discussions about the war, including eyewitness accounts of the war from the viewpoint of soldiers, protestors, and Vietnamese citizens;
- making a virtual visit to an exhibition on the Vietnam War at the Smithsonian Museum; and
- establishing a keypal online relationship with Vietnamese and U.S. students and their families.

While the groups worked, the teachers and the other professionals in the room helped them. When computers froze because students tried to download too much information, they helped students reboot them. They also aided students who had difficulty accessing information from websites by using an Internet screen reading program that read the text and images aloud and reformatting the text and images so that they were easier for students with reading difficulties to read.

Ms. Taravella and Ms. Camac also allowed each group to choose its own final product. Group projects included writing and making a video and podcast of a play about the war, preparing a presentation about the war using presentation software and digital photos, conducting an online survey of the community's knowledge of the Vietnam War, and cleaning a memorial to Vietnam Veterans and the peace movement. All students helped develop their group's project. Tom, a student with a severe disability, used his assistive communication system to speak lines in his group's play and Marta, a second language learner, helped her group translate their community survey into Spanish.

The teachers and their students used the class's web page to create a weblog that provided an ongoing summary of the class's learning activities that also included digital photos of the groups' projects with accompanying narration. They were pleased when they received e-mail messages from other teachers and their students' families commenting on the students' products and requesting to use activities from their unit.

- What strategies did Ms. Taravella and Ms. Camac use to differentiate instruction for their students?

Source: From *Creating Inclusive Classrooms: Effective and Reflective Practices* (6th ed.) (p. 372). 2008. By S. J. Salend. Upper Saddle River, NJ: Pearson.

TIPS FOR ADAPTING A LESSON FOR JAKE

Since Jake's primary limitations include a short attention span, impulsive movement, and being easily distracted (as described in the chapter-opening vignette), the teacher's adaptations listed in his 504 plan and those recommended here should limit the impact of these challenges and help Jake make the good grades he needs to go to college.

Jake's teacher should:

- allow Jake to sit by students who generally remain on task;

- provide a copy of notes and overheads;

- color-code or underline important concepts;

- give Jake permission to leave the room occasionally or to walk in back of the room to provide authorized movement and not create a disturbance;

- take tests in a distraction-reduced environment and give extra time as needed;

- check often for understanding and review;

- vary activities.

Students should practice planning as an organizational strategy. Before being given an assignment such as a term paper, students should practice deciding how to break the task into small parts and how to complete each part. Students should also practice estimating how much time is needed for various activities so they can establish appropriate and realistic goals. Outlining skills can also help with organization and planning. Students may want to use a word processor to order their ideas and to help organize their work.

Self-Management   The primary goal of programs that teach self-management or self-control is to "make children more consciously aware of their own thinking processes and task approach strategies, and to give them responsibility for their own reinforcement" (Reeve, 1990, p. 76). Here are some advantages of teaching self-control:

- It saves the teacher's time by decreasing the demand for direct instruction.
- It increases the effectiveness of an intervention.
- It increases the maintenance of skills over time.

Polloway and Patton (2005) cite four types of self-regulation: self-assessment, self-monitoring, self-instruction, and self-reinforcement. In self-assessment, the individual determines the need for change and also monitors personal behavior. In self-monitoring, the student attends to specific aspects of his or her own behavior. While learning to self-monitor, a student can be given a periodic beep or other cue to signal that it is time for him or her to evaluate "on" or "off" task behavior. In self-instruction, the student cues himself or herself to inhibit inappropriate behaviors or to express appropriate ones. In self-reinforcement, the student administers self-selected reinforcement for an appropriate behavior that has been previously specified. Figure 8.9 contains a self-management strategy used to help students deal with anger. Figure 8.10 provides a self-monitoring sheet for the student to use to reflect on his or her use of the strategy. Eventually the student will begin to automatically self-monitor and will begin to use the appropriate response to situations that previously triggered an inappropriate display of anger. Other behaviors commonly targeted for self-regulation include completing assignments, appropriate classroom behavior (such as staying in one's seat), accuracy of work (such as percent correct), and staying on task.

■ Cuing or signaling students is one method that teachers can use to help get their attention.

FIGURE 8.9

A self-management strategy for dealing with anger.

Source: From "Collaborating to Teach Prosocial Skills," by D. H. Allsopp, K. E. Santos, and R. Linn, 2000, *Intervention in School and Clinic, 35*(3), p. 145.

1. **W**ATCH for the "trigger."
   ▶ Count to 10.
   ▶ Use relaxation techniques.

2. **A**NSWER, "Why am I angry?"

3. **I**DENTIFY my options.
   ▶ Ignore the other person.
   ▶ Move away.
   ▶ Resolve the problem.
   ▶ "I feel this way when you . . ."
   ▶ Listen to the other person.
   ▶ Talk to the teacher.

4. **T**RY an appropriate option for dealing with my anger.

Learning Strategies   Deshler and Lenz (1989) define a learning strategy as an individual's approach to a task. It includes how an individual thinks and acts when planning, executing, or evaluating performance. The learning strategies approach combines what is going on in an individual's head (cognition) with what a person actually does (behavior) to guide the performance and evaluation of a specific task. All individuals use strategies; however, not all strategies are effective. Strichart and Mangrum (2010) recommend this approach to assist students who are inefficient learners.

Babkie and Provost (2002) encourage teachers and students to create their own strategies or cues to teach a difficult concept or behavior. A key word is identified that specifies the targeted area. A short phrase or sentence that tells the student what to do is written for each letter in the key word. Figure 8.11 shows a strategy developed to cue students to organize homework.

Social Skills   Because students with ADHD often do not exhibit good problem-solving skills and are not able to predict the consequences of their inappropriate behavior, specific and direct instruction in social skills may be necessary. Although it is better for students to

FIGURE 8.10	A Self-Monitoring Sheet for Dealing with Anger		
What was the trigger?	Why was I angry?	Did I identify my options?	What option did I choose and was it successful?
1.			
2.			
3.			
4.			
5.			

FIGURE 8.11	A Learning Strategy for Homework

Organization: **HOMEWORK**
Have a place to work
Organize assignments according to difficulty
Make sure to follow directions
Examine the examples
Weave my way through the assignments
Observe work for errors and omissions
Return work to school
Keep up the effort!

Source: From "Select, Write, and Use Metacognitive Strategies in the Classroom" (p. 174) by A. M. Babkie and M. C. Provost, 2002, *Intervention in School and Clinic,* 37(3).

be able to assess their own inappropriate behavior and adjust it to acceptable standards, many students may need social-skills training first. For example, students who misread or totally miss social cues can benefit from role-playing situations where problems have previously occurred. A fight on the playground, inappropriately interrupting a teacher, or a shoving incident in the lunchroom are examples of situations in which reenacting the event under controlled circumstances allows students to proactively rehearse correct responses for future social encounters. Repeated opportunities to practice appropriate social skills may be needed for the correct responses to be internalized (Sharpe, 2008).

Promoting Inclusive Practice

Barkley (2006) suggests that the education of the school staff, peers, the family, and the individuals with ADHD is one of the most important interventions. He also reports that parent training in child management is helpful, particularly when children are preadolescent, and that family therapy is often needed to improve communication, especially with teens. Two critical features for successful inclusion of students with ADHD are the skills and behaviors of their teachers and the understanding and acceptance of the general education peers.

Community-Building Skills for Teachers   One of the most important elements in promoting success for children with ADHD is the teacher. Fowler (1992a) suggests that success for children with ADHD might vary from year to year, from class to class, and from teacher to teacher. She reports that" the teacher" is the most commonly cited reason for a positive or negative school experience. She cites the following 17 characteristics of teachers as likely indicators of positive learning outcomes for students with ADHD; the effectiveness of these traits is timeless:

1. positive academic expectations
2. frequent review of student work
3. clarity of teaching (e.g., explicit directions, rules)
4. flexibility
5. fairness
6. active interaction with the students
7. responsiveness
8. warmth
9. patience
10. humor
11. structured and predictable approach

12. consistency
13. firmness
14. positive attitude toward inclusion
15. knowledge of and willingness to work with students with exceptional needs
16. knowledge of different types of effective interventions
17. willingness to work collaboratively with other teachers (e.g., sharing information, requesting assistance as needed, participating in conferences involving students). (p. 17)

Resources for Developing Awareness in Peers   Teachers with the traits in the preceding list will provide a positive role model for general education students in how to understand and accept children with ADHD. Teachers should confer with parents and the child with ADHD to obtain advice on explaining ADHD to other students in the classroom. The child with ADHD may wish to be present during the explanation or even to participate in informing his or her classmates. The following books and publications may help introduce this topic to students with ADHD and their peers:

Eagle Eyes: A Child's View of Attention Deficit Disorder (1996)
By J. Gehreet
Fairport, NY: Verbal Images Press (ages 5–12)

Eddie Enough! (2000)
By D. Zimmett
Bethesda, MD: Woodbine House

Eukee the Jumpy, Jumpy Elephant (1995)
By C. Corman and El Trevino
Plantation, FL: Specialty Press (ages 3–8)

Joey Pigza Swallowed the Key (1998)
By J. Gantos
New York: Farrar, Strauss, and Giroux (ages 9–12)

Taking ADHD To School (1999)
By E. Weiner
Valley Park, MO: JayJo Books (ages 5–10)

Who Took My Shoe? (2003)
By K. Emigh
Arlington, TX: Future Horizons (ages 5–10)

Zipper, the Kid with ADHD (1997)
By C. Janover
Bethesda, MD: Woodbine House (ages 8–13)

Collaborating with Parents of Students with ADHD   Evelyn Green, former president of the CHADD National Board of Directors and a parent of a child with ADHD, stresses the importance of teachers and other professionals in supporting and helping parents. In an interview (Chamberlain, 2003), she offers the following insight:

> I think professionals are not always sympathetic to the fact that for most parents, it is initially devastating when they discover that their child is not the "perfect" little person that they have dreamed about. But it isn't hopeless and doesn't have to remain devastating if you use a strength-based approach, if you help the child discover her or his talents and strengths and build from there. Professionals can be extremely helpful to parents in getting over the initial feelings of helplessness and in finding the child's strengths. . . . Parents absolutely have to have somebody who knows and understands, who does not blame them . . . who will let you know that there is a next step to get to and whatever challenges you are facing now will pass. Having that kind of support system has certainly been one of our [family's] keys to success.

Brandes (2005) stresses the importance of keeping parents involved in their child's education through meaningful communications. She offers these recommendations to promote healthy relationships based on respect:

- Be an active listener, sit or stand beside parents, and give them your undivided attention.
- Take notes while talking with parents and review them for accuracy as they leave; recap the meeting.
- View a challenging parent as an opportunity to grow. Be respectful when working with angry parents, write down their concerns, and do not be defensive.
- Share specific behavioral and curricular goals early and provide their relevance.
- Communicate regularly and often; always share some of the positive events from school; let parents know how much you appreciate their support and follow-through at home; specify future communications.

SUMMARY

Basic Concepts about ADHD

- Children and adults with ADHD often have serious challenges in academic and non-academic environments due to their difficulties with inattention, hyperactivity, and/or impulsivity.
- The legal basis for service delivery and protection for students with ADHD comes from IDEA and Section 504 of the Rehabilitation Act of 1973.
- Under IDEA, students with ADHD may be served through the category of "other health impaired" because attention deficits are considered a chronic and acute condition that limits alertness and adversely affects educational performance.
- The diagnosis of ADHD is primarily based on the presence of inattention, hyperactivity, and impulsivity and specific criteria listed in the DSM-IV-TR.
- Many theories exist to explain the cause of ADHD; however, the presence of ADHD is considered to be primarily influenced by genetic and environmental factors.

Characteristics of Students with ADHD

- For the majority of individuals, ADHD manifests itself across the life span.
- Characteristics include limited sustained attention, reduced impulse control, excessive task-irrelevant activity, disorganization, forgetfulness, time-management problems, limited self-talk and behavior control, and greater-than-normal variability during task performance.

Effective Inclusive Practices for Students with ADHD

- To be effective in working with students with ADHD, teachers must collaborate with families and professionals outside of education.
- A continuum of placement options is available to students with ADHD; however, the majority of students with ADHD spend all or most of the school day in general education classes.
- An individual accommodation plan or IEP is written collaboratively with parents, professionals, and, when possible, the student to identify interventions that will create success in the general education classroom.
- Medication is frequently used to enhance the educational and social experience of children and adults with ADHD.
- Teachers play an important role in monitoring both positive outcomes and negative side effects of students taking medication for ADHD.

- Effective teachers for students with ADHD provide positive classroom environments, frequently review student work, and are flexible, fair, responsive, warm, patient, consistent, firm, and humorous. They develop a knowledge of the strengths and needs of their students with ADHD and are knowledgeable about different intervention strategies.
- Classroom adaptations include environmental management techniques, instructional adaptations, and student-regulated strategies.
- Techniques used to manage the classroom environment include strategies for group management, physical arrangement of the room, and individual behavior-management techniques.
- Through instructional adaptations, teachers modify their behavior to include novel and stimulating activity, to provide structure and consistency, to allow physical movement as frequently as possible, to include cooperative learning activities, and to give both spoken and written direction.
- Typically the curricular goals for students with ADHD are shared by their general education peers; however, it may be important to differentiate instruction and assessment techniques for optimal learning and performance for students with varying levels of ability, attention, and achievement.
- Student-regulated strategies include study and organizational tactics, self-management techniques, learning strategies, and social skills training.

PEARSON
myeducationlab

The MyEducationLab for this course can help you solidify your comprehension of Chapter 8 concepts.

- Gauge and further develop your understanding of chapter concepts by taking the quizzes and examining the enrichment materials on the Chapter 8 Study Plan.
- Visit Topic 14, Learning Disabilities and Attention Deficit/Hyperactivity Disorder, to:
  - Connect with challenge-based interactive modules, case study units, and podcasts that provide research-validated information about working with students in inclusive settings by visiting the IRIS Center Resources
  - Explore Assignments and Activities, assignable exercises showing concepts in action through video, cases, and student and teacher artifacts
  - Practice and strengthen skills essential to quality teaching through the Building Teaching Skills and Dispositions lessons

9

Teaching Students with Autism Spectrum Disorders

Gena P. Barnhill and Ed Polloway

ANDREA'S parents noted something different about their child when she was about 2 years old. Up until that time she had developed perfectly. She walked at 13 months, started babbling at about 7 months, and loved to play with adults and other children. Then between 18 months and 2 years things began to change. Andrea's babbling stopped and she no longer used the words she had developed (e.g., mama, daddy, cup, and kitty). She stopped paying any attention to other children and adults. Her parents were frustrated by her inability to potty train. When she was about 3 years old, her parents took her to a medical center, and the diagnosis was autism. Andrea was placed in a preschool program and has been in special education services ever since. In kindergarten and first grade, she was placed in a self-contained special education classroom. During these two years, Andrea seemed to regress and started picking up some of the other children's stereotypical, self-stimulating behaviors. Her parents convinced the school to place Andrea in the regular second grade, with supports. Now, in December, Andrea is doing very well. While she has limited oral language, she enjoys being with her peers and is able to do much of the academic work with the assistance of a paraprofessional.

QUESTIONS TO CONSIDER

1. Is there a preferred placement for children with autism?
2. What kinds of supports should be available for Andrea to facilitate her success in the general education classroom?
3. How can the schools provide the necessary supports to make inclusion work for students with ASD?

Visit the MyEducationLab for this course to enhance your understanding of chapter concepts with a personalized Study Plan. You'll also have the opportunity to hone your teaching skills through video-based Assignments and Activities, IRIS Center Resources, and Building Teaching Skills and Disposition lessons.

This chapter provides an introduction and discussion of autism spectrum disorders (ASD). Given the clear trend toward increased prevalence of ASD reported by the U.S. Department of Education (USDOE, 2009) and the unique learning challenges faced by students so identified, teachers must have a clear understanding of the condition and its implications for education. A multidisciplinary approach to meeting the needs of students with ASD will be the key to successful education.

BASIC CONCEPTS ABOUT AUTISM

Autism spectrum disorders are pervasive developmental disorders (PDD) that primarily affect social interactions, language, and behavior. Although autism has been glamorized by several movies, such as *Rain Man* (1988), most students with this condition do not have such special abilities. The characteristics displayed by individuals with autism vary significantly; some individuals are able to assimilate into community settings and activities, whereas others have major difficulties achieving that goal (Scheuermann & Webber, 2002). Needless to say, "children and youth with ASD are a particularly unique group, even when compared with other children with disabilities" (Simpson, 2001, p. 68).

In general, PDD and ASD are both considered to be "umbrella" concepts. The term *pervasive developmental disorder* was first used in the DSM in 1980, while the term *autism spectrum disorder* was initially coined in 1988. Thus, they are inclusive of the conditions of autism, Asperger syndrome (AS), Rett syndrome, childhood disintegrative disorder, and pervasive developmental disorder not otherwise specified (PDD-NOS). Rett syndrome occurs mostly in girls who develop normally for the first 5 months of life and then deceleration of head growth occurs between 5 and 48 months, along with loss of purposeful hand movements between 5 and 30 months, which is followed by stereotypical hand-wringing or hand-washing movements. Childhood disintegrative disorder is extremely rare, occurs mostly in boys, and is characterized by a marked regression in multiple areas of functioning after a period of normal development for 2 to 10 years (American Psychiatric Association; APA, 2000). PDD-NOS, sometimes referred to as atypical autism, is a category used "when there is a severe and pervasive impairment in the development of reciprocal social interaction associated with impairment in either verbal or nonverbal communication skills or with the presence of stereotyped behavior, interests, activities" and the criteria are not met for another disorder (APA, 2000, p. 84). In education, there is a strong consensus for the use of ASD, and thus it will be the term used in this chapter.

The study of autism has had a controversial history since the condition was first described by Leo Kanner in 1943 (Webber & Scheuermann, 2008). Some of the early controversy centered on attempts to relate the cause of autism to poor mother-child bonding. Some professionals once believed that children with autism made a conscious decision to withdraw from their environment because of its hostile nature. Eventually this hypothesis was disproved in the 1960s, but it caused a great deal of guilt, confusion, and misunderstanding. At that time, research into child development and language disorders and the work of Kanner and Rutter and his colleagues suggested viewing autism as a disorder of development starting from birth or in the early childhood years (Wing, 1996). In 1980, autism was first introduced in the DSM III as a new classification of childhood onset disorders separate from childhood schizophrenia. Data support biological factors such as genetics and dysfunction in the brain system in the development of autism (Volkmar & Klin, 2005).

Prior to 1990, children with autism were eligible for special education services only under the category of "other health impaired." Parents and others subsequently and successfully advocated that children with this disability deserved their own category. AS, one of the conditions under the umbrella of ASD that has received a great deal of attention since the 1990s, was first described in 1944 by Hans Asperger (Griswold, Barnhill, & Myles, 2002) but his work did not receive much attention in the English language until Wing published her case history of the syndrome in 1981. In 1994 the American Psychiatric Association (APA) recognized AS as a unitary disorder under the category "Pervasive Developmental Disorders" in the DSM-IV (APA, 1994). The DSM-IV was later revised in 2000 and, although the criteria for Asperger's disorder (commonly referred to as AS) were not changed, additional text was provided to describe the condition.

As discussed in the "Prevalence" section on page 290, the epidemic-like recent increases in the number of people identified as having autism has given rise to new societal challenges that require a response on a greater scale than would have been anticipated even in the mid-1990s. Steuernagel (2005) highlighted the policy implications as related to the need for:

- Enhanced teacher training
- Support for general education teachers to promote successful inclusion
- Increased vocational rehabilitation services for adults
- Increased commitment to research on etiology
- Advanced understanding of effective interventions for use by parents and teachers

Definition, Identification, and Eligibility

It is important to be familiar with three key definitions: the one in IDEA, primarily used by educators, and the ones for autism and AS found in the DSM-IV-TR (APA, 2000), used more often by psychologists and medical professionals. IDEA defines autism as

> (i) a developmental disability significantly affecting verbal and nonverbal communication and social interaction, generally evident before age three, that adversely affects a child's educational performance. Other characteristics often associated with autism are engagement in repetitive activities and stereotyped movements, resistance to environmental change or change in daily routines, and unusual responses to sensory experiences.
>
> (ii) Autism does not apply if a child's educational performance is adversely affected primarily because the child has an emotional disturbance, as defined in paragraph (c)(4) of this section.
>
> (iii) A child who manifests the characteristics of autism after age three could be identified as having autism if the criteria in paragraph (c)(1)(i) of this section are satisfied. [34 CFR § 300.8(c)(1)]

Figure 9.1 provides the DSM-IV-TR definition and diagnostic criteria of autism, and Figure 9.2 provides the DSM-IV-TR definition and diagnostic criteria of AS.

Within this chapter, the following referents are used: **ASD** to reflect broad considerations across the spectrum of the disorders, **autism** to be broad-based unless specified as being in specific reference to the autistic subtype under ASD, and **Asperger syndrome** to reflect only this specific subtype.

FIGURE 9.1 — Definition of Autism

A. A total of six (or more) items from (1), (2), and (3), with at least two from (1), and one each from (2) and (3):

(1) qualitative impairment in social interaction, as manifested by at least two of the following:
  (a) marked impairment in the use of multiple nonverbal behaviors such as eye-to-eye gaze, facial expression, body postures, and gestures to regulate social interaction
  (b) failure to develop peer relationships appropriate to developmental level
  (c) a lack of spontaneous seeking to share enjoyment, interests, or achievements with other people (e.g., by a lack of showing, bringing, or pointing out objects of interest)
  (d) lack of social or emotional reciprocity

(2) qualitative impairments in communication as manifested by at least one of the following:
  (a) delay in, or total lack of the development of spoken language (not accompanied by an attempt to compensate through alternative modes of communication such as gesture or mime)
  (b) in individuals with adequate speech, marked impairment in the ability to initiate or sustain a conversation with others
  (c) stereotyped and repetitive use of language or idiosyncratic language
  (d) lack of varied, spontaneous make-believe play or social imitative play appropriate to developmental level

(3) restricted repetitive and stereotyped patterns of behavior, interests, and activities, as manifested by at least one of the following:
  (a) encompassing preoccupation with one or more stereotyped and restricted patterns of interest that is abnormal either in intensity or focus
  (b) apparently inflexible adherence to specific, nonfunctional routines or rituals
  (c) stereotyped and repetitive motor mannerisms (e.g., hand or finger flapping or twisting, or complex whole-body movements)
  (d) persistent preoccupation with parts of objects

B. Delays or abnormal functioning in at least one of the following areas, with onset prior to age 3 years: (1) social interaction, (2) language as used in social communication, or (3) symbolic or imaginative play.

C. The disturbance is not better accounted for by Rett's Disorder or Childhood Disintegrative Disorder (two pervasive developmental disorders characterized by impairment in the development of reciprocal social interaction).

Source: From *Diagnostic and Statistical Manual of Mental Disorders-TR* (4th ed., p. 75), 2000. Washington, DC: American Psychiatric Association. Used by permission.

FIGURE 9.2	Definition of Asperger Disorder

A. Qualitative impairment in social interaction, as manifested by at least two of the following:
   1. marked impairment in the use of multiple nonverbal behaviors such as eye-to-eye gaze, facial expression, body postures, and gestures to regulate social interaction
   2. failure to develop peer relationships appropriate to developmental level
   3. a lack of spontaneous seeking to share enjoyment, interests, or achievements with other people. (e.g., by a lack of showing, bringing, or pointing out objects of interest to other people)
   4. lack of social or emotional reciprocity
B. Restricted repetitive and stereotyped patterns of behavior, interests, and activities as manifested by at least one of the following:
   1. encompassing preoccupation with one or more stereotyped and restricted patterns of interest that is abnormal in intensity or focus
   2. apparently inflexible adherence to specific, nonfunctional routines or rituals
   3. stereotyped and repetitive motor mannerisms (e.g., hand or finger flapping or twisting, or complex whole-body movements)
   4. persistent preoccupation with parts of objects
C. The disturbance causes clinically significant impairment in social, occupational, or other important areas of functioning.
D. There is no clinically significant general delay in language (e.g., single words used by age 2 years, communicative phrases used by age 3 years).
E. There is no clinically significant delay in cognitive development or in the development of age-appropriate self-help skills, adaptive behavior (other than social interaction), and curiosity about the environment in childhood.

Source: From *Diagnostic and Statistical Manual of Mental Disorders-TR* (4th ed., p. 84), 2000. Washington, DC: American Psychiatric Association. Used by permission.

Identification of Children with ASD

A number of problems are related to the identification of children with ASD. As noted by the National Research Council (NRC, 2001), these include:

- "There is no one single behavior that is always typical of . . . ASD and no behavior that would automatically exclude an individual from diagnosis of ASD" (NRC, 2001, p. 2).
- The presenting features of ASD can vary considerably across children and within a particular child over time.
- The severity of symptoms, age of onset, and the presence of features such as intellectual disability and language delay vary for individuals with ASD.

Another problem in identifying children with autism is the large, diverse group of professionals involved in evaluation and diagnosis (e.g., pediatricians, speech–language pathologists, psychologists, social workers). Working with such a large group of individuals can cause logistical problems. Diverse definitions and eligibility criteria, different funding agencies, and varying services complicate the process of identifying and serving these children and adults. The Rights & Responsibilities feature summarizes some of the legal decisions concerning the rights of students with autism; a number of the cases relate to diagnostic as well as service issues.

Finally, the process of identification is further complicated by professional and parental disagreement as to whether ASD reflects a continuum of disorders or several discrete categories, as are found in the DSM-IV-TR (APA, 2000). Volkmar (2004) refers to "clumpers" (i.e., those who will include AS under ASD because all have social deficits) and "splitters" (e.g., those who keep Asperger on its own because of advanced language and higher cognitive functioning). The National Research Council (2001) recommended that children with any autistic spectrum disorder, no matter what their level or severity of function, should be eligible for special education services within the category of autistic spectrum disorders "because of their shared continuities and their unique social difficulties, as opposed to other terminology used by school systems, such as other heath impaired, socially maladjusted, significantly developmentally delayed, or neurologically impaired" (pp. 213–214).

RIGHTS & RESPONSIBILITIES

SELECTED COURT DECISIONS RELATED TO INTERVENTIONS FOR STUDENTS WITH ASD

- **Delaware County IU#25 v. Martin K. (1993)** When programs are new or considered pilot programs, programs with documented benefits will be considered more effective.

- **Hartmann v. Loudoun County Board of Education (1997)** A student's IEP should reflect individual needs; an IEP that strictly focuses on a singular emphasis, such as social skills training, will likely be considered inappropriate.

- **Johnson v. Independent School District No. 4 of Bixby (1990)** In addition to regression/recoupment, other factors that must be included when determining the need for an extended school year for students with autism are the degree of impairment, the ability of the child to interact with others, the child's rate of progress, and professional opinion predicting the student's progress toward goals.

- **Byron Union School District 35, IDELR 49 (SEA CA 2001)** A district hearing officer ruled that an 11-year-old student with autism did not require placement in a special day class to receive a free appropriate public education. Evidence and testimony supported the fact that the student was able to benefit from academic instruction in the general education classroom and therefore did not need to be placed in the special school.

- **West Des Moines Community School District, 36 IDELR222 (SEA-IA, 2002)** A 14-year-old boy with AS who was also in-

tellectually gifted had difficulty with social skills, friendship relationships, eye-contact maintenance, conversation interactions, and eccentric behavior. The hearing officer and review panel held that the schools needed to focus not just on his academic strengths but also on the need for gifted education and related social skills training.

- **Sanford School Committee v. Mr. and Mrs. L., No. CIV.00–CV113 PH (D. Me.2001)** A student with autism was found to be denied his free appropriate public education when an IEP was developed that did not take into consideration his needs. In developing the IEP, it was determined that the district never considered whether the proposed placement would meet the needs of the student.

- **West Des Moines Community School Dist., 36 IDELR 222 SEA(IA, 2002)** In this case, a federal judge ruled that a child with AS has a disability and is thus entitled to special education services even though he or she is performing well in the classroom (e.g., appropriate behaviors, homework completion, test performance).

Sources: Adapted from: 1. "Interventions for Children and Youth with Autism: Prudent Choices in a World of Exaggerated Claims and Empty Promises," by L. J. Heflin and R. Simpson, 1998, *Focus on Autism and Other Developmental Disabilities, 13*, pp. 212–220. 2. "Legal Issues," by S. Gorn (pp. 257–274), in *Asperger's Syndrome. Intervening in Schools, Clinics, and Communities,* edited by L. J. Baker and L. A. Welkowitz, 2005. Mahwah, NJ: Erlbaum.

Addressing the question of an autism continuum versus discrete categories, Tryon, Maves, Rhodes, and Waldo (2006) presented data on 22 children who had been identified as having AS. They found that 20 met the DSM-IV-TR criteria for autism and that none met the criteria for AS. They cited their data as consistent with:

> the mounting empirical evidence that Asperger's disorder is high-functioning autism [and thus encouraged that] Asperger's disorder be deleted from the next version of the *DSM*. High- and low-functioning autism would continue to be indicated, as before, by an Axis I diagnosis of autism with an Axis II diagnosis of <intellectual disabilities> for low-functioning autism, and no Axis II diagnosis of <intellectual disabilities> for high-functioning autism. According to the DSM-IV-TR, a child can still have autism even without language or cognitive delays, and a diagnosis of autism takes precedence over Asperger's disorder. If a child meets DSM-IV-TR autism criteria, the child cannot have Asperger's disorder. (p. 4)

The debate concerning whether to keep AS a separate diagnostic category in the new DSM-V continues. Baron-Cohen, director of the Autism Research Center at Cambridge University, stated that until we know if AS is genetically identical or different from classical autism, we should keep it as a separate category. Furthermore, he reported that science has not been able to determine if there is a biological difference between AS and autism. Baron-Cohen's first candidate gene study of AS identified 14 genes associated with the syndrome (Baron-Cohen, 2009). On the other hand, Catherine Lord, director of the Autism and Communication Disorders Centers at the University of Michigan, argued, "Nobody has been able to show consistent differences between what clinicians diagnose as Asperger syndrome and what they diagnose as mild autistic disorder" (Wallis, 2009b). She went on to comment, "Asperger's means a lot of different things to different people. It's confusing and not terribly useful" (Wallis, 2009b).

Early Identification   A critical concern in the field of ASD is early identification. The common challenge has been to determine how early autism can be detected. Goin and Myers (2004) indicated that, although there were better detection rates during the second year, nevertheless, some developmental anomalies may be noticed in year one. They stressed the value of multiple sources, including home videos, early screening devices, and parental reports.

The key characteristics identified in the literature (e.g., Goin & Myers, 2004; Gomez & Baird, 2005; Webber & Scheuermann, 2008; Zwaigenbaum, Bryson, Roberts, Brian, & Szatmari, 2005) for earliest detection include lack of eye contact and limited social skills; lack of joint attention or sharing of social experiences; differences in postural and motoric characteristics; lack of responsiveness to others and to one's own name; a pattern of solitary or unusual play; marked passivity; fixation on objects; delayed expressive and receptive language, including gestural communication; and difficulties in self-regulation that may be reflected in, for example, impulsivity, irritability, and interference with the formation of attachments.

Causes of Autism Spectrum Disorder

There is no single specific cause of autism, but a variety of factors can result in this disability. Organic factors such as brain damage, genetic links, and complications during pregnancy may be contributors to this condition, though in most cases no single cause and no genetic, metabolic, or radiographic markers help in the diagnosis or predict the severity of symptoms (Bauman & Kemper, 2005; Rogers & Dawson, 2010). Moreover, "there is currently no autism signature in the brain—no difference that is universally present in people who have autism, and only in them" (Rogers & Dawson, 2010, p. 8). In general, autism occurs across all segments of society (Volkmar & Klin, 2005) and U.S. prevalence rates are similar to rates reported in England, Japan, Sweden, and Canada (Wallis, 2009a).

The study of causation reflects a continued focus on efforts to unravel complexity. While the "cold mother" theory has long been discredited, the precise causative mechanism remains elusive. Most accepted models suggest a combination of a genetic base influenced by environmental events. The genetic role is presumed to create a predisposition for ASD. However, genetics alone cannot explain the recent rapid increases in prevalence.

The common assumption is that autism is related to abnormalities in brain structure or function. According to the ASA (2008):

> Brain scans show differences in the shape and structure of the brain. . . . In many families there appears to be a pattern of autism or related disabilities, further supporting a genetic basis to the disorder. While no one gene has been identified as causing autism, researchers are searching for irregular segments of genetic code that children with autism may have inherited. It also appears that some children are born with a susceptibility to autism, but researchers have not yet identified a single "trigger" that causes autism to develop. (Medical Components of ASD, para. 1)

Environmental factors that have been hypothesized include toxins, heavy metals, and infections. One area of debate has related to the measles-mumps-rubella (MMR) vaccine. It is within post-hoc case studies that the argument was made based on the presence of thimerosal (mercury preservative) within the MMR vaccine and the possibility that millions of children were exposed to mercury levels above EPA guidelines. The Institute of Medicine of the National Academies concluded that "the body of epidemiological evidence favors a rejection of a causal relationship between thimerosal-containing vaccines and autism". . . and "between the MMR vaccine and autism" (Immunization Safety Review Committee of the Institute of Medicine, 2004). Harris (2010) reported that the *Lancet* officially retracted the original study that allegedly linked the MMR with autism.

Prevalence

Autism historically has been considered a low-incidence disability. Moreover, 30 years ago it was unusual to have a student with autism in the public schools (McKenna, 2007). However, the number of children identified over the past few years has increased dramatically and it certainly can be argued that autism is no longer low incidence (Simpson, 2004). The incidence of autism varies directly with the definition used.

The Centers for Disease Control (CDC, 2009) most recently indicated that current prevalence rates of ASD are 1 in 110 children in the United States. Furthermore, they concluded that ASD occurs in all racial, ethnic, and socioeconomic groups and is four to five times more likely to occur in boys than girls. Kogan et al. (2009) indicated even higher rates of 110 per 10,000 (1.1%, or 1 in 91) in their study of parent-reported diagnosis of ASD among children aged 3 to 17. This represents an estimated 673,000 children in the United States. The Autism Society of America (ASA, 2008) reported an estimated 1.5 million Americans may have some form of autism and, based on an increase in prevalence of 10 to 17% per year, as many as 4 million Americans may be affected in the next decade. Children with autism represent the fastest-growing group of students served through special education (Ludlow, Keramidas, & Landers, 2007).

The USDOE (2009) reported that the percentage of children ages 6 to 17 in the schools served under the category of autism was 0.32%. Across individual states, the range was from 0.70% (Oregon) to 0.11% (New Mexico).

Part of the confusion as to whether autism rates have truly increased is that the term *incidence* is often incorrectly assumed to be synonymous with *prevalence. Incidence rates* are used for causal research and refer to the number of new cases of a disease occurring over a specified time in persons at risk for developing the disease in a given population. Only three epidemiological studies investigating incidence rates of autism have been conducted and they did demonstrate an upward trend in incidence over short periods of time. However, most of the studies have reported *prevalence rates*, a measure used in cross-sectional research that indicates the proportion of individuals in a given population who have the disorder at the time of the research. Prevalence information is useful for planning and estimating needs. However, time trends in autism are difficult to gauge from prevalence rates and even in the absence of a change in incidence, prevalence rates can increase because of methodological reasons (Fombonne, 2005).

Several reasons (Fombonne, 2005; Grinker, 2007; Wallis, 2009a) are postulated for the significant increase in the rates of autism. They include:

- Greater awareness of ASD by parents, pediatricians, and educators
- Broader definitions of ASD
- Earlier diagnosis of ASD, which can now be identified by age 2 in many cases
- Increased availability of special services and interventions
- Autism is no longer confused with childhood schizophrenia
- Diagnostic reclassification (e.g., some individuals formerly diagnosed with mental retardation now are diagnosed with autism)
- Epidemiological methods have changed
- Autism is now being used for individuals with medical disorders and this was not the case in Kanner's day
- General overall population increase

Gender and Ethnicity

One area of note is gender variability. For example, according to the U.S. Department of Education (2005), 83% of all children between the ages of 6 and 12 identified as having autism were male; for ages 13 to 17, the comparable figure is 84.8%.

In terms of racial and ethnic composition, the U.S. Department of Education (2009) reported the following ethnic percentage breakdown within the category of autism with comparative data for all students with disabilities across categories provided in parentheses: 0.70% for Native Americans/Alaskans (1.5%); 5.1% for Asian/Pacific Islanders (2.1%);

15.4% for African Americans (20.5%); 11.0% for Hispanic (17.2%); and 67.7% for White, non-Hispanics (58.7%). By comparing these two sets of data, it can be noted that the percentage of children identified as having autism by ethnic group is generally less for each group with the exception of higher school prevalence rates for Asian/Pacific Islanders and European Americans.

Educational Environments

For preschool students with ASD (ages 3 to 5), the USDOE (2009) reported that 17.6% were served in an early childhood setting; 52.8% were served in an early childhood special education setting; 1.7% received services in a home-based program; 19.7% received part-time services in an early childhood and part-time special education setting; 0.03% were served in a residential facility; 5.2% were served in a separate school; 1.0% were served through itinerant services provided outside of the home; and 1.9% were served in a reverse mainstreaming program.

For students ages 6 to 21, the same source reported that 29.1% were in the regular classroom for 79% or more of the day, 17.7% were served outside of the regular classroom between 21 and 60% of the time, and 41.8% were served outside of the regular classroom over 60% of the time. Further, 5.5% were served in public separate facilities and 4.7% in private separate facilities. In terms of residential placement, 0.8% were served in public or private residential facilities and 0.4% were served within the home or in a hospital environment. In general, a larger percentage of students ages 6 to 11 tend to be educated in general education-based programs and fewer served in separate facilities than students between the ages of 12 and 21, who are more often served in restrictive settings.

CHARACTERISTICS OF INDIVIDUALS WITH ASD

Individuals with ASD are a heterogeneous group of people that display a wide variety of abilities and present with different strengths and challenges (Barnhill, 2011). However, many of the associated characteristics fall into the following three core deficit areas commonly referred to as the triad of deficits: (1) communication (verbal and nonverbal), (2) socialization, and (3) repetitive behavior, interests and activities (Heflin & Alaimo, 2007). Cognitive and perceptual impairments *may manifest* as literal, here-and-now thinking, a tendency to over-select irrelevant stimuli and miss the salient features in the environment, lack of imaginary play, good rote memory, and obsessive need for sameness and repetition. In addition, sensory processing deficits may manifest in one or more of the following ways: intense fear reactions to new situations, people, or changes and loud noises; underresponsive to pain; appear to be deaf or blind when they are not; tactile defensiveness; and specific food and clothing preferences (Webber & Scheuermann, 2008).

Several theories have been proposed to explain the social cognitive deficits associated with ASD. Happe and Frith (2006) proposed that, currently, the most plausible explanation is to consider autism the result of irregularities affecting core cognitive processes including executive dysfunction, theory of mind, and central coherence. One of the challenges is that the deficits associated with these theories exist in varying degrees for individuals with ASD and these deficits may not be exclusive to ASD. *Executive function* is defined as "the ability to regulate one's behavior through working memory, inner speech, control of emotions and arousal levels, and analysis of problems and communication of problem situations to others" (Hallahan, Kauffman, & Pullen, 2009, p. 569). Ozonoff and Schetter's (2007) review of the research revealed that persons with ASD experience executive function impairments at a high rate. *Theory of mind* is "the ability to recognize and understand other people's thoughts, feelings, desires, and intentions in order to make sense of their behavior and to be able to predict what they will do next" (Buron & Wolfberg, 2008, p. 377). These difficulties can lead to the person with ASD experiencing challenges explaining the impact of other's behaviors as well as understanding the impact of his or her behavior on others. Furthermore, there may be challenges comprehending emotions, understanding the perspective of others, making inferences, knowing when to use social conventions, understanding when bullying is occurring and differentiating fact from fiction (Barnhill, in press). *Weak central coherence* theory refers to a processing bias for details and a relative failure to get the gist or "see the forest from the trees" perspective. It does not explain the primary social challenges of ASD, but the primary focus on details may further impede already abnormal social functioning. It also may explain why generalization of skills for individuals with ASD is so problematic. The relationship between central coherence and theory of mind is currently unclear and it is being investigated (Happe & Frith, 2006).

The challenge of making generalizations is that the individual variance within ASD is so significant. For example, while the characteristics associated with autism are pervasive communication and social disabilities, Asperger syndrome is typically described as follows:

- Limited social interaction
- Repetitive behaviors and overly focused interests
- Significant impairment in social, occupational, or other functioning areas
- No significant delay in language, self-help, adaptive behavior (other than social), and cognition

While students classified as having AS share a number of characteristics with children with autism, they also display some unique features, as noted by Myles and Simpson (1998, p. 3): "Clinical features of Asperger syndrome include social interaction impairments, speech and communication characteristics, cognitive and academic characteristics, sensory characteristics, and physical and motor-skill anomalies." Although individuals with AS usually have average to above average intelligence, they may demonstrate academic difficulties because they lack higher-level thinking and comprehension skills, tend to be very literal, and often have challenges applying and generalizing skills (Barnhill, 2001).

Behavioral Patterns

Scheuermann and Webber (2002) describe the characteristics of autism by using two broad groups: behavioral deficits and behavioral excesses:

1. **Behavioral deficits**
   - Inability to relate to others
   - Lack of functional language
   - Sensory processing deficits
   - Cognitive deficits
2. **Behavioral excesses**
   - Self-stimulation
   - Resistance to change
   - Bizarre and challenging behaviors
   - Self-injurious behaviors

Specific to AS, Myles and Simpson (2002) noted that in the social domain, individuals are "typically thought to be socially stiff, socially awkward, emotionally blunted, self-centered, deficient at understanding nonverbal social cues, and inflexible. . . . Although they are well known for their lack of social awareness, many students with AS are aware enough to sense that they are different from their peers . . . self-esteem problems and self-concept difficulties are common" (p. 133).

Academic, Linguistic, and Cognitive Considerations

Academic difficulties are commonly noted in students with ASD, although there is wide variance in achievement levels. The U.S. Department of Education (2005) provided summative academic data on a variety of academic tasks. Within these data sets, they note the following: "For the standardized assessments, each student's performance is associated with a percentile score which reflects the proportion of the individuals of that student's age in the general population who received a lower score on that assessment. The [data] indicate the proportion of students whose percentile rank on the assessment fell within a given percentile range (e.g., 0–20, 21–60, 61–100) . . . and provide comparative samples for students with specific disabilities as compared to the general population" (p. 57). The academic data are as follows:

1. **Letter-word identification** measures reading skills in identifying isolated letters and words: 49% of children with autism fall into the bottom 20% of students in the general population while only 19% are in the upper 40% (p. 57).
2. **Passage comprehension** measures the student's skill in reading a short passage and identifying a missing key word; student must exercise a variety of comprehension and vocabulary skills: 66% of students fall into the lower 20% and only 8% in the upper 40% (p. 58).
3. **Calculation** measures the student's ability to perform mathematical calculations: 49% of students with autism fall into the lower 20% and 18% are in the upper 40% (p. 59).
4. **Applied problems** measures the ability to analyze and solve problems in mathematics: 65% of students with autism fall into the lowest 20% of the general population while only 12% are within the upper 40% (p. 60).

Although many characteristics associated with autism present as negative academic traits, some children with autism present some positive, as well as unexpected, characteristics. For example, Tirosh and Canby (1993) describe children with autism who also have hyperlexia that is defined as "an advance of at least one standard deviation (SD) in the reading over the verbal IQ level" (p. 86). For these children, spelling and contextual reading also may be advanced.

Some children with autism display unique splinter skills, or islands of precocity where they display areas of giftedness: "Common splinter skills include (1) calendar abilities, such as being able to give the day of the week for any date you might provide (e.g., May 12, 1896); (2) the ability to count visual things quickly, such as telling how many toothpicks are on the floor when a box is dropped; (3) artistic ability, such as the ability to design machinery; and (4) musical ability, such as playing a piano" (Scheuermann & Webber, 2002, p. 9).

For students with AS, areas of strength may include oral expression, reading recognition, rote-based skills, and general fund of information while difficulties may include reading comprehension, listening comprehension, written expression including graphomotor and organization skills, mathematics, problem solving, and language-based critical thinking (Griswold et al., 2002; Whitby & Mancil, 2009). As students get older and reading instruction focuses more on comprehension of abstract concepts and the ability to make inferences, comprehension difficulties become more pronounced. Myles and colleagues (2002) found that students with AS typically performed better on rote-based comprehension questions than on inference comprehension questions and when asked to read silently, they performed lower than they did when they read out loud. Myles and Simpson (2002, p. 135) cautioned that "these students often give the impression that they understand more than they do. . . . Their pedantic style, seemingly advanced vocabularies, parrot-like responses, and ability to word call may actually mask deficits in higher order thinking and comprehension."

Barnhill (2002) noted that students with AS often exhibit potential strengths in the areas of grammar, vocabulary, rote memory, absorbing facts, and honesty (often to a fault). At the same time, certain characteristics may have a negative impact on academic performance. These characteristics include insistence on sameness, impairment in social interaction, a restricted range of interests, poor concentration, poor motor coordination, academic difficulties, and emotional vulnerability (Safran, 2002; Williams, 1995).

Table 9.1 shows the similarities and differences of the behavioral characteristics of children with AS and children with autism. It provides summative information to the discussion on characteristics and helps to further delineate distinctions between these populations.

TABLE 9.1

Behavioral Comparison of Asperger Syndrome and Autism

	ASPERGER SYNDROME	AUTISTIC SYNDROME
1. Intelligence measures		
Standardized scores	Average to high average range	Borderline through average range
2. Language		
Pragmatic language	Normal development	Delayed onset, deficits
a. Verbal	Deficits can be observed	Delayed and disordered
b. Nonverbal	Deficits (e.g., odd eye gaze)	Deficits can be severe
3. Communication		
Expressive	Within normal limits	Deficits can be observed
Receptive	Within normal limits	Deficits can be observed
4. Social responsiveness		
Attachment		
a. Parents	Observed responsiveness	Lack responsiveness
b. Caregivers	Observed responsiveness	Lack responsiveness
c. Peers	Observed responsiveness	Lack responsiveness
Interactions		
a. Initiations to peers	Frequent, poor quality	Minimal frequency
b. Positive responses to peers	Frequent, awkward, and pertains to self-interests	Minimal frequency
c. Symbolic play	No impaired symbolic play	Absence of symbolic play
d. Reciprocal play	Observed but awkward	Minimal frequency
e. Coping	Deficits observed in quality	
f. Friendships	Minimal frequency	Minimal frequency
g. Requests for assistance	Observed but awkward	Minimal frequency
Self-regulation		
a. Emotional empathy	Observed but awkward	Deficits can be observed
b. Emotional responsiveness	Observed but could be extreme	Aloof, indifferent

Source: Adapted from "Asperger Syndrome and Autism: A Literature Review and Meta-Analysis, by E. McLaughlin-Cheng, 1998, *Focus on Autism and Other Developmental Disabilities, 13,* p. 237. Used by permission.

Figure 9.3 presents a summary of the school-relevant characteristics of students with autism accompanied by their educational implications. Figure 9.4 then presents similar information as relevant to AS.

Educational Outcomes

The USDOE (2009) provides information on adolescents exiting from special education. These national data indicate that there has been a gradual increase in the number of children with ASD who have graduated with a standard diploma, with an increase from 35.5% in 1995 to 58.5% in 2004. Conversely, the number of students with autism dropping out of school has decreased from 33.6% in 1995 to 13.2% in 2004.

While difficulty in social relationships and verbal and nonverbal communication are common characteristics and are coincidentally critical in the workplace, nevertheless there is evidence that individuals with autism can be successful in the community work environment. Further, some characteristics (e.g., memory, tolerance for repetition) may be beneficial for certain types of tasks (Hagner & Cooney, 2005). A key aspect for success is the presence

FIGURE 9.3	Autism: Characteristics and Implications	
Characteristics	**Possible Problem Areas**	**Educational Implications**
Social Interaction Deficits	• Lack of joint attention in infancy • May not respond to name and may appear deaf • Oblivious to others and appears to be in own world • Little or no eye contact • No reciprocal friendships • May treat people as objects (e.g., use another person's hand to reach an object up high) • Resistance to being cuddled or touched	Teach Joint Action Routines (JARS) to engage student. Follow the child's lead to determine preferences that can be used to engage student socially. Understand that student may be unable to look and listen at the same time. Consider peer intervention packages to assist with social skills training. Consult with family and occupational therapist regarding resistance to being touched to brainstorm strategies.
Speech and Language Communication Difficulties	• Deficits may include mutism, echolalia (immediate or delayed) and perseveration of a specific topic • Does not understand communicative intent • Does not demonstrate communicative reciprocity • Difficulty with language comprehension • Idiosyncratic speech • Unusual prosody • Deficits in nonverbal communication • Literal, rigid use of language with typically immature grammar	Do not discourage echolalia. Focus on teaching functional, spontaneous communication. Frequently conduct a reinforcer inventory to determine student's preferences and use these preferences as reinforcers to teach language skills. Teach student how to request and initiate social interactions through the use of PECS or mand training. Consider using Social Stories™ (Gray 2004), Power Cards (Gagnon, 2001), Comic Strip Conversations (Gray, 1994), and/or video modeling to teach language skills. Provide direct instruction on multiple meaning words and idioms and nonverbal communication. Recognize that the student may parrot what has been heard, but does not necessarily understand what was repeated.
Stereotypic Behaviors	• Obsessive adherence to a few routines or activities • Preoccupation with a few objects or parts of objects (e.g., fans or spinning the wheels of a toy truck rather than playing with it appropriately) • Repetitive motor mannerisms such as rocking, spinning or hand flapping • May experience tantrums and aggression • May engage in self-injurious behaviors	Provide a predictable and safe environment. Minimize transitions. Capitalize on student's visual strengths and provide visual supports to aid in transitions. Teach appropriate play skills with peers and object uses through direct instruction and JARS. Determine the function of the behavior and teach a more appropriate replacement behavior to meet that function.

(continued)

Characteristics	Possible Problem Areas	Educational Implications
Cognitive and Perceptual Challenges	• Literal, restricted and inflexible patterns of thinking • Tendency to overselect irrelevant stimuli in environment and not focus on relevant stimuli • Obsessive need for sameness; resistance to change • Problems with abstract thinking, but typically have good rote memory • Lack imagination and appropriate play • Exhibits problems with social cognition • Lack of motivation and curiosity regarding environment • Occasionally may demonstrate extraordinary skills in a specific area • Frequently have intellectual disability	Use Social Stories™ (Gray 2004) to teach others' perspecives and social cognition skills and offer role playing opportunities. Teach students to focus on multiple cues. Use priming to increase familiarity with materials before introduced at school. Provide structure through visual supports to assist with planning, goal selection and organization skills. Provide choices throughout the day and reward student task attempts to increase motivation. Provide concrete examples to increase understanding. Capitalize on student's strengths and good rote memory.
Sensory Processing Issues	• Extreme fear to some auditory stimuli and to new situations, people, changes and surprises • May appear deaf and blind • Extreme partiality to distinct clothing and food • Tactilely defensive • Oversensitivity or undersensitivity to pain	Consult with the occupational therapist to determine sensory issues and to provide appropriate accommodations. Provide a predictable and safe environment. Respect food and clothing preferences. Modify the environment by changing antecedents that may trigger problem behavior.

Sources: Adapted from *Educating Students with Autism: A Quick Start Manual* by J. Webber & B. Scheuermann (2008). Austin, TX: PRO-ED (and) "What is Autism?" by Autism Society of America, 2008. Retrieved from: http://www.autism-society.org/site/PageServer?pagename=about_whatis_char

of effective supports in the workplace. It can be generalized that this would also be true for vocational placement programs that may be used for secondary-school-level students with autism.

The National Longitudinal Transition Study 2 (NLTS2) reported that nearly all of the 1,000 students with autism in grades 7 and above surveyed in the United States received accommodations, modifications, supports, technology aids or related services. Additional time to complete assignments and tests and modified tests and assignments were the most frequent accommodations provided. Technology aides were used less frequently than were other supports and speech-language services were the most frequently reported services accessed. Furthermore, 92% of students with ASD took at least one academic subject in a given semester. Ninety percent of these students took mathematics, 89% took language arts, 69% took social studies, 67% took science and 12% took foreign language. On average, academic courses represented 46% of the courses students with autism took in a particular semester while 77% also took vocational education courses in a particular semester. Students also took courses in general education settings and special education settings, although on average general education courses comprised one-third of the type of courses taken and special education courses comprised 62% (National Center for Education Research, 2007). The Personal Spotlight provides a case study of a secondary student with AS, including postsecondary transition goals.

FIGURE 9.4	Asperger Syndrome: Characteristics and Implications	
Characteristics	**Possible Problem Areas**	**Educational Implications**
Reciprocal Social Interaction	• May have few or no friends • Does not understand give and take of social interaction and instead monologues or lectures • May not understand nonverbal cues such as eye gaze, facial expressions and body language • May not spontaneously seek interactions with others because does not know how to interact or has no interest in interacting • May display socially inappropriate behaviors because does not understand social conventions	Provide direct social skill instruction on friendship making skills and conversation skills, which includes modeling (live and/or video) appropriate skills, allowing person to role play, and providing feedback, as well as working toward maintenance and generalization of skills taught. Use SENSE (McAffee, 2002) to teach nonverbal behavior (i.e., **S**pace, **E**ye Contact, **N**odding, **S**tatements of Encouragement, **E**xpressions). Engage student in problem solving to analyze social situations, understand cause and effect and determine alternate responses using "When . . . then . . ." or "If . . . then . . . format.
Language	• Displays difficulty in pragmatic or social aspect of language, but typically no difficulties in grammar or language development • Uses language to convey facts and information about special interests • Demonstrates challenges beginning, maintaining and ending conversations • Is unsure how to request help and make comments • May have unusual prosody and speak in a robotic manner or with a flat tone • May have difficulty modulating voice volume • Experiences challenges with abstract language, idioms, expressions and makes literal interpretations	Provide direct instruction on pragmatic language including using social niceties, initiating, beginning, and ending conversations, and voice control with time to role play and receive feedback, as well as opportunities to work toward maintenance and generalization of skills taught. Consider using Social Stories™ (Gray 2004), Power Cards (Gagnon, 2001), Comic Strip Conversations (Gray, 1994), and/or video modeling to teach language skills. Provide direct instruction on multiple meaning words and idioms. Recognize that the student may parrot what has been heard, but does not necessarily understand what was repeated.
Narrow Interests and Insistence on Specific Routines	• Sees rules as black and white • Has few interests, but the existing interests are all encompassing in intensity and focus • Insists on following specific rituals and routines that interfere with functioning and make transitions to other activities challenging • May experience meltdowns or tantrums as a result of changes in routine or lack of understanding of the expected situation	Provide a predictable and safe environment. Minimize transitions. Capitalize on student's visual strengths and provide visual supports to aid in transitions. Do not allow student to perseveratively talk about their special interest by limiting this to a specific time and place. Provide assignments that will help expand or broaden the current perseverative interest (e.g., if interested in trains, have student research trains in a specific country for social studies). Watch for subtle signs of student's discomfort and intervene immediately to avoid meltdowns; use the Incredible 5-Point Scale (Buron, 2003) to teach recognizing feelings.

(continued)

FIGURE 9.4	Asperger Syndrome: Characteristics and Implications *(continued)*

Characteristics	Possible Problem Areas	Educational Implications
Cognitive Challenges	• Demonstrates difficulties with theory of mind (mindblindness) • May have problems with central coherence or seeing the gestalt or big picture • Displays executive functioning difficulties • Exhibits problems with social cognition • Typically demonstrates average to above average intelligence	Use Social Stories™ (Gray 2004) to teach others' perspectives and social cognition skills and offer role playing opportunities. Teach students to focus on multiple cues. Provide structure through visual supports to assist with planning, goal selection, and organization skills. Teach self-management skills through use of checklists, wrist counters, prompts, and tokens. Capitalize on student's intellectual strengths.
Motor Clumsiness	• Demonstrates difficulty with gross motor skills such as an awkward gait, poor balance, difficulty coordinating motor movements • Demonstrates difficulty with fine motor skills such as writing	Provide accommodations in physical education class for gross motor skill deficits and offer adult supervision on the playground to assist student with less well-developed motor skills to be a part of group games. Allow students to use keyboarding if handwriting is too laborious. Some students perform better with cursive writing than with printing.
Sensory Sensitivities	• May exhibit oversensitivity or under-sensitivity in 1 or more of following areas: tactile, visual, auditory, gustatory, olfactory, vestibular (sense of balance), proprioception (body position)	Consult with the occupational therapist to determine sensory issues and to provide appropriate accommodations.

Sources: Adapted in part from "The Six Characteristics of Asperger's Syndrome." Retrieved from: http://school.familyeducation.com/learning-disabilities/56315.html and *Asperger Syndrome and Sensory Issues: Practical Solutions for the Real World* by B. S. Myles, K. T. Cook, N. E. Miller, L. Rinner, & L. A. Robbins (2000). Shawnee Mission, KS: Autism Asperger Publishing.

☷ PERSONAL SPOTLIGHT ☷

SECONDARY STUDENT WITH ASPERGER SYNDROME

BRYCE STEVENS is a 17-year-old student who just completed his sophomore year of high school. His mother reports that she did not have any complications during her pregnancy, but when Bryce was born, he had a low Apgar score of 3 at 1 minute and then an Apgar score of 7 at 5 minutes. Examinations revealed that Bryce's lungs were clear and no further complications were noted; therefore, he was discharged from the hospital with his mother 48 hours later.

Mrs. Stevens stated that Bryce achieved developmental milestones within normal limits. Moreover, she indicated that he did not have any friends during elementary school, but this did not seem to bother him. His teachers reported that he was fidgety, had difficulty maintaining attention in class, and often acted impulsively by blurting out comments without first thinking. He achieved satisfactory grades in most subject areas and excellent grades in spelling up through third grade. He also tended to touch other children a lot and his teachers continually reminded him to use his words to gain his peers' attention instead of touching them, especially since he had an excellent vocabulary. In fact, he often spoke like a "little professor" and corrected his teachers' grammar. His avid interest in dinosaurs changed to an intense interest in meat-eating plants in fourth grade. It was at this time that he began refusing to complete work at school that did not interest him.

His mother thought that he may have started experiencing problems at this time because she and her husband were going through divorce proceedings. She brought Bryce to counseling during his fourth-grade year and the psychologist diagnosed him as having Asperger syndrome and attention deficit hyperactivity disorder. Mrs. Stevens sought help from the school district when Bryce received these diagnoses. He was determined eligible for special education services during fourth grade and he began receiving services to assist with reading comprehension, organizational skills, and social skills.

Bryce has continued to receive special education resources services while remaining in general education classes most of the school day. These services address reading comprehension, organization, and social skills. Social skills instruction has focused on beginning, maintaining and ending conversations; dealing with bullying; relaxation techniques; and reading verbal and nonverbal cues. Progress has been noted and Bryce is able to maintain a conversation for six conversation turns if it is a topic he is interested in discussing. Organizational skills continue to be an issue and even with visual supports, Bryce typically misses at least one step in a five-step task sequence.

Assessment results indicate that Bryce's word-decoding skills are on the college level; reading comprehension skills are at about an eighth-grade level. Math skills are commensurate with his above average IQ and spelling remains an area of significant strength for Bryce. Bryce's report card at the end of his sophomore year revealed a cumulative grade point average of 3.3. Areas of strength were science and math and areas of weakness were in physical education, public speaking, and typing.

Results of an occupational therapy assessment indicate that sensory differences, especially tactile, auditory, and proprioceptive (knowing where his body is in space) are having an impact on his performance in the classroom. Bryce demonstrates acute hearing ability and often hears noises before others do (e.g., an airplane or approaching train). The fluorescent lights in the classroom reportedly irritate him and make it hard for him to concentrate. He has difficulty maintaining an erect posture, has fallen out of his seat on numerous occasions, and often appears fatigued. He prefers a quiet learning environment with subdued lighting and prefers not to eat in the cafeteria. During lunch period, he requests a library pass and he researches topics on botany. Bryce reports that he wants to be a botanist and earn a doctorate degree in botany. He is still interested in the study of meat-eating plants and he reports that he has over 200 species at home in the greenhouse his parents built for him.

According to parent and teacher reports, Bryce experiences "meltdowns," which involve him shutting down, as evidenced by refusal to work and communicate and curling into a fetal position at home and at school approximately once a month. These meltdowns seem to need to run their course and at school he goes to the nurse's office until he recovers. His teachers have reported that he will resume work if they do not place any demands on him for about 20 minutes and allow him to first make outlines of his latest botany research. He is reinforced with additional time on the computer when he has completed all of his class assignments and this behavioral strategy has appeared to work well at school. His mother reports that he is difficult to motivate at home and he needs to be reminded frequently to complete simple chores such as taking out the garbage and mowing the lawn. He currently has no plans regarding where he would like to live or where he would like to go to college, except to indicate that the school needs to have an excellent botany program. Bryce has never been away from home except to go on vacation with one of his parents. He currently has no friends.

Bryce is a client of Vocational Rehabilitation Services and is scheduled for a functional vocational assessment that will also include driving and life skills assessment. He and his mother met with the school staff to complete a self-determination checklist. Areas targeted for skill development include establishing and maintaining relationships with peers, leading his IEP meeting, and self-advocating for supports and accommodations he needs in multiple settings. He is currently receiving social skills training in a small group format targeting friendship skills and dealing with frustration. In addition, he is receiving instruction on completing college applications and interviewing skills. Bryce will complete three interviews of employees in the field of botany to gain more information on work requirements in his field of interest. The IEP team (including Bryce and his mother) developed the following postsecondary transition goals:

Employment: Bryce will be employed in a field of work related to botany and horticulture after graduation from college.

Further Education: Bryce will enroll in a college program and major in botany after graduation from high school.

Independent Living: Bryce will live and work in a community of his choice after graduation from high school. Bryce will use electronic and nonelectronic methods to organize his daily schedule across settings, for long-term planning, and for prompting and reminders.

EFFECTIVE INCLUSIVE PRACTICES

Challenges for General Education

Students with autism present significant challenges to classroom teachers. Traditionally, students with these characteristics likely were not considered for placement in inclusive settings; however, they are much more likely to be in general education classrooms at this time.

A key challenge of the successful inclusion of students with ASD in the general education classroom is the incorporation of key curricular needs into the educational programs for these students. Therefore, when these students are placed in the general education classroom, there will likely be a need for attention to curricular differentiation. This differentiation is reflected in the priority educational goals for students with ASD, which include the following:

- To develop basic language and social skills
- To provide academic instruction consistent with cognitive level
- To teach functional skills for postschool success
- To tie instruction to parental education, such as to encompass behavioral interventions to enhance social and functional skills (Forness, Walker, & Kavale, 2003).

Considered more broadly, Egel (1989) emphasized two important principles that should inform educational programs for students (across age levels) with autism: the use of functional activities and an effort to make programs appropriate for the student's developmental level and chronological age. Children with autism grow up to be adults with autism; the condition cannot be cured. As a result, educational programs should promote *functionality* in order to help these students deal with the daily needs that will extend throughout their lives. Educators should ask themselves the following questions:

1. Does the program teach skills that are immediately useful?
2. Will the materials used be available in the student's daily environment?
3. Will learning certain skills make it less likely that someone will have to do the task for the student in the future?

Programs for students with autism should also be *age appropriate and developmentally appropriate*. The individual's chronological age and developmental status must be considered together. Sometimes incongruence exists between these two realms, making program planning a challenge (McDonnell, Hardman, & McDonnell, 2005). In this case, developmentally appropriate materials must be modified to make them as age appropriate as possible. The nearby IEP Goals and Objectives for Andrea are developmentally appropriate for her. Finally, the goals for educational services should be *personal independence and social responsibility* to the extent possible (NRC, 2001).

Evidence-Based Interventions

The increased attention to students with ASD has led to the identification of specific evidence-based interventions. The National Autism Center (NAC, 2009a, b, c) completed a standards project initiative that sought to identify the level of current research for educational and behavioral treatments for persons with ASD; assist parents, caregivers, educators, and service providers in understanding how to incorporate essential information in making treatment decisions; and identify limitations in the existing treatment research for individuals with ASD. The NAC included 775 studies that met the criteria to be reviewed "in terms of the quality of the research design, dependent measure, treatment fidelity, participant ascertainment, and generalization" (Wilcyznski, 2010, p. 24). This yielded 38 treatments that were classified as: (a) *established treatments* if a sufficient number of high-quality studies were published to allow scholars to confidently conclude that they produced beneficial outcomes for individuals with ASD less than 22 years old; (b) *emerging treatments* if there was some evidence of effectiveness but not enough high-quality studies to demonstrate effectiveness;

IEP GOALS AND OBJECTIVES FOR ANDREA

Appropriate goals and objectives might include the following:

GOAL 1   To reproduce written materials

    Objective 1: Given a set of letter and word templates, Andrea will be able to trace the letters and words on four of five trials.

    Objective 2: Given a set of letters and words on a piece of paper, Andrea will be able to write the letters and words on four of five trials.

    Objective 3: Given the assignment to write her name, Andrea will write her name accurately on four of five trials.

GOAL 2   To participate in group activities

    Objective 1: During a recess game, Andrea will be able to remain with a selected group on four of five trials without disruptions or leaving the group.

    Objective 2: Given the opportunity to participate in a cooperative learning activity, Andrea will do so for at least 10 minutes, without any inappropriate behaviors on four of five trials.

GOAL 3   To increase expressive vocabulary

    Objective 1: Given an opportunity to express herself verbally, Andrea will increase her expressive vocabulary by ten words over a 2-week period.

    Objective 2: Given the need to go to the bathroom, Andrea will verbally communicate the need to go to the bathroom appropriately on five of five trials.

---

or (c) *unestablished treatments* if there were no studies published or the studies that were published did not demonstrate reliable evidence of effectiveness. A fourth category for *ineffective or harmful treatments* was developed but no treatments had sufficient evidence specific to ASD to meet criteria. (Note: These findings were reported in documents that can be downloaded in PDF format from the NAC's website: www.nationalautismcenter.org.)

Six age groups were identified between 0 and 21 years. Favorable outcomes included an increase in skills in academic, communication, higher cognitive functions, interpersonal, learning readiness, motor, personal responsibility, play, and self-regulation. The favorable outcomes included a decrease in behaviors in the following areas: problem behaviors; restricted repetitive, nonfunctional behavior, interests, or activities; sensory/emotional regulation; and general symptoms (see Table 9.2). The NAC (2009c) classified 11 treatments as established treatments, 22 as emerging, and 5 as unestablished.

The majority of the established treatments were developed from the behavioral literature. The use of applied behavior analysis (ABA) strategies is discussed more fully under the section entitled *Classroom Adaptation.* Table 9.3 lists the 11 established treatments with selected examples of each.

The following selected interventions were among the 22 treatments determined to be emerging by the NAC (2009b, 2009c): augmentative and alternative communication devices, cognitive-behavioral intervention package, exercise, imitation-based interaction, language training (production and understanding), massage/touch therapy, music therapy, peer-mediated instructional arrangement, picture exchange communication system (see below), sign instruction, social skills package, structured teaching, technology-based treatment, and theory of mind training.

Five treatments were rated as unestablished (NAC, 2009b, 2009c) and additional cautionary statements were provided for two of these: facilitated communication and the gluten- and casein-free diet. For a third, academic intervention, studies reviewed included personal instruction, paired associate, picture-to-text matching, answering pre-reading questions, completing cloze sentences, sentence combining, speech output and orthographic feedback, and handwriting training. Only 10 academic studies met the Scientific

TABLE 9.2

Established Treatments with Favorable Outcomes Reported

SKILLS INCREASED

ACADEMIC	COMMUNICATION	HIGHER COGNITIVE FUNCTIONS	INTERPERSONAL	LEARNING READINESS
Behavioral Package	Antecedent Package Behavioral Package CBTYC Joint Attention Modeling NTS Peer Training PRT	CBTYC Modeling	Antecedent Package Behavioral Package CBTYC Joint Attention Modeling NTS Peer Training PRT Self-management Story-based	Antecedent Package Behavioral Package NTS

MOTOR	PERSONAL RESPONSIBILITY	PLACEMENT	PLAY	SELF-REGULATION
CBTYC	Antecedent Package Behavioral Package CBTYC Modeling	CBTYC	Antecedent Package Behavioral Package CBTYC Modeling NTS Peer Training PRT	Antecedent Package Behavioral Package Schedules Self-management Story-based

BEHAVIORS DECREASED

PROBLEM BEHAVIORS	RESTRICTED, REPETITIVE, NONFUNCTIONAL BEHAVIOR, INTERESTS, OR ACTIVITIES	SENSORY/ EMOTIONAL REGULATION	GENERAL SYMPTOMS
Antecedent Package Behavioral Package CBTYC Modeling Self-management	Behavioral Package Peer Training	Antecedent Package Behavioral Package Modeling	CBTYC

AGES

0–2	3–5	6–9	10–14	15–18	19–21
Behavioral CBTYC Joint Attention NTS	Antecedent Behavioral CBTYC Joint Attention Modeling NTS Peer Training PRT Schedules Self-management	Antecedent Behavioral CBTYC Modeling NTS Peer Training PRT Schedules Self-management Story-based	Antecedent Behavioral Modeling Peer Training Schedules Self-management Story-based	Antecedent Behavioral Modeling Self-management	Behavioral

TABLE 9.2 *(continued)*

DIAGNOSTIC CLASSIFICATION

AUTISTIC DISORDER		ASPERGER'S SYNDROME	PDD-NOS
Antecedent	Peer Training	Modeling	Behavioral Package
Behavioral	PRT	Story-based	CBTYC
CBTYC	Schedules		Joint Attention
Joint Attention	Self-management		Modeling
Modeling	Story-based		NTS
NTS			Peer Training

Note: Antecedent=Antecedent Package; Behavioral=Behavioral Package; CBTYC=Comprehensive Behavioral Treatment for Young Children; Joint Attention=Joint Attention Intervention; NTS=Naturalistic Teaching Strategies; Peer Training=Peer Training Package; PRT=Pivotal Response Treatment; Story-based=Story-based Intervention Package.

Merit Rating Scale criteria to be included. The NAC (2009a) acknowledged that there are more treatments that would fall into this category but that either no research was published or it was published in a nonpeer-reviewed journal.

It is critical to note that the NAC (2009b) reported, "Research findings are not the sole factor that should be considered when treatments are selected" (p. 25) and "even among Established Treatments, universal improvements cannot be expected to occur for all individuals on the autism spectrum" (NAC, 2009c, p. 43). The authors also caution that established treatments should not be avoided for specific age groups or ASD subgroups just because favorable outcomes have not been extended to these groups at this time.

Most importantly the NAC (2009b) recommendations for educators included:

1. Give important consideration to established treatments.
2. Do not typically begin intervening with emerging treatments. However, they do warrant important consideration if established treatments are determined to not be appropriate by the decision-making team.
3. Consider unestablished treatments only after additional research has been conducted and demonstrates their effectiveness for individuals with ASD because currently there is either no research support or the research does not provide evidence to draw firm conclusions about the effectiveness of these treatments.
4. Remember that treatment selection is complicated and that the person's unique history and needs and family preferences and values need to be considered before selecting an intervention.
5. Make treatment decisions based on data.

Special Considerations: Early Intervention Programs

Research strongly supports the importance of effective early intervention practices for students with autism. Hume, Bellini, and Pratt (2005) noted that these practices "appear to reduce the debilitating impact of autism [and] young children with autism may make gains more quickly than young children with other severe neuro-developmental disorders. The results of a retrospective study corroborated the belief that children with autism have significantly better outcomes when an intervention begins before age 5" (p. 195).

Results of a National Institute of Mental Health (NIMH) funded randomized, controlled clinical trial of the Early Start Denver Model (ESDM) revealed that core symptoms of autism were diminished based in clinical diagnosis in 48 toddlers between the ages of 18 months and 30 months after 2 years of treatment using ESDM (Dawson et al., 2010). Furthermore, findings demonstrated an increase in the toddlers' learning composites, adaptive behavior, and expressive and receptive language skills. ESDM "refines, adapts, and extends downward

TABLE 9.3

Established Interventions

INTERVENTION	DESCRIPTION
Antecedent Package	Involves cost-effective, time-efficient strategies that modify environmental events that typically precede target behaviors and includes: behavior chain interruption; choice; priming; noncontingent reinforcement; errorless learning; social comments, adult presence; incorporating echolalia, special interests, thematic activities, or obsessive behaviors into tasks; contriving motivational operations; environmental modification of tasks; and time delay.
Behavioral Package	Involves reducing problem behavior and teaching functional replacements by applying principles of behavior change including: behavioral sleep package, behavioral toilet training/dry bed practice, mand training, discrete trial teaching, differential reinforcement strategies, successive approximations, functional communication training, contingency contracting, contingency mapping, shaping, task analysis, token economy, instructional fading, and generalization training.
Comprehensive Behavioral Treatment for Young Children (CBTYC)	Includes combination of ABA procedures (e.g., discrete trial teaching, incidental teaching) for children under age 8 in various settings such as center-based or home-based programs.
Joint Action Intervention	Entails interventions that build foundational skills included in regulating behavior of others. It often includes teaching child to respond to nonverbal social bids of others or to initiate joint attention interactions to share mutual interest in object, activity or experience. Examples: pointing to objects, showing items to others and following eye gaze.
Modeling	Involves adults or peers giving demonstration of target behavior for individual with ASD to imitate. Examples: live modeling, video modeling, and self-modeling where person with ASD is model and video is edited by educator so that student appears successful in performing targeted task or behavior independently.
Naturalistic Teaching Strategies (NTS)	Entails primarily child-directed interactions to teach functional skills in natural environment through direct and natural consequences, use of variety of materials, and programming common stimuli. The adult takes advantage of student's motivation by following his/her interest.
Peer Training Package	Focuses on teaching children w/o disabilities to facilitate play and social interactions with children with ASD. Examples: peer networks, Circle of Friends, Integrated Play Groups, and peer-mediated social interactions.
Pivotal Response Treatment (PRT)	Involves targeting "pivotal behavioral areas that may have a watershed effect on the development of many other skills" (NAC, 2009a, p. 58). Examples: social communication, self-initiation, self-management, and responding to multiple cues. Parent involvement is key aspect.
Schedules	Uses task list typically in form of pictures, typed words, or 3-D objects that provide series of steps or activities needed to complete specific activity.
Self-management	Promotes independence by teaching behavior regulation through recording occurrence/nonoccurrence of behavior and receiving reinforcement for doing this. Some tools: checklists, wrist counters, visual prompts, and tokens.
Story-based Intervention Package	Includes written materials designed to increase independence similar to written scripts and self-management. Most well known is Social Stories™, which provides information on who/what/when/where/why of target behavior and teaches perspectives of others.

Source: Adapted from National Autism Center (2009c). *National standards report.* Randolph, MA: Author.

in age, the original Denver Model for preschoolers with ASD ages 24–60 months" and it "is a comprehensive, early intervention approach for toddlers with autism ages 12–36 months and continuing until ages 48–60 months" (Rogers & Dawson, 2010, p. 1). Rogers and Dawson concluded that their results compared favorably with those published by Lovaas (1987) and their toddlers also showed "larger and more widespread changes" than those from the randomized control trial of Lovaas's method published by Smith, Groen, and Wynn in 2000, and their treatment approach included fewer hours. Although Dawson and Rogers report that the ESDM needs to be independently replicated, their 2010 results were consistent with earlier positive findings from Denver Model research.

The National Research Council (NRC, 2001) recommended that the following six types of interventions should have priority, particularly in the early education of children with ASD:

- Functional, spontaneous communication needs as the primary focus
- Social instruction throughout the day in multiple settings
- Play skills with peers and instruction in appropriate toy and object use
- Functional behavioral assessment and proactive approaches for problem behaviors
- Cognitive skill development focusing on generalization and maintenance of skills
- Functional academic skills

Furthermore, the NRC (2001) indicated that the following six features are critical in programs serving young (preschool) children with ASD:

- Entry into program as soon as an ASD is seriously contemplated
- Active instructional engagement for at least 25 hours per week, 5 days per week with full-year programming
- Repeated teaching in 15–20 minute intervals in one-on-one or small group
- Inclusion of parents and parent training
- Low child/teacher ratios with no more than 2:1 children to adults
- Ongoing program and student evaluations

Promoting Inclusive Practices

Growing evidence shows that placing children with autism with their peers who are nondisabled in general education settings, with appropriate supports, can make a significant difference in their behaviors (and their learning). A key reason is that appropriate role models in general education are very important. Peers can provide a basis for students with ASD to understand social situations and develop the ability to respond in a socially appropriate fashion. An encouraging finding was reported by Boutot and Bryant (2005, p. 14), who found that "students with autism in inclusive settings are [just] as accepted, visible, and members of peer groups, as well as both their peers without disabilities and those with other disabilities."

■ Self-management is a promising intervention strategy for children with autism.

Ruble and Dalrymple (2002) suggest a variety of environmental supports that can facilitate the success of students with autism in inclusive settings. These supports that are relevant to classroom situations are listed in Figure 9.5.

An established intervention strategy that has the potential to promote successful inclusion for children with autism is self-management—implementing a variety of techniques that assist in self-control. See the nearby Differentiated Instruction—Elementary boxed reading for further information.

Inclusion: Students with Asperger Syndrome

As Myles and Simpson (2002) noted, students with AS are educated primarily in general education classrooms. This placement seems particularly appropriate for these students, and clearly they have the capacity to benefit significantly from academic instruction in general

---

FIGURE 9.5	Environmental Supports for Children with Autism

Communicating to the person (receptive language supports)

- Slow down the pace.
- State positively what to do (e.g., "Let's walk" instead of "Stop running").
- Provide more information in visual format.

Encouraging communication from the person (expressive language supports)

- Pause, listen, and wait.
- Encourage input and choice when possible.
- Provide alternative means, such as written words or pictures, to aid communication.
- Encourage and respond to words and appropriate attempts, rather than to behavior.

Social supports

- Build in time to watch, encourage watching and proximity.
- Practice on specific skills through natural activities with one peer.
- Structure activities with set interaction patterns and roles.
- Provide cooperative learning activities with facilitation.
- Facilitate recruitment of sociable peers to be buddies and advocates.

Expanding repertoires of interests and activities

- Capitalize on strengths and individual learning styles.
- Over time, minimize specific fears and frustrations.
- Use rehearsal with visuals.

Source: From "COMPASS: A Parent-Teacher Collaborative Model for Students with Autism," by L. A. Ruble & M. J. Dalrymple, 2002, *Focus on Autism and Other Developmental Disabilities, 17,* p. 76. Used with permission.

---

education programs. In fact, contrary to conventional wisdom about inclusion, students with AS may experience more difficulty through inclusion in the nonacademic portions of the day (e.g., lunch, recess) than in the academic portions.

Just as there is no single method to teach children with ASD in general, there is also not a preferred educational intervention for children with AS. Teachers must address several issues when dealing with these children and develop effective strategies for each child on an individual basis. Areas that should be considered include using visual strategies, which takes advantage of their more intact learning modality; using structural strategies, such as preparing students for changes in schedules and routines; and providing an instructional sequence that follows a logical progression for learning (Myles & Simpson, 1998).

Barnhill (in press) provided the following tips for working with students with AS:

- Provide opportunities for direct social skill instruction in the following areas: interpreting nonverbal communication and responding to social cues, making friends, dealing with frustration, and learning how to participate in a conversation.
- Use visual reminders such as visual scripts or Social Stories™ to prompt social skills and to prepare for changes in routines.
- Teach cause and effect concepts (e.g., When . . . then.).
- Provide a predictable and safe environment in a manner that avoids triggering rages and guards the student from bullying and teasing.
- Gain the student's attention before giving brief and concrete instructions.
- Use direct instruction to teach multiple meaning words and idioms.
- Check for understanding. Do not assume comprehension just because the student parrots what has been heard or because child can decode words. Comprehension skills are frequently not as strong as decoding and verbal skills.
- Capitalize on special interests to broaden student's repertoire of interests.

Differentiating Elementary Instruction

TEACHING SELF-MANAGEMENT SKILLS

Teaching students with autism to increase their self-management skills is an area that is appropriate for many of these students. The following provides examples of self-management goals and supports that could help students achieve these goals:

Goal 1: To independently transition from one activity to another using a picture/word schedule

Supports

- Imitate peers
- Learn by observing
- Provide visual supports including schedule for the day, steps in each activity, completion of activity, and time to move
- Train peers in how to use schedule
- Peer models

Goal 2: To stay in bounds at recess

Supports

- Imitate skills
- Learn by observing

- Teach and practice skills
- Use flags to show playground boundaries
- Use peers to model staying within boundaries
- Reinforce appropriate behaviors

Goal 3: To work quietly during individual work time

Supports

- Imitation skills
- Academic ability
- Motivation to do what other students are doing
- Peer models
- Visual reminders about being quiet
- Social story for quiet work
- Positive reinforcement for appropriate behaviors

Source: Adapted from "COMPASS: A Parent-Teacher Collaboration Model for Students with Autism," by L. A. Ruble and M. J. Dalrymple, 2002, *Focus on Autism and Other Developmental Disabilities, 17,* pp. 76–83.

- Limit opportunities for excessive talk about perseverative interests by allowing specific times during the day and a limited amount of time to verbally share special perseverative interests.
- Consult with parents when designing the educational program so that the student will experience success across environments.
- Consider accommodations for writing challenges.

CLASSROOM ADAPTATIONS

The development of successful special education programs for students with ASD will require specific attention to classroom adaptations that include behavioral considerations along with instruction on curricular foci. In addition, there are also medical considerations that may result in adaptations. While classroom teachers will not be expected to implement all of the adaptations described here, it is nevertheless important to be familiar with these interventions in order to effect successful collaboration with other professionals serving the students.

Behavioral Adaptations

A critical area of concern for students with ASD will be the implementation of effective behavioral intervention programs, typically included within the generic area of applied behavior analysis. Dunlap, Kern, and Worcester (2001) indicated that applied behavioral analysis (ABA) contributes to the philosophy and mission of special education because it places importance on individualization, is scientifically based, documents replicable instructional strategies, emphasizes function over topography of behavior, and is a dynamic discipline based on a methodology of persistent experimentation. It is important to note that the principles and methods of ABA have been used to effectively teach everyone, not just individuals with ASD. This is especially significant given the importance of UDL to benefit students of all ages and abilities. There have been many arguments concerning the use of ABA with children with ASD. However, most of these arguments are really about whether or not discrete trial training (DTT), which is a specific ABA strategy, can enable children with ASD to attain the normal educational and intellectual functioning that Lovaas (1987) portrayed in his research (Heflin & Alaimo, 2007). The effectiveness of the science of ABA is supported by abundant research, and ABA is cited as the methodology that has empirically demonstrated the most effective treatment outcomes for individuals with ASD (Green, 1996). There are many ABA strategies that are effectively and scientifically validated for individuals with ASD, including reinforcement, discrete trials, prompting, shaping, antecedent interventions, and functional behavioral assessment (Heflin & Alaimo, 2007).

Typical children learn by watching others and imitating what they do. Their behaviors are maintained by natural consequences in their environment, such as teacher and parent approval and attention. However, children with autism frequently lack the imitation skills needed to begin learning. Therefore, their instruction needs to focus on how to learn. Learning becomes possible when their learning environment is systematically and precisely structured (Zager & Shamow, 2005). Dawson and Osterling (1997) recommended that curriculum content include teaching the child to (a) attend to elements in his or her environment that are essential for learning, (b) imitate others, (c) comprehend and use language, and (d) socially interact with others, particularly peers. Green (2001) stated that the overarching goal of a quality ABA program is to teach students with ASD how to learn from typical environments and how to act in ways that will consistently produce positive outcomes for the students and those around them.

Reinforcement   Reinforcement refers to consequences that follow a behavior and either maintain or increase the occurrence of such behavior (Heflin & Alaimo, 2007). Reinforcers are unique to the individual and to the setting and can vary frequently, even with the same child. An effective instructional program needs to focus on developing an inventory of reinforcers for each student and a method for clearly delineating the conditions under which these reinforcers are selected and distributed. Therefore, teachers need to be "good contingency managers" and clearly indicate the conditions necessary for reinforcement (Zager & Shamow, 2005, p. 305). Watching the child's behavior gives important clues as to the effects of the consequences. Also giving the child access to many items and seeing which ones the child likes and dislikes provides valuable information to develop a list of reinforcers. In addition, parents can often provide a list of preferred items. Positive attention and social praise may not function as effective reinforcers for students with ASD. However, by repeatedly pairing praise with the student's strongly valued reinforcers, positive attention will gradually become valuable and maintain performance. Later, new items and events can develop into reinforcers by pairing them with these newly acquired secondary reinforcers. Then students with ASD can be brought under the control of the same reinforcers that control the behavior of typically developing children (Zager & Shamow, 2005).

Discrete Trial Training   The ABA approach that has been studied the most is discrete trial training (DTT). A discrete trial is a small unit of teaching implemented by a teacher who works one-on-one with a student in a distraction-free environment for 5 to 20 seconds. The teacher presents the discriminative stimulus, which is a short, clear instruction or question such as "Do this" or "Match with same." The student then responds with a correct or incorrect response to the discriminative stimulus. This is followed by a consequence (Smith, 2001). If the response is correct, the teacher may reinforce with a stimulus selected from the reinforcer inventory conducted earlier. If the response is incorrect and the teacher is using errorless teaching, he or she will immediately provide the student with the correct answer and then present another trial after briefly pausing for 1 to 5 seconds. This time between trials is referred to as the inter-trial interval. DTT is especially helpful for teaching children with ASD to add new forms of behavior and new discriminations. It is also used in teaching imitation, receptive and expressive language, conversation, sentences, grammar, and syntax. Additionally, it is implemented to expand children's skills such as daily living skills and managing disruptive behavior. Furthermore, Smith (2001) cautioned that DTT must be used with other strategies to enable children to initiate the use of their skills and display them across settings (maintenance and generalization). He also reported that at the beginning of intervention, students may need many hours of DTT each week, although there is controversy over how much time is appropriate. Teachers also need to be trained to implement DTT appropriately. Smith (2001) concluded that "despite these limitations, DTT is one of the most important instructional methods for children with autism" (p. 86).

Shaping   Skill building can be promoted by using shaping to develop new behavioral repertoires. If teachers wait for the desired skills to be demonstrated by the student, and these skills occur with a low frequency or are not in the student's repertoire, it will not be possible to wait for the skill to occur to provide reinforcement. Instead, the teacher can differentially reinforce successive approximations of a skill or behavior, thereby shaping the behavior from the initial approximation to the final response. The desired skill is broken down into smaller, easier to accomplish steps, and a hierarchy is developed. If the student is successful at performing the first step, then the criterion for reinforcement is shifted to the next intermediary step and reinforcers for previous responses in the hierarchy are withheld. Reinforcing the successive approximations is continued until the final response of the skill is attained (Zager & Shamow, 2005).

Antecedent Interventions   Antecedent strategies are considered proactive in that they modify the discriminative stimuli for appropriate and inappropriate behavior and can be used to decrease problem behavior and increase learning opportunities. Priming, delivering prompts, and using picture schedules (see Table 9.3) are three antecedent procedures that have been used specifically with children with ASD in general education classrooms. *Priming*, also sometimes referred to as pre-practice, has been documented as an effective classroom strategy for students with ASD (Harrower & Dunlap, 2001). The teacher or parent previews the information or activity that the child might have difficulty with before the child participates in that activity. For example, if the child is having some challenges participating in group story time when the teacher reads to the whole class, the story could be read to the child individually before he or she experiences the story with the entire class (Harrower & Dunlap, 2001).

 Prompts are additional supports that increase the probability that a response is learned (Heflin & Alaimo, 2007). The most intrusive type of prompt is a hand-over-hand prompt where the teacher puts his or her hands over the student's hands to guide the student through the skill movements. Other types of prompts are partial physical prompts, where the teacher may just touch the student's elbow to initiate the response, or gestural prompts, where the teacher signals the student by using a gesture to initiate performance of a skill. Other times verbal prompts and/or visual cues or prompts can be used to assist the student to perform the skill. Although prompts can increase the rate and accuracy of learning skills, they can also lead to the student becoming dependent or waiting for the prompt before initiating a behavior or skill. Therefore, the teacher needs to learn to systematically fade the prompts (Heflin & Alaimo, 2007).

Functional Behavioral Assessment (FBA)   FBA is a problem-solving process that is used to determine the purpose of behavior so that appropriate strategies can be selected to address problem behavior. For example, if the function of the target behavior is escape from academic tasks, time out is typically not an effective extinction procedure because it allows the student to escape the academic task. Instead, escape is put on extinction by not allowing the student to escape the academic task. Sometimes the teacher can physically guide the student to complete the work and model how the academic task should be completed by providing as much assistance as possible to support the student in complying until behavioral momentum is achieved. The teacher, at another time, can analyze what was challenging about the task and modify the task so that it is not as difficult for the student the next time it is presented. The teacher also can provide the student choices, warn the student that a new task is going to happen, vary the academic tasks by interspersing harder tasks with easier tasks, and alter the pace of instruction. The student can also be taught appropriate ways to ask for a break so that he or she does not need to continue misbehaving in order to escape academic tasks. These are all appropriate strategies if the function of the target behavior is escape. The teacher can inadvertently reinforce the inappropriate target behavior if an assessment to determine the function or purpose of the behavior is not conducted (Barnhill, 2005).

Instructional Adaptations

A number of effective, broad-based educational practices were identified by Iovannone and colleagues (2003). These include:

1. Individualized services and supports for both the family and the child
2. The systematic instruction of meaningful skills
3. Reliance on data-based decision-making in educational programs
4. The creation of structured learning environments
5. The implementation of specialized curriculum for language and social skills
6. The application of a functional approach to understanding problem behavior

The Differentiated Instruction—Secondary boxed reading provides an analysis of each of these core elements of effective interventions. These interventions provide overall guidance for program development.

Differentiating Secondary Instruction

APPROPRIATE ADAPTATIONS FOR STUDENTS WITH ASD

Yell, Drasgow, and Lowrey (2005), drawing on the research review of Iovannone and colleagues (2003), outlined the six core elements of effective practices in education for those with autism.

1. **Individualized supports and services:** Must be tailored to meet the unique individual needs and family characteristics of each student. Individualized programming includes (a) considering family preferences when selecting curriculum, (b) developing programming that reflects a student's preferences and interests, and (c) determining the appropriate intensity and level of instruction on the basis of the student's strengths and weaknesses.

2. **Systematic instruction:** Teaching based on identifying desirable learning outcomes, developing specific and focused teaching strategies to achieve these outcomes, consistently implementing the teaching strategies, and using information about student performance to guide daily instructional decisions.

3. **Comprehensible and structured learning environments:** Allow students to predict their daily routine and respond appropriately to behavioral expectations during different activities.

4. **Specific curriculum content:** Must include and emphasize language and social interaction, because these are the primary challenges for students with ASD.

5. **Functional approach to problem behavior:** Represents a movement away from punishment-based approaches that emphasize obedience and compliance and toward instruction that emphasizes useful skill development.

6. **Family involvement:** Improves programming because family members know their child best, spend the most time with him or her, and have an immense influence on their child. It is crucial that they are active participants in developing and implementing their child's educational programming.

Source: From "No Child Left Behind and Students with Autism Spectrum Disorders," by M. L. Yell, E. Drasgow, and K. A. Lowrey, 2005. *Focus on Autism and Other Developmental Disabilities, 20,* pp. 130–139.

TIPS FOR ADAPTING A LESSON FOR ANDREA

Andrea's teacher can:

- Make sure that Andrea is attending before starting instruction.
- Make classroom instructions clear and brief.
- Make sure instruction is appropriate and relevant.
- Be consistent with directions.
- Use effective prompts.
- Fade prompts when/as appropriate.

- Make consequences to behavior and academic performance contingent on appropriate responses and immediate, consistent, and clear.

Change consequences if they are determined to be ineffective.

Source: Adapted from *Autism: Teaching Does Make a Difference*, by B. Scheuermann and J. Webber, 2002. Belmont, CA: Wadsworth.

Regardless of the specific intervention used, professionals who develop programs for children with autism should ask these questions (Heflin & Alaimo, 2007):

1. What are the anticipated outcomes of the programming option?
2. What are the potential risks?
3. How will the option be evaluated?
4. What proof is available that the option is effective?
5. What other options would be excluded if this option is chosen?

The Tips for Adapting a Lesson for Andrea box presents examples of the instructional adaptations that might be appropriate for her.

Selected Curricular Adaptations

Social Stories™   Social Stories™ were first introduced as an intervention by Carol Gray in 1991. Research conducted by the NAC (2009a, 2009c) indicates that there is enough empirical support to consider them as an established treatment for children with autism and AS ages 6 to 14 years. "A Social Story™ describes a situation, skill, or concept in terms of relevant social cues, perspectives, and common responses in a specifically defined style and format" (Gray, 2004, p. 2). One of the most common misconceptions regarding Social Stories™ is that their goal is to change a person's behavior. Gray (2004) reported that this is not the case, but rather that Social Stories™ focus on the underlying causes of the child's frustrations and attempt to increase his or her understanding of events and expectations. For more information and additional resources on Social Stories™ see www.thegraycenter.org (see Figure 9.6).

PECS   A popular low-technology approach used worldwide for persons who lack functional speech is the **picture exchange communication system (PECS)**. Sulzer-Azaroff, Hoffman, Horton, Bondy, and Frost (2009) reported that results of research suggest that "intensive PECS training and maintenance across time and settings for up to 2 years can enable many participants to attain a functional communicative repertoire" (p. 98). PECS uses the principles of "broad-spectrum applied behavior analysis" (Frost & Bondy, 2002, p. vii) and focuses on the development of functional communication skills, independent of communication modality. Children are taught how to exchange picture symbols with a communicative partner to make varied social requests, such as to request a type of food, a classroom activity, or refer to a scheduled event. The communicative partner instantly honors the picture exchange as a request. PECS is based on the Pyramid Approach to Education. The base of the Pyramid Approach includes teaching functional objectives, powerful reinforcement systems, functional communication and social skills, and preventing and reducing contextually inappropriate behaviors. The top elements of the Pyramid Approach include generalization, creating effective lessons, precise teaching strategies, and reducing and correcting errors. Collecting and analyzing data to make decisions is critical to the model (Frost & Bondy, 2002, pp. 4–19). The phases for using PECS are shown in Figure 9.7.

FIGURE 9.6

Sample social story.

Source: From "Teacher-Researcher Partnerships to Improve Social Behavior Through Social Stories," by E. Agosta, J. E. Graetz, M. A. Mastropieri, and T. E. Scruggs, 2004, *Intervention in School and Clinic, 39,* p. 283.

Every day we sit in circle.

All the children sit quietly.

Sometimes in circle, I want to scream.

I will try to sit quietly.

It makes my teacher happy when I sit quietly and do not scream. She says, "Good job, Robert!"

Alternative and Medical Interventions

Other approaches to treatment may involve complementary and alternative medical treatments and drug therapies. Umbarger (2007) reported that "one of the unfortunate realities for treating the symptoms associated with ASD is that we know more about what does not work than we do about those interventions that are truly effective" (p. 440).

Currently, evidence does not support the use of facilitated communication, auditory integration training, secretin, dietary interventions, heavy-metal chelation, and dolphin-assisted therapy for individuals with autism. Furthermore, more scientific evidence is needed for the following strategies: vitamin B interventions, music therapy, hippotherapy, and therapeutic riding (Umbarger, 2007).

For students with ASD, Broun and Umbarger (2005) noted the following behaviors that impact quality of life, and thus may warrant medical interventions:

- Aggression that has moved beyond what can be tolerated or has become significantly less manageable.
- Self-injurious behavior that poses a threat to her/his health and safety and/or significantly interferes with the activities of daily living.
- Obsessions/compulsions that significantly interfere with the child's participation in the activities of daily living or safety.
- Ongoing, unsafe impulsivity that may include running, climbing, mouthing, or eating inappropriate objects. (p. 1)

FIGURE 9.7	Phases in Using a Picture Exchange Communication System (PECS)

Phase I: How to Communicate
Child is shown one picture at a time and learns how to exchange an item for a picture. Two trainers needed—one to physically prompt and one to be communicative partner

Phase II: Distance and Persistence
The communicative partner shapes the child's behavior by moving farther away or by placing the child's pictures farther away to increase persistence in requesting in a variety of settings and with a variety of partners.

Phase III: Picture Discrimination
Child is required to select the appropriate picture from an assortment of pictures and hand it to a communication partner.

Phase IV: Sentence Structure
Child learns to use sentence strips to make requests to a variety of partners.

Phase V: Responding to "What do you want?" (Responsive Requesting)
This is the first time that the adults ask the child what he or she wants and the child responds spontaneously.

Additional attributes are added to the child's repertoire.
Phase VI: Commenting
The goal is for child to exhibit responsive, spontaneous commenting by answering "What do you want?" "What do you see?" "What do you have?" "What do you hear?" "What is it?" (p. 223).

Source: Adapted from: *The Picture Exchange Communication System Training Manual,* by L. Frost and A. Bondy, 2002. Newark, DE: Pyramid Educational Products.

Hendren and Martin (2005) aptly describe the current state of affairs with regard to psychotropic medication:

> Psychotropic medications can be an important part of an effective treatment plan for individuals with ASD. Generally, a comprehensive treatment plan involves behavioral interventions, education for the family, special education services, and sometimes speech, occupational therapy, and other services as well. Improvement in symptoms as a result of these interventions plus pharmacotherapy can result in ... better responses from the environment, leading to additional gains for the youngster with ASD. However, although psychiatric medications are widely used in the ASD population, they have not been systematically studied in great detail. Careful monitoring of their use by experienced practitioners and further research are warranted. (p. 75)

No specific drugs are recommended for the direct treatment of core symptoms associated with ASD (Forness et al., 2003). Consequently, medical interventions are most often used for secondary symptoms, such as aggression or self-injurious behavior (SIB). The process recommended to address specific symptoms with psychotropic medication is to test one drug at a time and to evaluate its effects by following accepted nondrug practices (e.g., the use of applied behavior analysis methodology). Kalachnik and colleagues (1998, cited in Schall, 2002) recommended that the use of psychotropic drugs (i.e., any substance prescribed to improve or stabilize mood, mental status, or behavior) should follow these principles:

- Use a multidisciplinary plan and team to coordinate treatment and care.
- Use only in response to a specific hypothesis regarding how the medication will change behavior.
- Obtain informed consent and develop alliances with the person and his or her parents.

FIGURE 9.8   Medication: Questions for Parents to Ask Physicians

- Why is the person taking medication?
- What behavior changes should occur if medication works?
- About how long should it be before behavior changes occur?
- What adverse side effects may occur?
- What should we do if side effects occur?
- What should we do if the people administering medication forget a dose?
- When and how should the medication be taken?
- When is it necessary or important to call the doctor?
- What information should we bring to our appointment so that the doctor can judge if the drug is working?

Source: From "A Consumer's Guide to Monitoring Psychotropic Medication for Individuals with Autism Spectrum Disorders," by C. Schall, 2002, *Focus on Autism and Other Developmental Disabilities, 17*, p. 231.

- Track outcomes by collecting data on behavioral disorders and quality of life.
- Observe for the presence or absence of side effects.
- Conduct ongoing reviews of the person's clinical status, behavior, and quality of life.
- Strive for administration of the lowest dose possible.

These same authors also identified these "don'ts" related to the use of psychotropic medication:

- Don't use psychotropic drugs in lieu of educational and other services.
- Don't use drugs in quantities that result in a decreased quality of life.
- Don't change drugs and doses frequently.
- Don't use multiple drugs that come from the same pharmaceutical category.
- Don't prescribe medications that are associated with addiction and/or serious side effects.
- Don't prescribe drugs without a regular schedule and eschew the use of drugs on an as-needed basis.

Figure 9.8 provides a list of questions that parents can ask physicians about medication.

SUMMARY

Basic Concepts about Autism Spectrum Disorders
- ASD is a pervasive developmental disability that primarily affects social interactions, language, and behavior.
- Autism is now considered to be caused by biological factors such as genetics and dysfunction in the brain system.
- A dramatic increase in the number of students with ASD has occurred in the past decade.

Characteristics of Individuals with ASD
- ASD is associated with the triad of difficulties associated with social interaction, communication, and repetitive patterns of behavior.
- Although many of the behavioral characteristics displayed by children with AS are similar to those displayed by children with autism, the former generally have higher cognitive development and more typical communication skills.

Effective Inclusive Practices for Students with ASD

- A number of specific interventions have been developed for students with ASD.
- Because the field of ASD has witnessed a number of "miracle cures," it is particularly important that evidence-based interventions be used.
- The National Autism Center (2009) has presented its analysis of interventions and classified treatments as established, emerging, and unestablished.

Classroom Adaptations for Successful Inclusion

- Growing evidence suggests that placing students with autism in general education classrooms results in positive gains.
- Specific adaptations include considerations from curriculum, instruction, behavioral interventions, and possible medical options.

**PEARSON
myeducationlab**

The MyEducationLab for this course can help you solidify your comprehension of Chapter 9 concepts.

- Gauge and further develop your understanding of chapter concepts by taking the quizzes and examining the enrichment materials on the Chapter 9 Study Plan.
- Visit Topic 18, Autism Spectrum Disorders, to:
  - Connect with challenge-based interactive modules, case study units, and podcasts that provide research-validated information about working with students in inclusive settings by visiting the IRIS Center Resources
  - Explore Assignments and Activities, assignable exercises showing concepts in action through video, cases, and student and teacher artifacts
  - Practice and strengthen skills essential to quality teaching through the Building Teaching Skills and Dispositions lessons

10

Teaching Students with Sensory Impairments

CHAPTER OBJECTIVES

After reading this chapter, you should be able to:

1. Provide an overview of students with sensory impairments.
2. Describe basic concepts of hearing impairment.
3. Describe characteristics of students with hearing impairments.
4. Describe effective inclusive practices for students with hearing impairments.
5. Describe classroom adaptations for students with hearing impairments.
6. Describe concepts of visual impairment.
7. Describe characteristics of students with visual impairments.
8. Describe effective inclusive practices for students with visual impairments.
9. Describe classroom adaptations for students with visual impairments.

AMANDA is 8 years old. She was diagnosed with a hearing impairment when she was 2-1/2 years old. While Amanda had appeared to develop typically for the first 12 months, her parents began to realize that she did not seem to respond to noises or voices. She also did not seem to start the "typical" babbling or trying to say words. Amanda was officially diagnosed as having a mild-moderate hearing loss when she was 36 months old. At that time she was referred for a preschool special education program where she received half-day services from a special education teacher and daily services from a speech–language pathologist.

Amanda has been included in general education classrooms since kindergarten. She has been wearing a hearing aid since the age of 3 and can utilize spoken language. Amanda spends 30 minutes a day with a speech–language pathologist, and is beginning to express herself orally fairly effectively. Her teacher, Ms. Jordan, and her classmates are able to understand most of what Amanda says. Still, she seems to be isolated from other children and often sits by herself in the lunchroom. Ms. Jordan has implemented a peer support system for Amanda in an effort to get her more included in the social aspects of the classroom.

Julie volunteered to serve as Amanda's peer support during classroom activities, and Jeremy serves as her peer support during recess and lunch. These two students have greatly facilitated Amanda's social inclusion.

Amanda is a low-average academic student. Her main difficulties are in reading and written expression, skills directly related to her hearing impairment. She does extremely well in math and really likes science. Amanda's IEP provides her with 30 minutes of resource room time daily, when she receives more intensive support for reading and written expression.

QUESTIONS TO CONSIDER

1. What kind of special skills does Amanda's third-grade classroom teacher need to meet Amanda's educational and social needs?
2. What can Ms. Jordan do to help Amanda improve her social skills?
3. What skills are critical for Amanda to be successful in higher grades?

Students with disabilities often considered "high-incidence" disabilities have been the focus in previous chapters. These disabilities, including learning disabilities, attention deficit disorder, emotional disturbance, and intellectual disabilities occur much more frequently than disabilities described in this chapter. As a result, some special education professionals dichotomize disabilities into *high-incidence* and *low-incidence*, depending on the likelihood of occurrence.

Sensory impairments, including hearing impairments and visual impairments, are typically considered low-incidence disabilities because they do not occur in many children.

Visit the MyEducationLab for this course to enhance your understanding of chapter concepts with a personalized Study Plan. You'll also have the opportunity to hone your teaching skills through video-based Assignments and Activities, IRIS Center Resources, and Building Teaching Skills and Disposition lessons.

CROSS-REFERENCE

Other low-incidence disabilities, including traumatic brain injury (TBI) and a host of physical and health problems that may be present in school-age children, such as cerebral palsy, spina bifida, AIDS, cystic fibrosis, epilepsy, and diabetes will be described in Chapter 11.

It is possible that many general education classroom teachers will teach their entire careers without encountering children with these problems. However, as a result of IDEA and the inclusion of students with a wide range of disabilities in general education classrooms, teachers need to have a general understanding of these conditions and how to support these students in the classroom.

AN OVERVIEW OF SENSORY IMPAIRMENTS

Sensory impairments is an overarching term used to describe individuals who have difficulties with their hearing and vision. Students with sensory impairments are often at a distinct disadvantage in academic settings because of the extent that hearing and vision are used in teaching and learning. Most of the activities in classes focus on visual or auditory activities; these are the primary ways teachers teach and students learn. Having limitations in these areas can cause substantial difficulties in the teaching and learning process.

There remains some debate regarding the best setting in which to provide services to students with visual and hearing impairments. Whereas many students with sensory impairments were historically served in residential settings, today most students with these conditions are placed in general education settings, similar to students with other disabilities (Moores, 2009a). While most of these students are capable of handling the academic and social demands of these settings, a variety of accommodations may be needed, ranging from minor seating adjustments to the use of sophisticated equipment for communicating, listening, or navigating, in order for them to be successful (Freiberg, 2005). Students with these impairments may also need the support of additional personnel (e.g., a sign-language interpreter, Braille instructor, or educational consultant).

General classroom teachers must have knowledge and skills about how to modify their classrooms and adapt instruction to meet these students' needs. In addition, they need to understand the psychosocial aspects of these types of disabilities. For some students with severe sensory problems, special consultants may also be needed to assist general education teachers. Ultimately, teachers must feel comfortable and confident that they can address the range of needs these students present.

The number of students (ages 6 to 21) with hearing or visual impairments who were officially identified and provided with special education or related services nationally for the school year 2001–2002 was only 97,067. These are small numbers, considering the total number of students in this age range of the school-age population. Furthermore, these groups represent a very small percentage of all students who are disabled. Regardless of the overall number of students with sensory impairments, having only one of these students in a classroom may seem overwhelming because of the substantial accommodations and modifications that may be needed to ensure academic and social success for this student. Students who have both vision and hearing losses present significant challenges for educators.

BASIC CONCEPTS ABOUT HEARING IMPAIRMENT

Hearing impairment is considered a hidden disability because individuals with this type of disorder frequently do not display any physical features that suggest an impairment is present. However, in any context where communicative skills are needed, hearing limitations become evident. Individuals who are not able to process information audibly are at a distinct disadvantage in schools, where oral language is a primary mode for teaching. Hearing loss has a significant impact on thought and learning (Miller, 2009).

Students with hearing disabilities pose a variety of challenges to the general classroom teacher. While students with mild hearing losses can generally be accommodated for in general classrooms, students with more severe hearing losses, classified as deaf, typically need more extensive supports, such as a sign-language interpreter and extensive technology.

Because most students with hearing impairments can function in general education settings more easily when certain accommodations are provided, it is critical for teachers to understand the nature of hearing impairments and know how to address the needs associated with these conditions. In addition to students receiving services as hearing impaired under IDEA, there may be other students with minimal hearing losses that are not severe enough to result in eligibility for special education services. These students may be at a distinct disadvantage in the general education classroom if the teacher does not recognize their problem (Kaderavek & Pakulski, 2002).

The importance of language acquisition and usage to the development of cognitive abilities and achievement in academic subject areas is unassailable (Polloway, Miller, & Smith, 2011). While the greatest effect of a hearing impairment is on a student's ability to use oral language, it is also important in learning and socialization (Miller, 2009).

There are numerous myths that teachers must address when teaching students with hearing impairments. These include (Williams & Finnegan, 2003):

1. Children who are deaf are not as intellectually capable as children who can hear.
2. Children who are deaf are "concrete" learners.
3. Most children who are deaf have parents who are deaf.
4. Having hearing parents educationally advantages children who are deaf.
5. All children who are deaf can lipread.
6. Using sign language negatively affects speech.
7. All children who are deaf can hear better with hearing aids.
8. There is *a* sign language that differs from spoken language.
9. Having interpreters in the general education classroom ensures access to instruction.
10. The condition of deafness imposes employment limitations. (p. 40)

Teachers must move beyond these myths if they are to successfully educate students with hearing impairments.

Definition, Identification, and Eligibility

Three terms are frequently used when describing students with hearing losses: hearing impairment, deafness, and hard of hearing. *Hearing impairment* is the generic term that has frequently been used to cover the entire range of hearing loss; whereas deafness describes a hearing loss that is so severe that speech cannot be understood through the ear alone, with or without aids. *Hard of hearing* describes individuals who have a hearing loss that makes it difficult, but not impossible, to understand speech through the ear alone, with or without a hearing aid (Moores, 2007). Some school systems use other terminology, such as *audibly impaired*, to describe people with hearing loss.

The degree of hearing impairment is often measured in decibel (dB) loss. Individuals with losses from 25 to 90 dB are considered hard of hearing, whereas those with losses greater than 90 dB are classified as deaf. Most schools use the definitions of hearing impairment found in IDEA. The federal definitions of deafness and hearing impairment are as follows:

- *Deafness* means a hearing impairment that is so severe that the child is impaired in processing linguistic information through hearing, with or without amplification, that adversely affects a child's educational performance (IDEA, 2004).
- *Hearing impairment* means an impairment in hearing, whether permanent or fluctuating, that adversely affects a child's educational performance but that is not included under the definition of deafness in this section (IDEA, 2004).
- *Minimal hearing loss*, which is not included in the federal definition of hearing impairment but which can cause problems for students, is defined as a loss of between 16 and 25 dB (Kaderavek & Pakulski, 2002).

Identification How students with hearing impairments are identified depends on the degree of their hearing loss. Students with severe losses are more easily recognized, while those with mild losses may go unrecognized for many years or even their entire school career because of the way they manifest their disability (Kaderavek & Pakulski, 2002). Some children with very mild hearing losses, which may not classify them for services under IDEA, may still need accommodations, even though they are not officially recognized as having a disability.

Teachers should be alert for children who display certain characteristics that could indicate deficits in hearing. Too often teachers and parents assume children are simply not listening when they do not respond to questions or directions, when in fact, they may not be hearing the information. Therefore, if students persistently ask for information to be repeated, do not respond to directions or questions, have articulation problems, or simply appear to not be listening, teachers should consider a referral for possible hearing loss.

Informal Assessment   Teachers have an ideal opportunity to conduct **informal assessments** related to hearing impairments. Informal assessment focuses on observing students for signs that might indicate a hearing loss. Table 10.1 lists indicators that, if recorded over a period of time, show that a student may need formal assessment. Often, careful observations and referral by teachers can spare a student months or years of struggle and frustration. While all students referred will not be found to have a significant hearing loss, teachers should continue to refer students who display certain characteristics to ensure appropriate identification of those who have hearing impairments.

Formal Assessment   If there is reason to believe that a child has a hearing impairment, a more formal assessment should be provided. The most common method of evaluating hearing is the use of **pure-tone audiometry**, in which sounds of different frequencies are presented at increasing levels of intensity. This assessment determines the hearing threshold of the student for different frequency pure tones in each ear. Another type of formal hearing assessment is **tympanometry screening**, also known as impedance audiometry. Tympanometry screening can detect defects in the middle ear, which could significantly impact education (Salvia & Ysseldyke, 2010).

Academic Assessment   The role of academic assessment has grown tremendously over the past 10 years, primarily due to the No Child Left Behind legislation requiring schools to show that students achieve annual yearly progress. Luckner and Bowen (2006) note that although students with hearing impairments may master academic work, assessments often do not accurately reflect this academic achievement. They further found that standardized tests may cause problems for this group of students because of their reading difficulties. Teachers and administrators must address this issue in order to accurately reflect the achievement of students with hearing impairments.

TABLE 10.1
Possible Indicators of Hearing Loss
Turns head to position an ear in the direction of speaker or noise
Asks for information to be repeated
Appears to be daydreaming and not paying attention
Does not respond when asked questions or given directions
Articulation problems
Difficulty with sounds and letters
Speaks in a loud voice
Pulls on ears
Frequent ear infections
Limited vocabulary

Eligibility   The eligibility of students for special education and related services as a result of having a hearing impairment is determined by the federal definition and criteria in IDEA. In order to receive special education services, students must meet one of the IDEA definitions of deaf or hearing impairment described previously. Teachers should not be concerned about specific eligibility criteria, but should refer students who display characteristics suggesting the presence of a hearing loss. The evaluation/eligibility committee will be responsible for making decisions on eligibility.

Classification of Hearing Impairment

Hearing impairment is frequently organized into four different groups: conductive hearing loss (mild loss in both ears), sensorineural hearing loss (caused by sound not being transmitted to the brain), mixed hearing loss, and central auditory hearing loss (Salvia & Ysseldyke, 2010). Table 10.2 describes each of these types of loss.

Prevalence and Educational Environments

Significant hearing impairments affect approximately three to four in every 1,000 births (Hear-It.org, 2010). Approximately 80,000 students were served in special education programs for students with hearing impairments during the 2006–2007 school year. This figure represents only about 0.2% of the total school population (National Center for Educational Statistics, 2010). Although the number of children with hearing impairments served under

---

TABLE 10.2

Types of Hearing Loss

TYPE OF LOSS	CHARACTERISTICS
Conductive Loss	Caused by abnormality of outer or middle ear
	Causes include excessive wax buildup, fluid, eardrum perforation
	Bone conduction is normal
	Most common type of hearing loss in school-age children
	Amplifying sounds with hearing aids and other devices is helpful
Sensorineural Loss	Loss due to dysfunction of inner ear
	Impacts bone and air-conduction hearing
	Does not respond to medical or surgical treatment
	Amplifying sounds with hearing aids and other devices is helpful
Mixed Loss	Combination of conductive and sensorineural losses
	Usually results from something that causes a conductive loss to a child who already has a sensorineural loss
	Often correctable with surgical or medical treatment
	Amplifying sounds with hearing aids and other devices is helpful
Central Auditory Loss	Caused by problems with the central auditory system
	May have problems with speech within a noisy environment
	May pass traditional hearing exams
	Experience difficulties with auditory memory, auditory sequential memory, phonetics, and reading comprehension
	May respond to various instructional strategies

Source: Information from Salvia & Ysseldyke (2010).

IDEA is small, the Centers for Disease Control and Prevention (CDC) estimated that as many as 15% of all children experience some degree of hearing loss (Crawford, 1998). This estimate includes those children with minimal hearing loss that does not result in eligibility for special education services (Kaderavek & Pakulski, 2002).

Students with hearing impairments are educated in all of the **continuum-of-placement options**, depending on their individual needs. These options range from general education classrooms to residential schools for the deaf. There is no single educational setting that is best for all students with hearing impairments. The placement decision for these students should be based on the unique needs of the student and the IEP process, not a philosophical position, such as inclusion.

The trend continues toward educating more students with hearing impairments in the general education classroom. During the fall 2004, approximately 67% of all students with hearing impairments were educated in general education classrooms for at least 40% of the school day (U.S. Department of Education, 2008). Fewer than 7% of these students were educated in residential settings, the most likely placement prior to the passage of Public Law 94–142 (U.S. Department of Education, 2008). There have actually been several states where residential schools for students with hearing impairments have closed (Moores, 2009b). The trend continues to be the inclusion of this group of students in general education, which in turn means the increased need for supports and services provided in inclusive settings. Types of supports that students with hearing impairments need resemble those needed by students with other disabilities, except for a few services specific to students with hearing problems.

Unfortunately, some students with hearing impairments served in general education classrooms may not receive appropriate educational services. Moores (2008) noted that some students served in general classrooms, with assistance from itinerant teachers who travel among several schools to provide support services, receive fewer interventions than needed. This underlines the importance of making placement decisions based on students' needs rather than implementing a model that does not take student needs into consideration.

Causation and Risk Factors

Many different factors can lead to hearing impairments. These include genetic causes, which accounts for approximately 50% of congenital hearing loss in children; prenatal impact, including infections during pregnancy; head trauma; childhood infections, such as measles; ear infections (Hear-It.org., 2010); toxic reaction to drugs, infections, prematurity, and Rh incompatibility (Moores, 2007); birth trauma (Chase, Hall, & Werkhaven, 1996); allergies (Lang, 1998); and noise-induced hearing loss (Haller & Montgomery, 2004). Knowing the specific cause of a hearing impairment is usually not important for school personnel because the cause rarely affects interventions needed by students.

CHARACTERISTICS OF STUDENTS WITH HEARING IMPAIRMENTS

The characteristics of students with hearing impairment vary greatly. Four categories of characteristics are especially meaningful to the classroom setting: psychological, communicational, academic, and social-emotional. Many of the characteristics presented by students with hearing impairments create unique problems for teachers. The Characteristics and Implications feature lists characteristics and educational implications for students with hearing impairments.

Significant Disabilities

Students with mild hearing impairments can typically be included in general education classes without a great deal of difficulty. For students who can receive and understand oral language, even if it is enhanced with technology such as hearing aids and other amplifica-

■ CHARACTERISTICS AND IMPLICATIONS: HEARING IMPAIRMENTS ■

AREA	POTENTIAL DIFFICULTIES	EDUCATIONAL IMPLICATIONS
Attention	Initial attention to directions/information Problems with auditory attention Attention span (length of time on task) Focus (inhibition of distracting stimuli) Selective attention (discrimination of important stimulus characteristics)	Provide cues that indicate important information is going to be provided. Provide oral information in short amounts. Provide information, such as directions and important information in written format. Provide information visually.
Memory	Problems with auditory memory Problems with vocabulary development	Stress meaningful content. Provide strategies instruction. Use multisensory presentation of information.
Oral Communication Problems	Difficulty understanding teachers Difficulty understanding peers	Create environment that encourages verbal communication. Provide information visually. Provide information in written format. Establish peer support systems. Teachers must use effective communication skills. Promote support from speech–language pathologists.
Language Development	Difficulty with receptive and expressive language Delayed acquisition of vocabulary and language rules Articulation of thoughts and feelings Possible interaction of cultural variance and language dialects	Provide alternative modes of communication. Create environment that encourages verbal communication. Encourage expression of thoughts. Provide appropriate language models. Provide opportunities for students to learn language for varied purposes and with different audiences.
Academic Deficiencies	Delayed acquisition of reading, writing, and mathematical skills Decoding of text Reading comprehension Math computation Problem-solving in mathematics Self-directed expressive writing	Use learning strategies to promote effective studying. Teach sight words including functional applications. Teach strategies for decoding unknown words. Provide strategies to promote reading comprehension and math problem solving. Develop functional writing skills. Adapt curriculum to promote success. Encourage and support independent reading. Encourage shared reading and writing. Teachers must use effective communication skills.
Social-Behavorial Interactions	Classroom behavior Peer acceptance Displaying emotions appropriately	Promote social competence through direct instruction of skills. Reinforce appropriate behaviors. Seek self-understanding of reasons for inappropriate behavior. Teach self-management, self-control. Organize peer support systems.

tion devices, instruction can take place with minimal accommodations and modifications. Even when dealing with these students, classroom teachers need to realize that reading levels are likely lower than for students without hearing impairments. Just because students with mild hearing impairments can process information aurally does not mean that they do not need accommodations.

Students with more severe hearing impairments present significant challenges to teachers. For many of these students, understanding and using oral language is not feasible. Therefore, the "critical intervention with students who are severely disabled and hearing impaired is to develop communication skills" (Westling & Fox, 2009, p. 351). The use of sign language may be the primary method of communication for this group of students. Many of these students may have interpreters in the classroom for real-time interpreting supports. When students have interpreters, teachers should keep these ideas in mind (www.as.wvu.edu/scidis/hearing.html, 2005):

- Speak directly to the student rather than to the interpreter.
- Signing may be distracting at first, but you and the other students will soon become accustomed to the interpreter's presence.
- Give the student and the interpreter outlines of the lecture or written material, in advance, so that they can become familiar with new technical vocabulary.
- Interpreters should not give their opinion of a student's progress, as this can violate the student's rights.
- Provide scripts of video and laser media when possible for both the interpreter and the student with a hearing disability (with or without captioning).
- The interpreter is not to answer lesson-related questions from the student with a hearing impairment. The student should direct all lesson-related questions to the instructor.
- The interpreter should stand closer to the section of the chalkboard that is being used by the instructor, thereby allowing the student to simultaneously see both the signs and the writing on the board.

Perspectives on Outcomes

Students with hearing impairments, like all students with disabilities, successfully complete high school and receive a diploma at a much lower rate than students without disabilities. During the 2006–2007 school year, 6,697 students with hearing impairments, ages 14 to 21, exited public schools. Of this number, 2,921, or approximately 44%, received a diploma; another 827, or 12.3%, received a certificate. The remaining students exited under less optimal conditions (28th Annual Report to Congress on the Implementation of the Individuals with Disabilities Education Act, 2009). Therefore, during the 2006–2007 school year, approximately 50% of students with hearing impairments received a diploma or certificate, compared to a rate of approximately 70% for students without disabilities.

Special Considerations

The most problematic issue for students with hearing impairments is the impact on their oral language skills and ability to communicate. With a significant amount of information transmitted using oral language, students with hearing impairments are at a major disadvantage both in receiving information as well as expressing themselves. For students with mild hearing impairments, the use of hearing aids and other amplification devices may be sufficient to enable them to be successful in educational settings. For this group of students, teachers need to have a basic understanding of hearing aids and other technological aids, as well as general accommodations that result in positive opportunities.

Students with more severe hearing losses create additional challenges for educators. For this group of students, amplification will not be sufficient for students to learn effectively. Many of these students require sign language interpreters to accompany them to their classes. Teachers need to know how to utilize sign language interpreters to maximize their benefit to the student.

EFFECTIVE INCLUSIVE PRACTICES FOR STUDENTS WITH HEARING IMPAIRMENTS

Including students with hearing impairments in general classroom settings presents unique opportunities for this group to become immersed in the "hearing" world.

Including students with hearing impairments in general education classrooms is definitely the trend and should remain so over the foreseeable future. This can present significant challenges for general education teachers. As a result, it is imperative that general classroom teachers develop a repertoire of skills that will enable them to successfully include this group of students.

Language is an important component of learning and instruction (Miller, 2009). As a result of the language limitations of students with hearing impairments, it is often difficult for teachers to use standard instructional methods effectively with this group of students. Teachers therefore have to rely on supports provided by special education staff and specialists in hearing impairments to meet the needs of these students.

Transition Considerations   Students with hearing impairments must be involved in their transition planning. Just like students with other disabilities, students with hearing impairments need to learn independent living skills that will facilitate their success as adults (Garay, 2003). While IDEA requires the involvement of students in the development of their IEP, certain steps must be taken to make this effective for students with hearing impairments. For example, materials need to be provided in writing and an interpreter must be present in cases where an interpreter is necessary for true involvement. Ensuring that students have access to verbal communications among committee members is imperative for active participation in the IEP/transition process.

Promoting Inclusive Practices

Students with hearing impairments vary greatly in their need for supports in the general education classroom. Students with mild losses, generally classified as hard of hearing, need minimal supports. In fact, these students resemble their nondisabled peers in most ways, with the primary exception being their difficulty in processing oral language. If amplification assistance can enable these students to hear clearly, they will need little specialized instruction in the general classroom setting (Dagenais, Critz-Crosby, Fletcher, & McCutcheon, 1994).

On the other hand, students with severe hearing impairments, those classified as deaf, present unique challenges to teachers. Specialized instructional techniques usually involve alternative communication methods; the use of interpreters is typically a necessity for these students. General education teachers must know how to utilize the services of an interpreter to facilitate the success of students with significant hearing losses. In doing so they must remember that interpreters are providers of a related service; they are not teachers (Heath, 2006).

Challenges for general classroom teachers resulting from students with hearing impairments are due primarily because of the language barrier that hearing loss often creates. As a result, teachers must rely on support personnel such as educational consultants who specialize in the area of hearing impairment, as well as interpreters, audiologists, and medical personnel, to assist them in their efforts to provide appropriate educational programs. Professionals, such as speech–language pathologists, deaf educators, and interpreters can greatly assist general classroom teachers when dealing with students with hearing impairments (Hanks & Velaski, 2003). See Figure 10.1 for potential sources of support.

Being an integral part of the inclusive school community is important for students with hearing impairments who receive their educational programs in public schools, especially for those placed in general education classrooms. Simply physically situating students in classrooms does not automatically make them included members of the class. This statement

FIGURE 10.1

Types of supports for students with hearing impairments in inclusive settings.

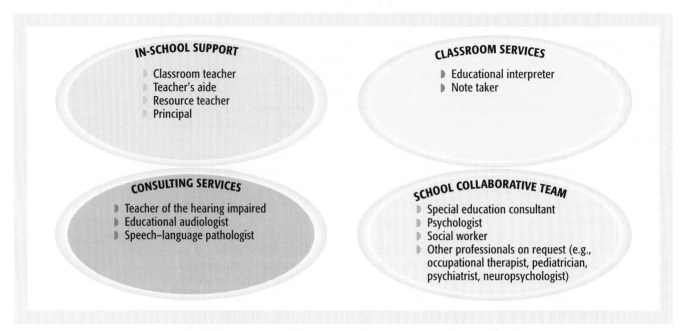

Source: From "Educational Management of Children with Hearing Loss," by C. Edwards, p. 306, in *Hearing Care for Children*, edited by F. N. Martin and J. G. Clark, 1996. Boston: Allyn & Bacon. Used by permission.

especially holds true for children with hearing impairments who have a very difficult time associating with the "hearing" culture (Andrews & Jordan, 1998). Students with hearing losses may tend to keep to themselves and withdraw from social activities (Hear-it.org., 2006). Therefore, teachers must ensure that these students become part of the community of the school and class and are socially accepted by their peers.

Teachers may have to orchestrate opportunities for interaction between students with hearing impairments and their nondisabled peers. These could include grouping, pairing students for specific tasks, assigning buddies, and establishing a circle of friends. Kluwin (1996) suggests using dialogue journals to facilitate this interaction. Students are paired (one hearing and one nonhearing) to make journal entries and then exchange them. Rather than assign deadlines, allow students to exchange journal entries whenever they want and reward students for making and exchanging journal entries. This approach encourages interactions among students with hearing impairments and their nondisabled peers without using a rigidly structured activity or assignment.

CLASSROOM ADAPTATIONS FOR STUDENTS WITH HEARING IMPAIRMENTS

Because the general education setting is appropriate for most students who are hard of hearing and for many students who are deaf, classroom adaptations for this group of students are generally the focus for academic supports. General and specific suggestions are clustered under four major areas: management considerations, curricular and instructional accommodations, social-emotional interventions, and technology.

Teachers must deliver instruction in a way that will benefit students with hearing impairments. Some suggestions include:

• Allow students to move about the classroom to position themselves for participation in ongoing events.

- Let students use swivel chairs.
- Reduce distracting and competing noise by modifying the classroom environment (e.g., carpeting on floor, corkboard on walls).
- Ensure that adequate lighting is available.
- Provide visual reminders indicating the amount of time left for an activity or until the end of class.
- Use cooperative learning arrangements to facilitate student involvement with hearing peers.
- Include a section of the lesson plan for special provisions for students with hearing impairments.
- Acquire or develop visually oriented materials to augment orally presented topics—use overhead projection systems when appropriate.
- Use homework assignment books and make sure that students understand their assignments.

CROSS-REFERENCE

Specific suggestions related to grouping, lesson planning, materials acquisition and adaptation, and homework systems can be found in Chapter 14.

Curricular Adaptations

All basic elements of effective instructional practice will benefit students with hearing impairments. However, certain specific ideas will enhance their learning experiences.

Communication Perhaps the most challenging aspect of teaching students whose hearing is impaired is making sure that they participate in communicational activities (i.e., teacher to student, student to teacher, student to student) in the classroom and that they are able to handle the reading and writing demands of the class. Language and communication tend to dominate the teaching of these students (Mayer et al., 2002). Students who have profound hearing loss must rely on alternative methods of communication, such as sign language or lip reading. Because these students typically do not become facile with standard forms of English, they can have significant problems in the areas of reading and writing. Unfortunately, research has found that many students with hearing impairments receive limited instruction in reading (Donne & Zigmond, 2008).

Studies have shown that auditory-verbal therapy programs can be effective for students with hearing loss. Dornan, Hickson, Murdoch, and Houston (2009) found that after a 21-month intervention program, students receiving interventions based on an auditory-verbal model compared favorably with students without hearing losses in their speech perception, auditory comprehension, oral expression, total language, and speech skills.

When students using some form of manual communication, usually **American Sign Language (ASL)**, are in general education classrooms, teachers are not required to learn this language. However, teachers should make an effort to know some of the more common signs and to be able to finger-spell the letters of the alphabet as well as the numbers 1 to 10. If students can communicate only by using sign language, an interpreter will most likely need to be present. Teachers should know basic information about the role and functions of an interpreter.

Still another form of communication that may be effective is **cued speech** (Stewart & Kluwin, 2001). Cued speech is a system of hand cues that enhances lip-reading. Eight different hand shapes represent consonant sounds and four hand positions represent vowel sounds. Using the hand signs near the lips provides students with cues that help with their lip-reading (Blasi & Priestley, 1998).

Teachers should be conscious of how well they are communicating with their students. The teacher's speech, location, and movement in the classroom can affect the facility with which a student with a hearing impairment can follow a discussion or lecture. The proper use of assistive equipment (e.g., amplification devices) can also make a difference.

Since the late 1980s there has been a movement to provide instruction to students with hearing impairments as if they were second language learners, using a bilingual educational model. Mayer (2009) points out that this model will not likely be effective with students with hearing losses because "the deaf learner differs from that of hearing second language learners in that being bilingual refers only to proficiency in the written form of the second language" (p. 326). While this has become a trend in some school districts, the model is unlikely to be successful with many of these students.

Social-Emotional Considerations

Classrooms constitute complex social systems. In addition to development of scholastic abilities and academic support skills, personal development is also occurring. Students need to learn how to get along with their peers and authority figures while they learn how to deal with their beliefs and emotions. Some of the available research suggests that students with hearing impairments develop similarly, socially and emotionally, to their hearing peers (Moores, 2001). However, other research suggests that students with hearing impairments are more likely than their nondisabled peers to have emotional-behavioral problems (Fellinger, Holzinger, Sattel, & Laucht, 2008). In a recent qualitative study, Hatamizadeh, Ghasemi, Saeedi, and Kazemnejad (2008) found that students with mild to moderate hearing losses rated themselves less competent than their nondisabled peers in the areas of (1) cognitive competence, (2) physical competence, (3) social-emotional competence, (4) school adjustment, and (5) communicative competence. Therefore, teachers need to be able to help students develop a realistic sense of their abilities, become more responsible and independent, interact appropriately with their peers, and enhance their self-concept and sense of belonging (Luckner, 1994). The following are some specific suggestions:

- Create a positive, supportive, and nurturing classroom environment.
- Encourage class involvement through active participation in classroom activities and interaction in small groups.
- Let students know that you are available if they are experiencing problems and need to talk.
- Help the students with normal hearing understand the nature of hearing impairment and what they can do to assist.
- Practice appropriate interactive skills.
- Encourage and assist students to get involved in extracurricular activities.
- Help them develop problem-solving abilities.
- Help students develop realistic expectations.
- Prepare students for dealing with the demands of life and adulthood.

Universal Design for Learning

Teachers need to utilize a host of practices that allow students to learn more effectively and efficiently. This can be accomplished with the principles of universal design for learning, which focuses on providing supports and reducing barriers found in the general education classroom (PCPID, 2007). One suggestion is the use of visually oriented material, which is especially valuable for students with hearing problems. Many classroom adaptations covered earlier in this chapter spring from the ideas of universal design, including the provision of advance organiz-

---

TIPS FOR ADAPTING A LESSON FOR **AMANDA**

The following are some ways to infuse concepts related to deaf students and self-advocacy throughout the school curriculum for Amanda.

Amanda's teacher should:

- Understand Amanda's strengths and weaknesses.
- Provide written copies of materials that are provided orally.
- Make sure that Amanda understands assignments.
- Encourage Amanda to use oral language and provide positive reinforcement to her when she speaks.
- Implement a buddy system so that Amanda has a partner during social activities.

- Routinely check to ensure that Amanda's hearing aid is working properly.
- Allow Amanda to sit near the front of the class and have students face Amanda when they are talking.
- Encourage Amanda to turn and watch students when they are talking.
- Collaborate with the speech therapist to find out what reinforcing activities can be done in the classroom to improve Amanda's use of oral language.

ers such as lecture outlines, and the use of visual aids like slides, diagrams, and multimedia. As mentioned previously, teachers should keep their face visible to students and maintain eye contact with the student, not the interpreter. The following are additional suggestions:

- Make sure students are attentive.
- Provide short, clear instructions.
- Speak clearly and normally—do not exaggerate the pronunciation of words.
- Avoid frequent movement around the classroom, turning your back on students while talking, and standing in front of a bright light source.
- Use gestures and facial expressions.
- If the student reads speech, male teachers should make sure that their mustache and beard are trimmed to maximize visibility.
- Check with students to confirm that they understand what is being discussed or presented.
- Encourage students to request clarification and to ask questions.
- Identify other speakers by name so that students can more easily follow a discussion among more than one speaker.
- Repeat the comments of other students who speak.
- Paraphrase or summarize discussions at the end of a class session.
- Write information when necessary.
- Have students take responsibility for making themselves understood.
- Preview new vocabulary and concepts prior to their presentation during a lecture.
- Utilize a variety of instructional formats, including demonstrations, experiments, and other visually oriented activities.
- Emphasize the main points covered in a lecture both verbally and visually.
- Provide summaries, outlines, or scripts of videotapes, videodiscs, or films.
- Let students use microcomputers for word processing and for checking their spelling and grammar.

Coteaching has been shown to be one effective method for teaching students with hearing impairments in general education classes. This model encourages general classroom teachers and teachers of students with hearing losses to combine their skills in an inclusive setting. "Coteaching allows teachers to respond to the diverse needs of all students, provides another set of hands and eyes, lowers the teacher–student ratio, and expands the amount of professional expertise that can be directed to student needs" (Luckner, 1999, p. 150).

The seating considerations discussed earlier in this chapter are classroom adaptations in keeping with the ideas of universal design.

Other Instructional Adaptations

Students with hearing impairments placed in general education classrooms often use technological devices to help them to maximize their communication abilities (Easterbrooks, 1999). Teachers need a working knowledge of these devices so that they can provide a supportive environment for their use and ensure that the student benefits from the equipment. See Figure 10.2 for a description of some of these devices.

Assistive Listening Devices   **Assistive listening devices (ALDs)** include hearing aids and other devices that amplify voices and sounds, communicate messages visually, or alert users to environmental sounds (Marschark, Lang, & Albertini, 2002). Children with even small hearing losses, those in the 16- to 25-dB range, may have problems hearing faint or distant speech without some amplification (Iskowitz, 1998).

Hearing aids are the predominant ALDs found in schools. These devices pick up sound with a microphone, amplify and filter it, and then convey that sound into the ear canal through a loudspeaker, also called a receiver (Marschark et al., 2002). They work very well with students who experience mild-to-severe hearing losses (Iskowitz, 1997). Educators must realize that hearing aids amplify sounds; they do not make the sound clearer. Often, students who use hearing aids must have auditory training to learn to use and discriminate the sounds (Deafness.about.com, 2006).

FIGURE 10.2	**Media, Materials, and Technology for Students with Hearing Losses**

Visual Technology, Media, and Materials	• Microcomputers and computer systems such as ENFI • Captioning systems • Computer-assisted note taking • Videotapes and interactive video discs • Instructional CDs and software • Telecommunication technology • Printed materials, programs, and packages
Auditory Technology, Media, and Materials	• Induction loops • FM systems • Programmable hearing aids • Soundfield amplification systems • Cochlear implants • Instructional CDs, interactive listening developmental program, and software • Audiocassette programs • Computer-based speech training systems

Source: From Bruce, Peyton, & Batson, 1993; Kaplan et al. (1993).

To assist students in maximizing the use of their ALDs, teachers should:

- Know what type of ALD a student uses
- Understand how the device works: on/off switch, battery function (e.g., selection, life span, insertion), volume controls
- Be able to determine whether a hearing aid is working properly
- Help students keep their hearing aids functioning properly (e.g., daily cleaning, appropriate storage)
- Make sure students avoid getting their hearing aids wet, dropping or jarring them, spraying hairspray on them, and exposing them to extreme heat (Shimon, 1992)
- Keep spare batteries on hand
- Ensure that the system is functioning properly
- Be sure that students turn the transmitter off when not engaged in instructional activities to prevent battery loss
- Perform daily troubleshooting of all components of the system (Brackett, 1990)
- Make sure background noises are minimized

Cochlear Implants   More than 20,000 individuals in the United States, including 10,000 children, have cochlear implants. Unlike hearing aids, which basically amplify sound, cochlear implants convert auditory signals into electrical impulses, which can therefore stimulate nerves in the inner ear (Schraer-Joiner & Prause-Weber, 2009). Students with cochlear implants may require different instructional interventions than those with hearing aids. For example, when teaching music to students with cochlear implants, Schraer-Joiner and Prause-Weber (2009) recommend that multisensory approaches are used, which can actually increase the level of student participation.

BASIC CONCEPTS ABOUT VISUAL IMPAIRMENT

Students with visual impairments comprise the smallest number of children in any one category served under IDEA, making up approximately 0.04% of the school population (U.S. Department of Education, 2006).

The development of concepts, the understanding of spatial relations, and the use of printed material depends on children's ability to use vision. Li (2004) notes that "vision is intimately involved with 70 to 80% of all tasks that occur in our educational programs" (p. 39). Thus children with visual problems have unique educational needs mandating the use of alternative teaching strategies, modified materials, and technology (Downing & Chen, 2003). Teachers may be able to use their usual instructional techniques with some modifications with students who have some functional vision. But for students who have very little or no vision, teachers will need to implement alternative techniques to provide effective educational programs. Students with visual impairments and additional disabilities create even more significant challenges for teachers (Li, 2009).

Many students with visual impairments can be successful in general education classrooms. However, teachers working with these students need to understand the nature of a particular student's vision problem to be able to choose appropriate accommodative tactics. They need basic information related to four categories: fundamental concepts of vision and visual impairment, signs of possible visual problems, typical characteristics of students with visual problems, and specific accommodative techniques for meeting student needs.

Definition, Identification, and Eligibility

Several different terms are associated with the concept of visual impairment; the following are those most frequently used and their definitions:

- *Visual impairment* is a generic term that includes a wide range of visual problems.
- *Blindness* has different meanings depending on context, resulting in some confusion. *Legal blindness* refers to a person's visual acuity and field of vision. It is defined as a visual acuity of 20/200 or less in the person's better eye after correction, or a field of vision of 20 degrees or less. An educational definition of *blindness* implies that a student must use Braille (a system of raised dots that the student reads tactilely) or aural methods to receive instruction (Freiberg, 2005). Only about 10% of all individuals with visual impairments are totally blind (Griffin, Williams, Davis, & Engleman, 2002).
- *Low vision* indicates that some functional vision exists to be used for gaining information through written means with or without the assistance of optical, nonoptical, or electronic devices (Freiberg, 2005).

Most students with low vision are capable of handling the demands of most classroom settings, often with some modifications. On the other hand, students who are blind (i.e., have very little or no vision) will need major accommodations to be successful in general education settings.

In addition to students in the preceding classifications, there is also a group of students with cortical visual impairment (CVI). CVI is defined as "impaired vision that is due to bilateral dysfunction of the optic radiations or visual cortex or both" (Roman et al., 2010, p. 69). It is estimated that 30 to 40% of children with visual impairment have CVI.; unfortunately, some of these students are not classified as having visual impairments, under IDEA, and therefore are not eligible for special education services. Roman and others (2010) believe that all students with CVI should be eligible for IDEA services.

Students with visual impairments can be easily identified if their visual loss is severe. However, students with milder losses might go several years without being recognized. Teachers must be aware of behaviors that could indicate a vision problem. Table 10.3 summarizes possible symptoms of vision problems.

Formal Assessment   Students are routinely screened for vision problems in schools. A more in-depth evaluation is conducted for those who display possible problems. The typical eye examination assesses two dimensions: visual acuity and field of vision. Visual acuity is most often evaluated by the use of a **Snellen chart**. Two versions of this chart are available: the traditional version using alphabetic letters of different sizes, and the other version using the letter E presented in different spatial arrangements and sizes for students who are unfamiliar with letters (Salvia & Yssledyke, 2010). While these charts can effectively

TABLE 10.3

Symptoms of Possible Vision Problems

Behavior	• Rubs eyes excessively
	• Shuts or covers one eye, tilts head, or thrusts head forward
	• Has difficulty in reading or in other work requiring close use of the eyes
	• Blinks more than usual or is irritable when doing close work
	• Holds books close to eyes
	• Is unable to see distant things clearly
	• Squints eyelids together or frowns
Appearance	• Crossed eyes
	• Red-rimmed, encrusted, or swollen eyelids
	• Inflamed or watery eyes
	• Recurring styes
Complaints	• Eyes that itch, burn, or feel scratchy
	• Cannot see well
	• Dizziness, headaches, or nausea following close eye work
	• Blurred or double vision

Source: From *Exceptional Learners: Introduction to Special Education* (9th ed., p. 343), by D. P. Hallahan and J. M. Kauffman, 2003. Boston: Allyn & Bacon. Used by permission.

determine the likelihood of children having vision problems, they might not detect near-vision problems.

Once identified as having possible vision problems, students should be referred for more extensive evaluations. Ophthalmologists, medical doctors, and optometrists (who specialize in evaluating vision and prescribing glasses) are typically involved in this more-extensive evaluation. These specialists determine the specific nature and extent of any vision problem.

Other formal assessments of vision focus on the functional use of vision. Examples of these types of assessments include functional-vision assessment and learning-media assessment. The learning-media assessment determines the efficiency with which students gather information from sensory modalities, the types of learning media used by students, and the media used for reading and writing (Salvia & Yssledyke, 2010).

Informal Assessment   In addition to formal assessment, there are numerous informal ways to assess students' vision, generally focusing on simple observation activities. By observing the child, teachers and other school personnel note behaviors that might indicate a vision loss or change in the child's vision. Once students are identified as having a problem, school personnel must be alert to any changes in the student's visual abilities.

Eligibility   IDEA guidelines for students with visual impairments are used in most states for eligibility. These guidelines focus on the visual acuity of students. Students with a 20/200 acuity or worse, in the better eye with best correction, are eligible as blind students, whereas those with a visual acuity of 20/70 to 20/200 are eligible as low-vision students. In addition to the visual acuity limitation, all students with disabilities served under IDEA must evidence need of special education services.

In addition to the educational challenges resulting from visual impairments, this group of disabilities also results in a substantial financial burden for school districts and society. Wong, Chou, Lamoureux, and Keefe (2008) determined that the annual economic impact of visual impairments in the United States ranged from $5.5 billion to $35 billion. The financial impact on schools is directly related to the level of visual impairment and the resulting intervention needs of each student.

Classification

While there are several different ways to classify individuals with visual impairments, a common method organizes visual problems as refractive errors (e.g., farsightedness, nearsightedness, and astigmatism); retinal disorders; disorders of the cornea, iris, and lens; and optic nerve problems. In addition to common refractive problems, which usually can be improved with corrective lenses, other visual problems include the following:

- *Strabismus*—improper alignment of the eyes
- *Nystagmus*—rapid involuntary movements of the eye
- *Glaucoma*—fluid pressure buildup in the eye
- *Cataract*—cloudy film over the lens of the eye
- *Diabetic retinopathy*—changes in the blood vessels of the eye caused by diabetes
- *Macular degeneration*—damage to the central portion of the retina, causing central vision loss
- *Retinitis pigmentosa*—genetic eye disease leading to total blindness (Smith, 2007)

Tunnel vision is the condition that occurs when individuals have only central vision. This condition results in individuals seeing as if they are looking through a long tube; they have little or no peripheral vision. Tunnel vision is caused by the deterioration of the retina.

The primary concern for educators is the functional impact of the vision loss. The student's usable residual vision and the time when the vision problem developed are issues for educators. Students should always be encouraged to use any residual vision they have. For example, if they can read print by holding it close, they should be encouraged to hold reading materials close. Likewise, if materials can be read with the aid of magnification devices, students should be encouraged to use those magnification aids. Students who are born with significant visual loss have a much more difficult time understanding some concepts and developing basic skills than students who lose their vision after they have established certain concepts. Once developed, individuals have a visual memory and therefore understand the basic concepts (Warren, 1994).

Prevalence and Educational Environments

While vision problems are common in U.S. society, corrective lenses allow most individuals to see very efficiently. However, some individuals have vision problems that are uncorrectable. As with hearing impairments, the number of individuals who have visual impairments increases with age. In the school-age population, approximately 0.04% of students are classified as visually impaired. During the Fall of 2004, 26,130 students, ages 6 to 21 were classified as having visual impairments in the United States (U.S. Department of Education, 2009).

Like students with hearing impairments, students with visual problems may be placed anywhere on the full continuum of placement options, ranging from general education classrooms to residential schools for students with visual impairments. Students must be evaluated individually to determine the appropriate educational placement. Although some totally blind students function well in general education settings, many are placed in more restrictive settings, including residential schools where they receive more extensive services.

The trend for placing students with visual impairment is toward more inclusive placements. During the Fall of 2004, approximately 72% of all students with visual impairments were served in general education classrooms at least 40% of each school day. Approximately 56% were in general classrooms more than 80% of the school day. During this same year, fewer than 7% were educated in residential schools (U.S. Department of Education, 2009).

Causation and Risk Factors

There are a variety of factors that can cause visual impairments. These include genetic causes, physical trauma, infections, premature birth, anoxia, and retinal degeneration. Vision problems are frequently genetic—notice the number of family members who wear glasses. Frequently more than one member of a family wears glasses, often the majority of the family. Physical trauma is another common cause of vision problems, caused most frequently by accidents. The leading cause of adult-onset blindness is diabetes.

CHARACTERISTICS OF STUDENTS WITH VISUAL IMPAIRMENTS

The predominant characteristic of students with visual impairments is their limited vision, which results in their inability to process information visually. The extent of their ability to process information visually becomes the critical factor related to education. Students who are capable of processing some information visually are at a major advantage over those who cannot process any information visually. Additional characteristics can be categorized as psychological, communicational, academic, and social-emotional. These characteristics, along with their educational implications, are listed in the Characteristics and Implications feature. In addition to these characteristics, another fact impacting students with visual impairments is their limited physical activity. A recent study determined that these students have low levels of physical activity (Ayvazoglu, Oh, & Kozub, 2006). In addition to the lower level of their motor activity, these students frequently display other motor deficiencies. The extent of motor deficiencies in students with visual impairments is related to (Houwen, Visscher, Lemmink, & Hartman, 2009):

- Degree of visual impairment
- Type of eye condition
- Age of onset
- Visual perceptual-motor variables
- Age of the student
- Gender
- Physical fitness
- Personality characteristics
- Opportunities for movement experience
- Nature of tasks

Significant Disabilities

There are degrees of visual impairment just as there are degrees of hearing impairment. The greater the visual loss, the more significant impact the loss will have on educational, social, and physical abilities. For example, students with residual vision can be assimilated into

Differentiating Elementary Instruction

PHYSICAL ACTIVITY OF CHILDREN WITH VISUAL IMPAIRMENTS

Research shows that individuals with visual impairments become less physically active with age. Physical activity among all individuals is linked to a variety of good physical and mental health. Ayvazoglu and colleagues (2006) identified the following ways to increase physical health among children with visual impairments:

- Promote peer involvement in physical activity.
- Ensure safety provisions are in place for family members.
- Provide children with visual impairments with the necessary skills to engage in physical activities.

- Involve family members in the physical activities of children.
- Provide school programs that are supportive of home activities.
- Focus school programs on fitness as well as recreational activities.

Source: "Explaining Physical Activity in Children with Visual Impairments: A Family Systems Approach," by N. R. Ayvazoglu, Hyun-Kyoung Oh, and Francis M. Kozub, 2006, *Exceptional Children, 72*, pp. 235–248.

■ CHARACTERISTICS AND IMPLICATIONS: VISUAL IMPAIRMENTS ■

AREA	POTENTIAL DIFFICULTIES	EDUCATIONAL IMPLICATIONS
Attention	Initial attention to directions/information Problems with visual attention Attention span (length of time on task) Focus (inhibition of distracting stimuli) Selective attention (discrimination of important stimulus characteristics)	Provide auditory cues that indicate important information is going to be provided. Provide oral information in short amounts. Provide information, such as directions and important information, in auditory format. Provide directions on tape recorder.
Memory	Problems with visual memory Problems with concept development	Stress meaningful content. Provide strategies instruction. Use multisensory presentation of information, primarily auditory and tactile.
Oral Communication Problems	Relatively unimpaired	None
Intellectual abilities	Relatively normal	None
Language Development	Difficulty with receptive and expressive language Delayed acquisition of vocabulary and language rules Limited visual cues related to language development	Create environment that encourages verbal communication. Encourage expression of thoughts. Provide appropriate language models. Provide opportunities for students to learn language for varied purposes and with different audiences.
Academic Deficiencies	Delayed acquisition of reading, writing, and mathematical skills Decoding of text Reading comprehension Math computation Problem-solving in mathematics Self-directed expressive writing	Use learning strategies to promote effective studying. Teach strategies for decoding unknown words for students with residual vision. Provide strategies to promote reading comprehension and math problem solving. Develop functional writing skills. Adapt curriculum to promote success. Encourage and support independent reading. Encourage shared reading and writing. Teachers must use effective communication skills. Teach Braille for students without residual vision. Use technology aids.
Social-Behavioral Interactions	Repetitive, stereotypical behaviors Social immaturity Withdrawn Unable to use nonverbal cues Peer acceptance	Promote social competence through direct instruction of skills. Reinforce appropriate behaviors. Seek self-understanding of reasons for inappropriate behavior. Teach self-management, self-control. Develop peer social support systems.
Orientation and Mobility Problems	Difficulty using spatial information Difficulty moving from one place to another	Provide orientation to classroom and building. Re-orient student when physical layout changes.

Differentiating Secondary Instruction

Students with visual and hearing impairments frequently display problems in their social skills. Therefore, teachers must incorporate social skills training in their daily lessons. Burden and Byrd (2006) give an example of how an inquiry problem-solving activity can help students improve their social skills. Steps in this process include:

Step 1: Students are presented with a problem that is important to them. The problem needs to be authentic and something that would motivate students to develop solutions.

Step 2: Students describe the problem and what prevents an easy solution to the problem.

Step 3: Students identify possible solutions to the problem. This could result from a group discussion into possible solutions to the problem.

Step 4: Students try solutions to the problem and gather information to determine the effectiveness of the solutions.

Step 5: Students analyze the results of their solutions and make a report about the problem-solving process.

Using an inquiry problem-solving model requires students to work together to find solutions. This required activity results in the development and improvement of social skills. Students with hearing and visual impairments may need accommodations throughout the process, but the end result will be the improvement of social skills.

most academic settings and tasks with limited supports whereas students with limited or no residual vision, similar to students who are classified as deaf, create major challenges for general classroom teachers. Some of these students will need to communicate through the use of Braille. For this group of students, educational consultants who provide support to the student and general classroom teacher may be needed.

Students with significant visual difficulties may also need supports in orientation and mobility. Orientation and mobility instructors are frequently available to consult with general classroom teachers and provide direct instruction to students with severe visual problems. Learning to travel from one point to another, something individuals without visual problems take for granted, can be a major challenge for this group of students.

Perspectives on Outcomes

Students with visual impairments receive a high-school diploma at a much lower rate than do students without disabilities. During the 2007–2008 school year, out of a total of 2,422 students, only 1,173 students with visual impairments, aged 14 to 21, received a high-school diploma. Another 32 students received a certificate. In other words, fewer than 50% of this group of students received a diploma or certificate (28th Annual Report to Congress on the Implementation of the Individuals with Disabilities Education Act, 2009). The fact that more than 25% of this group of students leaves school without a diploma has a negative impact on their ability to work successfully, assimilate into the community, and live independently.

Special Considerations

As noted, the key consideration for teaching students with visual impairment is their level of residual vision. Students who can read print are significantly easier to integrate into a general classroom than those who must process information using other formats. The majority of students with visual impairments have functional residual vision. Therefore, a key component of the educational intervention program is to provide supports to encourage and facilitate students' use of their residual vision. Magnification devices, technological supports, and other aids can greatly enhance visual images, making it more likely that this group of students can be successful in general education classrooms.

For students with more severe disabilities, Braille, or some other alternative communication system, along with orientation and mobility supports, are critical. This group of students needs substantially more support efforts than those with milder forms of visual impairment. That said, students with visual impairments are generally capable of content mastery; the key is providing accessible inputs.

EFFECTIVE INCLUSIVE PRACTICES FOR STUDENTS WITH VISUAL IMPAIRMENTS

Students with visual impairments can be successfully educated in general classroom settings. (See the nearby Rights and Responsibilities feature.) Those who are capable of reading print, with modifications, often require minimal curricular changes; those who must read using Braille require significant changes. For students who can read print, teachers must still make modifications in many day-to-day activities and in how they provide instruction in reading (Parker & Pogrund, 2009). These accommodations may be as simple as ensuring appropriate contrast in printed materials and having students sit in a place that will optimize their vision, or they could require extensive changes in teaching methods.

In order to meet the needs of students with visual impairments, collaboration with a vision specialist may be necessary, particularly when students present significant learning challenges (Corn, 2007). Examples of specialists and their roles include:

- Vision specialists to work with students on specific skills, such as Braille;
- Orientation and mobility instructors to teach students how to travel independently;
- Adaptive physical education instructor to help modify physical activities for the student with visual impairment.

Regardless of the support of professionals collaborating in the educational program for a particular child, it is always best if the individual who plans the interventions is the one who carries it out (Holbrook, 2008). Trying to implement IEP goals and objectives without having input in their development can present significant challenges.

Because many students with visual impairments need one-on-one instruction in some subject areas, the use of paraprofessionals can be extremely helpful. Unfortunately, many general classroom teachers and special education teachers do not know how to best utilize paraprofessionals in the delivery of instruction. Lewis and McKenzie (2009) suggest a number of competencies needed by teachers when supervising paraprofessionals who provide instruction to students with visual impairments. These include:

- Communication skills
- Planning and support

RIGHTS & RESPONSIBILITIES

ACCESS TO INSTRUCTIONAL MATERIALS

IDEA 2004 adds language related to access to instructional materials. IDEA 1997 did not refer to this topic. Section 612(a)(23) of IDEA 2004 states:

1. States must adopt the National Instructional Materials Accessibility Standard (NIMAS) to provide instructional materials to blind persons or those with disabilities in relation to print.
2. States do not have to coordinate with the National Instructional Materials Access Center (NIMAC), but must assure that they will provide materials to blind or print-disabled individuals in a timely manner.
3. If state coordinates with NIMAC, no later than two years after enactment of IDEA 2004 the state must contract with publishers to provide electronic files of print instructional materials to NIMAC using the NIMAS or must buy materials in specialized formats.

IEP GOALS AND OBJECTIVES FOR AMANDA

Goals and objectives for Amanda, whom you met in the introductory vignette, might include the following. IDEA 2004 does not require objectives. Objectives are provided here to give examples of how interventions might be directed toward goals:

GOAL 1   To improve literacy skills, including reading and writing.

Objective 1: Amanda will improve her reading level by 1.5 grade levels by the end of the year.

Objective 2: Amanda will improve her written expression skills by 1.5 grade levels by the end of the year.

Objective 3: Amanda will improve her comprehension skills by 1.5 grade levels by the end of the year.

GOAL 2   To develop better social skills.

Objective 1: Amanda will interact with peers during recess at least 50% of the time.

Objective 2: Amanda will initiate conversations with peers at least 50% of the time during classroom communication time.

Objective 3: Amanda will be selected by three peers as part of a group often for different social activities at least once each week.

- Modeling
- Public relations
- Training
- Management of paraeducators

Counselors, school health personnel, and vocational specialists may also provide support services for general education teachers. Also, school personnel should never forget to include parents in helping develop and implement educational supports for students with visual impairments.

CLASSROOM ADAPTATIONS FOR STUDENTS WITH VISUAL IMPAIRMENTS

Certain classroom accommodations will enhance the quality of programs for students with visual problems. The following sections recommend ways to address the needs of these students, organized according to general considerations, curricular and instructional accommodations, and social-emotional interventions.

General Considerations

As with all students with disabilities, the unique needs of students with visual impairments must be considered when developing and implementing programs (Desrochers, 1999). The nature of their disability has a significant impact on how instruction should be provided; however, some general practices apply for most, if not all, students with these problems (Parker & Pogrund, 2009). These practices include:

- Ask the student if assistance is needed.
- Do not assume that certain tasks and activities cannot be accomplished without accommodations or modifications.
- Include students with visual impairments in all activities that occur in the class.
- Use seating arrangements to take advantage of any vision the child can use.
- Encourage the use of residual vision.

Remember that many characteristics of students with visual impairments (i.e., intelligence, health) may not be negatively affected by the vision problem.

The physical layout of the classroom can be a major consideration in providing inclusive educational opportunities for students with visual impairments. In order for students to navigate successfully in the classroom and building, they need to have an understanding of the physical layout of the building and classroom. Teachers need to orient these students to the classroom and building by taking them around these spaces and noting certain features, such as the location of desks, tables, doorways, stairs, and materials. A clock orientation approach is a useful means for this orientation. If the classroom arrangement is changed, a reorientation should occur.

Appropriate seating is extremely important for this group of students, especially those who are able to use their existing vision. Placement of the student's desk, lighting, glare, and distractions should be considered in situating such students in the classroom. Teachers should plan ahead to adapt instruction to the needs of students with visual impairments. Class schedules must allow extra time for students who use large-print or Braille materials, as it takes longer to use these materials. Test-taking procedures may need to be modified. Modifications might involve preparing an enlarged version of the test, allowing extra time, or arranging for someone to read the test to the student.

■ Classmates can assist students with visual problems in areas such as mobility.

Study skills instruction in areas such as note taking, organizational skills, time management, and keyboarding may be an important intervention for some students. These skills become increasingly important as students move to middle school and high school. The following are some specific accommodation suggestions:

- Assign a classmate to assist students who may need help with mobility in emergency situations.
- Teach all students in the class the proper techniques of being a sighted guide.
- In advance, inform staff members at field-trip sites that a student with a visual problem will be part of the visiting group.
- Tell students with visual problems that you are entering or leaving a room so that they are aware of your presence or absence.
- Have all students practice movement patterns that you expect of them, to maintain an orderly classroom.
- Orient students to the physical layout and other distinguishing features of the classroom.
- Maintain consistency in the placement of furniture, equipment, and instructional materials—remove all dangerous obstacles.
- Keep doors to cabinets, carts, and closets closed.
- Assist students in getting into unfamiliar desks, chairs, or other furniture.
- Eliminate auditory distractions.
- Seat students to maximize their usable vision and listening skills—often a position in the front and center part of the room is advantageous.
- Seat students so that they are not looking into a source of light or bothered by glare from reflected surfaces.
- Ensure that proper lighting is available.
- Create extra space for students who must use and store a piece of equipment (e.g., Brailler, notebook computer).
- As a special section of the lesson plan, include notes for accommodating students with visual problems.

Curricular and Instructional Considerations

One of the biggest instructional challenges for teachers is how to convey primarily visual material to students with limited vision. Educators need to be creative in making visual material understandable for students who have limited visual abilities. As a result of the wide array of curricular options for these students, teachers must decide what to teach as they consider different skills possessed by students and the amount of time available for instruction.

Teachers who are successful teaching students with visual impairments need to possess certain characteristics. Holbrook (2008) identified the following characteristics as important for providing reading instruction to this group of students. Many of the characteristics would apply when teaching any subjects.

- Creativity, flexibility, and other characteristics of good teachers
- Ability to teach subject matter
- Understanding and knowledge about what is being taught
- Understanding and knowledge about the impact of the visual limitations of the student on learning the content

Materials and Equipment   Special materials and equipment can enhance the education of students who have visual impairments. Some materials (e.g., large-print materials) are not appropriate for all and must be considered in light of individual needs. Vision specialists can help teachers select appropriate materials and equipment.

For students who need to learn how to use tactile strategies, teachers may need to adapt materials to a tactile format. Some considerations for developing tactile adaptations include (Downing & Chen, 2003):

1. Identify the objective of the lesson or the instructional concept.
2. Select the materials to convey this concept.
3. Close your eyes and examine the material with your hands.
4. Take a tactile perspective, not visual, when deciding how and what to present.
5. If the entire concept (e.g., house) is too complicated to represent through a tactile adaptation, then select one aspect of the concept (e.g., key) for the tactile representation.
6. Consider the student's previous tactile experiences. What items has he or she examined? How does the student examine materials through the sense of touch?
7. Decide how the item will be introduced to the student.
8. Identify what supports the student needs to tactilely examine the item.
9. Decide what language input (descriptive words) will be used to convey the student's experience of the material. (p. 59)

Some of the materials used in general education classrooms may pose difficulties for students with vision problems because of the size and contrast of print materials. Print size can generally be taken care of with magnification devices or even font sizes; however, little can be done to enhance the poor contrast often found on photocopies. Consider these points when using photocopies:

- Avoid using both sides of the paper (ink often bleeds through, making it difficult to see either side).
- Avoid old or light worksheet masters.
- Avoid worksheet masters with missing parts or creases.
- Give the darkest copies of handouts to students with visual problems.
- Do not give a student with a visual impairment a poor copy and say, "Do the best you can with this."
- Copy over lines that are light with a dark marker.
- Make new originals when photocopies become difficult to read.
- Avoid the use of colored inks that may produce limited contrast.
- Do not use colored paper—it limits contrast.

Concrete materials may also be helpful for teachers. However, teachers need to remember that concrete representations of large, real-life objects may not be helpful for young students, who may not understand the abstract notion of one thing representing another. Teachers must carefully ensure that all instructional materials for students with visual impairments are presented in the appropriate medium for the particular student (Corn et al., 1995).

Various optical, nonoptical, and electronic devices are also available for classroom use. These devices help students by enlarging existing printed images. If these devices are recommended for certain students, teachers will need to learn about them to ensure that they are used properly and to recognize when there is a problem. Teachers should practice the use of optical and electronic devices with students after consultation with a vision specialist.

Some students with more severe visual limitations use Braille as their primary means of working with written material. They may use instructional materials that are printed in Braille and may also take notes using it. Through the use of computers, a student can write in Braille and have the text converted to standard print. The reverse process is available as well. If a student uses this system of communication, the teacher should consult with a vision specialist to understand how it works.

Following are some specific accommodation suggestions:

- Call students by name, and speak directly to them.
- Take breaks at regular intervals to minimize fatigue in listening of using a Brailler or optical device.
- Ensure that students are seated properly so that they can see you (if they have vision) and hear you clearly.
- Vary the type of instruction used, and include lessons that incorporate hands-on activities, cooperative learning, or the use of real-life materials.
- Use high-contrast materials, whether on paper or on the chalkboard—dry-erase boards might be preferable.
- Avoid using materials with glossy surfaces and, if possible, dittoed material.
- Use large-print materials only after other methods have been attempted and proved unsuccessful.
- Use environmental connectors (e.g., ropes or railing) and other adaptations for students with visual problems for physical education or recreational activities (Barraga & Erin, 1992).
- Avoid using written materials with pages that are too crowded.

Social-Emotional Considerations

Although the literature is mixed on whether students with visual impairments are less well-adjusted than their sighted peers (Hallahan & Kauffman, 2010), there is evidence that some students with this disability experience social isolation (Huurre, Komulainen, & Aro, 1999). As a result, many students with visual problems will benefit from attention to their social and emotional development. Social skill instruction may be particularly useful (Sacks, Wolffe, & Tierney, 1998). However, because social skills are typically learned through observing others and imitating their behaviors, it is difficult to teach these skills to students who are not able to see.

Concern about emotional development is warranted for all students, including those with visual problems. Teachers should make sure that students know that they are available to talk about a student's concerns. A system can be developed whereby a student who has a visual impairment can signal the need to chat with the teacher. It is extremely important that teachers are accessible and let students know that someone is concerned about their social and emotional needs..

The following are some specific accommodation suggestions:

- Encourage students with visual problems to become independent learners and to manage their own behaviors.
- Create opportunities for students to use tactile learning (Downing & Chen, 2003).
- Reinforce students for their efforts.
- Help students develop a healthy self-concept.
- Provide special instruction to help students acquire social skills needed to perform appropriately in classroom and social situations.
- Teach students how to communicate nonverbally (e.g., use of hands, etc.).
- Work with students to eliminate inappropriate mannerisms that some students with visual impairments display.

Universal Design for Learning

Students with visual impairments, like those with hearing impairments, need to be part of the school community. Many can be included without special supports. However, for others teachers may need to consider the following (Amerson, 1999; Desrochers, 1999; Torres & Corn, 1990):

- Remember that the student with a visual impairment is but one of many students in the classroom with individual needs and characteristics.
- Use words such as *see, look*, and *watch* naturally.
- Introduce students with visual impairments the same way you would introduce any other student.
- Include students with visual impairments in all classroom activities, including physical education, home economics, and so on.
- Encourage students with visual problems to seek leadership and high-visibility roles in the classroom.
- Use the same disciplinary procedures for all students.
- Encourage students with visual problems to move about the room just like other students.
- Use verbal cues as often as necessary to cue the student with a visual impairment about something that is happening.
- Provide additional space for students with visual impairments to store materials.
- Allow students with visual impairments to learn about and discuss with other classmates special topics related to visual loss.
- Model acceptance of visually impaired students as an example to other students.
- Encourage students with visual impairments to use their specialized equipment, such as a Braille writer.
- Discuss special needs of the child with a visual impairment with specialists, as necessary.
- Always tell a person with a visual impairment who you are as you approach.
- Expect the same level of work from students with visual impairments as you do from other students.
- Encourage students with visual impairments to be as independent as possible.
- Provide physical supports for students with concomitant motor problems.

In your efforts to promote a sense of community, consider that some students with visual impairments may have different cultural backgrounds than the majority of students in the school. School personnel must be sensitive to different cultural patterns. Bau (1999) noted seven cultural values that could have an impact on the provision of services to students with visual impairments: communication, health beliefs, family structure, attitude toward authority, etiquette, expectations of helping, and time orientation. To communicate clearly with a family that speaks a different language, you may need to use a language interpreter. Being sensitive to the culture and family background of students with visual impairments facilitates the delivery of appropriate services.

Other Instructional Adaptations

Like students with hearing impairments, those with visual problems often use technological devices to assist them in their academic work and daily living skills. Low-vision aids include magnifiers, closed-circuit televisions, and monoculars. These devices enlarge print and other materials for individuals with visual impairments and take advantage of environmental cues, color and contrast, illumination, and space. Since the early 1960s there has been a significant increase in technology that can be used to support individuals with low vision (Griffin et al., 2002). Unfortunately, many students with visual impairments who could benefit from assistive technology do not have access to it. Kelly (2009) found that only 29 to 41% of students with visual impairments who would most likely benefit from the use of assistive technology were actually using it. This is an unfortunate finding. Schools that make this technology available to students are providing a supportive school environment (Kelly, 2009).

PERSONAL SPOTLIGHT

BONNIE LAWRENCE has been an orientation and mobility specialist for students with visual impairments for more than 20 years. During this time she has seen the number of students with visual impairments served in general education classrooms increase dramatically. "When I first started providing orientation and mobility services, most school districts did not have any students who were visually impaired." As a result of the limited numbers of students, Bonnie had to travel great distances to provide services for students who did receive services in local school districts. Also, many of the students served in these districts were not totally blind but had various degrees of residual vision.

Over the past few years, the population of students with visual impairments has changed dramatically. More students with visual impairments than ever before are placed in their local school districts. General classroom teachers are becoming responsible for more of these students' educational programs, and more of these students are exhibiting significant vision loss. The result is that schools need the services of itinerant specialists more than ever. "I never thought I would see the day when so many students with visual impairments were placed in public school programs. Now it's simply the way it is most of the time." For the most part, Bonnie believes the inclusion of these students work well. She noted that there are some teachers who still believe that these students do not belong in their local schools; however, she says that this is not as likely now as before and that most of these students are accepted and well received by their teachers and peers. To sum of her feelings about the increased inclusion of students with visual impairments, Bonnie only says, "it is a very, very good thing."

Many other technological devices are used by students with visual impairments. While access to the Internet is relatively easy for students without visual problems, many students with visual impairments may have difficulty. Certain technological devices can make access to the Internet available. Braille printers and speech input/output devices can help achieve access. Access and computer training can give students with visual impairments a vast resource that can have a profound positive impact on their education (Heinrich, 1999).

One area of technology for individuals with visual impairments is electronic mobility aids. Individuals with visual impairments are 10 times more likely to use the white cane than a dog guide; however, the white cane is not an adequate mobility device if the individual using it lacks extensive training with an orientation and mobility specialist. Electronic mobility devices were first developed after World War II; devices became commercially available in the 1960s. Roentgen, Gelderblom, Soede, and de Witte (2008) identified 146 different systems, products, and devices that could be classified as electronic mobility aids. These include devices that classified as obstacle detection and orientation as well as others that are simply used as navigation aids (Roentgen et al., 2008). Individuals who are adequately trained in the use of these types of aids have a definite advantage over others who do not have such devices.

SUMMARY

Overview of Sensory Impairments

- Many students with sensory deficits are educated in general education classrooms.
- For students with sensory impairments to receive an appropriate education, various accommodations must be made.
- Students with hearing and visual problems represent a very heterogeneous group.

Basic Concepts of Hearing Impairments

- Most students with hearing impairments can function in general education settings.
- Hearing impairment includes deaf and hard of hearing.

- Most students with hearing impairments have some residual hearing.
- Hearing levels are measured in decibels.

Characteristics of Students with Hearing Impairments

- Characteristics of students with hearing impairments vary greatly.
- Students with severe hearing impairments present significant challenges for teachers.
- Language problems present the most significant challenge for students with hearing impairments.

Effective Inclusive Practices for Students with Hearing Impairments

- The effect of a hearing loss on a student's ability to understand speech is a primary concern of teachers.
- An audiometric evaluation helps to determine the extent of a hearing disorder.
- Several factors should alert teachers to a possible hearing loss in a particular student.

Classroom Adaptations for Students with Hearing Impairments

- Teachers in general education classrooms must implement a variety of accommodations for students with hearing impairments.
- The seating location of a student with hearing loss is critical for effective instruction.
- Specialized equipment, such as hearing aids, may be necessary to ensure the success of students with hearing losses.
- The most challenging aspect of teaching students with hearing problems is making sure that they participate in the communicational activities that occur in the classroom.
- Teachers need to encourage interaction between students with hearing impairments and their nondisabled classmates (e.g., grouping, assigning buddies).

Basic Concepts about Visual Impairment

- Vision plays a critical role in the development of concepts such as understanding the spatial relations of the environment.
- Teachers must use a variety of accommodations for students with visual disabilities.
- Most students with visual disabilities have residual or low vision.
- Refractive errors are the most common form of visual disability.
- Visual problems may be congenital or occur later in life.

Characteristics of Students with Visual Impairments

- Students with low vision are easier to accommodate than students classified as being blind.
- Students with visual impairments present a wide variety of characteristics.
- Social skills are often a weakness for students with visual impairments.
- For students needing Braille instruction, special support teachers should be available.

Effective Inclusive Practices for Students with Visual Impairments

- The most educationally relevant characteristic of students who have visual impairments is the extent of their visual efficiency.
- Special materials may be needed when working with students with visual problems.
- Using large-print and nonglare materials may be sufficient accommodation for many students with visual disabilities.
- Provide ample storage space for students' materials.
- Allow students additional time—it takes more time to read Braille and large-print materials.

Classroom Adaptations for Students with Visual Impairments

- A very small number of students require instruction in Braille.
- Specialists to teach Braille and develop Braille materials may be needed to successfully place students with visual disabilities in general education classrooms.
- Academic tests may need to be adapted when evaluating students with visual disabilities.
- Facilitate all technology needed by students.

myeducationlab

The MyEducationLab for this course can help you solidify your comprehension of Chapter 10 concepts.

- Gauge and further develop your understanding of chapter concepts by taking the quizzes and examining the enrichment materials on the Chapter 10 Study Plan.
- Visit Topic 20, Sensory Impairments, to:
  - Connect with challenge-based interactive modules, case study units, and podcasts that provide research-validated information about working with students in inclusive settings by visiting the IRIS Center Resources
  - Explore Assignments and Activities, assignable exercises showing concepts in action through video, cases, and student and teacher artifacts
  - Practice and strengthen skills essential to quality teaching through the Building Teaching Skills and Dispositions lessons

11

Teaching Students with Low-Incidence Disabilities

CHAPTER OBJECTIVES

After reading this chapter, you should be able to:

1. Define and describe low-incidence disabilities.
2. Define and describe students with other health impairments.
3. Define and describe students with physical impairments.
4. Define and describe students with traumatic brain injury.
5. Describe the role of general classroom teachers when they are working with students with low-incidence disabilities.

FRANK was a very bright, precocious 6-year-old first-grader. He was reading and doing math above grade level and was socially very mature. He was one of the most popular students in Ms. Bond's classroom. Over the Christmas holidays, Frank fell out of a tree where he and some friends were playing. He was rushed to the emergency room unconscious. He remained hospitalized for 3 weeks, diagnosed with a closed head injury. Frank was then moved to a residential rehabilitation facility for children with head injuries. He remained in the rehabilitation hospital until April when he was released to home.

Frank's parents and the school agreed that he should repeat first grade because he was having some lingering effects from his head injury. He exhibited problems with memory, had occasional behavior outbursts, did not get along well with his peers, and had lost many of the academic skills he had developed during first grade. Ms. Bond would be his teacher again, since she knew him from the previous year. When school started, Frank was somewhat apprehensive about going. He had difficulty paying attention, displayed some hyperactive behaviors,

and had problems with short-term memory skills. His social skills were very immature and he did not have any friends. After 6 weeks, Ms. Bond referred him for special education. After a comprehensive evaluation, Frank was determined eligible for special education services under the category of traumatic brain injury.

QUESTIONS TO CONSIDER

1. What kind of special skills does Frank's first-grade classroom teacher need to meet Frank's educational and social needs?
2. What are Frank's major problems that need to be addressed if he is to make progress during the first grade and be prepared for promotion to second grade?
3. What can Frank's teacher do to help him improve his social skills?
4. What academic skills are critical for Frank to have for him to be successful in higher grades?

LOW-INCIDENCE DISABILITIES

Many health and physical disabilities present in children result in a need for special education and related services. Similar to sensory impairments, these disabilities are significantly less prevalent than disabilities such as learning disabilities and intellectual disabilities. As a result, they are considered *low-incidence disabilities*. Although teachers are less likely to have a student with one of these disabilities, only one or two of these children in a classroom can present major challenges for teachers due to their unique needs.

Two of the major categories identified under IDEA that fall into the low-incidence grouping are *other health impaired* and *orthopedically impaired*. These two categories serve as umbrella terms for myriad conditions, such as childhood cancer, asthma, and cerebral palsy. Traumatic brain injury is also considered a low-incidence disability. Teachers who

Visit the MyEducationLab for this course to enhance your understanding of chapter concepts with a personalized Study Plan. You'll also have the opportunity to hone your teaching skills through video-based Assignments and Activities, IRIS Center Resources, and Building Teaching Skills and Disposition lessons.

Differentiating Elementary Instruction

INCREASING PEER INTERACTIONS FOR STUDENTS WITH LOW-INCIDENCE DISABILITIES VIA TRAINING FOR PARAPROFESSIONALS

Peer interactions among individuals with disabilities and their nondisabled peers can be increased by training paraprofessionals to facilitate such interactions. Four topics in the training activities include:

1. Enhance paraprofessionals' perspective of their social interactions. Paraprofessionals should complete a worksheet to reflect their own social relationships and that of the students they work with.
2. Establish the importance of peer interactions. The importance of peer interactions should be discussed with paraprofessionals.

3. Clarify the paraprofessional's role in facilitating interactions. Discussions about how paraprofessionals could facilitate interactions can help them understand their important role in facilitating such interactions.
4. Increase paraprofessionals' knowledge base. Specific strategies for enhancing interactions should be presented and discussed. Examples of such strategies should be provided.

Source: From "Increasing Peer Interactions for Students with Severe Disabilities via Training for Paraprofessionals," J. N. Causton-Theoharis and K. W. Malmgren, 2005, *Exceptional Children, 71,* pp. 431–444.

work with children with these conditions often need the assistance of specialists when implementing appropriate programs because of the unique needs these disabilities present. General classroom teachers are generally often not equipped to address the needs of many of these students without the assistance of other professionals.

Because of the specialized nature of many of the problems exhibited by students with low-incidence disabilities, schools and state education agencies frequently provide support personnel for teachers and students to help address the needs of these students. Behavioral specialists, psychologists, physical therapists, occupational therapists, nurses, and other health personnel are often available to provide services to students and support for their

PERSONAL SPOTLIGHT

DIFFERENTIATED INSTRUCTION: NOT JUST FOR GIFTED STUDENTS

JANIE ELDRIDGE is an itinerant teacher for children who are gifted and talented. Her primary duties include identifying students for the program and supporting teachers to develop and implement appropriate programs for their students. Janie is a firm believer in differentiated instruction. In fact, she supports using differentiated instruction for all students, ranging from gifted to intellectually disabled. Because many students with health and physical impairments are placed in general classrooms, and most are intellectually capable of achieving academic success in these classrooms, Janie believes that using differentiated instruction with this group of students would be ideal. "I think differentiated instruction would work extremely well with students with cerebral palsy, spina bifida, asthma, cystic fibrosis, and any other physical or health prob-

lems because teachers simply need to differentiate how they teach this group of students. They can definitely learn; teachers must teach them differently."

Janie notes that while differentiated instruction works with all students, it would be very easy to implement with students who have health and physical problems because they would need minimal differences from the majority of their peers. "Unfortunately," notes Janie, "too many teachers think that differentiated instruction is for gifted students. It's not! It is for all students and the sooner teachers begin to adapt differentiated instruction techniques, the sooner all students will be successful in regular classrooms." Janie is a strong advocate for all students, and she really means *all students.* She sees differentiated instruction as the very best way to support all students together in inclusive classrooms, not just students classified as gifted and talented.

■ CHARACTERISTICS AND IMPLICATIONS: LOW-INCIDENCE DISABILITIES ■

DISABILITY	POTENTIAL DIFFICULTIES	EDUCATIONAL IMPLICATIONS
Traumatic Brain Injury	Attention problems Emotional lability Aggressiveness Physical limitations Speech and language deficits Slower to respond/react	Use attention-focusing strategies. Implement behavior management planning. Provide physical access. Provide speech-language supports. Use task analysis to break down assignment. Provide extra time. Implement social skills training. Teach self-determination skills.
Orthopedic Impairments	Physical access problems Physical limitations Social skill problems	Provide physical access. Provide accommodations for physical limitations. Collaborate with related services personnel and family. Implement social skills training. Teach self-determination skills. Utilize available technology.
Other Health Impairments	Health-related issues Social skill problems	Collaborate with health professionals and family. Ensure universal precautions. Teach self-determination skills.
Severe Intellectual Disabilities	Difficulty with all academic tasks Social skills deficits	Implement functional curriculum. Focus on needed, daily living skills. Teach self-determination skills. Implement social skills training. Utilize task analysis. Provide frequent reinforcement.

teachers (Wadsworth & Knight, 1999). Without their involvement many students would not receive appropriate educational and support services and might not be able to receive educational opportunities in inclusive settings.

Teachers should also work hard on getting peers involved in educational programs for these students. Students with low-incidence disabilities are typically placed in general classroom settings because, academically, they are capable of achieving success. However, they will likely have social skills deficits and may need peer support to enhance their social skills. See the Differentiated Instruction—Elementary boxed reading, which focuses on how to increase peer involvement with students who experience low-incidence disabilities.

Regardless of the specialized needs of students with low-incidence disabilities, most with health and physical problems are very capable of achieving in inclusive classrooms. See the Personal Spotlight, which supports the use of differentiated instruction with students who have low-incidence disabilities. See the nearby characteristics and implications feature for low-incidence disabilities.

OTHER HEALTH IMPAIRMENTS

The category of *other health impairments* is similar to *orthopedic impairments* in that it is an umbrella group of conditions. IDEA 2004 defines other health impairments as "having limited strength, vitality or alertness, due to chronic or acute health problems such as a heart condition, tuberculosis, rheumatic fever, nephritis, asthma, sickle cell anemia, hemophilia, epilepsy, lead poisoning, leukemia, or diabetes that adversely affects a child's educational performance" (300.7(b)(8)). In 2006–2007, schools served 611,000 students as other health impaired (National Center for Education Statistics, 2008).

The primary role of educators when dealing with students with other health impairments is to support health professionals and parents and provide accommodations needed as a result of the health problems. Physicians and other healthcare professionals typically provide the primary interventions for many of these students. Educators must develop a thorough understanding of these conditions so they will be able to provide any necessary supports the student may need. For example, although teachers and other educators do not provide direct, health-related services to students with diabetes, they do need to understand the condition and the resulting needs of the student with diabetes. From time to time there may be situations that can result in life-threatening situations for students with some of these disorders. Teachers have to understand these conditions and know specific interventions that can be critical to provide. For example, if a student with epilepsy has a gran mal seizure, teachers and other school personnel need to know what actions they should take to minimize any dangers to the students.

Asthma

Of the approximately 20 million individuals affected by asthma in the United States, 9 million are children (National Institutes of Health, 2010). Asthma is the most common chronic illness in children—the rate of asthma in children is one in 13 and increasing (Managing Asthma in the School Environment, 2005). Hospitalizations due to asthma have increased about 30% over the past 20 years, and each year approximately 5,000 individuals die from asthma (MedicineNet.com, 2010). In addition, asthma is the leading cause of school absenteeism (U.S. Department of Education, 2003).

Asthma is the result of the body's antibodies reacting to antigens and causing swelling, mucus secretion, and muscle tightening in the lungs (Best, 2006). This can cause repetitive episodes of coughing, shortness of breath, and wheezing. There are numerous substances that can trigger an asthma episode, including dust, cigarette smoke, mold, dust mites, and animal dander. While some asthma is mild and can be controlled by simply inhaling medication, severe attacks can be very dangerous and should be taken seriously by school personnel. A severe asthmatic attack can result in death.

The best way to deal with asthma is to prevent an asthma episode. This means that school personnel should focus on taking actions to minimize asthma triggers. These include (1) controlling animal allergens, (2) cleaning up mold and controlling moisture, (3) controlling cockroach and pest allergens, (4) eliminating secondhand smoke exposure, and (5) reducing exposure to dust mites (Managing Asthma, 2005). The U.S. Department of Education (2003) published a handbook for schools on how to manage asthma. Suggestions for the classroom teacher include:

- Consult with principal and school nurse for policies and procedures for dealing with students who have chronic health problems, such as asthma.
- Understand your role in implementing a student's asthma action plan, including knowing when to seek medical assistance for children.
- Develop and implement a procedure for students to complete missed school work.
- Monitor students to ensure that their asthma is not interfering with school work; report such events to parents and school health professionals.
- Inform school administrators, nurses, and parents if student's behavior or academic performance changes.
- Encourage students to participate in physical activities and field trips.
- Be aware of signs of uncontrolled asthma.
- Inform school nurse in situations where asthma is not controlled properly.
- Understand asthma triggers and attempt to minimize them in the classroom.
- Understand warning signs of an asthma episode and what actions should be taken.

Schools should be proactive in dealing with asthma. As such, they need to know whether or not their school is prepared to deal with students with asthma. The National Heart, Lung, and Blood Institute (1998) recommends that schools ask the following questions to determine their readiness to deal with asthma:

1. Is the school free of tobacco smoke all of the time, including during school-sponsored events?
2. Does the school maintain good indoor air quality?
3. Is a school nurse in the school all day, every day?
4. Can children take medicines at school as recommended by their doctor and parents?
5. Does the school have an emergency plan for taking care of a child with a severe asthma attack?
6. Does someone teach school staff about asthma, asthma management plans, and asthma medicines?
7. Do students with asthma have good options for fully and safely participating in physical education class and recess? (p. 168)

Childhood Cancer

Childhood cancer occurs in approximately 1 in 330 children before the age of 19 years, affecting more than 12,500 children and adolescents every year (American Cancer Society, 2002; National Childhood Cancer Foundation, 2003). Childhood cancer can take several different forms. The most common forms of cancer in children are leukemia, brain cancer, and tumors of the central nervous system. These account for more than half of all childhood cancer. The most common form of childhood cancer is leukemia, affecting approximately one-third of all children who have childhood cancer (National Cancer Institute, 2010). Although the prevalence of cancer has increased over the past 20 years, the rate of cure has increased even more. The 5-year survival rate for all childhood cancers increased from 58.1% in 1975–1977 to 79.6% in 1996–2003 (National Cancer Institute, 2010). Treatment of cancer includes chemotherapy, radiation, surgery, and bone marrow transplantation.

■ Teachers who have students with cancer should learn about the child's illness from medical personnel.

Obviously, the primary treatment for children with cancer focuses on medical interventions. However, there are supports and interventions that schools should provide. The extent to which schools provide appropriate assistance to students with cancer depends on their understanding of the condition and the variety of supports that can be provided (Spinelli, 2004). Suggestions for teachers and administrators who have students with cancer include (American Cancer Society, 2010):

- Maintain communication between school and family.
- Encourage the student to attend classes when possible.
- Learn about the child's diagnosis.
- Learn about the treatment the child is receiving and any possible side effects to the treatment.
- Encourage the student to continue to complete school work.
- Provide supports and accommodations for the student.
- Determine if the child should receive IDEA or 504 supports.
- Understand that the student may display learning problems not displayed before the diagnosis.

In addition to these suggestions, teachers should also be prepared to deal with the long-term impact of the cancer and possible death of the student. While survival rates have improved dramatically, there are still many children who die annually from cancer. Being prepared, and having your other students prepared, could assist in the grieving process if the child dies as a result of the disease.

Cystic Fibrosis

Cystic fibrosis is an inherited, fatal disease that results in an abnormal amount of mucus throughout the body, most often affecting the lungs and digestive tract. This results in the blockage of air sacs in the lungs, causing air to be trapped in the lungs, which then overinflate and collapse (Best, 2006). Cystic fribrosis affects approximately 30,000 children and adults in the United States; 1,000 new cases are diagnosed each year (Cystic Fibrosis Foundation, 2010). Although life expectancy for children with cystic fibrosis at one time was only in the teens, the current median age of individuals with this condition is 37 years (Cystic Fibrosis Foundation, 2010).

As the disease progresses, it greatly affects stamina and the student's physical condition. While health professionals provide primary interventions and services to children with cystic fibrosis, teachers play a very important role in their support. One role for teachers is to make sure that these children take special medication before they eat. Children with cystic fibrosis take a great deal of medication. Here are some specific suggestions for dealing with students with this disease:

- Prepare students in class for the realities of this disease (e.g., coughing, noncontagious sputum, gas).
- Learn how to clear a student's lungs and air passages, as such assistance may be needed after certain activities.
- Know the medications a student must take and be able to administer them (e.g., enzymes, vitamins).
- Consider restricting certain physical activities.
- Inquire about the therapies being used with the student.
- Support the implementation of special diets if needed.
- Provide opportunities for students to talk about their concerns, fears, and feelings.
- Ensure that the student is included in all class activities to whatever extent is possible.
- Prepare students for the eventual outcome of the disease by discussing death and dying.

The primary therapy for individuals with cystic fibrosis focuses on clearing the airways of the excess mucus. Airway clearance techniques are used to clear the air passages. Some of these techniques require the assistance of a third person, such as a family member, friend, or teacher (Cystic Fibrosis Foundation, 2010). Many individuals with cystic fibrosis are undernourished. Therefore, nutrition becomes a very important factor in maintaining good health for this group of individuals. School personnel need to work as a team to ensure proper airway clearance technique strategies are available, as well as appropriate nutrition (Cystic Fibrosis Foundation, 2010).

Dual Sensory Impairment

CROSS-REFERENCE

Students with dual sensory impairments are also discussed briefly in Chapter 10.

Students who have visual impairments or auditory impairments create unique problems for educators. When students present deficits in both sensory areas, resulting in their having dual sensory impairment, their needs become extremely complex. Although the term *deaf-blind* continues to be found in federal legislation and regulations, including IDEA, the terms **dual sensory impairment** or **multiple sensory impairments** are considered more appropriate (Marchant, 1992). For purposes of being eligible for special education services under IDEA, deaf-blind is still the label for such students.

Students who are classified as being deaf-blind may have their primary impairment in either vision or hearing. They typically are blind or deaf with minimal impairment in the other sense, or they may have milder degrees of visual and auditory impairments that do not classify as blindness or deafness. The Helen Keller National Center estimates that about 94% of such individuals have some hearing or vision, which can be used to enhance their educational programs (Marchant, 1992). During the 2000–2001 school year, only 1,320 students nationwide were identified as being deaf-blind and served in special education programs (U.S. Department of Education, 2003).

Individuals classified as being deaf-blind are very heterogeneous. Their characteristics represent those exhibited by students who only have visual or hearing impairments, but have an overlap of these two disabilities. The result is significant educational needs. Obviously, when students are blind, but have good auditory skills, teachers can focus on teaching them using oral language. Likewise, students who are deaf but have good vision can be taught using visual strategies. Students deficient in both of the senses present major challenges to teachers. Wolfe (1997) suggests the following educational techniques for teachers to use when working with students classified as deaf-blind:

- Use an ecological approach to assessment and skill selection to emphasize functional needs of students.
- Use a variety of prompts, cues, and reinforcement strategies in a systematic instructional pattern.
- Use time-delay prompting, increasing the time between prompts.
- Use groups and cooperative learning strategies.
- Implement environmental adaptations, such as enlarging materials, using contrasting materials, altering seating arrangements, and reducing extraneous noises to maximize the residual hearing and vision of the student.

Diabetes

There are currently approximately 23.6 million children and adults, or 7.8% of the population, with diabetes in the United States. This includes nearly 200,000 children under the age of 20. In addition, approximately 2 million adolescents aged 12 to 19, or 1 in 6, are overweight and are considered pre-diabetic. In 2006 diabetes was listed as the seventh-leading cause of death in the United States. Individuals with diabetes are at risk for many other major health conditions, including blindness, high blood pressure, stroke, kidney disease, nervous system disease, and amputations (American Diabetes Association, 2010).

Diabetes is a metabolic disorder in which the pancreas cannot produce sufficient insulin to process food (American Diabetes Association, 2010). Many Americans suffer from **type II**, or **adult-onset**, diabetes. Individuals with this type of diabetes produce some insulin. The more serious form of diabetes, **type I**, or **insulin-dependent**, occurs in children; approximately one in every 400 to 600 people under the age of 20 have type I diabetes. Type I diabetes accounts for approximately 5 to 10% of all diabetes (Helping the Student, 2003). Individuals with type I diabetes do not produce any insulin and must therefore have insulin added to their bodies daily.

A primary role for teachers is to keep students with diabetes safe at school. This includes being alert to possible symptoms of diabetes for students who have not been diagnosed. Symptoms include increased thirst, appetite, and urination; weight loss; fatigue; and irritability. For children identified as having diabetes, teachers must monitor their diet and physical activity, and be aware of symptoms indicating that a child has too much or too little insulin. Figures 11.1 and 11.2 describes a quick reference plan for students with diabetes with too much insulin (hypoglycemia) and too little insulin (hyperglycemia), and actions that need to be taken in each situation. Children with type I diabetes must take daily injections of insulin or have an insulin pump. School personnel must have knowledge of the special dietary needs of these children and understand their need for a daily activity regimen.

Specific things that teachers should do when they have students with diabetes in their classroom include (Getch, Bhukhanwala, & Neuharth-Pritchett, 2007):

1. Attend diabetes education training programs.
2. Become familiar with student's healthcare plan for management of diabetes at school and school-sponsored events.
3. Become aware of how to handle emergency situations for individual students.
4. Be alert to recognize signs and symptoms of hypoglycemia and hyperglycemia.
5. Encourage the students with diabetes to participate fully in school activities and events.
6. Prepare substitute teachers to handle emergencies or know whom to notify in case of emergencies.
7. Provide accommodations for educational issues related to hyperglycemia and hypoglycemia, as those conditions can impair thinking for several hours.

FIGURE 11.1

Quick reference emergency plan for a student with diabetes (low blood sugar).

Quick Reference Emergency Plan
for a Student with Diabetes
Hypoglycemia
(Low Blood Sugar)

| Photo |

Student's Name

Grade/Teacher   Data of Plan

Emergency Contact Information:

Mother/Guardian   Father/Guardian

| Home phone | Work phone | Cell | Home phone | Work phone | Cell |

School Nurse/Trained Diabetes Personnel   Contract Number(s)

Never send a child with suspected low blood sugar anywhere alone.

Causes of Hypoglycemia
- Too much insulin
- Missed food
- Delayed food
- Too much or too intense exercise
- Unscheduled exercise

→

Onset
- Sudden

↓   ↓

Symptoms

Mild
- Hunger
- Shakiness
- Weakness
- Paleness
- Anxiety
- Irritability
- Dizziness
- Sweating
- Drowsiness
- Personality change
- Inability to concentrate
- Other: _____ _____

Circle student's usual symptoms.

Moderate
- Headache
- Behavior change
- Poor coordination
- Blurry vision
- Weakness
- Slurred Speech
- Confusion
- Other: _____ _____

Circle student's usual symptoms.

Severe
- Loss of consciousness
- Seizure
- Inability to swallow

Circle student's usual symptoms.

↓   ↓   ↓

Actions Needed

Notify School Nurse of Trained Diabetes Personnel. If possible, check blood sugar, per Diabetes Medical Management Plan.
When in doubt, always TREAT FOR HYPOGLYCEMIA.

↓   ↓   ↓

Mild
- Student may/may not treat self.
- Provide quick-sugar source.

  3-4 gluscose tablets

  or

  4 OZ, juice

  or

  6 OZ, regular soda

  or

  3 teaspoons of glucose gel
- Wait 10 to 15 mintues.
- Recheck blood glucose.
- Repeat food if symptoms persist or blood glucose is less than _____.
- Follow with a snack of carbohydrate and protein (e.g., cheese and crackers).

Moderate
- Someone assists.
- Give student quick-sugar source per MILD guidelines.
- Wait 10 to 15 minutes.
- Recheck blood glucose.
- Repeat food if symptoms persist or blood glucose is less than _____.
- Follow with a snack of carbohydrate and protein (e.g., cheese and crackers).

Servere
- Don't attempt to give anything by mouth.
- Position on side, if possible.
- Contact school nurse or trained diabetes personnel.
- Administer glucagon, as prescribed.
- Call 911.
- Contact parents/guardian.
- Stay with student.

FIGURE 11.2

Quick reference emergency plan for a student with diabetes (high blood sugar).

Quick Reference Emergency Plan
for a Student with Diabetes
Hyperglycemia
(High Blood Sugar)

| Photo |

Student's Name

Grade/Teacher   **Data of Plan**

Emergency Contact Information:

Mother/Guardian   **Father/Guardian**

| Home phone | Work phone | Cell | Home phone | Work phone | Cell |

School Nurse/Trained Diabetes Personnel

Contract Number(s)

Causes of Hypoglycemia
- Too much food   • Illness
- Too little insulin   • Infection
- Decreased activity   • Stress

→

Onset
- Over time—several hours or days

↓   ↓

Symptoms

↙   ↓   ↘

Mild
- Thirst
- Frequent urination
- Fatigue/sleepiness
- Increased hunger
- Blurred vision
- Weight loss
- Stomach pains
- Flushing of skin
- Lack of concentration
- Sweet, fruity breath
- Other: _____

Circle student's usual symptoms.

Moderate
- Mild symptoms plus:
- Dry mouth
- Nausea
- Stomach cramps
- Vomiting
- Other: _____

Circle student's usual symptoms.

Severe
- Mild and moderate symptoms plus:
- Labored breathing
- Very weak
- Confused
- Unconscious

Circle student's usual symptoms.

↓   ↓   ↓

Actions Needed
- Allow free use of the bathroom.
- Encourage student to drink water or sugar-free drinks.
- Contact the school nurse or trained diabetes personnel to check urine or administer insulin, per student's Diabetes Medical Management Plan.
- If student is nauseous, vomiting, or lethargic, _____ call the parents/guardian or _____ call for medical assistance if parent cannot be reached.

Source: From *U.S. Department of Health and Human Services.* (2003). Helping the student with diabetes succeed: A guide for school personnel.

8. Communicate appropriate events to the school nurse, school counselor, and parents.
9. Help the other students in the class empathize with the child who has diabetes while respecting the child's needs for privacy. (p. 50)

Epilepsy

Epilepsy is a neurological disorder that results in individuals having seizures. The condition is also called seizure disorders. A seizure occurs when there is a strong, electrical surge to all or parts of the brain. Individuals are diagnosed with epilepsy after suffering at least two seizures. Approximately 3 million people in the United States have epilepsy, including 326,000 children under the age of 15 (Epilepsy Foundation, 2010). Each year there are an additional 200,000 individuals diagnosed with epilepsy. Approximately 45,000 children under the age of 15 experience their first seizure each year. Other facts related to epilepsy include (Epilepsy Foundation, 2010):

- Epilepsy occurs in males slightly more than in females.
- Prevalence of epilepsy increases with age.
- Epilepsy occurs more frequently in racial minorities than in Caucasians.
- A higher prevalence of epilepsy exists among individuals with disabilities than those without disabilities.
- 10% of Americans will experience at least one seizure during their lifetime.

Unlike most other disabilities, there are no common characteristics shared by individuals with epilepsy. Individuals with epilepsy display the same characteristics as individuals without epilepsy. There are several different types of epilepsy, determined by the impact of abnormal brain activity. However, more importantly, educators need to know what actions to take in case students have seizures in their classroom. The seizures exhibited by individuals with epilepsy vary in their impact on an individual. Seizures are impossible to predict; they occur without any pattern and are brief, usually lasting only a few minutes, and manifest in the same manner each time (Epilepsy.com, 2007).

Most individuals with epilepsy can control their seizures with medication. However, even people who respond well to medication may have occasional seizures. Therefore, teachers and other school personnel must know what actions to take should a person experience a generalized seizure. Often, individuals will exhibit signs that they are beginning to have a seizure. These signs could include staring spells, ticlike movements, rhythmic movements of the head, purposeless sounds and body movements, head drooping, lack of response, eyes rolling upward, and chewing and swallowing movements (Epilepsy Foundation, 2010).

Once a student begins to have a seizure there is nothing that can prevent the seizure from occurring. Figure 11.3 summarizes actions that should be taken when a child has a seizure. Teachers, parents, or others need to record behaviors that occur before, during, and after the seizure because they may be important to treatment of the disorder. One way of keeping this information is to have a seizure record for students who have epilepsy. This record can include (1) date and time the seizure started, (2) behaviors before the seizure, (3) body parts involved in the seizure, (4) ending time and recovery period, and (5) behaviors during the recovery period (CHOC Epilepsy Center, n.d.).

Some children will also have petit mal seizures. These seizures are similar to staring spells and can occur multiple times during the day. Unlike a generalized seizure, petit mal seizures do not result in loss of consciousness. Often, students are accused of daydreaming when, in fact, they are having petit mal seizures. Teachers who suspect a child is having petit seizures should notify the school nurse and the child's parents so the child can be medically evaluated to determine if petit mal seizures are occurring.

HIV and AIDS

Human immunodeficiency virus (HIV) occurs when the virus attacks the body's immune system, leaving an individual vulnerable to infections or cancers. In its later stages, HIV infection becomes **acquired immunodeficiency syndrome (AIDS)**. Two of the fastest-growing groups contracting HIV are infants and teenagers (Johnson & Jefferson-Aker, 2001).

FIGURE 11.3	Steps to Take When Dealing with a Seizure

During a generalized tonic-clonic seizure (grand mal), the person suddenly falls to the ground and has a convulsive seizure. It is essential to protect him or her from injury. Cradle the head or place something soft under it, a towel or your hand for example. Remove all dangerous objects. A bystander can do nothing to prevent or terminate an attack. At the end of the seizure, make sure the mouth is cleared of food and saliva by turning the person on his or her side to provide an open airway and allow fluids to drain. If the person assisting remains calm, the person having the seizure will be reassured when he or she regains consciousness.

Breathing almost always resumes spontaneously after a convulsive seizure. Failure to resume breathing signals a complication of the seizure such as a blocked airway, heart attack, or severe head or neck injury. In these unusual circumstances, CPR must start immediately. If repeated seizures occur, or if a single seizure lasts longer than five minutes, the person should be taken to a medical facility immediately. Prolonged or repeated seizures may suggest status epilepticus (nonstop seizures), which requires emergency medical treatment.

When providing seizure first aid for generalized tonic-clonic seizures, these are the key things to remember:

- Keep calm and reassure other people who may be nearby.
- Don't hold the person down or try to stop his or her movements.
- Time the seizure with your watch.
- Clear the area around the person of anything hard or sharp.
- Loosen ties or anything around the neck that may make breathing difficult.
- Put something flat and soft, like a folded jacket, under the head.
- Turn him or her gently onto one side. This will help keep the airway clear. Do not try to force the mouth open with any hard implement or with fingers. It is not true that a person having a seizure can swallow his or her tongue. Efforts to hold the tongue down can injure teeth or jaw.
- Don't attempt artificial respiration except in the unlikely event that a person does not start breathing again after the seizure has stopped.
- Stay with the person until the seizure ends naturally.
- Be friendly and reassuring as consciousness returns.
- Offer to call a taxi, friend, or relative to help the person get home if he or she seems confused or unable to get home by himself or herself.

Source: From "First Aid for Generalized Tonic Clonic (Gran Mal) Seizures." Epilepsy Foundation website. www.epilepsyfoundation.org. Used with permission.

In 2008 there were 2.1 million children living with HIV worldwide. More than 430,000 new cases were diagnosed during 2008. The number of children affected by HIV in the United States is much less than in the rest of the world, particularly sub-Saharan Africa, where the largest number of AIDS cases occur. In the United States in 1992, there were almost 1,000 new cases among children; there were only 100 in 2000. However, the number of cases among adolescents continues to cause concern. The Centers for Disease Control and Prevention reported more than 4,000 cases among adolescents, ages 13 to 19, through June 2001 (HIV Infosource, 2010). As of September 1996, 7,472 cases of AIDS in children under age 13 years were reported to the CDC (Centers for Disease Control, 1997).

HIV/AIDS is transmitted through the exchange of blood, semen, or other body fluids. Most children contract the virus from their mothers during pregnancy, birth, or when breastfeeding. Most students who are HIV positive are able to attend school (Cohen et al., 1997). These students can display a variety of academic, behavioral, and social-emotional problems.

Teachers need to take precautions when dealing with children with HIV/AIDS, hepatitis B, or any other blood-borne pathogen (see Figure 11.4 for specific precautions). Some suggestions for teachers include:

- Follow the guidelines (universal precautions) developed by the CDC and the Food and Drug Administration for working with HIV-infected individuals (Figure 11.4).

| FIGURE 11.4 | Universal Precautions for Prevention of HIV, Hepatitis B, and Other Blood-Borne Pathogens |

The CDC and the Food and Drug Administration (1988) published guidelines designed to protect healthcare workers and to ensure the confidentiality of patients with HIV infection. These guidelines include the following information that is useful for classroom teachers.

- Blood should always be handled with latex or nonpermeable disposable gloves. The use of gloves is not necessary for feces, nasal secretions, sputum, sweat, saliva, tears, urine, and vomitus unless they are visibly tinged with blood. Handwashing is sufficient after handling material not containing blood.

- In all settings in which blood or bloody material is handled, gloves and a suitable receptacle that closes tightly and is childproof should be available. Although HIV does not survive well outside the body, all spillage of secretions should be cleaned up immediately with disinfectants. This is particularly important for cleaning up after a bloody nose or a large cut. Household bleach at a dilution of 1:10 should be used. Only objects that have come into contact with blood need to be cleaned with bleach.

- When intact skin is exposed to contaminated fluids, particularly blood, it should be washed with soap and water. Handwashing is sufficient for such activities as diaper change; toilet training; and clean-up of nasal secretions, stool, saliva, tears, or vomitus. If an open lesion or a mucous membrane appears to have been contaminated, AZT therapy should be considered.

Source: From *AIDS Surveillance Report* (p. 7), Centers for Disease Control, 1988. Atlanta, GA: Author. Used by permission.

- Ask the student's parents or physician whether there are any special procedures that must be followed.
- Discuss HIV/AIDS with the entire class, providing accurate information, dispelling myths, and answering questions.
- Discuss with students in the class that a student's skills and abilities will change over time if he or she is infected with HIV/AIDS.
- Prepare for the fact that the student may die, especially if AIDS is present.
- Ensure that the student with HIV/AIDS is included in all aspects of classroom activities.
- Be sensitive to the stress that the student's family is undergoing.

Children with HIV have social, psychological, and emotional needs as well as physical and health care needs (Avert, 2010). This is one area where teachers and other school personnel can provide extensive supports. Still another important role that teachers can play is to develop and implement an HIV/AIDS prevention education program (Sileo, 2005).

Tourette Syndrome

Tourette syndrome (TS) is a neurological disorder that results in multiple motor and verbal tics. The condition is genetically transmitted, with parents having a 50% chance of passing the gene to offspring. Tourette syndrome develops before the age of 18 (Facts about Tourette Syndrome, 2006). There are an estimated 200,000 individuals in the United States with the most severe form of Tourette syndrome; as many as one in 100 may have milder symptoms of the condition. Tourettes typically manifests itself between the ages of 7 and 10, with the worst symptoms occurring during adolescence. For many adults, symptoms become severe. The condition occurs in males three to four times as often as in females (National Institute of Neurological Disorders and Stroke, 2010). In a national study in 2007, the Centers for Disease Control reported that 3 per 1,000 individuals were reported by parents to have been diagnosed with Tourette syndrome.

There are numerous tics associated with individuals with TS; for example (Christner & Dieker, 2008):

- Clearing of throat
- Coughing
- Stuttering
- Repeating words or phrases

- Shouting
- Grunting
- Spitting
- Barking or other animal noises
- Blinking eyes
- Rolling eyes
- Moving jaw
- Rocking back and forth
- Making facial grimaces/movements/twitches
- Biting nails and lip
- Picking at skin and pinching
- Flailing arms

The condition is manifested in several characteristics that negatively impact educational success, including incomplete work, illegible or poor quality of work, inattention, disorganization, and difficulty understanding and following directions (Prestia, 2003).

The most important role for school personnel when working with students with Tourette syndrome is to be understanding. Monitoring medication and participating as a member of the interdisciplinary team are also important roles for teachers and other school personnel.

PHYSICAL IMPAIRMENTS

Physical Impairments

Disabilities related to physical impairments are placed under the umbrella category of orthopedic impairments in IDEA. These include disorders that "hinder physical mobility or the ability to use one or more parts of the skeleton-muscular system of the body" (Freiberg, 2005, p. 169). Under IDEA 2004, an orthopedic impairment must be severe and must adversely affect a child's educational performance. It includes impairments caused by congenital anomaly (e.g., clubfoot, absence of some member, etc.), impairments caused by disease (e.g., poliomyelitis, bone tuberculosis, etc.), and impairments from other causes (e.g., cerebral palsy, amputations, and fractures or burns, that cause contractures) [300.7(b)(7)]. During the 2006–2007 school year, public schools served 69,000 students with orthopedic impairments (National Center for Education Statistics, 2008). There are too many orthopedic impairments to describe, so the remainder of this section will focus on some of the more prevalent ones.

The primary need of students with orthopedic impairments focuses on ensuring physical access and other physical interventions. Physical therapists, occupational therapists, and other health-related professionals are often directly involved in providing services and supports for these students. The role of educators is often to collaborate with these professionals and create a positive learning environment for students. Teachers and other school personnel should become familiar with the various interventions provided by specialists and provide any supportive interventions that may be helpful, as well as any modifications that need to be made to ensure physical accessibility. See the nearby Rights & Responsibilities feature related to physical accessibility.

Amputations

An amputation is the partial or total absence of an arm or a leg. Amputations can be congenital, present at birth, or acquired after birth. Tooms (2010) reported that 60% of all childhood amputations are congenital and 40% are acquired. Congenital amputations are birth defects and many have no known cause. Acquired amputations are usually secondary to trauma or disease; trauma is responsible for double the number caused by disease. The leading causes of acquired amputations include accidents with power tools and machinery, vehicular accidents, gunshot wounds, and explosions. Loder (2004) studied a group of children with

RIGHTS & RESPONSIBILITIES

The Americans with Disabilities Act Accessibility (ADAAG) Guidelines provides accessibility detailed guidelines for buildings. The following provides a small section of the guidelines related to the application of section four, accessible elements and spaces: scope and technical requirements. A complete set of guidelines is available at www.access-board.gov/adaag

4.1.1* Application.

(1) General. All areas of newly designed or newly constructed buildings and facilities and altered portions of existing buildings and facilities shall comply with section 4, unless otherwise provided in this section or as modified in a special application section.

(2) Application Based on Building Use. Special application sections provide additional requirements based on building use. When a building or facility contains more than one use covered by a special application section, each portion shall comply with the requirements for that use.

(3) * Areas Used Only by Employees as Work Areas. Areas that are used only as work areas shall be designed and constructed so that individuals with disabilities can approach, enter, and exit the areas. These guidelines do not require that any areas used only as work areas be constructed to permit maneuvering within the work area or be constructed or equipped (i.e., with racks or shelves) to be accessible.

(4) Temporary Structures. These guidelines cover temporary buildings or facilities as well as permanent facilities. Temporary buildings and facilities are not of permanent construction but are extensively used or are essential for public use for a period of time. Examples of temporary buildings or facilities covered by these guidelines include, but are not limited to: reviewing stands, temporary classrooms, bleacher areas, exhibit areas, temporary banking facilities, temporary health screening services, or temporary safe pedestrian passageways around a construction site. Structures, sites and equipment directly associated with the actual processes of construction, such as scaffolding, bridging, materials hoists, or construction trailers are not included.

(5) General Exceptions.

(a) In new construction, a person or entity is not required to meet fully the requirements of these guidelines where that person or entity can demonstrate that it is structurally impracticable to do so. Full compliance will be considered structurally impracticable only in those rare circumstances when the unique characteristics of terrain prevent the incorporation of accessibility features. If full compliance with the requirements of these guidelines is structurally impracticable, a person or entity shall comply with the requirements to the extent it is not structurally impracticable. Any portion of the building or facility which can be made accessible shall comply to the extent that it is not structurally impracticable.

(b) Accessibility is not required to or in:

(i) raised areas used primarily for purposes of security or life or fire safety, including, but not limited to, observation or lookout galleries, prison guard towers, fire towers, or fixed life guard stands;

(ii) non-occupiable spaces accessed only by ladders, catwalks, crawl spaces, very narrow passageways, tunnels, or freight (non-passenger) elevators, and frequented only by service personnel for maintenance, repair, or occasional monitoring of equipment; such spaces may include, but are not limited to, elevator pits, elevator penthouses, piping or equipment catwalks, water or sewage treatment pump rooms and stations, electric substations and transformer vaults, and highway and tunnel utility facilities;

(iii) single occupant structures accessed only by a passageway that is below grade or that is elevated above standard curb height, including, but not limited to, toll booths accessed from underground tunnels;

(iv) raised structures used solely for refereeing, judging, or scoring a sport;

(v) water slides;

(vi) animal containment areas that are not for public use; or

(vii) raised boxing or wrestling rings.

Source: From www.access-board.gov/adaag

---

amputations and found that lawn mowers and farm machinery were involved in a large percentage of childhood amputations. Approximately two-thirds of all pediatric amputations resulting from trauma affect fingers and thumbs (Dotinga, 2010). More than half of amputations resulting from disease are the result of malignant tumors. Other statistical data related to amputations include (Hostetler, Schwartz, Shields, Xiang, & Smith, 2005):

- The average age of childhood amputation was 6.18 years.
- Males experience 65.5% of amputations.
- Finger amputations account for more than 90% of amputations.

The educational implications of amputations are directly related to the location and extent of the amputation. For example, students who are right-handed would be much less affected by an amputation of the left hand than an amputation of the right hand. Students with a double leg amputation would have much more difficulty adjusting to mobility issues than students with only a single leg amputation.

The primary objective of interventions for students with amputations targets accessibility. Educators need to make sure that students can access classrooms, playgrounds, gyms, cafeterias, and other areas of the school. Also, teachers may need to provide alternative options for students to complete written academic work if amputations affect their upper extremities. In addition to accommodations related to accessibility, teachers and other school personnel need to address emotional and social issues that could result from an amputation.

Cerebral Palsy

Cerebral palsy (CP) is a disorder of movement or posture. The condition is caused by brain damage and primarily affects the ability to control muscles and coordination (United Cerebral Palsy, 2006). Cerebral palsy is not (1) progressive—it does not become more severe as the child ages; (2) communicable—it cannot be transmitted from one individual to another, nor (3) curable. Although students with cerebral palsy cannot be cured, education, therapy, and applied technology can help them lead productive lives.

Every year, approximately 5,000 babies are born with CP and an additional 1,200 to 1,500 young children develop the condition (Best & Bigge, 2006). Anything that causes brain damage can result in cerebral palsy. This includes lack of oxygen before, during, or after birth, infections such as encephalitis and meningitis, and physical trauma. Additionally, there are many cases of cerebral palsy without a known cause. Cerebral palsy can be classified using several different models. The two used most frequently classify individuals by (1) the location of the disorder and (2) how it affects movement (Best & Bigge, 2006). Table 11.1 describes the different types of cerebral palsy according to two classification systems.

In addition to the characteristics associated with the type of cerebral palsy, students with cerebral palsy display a variety of other characteristics. Two of the most common include oral language problems and learning difficulties. Students with cerebral palsy who exhibit oral communication problems may need a speech–language pathologist to provide direct interventions. Teachers and other educators need to collaborate with these professionals to provide language supports in the classroom.

While students with cerebral palsy have a greater frequency of intellectual disabilities than students without cerebral palsy, many students have average or even above-average intelligence. Still, some of these students exhibit learning problems.

TABLE 11.1

Classification of Cerebral Palsy

CLASSIFICATION BY LOCATION	CLASSIFICATION BY MOVEMENT
A. *Monoplegia:* one limb B. *Paraplegia:* legs only C. *Hemiplegia:* one-half of body D. *Triplegia:* three limbs (usually two legs and one arm) E. *Quadriplegia:* all four limbs F. *Diplegia:* more affected in the legs than in the arms G. *Double hemiplegia:* arms more involved than the legs	A. Spasticity: uncontrolled muscle contractures B. Athetosis: uncontrolled muscle movement C. Rigidity: severe form of spasticity D. Ataxia: problems with balance E. Tremor: mild form of athetosis

The primary interventions needed for children with cerebral palsy focus on their physical needs. Physical therapy, occupational therapy, and even surgery often play a part. In addition to supporting these specialists, along with speech–language pathologists, other specific suggestions for teachers include:

- Create a supportive classroom environment that encourages participation in every facet of the school day.
- Allow extra time for students to move from one location to another.
- Ask students to repeat verbalizations that may be hard to understand because of their speech patterns.
- Provide many real-life activities.
- Learn the correct way for the student to sit upright in a chair or wheelchair and know how to use adaptive equipment (e.g., prone standers).
- Understand the functions and components of a wheelchair and any special adaptive pieces that may accompany it.
- Encourage students to use computers that are equipped with expanded keyboards if necessary or other portable writing aids for taking notes or generating written products.
- Consult physical and occupational therapists to understand correct positioning, posture, and other motor function areas.

Assistive technology (AT) can also play a significant role in the education of students with cerebral palsy. One area of assistive technology that provides communication assistance for individuals with cerebral palsy is augmentative and alternative communication (AAC). The use of voice output communication aids can be extremely useful for students; however, assessing their needs in this area is difficult (Clarke & Wilkinson, 2008). When determining what assistive technology is needed, school personnel must collaborate with family members. Areas where family members can play a critical role include AAC device selection, understanding the knowledge and skills necessary for AAC use, dealing with barriers to learning AAC, and teaching individuals how to use AAC (McNaughton et al., 2008). After determining what AAC is needed, school personnel can develop a plan of action to implement appropriate AT supports.

Muscular Dystrophy

Muscular dystrophy is a group of more than 30 genetic diseases characterized by progressive weakness and eventual death of muscle fibers that control movement. The most common and most serious form of muscular dystrophy is **Duchenne dystrophy**. In this type of muscular dystrophy, fat cells and connective tissue replace muscle tissue. Symptoms first appear between the ages of 3 and 5 years, and progress rapidly. By age 12, most are unable to walk and must use a respirator as the disease progresses (Neurological Institute of Neurological Disorders and Stroke, 2010). This form of muscular dystrophy is a terminal condition; most individuals die during young adulthood. The condition is genetically transmitted and affects approximately one in every 3,500 male births. Females carry the gene but are not affected (Best, 2006).

Students with muscular dystrophy face numerous physical, academic, and social challenges. These include fatigue, learning disabilities, difficulty with written assignments, general mobility issues, and dealing with the social demands of childhood (Muscular Dystrophy Association, 2005). The condition is progressive, so teachers must adapt their level of supports as the disease worsens. The primary role for teachers is to modify their classrooms to accommodate the physical needs of these students. Specific suggestions for teachers include:

- Be prepared to help the student deal with the loss of various functions.
- Involve the student in as many classroom activities as possible.
- Using assistive techniques that do not hurt the individual; help the student as needed in climbing stairs or in getting up from the floor.
- Understand the functions and components of wheelchairs.
- Monitor the administration of required medications.

- Monitor the amount of time the student is allowed to stand during the day.
- Be familiar with different types of braces (e.g., short leg, molded ankle-foot) students might use.
- Prepare other students in class for the realities of the disease.

Spina Bifida

Spina bifida is a neural tube defect characterized by bones in the spinal column (vertebrae) not connecting properly. Spina bifida occurs in about 3,000 pregnancies each year; currently there are an estimated 70,000 people in the United States with this disorder (Spina Bifida Association, 2006). There are different types of spina bifida: occult spinal dysraphism, spina bifida occulta, meningocele, and myelomeningocele (Spina Bifida Association, 2010).

Occult spinal dysraphism occurs when the spinal cord does not grow correctly. Children who have this form of spina bifida frequently have a small dimple on their back. Surgery may be necessary to prevent nerve damage from occurring (Spina Bifida Association, 2010). The least serious form of spina bifida is **spina bifida occulta**. In this type, the vertebral column fails to close properly, leaving a hole in the bony vertebrae that protect the delicate spinal column. Other than monitoring by a physician, children with this form of spina bifida do not usually need any additional interventions. **Meningocele** is similar to spina bifida occulta in that the vertebral column fails to close properly, leaving a hole in the bony vertebrae. Skin pouches out in the area where the vertebral column is not closed. In meningocele, the outpouching does not contain any nerve tissue, and surgically removing the outpouching and closing the opening usually results in a positive prognosis without any problems. **Myelomeningocele** is the most common and most severe form of spina bifida. It is similar to meningocele but has one major difference: nerve tissue is present in the outpouching. Because nerve tissue is involved, this form of spina bifida generally results in permanent paralysis and loss of sensation. Incontinence is also a possible result of this condition (Best, 2006).

School personnel must ensure appropriate use of wheelchairs and make accommodations for limited use of arms and hands. Although the primary impact of spina bifida is physical, a common characteristic of children with spina bifida that teachers must also address is nonverbal learning disorders (Russell, 2004).

Teachers should do the following when working with a child with spina bifida:

- Inquire about any acute medical needs the student may have.
- Learn about the various adaptive equipment a student may be using.
- Maintain an environment that assists the student who is using crutches by keeping floors from getting wet and removing loose floor coverings.
- Understand the use of a wheelchair as well as its major parts.
- Learn how to position these students to develop strength and to keep sores from developing in parts of their bodies that bear their weight or that receive pressure from orthotic devices they are using. Because they do not have sensation, they may not notice the sores themselves. Healing is complicated by poor circulation.
- Understand the process of **clean intermittent bladder catheterization (CIC)**, as some students will be performing this process to become continent and avoid urinary tract infections. The process involves insertion of a clean catheter through the urethra and into the bladder, must be done four times a day, and can be done independently by most children by age 6.
- Be ready to deal with the occasional incontinence of students. Assure the student with spina bifida that this is not a problem and discuss this situation with other class members.
- Learn how to deal with the special circumstances associated with students who use wheelchairs and have seizures.
- Ensure the full participation of the student in all classroom activities.
- Help the student with spina bifida develop a healthy, positive self-concept.
- Notify parents if there are unusual changes in the student's behavior or personality or if the student has various physical complaints such as headaches or double vision—these may indicate a problem with increased pressure on the brain (Deiner, 1993).

TRAUMATIC BRAIN INJURY

Traumatic brain injury (TBI) is defined by IDEA (2004) as an acquired injury to the brain caused by an external physical force, resulting in total or partial functional disability or psychosocial impairment, or both, that adversely affects a child's educational performance. The term applies to open or closed head injuries resulting in impairments in one or more areas, such as cognition, language, memory, attention, reasoning, abstract thinking, judgment, problem solving, psychosocial behavior, physical functions, information processing, speech, and sensory, perceptual, and motor abilities. The term does not apply to brain injuries that are congenital, degenerative, or induced by birth trauma. An open head injury occurs when the skull is broken or penetrated; a closed head injury occurs when the head receives trauma but there is no skull break or penetration. TBI was added as a specific disability category under IDEA in 1990.

Traumatic brain injury is very common among children, being the most common cause of death and disability among children in the United States. The Brain Injury Association of America says that 14 million individuals in the United States suffer a TBI every year. Of this number, 50,000 die and an additional 235,000 are hospitalized. It has been estimated that every 23 seconds, one person suffers a TBI. During the 2006–2007 school year, 25,000 students were served in special education programs because of TBI (National Center for Education Statistics, 2010). Since the number of children served as TBI is significantly fewer than the number of children who suffer from TBI, there are many children with TBI who are not in special education. This fact makes it even more important that general classroom teachers understand this disability because they may have students in their classes who have experienced a TBI but who are not eligible for special education. Students are only eligible for special education services if the TBI results in their needing special education. It is possible for a student to suffer a TBI and exhibit various problems associated with the TBI without needing special education.

TBI can result from a wide variety of causes, including a bump, blow, or jolt to the head. In some cases, a penetration of the skull causes the TBI. It should be noted that all head injuries do not result in a TBI (Centers for Disease Control and Prevention, 2010). A TBI affects a wide variety of a child's functioning, including cognition, learning, behavior, personality, and social interactions (Glang et al., 2008). Characteristics can include intellectual changes; sensory, coordination, and attention problems; emotional ability; aggressiveness; and depression (Best, 2006). The social-emotional and intellectual deficits caused by the injury may persist long after physical capabilities recover. As a result, teachers must guard against minimizing an injury because it presents no visible evidence and because many children may exhibit typical behaviors. There are numerous academic implications resulting from a TBI. These include (About.com: Special Education, 2010):

- Difficulty with logic, thinking, and reasoning
- Slower to respond, react, and complete activities and tasks
- Difficulty focusing attention
- Physical limitations
- Inappropriate social behaviors
- Difficulty remembering
- Frequently puzzled or challenged by grade level work
- Difficulty learning
- Speech and language deficits

The prognosis for recovery from a TBI depends on many variables, including the severity, location, and extent of the injury; immediacy of treatment; chronological age of the individual; and extent of time a student may have been in a coma (Best, 2006). The extent of recovery from the injury is also influenced by the nature of rehabilitative and educational intervention. Some students with TBI will achieve academic success, whereas others will have long-term lingering effects of their injury and need special education services indefinitely.

IEP GOALS AND OBJECTIVES FOR FRANK

GOAL 1: To improve his behavior in the classroom and playground

Objective 1: During calendar time in the morning, Frank will sit at his place on the mat and attend to the teacher for a minimum of 5 minutes without interrupting his neighbor or the class.

Objective 2: During transition period before and after lunch and recess, Frank will line up quietly without bothering his classmates 4 out of 5 days.

Objective 3: During recess, Frank will participate in group activities without hitting his classmates or displaying temper tantrums four out of five days.

GOAL 2: To improve his oral communication and social skills

Objective 1: Given a topic, Frank will take three turns in a conversation without changing the topic in three out of four times.

Objective 2: When asked a specific question, Frank will make eye contact and respond to the question four out of five times.

Objective 3: When asked to give a report of what he does over the weekend, Frank will stand, face the classroom, and give a coherent report three out of four Mondays.

GOAL 3: To improve his short term memory skills

Objective 1: After learning memory strategies, Frank will recall the names of five planets two days each week for two weeks.

Objective 2: Given a homework assignment grid, Frank will make notes daily regarding homework to be completed the following evening five out of five days.

Objective 3: Given a list of five steps in a direction, Frank will follow each step appropriately four out of five times

Classroom Adaptations for Students with TBI

Children who suffer a TBI are provided a wide variety of services by many different professionals. Some with more severe injuries may need services in a rehabilitation or hospital facility. Although the level of services in these programs is excellent, the transition of students from these facilities to school settings can be problematic and requires coordination among a number of people. Interventions for students with TBI, regardless of setting, involve the efforts of professionals from many different disciplines, making coordination of services a key factor in their education. Depending on the nature of the TBI, interventions could include intellectual behavioral therapy, neuropsychological rehabilitation (Shotton, Simpson, & Smith, 2007), environmental modifications, flexible programming, and academic retraining and accommodations (Arroyos-Jurado & Savage, 2008). See the nearby feature listing Frank's IEP goals and objectives and the adapting instruction feature.

TIPS FOR ADAPTING A LESSON FOR FRANK

- Use a multisensory approach—visual, auditory, and kinesthetic activities.
- Review the previous lesson before starting the new lesson.
- Present difficult information in a simple, organized manner.
- Break down assignments into a series of smaller assignments.
- Provide extensive feedback in written and oral forms.
- Break down teaching steps using task analysis.
- Provide clues but allow students to problem solve to find the correct answer.
- Teach various strategies, such as mnemonic strategies.
- Provide outlines and other advance organizers.

Source: From Keyser-Marcus et al. (2002).

TABLE 11.2

Best Practices for Children with TBI

- Become informed, work with the parents to understand as much as you can about the child.
- Exercise patience and lower your expectations.
- Set the student up for success.
- Repeat instructions and directions as needed and provide one direction at a time.
- Allow the student more time to complete tasks and reduce the workload if needed.
- Activities/tasks requiring the student to concentrate for long periods of time should be avoided.
- It's important to remember that the student takes a longer amount of time to process information.
- Be sure to have consistent routines and rules.
- Keep distractions to a minimum.
- Remember to assess this student with an approach that will meet his/her needs —i.e., additional time, more observation, etc.
- Make sure the IEP is in place and that it is flexible—a working document.
- Each child with TBI is unique in needs.
- The child may require a modified schedule and or a behavioral plan.
- The child may need direct support in organizational strategies.

Source: From About.com: Special Education (2010).

There are numerous instructional strategies that have been effective with students with TBI. Some of these include using a multisensory approach, teaching compensatory strategies, using advance organizers, and providing learning materials in a variety of different formats (Keyser-Marcus et al., 2002). Table 11.2 gives a list of best practices for teachers.

ROLE OF GENERAL CLASSROOM TEACHERS AND STUDENTS WITH LOW-INCIDENCE DISABILITIES

As a result of inclusion, general classroom teachers are very involved in the educational programs of students with disabilities, including those with low-incidence disabilities. Although most of the students included in general education classrooms have higher-incidence disabilities, including learning disabilities, intellectual disabilities, and attention deficit hyperactivity, there will be times when students with health and physical problems will be included. The primary role for teachers when working with students who have high-incidence disabilities is to provide academic supports, because most of these students have academic difficulties. Teachers therefore are primarily focused on academic accommodations and modifications that will facilitate learning.

The primary role of general classroom teachers when they are working with students who are experiencing health and physical disabilities is academic instruction; however, many of these students are academically capable and do not need academic supports. Their primary needs focus on physical access and accommodations and healthcare supports. Both of these areas require teachers to work with teams of health professionals and related services personnel to ensure appropriate educational opportunities for students. Members of these teams could include nurses, nutritionists, occupational and physical therapists, physicians, psychologists, special education teachers, speech–language pathologists and parents (Heller et al., 2000): Classroom teachers participate in the education of students with physical and health needs in a variety of ways. A key area deals with the equipment that many of

Differentiating Secondary Instruction

Students with orthopedic impairments and other health impairments face significant challenges throughout their public school years, but even more challenges after exiting school. Independent living skills, employment skills, and social skills will all have a huge impact on the success of young adults as they enter into adulthood. Individuals with orthopedic and health disabilities need to be involved in their own transition planning. Konrad (2008) lists 20 different ways to involve students in the IEP process:

1. Use your resources.
2. Develop an IEP scavenger hunt that requires students to find things in their own IEPs.
3. Assign students the task of evaluating their IEPs to make sure they contain all the requirements of the law.
4. Have students read fiction books featuring characters with disabilities and identify strengths and weaknesses of the characters.
5. Work with students to help them develop vision statements for themselves.
6. Get students involved in the assessment process.
7. Have students write letters inviting meeting participants to attend.
8. Use commercial programs such as The Self-Advocacy Strategy to help students identify potential needs, goals, and services.
9. Involve students in preparing the meeting.
10. Have students write paragraphs about their strengths and needs.
11. Have students take each need statement and turn it into an "I will" statement.
12. Require students to meet with their parents before their IEP meeting to review the draft.
13. Keep in mind that there is a range of options for involving students in IEP meetings.
14. Use published curricula such as *The Self-Directed IEP*.
15. Provide students with several opportunities to rehearse for their meeting.
16. Have each student create a fact sheet that summarizes his or her IEP for general education teachers.
17. Teach students self-advocacy and self-recruitment skills.
18. Provide students with access to their IEP files.
19. Teach students to self-monitor and self-evaluate their progress.
20. Have students develop first-person progress reports to share with their parents and the IEP team.

Source: From M. Konrad (2008). "Involve students in the IEP process." *Intervention in School and Clinic, 43,* 236–237. Used with permission.

these students may use. Areas where teachers could be involved include "(a) assessing the need for adaptive equipment and evaluating adaptive equipment use, (b) monitoring equipment and its use, (c) assisting the student in using the adaptive equipment, and (d) cleaning and caring for the equipment" (Heller et al., 2000, p. 12). Teachers would need support for several of these activities. As a result, they need to work with specialists in learning how to complete some of these tasks. Teachers also need to encourage students with low-incidence disabilities to become involved in their educational programming, especially as students get older. See the nearby Differentiated Instruction—Secondary boxed reading for suggestions for getting students involved in their IEP development.

Much of what teachers do when dealing with students who have physical and health needs is monitor their use of equipment and their overall health. Keeping checklists related to medication, effectiveness of equipment, and general observations concerning a student's overall health can be helpful. For example, teachers need to monitor students who have asthma to ensure that they do not need any interventions. An asthma action plan can provide teachers with detailed information about what actions need to be taken if certain conditions occur. Figure 11.5 provides a sample of an asthma action plan.

Regardless of specific actions, teachers need to be involved in all aspects of a child's educational program. For students with physical and health problems, this involvement is primarily as a team member with a group of health and related services personnel. Participating in team meetings, implementing various supports, and monitoring children are the primary areas in which teachers will be involved with students with these disabilities.

FIGURE 11.5

Asthma Action Plan

For: _____ Doctor: _____ Date: _____

Doctor's Phone Number _____ Hospital/Emergency Department Phone Number _____

GREEN ZONE

Doing Well

- No cough, wheeze, chest tightness, or shortness of breath during the day or night
- Can do usual activities

And, if a peak flow meter is used,

Peak flow: more than _____
(80 percent or more of my best peak flow)

My best peak flow is: _____

Take these long-term control medicines each day (include an anti-inflammatory).

Medicine	How much to take	When to take it
_____	_____	_____
_____	_____	_____
_____	_____	_____

| Before exercise | □ 2 or □ 4 puffs | 5 to 60 minutes before exercise |

YELLOW ZONE

Asthma Is Getting Worse

- Cough, wheeze, chest tightness, or shortness of breath, or
- Waking at night due to asthma, or
- Can do some, but not all, usual activities

-Or-

Peak flow: _____ to _____
(50 to 79 percent of my best peak flow)

First ⬆

Add: quick-relief medicine—and keep taking your GREEN ZONE medicine.

_____ □ 2 or □ 4 puffs, every 20 minutes for up to 1 hour
(short-acting beta₂-agonist) □ Nebulizer, once

Second ⬆

If your symptoms (and peak flow, if used) return to GREEN ZONE after 1 hour of above treatment:
□ Continue monitoring to be sure you stay in the green zone.

-Or-

If your symptoms (and peak flow, if used) do not return to GREEN ZONE after 1 hour of above treatment:

□ Take: _____ □ 2 or □ 4 puffs or □ Nebulizer
(short-acting beta₂-agonist)

□ Add: _____ _____ mg per day For _____ (3–10) days
(oral steroid)

□ Call the doctor □ before/ □ within _____ hours after taking the oral steroid.

RED ZONE

Medical Alert!

- Very short of breath, or
- Quick-relief medicines have not helped, or
- Cannot do usual activities, or
- Symptoms are same or get worse after 24 hours in Yellow Zone

-Or-

Peak flow: less than _____
(50 percent of my best peak flow)

Take this medicine:

□ _____ □ 4 or □ 6 puffs or □ Nebulizer
(short-acting beta₂-agonist)

□ _____ _____ mg
(oral steroid)

Then call your doctor NOW. Go to the hospital or call an ambulance if:
- You are still in the red zone after 15 minutes AND
- You have not reached your doctor.

⬆

DANGER SIGNS ■ **Trouble walking and talking due to shortness of breath** ■ **Take** □ 4 or □ 6 puffs of your quick-relief medicine AND
■ **Lips or fingernails are blue** ■ **Go to the hospital or call for an ambulance** _____ (phone) **NOW!**

SUMMARY

Define and Describe Low-Incidence Disabilities

- Low-incidence disabilities are those that occur infrequently and include sensory impairments, orthopedic impairments, and other health impairments.
- Teachers may have very few children with low-incidence disabilities.
- Due to the significant, unique needs of children with low-incidence disabilities, teachers often need supplemental professional support to appropriately serve these children.

Define and Describe Students with Other Health Impairments

- Students with health problems qualify for special education under the other health impaired category of IDEA.
- Other health impairments include having limited strength, vitality, or alertness caused by chronic or acute health problems.
- Examples of conditions classified under other health impaired are asthma, diabetes, epilepsy, and cancer.
- Asthma affects many children; teachers primarily need to be aware of medications to control asthma, side effects of medication, and the limitations of students with asthma.
- The survival rates for children with cancer have increased dramatically over the past 30 years.
- Teachers need to be prepared to deal with the emotional issues surrounding childhood health problems and death issues.
- Cystic fibrosis is a terminal condition that affects the mucous membranes of the lungs.
- Juvenile diabetes results in children having to take insulin injections daily. Diet and exercise can help children manage diabetes.
- Epilepsy is caused by abnormal activity in the brain that is the result of some brain damage or insult.
- Teachers need to keep up to date with developments in HIV/AIDS prevention and treatment approaches.
- Tourette syndrome is a neuropsychiatric disorder that is characterized by multiple motor tics, inappropriate laughter, rapid eye movements, winks and grimaces, and aggressive behavior.

Define and Describe Students with Physical Impairments

- Children with physical needs are entitled to an appropriate educational program as a result of IDEA under the category of orthopedic impairment.
- Students classified as orthopedically impaired include those with cerebral palsy, spina bifida, amputations, and other disorders that impact on physical mobility or the ability to use one or more physical parts of the body.
- Physical impairments are considered low-incidence disabilities.
- The severity, visibility, and age of acquisition affect the needs of children with physical impairments.
- Students with physical problems display a wide array of characteristics and needs.
- Students with physical problems qualify for special education under the orthopedically impaired category of IDEA.
- CP is a condition that affects muscles and posture; it can be described by the way it affects movement or which limb is involved.
- Muscular dystrophy is a term used to describe several different inherited disorders that result in progressive muscular weakness and may cause death.

- Spina bifida is caused by a failure of the spinal column to close properly; this condition may result in paralysis of the lower extremities.
- Physical therapy is a critical component of treatment for children with CP. Accessibility, communication, and social-emotional concerns are the primary areas that general educators must attend to.

Define and Describe Students with Traumatic Brain Injury

- TBI is one of the newest categories recognized by IDEA as a disability category eligible for special education services.
- Children with TBI exhibit a wide variety of characteristics, including emotional, learning, and behavior problems.
- Teachers need to maintain as high a level of expectation as possible for students with TBI.
- Teachers must familiarize themselves with any specific equipment or medications that students with TBI might need and modify the classroom accordingly.

Describe the Role of General Classroom Teachers

- General classroom teachers provide educational interventions and support services for students with physical and health disabilities.
- Teachers must work closely with health and related services personnel.
- Assessing the needs of students for adaptive equipment is a role for general classroom teachers.
- Teachers need to know how to help students use adaptive equipment as well as how to provide cleaning and maintenance of the equipment.
- Monitoring students with physical and health disabilities is a key role for classroom teachers.

PEARSON
myeducationlab

The MyEducationLab for this course can help you solidify your comprehension of Chapter 11 concepts.

- Gauge and further develop your understanding of chapter concepts by taking the quizzes and examining the enrichment materials on the Chapter 11 Study Plan.
  - Connect with challenge-based interactive modules, case study units, and podcasts that provide research-validated information about working with students in inclusive settings by visiting the IRIS Center Resources:
  - Explore Assignments and Activities, assignable exercises showing concepts in action through video, cases, and student and teacher artifacts
  - Practice and strengthen skills essential to quality teaching through the Building Teaching Skills and Dispositions lessons

12

Teaching Students with Speech and Language Disorders

DAVID is an 8-year-old who recently began stuttering in the classroom. At first, David's second-grade teacher, Mr. Parker, wasn't concerned because David's dysfluencies were infrequent and short, both in duration and in intensity. But lately, it seems to be becoming more of a problem. Mr. Parker has noticed that David has stopped participating in class and that he doesn't seem to be playing with his friends on the playground like he used to.

Mr. Parker called David's parents to schedule a parent-teacher conference. At the conference, David's parents said that they had also noticed David's stuttering, but that it didn't seem as severe at home as at school. They were very concerned about how David's stuttering might affect his educational, emotional, and behavioral development. They indicated that there was a history of disfluency in their family, and they knew how important it was that David begin receiving therapy as soon as possible.

Mr. Parker and David's parents requested an in-depth evaluation by the school's speech–language pathologist, Mrs. Woods. Mrs. Woods began by chatting with David about his stuttering. David said that he was aware of his stuttering and that he was really embarrassed and ashamed of it. He said that his stuttering was worse when he talked to his friends and when he talked on the phone or with adults with whom he was less familiar. David was clearly upset about his stuttering and even began crying during one part of the interview.

After completing the interview with David, as well as the formal assessment, Mrs. Woods scheduled the IEP meeting. At the meeting, she recommended that David begin receiving speech therapy services three times weekly for 30 minutes each session. David would join a small group of two other boys from his school who were also stuttering. Mrs. Woods gave David's parents and Mr. Parker some brochures and pamphlets that provided information about stuttering, speech therapy, and how to help David communicate better in school and at home. The IEP team agreed on David's goals and objectives for the coming school year, and discussed how to modify lessons to help David participate to the fullest extent possible.

QUESTIONS TO CONSIDER

1. What should Mr. Parker tell the students in his classroom about stuttering?
2. What could Mr. Parker and Mrs. Woods do to help David better interact with his peers in settings other than the classroom?
3. Should Mr. Parker expect David to give oral reports in front of the class? Why or why not?
4. Why would asking David to "slow down" or "relax" not help him to speak more fluently?

For most of us, the ability to communicate is a skill we take for granted. Our communication is effortless and frequent. In one day, we might share a story with family members, discuss problems with our coworkers, ask directions from a stranger on the street, and telephone an old friend. When we are able to communicate easily and effectively, it is natural to participate in both the commonplace activities of daily living and the more enjoyable experiences that enrich our lives.

However, when communication is impaired, absent, or qualitatively different, the simplest interactions can become difficult or even impossible. Moreover, because the communication skills that most of us use fluently and easily almost always involve personal interactions with others, disorders in speech or language can also result in social problems. For children, these social problems are most likely to occur in school. School is a place not only for academic learning, but also for building positive relationships with teachers and enduring friendships with peers. When a student's communication disorder, however mild, limits these experiences, makes him or her feel different and inadequate, or undermines confidence and self-esteem, the overall impact can be devastating.

BASIC CONCEPTS ABOUT SPEECH AND LANGUAGE DISORDERS

Speech and language disorders can be considered within the broader context of communication disorders.

Definition, Identification, Eligibility

Speech and **language** are interrelated skills, tools that we use to communicate and learn. Heward (1995) defines the related terms this way:

> Communication is the interactive exchange of information, ideas, feelings, needs, and desires. It involves encoding, transmitting, and decoding messages. Each communication interaction includes three elements: (a) message, (b) a sender who expresses the message, and (c) a receiver who responds to the message. . . . Language is a formalized code used by a group of people to communicate with one another . . . Speech is the oral production of language. Although it is not the only vehicle for expressing language (e.g., gestures, manual signing, pictures, and written symbols are also used), speech is the fastest, most efficient method of communication by language. . . . Speech is also one of the most complex and difficult human endeavors. (pp. 297–299)

Various cultures develop and use language differently, and the study of language is a complex topic. The **American Speech-Language-Hearing Association (ASHA)** includes the following important considerations in its discussion of language: language evolves within specific historical, social, and cultural contexts; language is rule-governed behavior; language learning and use are determined by the interaction of biological, cognitive, psychosocial, and environmental factors; and effective use of language for communication requires a broad understanding of human interactions, including associated factors such as nonverbal cues, motivation, and sociocultural roles. AHSA (1993) defines a "communication disorder" as:

> An impairment in the ability to receive, send, process, and comprehend concepts or verbal, nonverbal and graphic symbol systems. A communication disorder may be evident in the processes of hearing, language, and/or speech. A communication disorder may range in severity from mild to profound. It may be developmental or acquired. Individuals may demonstrate one or any combination of the three aspects of communication disorders. A communication disorder may result in a primary disability or it may be secondary to other disabilities.

As can be seen from examining the definition, communication disorders include speech, language, and hearing. Under IDEA, hearing issues are addressed under the category of "hearing impairment" and the term "speech and language impairment" (SLI) is used for those students who have these types of communication disorders.

Because language development and use are such complicated topics, determining what is normal and what is disordered communication is also difficult. With this in mind, Silverman & Miller (2006) note that additional considerations should be recognized and understood in relation to the ASHA definition. They suggest that for a condition to be truly a disorder, the following two conditions be evident:

- There has to be something noticeably different about how the person looks or listens. If the person is not aware of the difference and most people would not detect it, he or

Visit the MyEducationLab for this course to enhance your understanding of chapter concepts with a personalized Study Plan. You'll also have the opportunity to hone your teaching skills through video-based Assignments and Activities, IRIS Center Resources, and Building Teaching Skills and Disposition lessons.

CROSS-REFERENCE

Hearing impairment is covered in Chapter 10.

she would not likely be looked upon as having a communication disorder. In this situation, the communication difference would not interfere with communication, call adverse attention to the person, or cause him or her to be self-conscious or maladjusted.

- The communicative deviation has to be regarded as "abnormal" by at least one person whose judgment is respected by the person who has it. The person can be a professional such as a speech language pathologist (SLP) or audiologist, a family member, a friend, or the person himself or herself (p. 16).

Emerick and Haynes (1986) offer another perspective for determining whether a communication difference is considered a disability. They suggest that a disorder exists when:

- The transmission or perception of messages is faulty.
- The person is placed at an economic disadvantage.
- The person is placed at a learning disadvantage.
- The person is placed at a social disadvantage.
- There is a negative impact on the person's emotional growth.
- The problem causes physical damage or endangers the health of the person (pp. 6–7).

Placement patterns for students with disabilities vary according to students' individual needs. Usually, it is safe to say that the milder the disability, the less restrictive the placement. Students with SLI are the most integrated of all students with disabilities. Since 1985, most students with SLI have been served in either general education classes or resource rooms. Similarly, students with SLI were more likely than students with other disabilities to be educated in regular classes for most of the school day. See the Rights & Responsibilities feature for more details.

Data from the Fall of 2004 indicate that 88.3% of students whose primary disability was speech and language impairments were in general education classroom placements for the greater part of the school day and 6.6% were served outside of general education for a part of the day (i.e., resource rooms) (U.S. Department of Education, 2006). The small proportion (4.7%) served in separate classes most likely represents students with severe language delays and disabilities. For classroom teachers, having students with speech and language impairments in their classes is more the rule than the exception.

Classification

Because so many students with speech and language impairments are included in general education classrooms, it is important that teachers be able to identify those students who may be displaying speech or language problems, be familiar with common causes of com-

RIGHTS & RESPONSIBILITIES

THE RIGHT TO "RELATED SERVICES" FOR STUDENTS WITH SPEECH PROBLEMS

Students with speech and language problems are generally served in general education classes. Many other students with disabilities have speech and/or language problems as a secondary disability (e.g., students with intellectual disabilities or students with autism). As a result, they need related services to address their speech/language issue. According to IDEA (2004), speech–language pathology services include:

- Identification of children with speech or language impairments;
- Diagnosis and appraisal of specific speech or language impairments;

- Referral for medical or other professional attention necessary for the habilitation of speech or language impairments;
- Provision of speech and language services for the habilitation or prevention of communication impairments; and
- Counseling and guidance of parents, children, and teachers regarding speech and language impairments. [34 CFR, 300.34(c)(15)]

munication disorders, know when problems are significant enough to qualify as a disorder and to require referral to other resources, and have some effective strategies for working with students in the general education environment.

In its definition of communicative disorders, ASHA (1993) describes both speech disorders and language disorders. **Speech disorders** include impairments of voice, articulation, and fluency. **Language disorders** are impairments of comprehension or use of language, regardless of the symbol system used. A language disorder may involve the form of language, the content of language, or the function (use) of language. Specific disorders of language form include **phonologic**, **syntactic**, and **morphologic** impairments. **Semantics** refers to the content or meaning of language, and **pragmatics** is the system controlling language function. Figure 12.1 contains the definitions of communication disorders as described by ASHA. The terms in this figure are discussed in more detail later in the chapter. The category of communication disorders is broad in scope and includes a wide variety of problems, some of which may overlap. It is not surprising that this group of disorders includes a large proportion of all students with disabilities.

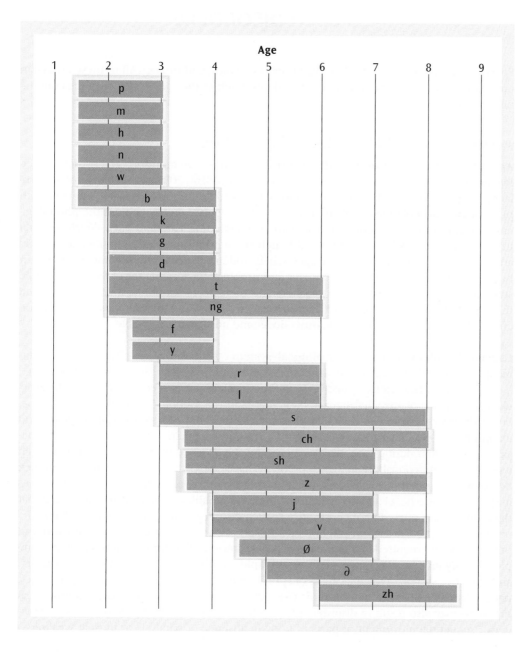

FIGURE 12.1

Ages at which 90% of all children typically produce a specific sound correctly.

Note: Average estimates and upper age limits of customary consonant production. The solid bar corresponding to each sound starts at the median age of customary articulation; it stops at an age level at which 90 percent of all children are customarily producing the sound. The ø symbol stands for the breathed "th" sound, as in *bathroom*, and the ∂ symbol stands for the voiced "th" sound, as in feather (Smith and Luckasson, 1992, p. 168).

Source: From "When Are Speech Sounds Learned?" by E. K. Sander, 1972, *Journal of Speech and Hearing Disorders, 37*, p. 62. Reprinted by permission of the American Speech-Language-Hearing Association.

Prevalence of Speech and Language Disorders

The second most common disability category of students ages 6 through 21 served under IDEA is speech or language impairment (U.S. Department of Education, 2006). These students have a disorder or delay in their ability to send or receive a message, to articulate clearly or fluently, or to comprehend the pragmatics of social interactions. Because many students have other conditions as their primary disability but still receive speech-language services, the total number of students served by **speech–language pathologists** is about 5% of all school-age children, two-thirds of whom are boys. In 2004, students with speech and language disorders constituted 18.8% of all students aged 6 to 21 with disabilities.

Of the more than 1 million students identified as speech or language impaired, about 90% (over 900,000) are 6 to 11 years of age (U.S. Department of Education, 2002). Thirty-four percent of students aged 6 to 11 who have been identified as requiring special education services are classified as having a speech or language impairment (SLI). For this reason, most of the suggestions in this chapter focus on that age group, although many of the language development activities would also be useful for older students.

SPEECH DISORDERS

Speech disorders include problems in phonology, voice, and fluency. All of these areas can create problems in the everyday lives of students whether they are in school, in the community, or at home.

Articulatory and Phonological Disorders

Articulatory and **phonological disorders** are the most common speech disorders, affecting about 10% of preschool and school-age children (ASHA, 2002a). In 2006, most speech-language pathologists who work in school settings (91%) reported serving students with phonological/articulation problems. The ability to articulate clearly and use the phonological code correctly is a function of many variables, including a student's age, developmental history, oral-motor skills, and culture. Although some articulatory and phonological errors are normal and acceptable at young ages, when students are older these same errors might be viewed as developmentally discrepant and problematic. As a matter of fact, by the time students begin kindergarten, their teachers and their peers should be able to understand them easily. Shames and Wiig (1990) has described the most common types of articulation errors: **distortions**, **substitutions**, **omissions**, and **additions** (see Table 12.1).

Causes of Problems in the Phonological System   Articulatory and phonological impairments can be either organic (i.e., having an identifiable physical cause) or functional (i.e., having no identifiable cause). Children with functional disorders account for 99% of the articulation caseloads of speech–language pathologists in the schools (ASHA, 1999). Some functional disorders may be related to the student's opportunities to learn appropriate and inappropriate speech patterns, including opportunities to practice appropriate speech, transient hearing loss during early development, and the absence or presence of good speech models. Some functional phonological problems have causes that may be related to complex neurological or neuromuscular deficits and might never be specifically identified. Differences in speech can also be related to cultural and linguistic variables. It is critical to understand that these differences often do not constitute a speech disorder (discussed later in the chapter).

Organic articulatory and phonological disorders are related to the neurological and physical abilities required in the process of producing speech sounds, which is a highly complex activity involving intricate, precise, and rapid coordination of neuromuscular, sensory, and cognitive systems. Organic causes of speech impairments may include hearing loss, cleft palate, dental malformations, or tumors (APA, 2000). Brain damage and related neurological problems may also result in disorders of speech production, such as verbal apraxia (disorder of sequential movement of parts of body in absence of paralysis or muscle weakness)

TABLE 12.1

The Four Kinds of Articulation Errors

ERROR TYPE	DEFINITION	EXAMPLE
Distortion	A sound is produced in an unfamiliar manner.	Standard: Give the pencil to Sally.
		Distortion: Give the pencil to Sally. (the /p/ is nasalized)
Substitution	Replace one sound with another sound.	Standard: The ball is red.
		Substitution: The ball is wed.
Omission	A sound is omitted in a word.	Standard: Play the piano.
		Omission: P_ay the piano.
Addition	An extra sound is inserted within a word.	Standard: I have a black horse.
		Addition: I have a balack horse.

Source: From *Human Communication Disorders* (3rd ed., p. 219) by G. H. Shames and E. H. Wiig, 1990, New York: Macmillan. Copyright © 1990 by Macmillan Publishing Company. Reprinted by permission.

and dysarthria (disorder due to paralysis, weakness, or lack of coordination of speech muscles). One good example is cerebral palsy. The severity of articulatory and phonological disorders can vary widely, depending in part on the causes of the disorders.

When Articulatory and Phonological Errors Are a Serious Problem Because we know the developmental patterns for normal sound production, we can recognize those children who are significantly different from the norm. The normal pattern of consonant sound production falls within relatively well-defined age limits (Sander, 1972). For example, children usually master the consonant /p/ sound by age 3, but may not produce a correct /s/ sound consistently until age 8. Although young children between ages 2 and 6 often make phonological errors as their speech develops, similar errors in older students would indicate a problem. At age 3 it might be normal for a child to say wabbit instead of rabbit. If a 5-year-old consistently makes the same error, it should be considered a problem, and the teacher should refer the student to a speech–language pathologist for evaluation. Figure 12.2 presents this pattern of normal development for production of consonants among speakers of Standard American English.

For a general education teacher, evaluating a student's phonological errors involves looking at the big picture—that is, how well the student is doing in class and whether the disorder is interfering with either overall academic performance or social development/adjustment. A few commonsense considerations may give some insight into whether the student has a serious problem and what, if anything, should be done about it:

- Take note of how understandable or intelligible the student's speech is.
- Consider how many different errors the student makes.
- Evaluate whether the speech errors might have an impact on the student's ability to read and write.
- Observe whether the articulation errors cause the student problems in socialization or adjustment.
- Consider whether the errors could be due to physical problems.

Voice Disorders

Vocal disturbances in children are actually quite common. **Voice disorders** are characterized by the abnormal vocal quality, pitch, loudness, resonance, or duration, given an individual's age and sex (ASHA, 1993). The early diagnosis and intervention of voice disorders is

FIGURE
12.2   Definitions of Communication Disorders from ASHA

I. A **communication disorder** is an impairment in the ability to receive, send, process, and comprehend concepts or verbal, nonverbal and graphic symbol systems. A communication disorder may be evident in the processes of hearing, language, and/or speech. A communication disorder may range in severity from mild to profound. It may be developmental or acquired. Individuals may demonstrate one or any combination of communication disorders. A communication disorder may result in a primary disability or it may be secondary to other disabilities.

  A. A *speech disorder* is an impairment of the articulation of speech sounds, fluency and/or voice.

    1. An *articulation disorder* is the atypical production of speech sounds characterized by substitutions, omissions, additions or distortions that may interfere with intelligibility.

    2. A *fluency disorder* is an interruption in the flow of speaking characterized by atypical rate, rhythm, and repetitions in sounds, syllables, words, and phrases. This may be accompanied by excessive tension, struggle behavior, and secondary mannerisms.

    3. A *voice disorder* is characterized by the abnormal production and/or absences of vocal quality, pitch, loudness, resonance, and/or duration, which is inappropriate for an individual's age and/or sex.

  B. A *language disorder* is impaired comprehension and/or use of spoken, written and/or other symbol systems. The disorder may involve (1) the form of language (phonology, morphology, syntax), (2) the content of language (semantics), and/or (3) the function of language in communication (pragmatics) in any combination.

    1. Form of Language
      a. *Phonology* is the sound system of a language and the rules that govern the sound combinations.
      b. *Morphology* is the system that governs the structure of words and the construction of word forms.
      c. *Syntax* is the system governing the order and combination of words to form sentences, and the relationships among the elements within a sentence.

    2. Content of Language
      a. *Semantics* is the system that governs the meanings of words and sentences.

    3. Function of Language
      a. *Pragmatics* is the system that combines the above language components in functional and socially appropriate communication.

  C. A *hearing disorder* is the result of impaired auditory sensitivity of the physiological auditory system. A hearing disorder may limit the development, comprehension, production, and/or maintenance of speech and/or language. Hearing disorders are classified according to difficulties in detection, recognition, discrimination, comprehension, and perception of auditory information. Individuals with hearing impairment may be described as deaf or hard of hearing.

    1. *Deaf* is defined as a hearing disorder that limits an individual's aural/oral communication performance to the extent that the primary sensory input for communication may be other than the auditory channel.

    2. *Hard of hearing* is defined as a hearing disorder, whether fluctuating or permanent, which adversely affects an individual's ability to communicate. The hard-of-hearing individual relies on the auditory channel as the primary sensory input for communication.

FIGURE 12.2	Definitions of Communication Disorders from ASHA *(continued)*

D. *Central auditory processing disorders* are deficits in the information processing of audible signals not attributed to impaired peripheral hearing sensitivity or intellectual impairment. This information processing involves perceptual, cognitive, and linguistic functions that, with appropriate interaction, result in effective receptive communication of auditorily presented stimuli. Specifically, CAPD refers to limitations in the ongoing transmission, analysis, organization, transformation, elaboration, storage, retrieval, and use of information contained in audible signals. CAPD may involve the listener's active and passive (e.g., conscious and unconscious, mediated and unmediated, controlled and automatic) ability to do the following:

- attend, discriminate, and identify acoustic signals;
- transform and continuously transmit information through both the peripheral and central nervous systems;
- filter, sort, and combine information at appropriate perceptual and conceptual levels;
- store and retrieve information efficiently; restore, organize, and use retrieved information;
- segment and decode acoustic stimuli using phonological, semantic, syntactic, and pragmatic knowledge; and
- attach meaning to a stream of acoustic signals through use of linguistic and nonlinguistic contexts.

II. Communication Variations

A. *Communication difference/dialect* is a variation of a symbol system used by a group of individuals that reflects and is determined by shared regional, social, or cultural/ethnic factors. A regional, social, or cultural/ethnic variation of a symbol system should not be considered a disorder of speech or language.

B. *Augmentative/alternative communication* systems attempt to compensate and facilitate, temporarily or permanently, for the impairment and disability patterns of individuals with severe expressive and/or language comprehension disorders. Augmentative/alternative communication may be required for individuals demonstrating impairments in gestural, spoken, and/or written modalities.

warranted, as they may lead to lifelong communication issues (Baker & Blackwell, 2004). It has been reported that 29% of school-based speech–language pathologists work with students who display voice/resonance problems. Because our voices are related to our identities and are an integral part of who we are and how we are recognized, we usually allow for a wide range of individual differences in voice.

There are two basic types of voice disorders: **phonation** and **resonance** (Heward, 2009). **Phonation** refers to the production of sounds by the vocal folds. Humans have two vocal folds, which are located in the larynx and lie side by side. When we speak, healthy vocal folds vibrate, coming together smoothly along the length of their surfaces, separating, and then coming together again. These movements are usually very rapid and are partially controlled by air pressure coming from the lungs. If the vocal folds do not meet and close together smoothly, the voice is likely to sound breathy, hoarse, husky, or strained. Chronic hoarseness is the most common phonatory disorder among children, affecting as many as 38% of the school-age population (Hooper, 2004). If a student's vocal folds are too tense or relaxed, or if the voice is produced by vibrating laryngeal structures other than the true vocal folds, the student might demonstrate a pitch disorder. Although pitch disorders occur infrequently in school-age populations, they can sometimes lead to devastating social-emotional consequences.

Disorders of **resonance** usually involve either too many sounds coming out through the air passages of the nose (hypernasality) or the opposite, too little resonance of the nasal passages (hyponasality). Hypernasality sounds like talking through one's nose or with a "twang," and hyponasality sounds like one has a cold or a congested nose. Because resonance is related to what happens to air that travels from the vocal folds into the throat, mouth, and nasal cavity, resonance problems can result when there are abnormalities in any of these structures or in the associated musculature.

Causes of Voice Disorders   Although voice disorders in school-aged children can have many causes, they most commonly result from vocal abuse or misuse, including shouting, screaming, talking loudly, making vocal sound effects, and throat clearing. Common child-hood health problems such as upper respiratory tract infections, allergies, asthma, and gastroesophageal reflux can worsen symptoms (Hooper, 2004). Voice disorders caused by abuse or misuse of the vocal folds affect boys more often than girls (ASHA, 2002a). Because some voice disorders can also be related to other medical conditions, the speech–language pathologist will refer students who evidence a voice disorder to an otolaryngologist (ear, nose, and throat doctor) for evaluation. Some examples of organic problems related to voice disorders include congenital anomalies of the larynx, Reye's syndrome, juvenile arthritis, psychiatric problems, Tourette syndrome, physical trauma to the larynx, and cancer. Because most of these conditions are relatively rare, it may be more likely that the student's voice disorder is a functional problem, perhaps resulting from learned speech patterns (Oyer, Crowe, & Haas, 1987).

When Voice Disorders Are a Serious Problem   Classroom teachers can help prevent voice disorders among their students by modeling and promoting healthy voice habits in the classroom, on the playground, and at home. Interestingly, teachers themselves are at higher risk for voice disorders than the general population and would greatly benefit from adopting good vocal hygiene (Merrill et al., 2004).

Studies have demonstrated that classroom teachers can consistently identify children with disordered and normal voices (Davis & Harris, 1992). A student who is suspected of having a voice disorder should be observed over the course of several weeks, because many symptoms of voice disorders are similar to those of other temporary conditions such as colds, seasonal allergies, or minor respiratory infections (Oyer et al., 1987). One way to get a meaningful measure of the student's speech during this time is to record him or her several times during the observation period. The recordings will be helpful to the speech-language pathologist and will provide a basis for comparison. Teachers might ask themselves the following questions before referring a student for evaluation of a voice disorder:

- Is the student's voice having such an unpleasant effect on others that the student is teased or excluded from activities?
- Does the student habitually abuse or misuse his voice?
- Is there a possibility that the voice disorder is related to another medical condition?
- Does the student's voice problem make him difficult for others to understand?
- Has there been a recent, noticeable change in the student's vocal quality?
- Might the voice quality be related to a hearing loss?

Speech-language pathologists are trained to provide treatment for voice disorders. The management of voice disorders depends on a number of variables; however, the primary goal of the SLP is straightforward, as indicated by Silverman and Miller (2006):

> The first goal in the process of voice rehabilitation is to restore the condition of the vocal folds to normal or, if is not possible, compensate for whatever abnormality is present. The primary goal of voice rehabilitation following a laryngectomy is restoring the condition of the larynx as much as possible or providing the person with an alternative way to phonate. (p. 120)

Read the nearby Personal Spotlight to find out more about the work of a speech-language pathologist.

Fluency Disorders

Fluency refers to the pattern of the rate and flow of a person's speech. Normal speech has a rhythm and timing that is regular and steady; however, normal speech patterns also include some interruptions in speech flow. We all sometimes stumble over sounds, repeat syllables or words, mix up speech sounds in words, speak too fast, or fill in pauses with "uh" or "you know."

PERSONAL SPOTLIGHT

SPEECH–LANGUAGE PATHOLOGIST

MARTHA DRENNAN has been a speech–language pathologist for eight years. She has been employed in both a large, urban district and a small, rural district. Currently she works for the Rison School District in Rison, Arkansas. One of the most significant changes Martha has observed in her field is that many children now receive speech-language services in a general education setting rather than being pulled out for services in a segregated, speech classroom. Martha likes this change. She notes that there are several advantages to providing services to these children in general classrooms rather than pulling them out. Among these advantages are that

- more students can be served because the speech–language pathologist can work with several students at the same time. Often an entire class is the target of a lesson conducted by the speech–language pathologist so that all students benefit.

- some students, especially older ones, do not feel the stigma of receiving services as part of their general education classroom whereas they did when they had to leave the room for speech.

Martha notes that many older students really resent having to go to the speech room. She especially sees serving students in the general education setting as beneficial for this group of students.

Despite benefits, there are also some negative factors associated with this newer service delivery model. Martha said that "some teachers would simply rather teach all the lessons in their classroom themselves because they feel like they do not have the luxury to give another teacher time."

Another negative to providing services in the general education classroom is that students with speech-language needs do not get the individual attention in general education classes that they would if they were to receive their services in the speech room.

Overall, Martha is very pleased with serving students with speech and language needs in general education classes. She noted that "virtually all general education teachers are very happy when you go into their classroom and provide a language lesson for all kids." She also stated that the collaboration needed to ensure an effective, smooth lesson requires time for general education teachers and speech–language pathologists to plan, something that seems to always be a problem.

Often normal dysfluencies of speech are related to stressful or demanding situations. When the interruptions in speech flow are so frequent or pervasive that a speaker cannot be understood, when efforts at speech are so intense that they are uncomfortable, or when they draw undue attention, the dysfluencies are considered a problem (Hallahan, Kauffman, & Pullen, 2009). Some of the key factors that distinguish normal from abnormal speech fluency include:

- Frequency of occurrence
- Duration of individual moments of dysfluency
- Amount of tension present
- Speakers' awareness of and attitude towards moments of dysfluency (Silverman & Miller, 2006, pp. 153–154)

Many young children, especially those between the ages of 2 and 4, demonstrate dysfluencies in the course of normal speech development. Parents and teachers may become concerned about young children's fluency, but most of the dysfluencies of early childhood begin to disappear by age 5. The most frequent type of fluency disorder is **stuttering**, which affects about 4 to 5% of school-age children, three times more often boys than girls (ASHA, 2008). Cluttering, another type of fluency disorder, occurs infrequently in school-age children. Disturbances of prosody and intonation are rare in children, and are often associated with other, more serious communication problems. The 2006 study conducted by ASHA reported that 69% of speech–language pathologists have caseloads that include students with fluency disorders.

Fluency problems usually consist of blocking, repeating, prolonging, or avoiding sounds, syllables, words, or phrases. In stuttering, these interruptions are frequently obvious to both the speaker and the listener. Often, they are very disruptive to the act of speaking, much more so than disorders of articulation or voice. When the speech dysfluencies occur, listeners may become uncomfortable and look away or try to finish the speaker's words, phrases,

TABLE 12.2

Interesting Characteristics of Stuttering

CONDITION	SITUATIONS
Those who stutter tend to be . . .	
. . . relatively fluent when . . .	• Reading in unison with another person • Speaking to an infant or an animal • Singing • Swearing or openly expressing anger • Speaking in any nonhabitual manner (e.g., overly loud voice; while engaged in rhythmic physical activity such as dancing)
. . . stutter a great deal when	• Speaking on the telephone • Speaking to people they regard as authority figures • Speaking in situations in which they anticipate stuttering and want to avoid dysfluencies • Speaking to people who are likely to react adversely • Desiring to communicate quickly (e.g., when giving an order to a waitress)

Source: From Silverman & Miller (2006).

or sentences. This discomfort is exacerbated when dysfluent speech is accompanied by unusual gestures, facial contortions, or other movements. Because stuttering can lead to such a pronounced interruption of normal speech and also has a profound impact on listeners, the disorder receives a lot of attention, even though it is not as prevalent as other communication disorders.

One of the mysteries related to dysfluencies is that individuals who stutter tend to be relatively fluent in certain situations and have major difficulties in others. Silverman and Miller (2006) identify some of these situations (see Table 12.2).

Causes of Stuttering   Although many causes of stuttering have been suggested over the years, the current thinking among professionals in the field of communication disorders is that there is no one cause for stuttering. Current theories regarding the possible causes of developmental stuttering include factors such as language development, motor skills, personality, and environment.

There seems to be no doubt that the children who stutter are very vulnerable to the reactions (e.g., attitudes, responses, and comments) of their teachers and peers. When considerable attention is focused on normal dysfluencies or when students begin to have negative feelings about themselves because of their stuttering, they may become even more anxious and their stuttering may get worse. Most students who stutter will benefit from intervention by a speech-language pathologist if they hope to avoid a lifelong problem that will affect their ability to communicate, learn, work, and develop positive interpersonal relationships.

When Fluency Disorders Are a Serious Problem   Although we know that many children will naturally outgrow their speech dysfluencies, we are unable to predict which children will not. Therefore, classroom teachers should be sure to refer any children who show signs of dysfluency so that a speech-language pathologist can evaluate them, and, if necessary, provide speech therapy. Teachers should consider the following questions when deciding whether speech dysfluencies are serious:

• Are the dysfluencies beginning to occur more often in the student's speech or beginning to sound more effortful or strained?
• Is there a pattern to situations in which the student stutters?

- Is the student experiencing social problems?
- Is the student concerned about his dysfluencies?
- Does the student avoid speaking because he is afraid he may stutter?

LANGUAGE DISORDERS

Language is the system we use to communicate our thoughts and ideas to others. Language is a code "whereby ideas about the world are expressed through a conventional system of arbitrary signals for communication" (Lahey, 1988, p. 2). The interrelationships of what we hear, speak, read, and write become our format for sharing information. For most of us, spoken language is the tool we use to communicate our ideas, but even the most articulate, fluent, pleasant speech would be useless without a language system that enables us to understand and be understood. Language is an integral component of students' abilities in reading, writing, speaking, and listening.

In recent years, the emphasis in the field of communication disorders has shifted to encompass an increased focus on language disorders. Language disorders often have a serious impact on academic performance. ASHA (1993) defines a language disorder as "the impaired comprehension and/or use of spoken, written, and/or other symbol system. The disorder may involve the form, content, and/or function of language in communication." Language impairment affects approximately 7% of children (Ziegler et al., 2005). Sixty-one percent of school-based SLPs provide services to students with specific language impairment (ASHA, 2006).

■ Stuttering is the most frequent type of fluency disorder, affecting about 2% of school age children, more often boys than girls.

More important for classroom teachers to recognize, however, is that remediation of language disorders will often be as much their responsibility as it is the speech–language pathologist's. Although remediation of speech problems is provided primarily in a therapeutic setting and then supported and reinforced by the classroom teacher, classroom teachers will often direct and manage the overall language development of their students in collaboration with the speech–language pathologist and other special education staff. Recent research has shown that some types of language disorders are best treated collaboratively in the classroom (McGinty & Justice, 2006).

We know that humans can communicate in several ways (speech, writing, gestures). We generally describe modes of communication as either **receptive language**, which involves receiving and decoding or interpreting language, or **expressive language**, which is the encoding or production of a message. Reading and listening are examples of receptive language; writing and speaking are forms of expressive language.

As with speech disorders, knowing the normal sequence of language development is important in working with students with language disorders. Some children may be delayed in their development of language but still acquire skills in the same general sequence as other children. Other children may acquire some age-appropriate language skills but have deficits in other specific areas. Table 12.3 shows the normal patterns of language development for children with language disorders and children without language disorders. Although teachers may refer to these general patterns of language development to judge students' overall progress, they should not expect every child to follow this precise sequence on these exact timelines.

Earlier in the chapter, some terminology related to language disorders was introduced. In addition, we refer to the dimensions of language and their related impairments in terms of form, content, and function (or use). Students can demonstrate impairments in any or all of these areas. Figure 12.3 describes these three major dimensions of language.

TABLE 12.3

Language Development for Children with Language Disorders and Without Language Disorders

LANGUAGE-DISORDERED CHILD			NORMALLY DEVELOPING CHILD		
AGE	**ATTAINMENT**	**EXAMPLE**	**AGE**	**ATTAINMENT**	**EXAMPLE**
27 months	First words	*this, mama, bye bye, doggie*	13 months	First words	*here, mama, bye bye, kitty*
38 months	50-word vocabulary		17 months	50-word vocabulary	
40 months	First two-word combinations	*this doggie more apple this mama more play*	18 months	First two-word combinations	*more juice here ball more TV here kitty*
48 months	Later two-word combinations	*Mimi purse Daddy coat block chair dolly table*	22 months	Later two-word combinations	*Andy shoe Mommy ring cup floor keys chair*
52 months	Mean sentence length of 2.00 words		24 months	Mean sentence length of 2.00 words	
55 months	First appearance of -ing	*Mommy eating*	24 months	First appearance of -ing	*Andy sleeping*
63 months	Mean sentence length of 3.10 words		30 months	Mean sentence length of 3.10 words	
66 months	First appearance of *is*	*The doggie's mad*	30 months	First appearance of *is*	*My car's gone!*
73 months	Mean sentence length of 4.10 words		37 months	Mean sentence length of 4.10 words	
79 months	Mean sentence length of 4.50 words		37 months	First appearance of indirect requests	*Can I have some cookies?*
79 months	First appearance of indirect requests	*Can I get the ball?*	40 months	Mean sentence length of 4.50 words	

Source: From "Language Disorders in Preschool Children" by L. Leonard, in *Human Communications Disorders: An Introduction* (4th ed.), p. 179, edited by G. H. Shames, E. H. Wiig, and W. A. Second, 1994, New York: Macmillan. Copyright © 1994. Reprinted with permission of Merrill, an imprint of Macmillan Publishing Company.

Types and Causes of Language Disorders

Various systems exist for classifying language disorders. Hegde (2010) identifies four major types of deficits: morphological, syntactic, semantic, and pragmatic. Naremore (1980) describes four categories of language disorders and includes some suspected causes of each (see Table 12.4). For children who are not deaf, a complete absence of language would likely indicate severe emotional disturbance or a severe developmental disorder such as autism.

Qualitatively different language is also associated with developmental disorders and emotional disturbance. A good example of this type of problem is the echolalic speech of children with autism, who may repeat speech they hear in a singsong voice and fail to use their spoken language in a meaningful way.

Delayed language occurs when a child develops language in the same approximate sequence as other children, but at a slower rate. Causes of delayed language include intellectual disability, hearing loss, or lack of stimulation or appropriate experiences. There is also substantial evidence for familial transmission of SLI. The incidence in families with a history of SLI is estimated at 20 to 40% (Choudhury & Benasich, 2003).

Sometimes language development is interrupted by illness or physical trauma. This type of language problem is increasingly common among children as a result of TBI. In general

FIGURE 12.3

Major dimensions of
language.

Form — rule systems used in oral language

Phonology—rules systems related to individual and combined sounds
(sounds are combined to form words)
Morphology—rule system related to construction of words
(units of meaning)
Syntax—ordering of words so they can be understood
(where words are placed in a phrase or sentence)

Content

Intent and meaning of language and its rule system
(words are used to describe and label objects or ideas)

Use

Purpose and setting of communication
and people communicated with dictate
the type of language used (children
speak differently to adults than to
children)

TABLE 12.4

Types of Language Disorders and Their Causes

TYPE	COMMONLY SUSPECTED CAUSATIVE FACTORS OR RELATED CONDITIONS
No Verbal Language Child does not show indications of understanding or spontaneously using language by age 3.	• Congenital or early acquired deafness • Gross brain damage or severe mental retardation/developmental disabilities • Severe emotional disturbance
Quantitatively Different Language Child's language is different from that of nondisabled children at any stage of development—meaning and usefulness for communication are greatly lessened or lost.	• Inability to understand auditory stimuli • Severe emotional disturbance • Learning disability • Mental retardation/developmental disabilities • Hearing loss
Delayed Language Development Language follows normal course of development, but lags seriously behind that of most children who are the same chronological age.	• Mental retardation • Experiential deprivation • Lack of language stimulation • Hearing loss
Interrupted Language Development Normal language development begins but is interrupted by illness, accident, or other trauma; language disorder is acquired.	• Acquired hearing loss • Brain injury due to oxygen deprivation, physical trauma, or infection

Source: Adapted from "Language Disorders in Children" by R. C. Naremore. In *Introduction to Communication Disorders,* p. 224, edited by T. J. Hixon, L. D. Shriberg, and J. H. Saxman, 1980, Upper Saddle River, NJ: Prentice-Hall. Used by permission.

education classrooms, teachers may encounter any or all of these types of language disorders ranging from very mild to severe. As stressed previously, many of the main challenges that these students present in the general education classroom will be associated with the demands of ongoing instruction. However, it will be extremely beneficial for teachers to work with the speech–language pathologist in relation to the language goals that have been written for these students.

Characteristics of Language Impairments

Some teachers may have an overall sense that a student is demonstrating language problems; others may not notice anything amiss. Wiig and Semel (1984) have identified some indicators of language problems as a function of school level:

Elementary level:
- Problems in following verbal directions
- Difficulty with preacademic skills
- Phonics problems
- Poor word-attack skills
- Difficulties with structural analysis
- Problems learning new material

Secondary level:
- Word substitutions
- Inadequate language processing and production that affects reading comprehension and academic achievement
- Inability to understand abstract concepts
- Difficulties connecting previously learned information to new material that must be learned independently
- Widening gap in achievement when compared to peers

The Characteristics and Implications feature provides a list of key characteristic areas, the educational implications that might arise, and some selected suggestions for addressing these potential problems. The feature considers areas beyond the language form and content with an emphasis on functional implications.

Children and youth who have language disorders sometimes develop patterns of interaction with peers, teachers, and family members that may result in behavior problems. The behavior problems might seem to have nothing to do with language problems but may in fact have developed in response to inabilities to read, spell, talk, or write effectively.

EFFECTIVE INCLUSIVE PRACTICES

Challenges for Teachers

Teachers must be careful to differentiate language differences from language disorders. Students' patterns of speech and use of language reflect their culture, socioeconomic status, and gender and may be different from that of some of their peers. It is extremely important not to mistake a language difference for a language disorder; however, a disorder must not be overlooked in a student with language differences. Variations in family structure, child-rearing practices, family perceptions and attitudes, regional dialects, and language and communication styles can all influence students' communication (Wayman, Lynch, & Hanson, 1990).

Acquiring English as a Second Language Students who are learning English as a second language (ESL) often exhibit error patterns that can look like language disorders when they are, in fact, part of the normal process of second-language acquisition (Roseberry-McKibbins & Brice, 2002). It is crucial that teachers of English language learners recognize

■ CHARACTERISTICS AND IMPLICATIONS: LANGUAGE DISORDERS ■

AREA	POTENTIAL DIFFICULTIES	EDUCATIONAL IMPLICATIONS
Language Development	Delayed acquisition of vocabulary and language rules Immature language for age	Provide appropriate language models. Provide opportunities for students to learn language for varied purposes and with different audiences.
Language Use	Limited vocabulary Language is not flexible	Teach specialized vocabularies (e.g., occupational vocabulary). Pre-teach vocabulary in lessons. Provide different situations where linguistic responses are required.
Expressive Language	Inability to articulate thoughts and feelings Problems indicating preferences and interests Language is incomprehensible	Allow additional opportunities for expressing thoughts. Make the student feel comfortable.
Receptive Language	Difficulty understanding classroom discussions Problems in following directions Struggle with questions that are asked	Teach strategies for listening and note taking. Recommend that the student ask that certain communications be repeated. Provide sufficient time for the student to process information. Provide suitable supplemental aids such as graphic organizers.
Pragmatic Language	Inability to communicate properly in social situations Problems in initiating and ending conversations Does not use typical greetings and good-byes Problems in taking turns when talking	Provide opportunities for students to interact with peers and adults. Teach specific skills. Role-play a variety of social situations.
Academic Performance	Difficulties understanding the language of the classroom Problems in comprehending vocabulary Problems in comprehending narrative and expository text	Include student in ongoing discussions. Provide wait-time for entire class before soliciting responses. Ask student—initially—questions for which you know he/she has a response.
Social-Emotional-Behavioral	Desire not to draw attention to self Lack of peer acceptance Poor self-concept Easily frustrated Inappropriate classroom behavior	Create a classroom climate where students feel accepted, valued, and able to interact. Encourage student. Remind student of what he/she can do well. Point out inappropriate behavior and why it is a problem. Teach appropriate behavior.
Metacognition	Inability to produce strategies to assist learning Not able to organize new information Inability to regulate behavior and make necessary changes	Teach various self-regulatory strategies. Provide aids to help with organization.

these patterns as language differences rather than language disorders in order to avoid unnecessary referrals:

- **Interference or transfer:** Students may make errors in English form because of the influence of structures or patterns in their native language.
- **Silent period:** Children who are learning a new language focus on listening to and attempting to understand the new language before trying out what they have learned. This silent period may last as long as a year in very young children and as briefly as a few weeks or months in older children.
- **Code switching or code mixing:** Students use words, phrases, or sentences from one language in the other language.

Relationship Between Communication Style and Culture   Culture has a strong influence on the style of communication. Many areas of communication style can be affected by factors including gender, status, dialect, and age roles; rules governing interruptions and taking turns; use of humor; and how to greet or leave someone (Erickson, 1992). Teachers must be aware of the many manifestations of culture in nonverbal communication as well.

Cultural differences in rules governing eye contact, the physical space between speakers, use of gestures and facial expression, and use of silence can cause dissonance between teachers and students of differing cultures. Walker (1993) described how differences such as directness of a conversation, volume of voices, and reliance on verbal (low-context) versus nonverbal (high-context) parts of communication affect attitudes toward the speaker. Teachers can respond to cultural differences in several ways. These suggestions are adapted from Walker (1993) and should be helpful for teachers who want to enhance both overall achievement and communication skills with students who are culturally or linguistically different:

- Try to involve community resources, including churches and neighborhood organizations, in school activities.
- Make home visits.
- Allow flexible hours for conferences.
- Question your own assumptions about human behavior, values, biases, personal limitations, and so on.
- Try to understand the world from the student's perspective.
- Ask yourself questions about an individual student's behavior in light of cultural values, motivation, and worldviews, and how these relate to his or her learning experiences.
- Remind yourself and your students to celebrate and value the cultural and linguistic differences among individuals in their school and community.
- Consult with the speech–language pathologist to understand how to differentiate between students who have language differences and those who have disorders. (p. 2)

Multicultural Considerations in Assessment   Assessment in the area of communication disorders is often complicated, just as it is for students with other disabilities. Because of the increasing numbers of students who are culturally and linguistically different and who require services in ESL or who are **limited English proficient (LEP)**, teachers should consult with personnel in special education, ESL, speech and language services, and bilingual education to obtain appropriate evaluation and programming services. Observation is an important form of assessment, particularly when assessing students who are linguistically different. In the 1999–2000 school year, speech–language pathologists reported that over one-fourth of their students were from a cultural or linguistic group different from their own, and 8.8% were English-language learners (Carlson, Brauen, Klein, Schroll, & Willig, 2002).

Because of the increasing number of students from cultural or linguistic minority groups in public schools, teachers are recognizing the need for information related to learning and communication styles as well as modifications to curriculum and instruction. Although many of these children will never be identified as having a speech or language disorder, teachers in general education must be aware that differences in language and culture can often impact a student's apparent proficiency in both oral and written communication.

PROMOTING INCLUSIVE PRACTICES FOR STUDENTS WITH SPEECH AND LANGUAGE DISORDERS

Until very recently, the traditional service delivery model for speech therapy included a twice-weekly, 30-minutes-per-session, pullout model in which speech–language pathologists worked with students in a small room away from the regular education classroom. Even though this model may still be appropriate with some students some of the time, there are other effective approaches for provision of speech-language therapy services in public school settings. Just as academic services to students with disabilities have become more and more integrated into general education programs, speech-language services are now following more inclusive models.

Service Delivery Options

This collaboration between regular and special education staff might involve speech–language pathologists visiting the class-room to work with individual students or with small groups, the teacher and speech–language pathologist teaching alternate lessons or sections of a particular lesson, or professionals coteaching the same lesson at the same time. The following delivery options have been recommended for the provision of speech and language services in the schools: **direct instruction (pullout)**, **classroom-based**, **community-based**, and **consultation** (ASHA, 1996). These service-delivery options can be implemented independently or in any combination to best meet the individual needs of the student. Recent evidence suggests that the influence of service-delivery models on the outcomes children achieve varies according to the type of disorder that is being addressed:

■ The cultural background of a child will influence many aspects of the style of communication that is used.

- The traditional pullout model is indicated for students who are in particular stages of the intervention process or for those who have very specific communication goals. Pullout services are often provided within the classroom or in the therapy room, and with individual students or in small groups.
- Classroom-based service-delivery options usually involve a collaborative effort between teachers and speech–language pathologists. This model is particularly appropriate at the preschool and kindergarten levels and in classrooms with large numbers of students who have been identified as having communication disorders or as being at risk. This collaboration can involve the speech–language pathologist providing individual or small-group instruction in the classroom or participating in team teaching or coteaching lessons with the classroom teacher.
- The community-based service-delivery model indicates that therapy services are being provided in more natural communication environments such as at home, on the playground, or in other age-appropriate community settings. Providing speech and language therapy in a community-based setting is ideal for students who have pragmatic language disorders, for those who need to generalize new skills to a variety of settings, and for students who are enrolled in vocational programs.
- Consultation is a model of service delivery in which the speech–language pathologist does not provide direct instruction to the student. Instead, the family, teachers, or other school staff are provided with assistance in the form of information, training, or resources to help the student reach specific communication goals. The provision of consultation services is indicated for those students who are working on generalization of communication skills or for those students who are receiving communication programming from other instructional staff.

Working Collaboratively with the Speech–Language Pathologist

The following list (Friend, 1992) demonstrates the various roles that members of an educational team might assume to implement speech and language interventions in the school setting:

- There is one primary provider of services to the student.
- One provider (speech-language pathologist) teaches others specific assessment or treatment strategies; other providers (e.g., teacher) implement the strategies.
- One provider provides services; the others assist side by side.
- One provider provides services at a learning center within a large group.
- Two providers implement interventions simultaneously during a codirected lesson (parallel teaching).
- One provider (teacher and curriculum) recommends to other providers suggestions of content and methods to incorporate into intervention; other providers (speech-language pathologists) implement recommendations (supplemental teaching).
- Other roles devised to meet the client's unique needs.

As schools try to maximize the positive impact of professional collaboration, it is important to recognize and overcome the barriers inherent in the process. The barriers to greater collaboration among speech-language professionals and teachers can include (Kerrin, 1996):

- Territorial obstacles ("This is my job; that is your job.")
- Time concerns ("When are general education teachers supposed to find the time to meet, plan, and modify?")
- Terror ("I'm afraid this new way won't work.")

Fortunately, Kerrin (1996) has also offered some good ideas for overcoming these obstacles. She suggests that team members try the following tips:

- Try to be flexible and creative when scheduling conferences.
- Encourage everyone involved to ask questions.
- Invite speech-language professionals into the classroom.
- Ask for assistance in planning.
- Maintain open, regular communication.
- Keep an open mind, a cooperative spirit, and a sense of humor.

LINC (Language IN the Classroom) LINC is a program adapted for use in many school districts (Breeding, Stone, & Riley, n.d.). The program philosophy holds that language learning should occur in the child's most natural environment and in conjunction with other content being learned. The development of students' language should relate to their world and should be a learning experience, not a teaching experience.

The purpose of the program is to strengthen the language system of those students in general education classrooms who need to develop coping and compensatory skills to survive academically. Another goal is to transfer language learned from the therapy setting to the classroom, thereby allowing children to learn to communicate, rather than merely talk. The teacher and the speech–language pathologist must both be present for the approach to be successful. The two professionals work together to plan unit lessons that develop language skills in students.

Hiller (1990) presents an example of how LINC works. His elementary school implemented classroom-based language instruction. At the beginning of the program, the speech-language pathologist visited each classroom for a specified amount of time each week (90 minutes) during the language arts period. The first 45 minutes were used for an oral language activity, often a cooking activity from the *Blooming Recipes* workbook (Tavzel, 1987). During the second 45 minutes, students wrote paragraphs. For example, after preparing peanut butter and raisins on celery ("Bumps on a Log"), students responded to the following questions:

- What was the name of the recipe we made?
- Where did we do our preparing?

- Who brought the peanut butter, celery, and raisins?
- How did we make "Bumps on a Log"?
- When did we eat "Bumps on a Log"?
- Why do you think this recipe is called "Bumps on a Log"?

Responses were written on the board. Students copied the responses in paragraph format.

Teachers and speech–language pathologists later extended the activities to teaching language lessons on current topics, team-teaching critical-thinking activities during science experiments, and team planning and teaching social studies units. Reports from Hiller and from other schools using LINC programs described better collaboration among professionals, more accurate language referrals, and increased interest in speech-language activities among the entire staff.

CLASSROOM ADAPTATIONS FOR STUDENTS WITH SPEECH AND LANGUAGE DISORDERS

This section of the chapter will provide a number of practical ways to address the needs of students with speech and language disorders within the context of the general education classroom. Thoughts to consider in the elementary classroom are highlighted in the Differentiating Elementary Instruction feature.

Ideas for Students with Speech Disorders

Establish and Maintain a Positive Classroom Climate Regardless of the type of speech disorder that students in general education classes demonstrate, it is crucial that teachers make every effort to create a positive, accepting, and supportive climate. This general suggestion is very important because it is a dimension that teachers are able to control. The following points are helpful for teachers to remember when dealing with children who have speech disorders:

- Talk with the student privately about his or her speech problems. Acknowledge your awareness of the problem, and stress your belief that his or her speech will improve with practice.

Differentiating Elementary Instruction

Many students have difficulty processing information to which they are listening. All students, for that matter, will experience problems from time to time. However, for students with a significant receptive language problem, doing so has functional impact, not only in the classroom, but also outside of school.

One of the most dramatic presentations on how it might feel to have difficulty processing information is demonstrated in the video, "How Difficult Can This Be? The F.A.T. City Workshop." The powerful video conveys the realities of the classroom faced by students with receptive language issues. The participants in the workshop clearly get the message of how this can be a problem. Richard Lavoie convincingly shows how difficult it truly can be.

Anyone who watches this video will come away with an appreciation of the obstacles faced by a student in a typical classroom situation. Moreover, teachers can easily determine ways to address processing problems by designing instructional lessons where all students are requested to "wait" to respond to a question until prompted to do so. In this way, students who need more time to process the question and develop a proper response have time to do so. Teachers may also want to alter the pace of instruction so that, while still engaging students, it allows students with processing issues an opportunity to keep up with the ongoing discussion and/or lecture.

- Encourage the student's family to actively support the student's educational and communication goals.
- Do not think of or refer to students with speech disorders in terms of their presenting issue (they are "students," not "stutterers").
- Work closely with the speech–language pathologist, following his/her suggestions and trying to reinforce specific communication skills.
- Encourage the student.
- Accept the student just as you would any other student in the class.
- Provide lots of opportunities for students to participate in activities that require oral participation.
- Give students lots of chances to model and practice appropriate speech.
- Maintain eye contact when the student speaks.
- Be a good listener.
- Don't interrupt the student (who stutters) or finish his or her sentence.
- When appropriate, educate other students in the class about speech disorders and about acceptance and understanding.

See Tips for Adapting a Lesson for David for specific recommendations for the student profiled in the chapter-opening vignette.

Help Students Learn to Monitor Their Own Speech Teachers can help students focus on using the skills they learn in speech therapy. After students have had success practicing their communication goals in the therapy setting, they can then practice, monitor their own performance, and earn reinforcement from the teacher or parents whenever specific criteria are met.

Pair Students for Practice If students are to master speech skills, they will need to practice the skills taught by the speech–language pathologist frequently in many different settings. One way for students to practice specific sounds is to use practice exercises like those in *Read the Picture Stories for Articulation* (Loehr, 2002, Figure 1.3). With a partner, students can use short periods of downtime, such as those between or before classes, to work on their articulation. First, the student is trained in the speech-therapy setting on a specific phoneme in a particular position of words; for example, the initial /s/ sound in seal. After the student has reached 90% mastery of the /s/ sound in the beginning of words, she or he then reads a story that is saturated with words beginning with the /s/ sound to a classmate. Each practice session should take no more than 5 minutes and will provide students with practice that is simple and fun. Both partners should be reinforced for their participation. This practice format can also be used at home with parents.

TIPS FOR ADAPTING A LESSON FOR **DAVID**

Based on the chapter-opening vignette, several adaptations are appropriate for David.

David's teacher should do the following:

- Do not complete sentences for David; be patient and allow him time to get the words out.
- Do not ask David to "slow down" or "relax"; these instructions are not helpful to him.
- During group instruction, call on David fairly early in the discussion and ask David questions that can be answered with relatively few words.

- Speak slowly during group instruction to help slow the pace of all interactions in class.
- Have the same academic expectations for David as for any other student in the class.
- Talk about stuttering with the class and with David just as you would any other matter. It is nothing to be ashamed of.

Teach Students Affirmations and Positive Self-Talk Students with speech disorders, especially stuttering, need to learn self-confidence and develop a positive attitude. These features are as important as mastery of specific speech skills. Research has supported the premise that we all talk to ourselves, and the more we talk to ourselves in certain ways, the more we think about ourselves in those same ways. Although negative **self-talk** is common among individuals who have speech disorders, it is possible to change negative patterns to more positive ones.

Affirmations like those suggested by Daly (1991) can help students to build their confidence. The goal of positive self-talk is to replace negative patterns, which might include the statements "I could never do that" or "I can never talk on the phone without stuttering" with positive statements, such as "I am positive and confident. I know that I can handle any speaking situation by being in control of my speech," and "I enjoy saying my name clearly and smoothly when answering the telephone." Whenever a student slips back into a negative frame of mind, encourage him or her to mentally erase the negative ideas and immediately think of something positive. Students should also write their affirmations in their own words, so that they will remember them easily and will more likely use them.

Differentiate Instruction and Materials A number of differentiating techniques can be used to address the needs of these students within the general education classroom. Referring to the interactive unit model for designing the way a teacher presents information in a classroom and the way the student has to respond, it is possible to design in-class instruction/activities in ways that consider the student's present levels of functioning.

The *Pre-Referral Intervention Manual-Third Edition* (PRIM) (McCarney & Wunderlich, 2006) presents numerous ways to intervene with students who demonstrate speech errors. Some of the suggestions include:

- Set up a system of motivators to encourage students' efforts.
- Highlight material to identify key syllables and words in a passage.
- Give students practice listening so that they can learn to discriminate among sounds, fluent speech patterns, and good vocal habits.
- Tape-record the students' reading so that they can evaluate themselves related to their communication goals.
- Reduce the emphasis on competition. Competitive activities may increase students' stress and result in even more speech errors.

Encourage Parents to Work with Their Children There are many ways to structure practice activities so that students can work at home with their parents. One program is described in the book *Oral-Motor Activities for School-Aged Children* (Mackie, 1996, Figure 11.4). This series of homework activities is designed to help build the skills that are prerequisite to producing sounds in words. They are designed to be an enjoyable approach to improving the coordination, sensory awareness, and muscle strength needed to produce the sounds of speech. By completing the activities, students assume responsibility for practicing skills learned in the therapy room in other environments. It is suggested that students complete one activity per day and have their parents discuss it with them and provide feedback and guidance.

Teach Students Their Own Strategies Many of the speech problems that students demonstrate when they are young can be corrected and modified with therapy. While the therapy is going on, the teacher should focus on giving students strategies for successful learning. The strategies are little "tricks of the trade" that students can use to maximize their academic and social strengths. Some of these strategies also require accommodations on the part of the teacher in structuring situations and requirements.

- Teach them to relax with breathing exercises or mental imagery.
- Encourage them to participate in groups in which responses do not have to be individually generated.
- Teach them to reinforce themselves by recognizing when they are doing well and by appreciating themselves.

IEP GOALS AND OBJECTIVES FOR DAVID*

GOAL 1: David will read in a variety of settings with normal fluency.

Objective 1: Given a short passage to read in the therapy setting, David will read the passage with normal fluency in 75% of trials.

Objective 2: Given a short passage at home, David will read the passage with normal fluency in 75% of trials.

Objective 3: Given a short passage in the classroom, David will read the passage with normal fluency in 75% of trials.

GOAL 2: David will learn techniques that facilitate fluent speech.

Objective 1: Given the opportunity to describe and demonstrate breathing techniques in the therapy setting and at home, David will do so appropriately in 70% of the trials.

Objective 2: Given the opportunity to demonstrate mastery of relaxation techniques in the therapy setting and at home, David will do so successfully in 70% of trials.

Objective 3: Given the opportunity to demonstrate the use of slow, easy speech in the therapy setting and at home, David will do so successfully in 70% of trials.

Objective 4: Given the opportunity to demonstrate the use of fluency-facilitating techniques in small groups in the classroom, David will do so successfully in 70% of opportunities.

*IDEA 2004 does not require short-term objectives except for students taking alternative assessments.

- Let them practice skills with a friend in real situations so that they are not afraid or nervous when it's the "real thing."
- Let them tape-record their own speech and listen carefully for errors so that they can discriminate between correct and incorrect sounds.
- Help them come up with strategies for dealing with specific people or situations that make them nervous (walking away, counting to ten before they speak, deep breathing, etc.).

The IEP Goals and Objectives for David feature includes examples of the strategies recommended for David to try on his own.

Adaptations for Students with Language Disorders

Numerous strategies can be used in general education classrooms to improve students' language skills and remedy language deficits. Teachers should consult with the speech–language pathologist and other special education personnel to differentiate instruction for students with language disorders. The following sections present some ways of differentiating instruction (i.e., structuring learning situations and presenting information) to enhance speech and language abilities.

Teach Some Prerequisite Imitation Skills   For young children, Nowacek and McShane (1993) recommend the following activities:

- Show a picture (of a girl running) and say, "The girl is running."
- Ask the student to repeat a target phrase.
- Positively reinforce correct responses.
- Present a variety of subject/verb combinations until the student correctly and consistently imitates them.

Give Students Opportunities for Facilitative Play   Facilitative play provides modeling for the students so that they can imitate and expand their own use of language. The following is an abbreviated sequence for this type of interaction (Nowacek & McShane, 1993):

- The teacher models self-talk in a play activity. ("I'm making the cars go.")
- The teacher elicits comments from the student and then expands on them. ("Yes, the cars are going fast.")
- The teacher uses "buildups" and "breakdowns" by expanding on a student's ideas, breaking them down, and then repeating them. ("Red car go? Yes, look at the red car. It's going fast on the road. It's going to win the race.")

Improve Comprehension in the Classroom   Clary and Edwards (1992) suggest some specific activities to improve students' receptive language skills:

- **Give students practice in following directions.** Begin with one simple direction, and then increase the length of the list of directions.
- **Have students pair up and practice descriptions.** Place two students at a table separated by a screen. Place groups of identical objects in front of both students. Have one describe one of the objects; the other must determine which object is being described. Reverse roles with new sets of objects.
- **Let students work on categorizing.** Orally present a list of three words. Two should be related in some way. Ask a student to tell which two are related and why (e.g., horse, tree, dog).

Encourage Students to Talk with Their Teachers and Peers   Sometimes students who are reluctant to speak require encouragement. In addition to encouraging them with positive social interactions, teachers might also have to structure situations in which students must use language to meet some of their needs in the classroom. The strategies that follow should prompt students to use language when they otherwise might not.

- Place items out of reach so that the child has to ask for them.
- When a child asks for an item, present the wrong item (e.g., the child asks for a spoon and you present a fork).
- Give a child an item that is hard to open so that he or she has to request assistance.
- When performing a task, do one step incorrectly (forget to put the milk in the blender with the pudding mix).
- Make items difficult to find.
- Give students an item that requires some assistance to work with (e.g., an orange that needs peeling).

Develop Pragmatic Language Skills   Pragmatic language simply can be understood to mean "how language is used socially to achieve some purpose" (Phelps-Terasaki & Phelps-Gunn, 2007). Having the opportunity to become more adept in social situations is beneficial to many students, especially those for whom the "use" of language is difficult. As a result, teachers can create opportunities for students to improve their skills. Gilliam and Miller (2006) offer a three-component way to conceptualize the areas where pragmatic skills are needed. Using this structure, some ideas for developing pragmatic skills are provided:

- **Classroom Interaction:**
  - Group activities that involve varying degrees of interaction
  - Presentations to the class
  - Lessons on how to ask questions
- **Social Interaction:**
  - Practice in how to begin conversations
  - Determination of how others are feeling
  - Practice in taking turns when talking with others
- **Personal Interaction:**
  - Discussion of how to express feelings
  - Practice using different types of figurative language

Use Naturalistic Techniques and Simulated Real-Life Activities to Increase Language Use   Often, the most effective techniques to instill language acquisition and use are those that will be easy for teachers to use and easy for students to generalize to everyday situations. Teachers can encourage generalization by using naturalistic and situational strategies and real-life activities:

- **Naturalistic techniques**
  - Try cloze activities. ("What do you need? Oh, you need paint and a _____. That's right, you need paint and a brush.")
  - Emphasize problem solving. ("You can't find your backpack? What should you do? Let's look on the hook. Is your coat there? What did we do to find your coat? That's right, we looked on the hook.")
  - Use questioning techniques. ("Where are you going? That's right, you are going to lunch.")
- **Simulated real-life activities**
  - Let students role-play a newscast or commercial.
  - Have students write and follow their own written directions to locations in and around the school.
  - Play "social charades" by having students act out social situations and decide on appropriate responses.
  - Have one student teach an everyday skill to another (e.g., how to shoot a basket).
  - Using real telephones, give students opportunities to call each other, and to give, receive, and record messages.

Encourage Students' Conversational Skills Through Story Reading   McNeill and Fowler (1996) give some excellent suggestions for helping students with delayed language development. Students with language development problems often do not get the results they want through their ordinary conversations, so they need more practice. What better way to practice effective language skills than through story reading! Students of all ages enjoy being read to, whether individually or in small groups while students are young, or in larger classes when they are in intermediate or secondary grades.

McNeill and Fowler suggest four specific strategies for teachers to use when reading stories aloud: praise the students' talk, expand on their words, ask open-ended questions, and pause long enough to allow students to initiate speaking. In addition, they emphasize taking turns, so that students have an opportunity to clarify their messages, hear appropriate language models, and practice the unspoken rules of communication.

McNeill and Fowler (1996) also recommend coaching parents in how to give their children opportunities to talk and how to respond when their children do talk. When parents pause, expand on answers, and ask open-ended questions that require more than just "yes" or "no" responses, they can become their children's best teachers.

Use Music and Play Games to Improve Language   Teachers should always try to have some fun with students. Using music and playing games are two ways language can be incorporated into enjoyable activities.

- **Music**
  - Use songs that require students to request items (e.g., rhythm sticks or tambourines passed around a circle).
  - Have picture symbols for common songs so that students can request the ones they like.
  - Use props to raise interest and allow students to act out the story (e.g., during "Humpty Dumpty" the student falls off a large ball).
  - Use common chants such as "When You're Happy and You Know It," and let students choose the action (e.g., clap your hands).
- **Games that require language comprehension and expression skills**
  - Play "Simon Says."
  - Play "Musical Chairs" with words rather than music. (Pass a ball around a circle. When the teacher says a magic word, the student with the ball is out.)
  - Use key words to identify and organize students. ("All the boys with red hair stand up. Everyone who has a sister sit down.")
  - Play "Twenty Questions." ("I'm thinking of a person." Students ask yes-or-no questions.)

Use Challenging Games with Older Students   Older students may require continued intervention to improve language skills. However, the activities chosen must be appropriate and not seem like "baby" games. Thomas and Carmack (1993) have collected ideas to involve older students in enjoyable, interactive tasks:

- Read fables or stories with morals. Discuss outcomes and focus on the endings.
- Do "Explain That." Discuss common idiomatic phrases, and help students discover the connection between the literal and figurative meanings (e.g., "She was on pins and needles").
- "Riddlemania" presents riddles to students and has them explain what makes them humorous.
- Have "Sense-Able Lessons." Bring objects to see, taste, hear, and smell, and compile a list of students' verbal comments. (p. 155)

For older students, vocabulary also becomes essential. The Differentiated Instruction—Secondary boxed reading explores this issue.

Adapt Strategies to Develop Students' Learning Tools   When facilitating language development for older students, help them develop their own strategies to use in challenging situations (Thomas & Carmack, 1993). Requiring them to use higher-order thinking skills will both require and stimulate higher-level language:

- Pair students to find word meanings. Use partners when working on categories such as synonyms or antonyms. Let students work together to master using a thesaurus.
- Teach students to categorize. Begin with concrete objects that they relate to easily, such as types of cars or names of foods, and then move to more abstract concepts such as feelings or ideas.
- Play reverse quiz games like "Jeopardy!" in which students have to work backward to think of questions for answers. (pp. 155–163)

Differentiating Secondary Instruction

It is important to not only increase the vocabulary of students, but also to make sure that they learn key vocabulary words that they will need in the future. Most students with language problems will eventually get jobs and it will be essential that they have an understanding of the vocuabulary that is associated with occupations and the workplace. Fisher, Clark, and Patton (2004) provided a context for addressing the vocabulary needs of older students:

Learning to understand new words or words used in a different way is the foundation children need to understanding their environments at home, in the community, and at school. Learning the vocabulary used by adults at home, in the community, and at school then becomes a major task for successful communication and learning in all aspects of a person's life. (p. 2)

Fisher and Clark (1992) identified a set of occupational vocabulary words that are needed by students, as they explore the world of work and the realities associated with it. Exam-

ples of this type of vocabulary, organized into four categories, include:

Person related: cooperation, dependable, experience, interests

Job application related: apply, employment, interview, qualification

General work related: benefits, harassment, on-time, policy, promotion, wages

Job setting related: accommodation, break, hazardous, safety, supervisor

Occupational vocabulary can be taught as part of a course on occupations or careers or other vocational guidance program provided by teachers or guidance personnel. This vocabulary can also be integrated into instructional lessons associated with general education classes such as reading, language arts/English, or social studies. Speech and language pathologists who are working with secondary-level students on pragmatic aspects of language are typically seeking topical areas that lead to the functional communication competence of students.

Use Storytelling and Process Writing   When children listen to and retell a story, they incorporate it into their oral language repertoire. McKamey (1991) has described a structure for allowing students to retell stories they had heard, to tell stories from their own experience, and to write down and illustrate their oral presentations. In process writing, students are instructed based on what they can already do. This and other balanced literacy approaches often allow students who have had negative language experiences to begin to succeed, to link written and spoken language, and to grow as communicators.

Augmentative and Alternative Communication (AAC)

According to ASHA (1993), augmentative/alternative communication (ACC) systems "attempt to compensate and facilitate, temporarily or permanently, for the impairment and disability patterns of individuals with severe expressive and/or language comprehension disorders."

The term **augmentative communication** denotes techniques that supplement or enhance communication by complementing whatever vocal skills the individual already has (Harris & Vanderheiden, 1980). Research has demonstrated that the use of communication devices does not inhibit the development of natural speech. Other individuals (e.g., those who are severely neurologically impaired and cannot speak) must employ techniques that serve in place of speech—in other words, alternative communication. According to Shane and Sauer (1986), the term **alternative communication** applies when "the production of speech for communication purposes has been ruled out" (p. 2). In 2004, almost 49% of speech–language pathologists in schools indicated that they served individuals who required AAC (ASHA, 2004).

AAC is a multimodal system consisting of four components (symbols, aids, techniques, and strategies) that can be used in various combinations to enhance communication. Communication techniques used in AAC are usually divided into either aided or unaided forms. Unaided techniques include nonverbal methods used in normal communication and do not require any physical object or entity to express information (e.g., speech, signing, gestures, and facial expressions). Aided communication techniques require a physical object, device, or external support to enable the individual to communicate (e.g., communication boards, charts, and mechanical or electrical devices). Because substantial numbers of individuals lack functional speech secondary to intellectual disabilities, traumatic brain injury, deafness, neurological disorders, or other causes, there has been increased demand for AAC in recent years. A student's communication skills and needs will change over time, as will the types of technology and methods available to support communication. Thus, the educational team should continually monitor and periodically reevaluate the usefulness of each AAC approach used by their students.

Types of AAC Devices/Systems   Students who cannot use spoken language can use a basic nonautomated communication device with no electronic parts. Examples include communication boards, charts, frames, and books that can be based on symbols, words, or letters. Typically, this kind of device will contain representations of common objects, words, phrases, or numbers and can be arranged in either an alphabetic or nonalphabetic format. For example,

YOU WILL SAVE YOURSELF SOME MONEY IF YOU CAN DESCRIBE THESE CARDS RATHER THAN INCLUDING THIS FIGURE.

Because they are easy to construct and can be modified to fit the student's vocabulary and communication context, nonautomated communication devices are very useful in communicating with teachers, family members, and peers. There are several commercially available sets of symbols, including the *Picture Communication Symbols* (Mayer-Johnson, 1986) and the *Oakland Schools Picture Dictionary* (Kirsten, 1981). Computer software programs that contain picture communication symbols can also be used to generate communication boards, picture schedules, instruction sheets, and other communication tools. Pictorial symbols are now available as applications on devices like the iPhone and iPad.

Electronic communication aids encompass a wide variety of capabilities, from simple to complex. Aids that produce voice are known as voice output communication aids, or VOCAs. A large number of different VOCAs are available that vary greatly in their level of sophistication and complexity. They range from aids that speak just one message to aids that provide access to keyboards for virtually unlimited messaging capacity. The voice output can be amplified, digitized, or synthetic speech. Often, a voice synthesizer is used to produce speech output, and written output is produced on printers or displays. Software, which is becoming increasingly sophisticated, can accommodate the many different needs of individuals who cannot produce spoken and/or written language. Some examples of electronic communication aids and their key features are shown in Table 12.5.

Because recent evidence has shown that everyone can communicate, the focus of contemporary AAC assessment and intervention is on developing and fine-tuning individualized

---

TABLE 12.5

Electronic Communication Aids and Their Key Features

BigMack

A large, colorful, single message digitizer

Record and re-record a message, song, sound, story line, or choice of up to 20 seconds.

A picture or label can easily be stuck to the large button.

Can be accessed by pressing anywhere on the large button or by a separate switch.

Can be used as a switch to control other devices, toys, or appliances.

Lightwriter SL35/SL40

A compact, portable keyboard will speak what is typed into it.

Text messages are displayed on the two-way screen, and synthesized speech is used.

Can be customized for people with more complex needs.

Add-ons such as key guards can be purchased, and a range of models are available.

Reduces keystrokes by using memory and word prediction.

ChatPC

Based on a palmtop Windows CE computer.

Housed in a durable case to give additional protection and additional amplification.

Has a color touchscreen, and over a hundred pages of messages can be programmed.

An onscreen keyboard is available, and this speaks out what is typed into it.

3,000+ symbols are supplied and can be supplemented with scanned or digital images.

Speech output can be digital or synthetic.

Changes can be made on the device or on a computer and then downloaded.

Dynavox

Touchscreen device offers word layouts, symbol layouts, or a combination of both.

Many preprogrammed page sets, suitable for users with a wide range of ability levels, are available.

Flexible layout can be thoroughly customized.

Symbol-supported word prediction encourages literacy.

DecTalk speech synthesis offers nine different voices.

Can be accessed via touchscreen, mouse, joystick, or switches.

Auditory and visual scanning modes are possible.

Built-in infrared for environmental controls and computer access.

methods that promote functional communication abilities in school, home, and community settings (Sevcik & Romski, 2000).

Caution: Facilitated Communication Facilitated communication (FC) is a process that has been used with individuals who have developmental disabilities, including autism. First introduced by Rosemary Crossley in Australia, FC usually involves having someone (a facilitator) support the arm or wrist of the person with autism, who then points to pictures, objects, printed letters, and words, or types letters on a keyboard. The keyboard is often connected to a computer so that the individual's words can be displayed or printed (Kirk, Gallagher, & Anastasiow, 1993). Supposedly, the support of the facilitator enables the individual to type out words and phrases.

Biklen (1990) has conducted much of the work done in FC and has reported anecdotal success with the procedure. However, results of objective research on the effectiveness of FC have found no conclusive evidence supporting the method. ASHA has issued a position paper on FC that cautions that the validity and reliability of this method have yet to be proven (ASHA, 1995).

SUMMARY

Basic Concepts about Speech and Language Disorders

- Although most people take the ability to communicate for granted, communication problems can result in difficulties in even the most simple of interactions and lead to problems in socialization and emotional adjustment. Speech and language are the interrelated, rule-governed skills that we use to communicate.
- About 2% of the school-age population has been identified as having speech or language impairments.
- Because most students with speech and language impairments are served in a regular classroom or resource room placement, having students with speech and language disorders in the classroom is more the rule than the exception.

Speech Disorders

- Speech disorders include impairments of phonology, voice, and fluency, with phonological disorders being the most common.
- Speech disorders can either be functional or organic in origin.

Language Disorders

- Language disorders can be expressive or receptive in nature and can affect the form, content, or use of language.
- Disorders of language can be classified into four basic categories: absence of verbal language, qualitatively different language, delayed language development, and interrupted language development.
- Significant language disorders directly impact a student's ability to interact with family, peers, and teachers.
- Augmentative and alternative communication options can facilitate the communicative abilities of people with severe speech and language disorders.

Effective Inclusive Practices

- Teachers should be aware of the influence that culture has on the style and nonverbal aspects of communication.

- Speech–language pathologists employ a variety of service-delivery models that can be used independently or in combination to meet the individual needs of each student. Most of these models involve some level of professional collaboration and consultation with the classroom teacher.
- The speech–language pathologist can work with the classroom teacher to make necessary modifications to the classroom environment, methodology, and curriculum to accommodate the needs of students with communication disorders in inclusive settings.
- Teachers and therapists need to work as a team to overcome common barriers to greater collaboration.

Classroom Adaptations for Students with Speech and Language Disorders

- Teachers can make numerous accommodation and modifications for students with speech disorders. For example, building a positive classroom environment is an important accommodation for these students.
- Specific, individualized intervention and instructional modifications (e.g., storytelling, facilitative play, classroom arrangement) are required.

PEARSON
myeducationlab

The MyEducationLab for this course can help you solidify your comprehension of Chapter 12 concepts.

- Gauge and further develop your understanding of chapter concepts by taking the quizzes and examining the enrichment materials on the Chapter 12 Study Plan.
- Visit Topic 17, Communication Disorders, to:
  - Connect with challenge-based interactive modules, case study units, and podcasts that provide research-validated information about working with students in inclusive settings by visiting the IRIS Center Resources
  - Explore Assignments and Activities, assignable exercises showing concepts in action through video, cases, and student and teacher artifacts
  - Practice and strengthen skills essential to quality teaching through the Building Teaching Skills and Dispositions lessons

13

Teaching Students with Special Gifts and Talents

CHAPTER OBJECTIVES

After reading this chapter, you should be able to:

1. Explain the basic concepts of giftedness.
2. Describe the characteristics of students with special gifts and talents.
3. Outline effective inclusive practices for students with special gifts and talents.
4. Describe appropriate classroom adaptations for students with special gifts and talents.

CARMEN is truly an amazing young woman. She was a student in classes for gifted/talented/creative students for 6 years, from the first to the sixth grade. Her story provides a glimpse of what giftedness might look like in a student. However, not all students who are gifted display the breadth of exceptionality that Carmen does.

Learning came very easily for Carmen, and she excelled in all subjects. However, mathematics was her personal favorite. When she was in the fifth grade, she successfully completed pre-algebra, and when she was a sixth grader, Carmen attended a seventh- and eighth-grade gifted mathematics class, where she received the highest grades in algebra. Carmen's writing skills were also well developed. Several of her essays and poems have already been published. When Carmen was a fourth grader, she presented testimony to a NASA board defending and encouraging the continuation of the junior astronaut program. After completing her first year of junior high school, Carmen was awarded two out of five academic awards given to seventh-grade students at her school for outstanding achievement in science and mathematics. As a tenth grader, she took the PSAT, and received a perfect score!

Carmen is also musically talented. When she was in second grade, a music specialist who came to school on a weekly basis informed her teacher that Carmen should be encouraged to continue with piano lessons because she demonstrated concert pianist abilities. When Carmen entered junior high school, she took up playing the clarinet in the band. At the end-of-the-year banquet, she received the top honor after being in the band for only one year.

Additionally, Carmen is psychomotorically talented. She is an accomplished gymnast, dances both the hula and ballet, has been a competitive ice-skater (an unusual sport for someone from Hawaii), played soccer for two years on champion soccer teams, and was a walk-on for her junior high's cross-country track team.

Carmen also has artistic strengths, demonstrates leadership abilities, has good social skills, and, wouldn't you know it, is simply beautiful.

Carmen's career goals have remained consistent for a long time. She wants to be either a dentist or an astronaut; she can probably be either one.

QUESTIONS TO CONSIDER

1. What kinds of challenges can students like Carmen create for teachers and for themselves?
2. How do individuals like Carmen, who are highly gifted, differ from other students who are gifted?
3. Should children like Carmen be included in general education classrooms all the time, separated from time to time, or provided with a completely different curriculum?

Children and youth such as Carmen, who perform or have the potential to perform at levels significantly above those of other students, have special needs as great as those of students whose disabilities demonstrably interfere with their performance. These needs are notable because most of these students are likely to spend much of their school day in general education settings, if they are attending public schools. As a result, teaching students who are gifted provides challenges to general education teachers that are certainly equal to those associated with meeting the needs of students with other special needs (McGrail, 1998). To feel confident to work with students who are gifted, classroom teachers should have basic information about giftedness and be able to implement some useful techniques for maximizing the educational experiences of these students.

Visit the MyEducationLab for this course to enhance your understanding of chapter concepts with a personalized Study Plan. You'll also have the opportunity to hone your teaching skills through video-based Assignments and Activities, IRIS Center Resources, and Building Teaching Skills and Disposition lessons.

Although there is no general agreement concerning the best way to educate students who are gifted and talented, many professionals argue that such students, especially highly gifted students, benefit from a curricular focus different from that provided in general education. Although some point out that gifted classes and special schools are more effective settings for highly gifted students (Clarkson, 2003), the vast majority of students who are gifted and talented, as noted, spend a considerable amount of time in general education settings. As a result, general education teachers are presented with the challenges of working with these students; however, these teachers are also privileged to receive some amazing rewards.

Although a set of exact competencies that general education teachers should have in working with students who are gifted has remained elusive over the years, certain ones have emerged recently. The National Association for Gifted Children and the Council for Exceptional Children (2006) has published a set of suggested standards to help guide the preparation of teachers who will work with students who are gifted and talented:

- Ability to differentiate curriculum and instruction to meet the needs and interests of these students, including the selection of appropriate methods and materials
- Ability to create an environment in which gifted and talented students can feel challenged, encouraged, and safe
- Knowledge and skills to promote thinking skills, develop creative problem-solving abilities of students, and facilitate independent research

The purpose of this chapter is twofold: to provide basic information about children and youth who are gifted, and to suggest practices for working with these students in inclusive settings. Many of the topics related to the education of students who are gifted and talented are worthy of discussion, particularly for those who will be working in gifted education; however, the focus of this chapter is to provide useful information for the general education teacher. This chapter is a primer only; confidence and competence in teaching students who are gifted come with study, experience, and ongoing professional development. More in-depth information about teaching students who are gifted can be found elsewhere (Clark, 2007; Colangelo & Davis, 2003; Coleman & Cross, 2005; Davis, Rimm, & Siegle, 2010; VanTassel-Baska & Stambaugh, 2005).

BASIC CONCEPTS ABOUT STUDENTS WITH SPECIAL GIFTS AND TALENTS

Students with exceptional abilities continue to be an underidentified, underserved, and too often, inappropriately served group. Unlike the situation for students with disabilities, no federal legislation *mandates* appropriate education for these students. Moreover, states and local school districts vary greatly in the type and quality of services provided.

Students who could benefit from special programming are often not identified because of several factors. Teachers in general education may not be aware of the characteristics that suggest giftedness, as only a few students are "highly" or "exceptionally" gifted and thus fairly recognizable. This oversight is particularly common for those students who differ from the general student populations because of culture, gender, low socioeconomic status, or disability. Historically, ineffective assessment practices have not identified gifted students coming from diverse backgrounds.

Fundamental Challenges

For students who are identified as gifted and talented, a common problem is a mismatch between their academic, social, and emotional needs and the programming they receive, especially when they remain in general education settings for much of their instructional day. In many schools, a limited amount of instructional time is devoted to special activities. The

point is reflected in the current focus on equity in education associated with the recent educational reform movement and on the need to address students who are below grade level, as accentuated by the No Child Left Behind Act. As Gallagher (1997) notes, "It is this value that leads one to heterogeneous grouping, whereby no one gets any special programming or privileges, and thus all are 'equal'" (p. 17). Furthermore, some gifted programming that exists today (e.g., pullout options) favors students who are gifted in the linguistic and mathematical areas only. In too many instances, students with gifts and talents do not receive the type of education in the general education classroom that addresses their cognitive, social, and emotional needs and interests.

In truth, many general education teachers simply are not prepared to deal with students who excel on any number of dimensions and are in their classes. Research has demonstrated that when teachers are provided training on various instructional techniques for use with gifted students, they can improve the way they differentiate their classrooms for this population (Robinson, Shore, & Enersen, 2007). Gifted students can intimidate some teachers, as seen in the anecdote depicted in Figure 13.1.

Services to students with gifts and talents remain controversial, partly because the general public and many school personnel hold misconceptions about these students. Hallahan, Kauffman, and Pullen (2009) highlight some of these misguided beliefs:

- **People with special intellectual gifts are physically weak, socially inept, narrow in interests, and prone to emotional instability or early decline.** *Fact:* There are wide individual variations, and most individuals with special intellectual gifts are healthy, well adjusted, socially attractive, and morally responsible.
- **Children with special gifts or talents are usually bored with school and antagonistic toward those who are responsible for their education.** *Fact:* Most children with special gifts like school and adjust well to their peers and teachers, although some do not like school and have social or emotional problems.
- **Students who have a true gift or talent for something will excel without special education. They need only the incentives and instruction that are appropriate for all students.** *Fact:* Some children with special gifts or talents will perform at a remarkably high level without special education of any kind, and some will make outstanding contributions even in the face of great obstacles to their achievement. But most will not come close to achieving at a level commensurate with their potential unless their talents are deliberately fostered by instruction that is appropriate for their advanced abilities. (p. 530)

It is this last point that general education teachers need to notice. Cautions about providing an appropriate education for students who are gifted in the general education

FIGURE 13.1	Classroom Experience

I was standing at the front of the room explaining how the earth revolves and how, because of its huge size, it is difficult for us to realize that it is actually round. All of a sudden Spencer blurted out, "The earth isn't round."

    I curtly replied, "Ha, do you think it's flat?"

    He matter-of-factly said, "No, it's a truncated sphere."

    I quickly changed the subject. While the children were at recess I had a chance to grab a soft drink in the teacher's lounge. While sipping my drink, I looked up the word "truncated" in the dictionary. I'm still not sure if he was right, but it sounded good: so good that I wasn't going to make an issue of it. Spencer said the darndest things.

Source: Blackbourn et al.

classroom have been noted by professionals in the field of gifted education (VanTassel-Baska & Stambaugh, 2005). Some of the more common barriers include:

- Teachers lacking sufficient subject matter knowledge
- Problems with classroom management when trying to differentiate instruction
- Misguided attitudes and beliefs about learning
- Inability to modify curriculum in such a way that it is appropriate for high-ability students
- The reality that differentiation is needed for an array of students with diverse learning needs
- Difficulty in obtaining and using appropriate instructional resources
- Lack of time to do adequate planning
- Lack of certain pedagogical skills (i.e., generating high-order thinking skills) that are needed for differentiating instruction for high-ability students—teachers were not taught how to provide this type of instruction.
- Inadequate administrative support

Many professionals in the field of gifted education find current services unacceptable and are frustrated by the lack of specialized programming for these students (Feldhusen, 1997). Undoubtedly, the programming provided in inclusive settings to students who are gifted should be improved. VanTassel-Baska (1997), highlighting key beliefs regarding curriculum theory, remarks that gifted students should be provided with curriculum opportunities that allow them to attain optimum levels of learning. In addition, these curriculum experiences need to be carefully planned, implemented, and evaluated. It is our belief that, with proper preparation on how to differentiate instruction for these students, the general education classroom can be a setting where students who are gifted can flourish, when the conditions are right.

Public Perceptions of Giftedness

The public in general has conceptions of individuals who are gifted. Many of the impressions that people have developed come from media images. While it might be claimed that the perceptions of individuals who are gifted are getting more positive, historically media images have portrayed individuals who were gifted in less favorable ways.

The portrayal of individuals who are gifted in movies is noteworthy. As Coleman and Cross (2001) note, too often the portrayal has negative connotations. They described the features of key characters in a number of notable movies, as highlighted in Table 13.1. The prob-

TABLE 13.1

Portrayal of Gifted Characters in Movies

MOVIE	YEAR	PORTRAYAL
Little Man Tate	1991	Dysfunctional
Searching for Bobby Fischer	1993	Dysfunctional
Powder	1995	Frail
Shine	1996	Bespectacled
The Nutty Professor	1996	Idealistic, misguided
Good Will Hunting	1997	Violent
A Beautiful Mind	2001	Psychiatric problems

Source: From *Being Gifted in School: An Introduction to Development, Guidance, and Teaching* (p. 3), by L. J. Coleman and T. L. Cross, 2001. Waco, TX: Prufrock Press. Copyright 2002 by Prufrock Press. Reprinted by permission.

lem with negative portrayals of individuals who are gifted is that it leads to inaccurate perceptions and attitudes, ultimately resulting in unfair, and often discriminatory, practices.

Another example of stereotyping that occurs is the use of various terms to describe children, adolescents, and even adults who are gifted and talented. Historically, terms such as "nerd" and "geek" have been used to refer disparagingly to this group of students. What might be an encouraging trend is that these terms may not carry the same virulence that they once did (Cross, 2005). This is most likely due to some very successful and public individuals, particularly in the technology fields, who might be associated with these terms and who have emerged in positive ways (think Bill Gates).

"Gifted" Defined

Our understanding of giftedness has changed over time, and the terminology used to describe it has also varied. The term **gifted** is often used to refer to the heterogeneous spectrum of students with exceptional abilities, although some professionals restrict the use of this term only to certain individuals who display high levels of intelligence. Other terms, such as *talented* and *creative*, are used to differentiate subgroups of gifted people. An emerging nomenclature is to refer to students as having special gifts and talents.

Gagné (1995) described the relationship of gifts and talents in the following way: "gifts," which are natural abilities that the person displays, have to be developed to become "talents." These talents are the result of proficiency that accrues through training and practice.

Historical Context   A number of attempts to define giftedness have been made. One of the earliest efforts, and one that has received a fair amount of attention, is the work of Terman that began in the early 1920s. Collectively the Terman work is titled *Genetic Studies of Genius*, and this research was still being conducted in recent times. Terman and colleagues identified 1,500 individuals with high IQs (i.e., over 140), collected data on their mental and physical traits, and also studied their lives longitudinally (Sears, 1979; Terman, 1926; Terman & Oden, 1959; Tomlinson-Keasey & Little, 1990). The research was important because it represented a major attempt to look closely at individuals who were exceptional and dispelled some early misconceptions relating to high intelligence and neurotic behavior. This work also provided some beginning conceptualizations of giftedness.

As Turnbull and Turnbull (2001) point out, however, Terman's work also led to some misconceptions. First, he equated genius with IQ, thus excluding other areas such as artistic ability. Second, Terman stressed the strong association of genius and genetics, thus precluding that some variability in intelligence can occur due to psychosocial factors and other life-related opportunities.

Throughout the years, other definitional perspectives emerged. Most of these were associated with federal legislation that recognized students who were gifted (e.g., the Elementary and Secondary Education Act; No Child Left Behind Act) or were developed by the U.S. Commissioner of Education (Marland, 1972). Attention was directed to this topic as a function of the creation of various professional organizations as well—for example, the American Association for the Study of the Gifted in 1946; the National Association for Gifted Children in 1954; and the Association for the Gifted, part of the Council for Exceptional Children, in 1958.

Federal Definition   The current definition of giftedness promoted by the U.S. Department of Education comes from the Jacob K. Javits Gifted and Talented Students Education Act of 1988 (reauthorized in 1994 and incorporated into the No Child Left Behind Act of 2001). This legislation does provide guidance about how to define this population. It contains many of the key concepts included in previous definitions:

> Children and youth with outstanding talent perform or show the potential for performing at remarkably high levels of accomplishment when compared with others of their age, experience, or environment. These children and youth exhibit high performance capability in intellectual, creative, and/or artistic areas, possess an unusual leadership capacity, or excel in

specific academic fields. They require services or activities not ordinarily provided by schools. Outstanding talents are present in children and youth from all cultural groups, across all economic strata, and in all areas of human endeavor. (U.S. Department of Education, 1993, p. 3)

A number of interesting observations can be made regarding this definition. First, attention is given to potential—students who have not yet produced significant accomplishments may be considered gifted. Second, there is no mention of giftedness in the psychomotor area (i.e., athletics) because this area is already addressed in existing school programs. Third, the need for special services or activities for these students is clearly stated, along with the observation that such intervention is not ordinarily provided. Finally, affirmation is given to the fact that students who are gifted come from a range of diverse backgrounds.

State Definitions   Because no federal mandates provide for gifted and talented education, it is up to the states to do so. The result is that programs and services vary greatly from state to state. Interestingly, only 28 states mandate some form of programs for students who are gifted (NAGC, 2009). Many states have adopted their own definitions of giftedness.

A Developmental Perspective   Attentive to the fact that changes occur with age, Coleman and Cross (2001) propose a definition that is considerate of developmental factors:

> The definition . . . differs from others by proposing a change in the criteria that describe giftedness, accounting for changes in abilities with advancing age in school. The criteria become narrower with increased age. This means that in early grades, giftedness would appear more in the areas of general ability or specific skills; but, as the child moves through the grades, evidence of ability and achievement would manifest within specific areas of study. . . . In this model, preadolescent gifted children have potential or demonstrated high ability in two areas: general cognitive ability and creative ability. Adolescent gifted children have demonstrated ability in abstract thinking, have produced creative works in some worthwhile area, and have demonstrated consistent involvement in activities of either type. (pp. 19–20)

This definitional perspective contains elements of the various conceptualizations of giftedness, as discussed in the next section.

Other Conceptualizations of Giftedness

Many different ways to understand gifts and talents have been presented in the professional literature. Three of the more popular conceptualizations include Renzulli's "three-ring" conception of giftedness, Sternberg's "triarchic theory" of intelligence, and Gardner's theory of "multiple intelligences."

Renzulli   One way to conceptualize giftedness is to consider the interaction of three interlocking clusters of traits (Renzulli, 1979; Renzulli & Reis, 1991) as essential elements associated with outstanding accomplishments. The three clusters are as follows; their interacting nature is depicted in Figure 13.2.

- High ability—including high intelligence
- High creativity—the ability to formulate new ideas and apply them to the solution of problems
- High task commitment—a high level of motivation and the ability to see a project through to its completion

These criteria are found in the two types of people who are truly gifted and noted in the U.S. Office of Education definition: those who produce and those who perform (Tannebaum, 1997).

Sternberg   A popular theory of intellectual giftedness has been developed by Sternberg (1991). His theory includes three types of abilities: analytic giftedness (i.e., ability to dissect a problem and understand its parts), synthetic giftedness (i.e., insight, intuitive creativity, or

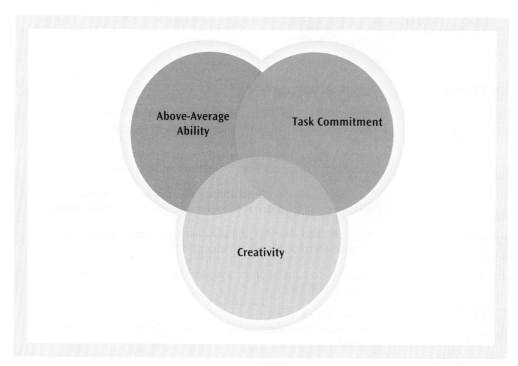

FIGURE 13.2

Renzulli's three-ring conception of giftedness.

Source: From *What Makes Giftedness?* (Brief #6, p. 10) by J. Renzulli, 1979. Los Angeles: National/State Leadership Training Institute. Reprinted by permission.

skill at coping with relatively novel situations), and practical giftedness (i.e., ability to apply aspects of analytical and synthetic strengths to everyday situations). All individuals demonstrate some blend of these three abilities. However, gifted individuals show high ability in one or more of these areas.

Gardner   Another perspective, constituting a broad theory of intelligence, has important applications for conceptualizing giftedness and for programming. Gardner and colleagues (Gardner, 1983; Gardner & Hatch, 1989) have developed a very popular model that proposes the idea of **multiple intelligences**. This model, which is most often used, comprises eight areas of ability. Originally the model included only seven areas, but an eighth area (naturalistic) was added. Three other "intelligences" have been discussed—they include spiritual intelligence, existential intelligence, and moral intelligence (Smith, 2002). Table 13.2 describes the features of each type of intelligence and provides a possible occupation/role that might be characteristic of a person with a high degree of a given intelligence.

If Gardner's ideas were followed closely, students would be assessed in all areas of intelligence. Accordingly, if they were found to have strengths in an area, students would be given opportunities to expand their interests, skills, and abilities accordingly. This conceptualization is attractive because it acknowledges some ability areas that are frequently overlooked in school settings and it recognizes the importance of different types of intelligences and gives them all equal status.

Concept of Creativity

Creativity is included as an element of the federal definition of giftedness, and it is a major part of Renzulli's three-ring model. The concept is difficult to pinpoint, yet its importance as it relates to individuals who are gifted makes it a current topic for debate and discussion. As Coleman and Cross (2001) note, this topic has been part of the ongoing discussion of gifted individuals ever since the publication in 1959 of Guilford's seminal work on this topic.

As indicated previously, the concept of creativity is somewhat elusive, and no one definition explaining it has become popular. The concept can be characterized by the phrase, "You know it when you see it." Coleman and Cross (2001) aptly describe the state of affairs:

A single accepted definition of creativity does not exist. In fact, neither is there universal agreement about what relevant attributes are needed to define an act as creative. The

TABLE 13.2

Multiple Intelligences

INTELLIGENCE	END STATES	CORE COMPONENTS
Logical–Mathematical	Scientist Mathematician	Sensitivity to, and capacity to discern, logical or numerical patterns; ability to handle long chains of reasoning
Linguistic	Poet Journalist	Sensitivity to the sounds, rhythms, and meanings of words; sensitivity to the different functions of language
Musical	Composer Violinist	Abilities to produce and appreciate rhythm, pitch, and timbre; appreciation of the forms of musical expressiveness
Spatial	Navigator Sculptor	Capacities to perceive the visual-spatial world accurately and to transform one's initial perceptions
Bodily–Kinesthetic	Dancer Athlete	Abilities to control one's body movements and to handle objects skillfully
Interpersonal	Therapist Salesperson	Capacities to discern and respond appropriately to the moods, temperaments, motivations, and desires of other people
Intrapersonal	Person with detailed, accurate self-knowledge	Access to one's own feelings and the ability to discriminate among them and draw upon them to guide behavior; knowledge of one's own strengths, weaknesses, desires, and intelligences
Naturalistic	Naturalist Park ranger	Affinity and appreciation for the wonders of nature

Source: Adapted from "Multiple Intelligences Go to School: Educational Implications of the Theory of Multiple Intelligences," by H. Gardner and T. Hatch, 1989, *Educational Researcher, 18*(8), p. 6. Copyright © 1989 by the American Educational Research Association. Reprinted by permission.

difficulty of selecting relevant attributes illustrates the problem of defining creativity. The terms originality and novelty pervade the literature on creativity. They express a quantitative and a qualitative standard, but they fail to say to what criterion a person is being compared. (p. 240)

The concept of creativity continues to receive wide attention, and efforts to better understand it and be able to apply it in meaningful ways within the context of education are warranted. A number of lists of traits associated with creativity or creative people have been generated (see Amabile, 1989; Neihart & Olenchak, 2002; VanTassel-Baska; 1981).

Prevalence and Origins of Giftedness

The number of students who display exceptional abilities is uncertain, particularly given the significant interstate variability in definitions and practices. Figures of 3 to 5% are typically cited to reflect the extent of giftedness in the school population (National Center for Education Statistics, 1989). The National Association for Gifted Children (NAGC, 2009) estimates that there are about 3 million students who are gifted (grades pre-kindergarten to 12).

The critical reader should also note the distinction between the number of students served and the number of students who might be gifted. Only certain types of gifted students can be served because of the methods used for identification. Another cautionary note is that such figures generally underestimate the number of gifted students who are ethnically or culturally different, or disabled. These subgroups are underrepresented in programs for students with exceptional abilities. Recent data indicate that there are more females than males in gifted programs (U.S. Department of Education, 2006).

Much professional discussion has focused on what contributes to giftedness in a person. Terman's early work made a strong case for genetics. Without question, research has shown that behavior is greatly affected by genetics. Although this notion is sometimes overemphasized, genetic factors do play a role in giftedness. Most researchers suggest that giftedness results from the interaction between biology and environment. In addition to genetic code, other biological factors, such as nutrition, also have an impact on an individual's development.

The environment in which a child is raised also affects later performance and intellectual abilities. Homes in which significant amounts of stimulation and opportunity to explore and interact with the environment exist, accompanied by high expectations, tend to produce children more likely to be successful scholastically and socially.

CHARACTERISTICS OF STUDENTS WHO ARE GIFTED

Students who are gifted demonstrate a wide range of specific aptitudes, abilities, and skills. Although they should not be overgeneralized or considered stereotypical, certain characteristics distinguish students who are gifted or talented. Teachers in general education classrooms must recognize and address these characteristics when they have students who are gifted in their classrooms. The Characteristics and Implications feature highlights some of the most common characteristics and provides some suggestions for addressing them within the context of the general education classroom.

An interesting phenomenon is the paradoxical negative effect of seemingly desirable behaviors displayed by gifted students. For instance, sincere, excited curiosity about a topic being covered in class can sometimes be interpreted as annoying or disruptive by a teacher or fellow students. These students' quick answers, along with their certainty that they are right, can be misconstrued as brash arrogance. Such behavior—while, at face value, features that most of us would love to have—can be misperceived as problem behavior for students who are gifted.

Some characteristics can outright be problematic for students who are gifted. For instance, characteristics such as uneven precocity, interpersonal difficulties (possibly due to cognitive differences), underachievement, nonconformity, perfectionism, and frustration and anger may indeed be negative features (Davis & Rimm, 1998). The desire for perfection, which was so often achieved in elementary school or high school, can become a debilitating personal feature when the student goes to college and is surrounded by others who are his or her equals.

Clark (2002) also points out that different levels of ability and performance exist within the ranks of those who are gifted. She distinguishes among students who would be considered typical or moderately gifted, those who are highly gifted, and those who are exceptionally gifted. Carmen, who was introduced at the beginning of the chapter, represents an individual who could be considered highly gifted. *Highly gifted* students "tend to evidence more energy than gifted individuals; they think faster and are more intent and focused on their interests and they exhibit a higher degree of ability in most of the traits . . . identified with giftedness" (Clark, 2002, p. 63). Clark describes *exceptionally gifted* as those who "seem to have different value structures . . . tend to be more isolated by choice and more invested in concerns of a meta-nature (e.g., universal problems) . . . seldom seek popularity or social acclaim" (p. 63). Both highly gifted and exceptionally gifted students pose significant challenges to educators in meeting their needs within the general education classroom. Most of the discussion in this chapter is directed toward the typical gifted student.

A notable characteristic that has important classroom implications is the gifted student's expenditure of minimum effort while still earning high grades (Reis & Schack, 1993). Many gifted students are able to handle the general education curriculum with ease. But the long-term effect of being able to excel without working hard might be a lack of the work habits needed for challenging programs at a later point in time (i.e., advanced placement classes in high school or the curriculum of an upper-tier college).

■ CHARACTERISTICS AND IMPLICATIONS: SPECIAL GIFTS AND TALENTS ■

AREA	CHARACTERISTICS	EDUCATIONAL IMPLICATIONS
Cognitive	High language development Advanced oral language skills Curiosity for learning new things Uneven precocity Problem-solving abilities	Provide opportunities for students to expand their language Provide opportunities for using oral language through debates and oral reports Provide opportunities for independent studies and other advanced learning opportunities Provide support for weak academic areas Provide problem-solving learning options
Affective	Idealism and sense of justice Leadership ability Popular among peers Difficulties with peers Nonconformity Frustration	Provide opportunities for expressing idealism Provide leadership opportunities Encourage students to serve as peer tutors and peer buddies Provide social supports Provide a structured learning environment Teach self-monitoring skills
Academic Development	High achievement in most academic areas Success without effort Possible boredom with classes Perfectionism Underachievement	Encourage learning beyond the regular curriculum Reinforce students for challenging themselves Reward students for effort, not perfectionism Identify areas of potential underachievement and reinforce learning effort in these areas
Arts	High interest in arts Exceedingly high skill in arts areas	Encourage study of arts Reinforce skills in arts and provide opportunities for expanding skills

Social-Emotional Considerations

Gifted students have the same physiological and psychological needs as their peers. In general, high-ability students seem to be as well adjusted as their peers in school (Neihart et al., 2002). In other words, most students with special gifts and talents do not experience more social and emotional problems than other students experience.

Yet, "The lives of gifted students are both the same as and different from other students' lives" (Cross, 1999, p. 33). They may also be dealing with perplexing concepts that are well ahead of the concerns of their peers. For instance, a gifted fourth-grade girl asked her teacher questions related to abortion—a topic with which she was already dealing conceptually. In addition, gifted students may be dealing with some issues that are different from those of their nongifted peers, such as stress, hypersensitivity, control, perfectionism, underachievement/lack of motivation, coping mechanisms, introversion, peer relationships, need for empathy, self-understanding, and self-acceptance (Smutny, Walker, & Meckstroth, 1997).

Perhaps the most important recommendation is for teachers to develop relationships with students that make them feel comfortable discussing their concerns and questions. Teachers can become important resources to gifted students, not only for advice, but also for information. Regularly scheduled individual time with a teacher can have important paybacks for both the student and the teacher.

Teachers may also find it beneficial to schedule weekly room meetings (Feldhusen, 1993b) or class councils (Kataoka, 1987) to identify and address social, procedural, or learning-related problems that arise in the classroom. The group discussion includes articulation of a problem; brainstorming and discussion of possible solutions; selection of an action plan; and implementation, evaluation, and reintroduction of the problem if the action plan is not effective.

Following are some specific suggestions for dealing with the social-emotional needs of gifted students:

- Know when to refer students to professionals trained to deal with certain types of emotional problems.
- Create a classroom atmosphere that encourages students to take academic risks and allows them to make mistakes without fear of ridicule or harsh negative critique.
- Provide time on a weekly basis, if at all possible, for individual sessions with students so that they can share their interests, ongoing events in their lives, or concerns.
- Maintain regular, ongoing communication with the families of gifted students, notifying them of the goals, activities, products, and expectations you have for their children.
- Require, and teach if necessary, appropriate social skills (e.g., appropriate interactions) to students who display problems in these areas.
- Work with parents on the personal development of students.
- Use different types of activities (e.g., social issues) to develop self-understanding and decision-making and problem-solving skills. Rosselli (1993) recommends the use of bibliotherapy (literature that focuses on children with disabilities).
- Teach gifted students how to deal with their "uniqueness."
- Recognize that gifted students may experience higher levels of social pressure and anxiety—for example, peer pressure not to achieve at a high level or lofty expectations originating internally or from others (Del Prete, 1996).

Identification, Assessment, and Eligibility

General education teachers need to know about the assessment process used to identify and confirm the existence of exceptional abilities. General education teachers play a crucial role in the initial stages of the process, for they are likely to be the first to recognize that a student might be gifted. For this reason, teachers should provide opportunities across the range of ability areas (e.g., multiple intelligences) for students to explore their interests and abilities, particularly at the preschool and elementary levels. Ramos-Ford and Gardner (1997) suggest that such opportunities may help students discover certain abilities that might otherwise go unnoticed.

RIGHTS & RESPONSIBILITIES

GIFTED CHILDREN'S BILL OF RIGHTS

Students who are gifted have often been overlooked. The public in general tends to perceive these students as already fortunate and devalues the need to provide more support and funding of programs for gifted students. In a related way, these students have needs that all too often are not given the attention they deserve. Some professionals (Clark, 2002) have developed lists of educational rights of these students. More recently, the National Association of Gifted Children has issued a "Bill of Rights" for these students. Written to students who are gifted, the rights are:

You have a right . . .

- . . . to know about your giftedness.
- . . . to learn something new everyday.

- . . . to be passionate about your talent areas without apologies.
- . . . to have an identity beyond your talent area.
- . . . to feel good about your accomplishments.
- . . . to make mistakes.
- . . . to seek guidance in the development of your talent.
- . . . to have multiple peer groups and a variety of friends.
- . . . to choose which of your talent areas you wish to pursue.
- . . . not to be gifted at everything.

The assessment process includes a sequence of steps, beginning with an initial referral (i.e., nomination) and culminating with the validation of the nomination by examining existing data and the collection of additional information (Oakland & Rossen, 2005). Schools typically send out announcements to all parents, notifying them that testing to screen for students who are gifted will occur and asking them if they would like for their son or daughter to be considered for this assessment. As mentioned, general education teachers also play a role in identifying gifted students. Efforts to identify children with gifts and talents should begin early. Although some children displaying exceptional abilities may be spotted very early (i.e., preschool years), many are not recognized until they are in school. For this reason, teachers need to be aware of classroom behaviors that gifted students typically display. A listing of such behaviors is provided in Table 13.3. Confirming that a student is gifted should involve "multiple identification criteria based on multiple sources" (Robinson et al., 2007, p. 235).

Teachers who recognize behaviors highlighted in Table 13.3 should determine whether a student should be evaluated more comprehensively. According to Robinson and colleagues (2007), "in the identification process, the teacher's greatest contribution is referral" (p. 243). Teachers should share their observations with the student's parents. Eventually, teachers may want to nominate the student for gifted services. Oakland and Rossen (2005) suggest that a nomination that "first informs, then educates, and then encourages teachers, parents, and students to become engaged" (p. 61) is most likely to identify a diverse range of students who might have gifts or talents.

Teachers can be involved in the next step in the assessment process as well. After a student has been nominated or referred, teachers should be part of the process of examining existing data. They can assemble information to help determine whether the student should receive special services. The following sources of information can contribute to understanding a student's demonstrated or potential ability: formal test results; informal assessments; interviews with teachers, parents, and peers; and actual student products. For example, a public elementary school may use various screening instruments to identify gifted students, including a standardized ability test, standardized creativity test, teacher observation form, student portfolio, and parent observation form. This phase should be followed by a set of nondiscriminatory evaluation procedures. Turnbull, Turnbull, and Wehmeyer (2010) provide a list of such techniques (see Table 13.4).

A helpful technique used in many school systems to determine the performance capabilities of students is **portfolio assessment**. Portfolios contain a collection of student-generated products, reflecting the quality of a student's work. They can also contain permanent products such as artwork, poetry, or videotapes of student performance (e.g., theatrical production, dance or music recital).

As VanTassel-Baska, Patton, and Prillaman (1989) point out, students who are culturally different and those who come from socially and economically disadvantaged backgrounds are typically overlooked in the process of identifying students for gifted programs. For the most part, this problem results from entry requirements that stress performance on standardized tests. When students obtain low test scores on standardized instruments that may be biased against them, exclusion results. Some methods exist for addressing this issue. It might be possible to develop local norms for tests (Oakland & Rossen, 2005). VanTassel-Baska and colleagues (1989) provide additional recommendations for improving the identification and assessment process:

- Use nontraditional measures for identification purposes.
- Recognize cultural attributes and factors in deciding on identification procedures.
- Focus on strengths in nonacademic areas, particularly in creativity and psychomotor domains. (p. 3)

It has also been difficult to identify and serve students who are twice exceptional—gifted *and* having a disability or ADHD. For instance, the problems that characterize a learning disability (e.g., problems in language-related areas) often mask high levels of accomplishment in other areas such as drama, art, or music. Special assessment considerations of this unique population, such as providing a range of opportunities to demonstrate capabilities across a range of areas (e.g., multiple intelligences), are warranted.

TABLE 13.3

Classroom Behaviors of Gifted Students

Does the child
- Ask a lot of questions?
- Show a lot of interest in progress?
- Have lots of information on many things?
- Want to know why or how something is so?
- Become unusually upset at injustices?
- Seem interested and concerned about social or political problems?
- Often have a better reason than you do for not doing what you want done?
- Refuse to drill on spelling, math, facts, flash cards, or handwriting?
- Criticize others for dumb ideas?
- Become impatient if work is not "perfect"?
- Seem to be a loner?
- Seem bored and often have nothing to do?
- Complete only part of an assignment or project and then take off in a new direction?
- Stick to a subject long after the class has gone on to other things?
- Seem restless, out of seat often?
- Daydream?
- Seem to understand easily?
- Like solving puzzles and problems?
- Have his or her own idea about how something should be done? And stay with it?
- Talk a lot?
- Love metaphors and abstract ideas?
- Love debating issues?

This child may be showing giftedness cognitively.

Does the child
- Show unusual ability in some area? Maybe reading or math?
- Show fascination with one field of interest? And manage to include this interest in all discussion topics?
- Enjoy meeting or talking with experts in this field?
- Get math answers correct, but find it difficult to tell you how?

- Enjoy graphing everything? Seem obsessed with probabilities?
- Invent new obscure systems and codes?

This child may be showing giftedness academically.

Does the child
- Try to do things in different, unusual, imaginative ways?
- Have a really zany sense of humor?
- Enjoy new routines or spontaneous activities?
- Love variety and novelty?
- Create problems with no apparent solutions? And enjoy asking you to solve them?
- Love controversial and unusual questions?
- Have a vivid imagination?
- Seem never to proceed sequentially?

This child may be showing giftedness creatively.

Does the child
- Organize and lead group activities? Sometimes take over?
- Enjoy taking risks?
- Seem cocky, self-assured?
- Enjoy decision making? Stay with that decision?
- Synthesize ideas and information from a lot of different sources?

This child may be showing giftedness through leadership ability.

Does the child
- Seem to pick up skills in the arts—music, dance, drama, painting, etc.—without instruction?
- Invent new techniques? Experiment?
- See minute detail in products or performances?
- Have high sensory sensitivity?

This child may be showing giftedness through visual or performing arts ability.

Source: From *Growing Up Gifted* (6th ed., p. 332), by B. Clark, 2002. Upper Saddle River, NJ: Merrill/Prentice Hall. Copyright 2002 by Pearson Education. Reprinted by permission.

After the student has been identified as gifted or talented and begins to participate in special programs or services, ongoing assessment should become part of his or her educational program. Practical and personal needs should be monitored regularly (Del Prete, 1996). Practical concerns, such as the monitoring of progress in academic areas and realization of potential in certain delineated areas, can be evaluated. Nevertheless, the personal needs of students who are gifted (e.g., feeling accepted and developing confidence), which should be addressed as well, may require additional time and effort.

Gifted students are not entitled to receive special services under IDEA, unless, of course, they also have a disability that significantly inhibits their ability to benefit from education. As a result, "special education" for gifted students is not guaranteed, even though it should be. Moreover, various due-process safeguards, as provided by IDEA, are not applicable to these students and their families.

TABLE 13.4

Nondiscriminatory Evaluation Procedures and Standards

ASSESSMENT MEASURES	FINDINGS THAT SUGGEST GIFTEDNESS
Individualized intelligence test	Student scores in the upper 2 to 3% of the population (most states have cutoff scores of 130 or 132 depending on test). Because of cultural biases of standardized IQ tests, students from minority backgrounds are considered if their IQs do not meet the cutoff but other indicators suggest giftedness.
Individualized achievement test	The student scores in the upper 2 to 3% in one or more areas of achievement.
Creativity assessment	The student demonstrates unusual creativity in work products as judged by experts or performs exceptionally well on tests designed to assess creativity. The student does not have to be academically gifted to qualify.
Checklists of gifted characteristics	These checklists are often completed by teachers, parents, peers, or others who know the student well. The student scores in the range that suggests giftedness as established by checklist developers.
Anecdotal records	The student's records suggest high ability in one or more areas.
Curriculum-based assessment	The student is performing at a level beyond peers in one or more areas of the curriculum used by the local school district.
Direct observation	The student may be a model student or could have behavior problems as a result of being bored with classwork. If the student is perfectionistic, anxiety might be observed. Observations should occur in other settings besides the school.
Visual and performing arts assessment	The student's performance in visual or performing arts is judged by individuals with expertise in the specific area. The student does not have to be academically gifted to qualify.
Leadership assessment	Peer nomination, parent nomination, and teacher nomination are generally used. However, self-nomination can also be a good predictor of leadership. Leadership in extracurricular activities is often an effective indicator. The student does not have to be academically gifted to qualify.
Case-study approach	Determination of student's giftedness is based on looking at all areas of assessment described above without adding special weight to one factor.

Source: From *Exceptional Lives: Special Education in Today's Schools* (p. 470), by R. Turnbull, A. Turnbull, and M. Wehmeyer, 2010. Upper Saddle River, NJ: Merrill/Pearson. Copyright 2010 by Pearson Education. Reprinted by permission.

Diversity Issues

As pointed out earlier, diversity issues remain an area of concern in the education of gifted students. Too few students who are culturally different from the majority of their peers are identified and served through programs for gifted students. "Culturally diverse children have much talent, creativity, and intelligence. Manifestations of these characteristics may be different and thus require not only different tools for measuring these strengths, but also different eyes from which to see them" (Plummer, 1995, p. 290). Teachers should look for certain behaviors associated with giftedness in children who come from diverse backgrounds. Torrence (1982) generated a list of behavioral strengths for assisting teachers and other school personnel in identifying students who are gifted and who come from diverse background. Some of the behaviors include:

- Ability to express feeling and emotions
- Ability to improvise with commonplace materials and objects
- Articulateness in role-playing, sociodrama, and storytelling
- Enjoyment of and ability in visual arts, such as drawing, painting, and sculpture
- Enjoyment of and ability in creative movement, dance, drama, etc.
- Enjoyment of and ability in music and rhythm

- Use of expressive speech
- Enjoyment of and skills in group or team activities
- Humor
- Originality of ideas in problem solving
- Problem-centeredness or persistence in problem-solving (p. 469)

Although much attention has been directed at the identification of students who come from a range of diverse backgrounds for gifted programming, it is noteworthy to realize that, for those who are identified, programming often has not been sensitive to their needs. As Plummer (1995) notes, few programs have the resources (i.e., personnel, materials) available to tap the interests and strengths of these students. Moore and Ford (2005) have raised the issue of retention of students from diverse backgrounds in special programs for students with gifts and talents. They point out that too many students of color do not fare well in these programs due to any combination of social and cultural barriers.

PROMOTING EFFECTIVE INCLUSIVE PRACTICES FOR STUDENTS WHO ARE GIFTED

The literature on providing effective services for students with exceptional abilities consistently stresses the need for **differentiated programming**. This concept simply means that learning opportunities provided to these students must differ according to a student's needs and abilities. Differentiation includes the settings where students learn, the content of what students learn, the materials used with students, the processes used in learning situations, the products that students develop, the behaviors of students in classroom settings, and the social/emotional aspects of students' lives.

VanTassel-Baska (1989) notes some of the mistaken beliefs that a number of educators have about educating students with exceptional abilities:

Cross-Reference

Differentiated programming is discussed in Chapter 4.

- A **"differentiated" curriculum for the gifted means "anything that is different from what is provided for all learners."** *Fact:* A "differentiated" curriculum implies a coherently planned scope and sequence of instruction that matches the needs of students and that typically does differ from the regular education curriculum.
- **All experiences provided for gifted learners must be creative and focused on process.** *Fact:* Core content areas are important areas of instructional focus.
- **One curriculum package will provide what is needed for the entire gifted population.** *Fact:* Students need a variety of materials, resources, and courses.
- **Acceleration, moving through the curriculum at a more rapid pace, can be harmful because it pushes children socially and leaves gaps in their knowledge.** *Fact:* This approach to meeting the needs of students with exceptional abilities is the intervention technique best supported by research. (pp. 13–14)

■ Methods that are effective with gifted students are also often useful for nongifted students.

Many professionals in the field of gifted education argue that the preferred setting for these students, particularly for highly and exceptionally gifted students, is not the general education classroom; they recommend differentiated programs delivered in separate classes for the greater part, if not all, of the school day. However, in reality students with special gifts and talents are more likely to spend a significant part of their instructional day in general education settings, possibly receiving some differentiated opportunities in a pullout program.

Concern has grown about the fact that few states require general education teachers to receive *any* preparation (preservice or in-service) in how to work with gifted students. Two statistics support this point: only five states require that all teachers at the preservice level receive training in gifted and talented education; 36 states do not require that general education teachers receive any training on the nature and needs of gifted students during any point in their teaching careers (NAGC, 2009).

Continuum-of-Placement Options

A variety of ways exist for providing educational programs to students who are gifted and talented. Figure 13.3 illustrates various options that might be considered for use with different types of gifted learners. Certain options, used more commonly in the public schools settings, include specialized grouping within the general education setting, independent study, various adjunct programs (e.g., mentorships, internships), special classes outside of general education, special schools, and special summer programs. Another option that some families have chosen is to place their son or daughter in a private school that specializes in providing differentiated programming for gifted students. The value of a particular option reflects the extent to which it meets an individual's needs. As Clark (2002) points out, all the options have some merit. None address the needs of all students with exceptional abilities; however, the general education classroom, as traditionally organized in terms of curriculum and instruction, is inadequate for true gifted education. For this reason, school systems should provide a range of programmatic alternatives.

Gifted students who are in general education classrooms for the entire instructional day can have some of their needs met through a variety of special provisions such as enrich-

FIGURE 13.3

Placement options for gifted students.

Source: From *Growing Up Gifted* (6th ed., p. 256), by B. Clark, 2002. Upper Saddle River, NJ: Merrill/Prentice Hall. Copyright 2002 by Pearson Education. Reprinted by permission.

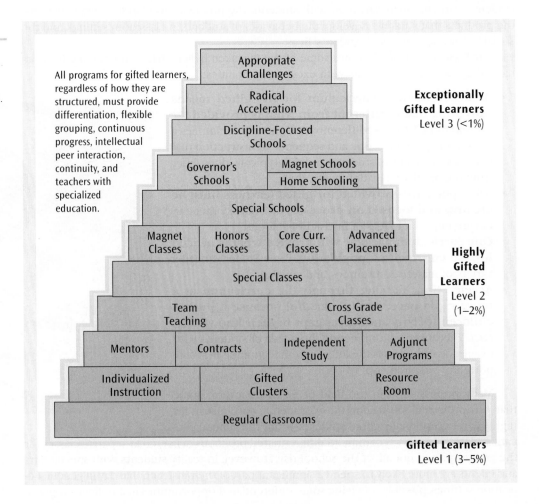

ment, certain acceleration options, or special grouping. The challenge for teachers is to coordinate these provisions with those required for other students in the classroom.

The idea of inclusion of students with gifts and talents in general education classes has been recognized as a reality for many students. The National Association for Gifted Children (NAGC, 1996) issued the following statement regarding this matter in a position paper on inclusion:

> NAGC maintains that gifted students, like other children with special needs, require a full continuum of educational services to aid in the development of the students' unique strengths and talents. One such option in that continuum of services for gifted students can be the regular classroom (inclusion). In such an inclusive setting there should be well-prepared teachers who understand and can program for these gifted students, and sufficient administrative support necessary to help differentiate the program to their special needs. There should be, for example, staff development to aid the general education teacher in understanding and instructing gifted students, provisions for teacher planning time, allowance for student independent study and access to a specialist in gifted education who can aid in differentiating the curriculum to meet the needs of advanced students.

In many schools, students who have been identified as gifted are pulled out for a specified period of time each day to attend a special class for gifted students. When they are in the general education setting, it may be possible for them to participate in an individualized program of study, apart from the regular curriculum. It should be noted that some parents make a conscious decision not to have their gifted children participate in the gifted programming offered by a school. This decision might be made for a number of reasons; sometimes it is made because the quality of the gifted programming is poor.

Students with special gifts and talents may also participate in various adjunct programs such as mentorships, internships, special tutorials, independent study, and resource rooms—many of which occur outside the general education classroom. For students at the secondary level, spending time in special programming for part of the day, attending heterogeneous classes, or attending a magnet school are other possibilities.

These programmatic options affect the role and responsibilities of the general education teacher. For much of the time, the general education teacher will be the primary source of differentiated instruction for these students. In other arrangements, the general education teacher may serve as a manager, coordinating the services provided by others. However, it is probable that most general education teachers will be responsible for providing some level of instruction to these students.

Realities of the General Education Classroom

More attention is being directed to the reality that most gifted students in public school settings will spend a significant amount of time in general education settings. Many innovative and useful techniques exist for addressing the needs of students in these inclusive settings. The section of the chapter on differentiating instruction will highlight many of the techniques. However, cautions remain in regard to meeting the needs of gifted students in general education settings.

In general education settings, students who are gifted or talented are sometimes subject to conditions that diminish the possibility of having their individual needs met. Some of the more common issues that can be problematic for gifted students include the following:

- Many gifted students have already mastered a significant amount of the material presented to them at the elementary level.
- When involved in group activities (i.e., cooperative learning), gifted students may end up doing all the work (Clinkenbeard, 1991).
- They are often subjected to more stringent grading criteria (Clinkenbeard, 1991).
- When they finish assignments early, they are given more of the same type of work or assigned more of the same types of tasks at the outset (Shaner, 1991).
- They are overused as coteachers to help students who need more assistance.

FIGURE 13.4

A personal experience.

Source: From *Exceptional Children in Focus* (p. 216), by J. R. Patton, J. Blackbourn, and K. Fad, 1996. Upper Saddle River, NJ: Merrill/ Pearson. Used by permission.

> Not long ago, I was invited to go on a "reef walk" with a class of gifted third- and fourth-graders. It was a very educational experience.
>
> While we were wading in shallow water, we came upon a familiar marine organism commonly called a feather duster (tube worm). Forgetting that these students had vocabularies well advanced of their nongifted age peers, I was ready to say something like, "Look how that thing hangs on the rock."
>
> Before I could get my highly descriptive statement out, Eddie, who always amazes us with his comments, offered the following: "Notice how securely anchored the organism is to the stationary coral?"
>
> All I could reply was "Yes. I did."

- Vocabulary use in the average classroom is inappropriate for advanced learners (Clark, 1996).
- Advanced levels of critical thinking are not typically incorporated into most lessons (Clark, 1996).
- Instructional materials in general education classrooms are frequently limited in range and complexity (Clark, 1996).
- Problem-solving strategies are not used often enough in ongoing lessons (Gallagher, 1997).

Unfortunately, most general education teachers are not provided with the necessary understanding, skills, and resources to deal appropriately with this population—an issue that will be addressed in more detail later in the chapter. This situation is exacerbated when teachers have to deal with a wide range of abilities and needs in their classrooms. The composition of the general education classroom in many of today's public schools requires a staggering array of teacher competence in providing differentiated instruction and addressing a wide range of social and emotional needs.

Teaching students who are gifted and who are in general education settings is challenging and can, at times, be intimidating. Read the personal experience described in Figure 13.4. This vignette illustrates the type of situation that easily can occur when working with these students. Some general education teachers can feel overwhelmed by the sophistication (in opening vignette, the vocabulary level) of these students.

Shaner (1991) remarks that a teacher who is working with a gifted student can be "intimidated by him or her, paralyzed with a fear of not being able to keep up, or threatened by the student's challenges to authority" (pp. 14–15). Teachers are also concerned about being asked questions they are unprepared to answer or challenged on points they may not know well. These are reasonable fears; however, they can be minimized by using these opportunities as a way to increase everyone's knowledge—a teacher's as well. The trick is knowing how to channel what appear to be teacher-challenging situations into positive experiences.

Programming Approaches for General Education Settings

A number of general approaches exist for designing programs for students who have exceptional abilities, as noted previously. While a variety of options might exist in any given school system, certain options are most commonly used. For instance, many elementary schools rely on a pullout program to provide enrichment-type experiences for students. At the secondary level, magnet schools and AP coursework are common examples of program options. Three types of programmatic approaches to addressing the needs of students who are gifted in general education classes can be implemented: acceleration, enrichment, and special grouping.

Acceleration   Acceleration refers to practices that introduce content, concepts, and educational experiences to gifted students sooner than for other students. Accelerations can be thought of as a way "in which the learner completes a course of study in less time than ordinarily expected" (Colemon & Cross, 2001, p. 298). This approach, if implemented properly, presents gifted students with more advanced materials appropriate to their ability and interests. There are many types of accelerative practices.

Specific accelerative techniques that have the most direct application in the general education classroom are continuous progress, self-paced instruction, subject-matter acceleration, combined classes, curriculum compacting, and curriculum telescoping. Table 13.5 describes these techniques in more detail. All of these practices require teachers to plan and implement instructional activities that are tailored to the needs of these students.

Other accelerative practices have a more indirect impact on ongoing activities in the general education classroom. Nevertheless, teachers should be aware of them. They include early entrance to school, skipping grades, mentorships, extracurricular programs, concurrent enrollment, advanced placement, and credit by examination.

Enrichment   Enrichment refers to techniques that provide topics, skill development, materials, or experiences that extend the depth of coverage beyond the typical curriculum. Coleman and Cross (2001) explain enrichment in the following way: "In its broadest interpretation, enrichment encompasses a number of modifications in standard educational practices. In its narrowest interpretation, enrichment means providing interesting and stimulating tributaries to the mainstream of school" (p. 298).

This practice is commonly used in general education classes to address the needs of students who move through content quickly. Many teachers' manuals and guides provide ideas on how to deliver enriching activities to students who finish their work quickly. Comprehensive lesson plans should include a section on "early finishers," which will often include gifted students, so that enriching activities are available for those who complete assignments before the rest of the class.

The distinction between acceleration and enrichment is, at times, blurred. Some enrichment activities ultimately involve acceleration (Southern & Jones, 1991). For instance, whenever topics of an advanced nature are introduced, a form of acceleration is actually being employed. There is, however, a distinction between materials or activities that are accelerated and involve a dimension of difficulty or conceptual complexity and materials or activities that provide variety but do not require advanced skills or understanding.

Special Grouping   Special grouping refers to the practice whereby gifted students of similar ability levels or interests are grouped together for at least part of the instructional day. One commonly cited technique is the use of cluster grouping within the general education classroom. This practice allows for interaction with peers who share a similar enthusiasm or have similar abilities, resulting in the students bringing different perspectives to topics and stimulating the cognitive and creative thinking of others in the group.

Addressing Student Needs

Addressing the needs of students with exceptional abilities in the context of the general education classroom is a monumental challenge. Current realities and probable trends in programming for gifted students suggest that general education will continue to be the typical setting in which they receive instruction. Thus, it is important that educators enrich the educational experiences of this population in these settings. To do so requires some thoughtful planning and revision to the modus operandi. First, classrooms need to be created where gifted students feel wanted and supported, in addition to having their instructional needs

TABLE 13.5

Range and Types of Accelerative Options

1. Early entrance to kindergarten or first grade	The student is admitted to school prior to the age specified by the district for normal entry to kindergarten or first grade.
2. Grade skipping	The student is moved ahead of normal grade placement. This may be done during an academic year (placing a third-grader directly into fourth grade), or at year end (promoting a third-grader to fifth grade).
3. Continuous progress	The student is given material deemed appropriate for current achievement as the student becomes ready.
4. Self-paced instruction	The student is presented with materials that allow him or her to proceed at a self-selected pace. Responsibility for selection of pacing is the student's.
5. Subject matter acceleration	The student is placed for a part of a day with students at more advanced grade levels for one or more subjects without being assigned to a higher grade (e.g., a fifth-grader going to sixth grade for science instruction).
6. Combined classes	The student is placed in classes where two or more grade levels are combined (e.g., third- and fourth-grade split rooms). The arrangement can be used to allow younger children to interact with older ones academically and socially.
7. Curriculum compacting	The student is given reduced amounts of introductory activities, drill review, and so on. The time saved may be used to move faster through the curriculum.
8. Telescoping curriculum	The student spends less time than normal in a course of study (e.g., completing a one-year course in one semester, or finishing junior high school in two years rather than three).
9. Mentorships	The student is exposed to a mentor who provides advanced training and experiences in a content area.
10. Extracurricular programs	The student is enrolled in course work or summer programs that confer advanced instruction and/or credit for study (e.g., fast-paced language or math courses offered by universities).
11. Concurrent enrollment	The student is taking a course at one level and receiving credit for successful completion of a parallel course at a higher level (e.g., taking algebra at the junior-high level and receiving credit for high school algebra as well as junior high math credits upon successful completion).
12. Advanced placement	The student takes a course in high school that prepares him or her for taking an examination that can confer college credit for satisfactory performances.
13. Credit by examination	The student receives credit (at high school or college level) upon successful completion of an examination.
14. Correspondence courses	The student takes high school or college courses by mail (or, more recently, through video and audio presentations).
15. Early entrance into junior high, high school, or college	The student is admitted with full standing to an advanced level of instruction (at least one year early).

Source: From *Academic Acceleration of Gifted Children* (Figure 1.1), by W. T. Southern and E. D. Jones, 1991. New York: Teachers College Press. Copyright © 1991 by Teachers College, Columbia University. All rights reserved. Used by permission.

met by appropriate programming. Second, appropriate programming needs to be identified and provided to gifted students who are currently underidentified. Third, it is essential that the necessary supports be provided to general education teachers to achieve desired outcomes for this group of students. Fourth, supports must be offered to parents and families. Finally, the way general education teachers are prepared must be examined to ensure that attention is given to the topic of giftedness.

PERSONAL SPOTLIGHT

SPECIAL EDUCATION TEACHER

JOY KATAOKA has taught students with special needs for ten years. She teaches students with many different types of disabilities, but believes that the most challenging teaching year she had was with students with learning disabilities, some of whom were also gifted. To meet the unique needs of these students, Joy had to develop an approach that met individual student needs while challenging their intellectual advancement. To do this, she selected a differentiated-integrated curriculum, which is a common approach for students classified as gifted. "I selected a broad-based theme that was implemented throughout the entire school year."

Using this model, learning activities and experiences were developed that related to the theme as well as to the basic skill needs of some of the students. For example, one year the theme "change" was chosen. Activities associated with this theme included the study of weather, seasons, the theory of continental drift, the theory of evolution, the Civil Rights movement, and people who made significant contributions to the Civil Rights movement. Conflict resolution in literature and factors that in-

fluence change in people were topics that were also included. In addition, students were also engaged in taking a scientific phenomenon, such as lightning, thunder, or rain, and researching how it was represented in mythology, examining the scientific explanation, and also looking at how different poets describe the scientific occurrence in poetry.

The implementation of the curriculum required some individualization. Basic concepts were presented to the entire class, and all students participated in class discussions. However, each student was evaluated based on what he or she could successfully accomplish. Gifted students were required to complete projects in much more detail and at a higher level of sophistication than students who were not gifted. However, all students had to meet certain basic or minimum requirements.

Joy noted that "although such a diverse group of learners in one classroom initially presented a challenge, this curricular approach turned out to be the most successful and productive teaching experience in my career." Inclusion often results in having to teach students with diverse needs and abilities. Teachers must analyze the situation and develop an approach that can meet the needs of all students.

Addressing the Needs of Special Populations

It is particularly important to address the needs of students who are typically underidentified as being gifted, such as students with disabilities, those who are economically disadvantaged, those who underachieve in school, and those who come from different ethnic or cultural backgrounds. Critical issues related to serving these groups focus on nurturing abilities of students in general education, recognizing their potential and discovering exceptional abilities in academic and nonacademic areas, and providing appropriate interventions. All of these issues are affected by the knowledge and skills of the general education teacher.

Some general suggestions for improving the nature of services include:

- **Nurture student development**
  - Create a supportive, caring, nurturing classroom environment, as noted earlier.
  - Establish high expectations for all students in the general education classroom.
  - Encourage all students to do their best.
  - Emphasize that everyone has strengths and areas needing improvement.
  - Identify areas of student interest. This effort often leads to recognition of areas where a student finds some degree of success.
- **Recognize hidden giftedness**
  - Regularly examine the qualitative aspects of students' performance on academic tasks.
  - Make sure that certain factors, such as a specific learning-related problem (e.g., memory problems) or English not being the student's first language, do not mask strength in a variety of areas.

- Use a variety of assessment techniques for screening and eligibility determination purposes.
- Seek parent input on students who are very shy and passive in class activities—these students are often overlooked.
- **Provide appropriate services**
  - Consider a student's personal style and cultural background in the selection of various programming options—for instance, heavy reliance on special ability group work may not be the best first choice for some students.
  - Be aware that some enrichment-related activities, while perhaps engaging, may be in conflict with a student's family and personal beliefs.

Communication with and Support for Parents and Families

In addition to the usual suggestion about the importance of establishing a good home-school collaborative arrangement, some parents of gifted students may need additional information and support. Cases exist where parents of highly gifted students did not recognize that their son or daughter might be gifted. These parents are likely to need information about their child as well as information about the different programming that might be available to address their child's needs.

Parents are faced with the same challenges arising from the gifted characteristics that teachers encounter in the classroom. Often these desirable characteristics can become points of contention. Parents can benefit from the advice of teachers in dealing with these student capabilities and in challenging their child at home during the time when the student is not in school.

Parents can also benefit from obtaining information about careers and further education. Most families are very familiar with the college selection process; however, some families are not, particularly those in which the parents may not have gone on to postsecondary education.

Support for the General Education Teacher

The responsibility to deliver a quality education to gifted students in general education settings rests on the shoulders of the instructional staff, quite often general education teachers. Given the realities of the general education classroom, teachers face a mighty challenge in meeting the needs of students with special gifts and talents. To maximize the chances of successfully addressing the needs of these students who are in general education settings, Coleman (1998) recommends that schools:

- Group students in teachable clusters—groups of 6 to 10 students whose instructional needs are similar.
- Reduce class size.
- Provide additional instructional resources.
- Modify schedules so that there are greater amounts of time available to work with gifted students.
- Provide additional support personnel.
- Require and/or provide training in working with gifted students.

School-based supports such as teacher assistance teams (Chalfant & Van Dusen Pysh, 1993) can also assist with addressing the needs of gifted students. When staffed properly, these teams become a rich resource of experience and ideas for dealing with myriad student needs. Parents also play an important, and often indirect, role in the school-based programs of their children. It is worthwhile to develop parents into good "dance partners" (i.e., to create and maintain positive relationships) in this process (Riley, 1999).

Teacher Preparation and Professional Development

To be a successful general education teacher of gifted students, a wide range of competencies are needed. The National Association for Gifted Children (2010) has made it clear that general education teachers do not receive adequate training to be able to address the needs of gifted students. Teacher training programs vary greatly in terms of the required coursework and the content of courses offered on teaching gifted students.

Maker (1993) highlighted the following personal features as important in teaching gifted students: commitment, belief that people learn differently, high expectations, organization, enthusiasm, willingness to talk less and listen more, facilitative abilities, creativity, and the ability to juggle. Others have discussed the personal characteristics desirable in teachers of students with special gifts and talents (see Davis & Rimm, 1998) or competencies that are desirable (NAGC, 1994).

It is important to acknowledge that "no one teacher can be expected to have complete expertise in meeting the needs of every type of learner" (Cline & Schwartz, 1999, p. 172). However, general education teachers should be exposed to some basic set of knowledge and skills to better address the needs of gifted students who will be in their classrooms. Research has validated that teachers who have had specialized training in addressing the needs of gifted students are more effective (Hansen & Feldhusen, 1994). Some of the basic knowledge/understanding areas and skills/competencies (Rogers, 1989) that general education teachers will need to have in order adequately address the needs of students who are gifted in their classes include:

- **Understanding of:**
  - The nature of giftedness
  - Educational needs of gifted students
  - Creativity and creative thinking strategies
  - Instructional materials and curriculum
- **Skills in:**
  - Instructional adaptation techniques
  - Instructional design strategies
  - Teaching strategy selection
  - Higher-order questioning
  - Group processes (p. 146)

CLASSROOM ADAPTATIONS FOR STUDENTS WHO ARE GIFTED

The notion of differentiated instruction is not a new idea, particularly to professionals who have worked in the field of special education for any length of time. However, the attention that has been given to it in recent years is welcome in that the underlying constructs have important implications for addressing a range of needs in today's classrooms. A differentiated classroom is "one in which a teacher provides a variety of avenues to content (what is taught), process (activities through which students come to understand what is taught), and products (how a student shows and extends what he or she has learned) in response to the readiness levels, interests, and learning profiles of the full range of academic diversity in the class" (Tomlinson, 1997, p. 34).

To be effective in providing an appropriate education to gifted students, teachers need to learn about the cognitive, social, and emotional needs of these students. Furthermore, teachers need a comprehensive long-term plan of education and must enjoy learning experiences that reflect this plan (Kitano, 1993). Teachers who will be working closely with these students are encouraged to consult resources that thoroughly discuss teaching gifted students in general education settings—see Maker (1993), Parke (1989), Ryser and McConnell (2003), Smutny, Walker, and Meckstroth (1997), or Winebrenner (2000).

Although special opportunities for enrichment, acceleration, and the use of higher-level skills are particularly beneficial to students with special gifts or talents, these opportunities can also be extended to other students when appropriate (Roberts, Ingram, & Harris, 1992). Many students in general education settings will find practices such as integrated programming (combining different subject matter) to be exciting, motivating, and meaningful.

Creating a Favorable Classroom Climate

First and foremost, teachers should strive to create classroom settings that foster conditions in which students with special gifts and talents feel comfortable and are able to realize their potential. The climate of any classroom is determined by the interaction among the teacher, the students in the class, and other regular participants in classroom dynamics. Clearly, however, the teacher plays a leading role in establishing the parameters by which a classroom operates and the foundation for classroom dynamics.

The degree to which a classroom becomes a community in which students care for one another and strive to improve the daily experience for everyone will depend on each class's unique dynamics. When a healthy and nurturing classroom context is established, students who are gifted can be important members of the classroom community. In such an environment, their abilities are recognized as assets to the class rather than something to be jealous of, envied, or despised.

To promote acceptance of students with special gifts and talents, teachers should strive to dispel prevailing stereotypes, as perpetuated by myths and misconceptions. Teachers should discuss the uniqueness of these students in terms of the diversity of the classroom, implying that everyone is different. The notion that we all have strengths and weaknesses is also useful.

As noted previously, many of the instructional strategies suggested for gifted students can also be used successfully with nongifted students (Del Prete, 1996). By taking this approach, teachers can accommodate the needs of students with gifts and talents without drawing undue attention to the special programming they are receiving.

Managing and Organizing Effective Classrooms

It is essential to organize and systematically manage the classroom environment. As noted earlier, teachers must create a psychosocial climate that is open to a "variety of ideas, materials, problems, people, viewpoints, and resources" (Schiever, 1993, p. 209). The learning environment should be safe, accepting, and supportive. It is also useful to design instructional activities that allow for extensive social interactions among all students in the class. Unfortunately, as reported by VanTassel-Baska and Stambaugh (2005), "classroom management is the most common concern that arises when educators attempt differentiation, and is one of the main reasons they quit within a few attempts" (p. 212).

Cross-Reference

Classroom management and organization are introduced in Chapter 4.

Classroom management and organization involve a number of critical areas. It includes issues such as setting classroom rules and procedures, managing behavior, and arranging the physical aspects of a classroom, as well as instructionally related topics such as grouping students and lesson planning.

Grouping gifted students for instructional purposes is not only useful, but often necessary, and can be done in a variety of ways. These might include cooperative cluster grouping on the basis of similar abilities or interests, dyads, or seminar-type formats. Gifted students should be afforded an opportunity to spend time with other gifted students, just as competitive tennis players must play opponents with similar or more advanced ability to maintain their skills.

Even though the merits of cooperative learning in classroom settings have been established, heterogeneous cooperative learning arrangements involving gifted students must be managed carefully, as there are some potential pitfalls. Teachers must guarantee that most of the work does not always fall on gifted students in such arrangements. Cooperative learning arrangements can be used effectively but need to be continually monitored and evaluated to ensure productiveness and fairness.

Teachers should develop effective procedures for planning lessons that include differentiated instruction and for keeping records in terms of monitoring the progress of all students, including gifted students who may be involved in a mix of enrichment and accelerated activities. A differentiated report card might be useful for conveying to parents more information about a gifted student's performance. In this type of report, qualitative information about student performance that parents will find extremely helpful in understanding the progress of their gifted son or daughter can be communicated.

The following are some specific management-related suggestions for dealing with gifted students in general education classrooms:

- Get to know gifted students early in the school year through interviews, portfolios of previous work, child-created portfolios, and dynamic assessment (test-teach-retest) (Smutny et al., 1997).
- Enlist parents as colleagues early in the school year by soliciting information and materials (Smutny et al., 1997).
- Require students with gifts and talents to follow classroom rules and procedures while allowing them to explore and pursue their curiosity when appropriate (Feldhusen, 1993a, 1993b).
- Provide reasonable rationales for certain classroom rules and procedures, as some gifted students may challenge their credibility.
- Include gifted students in the development of class procedures that emerge during the course of a school year (e.g., introduction of animals in the room).
- Use cluster seating arrangements rather than strict rows (Feldhusen, 1993a).
- Identify a portion of the room where special events and activities take place and where stimulating materials are kept.
- Include instructional ideas for gifted students within *all* lesson plans.
- Let students who are working in independent arrangements plan their own learning activities (Feldhusen, 1993a).
- Use contracts with students who are involved in elaborate independent study projects to maximize communication between teacher and student (Rosselli, 1993).
- Involve students in their own record keeping, thus assisting the teacher and developing responsibility.
- Use periodic progress reports, daily logs, and teacher conferences to monitor and evaluate students who are in independent study arrangements (Conroy, 1993).

Curricular and Instructional Considerations

General education teachers have no choice these days other than to develop instructional lessons that consider a range of abilities and interests. For students with special gifts and talents, instructional activities can be qualitatively, and even quantitatively, different from those assigned to the class in general—or completely different if certain accelerative options are being used. This section provides a number of suggestions for addressing the needs of students with special gifts and talents in general education settings. It is not meant to be an exhaustive list of examples; however, the examples that are provided do show how the needs of these students can be met.

Whole-Group Activities   When designing instructional activities for the entire class, teachers can use the following series of questions offered by Kitano (1993) to guide planning for gifted students:

- Do the activities include provisions for several ability levels?
- Do the activities include ways to accommodate a variety of interest areas?
- Does the design of activities encourage development of sophisticated products?
- Do the activities provide for the integration of thinking processes with concept development?
- Are the concepts consistent with the comprehensive curriculum plan? (p. 280)

Curriculum Compacting   An accelerative technique that can be used effectively with gifted students in general education classes is **curriculum compacting**, which allows students to cover assigned material in ways that are faster or different. As Renzulli, Reis, and Smith (1981) point out, this process involves three phases: (1) the assessment of what students know and the skills they possess; (2) identification of various ways of covering the curricular material in alternative ways; and (3) suggestions for enrichment and accelerative options. Based on the Rezulli et al. model, Ryser and McConnell (2003) developed a structure for compacting the curriculum for students who can move through material at a quicker rate than most of the students in a typical general education classroom. This resource is depicted in Figure 13.5.

Enrichment Activities   Another recommended way to address the needs of gifted students within the context of the general education classroom is to use **enrichment techniques**. Figure 13.6 provides an example of enrichment by showing how the play *Romeo and Juliet* can be taught, keeping in mind the needs of both nongifted and gifted students who are participating in this same lesson. This example, developed by Shanley (1993), shows how the content of the play and the activities used by the teacher can be adapted for gifted students.

Higher-Order Thinking Skills   Throughout the literature on teaching students who are gifted is a heavy emphasis on providing instructional opportunities for students to exercise higher-order thinking skills. Robinson and colleagues (2007) note, "in teaching for thinking, the concern is not how many answers students know, but what they do when they do not know; the goal is not merely to reproduce knowledge, but to create knowledge and grow in cognitive abilities" (p. 101). It is essential that general education teachers incorporate higher-level thinking into their lessons for these higher-ability students. For example, teachers should include questions that are open-ended and of varying conceptual levels in class discussions.

FIGURE 13.5

Curriculum compacting form.

Source: From *The Revolving Door Identification Model* (p. 79), by J. Renzulli, S. Reis, and L. Smith, 1981. Mansfield Center, CT: Creative Learning Press. Reprinted with permission from Creative Learning Press, copyright © 1981.

Individual Educational Programming Guide

The Compactor

Name _____   Age _____   Teacher(s) _____   Individual conference dates and persons participating in planning of IEP

School _____   Grade _____   Parent(s) _____

Curriculum areas to be considered for compacting. Provide a brief description of basic material to be covered during this marking period and the assessment information or evidence that suggests the need for compacting.	*Procedures for compacting basic material.* Describe activities that will be used to guarantee proficiency in basic curricular areas.	*Acceleration and/or enrichment activities.* Describe activities that will be used to provide advanced-level learning experiences in each of the regular curricula.

FIGURE 13.6

Adapting curricular content for teaching *Romeo and Juliet.*

APPROPRIATE CONTENT FOR REGULAR STUDENTS

1. Discuss qualities of drama that make drama a unique genre of literature.
2. Discuss terms used in discussion of drama, such as aside, soliloquy, prologue, epilogue, dramatic irony, and foreshadowing.
3. Discuss overview of Elizabethan time period, political system, and the role of arts in the society.
4. Distinguish between Shakespeare's time period and setting of the play, giving brief explanation of Verona's social and political characteristics.
5. Discuss structure of Shakespeare's plays, using terms such as act, scene, and line count.
6. Discuss Shakespeare's language and such terms as puns and asides.
7. Discuss main plot, characterization, conflict, and ending of the play.

POSSIBLE ASSIGNMENTS:
a. Write an "updated" scene from *Romeo and Juliet,* stressing the same relationships, but making the scene's setting, names, language more contemporary.
b. Act out the original or rewritten scenes with emphasis on staging considerations.

ROMEO AND JULIET

APPROPRIATE CONTENT FOR GIFTED STUDENTS

1. Arrange students in small groups to read play at rate appropriate to level of understanding.
2. Provide reference material dealing with Elizabethan time period, political and social characteristics, English theater, and time period information about Verona and play's setting.
3. Provide reference material on critical analysis of *Romeo and Juliet.*
4. Encourage awareness of concepts found in play, such as decision making, personal identity, interpretation of the law.
5. Complete a Taba Teaching Strategy (Application of Generalization or Resolution of Conflict), stressing concepts as areas for individual research.
6. Facilitate student research and projects on conceptual subject matter from play.

POSSIBLE ACTIVITIES:
a. Visit and interview local agency for counseling youth or counseling for suicide prevention.
b. Become involved in local drama group.
c. Write an original play dealing with similar or related concepts found in *Romeo and Juliet.*

Source: From "Becoming Content with Content" (p. 74), by R. Shanley, in *Critical Issues in Gifted Education: Vol. 1. Defensible Programs for the Gifted,* edited by C. J. Maker, 1993. Austin, TX: PRO-ED. Used by permission.

Table 13.6 provides an example of the different levels of questions that can be generated in regard to a lesson about George Washington Carver. The table provides a variety of types of questions accompanied by what the intent of the question is. The third column shows an actual example of each type of question for this particular lesson. Similar questions can be generated for any number of lessons.

Instructional Tactics   The following are more specific suggestions related to instructional strategies:

- Balance coverage of basic disciplines and the arts (Feldhusen, 1993a).
- Consult teacher/instructor guides of textbook series for ideas for enrichment activities.
- Incorporate Internet-based activities into lessons.
- Acquire an array of different learning-related materials for use with gifted students. These can include textbooks, magazines, artifacts, software, Internet sources, and digital media (CDs, DVDs), as well as other types of media.
- Include time for independent study; use independent study contracts (Pugh, 1999).
- Teach research skills (data-gathering and investigative techniques) to gifted students so they can develop their independent study abilities (Reis & Schack, 1993).
- Use integrated themes for interrelating ideas within and across domains of inquiry (Van-Tassel-Baska, 1997). This type of curricular orientation can be used for all students in the general education setting, with special activities designed for gifted students.
- Allocate time for students to have contact with adults who can provide special experiences and information to gifted students (e.g., mentors).
- Avoid assigning regular class work that gifted students will miss when they spend time in special programs.

TABLE 13.6

Question Analysis Chart for a Class Discussion on George Washington Carver

QUESTION TYPE	EXPLANATION	EXAMPLE
1. Data-recall questions	Requires remembering	What was the name given to George Washington Carver's laboratory?
2. Naming questions	Lacks insight	Name 10 peanut products developed by George Washington Carver.
3. Observation questions	Requires minimal understanding	What obstacles did George Washington Carver overcome as a black scientist?
4. Control questions	Modifies behavior	How will you remember George Washington Carver's scientific contribution to the farming community?
5. Pseudoquestions	Conveys expected answer	Were George Washington Carver's accomplishments inspirational to black people?
6. Hypothesis-generating questions	Involves speculation	Would George Washington Carver have been famous if he were white?
7. Reasoning questions	Requires rationale	Why did George Washington Carver want to preserve the small family farm?
8. Personal-response questions	Invites personal opinions	What, in your opinion, was George Washington Carver's greatest accomplishment?
9. Discriminatory questions	Requires weighing of pros and cons	Which of George Washington Carver's discoveries was the most significant, those evolving from the sweet potato or the peanut?
10. Problem-solving questions	Demands finding ways to answer questions	If you were to design a memorial for George Washington Carver, what sources would you study for inspiration?

Source: From "Process Differentiation for Gifted Learners in the Regular Classroom: Teaching to Everyone's Needs" (p. 151), by H. Rosselli, in *Critical Issues in Gifted Education: Vol. 3. Programs for the Gifted in Regular Classrooms,* edited by C. J. Maker, 1993. Austin, TX: Pro-Ed. Used by permission.

- Manage classroom discussions so that all students have an equal opportunity to contribute, feel comfortable doing so, and understand the nature of the discussion.
- Use standard textbooks and materials carefully, as gifted students will typically be able to move through them rapidly and may find them boring.
- Ensure that gifted students have access to technology, especially various types of software applications (e.g., word processing, spreadsheets, databases, presentation, photo editing) and various interactive/telecommunications options (e-mail, mailing lists, discussion groups, bulletin boards).

Demonstration of Mastery and Production Differentiation   Another area where differentiation can be used is related to how students demonstrate their mastery of a lesson or topic. Students can benefit by being given a choice from a menu of ways that they can demonstrate their mastery of an assignment. Teachers can provide a range of options for demonstrating student mastery of curricular/instructional objectives—for instance, consider a range of options for final product development. Figure 13.7 presents an extensive list of different types of products that students can use to demonstrate that they have learned a concept or topic.

Career Development

Gifted and talented students need to learn about potential careers that await them. They are often able to engage careers at an earlier time than other students because they may

FIGURE 13.7   Outlet Vehicles for Differentiated Student Products

Literary
Literary magazine (prose or poetry)
Newspaper for school or class
Class reporter for school newspaper
Collections of local folklore (*Foxfire*)
Book reviews of childrens' books for children, by children
Storytelling
Puppeteers
Student editorials on a series of topics
Kids' page in a city newspaper
Series of books or stories
Classbook or yearbook
Calendar book
Greeting cards (including original poetry)
Original play and production
Poetry readings
Study of foreign languages
Organizer of story hour in local or school library
Comic book or comic book series
Organization of debate society
Monologue, sound track, or script

Mathematical
Contributor of math puzzles, quizzes, games for children's sections in newspapers, magazines
Editor/founder of computer magazine or newsletter
Math consultant for school
Editor of math magazine, newsletter
Organizer of metrics conversion movement
Original computer programming
Programming book
Graphics (original use of) films

Media
Children's television show
Children's radio show
Children's reviews (books, movie) on local news shows
Photo exhibit (talking)
Pictorial tour
Photo essay
Designing advertisement (literary magazine)
Slide/tape show on self-selected topic

Artistic
Displays, exhibits
Greeting cards
Sculpture
Illustrated books
Animation
Cartooning

Musical, Dance
Books on life of famous composer
Original music, lyrics
Electronic music (original)

Musical instrument construction
Historical investigation of folk songs
Movement–history of dance, costumes

Historical and Social Sciences
Roving historian series in newspaper
"Remember when" column in newspaper
Establishment of historical society
Establishment of an oral history tape library
Published collection of local folklore and historical highlight stories
Published history (written, taped, pictorial)
Historical walking tour of a city
Film on historical topic
Historical monologue
Historical play based on theme
Historical board game
Presentation of historical research topic (World War II, etc.)
Slide/tape presentation of historical research
Starting your own business
Investigation of local elections
Electronic light board explaining historical battle, etc.
Talking time line of a decade (specific time period)
Tour of local historical homes
Investigate a vacant lot
Create a "hall" of local historical figures
Archaeological dig
Arthropological study (comparison of/within groups)

Scientific
Science journal
Daily meteorologist posting weather conditions
Science column in newspaper
Science "slot" in kids television show
Organizer at a natural museum
Science consultant for school
"Science Wizard" (experimenters)
Science fair
Establishment of a nature walk
Animal behavior study
Any prolonged experimentation involving manipulation of variables
Microscopic study involving slides
Classification guide to natural habitats
Acid rain study
Future study of natural conditions
Book on pond life
Aquarium study/study of different ecosystems
Science article submitted to national magazines
Plan a trip to national parks (travelogue)
Working model of a heart
Working model of a solar home
Working model of a windmill

Source: From "Differentiating Products for the Gifted and Talented: The Encouragement of Independent Learning," by S. M. Reis and G. B. Schack, in *Critical Issues in Gifted Education: Vol. 3. Programs for the Gifted in Regular Classrooms,* edited by C. J. Maker, 1993. Austin, TX: PRO-ED. Used by permission.

participate in accelerated programs that necessitate early decisions about career direction. Students should learn about various career options, the dynamics of different disciplines, and the educational requirements necessary to work in a given discipline.

Teachers can select different ways to address the career needs of students. One way is to ensure that gifted students have access to mentor programs, spending time with adults who are engaged in professional activities that interest them. Another method is to integrate the study of careers into the existing curriculum by discussing various careers when appropriate and by requiring students to engage in some activities associated with different careers. Students can become acquainted with a number of different careers while covering traditional subject areas and through the use of various print and online resources.

Career counseling and guidance are also recommended. As Hardman and colleagues (1993) point out, because of their multiple exceptional abilities and wide range of interests, some gifted students have a difficult time making career choices or narrowing mentorship possibilities. These students should spend some time with counselors or teachers who can help them make these choices and other important postsecondary decisions.

FINAL THOUGHT

If the topics and issues presented in this chapter are addressed correctly, we will do a great service to students with exceptional abilities. Furthermore, students with special gifts and talents should be entitled to a set of educational rights, as the National Association of Gifted Children (2008) has proposed (see "Rights & Responsibilities on page 414). It is only when these conditions are met that teachers will be able to "stimulate the imagination, awaken the desire to learn, and imbue the students with a sense of curiosity and an urge to reach beyond themselves" (Mirman, 1991, p. 59).

SUMMARY

Explain the Basic Concepts of Giftedness

- Definitional perspectives of giftedness and intellectual abilities vary and contribute to some of the problems related to identification, eligibility, and service delivery.
- A key component of most definitions is the student's remarkable potential to achieve at levels above that of peers, as well as high ability, high task commitment, and high creativity.
- The federal definition of giftedness (Jacob K. Javits Gifted and Talented Students Education Act of 1988) (reauthorized in 1994 and 2001) stresses high levels of accomplishment and performance capability in a number of areas.
- The notion of multiple intelligences suggests that there are different areas where one can show high ability.

Describe the Characteristics of Students with Special Gifts and Talents

- Gifted students can excel in a wide range of areas including academic, social, leadership, arts, and athletics.
- Some characteristics of gifted students can become problem areas for them within the general education classroom.

Outline Effective Inclusive Practices for Students with Special Gifts and Talents

- Gifted students continue to be an underidentified, underserved, and often inappropriately served segment of the school population. A host of misconceptions exist in the minds of the general public about these individuals.
- Gifted students need to be afforded range of placement options, one of which is the opportunity to receive an appropriate education in the general education classroom.

Describe Appropriate Classroom Adaptations for Students with Special Gifts and Talents

- Content and instructional techniques need to be differentiated for gifted students.
- Techniques such as curriculum compacting and AP coursework are examples of acceleration techniques that schools use to address the needs of gifted students.

PEARSON
myeducationlab

The MyEducationLab for this course can help you solidify your comprehension of Chapter 13 concepts.

- Gauge and further develop your understanding of chapter concepts by taking the quizzes and examining the enrichment materials on the Chapter 13 Study Plan.
- Visit Topic 1, Inclusive Practices, to:
  - Connect with challenge-based interactive modules, case study units, and podcasts that provide research-validated information about working with students in inclusive settings by visiting the IRIS Center Resources
  - Explore Assignments and Activities, assignable exercises showing concepts in action through video, cases, and student and teacher artifacts
  - Practice and strengthen skills essential to quality teaching through the Building Teaching Skills and Dispositions lessons

14

Teaching Students Who Are At Risk

After reading this chapter, you should be able to:

1. Describe basic concepts of students who are at risk.
2. Describe the select at-risk groups.
3. Discuss effective inclusive practices for students at risk.

ALEVA *is a 9-year-old girl who is currently in third grade; she was retained once in kindergarten. Mr. Sykes, her teacher, referred Aleva for special education, but the assessment revealed that she was not eligible. Although her intelligence is in the low-average range, she does not have intellectual disability or any other qualifying disability.*

Aleva has significant problems in reading and math. Although she seems sharp at times, she is achieving below even her own expected level. Her eyes fill with tears of frustration as she sits at her desk and struggles with her work.

She frequently cries if Mr. Sykes leaves the classroom; she is very dependent on her teacher. Even though on rare occasions a few of the other girls in the classroom will include her, she is typically teased, ridiculed, and harassed by her peers. She has been unable to establish and maintain meaningful relationships with her classmates and adults. Aleva's attempts to win friends are usually couched in a variety of undesirable behaviors, yet she craves attention and friendship. She just does not demonstrate the appropriate social skills requisite of her age.

Aleva lives with her mother and 5-year-old brother in a small apartment. Her mother has been divorced twice and works as a waitress at a local restaurant. Her mother's income barely covers rent, utilities, groceries, and other daily expenses. When her mother gets the chance to work extra hours at the restaurant, she will do so, leaving Aleva in charge of her brother. Although Aleva's mother appears interested in her schoolwork, she has been unable to get to a teacher's meeting with Mr. Sykes, even though several have been scheduled. Her interest in helping her daughter with her homework is limited by the fact that Aleva's mother did not complete school and does not have a great command of the content that she is studying.

Mr. Sykes knows that Aleva is not likely to qualify for special education services under IDEA; however, he also recognizes that Aleva could benefit from assistance, particularly in reading and in social areas.

QUESTIONS TO CONSIDER

1. What types of interventions does Aleva need? What services would you recommend?
2. Should Aleva be considered for special education?
3. What can teachers do with Aleva and students like her to prevent failure?

BASIC CONCEPTS ABOUT STUDENTS WHO ARE AT RISK

Visit the MyEducationLab for this course to enhance your understanding of chapter concepts with a personalized Study Plan. You'll also have the opportunity to hone your teaching skills through video-based Assignments and Activities, IRIS Center Resources, and Building Teaching Skills and Disposition lessons.

The movement to include students with special needs in general education has made substantial progress during the past several years. One beneficial result has been the recognition that many students who are not found eligible for special education services may need, and can benefit from, special interventions and supports. Although certain students like Aleva may not manifest problems severe enough to result in a disability classification, these students nevertheless are at risk for developing academic and behavior problems that could limit their success in school and as adults.

Aleva is a good example of a child who is already experiencing some problems that are limiting her ability to succeed in school, and she is at risk for developing major academic and behavior problems. In the current system, children like Aleva are not likely to be provided with special education and related services under IDEA or Section 504. The result, too often, is that Aleva and children like her find school to be frustrating and basically an undesirable place to be. Ultimately, these students may drop out of school and experience continuing challenges as adults.

Definition

The term *at risk* is often used to describe children who have personal characteristics, or who live in families that display characteristics, that are associated with problems in school. Using education as a frame of reference, children and youth **at risk** are *students who are in situations that can lead to academic, personal, and behavioral problems that could limit their success in school and later in life.*

Some professionals have championed the idea that a better term to use to describe these students is *placed at risk*. The argument for doing so is that the focus is taken off the student and placed more on situational features that contribute to their educational outcomes not being the same as their peers (Keogh, 2000). The philosophy behind the use of the term "children and youth placed at risk" was articulated by the Center for Research on the Education of Students Placed at Risk (2001): "The philosophy . . . is that students are not inherently at risk but rather are placed at risk of educational failure by many adverse practices and situations" (p. 11). This alternative term is attractive because it refocuses attention away from the individual. However, some at-risk situations are more directly associated with the person (e.g., suicidal tendencies that result from depression). A balance needs to be achieved in the use and implication of the term "at risk."

Students identified as being at risk often may have difficulty learning basic academic skills and may exhibit unacceptable social behaviors. They represent a very heterogeneous group (Davis, 1995). Unlike students with disabilities, who have historically been segregated full time or part time from their age peers, students who are considered at risk have traditionally been fully included in educational programs. Unfortunately, rather than receiving appropriate interventions, they have been neglected in the general education classroom and, thus, experienced failure.

Although often not eligible for special education and related services, students who are at risk need special interventions. Such efforts need to be preventative in terms of behavior problems, drug and alcohol abuse problems, grade retention, and dropping out of school. School personnel need to recognize students who are at risk for failure and develop appropriate programs to facilitate their success in school and in society.

While certain factors can increase the vulnerability of students becoming at risk, it is important to recognize that this phenomenon is not only associated with students who are poor or educationally disadvantaged in some other way. Barr and Parrett (2001) underscored this point when they stated: "any young person may become at risk . . . the risks now facing our youths have become a matter of life and death. It is now clear that students who are at risk are not limited to any single group. They cut across all social classes and occur in every ethnic group" (p. 2).

Prevalence and Factors Related to Being At Risk

Many factors place students at risk for developing school-related problems. These may include, for example, poverty, homelessness, single-parent homes, death of a significant person, abusive situations, substance abuse, teen pregnancy, sexual identity issues, delinquency, refugee, and unrecognized disabilities. For example, one factor is preterm birth (i.e., 22–36 weeks of gestation). In the United States, 12.4% of births in 2004 were identified as preterm, which represents the highest rate when compared to rates in 18 European countries (MMWR, 2009).

Although the presence of one or more of the factors noted above often makes failure more likely for students, it is important not to imply that every student who might possess these factors is at risk for school problems. Likewise, we must refrain from labeling every child who is poor or who lives with a single parent as an at-risk student. Many students are

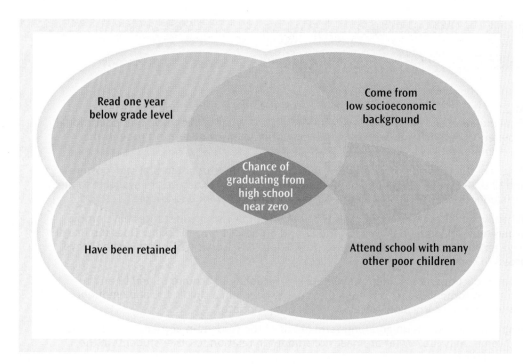

FIGURE 14.1

Research on third-grade students.

Source: From *Policy Perspectives Increasing Achievement of Students Who Are At Risk at Each Grade Level,* by J. M. McPartland and R. E. Slavin, 1990. Washington, D.C.: U.S. Department of Education. Cited in *Hope at Last for At-Risk Youth* (p. 10), by R. D. Barr and W. H. Parrett, 1995. Boston: Allyn & Bacon. Used by permission.

very resilient even when faced with some difficult life situations. Although overly simplistic conclusions should not be drawn concerning students at risk, research identifies certain factors as having a clear correlation with school problems.

According to Barr and Parrett (1995), it is possible to predict, with a high degree of accuracy, which students at the third grade are likely to drop out of school at a later point in time. Figure 14.1 depicts the relationship between four factors that are strong predictors of school failure. Even when children are strongly indicated as being at risk, school personnel must be cautious about predicting their actual abilities and potential for achievement. Such care is particularly important when considering students from ethnically, culturally, and linguistically different backgrounds who appear to be experiencing school-related difficulties. Caution must be exercised when initially considering special education referral for students from such backgrounds; some key issues need to be considered (see Table 14.1). Addressing these issues will decrease the likelihood of referring students for special education programs when in-class interventions might be effective.

SELECT AT-RISK GROUPS

This section explores the challenges that ten at-risk groups—children living in poverty, children who are refugees, homeless children, children from single-parent homes, children who suffer significant losses, children who are abused or neglected, children who abuse substances, children who become pregnant, children who are gay or lesbians, and children who become delinquents—present to school-based personnel. Each group is briefly discussed and an overview of the implications for school personnel is noted.

Students Who Grow Up in Poverty

Poverty is a social condition associated with many different kinds of problems. Poverty has been related to crime, physical abuse, and learning, behavior, and emotional problems. It is arguably the primary factor associated with children being at risk for academic failure.

TABLE 14.1

Issues to Consider before Referring Students from Culturally Diverse Backgrounds
for Special Education Programs

Stage of language development:	At what stage of language proficiency, oral and written, is the student in L1 (student's first language) and L2 (student's second language)? What impact have past educational experiences had on language development? Will the environment facilitate further development?
Language skills:	What are the particular strengths and weaknesses of the student in oral and written L1 and L2 skills? What curriculum materials and instructional expertise are available to meet the student's needs? What skills are the parents able to work on at home?
Disability/at-risk status:	What impact does the student's specific disability or at-risk circumstances have on the acquisition of language skills in L1 and L2 and on other academic skills? Does the teacher have an adequate knowledge base to provide effective services? Does the school have access to community supports?
Age:	What impact does the student's age have on the ability to acquire L1 and L2 and to achieve in content areas? Is there a discrepancy between a child's age and emotional maturity? Is the curriculum developmentally appropriate?
Needs of the student:	What are the short-term and long-term needs of the student in academic, vocational, and community life? What are needs of student in relation to other students in the environment?
Amount of integration:	How much time will be spent in L1 and L2 environments? Will the student be able to interact with students who have various levels of ability?
Personal qualities:	How might the student's personality, learning style, and interests influence the acquisition of L1 and L2, achievement in content areas, and social-emotional growth? How might personal qualities of the student's peers and teacher influence learning?

Source: From *Assessment and Instruction of Culturally and Linguistically Diverse Students with or At Risk of Learning Problems* (pp. 221–222), by V. Gonzalez, R. BruscaVega, and T. Yawkey, 1997. Boston: Allyn & Bacon. Used by permission.

Unfortunately, poverty is a fact of life for many families. The poverty rate in the United States is higher than for 22 other nations classified as "developed." Figure 14.2 illustrates poverty trends for the years 1980 to 2007.

The United States Forum on Child and Family Statistics (FCFS, 2009) reported the following data from 2007:

- Children (age 0–17) living in poverty: 18%
- Ethnic poverty rates for children: 10% White, 35% Black, and 29% Hispanic
- In married-couple families, the rate of poverty for children: 9% vs. 43% in female householder families
- The percentage of children living in families classified as "extreme poverty": 7.4%

The highest percentage of any age group that lives in poverty is for those who are age 18 or younger. Figure 14.3 illustrates the statistics for three age groups. The scenario is even more gloomy for children under the age of 6:

> Children under 6 have been particularly vulnerable to poverty. In 2002, the poverty rate for related children under 6 was 18.5 percent, unchanged from 2001. Of children under 6 living in families with a female householder, no spouse present, 48.6 percent were in poverty, five times the rate of their counterparts in married-couple families (9.7 percent). (Proctor & Dalaker, 2003, p. 7)

Strand and Lindsay (2009), summarizing data from the U.S. Census Bureau (2006), noted that the percentages of individuals living in poverty within specific ethnic groups were as follows: 8% of Whites, 11% Asians, 22% Hispanics, and 25% for both African Americans and Native Americans. They further noted that "socioeconomic disadvantage may have a direct

FIGURE 14.2

Percentage of related children ages 0–17 living in poverty by family structure, 1980–2007.

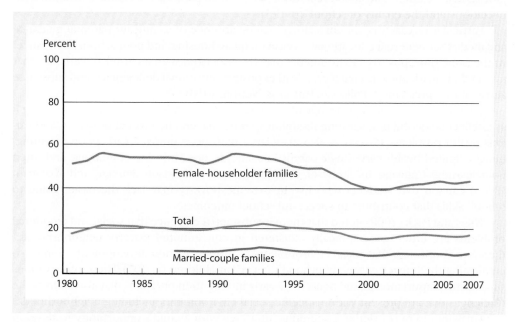

Note: Estimates for related children ages 0–17 include children related to the householder (or reference person of an unrelated subfamily) who are not themselves a householder or spouse of the householder (or family reference person). In 2007, the average poverty threshold for a family of four was $21,203.

Source: From Forum on Child and Family Statistics, 2009 from the U.S. Census Bureau, Current Population Survey, Annual Social and Economic Supplements.

FIGURE 14.3

Poverty rates by age: 1959 to 2002.

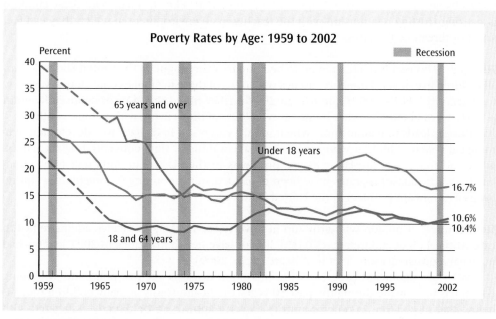

Note: The data points represent the midpoints of the respective years.
Data for people 18 to 64 and 65 and older are not available from 1960 to 1965.

Source: From U.S. Census Bureau, Current Population Survey, 1960–2003 Annual Social and Economic Supplements.

influence on children's development, through limited resources and increased risk for range of health and developmental problems, including low birth weight and increased risk for injuries and ill health … and an indirect influence through parental education, educational expectations, and the quality of school" (p. 175).

Particular risk factors (or correlates) include absence of significant parental guidance and mediation, maternal educational level, inadequate housing, and poor school attendance. At the same time, poverty environments may be associated with a cluster of variables that may include inadequate prenatal care, lead exposure, nutritional deficiencies, and substance abuse during pregnancy (Polloway, Patton, & Nelson, 2010).

Poverty is associated with a range of learning problems (Adelman & Taylor, 2002) as well as intellectual disabilities, learning disabilities, emotional and behavioral disorders, and various health problems. Poverty is also associated with poor prenatal care, poor parenting, hunger, limited health care, single-parent households, poor housing conditions, and often homelessness (Yamaguchi, Strawser, & Higgins, 1997). Evertson, Emmer, and Worsham (2006) caution that students who live in extreme poverty may lack the basic "going to school" skills that contribute to successful school outcomes.

Niles and Peck (2008) noted that there is substantial evidence that social and emotional problems are often "geographically cloistered in concentrated poverty neighborhoods," therefore confirming that social environments … influence child development … and also confirming the impact of "neighborhood effects" on children (p. 307). These observations support the importance of, and benefits of, early intervention programs that also address the challenges that are present within specific social environments, including neighborhoods.

Growing up in restricting conditions interferes with a child's opportunity to develop and mature. The consequences of an unstimulating environment must be diminished through intervention (Polloway, Smith, & Antoine, 2010).

Elders (2002) remarked that most children who are poor will be members of only one club in their lives—the "Five-H Club." Members carry the following credentials—they are hungry, "healthless," homeless, hugless, and hopeless. Using hyperbole, Elders accentuated some of the key issues confronting many children living in poverty. Most important, all of these issues are addressable. Her reference to "hugless" was meant to stress the need in their lives to have an array of people who sincerely care and show it—it was not meant to imply that all children who live in poverty are devoid of love at home. Her point regarding "hope" merely pointed to the need to provide children and youth with promise and motivation to make changes. Evertson and colleagues (2006) note that "a key to success for these children is a strong, trusting relationship with the teacher in an environment in which they can feel safe, not threatened or stressed" (p. 215).

Hunger   Thousands of children go to bed hungry every night. In the United States, 17% of all children live in "food-insecure" homes with 0.9% of these in families considered "very low food security" (FCFS, 2009). The data in 2007 further noted that 43% of children living in poverty were in food-insecure homes as were 32% of those living with a single mother.

Hunger leads to malnutrition, which in turn can result in damage to a developing neurological system. Children who are hungry have a difficult time concentrating on schoolwork and frequently display behavior problems in the classroom. Although free school lunch and breakfast programs have been expanded, hunger among schoolchildren still remains a significant problem in the United States.

Health Care   Children who grow up in poverty are unlikely to receive adequate health care. About 11% of children (ages 0–17) did not have health insurance in 2007, and 6% had no usual (consistent) source of healthcare (FCFS, 2009).

Although significant progress with childhood diseases such as polio and whooping cough has been made during the past 50 years, the health status of many children today is below that of children in other countries. Poverty appears to be directly associated with many of the health problems experienced by children today (Healthy People 2000, 1992). Just as children who are hungry have difficulties concentrating, children who are unhealthy may miss school and fall behind academically.

The 2009–2010 political debate on healthcare reform certainly reflected, in part, the fact that the United States is among the few developed nations without universal health care. Rothstein (2009) pointed to the impact of "vast differences in children's health and health care" (p. 6). This reality, he noted, may then be reflected in lack of dental care, undiagnosed problems in vision, inadequate nutrition, higher rates of asthma, and potentially increased exposure to lead in the environment.

Special Consideration: Children Who Are Refugees

According to the United States Bureau of Population, Refugees, and Migration, "a refugee is a person who has been forced from his or her home and crossed an international border for safety. He or she must have a well-founded fear of persecution in his or her native country, on account of race, religion, nationality, membership in a particular social group, or political opinion (n.d., p. 1). Refugees typically also include individuals who are seeking asylum and others who have been forced to migrate (Stevenson & Willott, 2007).

Although children who are refugees are certainly not necessarily associated with poverty environments, we include this topic here to highlight the fact that American schools are increasingly challenged by the need to provide effective education for an increasing number of refugee children who are now in the schools and, in many cases, also may experience difficulties similar to those of children who were born in the United States but have grown up in a poverty environment.

Stevenson and Willott (2007) noted that "many of the barriers to educational achievement experienced by refugee children are shared by other minority or disadvantaged groups. These include poverty . . ., experience of trauma, violence or threat . . ., interrupted education . . . and language difficulties" (p. 672).

Implications for School Personnel   Unfortunately, school personnel cannot do much to alleviate the base cause of poverty experienced by students. However, teachers can reduce the impact of poverty on achievement and behavior by:

- Recognizing the impact that poverty can have on students
- Making all students in the classroom feel important
- Establishing a strong, trusting relationship
- Avoiding placing students in situations in which limited family finances become obvious to other students
- Initiating and coordinating with school social workers or other school personnel who can work with family members to secure social services
- Realizing and preparing for the reality that students may not have supplies and other equipment required for certain class activities, and seeking contingency funds or other means that could be used to help pay for these items

See the Personal Spotlight feature, which further highlights this issue.

Students Who Are Homeless

Wilder, Okiakor, and Algozzine (2003) stated that "the success of any society can be ascertained by how it treats its members who have the greatest needs" (p. 9). One area in particular that does not reflect well on current society is the reality of homelessness. Homelessness has been a challenge in this country for centuries, including after traumatic historical events such as the Civil War and the Great Depression (Aviles de Bradley, 2008), after major hurricanes such as Katrina and Rita in 2005 (Pane, McCaffrey, Kalra, & Zhou, 2008), and on a regular basis even when no specific societal traumatic events have occurred. Given the fact that 43% of U.S. households report having housing challenges (i.e., shelter cost burden, crowding, physically inadequate housing) (FCFS, 2009), it is not surprising that homelessness is a major issue in our country.

The federal definition of a person who is homeless includes: "1. An individual who lacks a fixed, regular, and adequate nighttime residence; 2. An individual who has a primary nighttime residence that is a supervised publicly or privately operated shelter designed to provide temporary living accommodation including welfare hotels, shelters, and transitional

PERSONAL SPOTLIGHT

SCHOOL COUNSELOR

SARA GILLISON has been a school counselor for seven years. During that time, she has worked in inner-city schools where poverty is a fact of life for many children. In the two schools where she serves as elementary counselor, approximately 35% of students qualify for a free or reduced lunch. Many of the problems that she deals with as the counselor are related to poverty.

"One of the most difficult things for me to do is identify with these families. Unlike most of my friends growing up, many of the students I see on a daily basis do not have many of the basic things they need. They may not have decent clothes, or even enough to eat at night. I have to try to remember every day that my life experiences are just different and try not to project onto my students and their families the same experiences I have had."

Sara notes that the poverty many of her students experience has a wide-ranging impact on their performances in school. She states, "Many of the children who come from obvious poverty are less likely to be prepared for school every day. They often appear to be tired and uninterested. I wonder, sometimes, how much rest they get at home." She notes that while some poor children do well in school, for most it is a struggle that closely relates to their struggle with everyday life.

Sara has had to attempt to understand the impact of poverty on the families she counsels. She notes, "The first time I tried to have a parent conference with a student who was not doing well, I could not understand why the mother or father would not come to a meeting. Finally I realized that not only did they feel uncomfortable because of their personal history of school problems, but also that they did not have transportation. Not having access to personal transportation is not something I used to think of. However, after working with students who come from impoverished backgrounds, one of the first things I try to find out is whether or not the family has a car or access to transportation, and whether or not they have a telephone."

The best advice she can give to teachers and other school people is to try to make these students feel good about themselves and experience success. "Success goes so far with all students," Sara notes, "but for students who are poor, school success can mean the difference between being a failure in life or making it."

housing for the mentally ill; an institution that provides a temporary residence for individuals intended to be institutionalized; or a public or private place not designed for or ordinarily used as, a regular sleeping accommodation for human beings." (U.S. Department of Housing and Urban Development, n.d., p.1).

According to the National Law Center on Homelessness and Poverty (2004), approximately 3.5 million people (1.35 million of them children) are likely to experience homelessness in a given year. Hall (2007) noted that "despite the fact that obtaining solid data on the number of homeless is a challenge, substantial evidence supports the theory that the number of children who are homeless in the United States has dramatically increased in recent years. By some accounts, the number has more than doubled in recent decades. And contrary to popular belief, the homeless population is not necessarily concentrated in urban areas" (p. 10).

While historically the homeless population has been often stereotypically viewed as being made up of older adults, often with mental illness or alcohol problems, 41% are families (National Coalition for the Homeless, NCH, 2009) and as many as 39% of all persons who are homeless are children—42% of these children are under the age of 5 (National Coalition for the Homeless, 2006). The NCH (n.d.) reported that in the United States, one in 50 children is homeless. Research data on homelessness also indicate that an increasing number of persons who are homeless are from ethnic and racial minorities. An estimated 30% of persons who are homeless are employed (Aviles de Bradley, 2008).

The consequences of homelessness have been summarized as follows by the NCH (n.d.):

"homelessness severely impacts the health and well being of all family members. Children without a home are in fair or poor health twice as often as other children, and have higher rates of asthma, ear infections, stomach problems, and speech problems....Children who are homeless also experience more mental health problems, such as anxiety, depression, and withdrawal. They are twice as likely to experience hunger, and four times as likely to have delayed development. These illnesses have potentially devastating consequences if not treated early." (p. 3)

The NCH (n.d.) further noted that "deep poverty and housing instability are especially harmful during the earliest years of childhood; alarmingly it is estimated that almost half of children sheltered are under the age of five.... School-aged children who are homeless face barriers to enroll in attending school, including transportation problems, residency requirements, inability to obtain previous school records, and lack of clothing and schools supplies." (p. 3).

The National Coalition for the Homeless (2006) underscored the impact that homelessness has on families:

> Homelessness is a devastating experience for families. It disrupts virtually every aspect of family life, damaging the physical and emotional health of family members, interfering with children's education and development, and frequently resulting in the separation of family members. (p. 1)

Homelessness is not a fringe issue (National Center for Homeless Education, 2005)—many persons are not that far away from being homeless. One catastrophe (e.g., a hurricane like Katrina) can change our lives dramatically.

Federal Backdrop   Federal legislation guides policy and practice in the United States. The McKinney-Vento Homeless Assistance Act (2001) defines "children who are homeless and youth" as follows:

(A) individuals who lack a fixed, regular, and adequate nighttime residence ..., and
(B) includes—
   (i)   children and youths who are sharing the housing of other persons due to loss of housing, economic hardship, or a similar reason; are living in motels, hotels, trailer parks, or camping grounds due to the lack of alternative accommodations; are living in emergency or transitional shelters; are abandoned in hospitals; or are awaiting foster care placement;
   (ii) children and youths who have a primary nighttime residence that is a public or private place not designed for or ordinarily used as a regular sleeping accommodation for human beings ...
   (iii) children and youths who are living in cars, parks, public spaces, abandoned buildings, substandard housing, bus or train stations, or similar settings; and
   (iv) migratory children who qualify as homeless for the purposes of this subtitle because the children are living in circumstances described in clauses (i) and (iii). (Section 725, Subtitle B, Title VII)

The 2001 revision of the McKinney Act was intended to "increase children's access, stability and support in school, including immediate enrollment, liaisons in all schools, and the right to stay in the (same) school for the duration of homelessness" (Aviles de Bradley, 2008, p. 267). The act requires that each state have on record a plan for the education of students who are homeless. Every local school system must designate someone as liaison for students who are homeless and must provide access to appropriate education for these students.

Presenting Issues   Poverty and the lack of affordable housing are directly associated with homelessness. Making minimum wage does not provide enough income for one to afford a one- or two-bedroom apartment at fair market rent (federally established standard). This situation has received national attention in the popular literature in books such as *Nickel and Dimed* (Ehrenreich, 2001). The complications that arise when a person is making only minimum wage, may not be employed full time, is a single parent, and has limited outside supports are devastating.

Elders (2002) noted that the added impact of not having a home greatly compounds problems of poverty. Children and youth who are homeless experience health problems, hunger, poor nutrition, academic achievement deficits, behavioral problems, fears and phobias, anxiety, anger, depression, low self-esteem, and embarrassment (Hall, 2007; Yamaguchi et al., 1997). In addition, children who are homeless are often embarrassed that they do not have a place to live.

Educationally, specific challenges associated with homelessness for children can include having an appropriate place to complete homework, lower scores on achievement tests, greater likelihood of grade retention, difficulty in making new friends through switching schools, and social isolation (Aviles de Bradley, 2008). In summary, "homeless school-age children have been characterized as the group that is the most at-risk of all" (p. 10).

School Mobility Considerations   A special concern often related to homelessness is the frequent movement between schools for individuals who have no consistent home. The lack of affordability of adequate housing in recent years has exacerbated this problem and placed an additional burden on children in terms of school achievement (Rothstein, 2009). For some students, this might result in their attendance at as many as three or four schools in a given academic year. Reviewing the research on movement between schools as related to homelessness, Aviles de Bradley (2008, p. 264) noted that "every time children and youth move from a stable environment they must enroll in the new school. This has significant detrimental effects on their education, as it has been found that every time a child changes schools, they are set back academically 4–6 months."

Pane et al. (2008, p. 170) noted that "conventional wisdom suggests that a high rate of mobility negatively affects students' lives, from their academic achievement to peer acceptance. It also suggests a negative impact on the classroom and the school, as a whole, by increasing teacher workload, weakening the social bonds between students, and interrupting the curriculum." These researchers, however, noted that school mobility may be caused by a full range of events including homelessness on the one hand, but also upward mobility between neighborhoods and cities on the other hand. Consequently, they noted that "the effects of student mobility are much more complex and depend on several factors, including family background, socioeconomic status, reasons for and timing of the move, and teacher and school preparedness." Pane and colleagues concluded that, while research did not confirm that mobility in and of itself results in achievement gains or losses, it is clear that the causes behind the mobility (as in the case of persons who are homeless having to switch schools repeatedly) are predictive of such losses.

Implications for School Personnel   Although some students who are homeless are able to stay in a shelter, many live on the streets, in cars, or in other public settings with their parents. Of course, school personnel can do little to find homes for these children. A key emphasis is to avoid putting students in situations in which their homelessness will result in embarrassment. For example, going around the room after the students' birthdays and having everyone tell about gifts they received may be very uncomfortable for students who do not have a home to go to after school.

It is also important to realize that parents of children who are homeless may do everything they can to hide the fact that their family is homeless, typically as a precaution to avoid Child Protective Services from removing their children. As a result, they are unlikely to inform school personnel of significant situations related to a student's life that would be beneficial to know. Certainly a key consideration by school personnel is to ensure that students have access to critical resources inclusive of adequate food, sufficient clothing, medical care, and emergency shelter as needed (Hall, 2007). In addition, another important consideration is to monitor attendance so that patterns of absences are understood and can appropriately be responded to.

The following recommendations for school personnel concern issues related to students who are homeless:

- Realize that a large percentage of these students will not attend school on a regular basis.
- Be vigilant and sensitive to students who might be homeless—the students may need services, but their families may fear that to get needed services, discovery is required and the forced breakup of the family might follow. A list of common signs of homelessness is presented in Figure 14.4.
- Monitor behavior and progress in the classroom, paying particular attention to physical, health, emotional, and social manifestations.
- Become a safe resource for students and their parents.

FIGURE 14.4	Common Signs of Homelessness

Lack of Continuity in Education
- Attendance at many different schools
- Lack of records needed for enrollment
- Gaps in skill development

Poor Health/Nutrition
- Lack of immunizations and/or immunization records
- Unmet medical and dental needs
- Chronic hunger (may hoard food)
- Fatigue (may fall asleep in class)

Transportation and Attendance Problems
- Erratic attendance or tardiness
- Inability to contact parents
- Numerous absences
- Avoidance of class field trips

Poor Hygiene
- Wearing the same clothes for several days
- Lack of facilities to stay clean

Not Ready for Class
- Lack of basic school supplies
- Concern for the safety of belongings
- Incomplete or missing homework

Social and Behavioral Cues
- Change in behavior
- "Old" beyond years
- Protective of parents
- Poor/short attention span
- Poor self-esteem
- Difficulty or avoidance of making friends
- Difficulty trusting people
- Need for immediate gratification

Reactions/Statements by Parent, Guardian, or Child
- Anger or embarrassment when asked about current address
- Mention of staying with grandparents, other relatives, friends, or in a motel

Note: Warning signs adapted from flyers developed by the Illinois and Pennsylvania Departments of Education.

Source: Adapted from National Center for Homeless Education www.serve.org/nche_web/warning.php

Hall (2007) listed specific strategies that teachers could employ within the classroom setting: providing a homelike environment within the classroom by striving for consistency in the arrangement of furniture within the classroom, including elements (student photographs, classroom pet, plans) that can provide a stable and warm environment for students, and establishing a predictable daily routine.

To work with parents who are homeless, teachers and other school personnel should consider the following:

- Arrange to meet parents at their place of work or at school.
- Offer to assist family members in securing services from available social service agencies.
- Do not require excessive school supplies that many families cannot afford.

Schools can use any of several program models when working with students who are homeless. Table 14.2 identifies several possible options.

TABLE 14.2

Program Models for the Education of Students Who Are Homeless

Outreach Programs District-based programs may employ a coordinator whose duties can include:

- Maintaining communication among schools, shelters, and social service agencies
- Visiting shelters to identify children who may need assistance with school enrollment
- Assisting families with referrals to appropriate agencies for accessing necessary services
- Providing students with clothing and school supplies
- Assisting with school transportation arrangements
- Conducting in-service training programs at school sites or to parent groups

District Schools Schools located in the area of shelters may provide special programs including:

- Assisting with the school registration process
- Assisting with applications for services such as free school meals and before- and after-school programs
- Providing a closet for free clothing and school supplies located at the school
- Assessing the student's present academic levels for appropriate classroom placement
- Tutoring and social skills programs for the student

Transition Room in Neighborhood Schools A classroom located in the student's school provides a temporary setting for children. Characteristics include:

- Providing a safe environment where children become acquainted with the school and teachers before moving into their permanent classrooms
- Emphasizing the emotional needs of the child
- Emphasizing the assessment of academic skills
- Providing assistance for the family as necessary
- Providing clothing and school supplies as needed

Transition and Shelter Schools These schools' purpose is to serve students who are homeless. When students are functioning well in this setting, they are moved into regular schools. In this setting the goals include:

- Providing intense and temporary assistance
- Working on basic skills
- Providing emotional support to help the children cope with stress in their lives
- Assisting with the basic needs of clothing, school supplies, food, and health services

After-School Programs Programs may include all or some of the following:

- One-on-one tutoring
- Help with homework
- Opportunities to build friendships
- Counseling and emotional support
- Recreation, field trips, and other leisure activities

Source: Adapted from "Children Who Are Homeless: Implications for Educators," by B. J. Yamaguchi, S. Strawser, and K. Higgins, 1997, *Intervention in School and Clinic, 33,* p. 94. Used by permission.

Students in Single-Parent Homes

The nature of the American family has changed dramatically in a relatively short period of time. According to the FCFS (2009), only 68% of children lived with two married parents. In 2007, 40% of births were to unmarried women. Figure 14.5 illustrates trends for parental presence in households from 1980–2008.

Many factors result in children being reared in single-parent homes, including divorce, death of a parent, significant illness of a parent, or a parent being incarcerated. And, as has been stated previously, being raised in a single-parent family does not imply that these families' situations are not healthy, nurturing, and encouraging. The reality is that when single parents are also living at poverty level or have other complications (e.g., substance abuse) in their lives, children and youth are placed at risk.

FIGURE 14.5

Percentage of children ages 0–17 by presence of parents in household, 1980–2008.

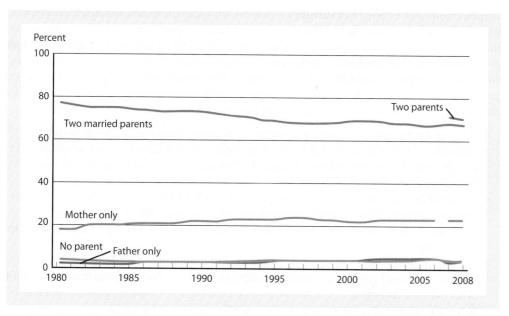

Note: Prior to 2007, *Current Population Survey* (CPS) data identified only one parent on the child's record. This meant that a second parent could only be identified if they were married to the first parent. In 2007, a second parent identifier was added to CPS. This permits identification of two coresident parents, even if the parents are not married to each other. In this figure "two parents" reflects all children who have both a mother and father identified in the household, including biological, step, and adoptive parents. Before 2007, "mother only" and "father only" included some children who lived with a parent who was living with the other parent of the child, but was not married to them. Beginning in 2007, "mother only" and "father only" refer to children for whom only one parent has been identified, whether biological, step, or adoptive.

Source: From Forum on Child and Family Statistics, 2009 from the U.S. Census Bureau, *Current Population Survey,* Annual Social and Economic Supplements.

It is estimated that half of all new marriages will end in divorce. Divorce is a disorganizing and reorganizing process, particularly when children are involved, and the process often extends over several years (Morgan, 1985).

Divorce offers the potential for growth and new relationships, but often creates problems for children and youth. Although some children cope well with the trauma surrounding divorce, others may experience significant problems. The central dilemma in many divorces is the conflict of interest between the child's need for continuity of the family unit and the parents' decision to break up the family that has provided the child's main supports. Children react in many different ways to divorce, including feeling guilt, developing anxiety, exhibiting social problems, experiencing grief, being angry, and displaying hostility.

Most single-parent homes are headed by mothers. The absence of a father figure may have a significant impact on the psychological development of a child. The absence of the father seems to affect the academic achievement of both boys and girls, with lower achievement correlating with limited presence of the father. In addition, as noted earlier, levels of food insecurity are markedly higher for female households than for two-parent homes (FCFS, 2009).

Although not nearly as prevalent as single-parent homes headed by mothers, the number of single-parent homes headed by fathers has increased significantly in recent years. The effects of growing up in a single-parent home headed by a father vary a great deal from child

■ More than one-quarter of all children live with a single parent, usually a mother.

to child. Fathers are likely to be more reliant on other adults in their support networks than are single-parent mothers.

Implications for School Personnel   Children who find themselves in single-parent families as a result of divorce, death, illness, or incarceration require a great deal of support. For many of these children, the school may be their most stable environment during a transitional phase of their lives. School personnel must develop supports to prevent negative outcomes, such as school failure, manifestation of emotional problems, or the development of behavior problems. An interview conducted with children residing in single-parent homes resulted in the following conclusions concerning the positive role schools can play (Lewis, 1992):

- Schools are a place of security and safety for students from single-parent homes.
- Students who lose parents due to death are often treated differently by school personnel than when the loss is from divorce. Unfortunately, the child's needs are similar in both situations.
- Teachers are the most important people in the school for children who are in single-parent homes because of their tremendous influence on self-esteem.
- Students want to be treated just as they were before they became part of a single-parent home.
- Trust with peers and teachers is the most important factor for students.
- School personnel need to be more sensitive to the new financial situation of families with only one parent.
- Keeping a log or diary is considered an excellent method for children to explore feelings and create opportunities for meaningful discussions.

There are many things schools should and should not do when dealing with students who are from single-parent homes (see Figure 14.6). For children whose parents are divorced, schools must consider the involvement of the noncustodial parent. To ensure that noncustodial parents are afforded their rights regarding their children, and to actively solicit the involvement of the noncustodial parent, school personnel should:

- Establish policies that encourage the involvement of noncustodial parents.
- Maintain records of information about the noncustodial parent.

FIGURE 14.6

Some DOs and DON'Ts when working with children with single parents.

Source: From "Meeting the Needs of Single-Parent Children: School and Parent Views Differ," by C. L. Wanat, 1992, *NAASP Bulletin, 76,* p. 47. Used by permission.

Some DOs
- Collect information about students' families.
- Analyze information about students' families to determine specific needs.
- Create programs and practices that address areas of need unique to particular schools.
- Include curricular areas that help students achieve success, such as study skills.
- Provide nonacademic programs such as child care and family counseling.
- Involve parents in determining appropriate roles for school and family.
- Take the initiative early in the year to establish a communication link with parents.
- Enlist the support of both parents, when possible.
- Provide a stable, consistent environment for children during the school day

Some DON'Ts
- Don't treat single parents differently than other parents.
- Don't call attention to the fact that a child lives with only one parent.
- Limit activities such as "father/son" night or other events that highlight the differences in a single-parent home.
- Don't have "room mothers," have "room parents."
- Don't overlook the limitations of single-parent homes in areas such as helping with projects, helping with homework, and so forth.

- Distribute information about school activities to noncustodial parents.
- Insist that noncustodial parents be involved in teacher conferences.
- Structure parent conferences to facilitate the development of a shared relationship between the custodial and noncustodial parents.
- Conduct surveys to determine the level of involvement desired by noncustodial parents (Austin, 1992).

Students Who Experience Significant Losses

The continued absence of one or both parents through separation or divorce is considered a loss. However, the loss created by the death of a parent or a sibling can result in significantly more emotional problems for children. Unlike children living in earlier centuries, when extended families often lived together and children actually observed death close at hand (e.g., a grandparent), often in the home environment, children of today are generally insulated from death. Therefore, when death does occur, especially that of a significant person in a child's life, the result can be devastating, often resulting in major problems in school.

Death of a Parent   When a child's parent dies, whether unexpectedly or over the course of a long illness, external events impinge on the child's life. The child is challenged to deal with the reality of the death itself, adapt to the resulting changes in the family, and contend with the perpetual absence of the lost parent.

Children respond in many different ways to a parent's death. Some responses are guilt, regression, denial, bodily distress, hostile reactions to the deceased, eating disorders, incontinence, sleep disturbances, withdrawal, anxiety, panic, learning difficulties, and aggression (Elizer & Kauffman, 1983; Van Eerdewegh, Bieri, Parrilla, & Clayton, 1982). It is also not unusual for sibling rivalry to become very intense and disruptive. Often, extreme family turmoil results from the death of a parent, especially when the parent who died was the controlling person in the family (Van Eerdewegh et al., 1982).

Death of a Sibling   A sibling plays an important and significant part in family dynamics, so the death of a sibling can initiate a psychological crisis for a child. Sometimes the grief of the parents renders them unable to maintain a healthy parental relationship with the remaining child or children, significantly changing a child's life situation.

When experiencing the death of a sibling, children frequently fear that they will die. When an older sibling dies, the younger child may revert to childish behaviors in hopes of not getting older, thereby averting dying. Older children often react with extreme fear and anxiety, especially if they are ignored by parents during the grieving period. Often these children become preoccupied with the questions about their own future.

Implications for School Personnel   For the most part, the best advice for teachers is to be aware of how the student who experiences loss is doing when in school. Equally important is to involve the school counselor. Some of the issues that may arise require intervention that is outside the training and expertise of most teachers. So, knowing about other school-based and outside school resources is valuable. Some communities are fortunate to have private, nonprofit organizations that have been established to help surviving members of a family deal with the ongoing terminal illness or death of a parent or sibling. School counselors should be aware of such community resources.

Students Who Are Abused and Neglected

Growing up in an abusive or neglectful family clearly places children at significant risk for a variety of pejorative outcomes, including school failure. Child abuse and neglect occur in families from every socioeconomic level, race, religion, and ethnic background. Family members, acquaintances, or strangers may be the source of the problem. Although there is no single cause that leads to abuse or neglect, many factors exist that add to the likelihood of these events occurring, including poverty, large family size, low maternal involvement with children, low maternal self-esteem, minimal father involvement, and a stepfather in the household (Brown, Cohen, Johnson & Salzinger, 1998).

Data from the National Child Abuse Statistics (adapted from Childhelp, n.d., p. 1) indicate the following:

- Almost five children die every day as a result of child abuse. More than three out of four are under the age of 4.
- 90% of child sexual abuse victims know the perpetrator in some way; 68% are abused by family members.
- Between 60 and 85% of child fatalities due to maltreatment are not recorded as such on death certificates.
- Child abuse occurs at every socioeconomic level, across ethnic and cultural lines, within all religions, and at all levels of education.
- 31% of women and 14% of men in prison in United States were abused as children.
- Over 60% of people in drug rehabilitation centers report abuse or neglect as a child.
- About 30% of abused and neglected children will later abuse their own children.
- About 80% of 21-year-olds abused as children met criteria for at least one psychological disorder.
- Abused children are 25% more likely to experience teen pregnancy.
- Children who experienced child abuse and neglect were 59% more likely to be arrested as a juvenile, 28% more likely to be arrested as an adult, and 30% more likely to commit violent crime.
- Children who have been sexually abused are 2.5 times more likely to develop alcohol abuse and 3.8 times more likely to develop drug addiction.

The two major categories addressed in this section are **abuse** and **neglect**. They are different yet are typically covered together in state statutes. Child abuse implies some type of overt, inappropriate action that results in negative outcomes for a child or adolescent. Neglect, however, refers to the omission or absence of basic behaviors that should be provided to children and youth and that also result in negative outcomes for the person. Each of these concepts has variations, as discussed below.

Data on the maltreatment of children indicate that the most frequently occurring type of maltreatment is neglect. In 2004, 62.4% of victims of maltreatment experienced neglect, 17.5% experienced physical abuse, 9.7% experienced sexual abuse, and 7.0% experienced psychological maltreatment. It should be noted that these data reflect reported cases and that the actual number of cases of maltreatment are higher due to many cases not being reported and confirmed (U.S. Department of Health and Human Services, 2006).

A variety of taxonomies exist for categorizing abuse and neglect with data from the federal government are organized into the following categories: physical abuse, neglect, medical neglect, sexual abuse, psychological or emotional maltreatment, and "other" (i.e., allows for variation in state reporting systems). The following discussion is organized around the two major concepts of abuse and neglect.

Abuse   There are three major types of abuse: emotional, physical, and sexual. **Emotional abuse**, sometimes referred to as psychological maltreatment, can be defined as "a pattern of behavior by parents or caregivers that can seriously interfere with a child's cognitive, emotional, psychological, or social development" (American Humane, 2004, p. 1). Emotional abuse, which accompanies all other forms of child abuse, can involve unreasonable demands placed on children by parents, siblings, peers, or teachers, or the failure of parents to provide the emotional support necessary for children to grow and develop (Thompson & Kaplan, 1999). Some examples of emotional abuse might include ignoring, rejecting, isolating, exploiting/corrupting, verbally assaulting, and terrorizing (American Humane, 2004).

Research has revealed that verbal abuse, by itself, can result in lowered self-esteem and school achievement (Solomon & Serres, 1999). Although difficult to identify, emotional abuse has several characteristics that may be exhibited by children who are being emotionally abused. These include:

- Absence of a positive self-image
- Behavioral extremes

- Depression
- Psychosomatic complaints
- Attempted suicide (see the nearby Differentiated Instruction—Secondary boxed reading for further information on suicide)
- Impulsive, defiant, and antisocial behavior
- Age-inappropriate behaviors
- Inappropriate habits and tics
- Inhibited intellectual or emotional development
- Difficulty in establishing and maintaining peer relationships
- Extreme fear, vigilance
- Sleep and eating disorders
- Self-destructive tendencies
- Rigidly compulsive behaviors (Gargiulo, 1990, p. 22)

Physical abuse is more easily identified than emotional abuse and is defined as "nonaccidental trauma or physical injury caused by punching, beating, kicking, biting, burning, or otherwise harming a child" (American Humane, 2003, p. 1). In addition to striking, other actions like violent shaking can potentially play a role in brain hemorrhage and retardation. Signs of a "shaken baby" include vomiting, seizures, blood pooling in the eyes, apnea (spells of interrupted breathing), irritability, sleeping difficulties, and drowsiness; outcomes may include hypertension, cerebral palsy, subcranial or subdural hemorrhages, coma, and death (Polloway, Smith, & Antoine, 2010).

Children who are physically abused are two to three times more likely than nonabused children to experience failing grades and to become discipline problems. They have difficulty with peer relationships, show physically aggressive behaviors, and frequently are substance abusers (Emery, 1989). Studies also show that children who suffer from physical abuse are likely to exhibit social skill deficits, including shyness, inhibited social interactions, and limited problem-solving skills. Deficits in cognitive functioning are also found in greater numbers in students who are abused than in their nonabused peers (Weston, Ludolph, Misle, Ruffins, & Block, 1990).

Sexual abuse is another form of abuse that puts children and youth at risk for school failure. Sexual abuse can be differentiated into three areas: "touching" sexual offenses (e.g., fondling, intercourse); "nontouching" sexual offenses (e.g., indecent exposure, exposing children to pornographic material); and "sexual exploitation" (e.g., prostitution, participating in the creation of pornographic material) (American Humane, 2003, p. 1).

Differentiating Secondary Instruction

Clearly one of the most critical concerns related to students at-risk within the school setting is the possible risk of suicide. As Peebles-Wilkins (2006) noted, "for youth between ages 15 and 24, suicide is more likely than any other reason to be the cause of death" (p. 195).

A number of specific risk factors are associated with suicide. These include "biological predisposition, depression, substance abuse, sexual-orientation-related factors, poor coping and interpersonal skills, stressful life events, and suicide in the family history (Peebles-Wilkins, 2006, p. 195).

Schools that are responsive to concerns about suicide, and perhaps have experienced occurrences, have increasingly developed specialized intervention programs. The goal of such programs is to eliminate or reduce the attempted suicides by adolescents. Peebles-Wilkins (2006) reported on one program that resulted in a 40% reduction in suicide attempts. This comprehensive program was designed to encourage help-seeking behavior by at-risk students while facilitating enhanced communication among students, teachers, and parents. She noted that through the technique of *acknowledge, care, and tell* (ACT), students were taught to recognize depression symptoms, note how these symptoms might relate to the potential for suicide, and subsequently alert an adult to concerns. As a consequence of such focused programs, more students come to the attention of schools and prevention is achieved.

The rate for sexual abuse of girls in the United States ranges from 15 to 32%, depending on the method of calculation used. Sexual abuse is more likely to occur in girls younger than the age of 15 (Vogeltanz et al., 1999). Children can be sexually abused by members of their own families as well as by strangers. Children who are sexually abused not only are at risk for developing problems during their school years, but also will typically manifest problems throughout their adulthood (Silverman, Reinherz, & Giaconia, 1996).

School personnel should be aware of typical symptoms of sexual abuse:

- Physical injuries to the genital area
- Sexually transmitted diseases
- Difficulty in urinating
- Pregnancy
- Aggressive behavior toward adults, especially a child's own parents
- Sexual self-consciousness
- Sexual promiscuity and acting out
- Inability to establish appropriate relationships with peers
- Running away, stealing, and abusing substances
- Using the school as a sanctuary, coming early, and not wanting to go home

Neglect Neglect refers to situations where a child is exposed to a substantial risk of harm. Neglect is much more difficult to recognize, as no visible physical signs of neglect are evident—unless physical harm also occurs. Signs of neglect are reflected through behaviors. Examples of neglect could include placing a child in an unsupervised situation that could result in bodily injury, failing to seek and obtain proper medical care for a child, or failing to provide adequate food, clothing, or shelter. As mentioned earlier, it is this last element that casts fear into the minds of parents who are homeless. The four major types of neglect (American Humane, 2003), are:

- *Physical neglect:* Generally involves the parent or caregiver not providing the child with the basic necessities (e.g., adequate food, clothing, shelter).
- *Educational neglect:* Failure of a parent or caregiver to enroll a child of mandatory school age in school or provide appropriate home schooling or needed special education training, thus allowing the child or youth to engage in chronic truancy.
- *Emotional neglect:* Includes actions such as engaging in chronic or extreme spousal abuse in the child's presence, allowing a child to use drugs or alcohol, refusing or failing to provide needed psychological care, constantly belittling the child, and withholding affection.
- *Medical neglect:* Failure to provide appropriate health care for a child (although financially able to do so), thus placing the child at risk of being seriously disabled or disfigured or dying. (pp. 1–2)

Implications for School Personnel The first thing that school personnel should be prepared to do when dealing with children and youth who might be abused or neglected is to report any incident to the appropriate agencies. In most states, school personnel and other professionals who work with children have a legal, as well as a moral, obligation to report suspected child abuse or neglect.

Failure to report a case is a punishable offense. School personnel need to understand their responsibility in reporting suspected abuse and know the specific procedures to follow when making such a report. In addition to reporting suspected cases of abuse, schools in general can do the following:

- Work with local government officials to establish awareness of child abuse and neglect as a priority in the community.
- Organize a telephone "hotline" service where parents or other caregivers can call for support when they believe a crisis is impending in their families.
- Offer parent education programs that focus on parenting skills, behavior management techniques, child-care suggestions, and communication strategies.

- Establish a local chapter of Parents Anonymous, a volunteer group for individuals who have a history of abusing their children.
- Develop workshops on abuse for concerned individuals and disseminate literature on the topic.
- Arrange visits by public health nurses to help families at risk for abuse after the birth of their first child.
- Provide short-term respite day care through a Mother's Day Out program.
- Encourage individuals to serve as foster parents in the community.
- Institute a parent-aide program in which parent volunteers assist single-parent homes by providing support.
- Make structured group therapy available to abuse victim. (Kruczek & Vitanza, 1999)

School-based personnel should consider the following suggestions:

- Provide a safe classroom where students can flourish.
- Be vigilant for the signs of abuse and neglect in students.
- Make yourself recognizable as a person in whom a student can confide very personal information—every student needs someone like this.
- Try not to show any extreme emotion when a student discloses information to you. Remain calm, interested, and reassuring.
- Report any suspected situations knowing that you are immune from civil or criminal liability as long as the report was made in good faith and without malice.
- Understand that a student who shares very personal information about being abused in all likelihood will ask you not to tell anyone—and yet you will have to do so. As a result, avoid promising to abide by any preconditions a student may ask of you.
- Understand that initially a student who confided information to you on which you had to take action will feel that you betrayed him or her. For a period of time your relationship with this child will be rough. Ultimately, the student is likely to come around and appreciate what you did.

Students Who Abuse Substances

Substance abuse among children and adolescents results in major problems and places students significantly at risk for school failure (Vaughn & Long, 1999). Students who are abusing substances have a much more difficult time succeeding in school than do their peers. While most people consider substance abuse to relate to the improper use of alcohol and drugs, it can also refer to the use of tobacco.

The substance that youths use the most is alcohol. According to data gathered by the National Institute on Drug Abuse (2006), 68.6% of high-school seniors reported using alcohol during the previous school year. Elders (2002) reported that a third of high-school students said that they engaged in binge drinking. The FCFS (2009) reported these data on binge drinking: 3% of students in eighth grade reported drinking five or more alcoholic beverages in a row within the *last two weeks*, 16% of tenth graders, and 25% of twelfth graders.

Table 14.3 shows the percentage of eighth-graders, tenth-graders, and twelfth-graders using drugs, by type of drug. The table provides information for four time frames: if ever used during one's lifetime, if used within past 12 months, if used within the past month, and if used daily.

After years of drug abuse education, the use of alcohol and certain drugs has not been significantly influenced. Another more alarming fact about substance abuse is that while the level of use by twelfth-graders has decreased or remained virtually constant, the level of use by younger students (eighth-graders) has increased significantly. For example, in 1991 only 3.2% of eighth-graders indicated that they had used marijuana or hashish during the previous 30 days. This number is now reported to be 6.6%. Nagel, McDougall, and Granby (1996) reported that boys have a tendency to use illegal drugs slightly more than do girls, but that girls actually use more over-the-counter drugs inappropriately than boys do.

While no factors are always associated with drug use in children and youth, some appear to increase the likelihood of such use. Parental factors—such as drug use by parents,

TABLE 14.3

Trends in Prevalence of Various Drugs for Eighth-Graders, Tenth-Graders, and Twelfth-Graders, 2004–2005

Note: [Bracketed figures in the tables below indicate statistically significant changes between 2004 and 2005.]

	8TH GRADERS		10TH GRADERS		12TH GRADERS	
	2004	2005	2004	2005	2004	2005
Any Illicit Drug Use						
lifetime	21.5	21.4	39.8	38.2	51.1	50.4
annual	15.2	15.5	31.1	29.8	38.8	38.4
30-day	8.4	8.5	18.3	17.3	23.4	23.1
Marijuana/Hashish						
lifetime	16.3	16.5	35.1	34.1	45.7	44.8
annual	11.8	12.2	27.5	26.6	34.3	33.6
30-day	6.4	6.6	15.9	15.2	19.9	19.8
daily	0.8	1.0	3.2	3.1	5.6	5.0
Inhalants						
lifetime	17.3	17.1	12.4	13.1	10.9	11.4
annual	9.6	9.5	5.9	6.0	4.2	5.0
30-day	4.5	4.2	2.4	2.2	1.5	2.0
Hallucinogens						
lifetime	3.5	3.8	6.4	5.8	9.7	8.8
annual	2.2	2.4	4.1	4.0	6.2	5.5
30-day	1.0	1.1	1.6	1.5	1.9	1.9
LSD						
lifetime	1.8	1.9	2.8	2.5	4.6	[3.5]
annual	1.1	1.2	1.6	1.5	2.2	1.8
30-day	0.5	0.5	0.6	0.6	0.7	0.7
Cocaine						
lifetime	3.4	3.7	5.4	5.2	8.1	8.0
annual	2.0	2.2	3.7	3.5	5.3	5.1
30-day	0.9	1.0	1.7	1.5	2.3	2.3
Crack Cocaine						
lifetime	2.4	2.4	2.6	2.5	3.9	3.5
annual	1.3	1.4	1.7	1.7	2.3	1.9
30-day	0.6	0.6	0.8	0.7	1.0	1.0
Heroin						
lifetime	1.6	1.5	1.5	1.5	1.5	1.5
annual	1.0	0.8	0.9	0.9	0.9	0.8
30-day	0.5	0.5	0.5	0.5	0.5	0.5
Tranquilizers						
lifetime	4.0	4.1	7.3	7.1	10.6	9.9
annual	2.5	2.8	5.1	4.8	7.3	6.8
30-day	1.2	1.3	2.3	2.3	3.1	2.9
Alcohol						
lifetime	43.9	[41.0]	64.2	63.2	76.8	75.1
annual	36.7	[33.9]	58.2	56.7	70.6	[68.6]
30-day	18.6	17.1	35.2	[33.2]	48.0	47.0
daily	0.6	0.5	1.3	1.3	2.8	3.1
Cigarettes (any use)						
lifetime	27.9	[25.9]	40.7	38.9	52.8	[50.0]
30 day	9.2	9.3	16.0	14.9	25.0	23.2
daily	4.4	4.0	8.3	7.5	15.6	[13.6]
1/2 pack +/day	1.7	1.7	3.3	3.1	8.0	[6.9]
Smokeless Tobacco						
lifetime	11.0	10.1	13.8	14.5	16.7	17.5
30-day	4.1	3.3	4.9	5.6	6.7	7.6
daily	1.0	0.7	1.6	1.9	2.8	2.5

TABLE 14.3 (*continued*)

	8TH GRADERS		10TH GRADERS		12TH GRADERS	
	2004	**2005**	**2004**	**2005**	**2004**	**2005**
Steroids						
lifetime	1.9	**1.7**	2.4	2.0	3.4	2.6
annual	1.1	**1.1**	1.5	**1.3**	2.5	**[1.5]**
30-day	0.5	**0.5**	0.8	**0.6**	1.6	**[0.9]**
Mdma						
lifetime	2.8	**2.8**	4.3	**4.0**	7.5	**[5.4]**
annual	1.7	**1.7**	2.4	**2.6**	4.0	**3.0**
30-day	0.8	**0.6**	0.8	**1.0**	1.2	**1.0**
Methamphetamine						
lifetime	2.5	**3.1**	5.3	**[4.1]**	6.2	**[4.5]**
annual	1.5	**1.8**	3.0	2.9	3.4	**[2.5]**
30-day	0.6	**0.7**	1.3	**1.1**	1.4	**[0.9]**
Vicodin						
annual	2.5	**2.6**	6.2	**5.9**	9.3	**9.5**
OxyContin						
annual	1.7	**1.8**	3.5	3.2	5.0	**5.5**

Source: Adapted from March 2006 National Survey on Drug Use and Health: National Findings. U.S. Department of Health and Human Services.

parents' attitudes about drug use, family management styles, and parent-child communication patterns—have an impact on children's drug use (Young, Kersten, & Werch, 1996). Additional cross-pressures—such as the perception of friends' approval or disapproval of drug use, peer pressure to use drugs, and the assessment of individual risk—also play a role (Robin & Johnson, 1996).

Implications for School Personnel   School personnel must be alert to the signs of substance abuse, whether the substance is alcohol, marijuana, inhalants, or some other drug of choice. The following characteristics, though they do not confirm abuse in and of themselves, can be associated with substance abuse:

- Inability to concentrate
- Chronic absenteeism
- Poor grades or neglect of homework
- Uncooperative and quarrelsome behavior
- Sudden behavior changes
- Shy and withdrawn behavior
- Compulsive behaviors
- Chronic health problems
- Low self-esteem
- Anger, anxiety, and depression
- Poor coping skills
- Unreasonable fears
- Difficulty adjusting to changes

Once a student is identified as having a substance abuse problem, a supportive classroom environment must be provided (Lisnov, Harding, Safer, & Kavenagh, 1998). This includes a structured program to build self-esteem and create opportunities for students to be successful. Referral to professionals who are trained to work with individuals who abuse substances is also recommended. Research has shown that substance-abusing adolescents do not respond positively to lecturing. Rather, successes appear to be related to the development of self-esteem and interventions that are supportive. School personnel involved with students who are substance abusers should consider establishing connections with Alcoholics Anonymous and Narcotics Anonymous to help provide support (Vaughn & Long, 1999).

Students Who Become Pregnant

Teenage pregnancy in the United States remains at a high rate and is the highest among Western industrialized nations. Approximately 34% of women become pregnant before age 20 with 80% of the pregnancies unintended (Family First Aid, n.d.). The number of births to females ages 15 to 17 was 22.2 per 1,000 in 2007 (FCFS, 2009). Many of these pregnancies were to unmarried women—the statistic overall for unmarried women is 40%. The percentage is much higher for teenage births (FCFS, 2009) (see Figure 14.7).

Breault and Trail (2005) reviewed the research on teenage pregnancy and state that the following characteristics are associated with a greater likelihood that a young woman may get pregnant: external locus of control, age at onset of sexual experience, socioeconomic status, level of education, mother's level of education, and ethnicity, race, locale, and family history of the teenage mother.

Although there are many unfortunate outcomes from teenage pregnancy, including an increased risk that the resulting child will have problems, one of the most prevalent is that the teenage mother will drop out of school (Trad, 1999). In an era of extensive sex education and fear of HIV/AIDS and sexually transmitted diseases (STDs), it appears that many adolescents continue to engage in unprotected sexual activity (Weinbender & Rossignol, 1996).

School personnel should get involved in teenage pregnancy issues before pregnancy occurs. Sex education, information about HIV, and the consequences of unprotected sex should be a curricular focus. Unfortunately, sex education remains controversial, and many schools refuse to get involved in such emotion-laden issues.

FIGURE 14.7

Percentage of all births to unmarried women by age of mother, 1980 and 2007.

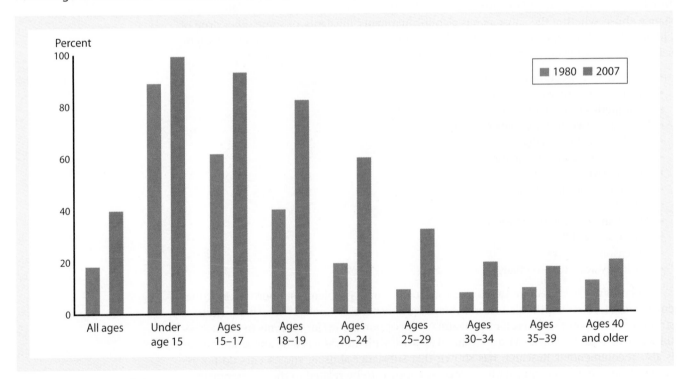

Note: Data for 2007 are preliminary.

Source: From Forum on Child and Family Statistics, 2009 from the National Center for Health Statistics, National Vital Statistics System.

Implications for School Personnel   In addition to having a pregnancy prevention program, school personnel can do the following to intervene in teenage pregnancy situations:

- Provide counseling and parent skills training for girls who become pregnant.
- Develop programs that encourage girls who are pregnant to remain in school—these programs need to include the availability of a school-based child-care program.
- Do not discriminate against students who become pregnant, have children, or are married.
- Work with families of girls who are pregnant to ensure that family support is present.
- Provide counseling support and parent skills training for boys who are fathers.

Students Who Are Gay, Lesbian, Bisexual, or Transgendered

One of the most vulnerable and overlooked groups who might be at risk comprises those students whose sexual identity differs from those around them. This group includes students who are **lesbian, gay, bisexual**, or **transgendered (LGBT)**. Johnson (n.d.) estimated that there are approximately 8.8 million persons who are LGBT in United States; the percentage estimate of 5% of the population is most often cited.

Students who are LGBT often have experienced some uncomfortable situations at school. A study conducted by the Gay, Lesbian, and Straight Education Network (GLSEN) (2005) found that they had experienced the following:

- 75.4% had heard derogatory remarks directed toward them frequently at school.
- 37.8% were physically harassed.
- 17.6% were physically assaulted (beaten, punched, kicked).
- LGBT students skipped school five times more often than the general population of students.

■ Students whose sexuality differs from those around them often remain unidentified as at risk.

The home environment for this population may also be an unsafe environment. This is especially true in cases where parents have a difficult time accepting a child who "comes out" or tells family members about this difference. Some LGBT youth may experience physical abuse at home.

Presenting Issues   Youth who are LGBT come to school feeling that few school staff understand their situation. Most school personnel do lack understanding of their needs and the daily dynamics of their lives at school. Most of the time, this lack of understanding is unintentional; sometimes it is not. This group of students in general is prone to being absent more frequently than their classmates and to dropping out of school more often as a result of their discomfort and lack of safety at school. Positive outcomes are achieved when schools have a staff that is supportive and understanding (GLSEN, 2005).

On a personal level, LGBT youth are at greater risk for depression and attempting suicide. They often feel alienated and isolated. Substance abuse is greater with this group. Furthermore, these students find themselves homeless more often than their straight peers, as they may be thrown out of their homes by parents. It should be noted that some LGBT students report very positive and productive school experiences.

Implications for School Personnel   A number of actions can be taken to improve the climate of acceptance for LGBT youth in schools:

- Include sexual orientation in all antiharassment and antidiscrimination policies.
- Educate all school-based personnel regarding LGBT issues.
- Commit resources to this issue.
- Have diversity days that include LGBT youth.
- Establish a clear antislur policy.
- Develop and disseminate positive images and resources (American Civil Liberties Union Freedom Network, n.d.).

Teachers play a key role. It would be helpful if teachers would:

- Recognize their own attitudes about this topic.
- Refer LGBT youth who are experiencing personal problems to personnel who are more comfortable with this issue than they are.
- Recognize their obligations to act on the behalf of LGBT youth when their rights are violated or policies are disregarded (e.g., harassment).
- Create and maintain a safe classroom environment.
- Let students know if they are a "safe" person with whom they can consult if they need to do so.
- Create and maintain a class environment where diversity is respected and different points of view are welcomed.
- Use language in the classroom that is sexual-orientation neutral.

Students Who Are Delinquents

Students who get into trouble with legal authorities are frequently labeled as *juvenile delinquents*. Morrison (1997) defines delinquency as "behavior that violates the rules and regulations of the society" (p. 189). The problem of delinquency is of significant magnitude. For example, in 2007, there were an estimated 2.2 million arrests of persons under the age of 18. Juveniles were the perpetrators of 26% of property crimes and 12% of violent crime arrests that year (Puzzancherra, 2009).

Juvenile delinquency often results in school failure; students who are involved in illegal activities often do not focus on school activities. Juvenile delinquency must be considered in conjunction with other factors related to students who are at risk, although the relationship of these factors may be difficult to discern. Juvenile delinquency is highly correlated with substance abuse and occurs in higher rates among poor children than among children who are raised in adequate-income environments. It is also more prevalent in single-parent homes (Morgan, 1994a).

Juvenile delinquency is frequently related to gang activity. Gangs currently represent a major problem for adolescents, especially in large, urban areas. In 1997, there were approximately 30,500 gangs in the United States with 816,000 gang members (National Youth Gang Center, 1999). Delinquent behaviors often disrupt school success. School personnel need to work with legal and social service agencies to reduce delinquency and academic failure. In addition, the educational needs of children with disabilities who are in the juvenile justice system must be met the same as for other children with disabilities (Robinson & Rapport, 1999).

Media reports in 2008 indicated that American incarceration rates are the highest in the world, with more than 1 in 100 citizens in jail. Certainly a key concern for students is to prevent behavioral occurrences that result in incarceration and, with it, significantly diminished positive adult outcomes.

Truancy Although not necessarily related to delinquency, one manifestation of school problems that is of consequence is missing school or truancy. The problem can be significant in certain schools, as reflected in a recent study by Henry (2007). She reported that 11% of students in eighth grade and over 60% of students in tenth grade reported recent truancy. The correlates of truancy identified included level of parental education, substantial unsupervised time outside of school, poor grades, lower educational aspirations, and substance abuse.

The problem of truancy illustrates the interrelationship of possible risk factors. While this chapter has endeavored to highlight specific factors, there is a danger that it consequently presents challenges in isolation. Therefore, it is particularly noteworthy that Henry (2007) found that "one of the most robust correlates of recent truancy is drug use. The idea that school-related problems (such as truancy) and substance use coexist has been incorporated into most of the theories that explain substance use and other problem behaviors . . .

we would expect that students who show a lack of commitment to school (as demonstrated by truancy, poor achievement, and low aspirations) will be more likely to demonstrate other problem behaviors, including drug use" (pp. 33–34).

EFFECTIVE INCLUSIVE PRACTICES FOR STUDENTS AT RISK

Challenges for General Education Teachers

The population of children and youth at risk is incredibly diverse. Many different professionals need to get involved in developing and implementing programs for this group of students. Nevertheless, general classroom teachers will continue to play a major role in the lives of students who are at risk. Because teachers and students spend a considerable amount of time together during the week, the importance of the teacher-student relationship is critical.

Effective programs are those that see through the myths that have evolved in relation to students who are at risk and have become barriers to successful efforts. Barr and Parrett (2001) identified myths that must be overcome.

1. **At-risk youth need slow learning.** *Fact:* They need to be academically challenged like all students.
2. **At-risk youth should be retained during the early grades until they are ready to move forward.** *Fact:* Research has shown that this can have disastrous effects.
3. **At-risk youth can be educated with the same expenditures as other students.** *Fact:* Additional programming that might be needed will require additional funds.
4. **Classroom teachers can adequately address the needs of at-risk youth.** *Fact:* Classroom teachers can contribute, but addressing the needs of students who are at risk requires a team effort.
5. **Some students can't learn.** *Fact:* Reaffirmation of this overriding education theme is often needed.
6. **Students who are having learning difficulties need special education.** *Fact:* A tendency to refer to special education must be balanced with the idea of addressing the needs of students at risk within the general education classroom with necessary assistance and supports.

Elders's (2002) thoughts about the key elements that should guide school-based efforts with at-risk students serve as an excellent touching-off point for educational efforts:

> They come to us like a sponge and we must ensure that they leave with four things. We want them to leave with that voice in the ear that can hear all of those less fortunate so that they can have compassion. We want them to leave with a vision in their eye that extends much farther than the eye can see. We want them to have a scroll in their hand, which is a good education, and a song in their heart to carry them through when things get tough, as we know they will. (p. 1)

Educational Strategies

Educational responses to meeting the needs of children at risk should be multifaceted. The following discussion addresses systemic, programmatic, and individual school-based considerations.

Systemic Considerations   Rothstein (2009, p. 5) noted that: "many of the curricular and school organizational reforms being pursued today have merit and should be intensified. Repairing and upgrading the scandalously decrepit school facilities that serve some lower-class children, raising salaries to permit the recruitment of more qualified teachers for lower-class children, reducing class sizes for lower-class children (particularly in the early

> ## TABLE 14.4
>
> ### Selected Protective Factors
>
> - Access to quality care at the prenatal, perinatal, and postnatal periods
> - Within the family, secure child-caregiver attachments, warm but demanding parenting style, parental level of education, parental employment, and high expectations for children
> - Within the school, positive and supportive teachers; a focus on building academic, social, emotional competencies; self-determination and internal locus of control; structured and programs; responsive learning environments sensitive to linguistic and cultural backgrounds; effective communication between school and home; and consistent transition planning
> - Within the community, access to pro-social organizations, opportunities for employment during high school, access to appropriate mentors and adult role models

grades), insisting on higher academic standards, holding schools accountable for fairly measured performance, creating a well-focused and disciplined school climate, doing more to encourage lower-class children to intensify their own ambitions—all of these policies, and others, can play a role in narrowing the achievement gap."

A key consideration is protective factors. Protective factors may "reduce risk and foster resilience . . . for children and families from circumstances that place them at risk (National Joint Committee on Learning Disabilities, 2006, p. 65). Selected examples of protective factors are presented in Table 14.4 (adapted from Murray, 2003 and NJCLD, 2006).

A major focus must be on effective early education programs. The benefits to children and families—and to society in general—are clear. For example, prekindergarten targeted programs for children at risk in Virginia have been estimated to have the potential to return to the state over $2.4 billion in benefits (Commonwealth Institute, February 2009).

Programmatic Adaptations There are four primary approaches to dealing with students who are at risk for failure in schools: prevention programs, compensatory education, intervention programs, and transition programs. Figure 14.8 depicts these four orientations.

FIGURE 14.8

Four approaches to education for students at risk.

Source: From Teaching in America (p. 193), by G. S. Morrison, 1997. Boston: Allyn & Bacon. Used by permission.

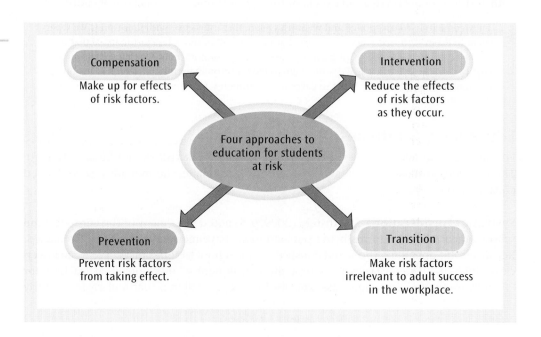

Compensation — Make up for effects of risk factors.

Intervention — Reduce the effects of risk factors as they occur.

Four approaches to education for students at risk

Prevention — Prevent risk factors from taking effect.

Transition — Make risk factors irrelevant to adult success in the workplace.

Prevention programs focus on developing appropriate skills and behaviors that lead to success and, if used, are incompatible with other undesirable behaviors. Prevention programs also attempt to keep certain negative factors from having an impact on students. Drug prevention programs, antismoking educational efforts, and sex education programs are examples of efforts designed to establish responsible behaviors and keep students from developing problem behaviors.

Compensatory education programs "are designed to compensate or make up for existing or past risk factors and their effects in students' lives" (Morrison, 1997, p. 192). Head Start and Chapter I reading programs are examples of efforts to reduce the impact of poverty on children (Morrison, 1997).

Intervention programs focus on eliminating risk factors. They include, for example, teaching teenagers how to be good parents and early intervention programs that target at-risk preschool children (Sexton et al., 1996).

Finally, **transition programs** are designed to help students see the relationship between what they learn in school and how it will be used in the real world. School-to-career programs, which help students move from school to work, are effective transition programs (Morrison, 1997).

After-school programs, along with involvement with various school-sponsored, extracurricular activities, provide schools with an opportunity to implement many of these strategies that are effective with students at risk. Many students who are at risk face extreme challenges in the afternoon hours following school. "School-age children and teens who are unsupervised during the hours after school are far more likely to use alcohol, drugs, and tobacco, engage in criminal and other high-risk behaviors, receive poor grades, and drop out of school than those children who have the opportunity to benefit from constructive activities supervised by responsible adults" (Safe & Smart, 1998, p. 5). After-school programs often combine prevention, intervention, and compensatory programs.

Individual School-Based Adaptations   At the individual school level, specific emphases must address the needs of students who are at risk. Table 14.5 provides a list of factors that

---

TABLE 14.5

Essential Components of Effective Programs

Positive School Climate	Choice, commitment, and voluntary participation
	Small, safe, supportive learning environment
	Shared vision, cooperative governance, and local autonomy
	Community partnerships and coordination of services
Customized Curriculum and Instructional Program	Caring, demanding, and well-prepared teachers
	Comprehensive and continuing programs
	Challenging and relevant curricula
	High academic standards and continuing assessment of student progress
	Individualized instruction: personal, diverse, accelerated, and flexible
	Successful transitions
Personal, Social, and Emotional Growth	Promoting personal growth and responsibility
	Developing personal resiliency
	Developing emotional maturity through service
	Promoting emotional and social growth

Source: From *Hope Fulfilled for At-Risk and Violent Youth: K–12 Programs That Work* (p. 73), by R. D. Barr and W. H. Parrett, 2001. Boston: Allyn & Bacon. Copyright 2001 by Allyn & Bacon. Reprinted by permission.

have been found to be essential to school programs where students at risk are learning effectively.

The movement to include students with disabilities in general education classrooms also provides an opportunity to meet the needs of students who are at risk as well. In an inclusive classroom, students are educated based on their needs rather than on their clinical labels. As a consequence, students who are at risk may benefit from the educational efforts, such as from cooperative teaching, that were implemented to meet the needs of all students.

Specific considerations that can help to address meeting the needs of all students include an emphasis on evidence-based instructional practices throughout all curricular areas. For example, direct instruction of core academic skills has been consistently supported, particularly for both students with disabilities and those who are at risk for school failure. Other important foci include an emphasis on teaching every child to read, reliance on one-on-one tutoring, extended day programs for students needing additional work, cooperative learning initiatives, and mentoring programs. Another important curricular emphasis should be on preparing teenagers for their roles as parents.

Several factors are associated with schools that provide effective programs for students who are at risk. The U.S. Department of Education has noted that some research-based school reform models have been very successful in improving the achievement scores of students who are at risk for school failure. Successful programs appear to share several characteristics (Tools for Schools, 1998):

- They provide a clear blueprint with specific instructions for the changes that are to be made by the school in order to improve its educational performance.
- They offer a system of guidance and technical assistance for schools and offer instructions on how the model can be scaled up at a large number of sites.
- The changes that the models propose for implementation are comprehensive, involving school organization, social relations (parental involvement, relationships between school staff and student), curriculum and instruction, and educational standards and goals.
- The models are flexible, which allows them to be implemented on variable time scales and with adaptations to meet local circumstances. (p. 2)

We conclude this discussion with mention of one program that has been used effectively in many schools—mentoring. Elementary, middle, and high schools design such programs to provide students with a positive personal relationship with an adult—something that many children and youth lack (Barr & Parrett, 2001). A mentor can be any person of any background who is committed to serving as a support person for a child or youth. Mentoring often serves as a key protective factor for children and youth and therefore helps to promote resilience.

Mentor programs range in scope from national programs such as Big Brothers/Big Sisters to programs developed by and for specific schools, such as a program wherein adults employed in the community have lunch with students (Friedman & Scaduto, 1995). Programs large and small have proved effective for many children. It is important to ensure that a positive match is made between the mentor and the child. Other features of successful mentor programs are listed in the nearby Differentiated Instruction—Elementary boxed reading.

Ethnic Disproportionality　While this chapter has focused on at-risk factors that are experienced across ethnic groups, it is important to note that ethnicity may correlate with specific factors as presented herein. As a consequence, schools continue to need to respond to issues of ethnic disproportionality. Certainly, a key consideration is that there remains an ethnic gap in terms of school completion—substantially more White students complete high school than do African American and Hispanic students (Morocco, Aguilar, Clay, Brigham, & Zigmond, 2006). With regard to identification as disabled, Strand and Aleva (2009) commented that "both over- and under-representation are problematic if they are associated

Differentiating Elementary Instruction

Components of Effective Mentoring Programs for Students At Risk

- **Program compatibility:** The program should be compatible with the policies and goals of the organization. . . . Program organizers should work closely with school personnel to ensure that the mentoring they provide complements the student's education.
- **Administrative commitment:** The program must be supported from the top as well as on a grass-roots level. In a school-based program, all school and district administrators, teachers, and staff must provide input and assistance. For a sponsoring business, the chief executive officer must view the program as important and worthy of the time and attention of employees.
- **Proactive:** Ideally the programs should be proactive; that is, not a quick-fix reaction to a crisis. Successful mentoring programs for youth work because they are well thought out, they have specific goals and objectives, and they exist within a larger realm of programs and policies that function together.
- **Participant oriented:** The program should be based on the goals and needs of the participants. These goals will determine the program's focus, recruitment, and training. . . .

- **Orientation:** An orientation should be provided for prospective participants. It will help determine interest and enthusiasm, as well as give prospective mentors and students an idea of what to expect. In addition, it will provide them with opportunties to help design the program.
- **Selection and matching:** Mentors and their proteges should be carefully selected and matched. Questionnaires are helpful in determining needs, areas of interest, and strengths.
- **Training:** Training must be provided for all participants, including support people, throughout the program. Assuming that because a person is knowledgeable, caring, and enthusiastic he or she will make a good mentor is a mistake. Training must be geared to the specific problems experienced by at-risk youth as well as different styles of communication.
- **Monitoring progress:** The program should be periodically monitored for progress and results to resolve emerging conflicts and problems.

Source: Adapted from *Mentoring Programs for At-Risk Youth* (pp. 5–6) by National Dropout Prevention Center, 1990, Clemson, SC: Clemson University.

with reduced access to the most appropriate forms of education, whether by inappropriate placement in special education programs for students who do not need such support and may then miss out on a mainstream curriculum or by a lack of support for students would benefit from special education provision. In either case, inappropriate matches may reduce student's educational opportunities" (p. 175).

To respond to disproportionality, Skiba and colleagues (2008) recommended that special attention be given to teacher preparation practices, improvements in behavior management strategies, increased emphasis on early intervention and prevention, increased usage of response-to-intervention/instruction strategies, reduced bias in assessment, increased community and family involvement, and reform of public policy in order to promote cultural responsive public school systems.

Certainly a particular concern in American schools is African American male students and their relative level of success. High-school graduation rates for these students are at a lower percentage compared to rates for students in general; this problem is particularly pronounced in urban school districts. In addition, a disproportionate number of minority male students are expelled from school each year (Livingston & Nahimana, 2006). Livingston and Nahimana (2006) posited that an understanding of the cultural context impacting on African American male students must include attention to issues emanating from poverty, education, fatherlessness, violence, racism, incarceration, and employment.

Schools must ensure that they do not discriminate against students who are at risk because of their race or socioeconomic status. The nearby Rights & Responsibilities feature focuses on this issue.

RIGHTS & RESPONSIBILITIES

NONDISCRIMINATORY ASSESSMENT

Under IDEA, schools are required to use nondiscriminatory practices when evaluating students because many children at risk experience poverty, come from single-parent homes, or are raised in homes where English is not the primary language. The case law supporting this requirement came out of the *Larry P. v. Riles* case first filed in 1972. The court in this case held that schools no longer may use standardized IQ tests for the purpose of identifying and placing African American children into segregated special education classes for students classified as "mild intellectual disabilities". . . .

The district court found that the Stanford-Binet, Wechsler, and Leiter IQ tests discriminate against African Americans on several grounds:

1. They measure achievement, not ability.
2. They rest on the "plausible but unproven assumption that intelligence is distributed in the population in accordance with a normal statistical curve" and thus are "artificial tools to rank individuals according to certain skills, not to diagnose a medical condition (the presence of retardation)."
3. They "necessarily" lead to placement of more African Americans than Whites into classes for students with mild or moderate mental retardation.

On appeal, the Ninth Circuit Court of Appeals affirmed the lower court decision and rejected the state's argument that tests are good predictors of academic performance, even if they have a discriminatory impact; found that the state did not use any means of diagnosing disability other than IQ tests; and agreed that inappropriate placement of children can result in a profound negative impact on their education (Turnbull & Turnbull, 2000, pp. 153–154).

SUMMARY

Basic Concepts about Students Who Are At Risk

- Students who are at risk may not be eligible for special education programs.
- Students who are at risk include those who are in danger of developing significant learning and behavior problems.

Select At-Risk Groups

- Poverty is a leading cause of academic failure.
- Poverty among children is increasing in the United States.
- Poverty is associated with homelessness, poor health care, hunger, and single-parent households.
- Hunger is a major problem in the United States.
- A large percentage of all homeless people are children.
- Students in single-parent homes face major problems in school.
- About 25% of all children live in single-parent homes.
- Divorce is the leading reason for which children live in single-parent homes.
- Schools must take into consideration the rights of the noncustodial parent.
- The death of a parent, sibling, or friend can have a major impact on a child and school success.
- Child abuse is a major problem in the United States and causes children to experience major emotional trauma.
- The most common type of child maltreatment is neglect.
- School personnel are required by law to report suspected child abuse.

- Drug use among students is on the increase after several years of decline.

- Teenage pregnancy continues to be a problem, despite the fear of HIV/AIDS and the presence of sex education programs.

- Attention to students who are lesbian, gay, bisexual, or transgendered is needed in schools, as this population still encounters a host of problems.

Effective Inclusive Strategies for Students At Risk

- Numerous programs and interventions have been proven to be effective in working with students who are at risk.

- Disproportionality remains a concern in school programs and is particularly significant with regard to students at risk as well as students with disabilities.

- Initiatives to be considered for students at risk can include major systemic efforts, programmatic initiatives, and individual school-based programs.

PEARSON
myeducationlab

The MyEducationLab for this course can help you solidify your comprehension of Chapter 14 concepts.

- Gauge and further develop your understanding of chapter concepts by taking the quizzes and examining the enrichment materials on the Chapter 14 Study Plan.

  - Connect with challenge-based interactive modules, case study units, and podcasts that provide research-validated information about working with students in inclusive settings by visiting the IRIS Center Resources

  - Explore Assignments and Activities, assignable exercises showing concepts in action through video, cases, and student and teacher artifacts

  - Practice and strengthen skills essential to quality teaching through the Building Teaching Skills and Dispositions lessons

15

Teaching Students with Special Needs in Elementary Schools

After reading this chapter, you should be able to:

1. Describe general curricular considerations for teaching students with special needs in elementary classrooms.

2. Identify curricular content emphases for academic, social skills, and transitional instruction.

3. Identify appropriate instructional strategies for inclusive classrooms.

JUSTIN is currently in Ms. Bennett's fifth-grade classroom. Justin has been in special education since being diagnosed as having learning disabilities in the second grade. While Justin's intellectual quotient is in the mid-90s, or average, his most recent academic tests reveal that he is only reading at the 2.3 grade level and spells at the 1.8 grade level. Obviously, Justin's need to improve his reading and spelling skills is critical if he is to achieve any degree of success in the fifth grade and beyond. In previous years, Justin has been included in his regular classroom and received only one hour of special education in the resource room daily, focusing primarily on reading skills. While this has been beneficial to Justin, his overall reading and spelling performance have not improved significantly since his diagnosis in the second grade.

This year Justin again is included in a regular classroom and receives one hour of resource room daily. Most of Justin's age peers are reading and spelling at or near grade level. This makes it difficult for Justin to achieve academic success and is also affecting his social skills. Ms. Bennett knows that this is a critical year for Justin to improve his reading and spelling levels if he has a chance to be successful in middle and high school. Justin's intellectual ability is sufficient for him to be academically suc-cessful; he simply needs to improve his reading and writing skills to a level that will allow him to be successful in general education classrooms. Since the beginning of the year, two months ago, Ms. Bennett has worked closely with the resource teacher to provide interventions in her classroom that support the interventions he is receiving in the resource room. She has also orchestrated social opportunities for Justin that have helped him become more socially accepted by his peers. In the two months since school began, Ms. Bennett has already seen some progress in his social skills.

QUESTIONS TO CONSIDER

1. What can Ms. Bennett do to continue to improve Justin's social skills and his social status in the classroom?

2. What strategies might be useful for Ms. Bennett to use to assist Justin's reading and spelling skills?

3. How can Ms. Bennett and the special education teacher collaborate to work more effectively with Justin?

4. What are realistic goals for Justin in reading and writing during the fifth grade?

Elementary school also offers an important beginning point for students with disabilities to profit from positive interactions with their peers who are not disabled. Preparation for successful life beyond the school setting requires the ability to learn, live, and work with a diversity of individuals. Thus, inclusion offers benefits both to students who are disabled and to their nondisabled peers. There is clearly no better time for inclusion to commence than in early childhood and throughout the primary and elementary grades.

The trend toward inclusion is reflected in Table 15.1. This analysis from Hoover and Patton (2005) reflects the changes in professional perspectives that have occurred over the past several decades. Furthermore, it highlights the core rationales for inclusive classrooms and the focus of curriculum.

Consistent with the trend reflected in Table 15.1, many young students with disabilities will receive a significant portion, or all, of their instruction in the general education

Visit the MyEducationLab for this course to enhance your understanding of chapter concepts with a personalized Study Plan. You'll also have the opportunity to hone your teaching skills through video-based Assignments and Activities, IRIS Center Resources, and Building Teaching Skills and Disposition lessons.

TABLE 15.1

Trends in Educational Placements of Special Education Students in Elementary and Secondary Schools

PREDOMINANT THEME	PRIMARY PLACEMENT(S)	PREVAILING THOUGHT TOWARD EDUCATION	PREDOMINANT VIEW TOWARD CURRICULUM
Separate special education is needed.	Self-contained classroom	Students who cannot benefit from general education would be best served in special classrooms.	Specialized curriculum and techniques are needed to effectively educate individuals with disabilities.
Effectiveness of separate special classrooms is questioned.	Self-contained classroom	Educators are questioning the practice and effects of educating students with disabilities in separate special classes.	The need for special curriculum and techniques for many students with disabilities is being questioned.
Education for many students with special needs does not occur in separate classrooms.	Resource rooms with some education in general education classrooms	Many learners may benefit from education in general education classrooms, requiring only some education in a special classroom.	Selected aspects of the general education curriculum are appropriate for learners with special needs.
Students with special needs may be educated appropriately in general education classrooms.	General education classrooms with some education in resource rooms	The least restrictive environment for many students termed "disabled" is education in the general education classroom.	Many students may benefit from the general education curriculum if proper adaptations and modifications are provided.
Students with disabilities should achieve full inclusion into general education.	Full integration into general education classrooms	The education of all students with disabilities is best achieved in the general education setting.	Continued expansion of integrated programs and curricula can be implemented in inclusive education settings.
Many diverse needs are to be met in inclusive settings.	Reaffirmation of full inclusion and full integration for students with special needs	The inclusive education setting is responsible for meeting an ever-increasing range of diverse needs.	Curriculum and instruction must be differentiated in collaborative ways to meet all diverse needs in the classroom.

Source: Adapted from *Curriculum Adaptations for Students with Learning and Behavior Problems: Principles and Practices for Differentiating Instruction* (p. 29), by J. J. Hoover and J. R. Patton, 2005. Austin, TX: Pro-Ed.

classroom. According to the National Center for Education Statistics (2009), 56.8% of all students with disabilities were served in general education for at least 79% of the school day, while an additional 22.4 percent were in regular classes for 40 to 79% of the day. Only 15.4% were served in more restrictive settings within the regular school or in separate school and/or residential settings (3.0%). These data reflect a clear trend across recent years. In 1989, only 31.7% of students with disabilities were served in regular classes for at least 79% of the time; 37.5% for 40 to 79% of the day, and 24.9% in more restricted settings. Thus, beginning at the elementary level, teachers must give careful attention to these students' educational needs.

The two critical questions in education are the question of curriculum (what?) and instruction (how?). Effective school programs begin with considerations of what information students need to learn and how best can they learn that information. The primary purpose of this chapter is to address these two concerns. The initial section outlines core curriculum considerations. The discussion that follows emphasizes instructional strategies that provide the means for achieving learning goals.

GENERAL CURRICULAR CONSIDERATIONS

Four general considerations provide a foundation for curriculum development. These include emphases on the general education (standards-based) curriculum, the need for a multitiered model of curriculum, universal design for learning, and the importance of comprehensive curriculum.

The curriculum for virtually all elementary students with special needs will be based on the **standards of learning**, as required in general by NCLB and as dictated by the particular state. The adoption of such standards, as consistent with the No Child Left Behind Act, has transformed the focus of educational programs for children with special needs. Table 15.2 provides an outline of key elements of standards-based education.

The core of the standards-based reform movement in recent years has been the focus on **content and performance standards**. As Pemberton, Rademacher, Tyler-Wood, and Cereijo (2006) note, "content standards define the knowledge and skills of students or what students should know and be able to accomplish as a result of their educational experiences. Performance standards define how well students should demonstrate the knowledge and skills" (pp. 283–284).

Providing further clarification, Wehmeyer (in press) referenced the work of the Committee on Goals 2000 and the Inclusion of Students with Disabilities (1997) in noting several ways in which standards could be made defensible for use with students with disabilities. Wehmeyer noted that content standards must reflect those skills that are critical to the success of students after leaving school; that these standards should be appropriate based on the age of the students; and that the standards-based curriculum should be taught to students with special needs while not effectively impacting on their opportunity to be taught, and acquire, functional behaviors and skills that are critical for community success.

TABLE 15.2

Elements of Standards-Based Education and Curriculum

ELEMENT	DESCRIPTION
Assessment closely linked to the curriculum	A significant alignment exists between the curriculum being taught and the skills and knowledge being assessed.
Comparison to standards, not other students	Standards-based curriculum emphasizes the development of standards, and the assessment reflects the level of proficiency for each student. Thus, the assessment compares students' proficiency levels with established standards and not with other students.
Alternative assessments used	Assessment of standards-based curriculum may include a variety of assignment strategies, such as constructed response, writing essays, authentic and real-life problem solving, or rubrics.
Achieving proficiency	NCLB requires that states and school systems annually monitor progress toward helping all students achieve proficiency of the standards, rather than simply reporting grouped, grade-level scores.
Application of results	Standards-based assessment results can be used to determine graduation requirements, hold educators accountable, and adapt curriculum. Results are no longer simply reported; rather, they are used for program improvement and documentation of progress toward full proficiency.
Inclusion of all students	Standards-based curriculum is designed to challenge all students to increase their expectations and proficiency levels. This includes English language learners and students with disabilities.

Source: From *Curriculum Adaptations for Students with Learning and Behavior Problems: Principles and Practices for Differentiating Instruction* (p. 21), by J. J. Hover and J. R. Patton, 2006. Austin, TX: Pro-Ed.

Response to Intervention

The emphases in standards-based curriculum and the need for students with special needs to have access to the general curriculum have provided the impetus for multitiered models for delivering instruction. One model that uses such a multitiered approach is Response to Intervention (RTI). The model provides interventions matched to students' needs. The greater the need of the student, the more intense the intervention (Shapiro & Clemens, 2009). Most RTI models include three levels of interventions, or tiers.

Tier I—High-quality core instruction: This tier refers to empirically validated and systematic instruction embedded in a challenging curriculum in the general education classroom. Universal design for learning (UDL) and differentiated instruction, for example, provide guidelines for vehicles to successfully implement Tier I interventions. For most elementary students, this is the core curriculum they will follow.

Tier II—High-quality, targeted supplemental instruction: The focus of Tier II is to provide supplemental supports in addition to the core program. Such instruction can be provided in the general education classroom or through a variety of pullout programs such as resource rooms. Specific examples of such programs are those that are identified as general education programs such as a collaborative teacher like Ms. Bennett, the special education teacher mentioned in the opening vignette. Students may also receive instruction in a small group of students with similar skill deficits; the intervention may be provided for longer sessions and occur more frequently. For many elementary students with special needs, this tier will provide the instructional supports they require. The discussion later in the chapter on adaptations provides numerous such examples. While this tier provides instructional supports beyond what most students in elementary grades need, it could still be considered a form of pre-referral interventions aimed at meeting the student's needs without more intensive interventions. The use of teacher assistance teams would be another Tier II strategy with the same goal.

Tier III—High-quality intensive intervention: Tier III is more consistent with the traditional concept of special education as modified to reflect scientifically validated instructional programs to teach relevant curricular content. Such programs typically are offered to students with more significant disabilities and may more often be delivered in specialized settings. Examples include certain remedial programs. However, many of these curricular goals can be achieved in general education as well.

Universal Design for Learning

A major emphasis at each of the three tiers is the importance of **universal design** for learning, a concept with its roots in architectural design. It is important to note here how this design relates to standards for learning.

A number of practices are consistent with this concept and are relatively straightforward and intuitive (Acrey, Johnstone, & Milligan, 2005). As a consequence, teachers are encouraged to design the learning environment by using basic original principles for universal design and architecture as a model (e.g., considering ways in which to make lessons more accessible to all in the same way that buildings can be made so).

To meet the needs of all students, including those with special needs, a curriculum that is based on universal design principles should be open-ended rather than close-ended. As Wehmeyer (in press) notes: "Close-ended standards are specific and require narrowly defined outcomes or performance indicators. Open-ended standards do not restrict the ways in which students exhibit knowledge with skills and focus more on the expectations that students will interact with the content, ask questions, manipulate materials, make observations, and then communicate their knowledge in a variety of ways." The differentiated instruction format lends itself to a number of positive outcomes. Teachers can better identify alternatives for presenting information, differentiating *what* students will learn. They can also provide multiple methods for acquiring and processing the information, differentiating *how* students will learn. Finally, differentiated instruction calls for a variety of methods (*output*) for students to demonstrate that learning has occurred (Tomlinson, 2005). The nearby Differenti-

Differentiating Elementary Instruction

When Mrs. Riley first began teaching third grade, she assumed that all students needed exposure to the same information; she created learning centers and sent every child to every center with instructions to complete every activity. After being introduced to differentiated instruction, she now designs a variety of centers based on her students' learning profiles, determined through her formal and informal assessment of their readiness. Even when students are assigned to a specific learning center, they can make choices about their work in ways that address their learning interests and learning preferences.

Today, for example, all students will be assigned to one of two reading/writing **learning centers.** Both centers focus on themes in biographies the students have read. At each center, students can choose to work alone, with a partner, or with a group of three or four peers assigned to their center. At one center, students select a person they've read about and make an annotated time line of the person's early life, selecting events that they think were most important in shaping the person's life. Then they choose to write a paper that explains their choices, draw a storyboard of the events, or act out the events one day during sharing time. Whatever way a student decides to express understanding, the focus must be on identifying themes in the life of the person about whom they read.

At the other, more complex reading/writing center, students select one of the biographies they've read, as well as a fic-tional work they've read about a young person. Then they write about some real-life events they and some of their third-grade friends have experienced. Finally, after looking in all three works for common themes about growing up, they design a method of showing how those themes are used in each setting. Mrs. Riley gives them three suggestions: theme trees, a matrix, and conversations between or among the subject of the biography, the fictional character, and a third grader. Some of the students go early in the day to one of these two reading/writing centers; after that, they work with differentiated math assignments at their desks. Other students experience this combination of activities in reverse order.

Interest centers are also available to students during the week. Offered at the same time as the biography-focused centers, some interest centers allow students to explore the skills of acting, learn how to make storyboards for advertisements and animated films, or use a laser disc to find out more about a famous person they're interested in. Mrs. Riley also offers interest centers on science- and math-related topics. Students select which interest centers to attend. Most interest centers in Mrs. Riley's classroom are available for two weeks or more.

Source: Adapted from *How to Differentiate Instruction in Mixed-Ability Classrooms* (2nd ed.) (pp. 28–29), by C.A. Tomlinson, 2005, Upper Saddle River, NJ: Pearson.

ated Instruction—Elementary boxed reading provides a glimpse into one classroom where the teacher uses learning and interest centers as a natural strategy for differentiation.

Comprehensive Curriculum

For all students, any consideration of curriculum also should include an outcomes orientation. Therefore, our concept of curriculum, even at the elementary level, must embrace consideration for the preparation for life after the completion of K–12 schooling. As a result, even though curriculum design is preordained by state standards in general education programs, it is nevertheless important to consider the concept of comprehensive curriculum. The concept takes into account the reality that students are enrolled in school on a time-limited basis. Educators must consider what will happen to their students in the future and consider the environments that students will need to adapt to in order to function successfully. Thus, curriculum design should be predicated on a focus on these subsequent environments (e.g., middle school, high school, college, community). The degree to which this subsequent-environments attitude permeates general education will significantly affect the ultimate success of students with disabilities taught in such settings (Polloway, Patton, & Serna, 2008).

An elementary-level comprehensive curriculum therefore should reflect responsiveness to the needs of the individual at the current time, the importance of achieving maximum interaction with peers while addressing critical curricular needs, and attention to relevant forthcoming transitional needs (e.g., transition from elementary to middle school) (Polloway et al., 2008).

CURRICULAR EMPHASES FOR ACADEMIC, SOCIAL SKILLS, AND TRANSITIONAL INSTRUCTION

Elementary students in general, and certainly most students with disabilities, primarily need scientifically validated instruction in reading, writing, and mathematics to maximize their academic achievement. These needs can typically be met by a developmental approach to instruction, supplemented as needed by a remedial focus for students who experience difficulty. In addition, students with special needs will also benefit from a curriculum that addresses social skills and transitional needs.

Reading Instruction

Reading problems are the foremost concern for all elementary teachers working in inclusive classrooms. Young students with special needs commonly experience difficulties in both the decoding processes inherent in word recognition and in reading comprehension. The *Report of the National Reading Panel: Teaching Children to Read* (NICHD, 2000) identified five specific areas of difficulty and synthesized the research on the effectiveness of materials and methods for each area. Following is a brief definition and summary of findings provided by Mercer and Pullen (2009) and Bursuck and Damer (2007):

Phonemic Awareness: Refers to the understanding that words and syllables can be broken down into the smallest units of sound, phonemes. Students demonstrate phonemic awareness skills by **segmenting** sounds in words (for example, the word "fish" contains the sounds /f/-/i/-/sh/) and **blending** sounds to say the word (for example, when the teacher says the sounds in "fish" separately, the student blends them together fast and responds with the correct word, "fish"). Research has demonstrated a strong relationship between phonemic awareness and the ability to read and spell.

Phonics: Refers to the alphabetic principle that a systematic relationship exists between written letters (graphemes) and their corresponding sounds (phonemes). Instruction in phonics helps students decode unknown words in print quickly. Research in this area confirms that a systemic and explicit approach to phonics instruction is more effective than nonsystematic (e.g., whole-language approach) and is particularly effective for struggling readers. Instruction provided in kindergarten and first grade is best and significantly improves spelling, word recognition, and comprehension.

Fluency: Refers to a reader's ability to read text accurately, using expression, and at a rate that promotes understanding. Research suggests that oral reading opportunities should be repeated and monitored to increase fluency; instruction in this area is particularly important for struggling readers who tend to spend so much time wrestling with word-by-word reading that comprehension suffers. Research does not support the efficacy of silent, independent reading in increasing fluency or overall reading achievement.

Vocabulary: Refers to developing an understanding of the meaning of words. Research suggests that direct instruction in vocabulary building is needed even though most of our understanding of word meaning is learned indirectly through everyday experience. Increasing a student's vocabulary positively affects a student's reading, writing and speaking. Figure 15.1 contains effective practices for teaching word recognition.

Comprehension: Refers to ultimate goal of reading instruction, decoding text accurately, with fluency, while understanding the meaning of the vocabulary. Specific strategies for improving comprehension are found in Figure 15.2.

Language Arts Programs   In a general sense, educators have responded to the need for quality instruction by selecting one (or a combination) of the three common approaches in elementary-level reading and language arts programs: **basal series**, **whole language**, and **direct instruction** .

Basal series, or graded class-reading texts, are the most typical means of teaching reading and, for that matter, other curricular domains including spelling and math, in the elementary school. Most reading basals are intended to meet developmental needs in reading.

FIGURE 15.1	Teaching Reading with Emphasis on Word Recognition

- Develop balanced programs that emphasize both decoding skills and comprehension skills.
- Determine whether students have sufficient phonological awareness skills to be able to use phonetic analysis as a decoding strategy.
- Develop phonological awareness skills by enhancing students' ability to differentiate, analyze, and blend sounds, and to tie this effort to word study.
- Teach word meanings directly and complement students' ability to recognize words with the ability to understand their meaning.
- Teach phonetic analysis conventions that have high levels of utility (i.e., have applicability to multiple words such as the "silent e" rule and the "two vowels together" format).
- Teach students word structures by providing opportunities for them to take advantage of structural analyses skills to focus on prefixes, suffixes, contractions, and compound words.
- Teach students to use context to enhance word recognition and comprehension. However, use caution in placing significant weight on contextual analysis because of the difficulties presented as students engage in reading with more difficult vocabulary. As this occurs, phonetic cues are likely to be more effective than context cues.
- Teach students to use a strategy for attacking unknown words in print so they can determine if it is important that they be able to say the word accurately (such as may not be the case with a proper noun), use phonetic analysis skills, and structural analysis, for example.
- Ensure that students have ample opportunity to read and encounter words, concepts, and knowledge through print.
- Provide motivational strategies for struggling readers that can relate to extrinsic strategies, such as the use of reinforcement, and intrinsic strategies related to student interest and self-management.
- Ensure that skills instruction is explicit, intensive, and ongoing to result in the acquisition, maintenance, and generalization of skills.

FIGURE 15.2	Teaching Reading Comprehension

- **Comprehension monitoring:** Readers learn how to be conscious of their understanding during reading and learn procedures to deal with problems in understanding as they arise.
- **Cooperative learning:** Readers work together to learn strategies in the context of reading.
- **Graphic and semantic organizers:** Readers learn to present graphically the meanings and relationships of the ideas that underlie the words in the text.
- **Story structure:** Readers learn to ask and answer "who, what, where, when, and why" questions about the plot and map out the timeline, characters, and events in stories.
- **Question answering:** Readers answer questions posed by the teacher and are given feedback on the correctness of their answers.
- **Question generation:** Readers ask "what, when, where, why, what will happen, how, and who" questions.
- **Summarization:** Readers attempt to identify and write the main idea that integrates the other meanings of the text into a coherent whole.
- **Multiple-strategy teaching:** Readers use several of these procedures and interact with the teacher over the text.

Source: Adapted from The National Reading Panel, 2000, pp. 4–6.

However, there is a multiplicity of programs, and it would be impossible to typify the focus of all basal series. Polloway, Miller, and Smith (2003) note that such series have both advantages and disadvantages. They note that on the positive side, basals contain inherent structure and sequence, a controlled vocabulary, a wide variety of teaching activities, and materials that provide preparation for the teacher. Weaknesses, however, include possible inappropriate pacing for an individual child, a common concern for certain skills to the exclusion of others, and the encouragement of group instructional orientation.

Whole-language approaches (i.e., programs that primarily emphasize meaning in the beginning of the reading process) at the primary and elementary levels dramatically increased in popularity in the 1990s. Whole-language programs attempt to break down barriers within the area of language arts between reading, writing, and speaking, as well as barriers between reading and other curricular areas, by stressing an integrated approach to learning. Polloway and colleagues (2008) provide examples of whole-language instruction:

- Orally sharing stories by the teacher
- Sustained silent reading
- Silent reading time segments in which students write responses to what they are reading and share this with other students or with the teacher in individual conferences
- Language experience activities in which children write stories in a group or individually to be used for future reading experiences
- Time set aside for large-group writing instruction followed by students' writing, revising, editing, and sharing their own writing
- Reading and writing activities that involve a content area theme such as science or social studies (pp. 16–17)

Although several aspects of this approach are both beneficial and enjoyed by students, the research reported by the National Reading Panel (2000) is more supportive of the benefits of systemic, direct instruction in each of the five areas identified previously. *Direct instruction* (i.e., the directive teaching of skills) has often been associated with a remedial perspective, although it clearly has played a significant preventive role as well. Often it has been tied to a focus on basic skills, which has typically constituted the core of most elementary special education curricula. In the area of reading, direct instruction programs are most often associated with a strong initial emphasis on decoding skills. Basic skills programs typically are built on the development of phonological awareness and subsequently phonetic analysis instruction. Research on beginning reading emphasizes the critical importance of children developing sound-symbol correspondences as a basis for subsequent reading success. Direct instruction in fluency, vocabulary building, and comprehension is also supported by scientific research (Polloway, Miller, & Smith, 2011).

Writing

Elementary-age children with special needs commonly experience problems with writing, especially with written expression. It is essential that they be given ample opportunities to write and that appropriate attention be given to handwriting and spelling. Unfortunately, too often instruction in writing is not a priority in many elementary classrooms. While there may be several reasons for this lack of attention, the most likely is the emphasis on reading and math, especially in light of the *No Child Left Behind* legislation. Elementary teachers need to become more proactive in teaching writing skills to all students because they are a key means of communication, whether it is electronic or manual (Polloway, Miller, & Smith, 2011). For students with disabilities, an emphasis on facilitating their ability to communicate in written language is very important to their success in school.

Teachers need to implement a formal writing program for their students. Having students write when it is convenient will unlikely provide them with sufficient opportunities to develop their writing skills. When developing instructional programs in writing, teachers should remember that writing (Polloway, Patton, & Serna, 2008):

- Is based on previous linguistic experiences
- Is a process and product

- Is a form of communication
- Must be tied to cognition
- Provides a unique opportunity for personal expression

There are several key stages of writing. These include (1) prewriting stage, (2) writing or drafting stage, and (3) post-writing stage (Polloway et al., 2008). During the prewriting stage, teachers should stimulate students to think about a topic and motivate them to write about it. They must also establish a purpose for writing. A good way to get students to start writing is to discuss topics that are motivating to the students. These could include activities they like to do, experiences they have had, or topics of interest based on students' age and ability levels.

The writing and drafting stage is when students actually put their thoughts and ideas into words. During this stage students learn the role of author: forming ideas, words, and phrases; and the secretarial role: ensuring legibility, spelling, punctuation, and grammar (Polloway et al., 2008). Both roles are important in the process, but a first step is getting students to form their ideas; the secretarial role usually follows the author role when getting students started in the writing process.

In order for students to improve their writing, they must have regular opportunities to do so. Daily journal writing is one means to ensure writing opportunities. Once the opportunity to write is established, emphasis should begin to focus on the mechanics. Opportunity to write, alone, will not lead to improvement. Teachers must balance students' learning skills without interfering with their desire to write (Polloway et al., 2008).

During the writing stage, vocabulary development, sentence development, paragraph development, and composition writing are developed. During the post-writing stage, students must proofread their work and make appropriate revisions and edits to ensure that the writing successfully communicates what is intended (Polloway et al., 2011). Too often, students complete a first draft of a writing assignment and assume it is a final product. Emphasis must be placed on multiple drafts that improve the quality of writing with each draft.

There are numerous strategies that have been developed to teach and improve writing. One common strategy is to teach students to use specific steps in completing a writing assignment. These could include (Study Guides and Strategies, 2009):

- Develop your topic
- Identify your audience
- Research your topic
- Organize and pre-write the paper
- Develop an initial draft and write a completed paper
- Revise the paper
- Proofread for final version

Figure 15.3 provides a list of practices associated with effective writing instruction.

See the nearby Selected IEP Goals and Objectives and Tips for Adapting a Lesson for Justin from the opening vignette.

TIPS FOR ADAPTING A LESSON FOR JUSTIN

When teaching a lesson that requires Justin to read text material for content, Ms. Bennett can use various strategies to help him learn unfamiliar words and become a better reader. Increasing Justin's vocabulary can greatly assist his reading fluency. One method Ms. Bennett can use to improve Justin's vocabulary is with a learning wall. Ms. Bennett starts a learning wall by identifying important words that are found in a passage students need to read and putting these words on the learning wall. Once the learning wall is developed, Ms. Bennett can have students guess the word after she provides clues that match the words on the learning wall (Faber, 2006). Another strategy that could help Justin become a better reader is the weekly vocabulary list. A weekly vocabulary list focuses on words students need to learn for a particular reading passage. The words are listed and practiced during the week and can be added to the student's vocabulary list.

FIGURE 15.3	Teaching Writing Skills

- Establish a writing environment where students understand that there is an audience for their work that includes teachers, other students, and individuals beyond the classroom.
- Encourage legible handwriting styles as alternatives to formal styles that may otherwise be taught to young children but abandoned by middle school. A helpful approach is to encourage a mixed script with cursive and manuscript forms blended together.
- After legibility has been achieved, focus instruction on maintenance through attention to continued legible work.
- Relate spelling instruction to emphases within the reading curriculum to take advantage of, for example, words that have significant personal interest, words from linguistic families, and words that are important for all writing efforts (i.e., high-frequency words).
- Beyond initial instruction, emphasize handwriting and spelling as tool subjects that can be improved in conjunction with writing skills.
- Avoid having students monitor errors only while writing and emphasize the importance of expression of ideas and error monitoring to take place during the postwriting stage.
- Teach writing through a process approach in which students learn the importance of, and strategies related to, prewriting, drafting, and postwriting (i.e., editing, revising) stages.
- Use learning strategies to promote student independence such as in areas inclusive of error monitoring and sentence, paragraph, and composition generation.
- Provide text structures, such as graphic organizers, to provide a model for students to follow in writing.
- Use student–teacher conferences to review student work and make recommendations for changes as related to both the craft (structure, mechanics) and content (ideas, themes) of written work.
- Have students write often so that they have an opportunity to develop skills and to reinforce interest.

Mathematics

Mathematics represents a third potentially challenging academic area for students with disabilities. The development of both **computational skills** and **problem-solving abilities** forms the foundation of successful math instruction and learning. In the area of computation, teachers should focus first on the students' conceptual understanding of a particular skill and then on the achievement of automaticity with the skill.

Problem solving can be particularly difficult for students with disabilities and thus warrants special attention. For learners with special needs, and for many other students as well, instruction in specific problem-solving strategies can greatly enhance math understanding. After a problem-solving strategy has been selected or designed, the strategy's steps should be taught and followed systematically so that students learn to reason through problems and understand problem-solving processes (see Figure 15.4). The potential benefits of including students with special needs in general education classrooms to study core academic areas also extend to other academic areas. Subjects such as science, social studies, health and family life, and the arts offer excellent opportunities for social integration, while effective instructional strategies can lead to academic achievement. Cooperative teaching (discussed later in the chapter) presents an excellent instructional alternative in these areas because it combines the expertise and resources of the classroom teacher with the talents of the special education teacher, rather than requiring them each to develop separate curricula in these respective curricular areas.

SELECTED IEP GOALS AND OBJECTIVES FOR JUSTIN

GOAL 1:

Objective 1: Justin will read and spell accurately 90% of words from the following word families, with 90% accuracy on weekly reading tests, during the first 9-week grading period.

"ake" family

Example:

rake   rakes   raked   raking   raker   rakers

"in" family

Example:

in   win   tin   twin   begin   pin   spin

"at" family

Example:

bat   cat   fat   hat   mat   pat   rat

Objective 2: Justin will read and spell accurately 90% of words with the following fancy patterns, with 90% accuracy on weekly reading tests, during the second 9-week grading period.

on - "un" sound   sample word - apron

ion - 'yun' sound   sample word - million

ous - "us" sound   sample word - nervous

GOAL 2:   Justin will develop social understanding skills

Objective 1: Justin will raise his hand and not begin talking until called on by the teacher 80% of the time during a specific class period.

Objective 2: Justin will be cooperative in small groups by taking turns, listening to peers, and letting others express their ideas 80% of the time.

Objective 3: Justin will take turns appropriately 80% of the time.

Source: AVKO Educational Research Foundation (2010); Cooperative Educational Service Agency No. 7 (2010).

Social Skills Instruction

As discussed in earlier chapters, virtually all students identified with intellectual disabilities or emotional and behavioral disorders, and many with learning disabilities, have difficulties related to the development of social skills. The challenge for classroom teachers is to find ways to incorporate this focus in their classes, such as by seeking assistance from a special education teacher or a counselor. Because performance in the social domain is often predictive of success or failure in inclusive settings, the development of social skills should not be neglected. All educators agree about the importance of social competence, but concern remains about the modest effects that social skills instruction has demonstrated in research (Kavale, 2001b).

A second consideration involves selecting a social adjustment program that promotes both social skills and social competence. Whereas social skills facilitate individual interpersonal interactions, social competence involves the broader ability to use skills at the right times and places, showing social perception, cognition, and judgment of how to act in different situations (Sargent, 1991). A focus limited to specific skill training may make it difficult for the child to maintain the specific social skills or transfer them to various settings. Third, a decision must be made as to who will teach social skills. Often initial instruction occurs in pullout programs (e.g., resource rooms) with generalization plans developed for transfer to the general education classroom. For inclusive classrooms, a useful strategy is the use of the complementary instructional model of cooperative teaching.

CROSS-REFERENCE

The effectiveness of social skills instruction is discussed in Chapter 8.

CROSS-REFERENCE

The complementary model of cooperative teaching is discussed in Chapter 2.

> **FIGURE 15.4**   Teaching Mathematics
>
> - Base instruction on a concrete/semi-concrete/abstract model in which initial instruction of a new skill is grounded in an understanding that comes through concrete representation and in which students learn to use visual representations (semi-concrete) to enhance skills and more abstract math to facilitate automaticity inclusive of accuracy and speed (e.g., through the reliance on numerals and mathematical symbols).
> - Ensure that prerequisite skills have been achieved in sequential fashion in mathematics (i.e., students should have 1-to-1 correspondence before counting and should have effective counting skills before addition).
> - Use math attack strategies as ways to learn, recall, and apply basic skills related to specific math operations (such as through the use of mnemonics to recall ways to perform multiplication, long division, and algebraic equations).
> - Teach problem-solving strategies that enable students to attack word problems and reach solutions (see, for example, Figure 15.2).
> - Place word problems in the context of real-life settings in which students are not directly cued as to the correct algorithm (operation) to be used, but rather are challenged to think about the task.
> - Present word problems that include distracters or extraneous information to teach students how to focus on relevant aspects for problem solutions.
> - Develop graduated word problems, such as through a matrix approach that enables students to enhance their skills in terms of the language structure of problems, the computational challenges, and the presence or absence of distracters, for example.

Transitional Needs

In addition to the academic and social components of the curriculum, career education and transition form an important emphasis even for younger children. For all elementary students, career awareness and a focus on facilitating movement between levels of schooling (i.e., vertical transitions) are curricular essentials.

Transition from Preschool to Primary School   Research on students moving from preschool programs into school settings has identified variables that predict success in school. Four such variables include early academic (i.e., readiness) skills, social skills, responsiveness to instructional styles, and responsiveness to the structure of the school environment (Polloway, Patton, Smith, & Roderique, 1992). Analyzing the new school environment can help a teacher determine the skills a student will need to make this crucial adjustment.

Academic readiness skills have traditionally been cited as good predictors of success at the primary school level. Examples include the ability to recognize numbers and letters, grasp a writing utensil, count to 10, and write letters and numbers. Yet, a clear delineation between academic readiness and academic skills is not warranted. Rather, to use reading as an example, it is much more productive to consider readiness as inclusive of examples of early reading skills, or what has been termed *emergent literacy*. Programming in this area should focus on academic activities that advance the processes of learning to read, write, and calculate.

Social skills consistent with the developmental attributes of other 5- and 6-year-olds are clearly important to success in the elementary school. It is particularly critical that students be able to function in a group. Thus, introducing small-group instructional activities in preschool programs prepares students to function in future school situations.

Developing responsiveness to instructional styles is another challenge for the young child. Because the instructional arrangement in the preschool program may vary significantly from that of the kindergarten or first-grade school program, providing instructional experiences that the student can generalize to the new school setting will be helpful; some learning activities in the preschool class should approximate those of kindergarten to provide the preparation.

Responsiveness to the daily learning environment is a fourth concern. Changes may include new transportation arrangements, extended instructional time, increased expectations of individual independence, and increased class size resulting in a reduction in individual attention. Teachers may set up opportunities for the preschoolers to visit kindergarten classes to familiarize them with the future environment.

Transition Curricular Considerations   Career education in general, and life-skills education in particular, have become major emphases among secondary school teachers, especially those who work with students who have disabilities. Yet, life-skills concepts should also be incorporated into elementary and middle school programs (Patton & Cronin, 1993; Patton & Dunn, 1998). Table 15.3 provides a matrix of topics that can be incorporated into an elementary-level life-skills curriculum. Even programs for young children should be designed to encourage positive long-term outcomes for all students.

Concepts and topics related to life skills can be integrated into existing subject areas, thus broadening the curriculum without the necessity of creating a new subject. This purpose can be accomplished in two ways. The first approach, augmentation, uses career–education oriented materials to supplement the existing curriculum. The second

TABLE 15.3

Life Skills in the Elementary School Curriculum

	CONSUMER ECONOMICS	OCCUPATIONAL KNOWLEDGE	HEALTH	COMMUNITY RESOURCES	GOVERNMENT AND LAW
Reading	Look for ads in the newspaper for toys.	Read books from library on various occupations.	Read the school lunch menu.	Find television listing in the *TV Guide*.	Read road signs and understand what they mean.
Writing	Write prices of items to be purchased.	Write the specific tasks involved in performing one of the classroom jobs.	Keep a diary of food you eat in each food group each day.	Complete an application to play on a Little League team.	Write a letter to the mayor inviting him/her to visit your school.
Speaking, Writing, Viewing	Listen to bank official talk about savings accounts.	Call newspaper in town to inquire about delivering papers in your neighborhood.	View a film on brushing teeth.	Practice the use of the 911 emergency number.	Discuss park playground improvements with the mayor.
Problem Solving	Decide if you have enough coins to make a purchase from a vending machine.	Decide which job in the classroom you do best.	Role-play what you should do if you have a stomachache.	Role-play the times you would use the 911 emergency number.	Find the city hall on the map. Decide whether you will walk or drive to it.
Interpersonal Relations	Ask for help finding items in a grocery store.	Ask a student in the class to assist you with a classroom job.	Ask the school nurse how to take care of mosquito bites.	Call the movie theater and ask the show times of a movie.	Role-play being lost and asking a police officer for help.
Computation	Compute the cost of a box of cereal with a discount coupon.	Calculate how much you would make on a paper route at $3 per hour for 5 hours per week.	Compute the price of one tube of toothpaste if they are on sale at three for $1.	Compute the complete cost of going to the movie (admission, food, transportation).	Compute tax on a candy bar.

Source: From "Curricular Considerations: A Life Skills Orientation," by J. R. Patton, M. E. Cronin, E. A. Polloway, D. R. Hutchison, and G. A. Robinson, 1989, in *Best Practices in Mild Mental Retardation,* edited by G. A. Robinson, J. R. Patton, E. A. Polloway, and L. Sargent, p. 31. Reston, VA: CEC-MR. Used by permission.

approach infuses relevant career-education topics into the lessons laid out in the existing curriculum.

Transition to Middle School   Elementary students with disabilities need to be prepared for movement to middle school or junior high school. To successfully make this vertical transition, students need an organized approach to their work, time-management and study skills, note-taking strategies, homework strategies, and the ability to use lockers.

Wenz-Gross and Siperstein (1998) similarly focused on transitional issues relative to students' success at the middle-school level. They concluded that interventions for students in middle school should emphasize developing coping skills for academic demands, peer stress, and relationships with teachers. Helping students develop time-management and organizational skills should also be a focus. To do so, teachers and parents should help these students prioritize multiple tasks and integrate and master the information needed at the middle-school level.

Students need to strengthen interpersonal skills so they can build more positive peer relationships. To assist students in these areas, schools should start teaching students self-management skills before middle school and add emphasis in this area in middle school, when peer relationships become so important. Students also need to be empowered to better deal with the problems experienced by adolescence.

A variety of instructional strategies can assist in the transition process: having middle school faculty visit elementary classes to discuss programs and expectations; viewing videotaped middle-school classes; and taking field trips to the middle school to get a sense of the physical layout, the changing of classes, and environmental and pedagogical factors (Jaquish & Stella, 1986). Cooperative planning and follow-up between both general and special education teachers at the two school levels will smooth the transition.

CROSS-REFERENCE

Further attention to transition into high school and into the community and/or postsecondary environments is provided in Chapter 16.

INSTRUCTIONAL STRATEGIES FOR INCLUSIVE CLASSROOMS

To successfully implement the curriculum, teachers should focus on strategies that are scientifically validated and produce significant gains in academic achievement. To be consistent with IDEA (2004) and NCLB (2002), effective instruction has now been defined as those practices that are research-based and empirically validated (Boardman, Arguelles, Vaughn, Hughes, & Klinger, 2005; Yell, Katsiyannis, & Shiner, 2006).

Although a variety of strategies are needed to reach this objective, three primary foci are to provide excellent instruction, to assess programs continuously, and to ensure instruction is intensive enough to guarantee learning. With regard to the first two, especially in reference to students with learning disabilities, Lloyd and Hallahan (2005) noted that "reasonably informed people ... argue strongly for explicit, systematic instruction that focuses on teaching students strategies for completing academic tasks and that includes monitoring of progress so instruction can be adjusted to maximize progress" (p. 135).

Deshler (2005) succinctly stated the third point in noting:

> Intensive instruction involves helping students maintain a high degree of attention and response during instructional sessions that are scheduled as frequently and consistently as possible. In other words, a key factor affecting learning is both the amount of time and instruction and how effectively each instructional moment is used to engage students in activities that contribute to their learning. Intensity during instruction is achieved by progressive pacing, frequent question-answer interactions, and frequent activities that require a physical response (e.g., pointing, writing, raising hands, repeating). Intensity can also be achieved through reflective or open-ended questions if the activities are focused on a process that engages interest and maintains the student's attention. (pp. 123–124)

In inclusive elementary-school environments, instruction also must be based on the realities of that environment. Successful programs thus reflect collaborative practices—both between teachers and among students.

Professional Collaboration

The successful elementary classroom is a model of collaboration. Both teachers and students benefit from supports from their peers.

Professional collaboration is a key component of effective elementary schools and a necessity for successful inclusion. Collaboration can occur in IEP meetings through cooperative teaching and within the prereferral (or child study) process.

Cooperative teaching potentially can help prevent or correct the learning problems of any student while effecting the remediation of identified deficits for students with disabilities. Cooperative teaching, perhaps the best vehicle for attaining successful inclusive classrooms, truly provides **supported education**, the school-based equivalent of supported work in which students are placed in the least restrictive environment and provided with the necessary support (e.g., by the special educator) to be successful. The nearby Personal Spotlight describes one approach to helping new teachers learn how to collaborate with other professionals.

Another key area for collaboration is through the prereferral process (also referred to as child-study or teacher assistance teams). According to Buck, Fad, Patton, and Polloway (2003), prereferral is best conceptualized as a problem-solving process aimed at meeting the needs of students who exhibit learning or behavioral problems. The process is typically carried out within a school by a team made up of various school personnel and sometimes joined by parents.

The objective of the prereferral process is to meet the challenges presented by students within the context of their classrooms. Teams review student cases and develop instructional and/or behavioral strategies to resolve problems. As Buck, Williams, Patton, and Polloway (in press) note, several assumptions are inherent in this team approach:

- Problems can be solved more effectively when they are clearly defined.
- Members of a team often can objectively perceive a student problem better than the referring teacher, who may be emotionally involved in the situation.
- A team of professionals is better able to develop intervention strategies than are one or two professionals.
- Many of the problems students have are complex and require the expertise of professionals from varied backgrounds and disciplines.
- Most learning and behavior problems are not indicative of a disability. With environmental manipulations, such problems can be reduced and eliminated without the need for special education services.

The prereferral process usually occurs in three stages:

1. A teacher or other school staff notices that a student is having difficulty in one or more areas (e.g., academics, social behavior, truancy).
2. The prereferral team attempts to analyze the student's difficulties.
3. Once the problem has been clearly defined, the prereferral team develops strategies to resolve the student's difficulties. In some cases, the team members may provide assistance to the teacher as he or she attempts to implement these strategies in the classroom.

Collaborative Learning

Cooperative learning (CL) is a key means of facilitating the successful inclusion of students with disabilities in general education classrooms. CL is categorized by classroom techniques that involve students in group learning activities, in which recognition and reinforcement are based on group, rather than individual, performance. Heterogeneous small groups work together to achieve a group goal, and an individual student's success directly affects the success of other students (Slavin, 1987).

A variety of formats can be used to implement cooperative learning. These include peer tutoring and group projects of various types.

Peer Tutoring Peer teaching, or peer tutoring, is a relatively easy-to-manage system of cooperative learning. It can benefit both the student being tutored and the tutor. Specific

CROSS-REFERENCE

Professional collaboration is covered in Chapters 1 and 2. Cooperative teaching is discussed also in Chapter 2.

PERSONAL SPOTLIGHT

TEACHER EDUCATOR

VAL SHARPE has taught in many educational settings. She notes: "It is the ongoing process of change in order to meet the needs of students with disabilities that has afforded me the opportunity for diversification as an educator." As a teacher educator, Val and her colleagues (e.g., Roberta Strosnider) have developed a "hands-on" approach to teaching methods courses in a professional development school (PDS) setting at Hood College.

During the teacher-training process, the future special educator is exposed to a variety of learning theories, adaptations, and modifications designed to facilitate instruction and enhance concept mastery. Within the PDS, the student is provided with multiple opportunities to practice these theories, adaptations, and modifications with children in the classroom setting. Initially, the Hood faculty teach a concept through modeling and incorporating the necessary adaptations and strategies that facilitate learning. The next step is for the student to practice teaching this concept to other future educators. Once the student acquires mastery of the concept, the student teaches this concept to children. This is the stage when the future educator is introduced to the collaborative process.

Val feels it necessary for future educators to be afforded the opportunity to become acquainted with this process through the implementation of various reality-based activities. After teaching the prerequisite skills and successful ingredients involved in the collaborative process, Val has students actively participate in this process using the following vehicles:

1. Students become knowledgeable about a variety of learning theories, adaptations, and modifications, and their implementation.

2. Students complete a collaborative worksheet.

3. Students are given an assignment to teach a lesson to a group of children within an inclusive setting. Using the collaboration process, decisions are made regarding appropriate topics for the lesson, as well as the necessary adaptations needed to facilitate the learning process. Via the collaborative process, the students then decide on the topic and develop a lesson plan. The lesson is then taught to the children. The implemented lesson is evaluated by the children, students, PDS teachers, and college supervisor.

4. Students reflect on this venture by referring back to their collaborative worksheet as well as discussing this experience with their classmates.

Throughout the student-teaching practicum, Val enables the students to utilize the collaborative process. These future educators are required to collaborate with parents in the form of a conference, collaborate with other teachers with regard to lesson development and implementation, collaborate with administrators in terms of scheduling and school policy, and collaborate with the multidisciplinary team in developing an IEP.

This hands-on approach to the collaborative process enables the future teacher to practice this process in a variety of settings. It is beneficial because it helps them make connections about the collaborative process. This approach incorporates the elements of good instructional practices through the use of modeling, repetition, guided practice, independent practice, and reflection. Future educators become familiar with the collaborative process and become comfortable using this process.

---

activities that lend themselves to peer tutoring include reviewing task directions, drill and practice, recording material dictated by a peer, modeling of acceptable or appropriate responses, and providing pretest practice (such as in spelling).

A research-based approach for using students as instructors is classwide peer tutoring, instructional strategies that involve students being taught by peers who previously were trained and are then supervised by teachers. Maheady, Harper, and Mallette (2003) identified the four primary components of *classwide peer tutoring (CWPT)* as follows: "competing teams; a highly structured tutoring procedure; daily point earning and public posting of people performance; and direct practice in the implementation of instructional activities. In using CWPT, the teacher's role changes from primary 'deliverer' of instruction to facilitator and monitor of peer-teaching activities" (p. 1).

CWPT is intended to be a reciprocal tutoring approach. That is, students assume roles as both tutor and tutee during individual instructional sessions. Further, the sessions are highly structured by the teacher to ensure that students are on task and focused on key instructional content.

As summarized by Seeley (1995), CWPT involves the following arrangements:

- Classes are divided into two teams that engage in competitions typically of one to two weeks' duration.
- Students work in pairs, both tutoring and being tutored on the same material in a given instructional session.
- Partners reverse roles after 15 minutes.
- Typical subjects tutored include math, spelling, vocabulary, science, and social studies.
- Teachers break down the curriculum into manageable subunits.
- Students accumulate points for their team by giving correct answers and by using correct procedures, and they receive partial credit for corrected answers.
- Individual scores on master tests are added to the team's total.

CWPT has been positively evaluated in terms of enhancing content learning, promoting diversity and integration, and freeing teachers to prepare for other instructional activities (King-Sears & Bradley, 1995; Maheady et al., 2003; Simmons, Fuchs, Hodge, & Mathes, 1994).

■ Classwide peer tutoring is one peer tutoring program that is effective in inclusive settings.

Another example of a successful peer tutoring approach is *peer-assisted learning strategies (PALS)*, described by Mathes and Torgesen (1998). In PALS, beginning readers are assisted in learning through paired instruction in which each member of the pair takes turns serving as a coach and a reader. The first coach is the reader who is at a higher achievement level who listens to, comments on, and reinforces the other student before the roles are reversed. These researchers found that the use of this approach enhanced students' reading by promoting careful attention to saying and hearing sounds, sounding out words, and reading stories. They recommended using the approach three times a week for approximately 16 weeks with each session lasting 35 minutes. The PALS program complements general education instruction by enhancing the academic engaged time of each student.

Kroeger and Kouche (2006) provided an example of a successful application of PALS to middle-school students in math. As they note, the benefits reflect "a world of students discussing and talking through math problems, regardless of ability levels or past experiences in math classes.... PALS is an effective intervention to increase engagement and opportunities to respond for all students" (p. 12).

Group Projects   Group projects allow students to pool their knowledge and skills to complete an assignment. The task is assigned to the entire group, and the goal is to develop a single product reflecting the contributions of all members. For example, in social studies, a report on one of the 50 states might involve making individual students responsible for particular tasks: drawing a map, sketching an outline of state history, collecting photos of scenic attractions, and developing a display of products from that state. The benefits of groups are enhanced when they include high, average, and low achievers.

The *jigsaw format* is an approach that involves giving all group members individual tasks to be completed before the group can reach its goal. Each individual studies a portion of the material and then shares it with other members of the team. For example, Salend (1990) discussed an assignment related to the life of Dr. Martin Luther King, Jr. in which each student was given a segment of his life to research (e.g., religious beliefs, protest marches, opposition to the Vietnam war). The students then had to teach others in their group the information from the segment they had mastered. In using this approach, teachers are cautioned to oversee the individual assignments within the group project and keep in mind the importance of distributing student expertise over aspects of the assignment.

Cooperative learning strategies offer much promise as inclusive practices. These approaches have been used successfully with low, average, and high achievers to promote the acquisition of academic and social skills and to enhance independence. The fact that CL appears to be effective in general education and special education classrooms would seem to support the benefits of its use with heterogeneous populations (McMaster & Fuchs, 2002). Cooperative learning also can enhance the social adjustment of students with special needs by helping to create natural support networks involving nondisabled peers, such as within the "circle of friends" approach discussed in Chapter 8.

At the same time, teachers should keep in mind that CL approaches are not the single solution for resolving the academic challenges faced by students with special needs. As McMaster and Fuchs (2002) conclude, the state of research in this area is such that CL is best seen as a "promising instructional strategy (rather than as) an unqualified effective approach" (p. 116). Thus, as with many classroom interventions, teachers are encouraged to assess the effectiveness of CL if they use it as a tool to promote the successful inclusion of students with special needs.

Instructional and Curricular Adaptations

In general, students with disabilities profit directly from the same types of teaching strategies that benefit all students. In particular, there are research-validated interventions reflecting classroom adaptations that are associated with successful learning outcomes for students with learning disabilities and other special needs. To promote successful inclusion, adaptations will frequently be needed both in terms of curriculum and instruction.

Wehmeyer (in press) notes that curriculum adaptations included "efforts to modify the representation of the curriculum content or to modify the student's engagement with the curriculum to enhance and progress" (p. 8). The complementary concept of instructional adaptation refers to ways in which teachers can design and deliver instruction and seek student responses to reflect learning in varied ways that enhance success for students with special needs.

Vaughn, Gersten, and Chard (2000) note that all students benefit when best practices for students with disabilities are used. They identify three general instructional features that stand out as producing the most significant impact on learning:

- Control of task difficulty (i.e., sequencing examples and problems to maintain high levels of student success)
- Teaching students in small interactive groups of six or fewer students
- Directed response questioning (i.e., involves the use of procedures that promote "thinking aloud" about text being read, mathematical problems to be solved, or about the process of composing a written essay or story) (p. 101)

It is useful to have a common set of definitions to build upon in discussing classroom adaptations. Polloway and colleagues (2002) provide the following differentiation between two types of adaptations. **Accommodations** refer to changes in processes in teaching and assessment, such as in the format of instructional presentations, as well as test practice and preparation activities. The concept of **modifications** refers to changes in content or standards. As a general pattern, Polloway and colleagues (2002) report that teachers are more willing to consider accommodations, whereas they express more reluctance to implement modifications.

Adaptations made to instructional programs in the general education classroom then form the keys to successful inclusion. As the traditional saying goes, special education is not necessarily special, it is just good teaching, and good teaching often means making appropriate modifications and accommodations.

A key component of successful inclusion is the likelihood that certain specific classroom interventions will be acceptable to the general education teacher. They may consider, for example, the helpfulness, desirability, feasibility, and fairness of the intervention, as well as how other students will perceive it in a particular setting. As Witt and Elliott (1985) note, the "attractiveness" of an intervention is important: If the treatment is not deemed acceptable, it is unlikely to be implemented.

In a review of research on adaptations, Scott, Vitale, and Masten (1998) summarize the types of adaptations that have been researched for their effectiveness. They use the qualifiers "typical" to refer to specific examples that are routine, minor, or applicable to an entire class, and "substantial" to refer to those that are tailored to the needs of individual students. Their categories (as adapted) are as follows:

- Adapting instruction: typical (concrete classroom demonstrations, monitoring classroom understanding); substantial (adjusting the pace to individual learners, giving immediate individual feedback, using multiple modalities)
- Adapting assignments: typical (providing models); substantial (breaking tasks into small steps, shortening assignments, lowering difficulty levels)
- Teaching learning skills: typical (study skills, note-taking techniques); substantial (learning strategies, test-taking skills)
- Altering instructional materials: substantial (using alternative materials, taping textbooks, using supplementary aids)
- Modifying curriculum: substantial (lowering difficulty of course content)
- Varying instructional grouping: substantial (using peer tutoring, using cooperative groups)
- Enhancing behavior: typical (praise, offering encouragement); substantial (using behavioral contracts, using token economies, frequent parental contact)
- Facilitating progress monitoring: typical (read tests orally, give extended test-taking time, give frequent short quizzes, provide study guides); substantial (retaking tests, obtaining direct daily measures of academic progress, modifying grading criteria) (p. 107)

The specific modifications and accommodations for students with disabilities in elementary classes, discussed next, will likely vary in terms of teacher acceptability. Many adaptations will prove beneficial to all students, not only to those with special needs. Teachers are encouraged to select strategies that appear applicable to a given situation and then evaluate their effectiveness.

Adaptations for Instructional Lessons

To facilitate learning, teachers must consider vehicles for the effective presentation of content to enhance successful listening. Adaptations in this area typically prove beneficial to all students. Some specific considerations include relating information to students' prior experiences and providing an overview before beginning, limiting the number of concepts introduced at a given time, and reviewing lessons before additional content is introduced.

In many instances, instructional tasks, assignments, or materials might be relevant and appropriate for children with disabilities but can present problematic reading demands. Teachers should consider options for adapting the task or the textual materials. Several suggestions that illustrate ways to assist students in processing reading content are:

- Previewing reading material with students to assist them in establishing purpose, activating prior knowledge, budgeting time, and focusing attention
- Preteaching vocabulary to ensure that students can use them rather than simply recognize them
- Using graphic organizers (e.g., charts, graphs) to provide an orientation to reading tasks or to supplement them

Adaptations can also enhance the ability of children to meet the written language demands of the inclusive classroom. For example, teachers can:

- Allow children to select the most comfortable method of writing (i.e., cursive or manuscript)
- Let students type or tape-record answers
- Provide the student with a copy of lecture notes, PowerPoint slides, or detailed outlines to guide note taking

Another key area is enhancing children's ability to follow instructions and complete work assignments. The following suggestions are adapted from *CEC Today* (1997):

- Get the student's attention before giving directions.
- Use alerting cues.
- Give one direction at a time.
- Quietly repeat the directions to the student after they have been given to the entire class.
- Check for understanding by having the student repeat the directions.
- Break up tasks into workable and obtainable steps, and include due dates.
- Post requirements necessary to complete each assignment.
- Check assignments frequently. (p. 15)

One type of adaptation warrants particular attention. Graphic organizers, advance organizers that provide visual models for presenting curricular content, have been widely promoted as a particularly efficacious approach to content learning for students with special needs (Wehmeyer, in press). As such, the widespread use of graphic organizers has become an important aspect of the application of universal design for learning, which was discussed earlier in the chapter. Strangman, Hall, and Meyer (n.d.) defined a graphic organizer as "a visual and graphic display that depicts the relationships between facts, terms, and/or ideas within a learning task. Graphic organizers are also sometimes referred to as knowledge maps, concept maps, story maps, cognitive organizers, advance organizers, or concept diagrams" (p. 2).

Graphic organizers can be developed for content in any instructional area. For example, graphic organizers can provide outlines for note taking from lectures, a template for organizing reports and speeches for oral presentation in class, a format for deriving key content information from reading assigned as homework, and a prompt to assist students in monitoring their own errors in writing as part of a proofreading strategy.

Cultural Diversity Considerations

Educators need to consider issues related to cultural diversity when working with elementary-age students with special needs. Students who come from different language backgrounds and whose families reflect values that differ from those of the majority culture must be treated with sensitivity and respect. Thus, teachers should often make adaptations to instruction so that it reflects effective responses to multicultural considerations.

Considerations of linguistic and cultural diversity must inform all aspects of curriculum design and should be reflected in instructional practices. The continued overrepresentation of minority children in high-incidence special education categories underscores the importance of this focus (e.g., Oswald, Coutinho, Best, & Singh, 1999). Because students with special needs benefit from direct, hands-on approaches to such topics, teachers should introduce specific activities that promote cultural awareness and sensitivity to develop students' appreciation of diversity at the elementary level and then lay the foundation for subsequent programming at the middle- and secondary-school levels.

Adapting the Classroom Environment

Two key considerations are time and physical arrangement. Time is a critical element and can be associated with special challenges for students with disabilities. Thus, adapting deadlines and other requirements can help promote success. When handled properly, these adaptations need not impinge on the integrity of the assignments or place undue burdens on the classroom teacher. Other examples include:

- Reviewing with students to reinforce routines
- Providing each student with a copy of the schedule
- Increasing the amount of time allowed to complete assignments or tests
- Teaching time-management skills

Changes in the classroom arrangement can also help children with special needs. Some specific examples include establishing a climate that fosters positive social interactions between students, using study carrels, and establishing high- and low-frequency areas for class work.

Developing Effective Homework Programs

Homework is an essential element of education, and educational reforms have led to its increased use by elementary general education teachers. Traditional research on the effectiveness of homework as an instructional tool suggests that it leads to increased school achievement for students in general, with particular benefits in the area of habit formation for elementary students (Cooper, 1989; Walberg, 1991).

Homework for students with disabilities presents several dilemmas for general education teachers. Epstein and colleagues (1997) recognized that communication concerning homework is often negatively affected by the inadequate knowledge base of general education teachers. Polloway, Epstein, Bursuck, Jayanthi, and Cumblad (1994) asked teachers to rate specific homework adaptations and practices that were most helpful to students with disabilities. Figure 15.5 summarizes these responses; each column reflects teachers' ratings from most to least helpful.

FIGURE 15.5	Teachers' Ratings of Helpfulness of Homework Adaptations and Practices

Most Helpful

- Communicate clear consequences about successfully completing homework.
- Begin assignment in class, and check for understanding.
- Communicate clear expectations about the quality of homework completion.
- Use a homework assignment sheet or notebook.
- Communicate clear consequences about failure to complete homework.
- Give assignments that are completed entirely at school.
- Begin assignment in class without checking for understanding.
- Assist students in completing the assignment.
- Make adaptations in assignment.
- Talk to students about why the assignment was not completed.
- Require corrections and resubmission.
- Call students' parents.
- Keep students in at recess to complete the assignment.
- Keep students after school to complete the assignment.
- Lower students' grades.
- Put students' names on board.
- Give praise for completion.
- Provide corrective feedback in class.
- Give rewards for completion.
- Monitor students by charting performance.
- Record performance in grade book.
- Provide additional teacher assistance.
- Check more frequently with student about assignments and expectations.
- Allow alternative response formats (e.g., oral or other than written).
- Adjust length of assignment.
- Provide a peer tutor for assistance.
- Provide auxiliary learning aids (e.g., calculator, computer).
- Assign work that student can do independently.
- Provide a study group.
- Provide extra-credit opportunities.
- Adjust (i.e., lower) evaluation standards.
- Adjust due dates.
- Give fewer assignments.

Least Helpful

Source: From "A National Survey of Homework Practices of General Education Teachers," by E. A. Polloway, M. H. Epstein, W. Bursuck, M. Jayanthi, and C. Cumblad, 1994," *Journal of Learning Disabilities, 27,* p. 504. Used by permission.

TABLE 15.4

Recommended Homework Practices

School-Based
- Require frequent written communication from teachers to parents.
- Schedule parent–teacher meetings in the evening.
- Provide release time for teachers to communicate with parents.
- Establish telephone hotlines.
- Establish after-school sessions to provide extra help.
- Institute peer tutoring programs.

Teacher-Directed
- Require and teach students to use homework assignment books.
- Assess students' skills related to homework completion.
- Involve parents and students in the homework process from the beginning of the school year.
- Establish an ongoing communication system with parents to convey information related to homework assignments.
- Coordinate homework assignments with other teachers.

- Present assignments clearly and provide timely feedback.
- Teach students techniques for managing their time more effectively.

Parent-Initiated
- Discuss homework assignments with their children daily.
- Attend parent–teacher conferences.
- Communicate views, concerns, and observations about homework to teacher(s) or other school personnel.
- Provide support to their child when doing homework by creating and maintaining an appropriate homework environment.

Student-Regulated
- Demonstrate a range of self-advocacy skills including the ability to ask for help when needed.
- Become an interdependent learner.
- Manage time more effectively.

Source: From "Home–School Collaboration about Homework: What Do We Know and What Should We Do?" by J. R. Patton, M. Jayanthi, and E. A. Polloway, 2001, *Reading & Writing Quarterly, 17,* p. 233.

Patton, Jayanthi, and Polloway (2001) reviewed the research on collaboration concerning homework and identified recommended practices that are respectively school-based, teacher-directed, parent-initiated, and student-regulated. These are listed in Table 15.4.

Developing Responsive Grading Practices

The assignment of grades is an integral aspect of education. Grading serves multiple purposes in contemporary education, as summarized in Table 15.5. Thus, grading practices have been subject to frequent evaluation and review, generating a number of problematic issues.

In a national survey of teachers, Bursuck and colleagues (1996) found that approximately 40% of general educators shared responsibilities for grading with special education teachers. This collaboration is timely because existing grading systems make success challenging for students who are disabled.

Further, these same researchers reported that elementary teachers evaluated adaptations and indicated that adaptations allowing for separate grades for process and product and grades indexed against student improvement were particularly helpful, whereas passing students "no matter what" or basing grades on effort alone was not. This finding is consistent with the distinction of accommodations versus modifications made by Polloway and colleagues (2002) noted earlier in this chapter.

A related issue is the feasibility of specific adaptations in general education. Bursuck and colleagues (1996) assessed this concern by determining whether teachers use these same adaptations for students with and without disabilities. Three of the four adaptations deemed most helpful for students with disabilities (i.e., grading on improvement, adjusting grades, giving separate grades for process and product) were also used by 50% or more of the teachers (regardless of grade level) with nondisabled students. Basing grades on less content and passing students no matter what are frowned on in both general and special education.

TABLE 15.5

Purposes of Grading

1. Achievements:	To certify and measure mastery of curricular goals and specific skills (e.g., learning standards).
2. Progress:	To indicate progress in learning over a specific period of time.
3. Effort:	To acknowledge and indicate the effort a student puts forth in learning.
4. Comparison:	To compare students in terms of their competence, progress, and effort.
5. Instructional planning:	To identify students' learning strengths and needs, and to group students for instruction.
6. Program effectiveness:	To examine the efficacy of the instructional program.
7. Motivation:	To motivate students to learn, to reward learning, and to promote self-esteem.
8. Communication:	To provide feedback to students, families, and others.
9. Educational and career planning:	To aid students, families, and school districts in determining the courses and educational services needed by students, placing students who enter the school district from another school district, and planning for the future (e.g., facilitate student advisement and career planning).
10. Eligibility:	To determine eligibility for graduation and promotion, and rank students in terms of their eligibility for certain programs and awards (e.g., honors programs, participation in extracurricular activities, grants, scholarships, rankings for college admission).
11. Accountability:	To provide measures of student achievement to the community, employers, legislators, and educational policy makers (e.g., grades provide employers with a point of reference concerning the aptitude and job skills of prospective employees).

Source: Adapted from "Grading Students in Inclusive Settings," by S. Salend and L. G. Duhaney, 2002, *Teaching Exceptional Children, 34,* pp. 13–14.

Questions of fairness also influence the discussion on grading (e.g., Are adaptations in grading made only for students with disabilities really fair to other students?). Bursuck and colleagues (1996) report that only 25% of general education teachers thought such adaptations were fair. Those who believed they were fair noted that students should "not be punished" for an inherent problem such as a disability, that adaptations for effort are appropriate because the students are "fighting uphill battles," and that adaptations allow students to "be successful like other kids."

Those teachers who thought adaptations unfair indicated that other students experience significant learning problems even though they have not been formally identified, that some students have extenuating circumstances (e.g., divorce, illness) that necessitate adaptations, and that all students are unique and deserve individual consideration (i.e., students both with and without disabilities may need specific adaptations). Finally, a minority of general educators believe that because classes have standards to uphold, all students need to meet those standards without adaptations (Bursuck et al., 1996).

Polloway and colleagues (2008) suggest these overall considerations about grading:

- Plan for special and general education teachers to meet regularly to discuss student progress.
- Emphasize the acquisition of new skills as a basis for grades assigned, thus providing a perspective on the student's relative gains.
- Investigate alternatives for evaluating content that has been learned (e.g., oral examinations for poor readers in a science class).
- Engage in cooperative grading agreements (e.g., grades for language arts might reflect performance both in the classroom and the resource room).

- Use narrative reports as a key portion of, or adjunct to, the report card. These reports can include comments on specific objectives within the student's IEP.
- Develop personalized grading plans for students. (Munk & Bursuck, 2001, 2004)

The Differentiating Instruction—Elementary Instruction on effective grading practices provides additional perspectives.

Differentiating Elementary Instruction

EFFECTIVE GRADING PRACTICES

Grading is a critical element of successful inclusion. Salend and Duhaney (2002) provided a series of recommendations, which include the following:

- **Communicating expectations and grading guidelines:** Student performance is enhanced when teachers clearly communicate their expectations to students and families and share their grading guidelines and criteria with them.

- **Informing students and families regarding grading progress on a regular basis:** Providing students and their families with ongoing information concerning current performance and grades helps all involved parties understand the grading guidelines. Ongoing sharing of students' grading progress facilitates the modifications of instructional programs so that students and families are not surprised by the grades received at the end of the grading period. It also prompts students to examine their effort, motivation, and attitudes, and their impact on their performance and grades.

- **Using a range of assignments that address students' varied learning needs, strengths, and styles:** Rather than assigning grades based solely on test performance or a limited number of assignments, many teachers determine students' grades by weighing a variety of student assignments (e.g., tests, homework, projects, extra credit, class participation, attendance, behavior, and other factors).

- **Employing classroom-based assessment alternatives to traditional testing:** Whereas grades are frequently determined by students' performance on tests, they also can be established on classroom-based assessment techniques, such as performance assessment, portfolio assessment, and curriculum-based measurement. By using performance assessment, teachers grade students on authentic products (e.g., creating and making things, solving problems, responding to stimulations) that demonstrate their skills, problem-solving abilities, knowledge, and understanding of the learning standards. Similarly, student portfolios and curriculum-based measurements that are linked to the learning standards serve as tools for grading students and guiding the teaching and learning process.

- **Providing feedback on assignments and grading students after they have learned something rather than while they are learning it:** Before grading students on an assignment or a test, teachers should provide a range of appropriate learning activities and give nongraded assignments that help students practice and develop their skills. As students work on these assignments, teachers should give them feedback and additional instructional experiences to improve their learning of the material, which is then assessed when they have completed the learning cycle.

- **Avoiding competition and promoting collaboration:** While grading on a curve results in a consistent grade distribution, it hinders the teaching and learning process by promoting competition among students. Therefore, educators minimize competition by grading students in reference to specific learning criteria and refraining from posting grades. Teachers also promote collaboration among students by structuring learning and assessments activities so that students work together and are graded cooperatively.

- **Designing valid tests and providing students with appropriate testing accommodations:** Teachers enhance the value of their tests and promote student performance by developing valid tests and providing students with appropriate testing accommodations. In designing valid tests, teachers select the content of the test so that it relates to the learning standards, the manner in which the content was taught, and the amount of class time devoted to the topics on the test. Teachers also carefully examine the format and readability of their tests and provide students with the testing accommodations outlined on their IEPs.

- **Teaching test-taking to students:** Instruction in test-taking skills helps students perform at their optimal levels by reducing testing anxiety and assisting them in feeling comfortable with the format of the test.

Source: Adapted from "Grading Students in Inclusive Settings," by S. Salend and L. G. Duhaney, 2002, *Teaching Exceptional Children, 34*(3), pp. 13–14.

SUMMARY

General Curriculum Considerations

- The curriculum for elementary students with disabilities should meet their current and long-term needs, facilitate their interactions with nondisabled peers, and facilitate their transition into middle school.

Curriculum Emphases for Academic, Social Skills, and Transitional Instruction

- Reading instruction should reflect emphases on both decoding skills and whole language to provide a comprehensive, balanced program.
- Math instruction should provide students with concrete and abstract learning opportunities and should stress the development of problem-solving skills.
- Teachers should select programs and strategies that focus on the social skills most needed by students in their classrooms.
- Life-skills instruction should be a part of the elementary curriculum through the use of augmentation, infusion, or an integrated curriculum.

Instructional Strategies for Inclusive Classrooms

- Cooperative teaching involves a team approach in which teachers share their talents in providing class instruction to all students. This requires a commitment to planning, time, and administrative support to reach its potential for success.
- Instructional adaptations should be evaluated against their "teacher acceptability" (e.g., helpfulness, feasibility, desirability, and fairness).
- Listening is a skill that requires conscious effort on the part of students and planned intervention strategies on the part of teachers.
- Reading tasks can be adapted through a variety of instructional strategies, such as clarifying intent, highlighting content, modifying difficulty level, and using visual aids.
- Written responses can be facilitated through modification of the response requirement.
- Cooperative learning affords teachers a unique opportunity to involve students with disabilities in classroom activities.
- Adaptations in class schedules or classroom arrangements should be considered to enhance the learning of students with disabilities.
- Educational programs should be designed to reflect the importance of motivation.
- Homework creates significant challenges for students with special needs; these should be addressed by using intervention strategies.
- Classroom grading practices should be flexible enough to facilitate inclusion.

PEARSON
myeducationlab

The MyEducationLab for this course can help you solidify your comprehension of Chapter 15 concepts.

- Gauge and further develop your understanding of chapter concepts by taking the quizzes and examining the enrichment materials on the Chapter 15 Study Plan.

- Visit Topic 10, Instructional Practices and Learning Strategies, as well as Topic 11, Reading, to:
  - Connect with challenge-based interactive modules, case study units, and podcasts that provide research-validated information about working with students in inclusive settings by visiting the IRIS Center Resources
  - Explore Assignments and Activities, assignable exercises showing concepts in action through video, cases, and student and teacher artifacts
  - Practice and strengthen skills essential to quality teaching through the Building Teaching Skills and Dispositions lessons

16

Teaching Students with Special Needs in Secondary Schools

CHAPTER OBJECTIVES

After reading this chapter, you should be able to:

1. Describe the secondary education curriculum.
2. Discuss the programs for students with disabilities in secondary schools.
3. Describe the key methods needed to facilitate success for students with special needs in the general education classroom.

JIM just turned 17 years old. While he seemed extremely happy about reaching this milestone in his life, his personality began to change. He gradually went from an easy-going eleventh-grade student to one who was more oppositional, lashing out occasionally at other students and teachers. Although he had always been close to his parents, they were having similiar problems with Jim at home. He wanted to stay in his room most of the time and was unusually resistant to helping around the house or talking about what was going on at school. He sat for hours pretending to do homework without making much progress, and his grades began to drop. In the past Jim had welcomed his parents' assistance in reading difficult content material, but now when they tried to help, he became agitated and refused the assistance. During a teacher–parent conference, it was decided that Jim needed counseling. After a bit of cajoling, an appointment was scheduled, and several sessions later, the counselor was able to get Jim to express his feelings. He was becoming overwhelmed by all of the "unknowns" in his life!

His driving test was coming up and he was afraid he would not be able to pass the written test, especially the part where he had to read a map. He had passed only the math and science portions of the exit exam; now reading and language were scheduled in the spring and he questioned whether he could make high enough scores to pass. Also, could he pass the academic courses that he needs to graduate? Would he go to college? What should he major in? Would someone be available to help in college, like his teachers and parents have helped in high school?

At least now the IEP team—and Jim—had the concerns identified. What could be done to help?

In a family session, Jim agreed to continue meeting with the counselor to explore these feelings, and a midyear IEP meeting was scheduled that included the counselor, general and special education teachers, Jim's parents, a vocational rehabilitation counselor, and Jim. The teacher agreed to teach Jim's skills in self-advocacy so he could access agencies and develop a network of support in his upcoming life after high school. The vocational rehabilitation counselor agreed to send Jim for a vocational assessment to determine his strengths, interests, and challenges. She also suggested that during the school breaks for the remaining year and a half, Jim job-shadow adults whose jobs held an interest for him. His parents agreed to work more with Jim on driving to obtain his permanent license, and the school assigned a driving instructor to add support and assist Jim in requesting accommodations for taking the written driving test. Insightful counselors, teachers, and parents, and a "relieved" student, turned this story into a positive ending.

QUESTIONS TO CONSIDER

1. What adolescent characteristics is Jim displaying?
2. What role did Jim's parents play in developing Jim's problems and solutions?
3. How did the legal requirement for a transition component of the IEP help Jim?
4. What could parents and teachers have done throughout Jim's school years to help prepare him to understand and address his transition challenges more effectively?

Secondary school can be a stressful setting for students with and without disabilities. Significant differences exist between elementary and secondary settings in terms of organizational structure, curricula, and learner characteristics. These differences create special challenges for successful inclusion. Certainly one concern is the gap found between the demands of the classroom setting and academics and the ability of many students with disabilities. Academically, this gap widens; many students with disabilities exhibit limited basic skills, study skills, and strategies, and therefore experience difficulty in performing higher-

FIGURE 16.1	Secondary Setting Demands

- Students need to be able to read a wide variety of content areas independently with fluidity and speed.
- Students are expected to have prerequisite content knowledge and skills.
- Students need to be able to learn from teachers who use lecture as their standard format and use a fast pace for introduction of new material.
- Students need to be able to learn with less contact time with the teachers than they had in elementary school (e.g., 50 minutes/day versus 350 minutes/day).
- Students need to have strong written language skills.
- Students need to be able to work independently with little immediate feedback or correction.
- Students need to be able to determine the importance of what is being said and take notes in a format that can be used later for review.
- Students need to be able to break a long-term task into parts, and complete each part prior to the due date.
- Students need to be able to keep track of their materials, their class requirements, and their schedules.
- Students are expected to pass high-stakes testing.

Source: From *Teaching Students with Mild- and High-Incidence Disabilities at the Secondary Level* (3rd ed., p. 6), by E. J. Sabornie and L. U. deBettencourt, 2009. Upper Saddle River, NJ: Merrill.

level cognitive tasks. Many will continue to need special education services. Figure 16.1 provides a list of the demands placed on students in a secondary setting.

A second concern is that teachers are often trained primarily as content specialists, yet are expected to present complex material in such a way that a diverse group of students can master the information. Secondary teachers are more likely to focus on teaching the content than on individualizing instruction to meet the unique needs of each student. Further, because there may be reluctance to differentiate grading systems or make other accommodations, it may become difficult for students with disabilities to experience success in general education settings.

A third challenge is the general nature of adolescence. Adolescence is a difficult and trying time for all young people, a developmental stage marked by dramatic psychological, physical and social changes (Sabornie & deBettencourt, 2009). For students with disabilities, the developmental period is even more challenging. Problems such as a lack of motivation associated with adolescence are exacerbated by the presence of a disability. Adolescents should be valued partners in all aspects of planning and implementing their instructional programs.

A fourth problem is the ongoing movement to reform schools, making high school more rigorous. For example, these changes may mean that all students will have to take more math and science courses or achieve a passing grade on a minimum competency test; students who do not pass these exams may receive a certificate of attendance or completion instead of a diploma. Such requirements may prove difficult to meet for many students who experience learning and behavior problems. As requirements increase in the core requirements, it becomes even more difficult to find class time to prepare students with disabilities for the challenges that they are going to face after high school as they transition to postsecondary education and/or employment, and pursue independent living.

Regardless of the difficulties associated with placing adolescents with special needs in general education programs, more students with disabilities are going to depend on their teachers in these classes to help develop and provide appropriate educational programs. Therefore, general education teachers and special education personnel in secondary schools must be prepared to collaborate to offer differentiated instructional opportunities in the core curriculum and to address transitional needs in order for these special students to benefit from their placement in general education settings.

Visit the MyEducationLab for this course to enhance your understanding of chapter concepts with a personalized Study Plan. You'll also have the opportunity to hone your teaching skills through video-based Assignments and Activities, IRIS Center Resources, and Building Teaching Skills and Disposition lessons.

SECONDARY EDUCATION CURRICULA

More curricular differentiation has been advocated at the secondary level to accommodate the individual needs and interests of the wide variety of students attending comprehensive high schools in the United States. At the same time, most high schools have a general curriculum that all students must complete to obtain a diploma. This curriculum, generally prescribed by the state education agency, includes science, math, social studies, and English. Often, state and local education agencies add areas such as art education, sexuality, drug education, and foreign languages to the required general curriculum.

Students have opportunities to choose curricular alternatives that are usually related to post-high-school goals. For example, students planning to go to college choose a college preparatory focus that builds on the general curriculum with higher-level academic courses and often the study of a foreign language. This college preparatory option helps prepare students for the rigorous courses found at college. Other students choose a vocational program, designed to help prepare them for specific job opportunities after high school. Still other students choose a general curriculum, with some course choices for students who would be willing to enter a variety of job fields not requiring postsecondary training. The curricular focus that students choose should be an important consideration because the decision could have long-term implications after the student exits school.

Special Education Curriculum in Secondary Schools

The curriculum for students with disabilities is the most critical programming consideration in secondary schools. Even if students have excellent teachers, if the curriculum is inappropriate to meet their needs, the teaching may be ineffective and students will not benefit from their education. The high-school curriculum for students with disabilities must be comprehensive. That is, it must:

- Be responsive to the needs and interests of individual students
- Facilitate maximum integration with nondisabled peers
- Facilitate socialization
- Focus on the students' transition to postsecondary settings

Determining Curricular Needs of Students

The curriculum for any student should be based on an appraisal of desired long-term outcomes and an assessment of current needs and selected to meet the individual needs of students. However, the dropout data for students with disabilities suggest that the needs of many of these students are not being met. Although the data on school completion reported from the National Longitudinal Transition Study has improved over the years, 28% of all students with disabilities are leaving high school without a regular diploma or certificate of completion (not a highly valued diploma). Students with behavioral-emotional disabilities have the lowest completion rate of 56%, still a 16% improvement from the original studies in 1987 (SRI, 2005). An important study by Bridgeland, DiIulio, & Morison (2006) found that there was no single reason identified for leaving school; however, the majority responded that the classes were not interesting. When asked what would have kept them in school, 81% cited teachers that kept learning interesting, and 81% wished for real-world learning opportunities with more time focused on the connection between school and work.

Unfortunately, school dropout rate is also tied to negative adult outcomes. Dropouts are more likely to be unemployed, receive public funds, live in poverty, serve a prison term, be divorced, and live an unhealthy lifestyle. Further, a noncompleter is estimated to earn an average of $9,200 a year less than their peers with a high-school diploma and a million dollars less across a lifetime of earnings compared to age peers who are college graduates (Bridgeland et al., 2006). Regardless of the efforts made in secondary schools to meet the individual needs of students with disabilities, many of these students seem unprepared to achieve success as young adults.

The Need for Transition Planning   To facilitate the planning process that would allow students with disabilities to have the optimum chance at success in their lives after high school, IDEA 2004 strengthened the transition planning process, and made it an essential responsibility for the IEP team and a continued legal requirement (see the Rights & Responsibilities feature).

The transition component of the IEP should focus on academic and functional achievement; the development helps individuals and their families focus on the future, building a bridge to further vocational training, a community or 4-year college education, or obtaining employment and living as independently as possible in a community. In the opening scenario, Jim's IEP team developed his Individualized Transition Plan (ITP) to support his desire to attend a community college after high school and to obtain his driver's license. To be successful, Jim also needed to gain an understanding of his legal rights and develop self-advocacy skills. He should be leading his IEP meeting! The transition portion of Jim's IEP is presented nearby.

When planning for a successful transition for a student, it is important to guide the student's thinking regarding his or her needs and preferences. Figure 16.2 contains interview questions that can assist the team in gathering the information that leads to transition goals.

A team of professionals, generally including a general and special education teacher, a vocational teacher, a representative from the local education agency and appropriate adult agencies, and the student's parents participate in developing the plan, but the student should be an active participant and, when possible, should lead the IEP meeting. His or her role might include planning the meeting, sending invitations, preparing the room, presenting his or her interests and goals, proposing activities, and interacting with parents and other team members to identify the objectives and activities that will most likely lead to the desired outcome (Steere & Cavaioulo, 2002). Teachers can then hold mock IEP meetings and provide feedback before the day of the actual meeting. The IEP team can identify services needed in a variety of categories including employment, living arrangements, leisure/recreational, transportation, financial services, postsecondary education, assistive technology, and medical services.

The overriding goal of the IEP and the ITP for secondary students is to achieve personal fulfillment as an adult. Every student's ITP will be tailored to individual needs; to be successful, students should identify and use all *needed* services and supports available to them. For some students that will include community agencies that will help them meet the demands of adulthood at their maximum potential. It is important to know the

RIGHTS & RESPONSIBILITIES

IDEA 2004: TRANSITION SERVICES

In 1990, with the reauthorization of the Individuals with Disabilities Education Act, transition became a critical mandate and component of the law. This mandate requires that schools provide a process for planning for students' attainment of future postschool outcomes through the development of an appropriate educational course of study. IDEA 2004 describes transition services as a coordinated set of activities for a student, designed within a results-oriented process, that is focused on improving the academic and functional achievement of the child with the disability to facilitate the child's movement from school to postschool activities, including postsecondary education, vocational training, integrated employment (including supported employment), continuing and adult education, adult services, independent living, and community participation. The coordinated set of activities is based on the individual child's needs, taking into account the child's strengths, preferences, and interests, and

includes instruction, community experiences, the development of employment and other postschool adult living objectives, and, when appropriate, acquisition of daily living skills and provision of a functional vocational evaluation [602(34)].

Transition Services
The IEP must include—

- For each student, with a disability beginning at age 16 (or younger if determined appropriate by the IEP team) appropriate, measurable postsecondary goals based upon age-appropriate transition assessments related to training, education, employment, and where appropriate, independent living skills.

- The transition services (including courses of study) needed to assist the child in reaching those goals [602(d)(1)(a–b)].

JIM'S IEP: TRANSITION

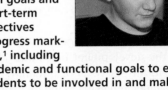

| Unique educational needs, characteristics, and measured present levels of academic achievement and functional performance (PLOPs). | Special education, related services and supplemental aids and services (based on peer-reviewed research to the extent practicable); assistive technology and modifications or personnel support. | Measurable annual goals and short-term objectives (progress markers),[1] including academic and functional goals to enable students to be involved in and make progress in the general curriculum and to meet other needs resulting from the disability. |

(Including how the disability affects student's ability to participate and progress in the general curriculum.)

(Including anticipated starting date, frequency, duration, and location for each.)

(Including progress measurement method for each goal.)

Instruction

Self-advocacy PLOP: Jim is unaware of his legal rights under Section 504 and ADA, and he is unable to request appropriate accommodations he would need in given situations, such as a large lecture class. He becomes embarrassed and anxious when discussing his disability and its affects on his school performance, and he becomes angry or tries to change the subject.

Community

Driver's license PLOP: Jim has been driving for a year on a learner's permit and is concerned that he cannot pass the written test required for his license, although he is confident of all his driving and related skills except map reading.

Employment and other

Not needed at this time. Jim intends to enroll in the computer network support program at Leland Community College (LCC) and is on track for a regular diploma. He is a tech lab assistant this year and is doing very well.

1. Small-group instruction from special ed teacher in relevant rights, procedures, and remedies under Section 504, ADA, and IDEA
   - Role playing in describing needed accommodations to employers, professors, and other adult life figures of authority.
   - Services to begin Tuesday, Sept. 15; two thirty-minute sessions weekly until goals are met.
   - (L&R) Protection and Advocacy will assist teacher and provide materials at no cost. (Verified by phone—M. Adams)
   - LCC Office of Disability Services will meet with Jim to set up an accommodation plan. (Verified by phone—S. Holvey)

2. Within two weeks from the date of this IEP, the driver training instructor will inform Jim about accommodations available in the state, if any, for licensing people with reading disabilities. Then she and Jim will develop a plan to follow through and that plan will be added to this IEP no later than Oct. 10.
   - (L&R) DMV will assist instructor and will provide information on test accommodations. (Verified by phone—J. Hill)
   - Instruction in map reading and route highlighting.

Goal 1: Given a 25-item objective test over basic rights and procedures under Section 504 and ADA, Jim will pass with a score of 75% or better.

Goal 2: In hypothetical role-play scenarios of disability-based discrimination, Jim will calmly and accurately explain to an employer, professor, or other representative of the postschool world his rights and remedies under Section 504 and ADA.

Goal 3: Given a real-world meeting with the Director of Disability Services at LCC, Jim will describe the effect of his disability in a school situation and will explain what accommodations help him to meet expectations.

Goal 4: Jim will become a competent driver in Jefferson state and will take the licensing exam on March 15. By March 1, given a practice exam administered under real-world conditions, Jim will score at least 70 percent.

Goal 5: Given a city map, Jim will accurately highlight six common routes he routinely follows and four routes he will use next year, when he is attending LCC, e.g., from his home to the mall, from his home to LCC, etc.

[1]For students who take an alternative assessment and are assessed against other than grade-level standards, the IEP must include short-term objectives (progress markers). For other students, the IEP may include short-term objectives. The IEP must—for all students—clearly articulate how the student's progress will be measured, and that progress must be reported to parents at designated intervals.

Source: From *Better IEPs: How To Develop Legally Correct and Educationally Useful Programs* (p. 145), by B. D. Bateman and M. A. Linden, 2007 Verona, WI: Attainment.

FIGURE 16.2	Sample Interview Questions

Profile and Family Life
- Tell me about yourself (age, where you live, etc.).
- Tell me about your family.
- Do your parents work?
- What kind of work does your father/mother do?
- Do you have brothers or sisters who work?
- What kind of work do they do?
- Have you always lived here, or did you move here?
- Tell me about the neighborhood that you live in.

Interests and Hobbies
- What do you like to do in your free time?
- What are your hobbies and interests?
- What do you like to do on weekends?
- Tell me about some enjoyable vacations that you have had.

School
- What are your favorite subjects in school?
- What are your least favorite subjects?
- Who are your friends in school?
- What do you like best about school? What do you like least?
- Are you involved in any extracurricular activities?

Finances
- Do you have a bank account?
- Do you earn an allowance?
- Do you know how to write a check?
- Do you know how to use a credit card/debit card?
- Do you know about costs such as electric service, phone service, and gas?

Mobility
- How do you get around your community?
- Where do you like to go?
- Do you have a driver's license or are you planning on getting one?

Employment
- Have you ever had a job?
- If you were going to get a summer job, what kind of job would you look for?
- What skills do you feel that you could build a career on?
- What are your interests in terms of employment?

Postsecondary Education
- Are you planning to go to college?
- If so, have you considered a major?
- Did anyone else in your family go to college?
- Have you ever visited a college campus?

Community Living
- Do you know how to cook?
- Do you do any chores at home? If so, what chores?
- Do you know how much it costs to rent an apartment?
- Do you like living with others?
- Do you like privacy?
- Do you know what to do if there is an emergency in your home?

Future Aspirations
- What do you see yourself doing in five years?
- What careers do you plan on exploring, and why?
- What steps do you feel you need to take now to help prepare you for your future career?
- Who could help you take the steps you described in the previous question, and how might they help you?

Source: From *Growing Up: Transition to Adult Life for Students with Disabilities* (pp. 37–38), by D. E. Steere, E. Rose, and D. Cavaiuolo, 2007. Boston: Allyn & Bacon.

collaborative role of each of these agencies and the requirements to qualify for services. Unlike the government-sponsored opportunity for all students to attend school (referred to as an entitlement program), receipt of services from many of the adult agencies are based on meeting eligibility requirements. For a list of agencies and a description of services, see Table 16.1.

Many challenges face educators as they try to implement methods to meet transition service needs of students with disabilities. High expectations must be maintained and students must remain on a full curriculum track, with additional opportunities as appropriate in vocational education, community work experience, service learning, and adult living skills (Johnson, 2002). A survey by Dunn, Chambers, and Rabren (2004) found that only 54% of students interviewed who had dropped out of school reported that school prepared them for what they wanted to do after high school; this was compared to 80% of students who did not drop out. Often when the curriculum fails a student, a favorite teacher can make the difference; however, these interviewers reported that 23% of the

TABLE 16.1

Common Community Agencies and the Transition Services They May Offer

AGENCY/PROGRAM* (PURPOSE AND FUNDING SOURCE)	EXAMPLES OF EMPLOYMENT SERVICES	EXAMPLES OF POSTSECONDARY EDUCATION SERVICES	EXAMPLES OF ADULT AND INDEPENDENT LIVING SERVICES
Vocational Rehabilitation Agency assists people with cognitive, sensory, physical, or emotional disabilities to attain employment and increased independence. Funded by federal and state money, VR agencies typically operate regional and local offices. VR services typically last for a limited period of time and are based on an individual's rehabilitation plan. If needed, an individual with disabilities can request services at a later time, and a new rehabilitation plan will be developed.	• Vocational guidance and counseling • Medical, psychological, vocational, and other types of assessments to determine vocational potential • Job development, placement, and follow-up services • Rehabilitation, technological services and adaptive devices, tools, equipment, and supplies	• Apprenticeship programs, usually in conjunction with Department of Labor • Vocational training • College training toward a vocational goal as part of an eligible student's financial aid package	• Housing or transportation supports needed to maintain employment • Interpreter services • Orientation and mobility services
Mental Health and Mental Retardation Agencies provide a comprehensive system of services responsive to the needs of individuals with mental illness or mental retardation. Federal, state, and local funding are used to operate regional offices; local funding is often the primary source. Services are provided on a sliding payment scale.	• Supported and sheltered employment • Competitive employment support for those who need minimal assistance		• Case management services to access and obtain local services • Therapeutic recreation, including day activities, clubs, and programs • Respite care • Residential services (group homes and supervised apartments)
Independent Living Centers help people with disabilities to achieve and maintain self-sufficient lives within the community. Operated locally, ILCs serve a particular region. ILCs may charge for classes, but advocacy services are typically available at no cost.	• Information and referral services • Connecting students with mentors with disabilities	• Advocacy training • Connecting students with mentors with disabilities	• Advocacy training • Auxiliary social services (e.g., maintaining a list of personal care attendants) • Peer counseling services • Housing assistance • Training in skills of independent living (attendant management, housing, transportation, career development) • Information and referral services • Connecting with mentors
Social Security Administration operates the federally funded program that provides benefits for people of any age who are unable to do substantial work and have a severe mental or physical disability. Several programs are offered for people with disabilities, including Social Security Disability Insurance (SSDI), Supplemental Security Income (SSI), Plans to Achieve Self-Support (PASS), Medicaid, and Medicare.	Work incentive programs which may include: • Cash benefits while working (e.g., student-earned income) • Medicare or Medicaid while working • Help with any extra work expenses the individual has as a result of the disability • Assistance to start a new line of work	• Financial incentives for further education and training	• Medical benefits • Can use income as basis for purchase or rental of housing

*Names of agencies or programs may differ slightly from state to state.

Source: From *Transition Planning: A Team Effort* (pp. 4–5), by S. H. de Fur, 2002. Washington, DC: NICHCY.

students who had dropped out responded that no one was helpful during their high-school program. Only 8% of those who did *not* drop out were *unable* to identify a helpful person.

Several have questioned the impact that heavy teacher workloads have had on the educational experiences of students. With the multiple tasks expected of both general and special education teachers, it is no wonder that there are many references in the literature to teacher burnout and attrition that will eventually impact student achievement (Wasburn-Moses, 2005). School personnel must prioritize the research needed to streamline teacher responsibilities and roles so that teachers can stay dedicated and physically and mentally healthy. One thing that can help is the collaboration between special and general education and other agencies to meet the needs of students.

PROGRAMS FOR STUDENTS WITH DISABILITIES IN SECONDARY SCHOOLS

Most secondary students with disabilities are currently included in general education classrooms for at least a portion of each school day. Therefore, the responsibility for these students becomes a joint effort between general education classroom teachers and special education personnel. Unfortunately, many of these students do not experience success in the general classroom setting. They frequently fail classes, become frustrated and act out, and may even drop out of school because they are not prepared to meet the demands placed on them by secondary teachers. Numerous reasons have been given as to why many students with disabilities fail in secondary classes. Notice that the explanations provided in the following list include placing the blame on general education teachers, special education personnel, and the students themselves:

- Lack of communication between special education personnel and classroom teachers
- Discrepancies between the expectations of classroom teachers and the abilities of students
- Students' lack of understanding about the demands of the classroom
- Classroom teachers' lack of understanding about students with disabilities
- Special education personnel's lack of knowledge about working with classroom teachers
- School policies that are inflexible

Figure 16.3 displays the frequent mismatch between the characteristics of students with disabilities and the academic and setting demands of high school.

Regardless of the reasons why some students with disabilities do not achieve success in general education settings, the fact remains that the majority will be taught in inclusive settings. Therefore, classroom teachers and special education personnel must improve their skills in working collaboratively to increase the chances that these students will be successful.

Collaborative Role of General Education Teachers   The primary role of general classroom teachers is to assume the responsibility for teaching content in particular classes or subject areas; they also have general responsibilities that include managing the classroom environment, providing instruction at an appropriate level and pace, using an appropriate curriculum, evaluating student success, and modifying instruction as appropriate. Most classroom teachers prefer to present new information to students using a technique that they feel confident implementing, one that compliments their own strengths and preferred learning style. To teach students with special needs effectively, teachers need to expand their instructional strategies as needed by individual students to differentiate the learning environment, the content, the techniques used to introduce students to new information, the methods the students are allowed to use to process that information, and the procedures/products used to measure that learning has occurred.

When teaching content courses, such as history and science, teachers should give students with disabilities the same opportunities to learn that they give other students,

> ### FIGURE 16.3 — Mismatch Between School Demands and Learner Characteristics
>
> **School Demands**
> - Gain information from lectures
> - Acquire information through secondary textbooks
> - Demonstrate knowledge through tests
> - Express information in writing
> - Use higher order thinking skills
> - Interact appropriately
> - Demonstrate motivation to learn
>
> **Characteristics of Learners**
> - Academic deficits
> - Thinking/reasoning deficits
> - Learning strategy deficits
> - Study skills deficits
> - Social interaction deficits
> - Motivation deficits
>
> *Source:* Adapted from *Students with Learning Disabilities* (7th ed., p. 532), by C. D. Mercer and P. C. Pullen, 2009, Upper Saddle River, NJ: Pearson.

remembering that the students with special needs would not be placed in the general classroom setting if the interdisciplinary team had not determined that he or she could benefit from that environment. In addition, teachers should ensure that all students have an opportunity to answer questions and a good chance to achieve at least moderate success in classroom activities. This is not a call for teachers to "give" students with disabilities passing grades, only a requirement that students with disabilities receive an equal chance at being successful through the use of differentiation strategies.

Within the classroom, teachers can do several things that will facilitate the success of students with disabilities. They must remember that students with disabilities, as well as those without disabilities, have different learning styles and needs, and therefore require, from time to time, some alteration of instruction. However, some basic principles of good teaching apply to all students. These are listed in Figure 16.4.

Salend (2008, p. 326) poses the following questions that teachers can use to develop specific teaching plans and to differentiate instruction successfully:

What are the themes or goals of the lesson?
What resources/materials will be used in teaching?
For how long and when will the activity or lesson occur?
Will students with and without disabilities participate in the same way?

■ General education teachers work collaboratively with special education personnel to develop and provide differentiated learning opportunities.

What technology, learning strategies, support, and accommodations might be needed to assure full participation?
Does the curriculum need to be modified or supplemented?
How can the activity or lesson be differentiated to address the students' interests, abilities, challenges, learning styles, language, cultural experiences, behavioral needs, and IEPs?

What Instructional Practices Are Best?

Kauffman, Mostert, Trent, and Hallahan (2002) suggest that good teaching (best instructional practice) is characterized by the following (and they provide a mnemonic, consisting of the first letters of each point—CLOCS-RAM—(for remembering the points)

1. *Clarity*—The student must know exactly what to do (i.e., have no doubt about what is expected).
2. *Level*—The student must be able to do the task with a high degree of accuracy (i.e., be able to get *at least* 80 percent correct), but the task must be challenging (i.e., the student should not easily get 100 percent correct repeatedly).
3. *Opportunities*—The student must have frequent opportunities to

respond (i.e., be actively engaged in the task a high percentage of the time).
4. *Consequences*—The student must receive a meaningful reward for correct performance (i.e., the consequences of correct performance must be frequent and perceived as desirable by the student).
5. *Sequence*—The tasks must be presented in logical sequence so that the student gets the big idea (i.e., steps must be presented and learned in order that the knowledge or skill is built on a logical progression or framework of ideas, which is a systematic curriculum).
6. *Relevance*—The task must be relevant to the student's life and, if possible, the student understands

how and why it is useful (i.e., the teacher attempts to help the student see why the task is important in the culture).
7. *Application*—The teacher helps the student learn how to learn and remember by teaching memory and learning strategies and applying knowledge and skills to everyday problems (i.e., teaches generalizations, not just isolated skills, and honors the student's culture).
8. *Monitoring*—The teacher continuously monitors student progress (i.e., records and charts progress and always knows and can show what the student has mastered and the student's place or level in a curriculum or sequence of tasks).

Source: From *Managing Classroom Behavior: A Reflective Case-Based Approach* (3rd ed., p. 7), by J. M. Kauffman et al., 2002. Boston: Allyn & Bacon. Copyright © 2002 by Pearson Education. Reprinted by permission of the publisher.

Do the students have choices? Is an additional motivational technique needed to increase interest and length of time in engagement?

Does the environment need to be differentiated to facilitate engagement?

What is the most effective method to evaluate content mastery?

Various accommodations and adaptations in instructional intervention and methods and materials that are useful in the learning process will be discussed later in the chapter.

Effective teachers constantly evaluate the impact of their teaching efforts. Figure 16.5 contains helpful questions to use for these self-reflections.

Teachers must also think carefully about how realistic their expectations are of students. Schumm, Vaughn, and Leavell (1994) developed the planning pyramid, which allows teachers to identify different degrees of learning to address individual needs and abilities. The philosophy is that all students will learn something but not all students will learn everything. Figure 16.6 shows a planning hierarchy developed for a science class; this format is helpful as it also provides teachers with a form to document the materials, instructional strategies/adaptations, and evaluations/products used in the lesson.

Both special education and general education teachers should do all they can to work effectively together. Open communication and dialogue is crucial if inclusion is to be successful. Communication among all individuals providing services to students with disabilities is the most important factor related to the success of inclusion.

Collaborative Role of the Special Education Teacher

The special education teacher plays an important role in the successful inclusion of students with disabilities in secondary schools. In addition to collaborating with general educators regarding curricula decisions, the special education teacher brings expertise in designing differentiated instruction and assessment strategies, classroom management techniques for the whole-class and for individuals, and knowledge of the legal requirements both educators must follow (Sabornie & deBettencourt, 2009). They may also provide direct instruction

FIGURE 16.5   Questions for Evaluating the Instructional Process

- *Student motivation*—Am I creating a context in which learning is valued?
- *Student attention*—Am I creating an environment in which students can and are encouraged to attend to the learning task?
- *Encouragement*—Am I creating a setting in which students are encouraged to take risks and be challenged by learning?
- *Modeling*—Are the students given the opportunity to watch, listen, and talk to others so that they can see how the knowledge or skill is learned?
- *Activating prior knowledge*—Am I getting the students to think about what they already know about a skill or topic, and are they given the opportunity to build upon that information in an organized fashion?
- *Rate, amount, and manner of presentation*—Are the new skills and knowledge being presented at a rate and amount that allows the students time to learn, and in a manner that gives them enough information yet does not overload them?
- *Practice*—Are the students given ample opportunity to practice?
- *Feedback*—Are the students given feedback on their work so they know how and what they are learning?
- *Acquisition*—Are the students given the opportunity to learn skills and knowledge until they feel comfortable with them and to the point they do or know something almost automatically?
- *Maintenance*—Are the students given the opportunity to continue to use their skills and knowledge so that they can serve as tools for further learning?
- *Generalization*—Are the students generalizing the skills and knowledge to other tasks, settings, and situations? Are the students, other teachers, or parents seeing the learning?
- *Application*—Are the students given the opportunity to apply their skills and knowledge in new and novel situations, thereby adapting their skills to meet the new learning experiences?

Source: From *Strategies for Teaching Students with Learning and Behavior Problems* (5th ed., p. 26), by C. S. Bos and S. Vaughn, 2002. Boston: Allyn & Bacon.

in areas not addressed in the general education curriculum and areas that support inclusive learning; these include preparing students for the challenges that occur daily in the general education environment and equipping them for future challenges in their lives after high school. Above all, special education teachers play a major support role for general classroom teachers. They should communicate regularly with classroom teachers and provide assistance through consultation or through direct instruction.

The specific roles of the special education teacher discussed further include counseling students for the personal crises that may occur daily and preparing students for content classes, the high-school graduation exam, postsecondary education, independent living, and, ultimately, employment. Special education teachers, general teachers, guidance counselors, vocational education teachers, and individuals from other agencies often collaborate in performing these roles.

Counseling for Daily Crises   Adolescence is a difficult time of change for all children. For children with disabilities, the period is even more challenging as they carry the joy and sorrow of adolescence as well as the stigma of a disability (Sabornie & deBettencourt, 2009). In U.S. society, students face the challenge of identifying career and life goals during a time of tremendous physical and social change. They also experience more exposure to drugs and alcohol as well as the possibility of school dropout, sexually transmitted diseases, depression, pregnancy, and AIDS. The increased tension, frustration, and depression can lead to a variety of behavior and emotional problems or suicide, the third-leading cause of death among adolescents and the leading cause of death in college students (Aseltine & DeMartino, 2004).

Special education teachers need to collaborate with general educators to help students deal with these problems. One innovative program being tried to increase access to the general education program and provide a support system for students with moderate or severe disabilities is the peer support program (Copeland et al., 2004). A student with a disability and a student without are partnered for shared activities that might be academic (e.g., tutoring functional academics and life skills) or nonacademic (e.g., "hanging out" between

FIGURE 16.6

A planning pyramid for a middle-school science lesson on weathering and erosion.

UNIT PLANNING FORM

Date: *Sept 1—30*   Class Period: *1.30—2.30*
Unit Title: *Weathering and Erosion*

What some students will learn.	• *How Earth looked during Ice Age* • *Disasters caused by sudden changes* • *Geographic examples of slow and fast changes*
What most students will learn.	• *Compare and contrast weathering and erosion* • *How humans cause physical and chemical weathering* • *Basic types of racks*
What ALL Students Should Learn.	• *Basic components of Earth's surface* • *Forces that change crust are weathering and erosion*

Materials/Resources:
Guest speaker on volcanoes
Video erosion and weathering
Rack samples
Library books — disasters, rock volcanoes, etc.
Colored transparencies for lectures

Instructional Strategies/Adaptations:
Concept maps
Cooperative learning groups to learn material in textbook
Audiotapes of chapter
Study buddies to prepare for quizzes and tests

Evaluation/Products:
Weekly quiz
Unit test
Learning logs (daily record of "What I learned)"
Vocabulary flask

Source: From *Teaching students who are exceptional, diverse, and at-risk in the general education classroom* (4th ed., p. 218) by S. Vaughn, C. Bos, & J. Schuum, 2007. Boston: Pearson.

classes and attending sporting events). The nondisabled peers report that the experience improved their knowledge of disabilities and allowed them to develop a friendship rather than simply offering help. It also gave them experience in advocating for someone else, gave them feelings of accomplishment, and was fun. The effect for students with disabilities is a decrease in alienation, a common problem for adolescents, especially those with disabilities (Brown, Higgins, & Paulsen, 2003). It is important for teachers to develop a nonthreatening classroom atmosphere where anxiety about learning is reduced and open lines of communication are maintained (Schloss, Schloss, & Schloss, 2007).

Preparing for High-School Content Classes   Inclusion in general education classes is extremely beneficial to students as they practice social skills in real-world environments and build friendships that can last a lifetime; however, inclusion also presents significant learning and behavioral challenges. The special education teacher should be aware of factors such as classroom teacher expectations, teaching styles, and the demands of the learning environment. One way special education teachers can help students deal with the "general education world" is to teach them how to self-advocate. To do so, students need to understand their specific learning problems. Special education teachers may need to have a discussion with students about the nature of their specific disabilities, because it is not uncommon for students in high school to have little understanding of their disability or the type of assistance they are receiving as a result. When asked if they receive special education services, they may respond with an honest "No, I just go to the resource class if I need help." This lack of information is not helpful when the longtime support in public school is removed.

Special educators must also communicate with their general education partners as to the unique abilities and challenges presented by each student, as well as the contents and provisions of each IEP. Their role also includes providing ongoing support and collaboration for the student and teacher, and frequent monitoring to ensure that the arrangement is satisfactory for both the student and the teacher.

Lenz and Deshler (2004) propose that effective teaching is based on making meaningful connections between teachers and students, students and students, and students and the content they need to learn. They challenge teachers to understand what their students already know as a result of prior learning as well as their life experiences, and to select content that is based on the general education standards but also is relevant to their future life goals. Finally, they recommend compensating for students' learning problems by using scientific research-based teaching methods to enhance instruction and explicitly teach students how to use and develop learning strategies so students learn how to learn. These strategies have been highlighted throughout the text and will be addressed again later in this chapter. An example of an effective strategy to help students prepare for and perform at their maximum level in a content area class is presented in Figure 16.7.

Preparing for the High-School Graduation Exam   Passing a high-school graduation exam as a requirement for receiving a regular diploma began in many states in the 1980s as part of the national reform movements in education. Students with disabilities may or may not be required to take the exam, depending on state regulations and local school district policies. In some states, students with disabilities are granted a regular high-school diploma without having to complete the examination; in others, students with disabilities who do not pass this "high-stakes" assessment are only awarded a certification of attendance or completion, even if they have passed all required classes.

One positive use of exit exam data is the identification of students who would continue to benefit from intense, direct instruction in scientific research-based intervention in reading, math or written expression. This is often the time that families and educators wish that remediation of basic skills had continued after elementary school, as these struggling readers are further penalized as they attempt to pass science, social studies, and even math sections of this written exam. High-school personnel can use this data and the results of standardized testing to implement RTI at the secondary level. A student's schedule can be adjusted to include one period a day of Tier II or Tier III level of instruction.

Special education teachers, in conjunction with classroom teachers, have two roles regarding the high-school graduation exam. On one hand, they are obligated to help the student prepare for the exam if it is the decision of the IEP team that the student should participate in this schoolwide assessment. On the other hand, the special education and general education classroom teachers may choose to focus on convincing the student and parents that time could more appropriately be spent on developing functional skills rather than on preparing for the graduation exam.

Preparing for Postsecondary Training   Students with disabilities should absolutely be encouraged to aim for a postsecondary education if they have the ability and motivation. One survey reported differences in positive outcomes in employment rates, salaries, and employment satisfaction between students with learning disabilities with and without postsecondary degrees (Madaus, Ruban, Foley, & McGuire, 2003). The National Council on Disability (2004) emphasized this in its 2002–2003 progress report:

> With unemployment among persons with disabilities remaining stubbornly high despite a variety of federal initiatives and public-private partnerships designed to improve the situation, and with long-term job prospects and income potential for people without college education looking increasingly grim, it should be more apparent than ever before that,

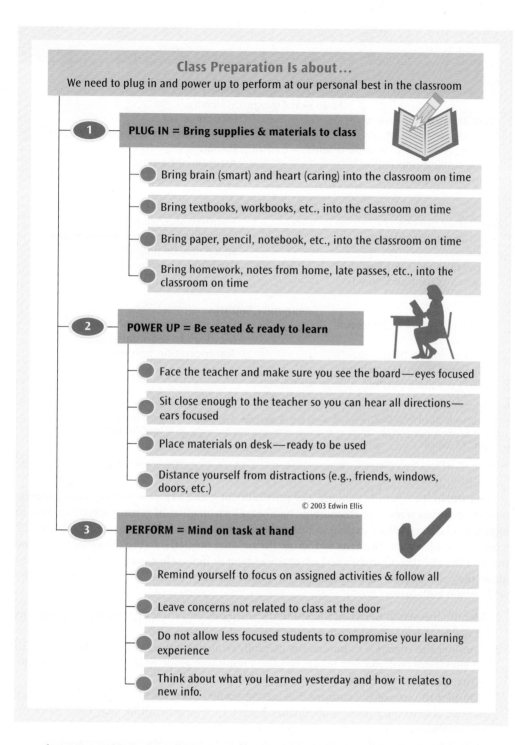

FIGURE 16.7

Sample hierarchic flowchart used to teach class preparation.

Source: From "Graphic Organizers: Tools to Build Behavioral Literacy and Foster Emotional Competency," by M. L, Rock, 2004, *Intervention in School and Clinic, 40*(1), p. 24.

wherever possible, higher education is key to the economic prospects and aspirations for independence of youth with disabilities. (p. 68)

Postsecondary education does not have to mean attending a 4-year institution. A community college, vocational-technical school, trade school/apprenticeships, or some other form of postsecondary education and training are other possibilities. Teachers, both general and special education, need to inform students about future employment trends and help them select a realistic career with employment potential. A variety of reports regarding the importance of education in the future for students with and without disabilities have concluded that very few jobs will be available for individuals deficient in reading, writing, and math. Technology will also play an increasing role for all individuals. Figure 16.8 provides the pros and cons of postsecondary options and community living.

FIGURE 16.8	Location Pros and Cons

Pros	Cons
Four-Year College/University	
Wide array of coursework	Less prevalent
Many clubs/organizations	Admissions and application process
Social sciences/medical departments	Tuition
Stable student population	Attitudinal barriers
Residential possibilities	
Community College	
Open-door policies	Transient student population
Nontraditional students	Limited access to potential peer support
Proximity	Space may be limited
Fellow graduates as peers	Attitudinal barriers
Lower costs (tuition waived)	
Community Settings	
Natural setting for students not going to college	Lack of access to same-age peers
Access to employment sites	May lead to segregated experiences
Daily living or social activities	Transportation barriers
Doesn't preclude possible college connections	

Source: From *Transitional Services for Students with Significant Disabilities in College and Community Settings: Strategies for Planning, Implementation and Evaluation*, p. 19 by M. Grigal, D. A. Neubert, and M. S. Moon, 2005, Austin, TX: Pro-Ed.

For Jim in the opening vignette, the possibility of going to a new school at the postsecondary level was terrifying. His parents had been instrumental in getting services set up in high school and suddenly everyone was talking to him about self-advocacy. Luckily the IEP team picked up on his concerns and wrote the training needed into the IEP. Refer to the portion of Jim's IEP that addresses self-advocacy as well as Jim's other transitional needs. Other ideas that are helpful in preparation for postsecondary education are summarized by Schloss and colleagues (2007):

1. Identify the match between the student's academic and career goals and the programs available at 2- and 4-year colleges and technical programs.
2. Consider the entrance requirements carefully. Some schools have open admission with a high-school diploma, and others require a minimum grade point average and specific scores on entrance exams.
3. Consider the size of the campus. Navigating smaller campuses may be easier, and they may be able to offer more individualized services. A larger campus may offer more extracurricular activities and a wider variety of courses.
4. Examine the cost and help the student and parents to identify financial resources.
5. Encourage families to meet with the director of the Office for Students with Disabilities to discuss services, policies, and procedures to document the disability and request appropriate accommodations. Students must also be taught self-advocacy skills so they can self-identify with their professors and talk to them before classes begin. (Madaus & Shaw, 2004)
6. Arrange for the student to shadow currently enrolled students.
7. Consider living arrangements available and begin to work with students and families to prepare for more independent living if the student will be leaving home.

With the proper documentation of need, students with disabilities may be eligible for a variety of services through their rights under Section 504 of the Rehabilitation Act of 1974; these may include such supports as tutors, note takers, books on tape, tape recording class, organizational skill remediation, early registration, speech-to-text technology, extended time on tests, test administered in a distraction reduced environment, breaks during testing, course substitutions, extended time to finish a program, and participation in support groups and counseling (Mercer & Pullen, 2009; Sabornie & deBettencourt, 2009).

Preparing for Independent Living   Independent living is a realistic goal for the vast majority of individuals with disabilities; however, for them to live successfully in today's complex, automated world, direct instruction in certain independent living skills may be required. This is also important in a student's transition program. The following areas may be problematic for people with disabilities:

- Sexuality
- Managing personal finances
- Developing and maintaining social networks
- Maintaining a home
- Managing food
- Employment
- Transportation
- Self-confidence and self-esteem
- Organization
- Time management
- Leisure activities

Special education teachers as well as general education teachers can help students with disabilities achieve competence in these areas. Although published materials are available to guide instruction in these areas, creative teachers can use community resources—gathering real materials from banks, libraries, restaurants, the local courthouse, and so forth—for developing their own program. These authentic life skills can then be infused into subjects such as math, science, or English to add interest and relevance for all students.

Preparing for Employment   The ultimate goal of all education is the employment of graduates at their maximum vocational potential. The passage of the Americans with Disabilities Act (ADA) in 1990 has made that dream a reality for millions of people with disabilities. The law encompasses areas of employment, transportation, public accommodations, and telecommunications, and prohibits discrimination against individuals with disabilities. ADA requires employers to make "reasonable accommodations" to assist people with disabilities in performing their jobs. Supported employment initiatives (i.e., providing job coaches to support workers on the job) have emerged as particularly powerful tools. Teachers need to help students prepare for employment by teaching them the necessary skills for vocational success. Inclusive vocational and technical programs in the high schools present a unique opportunity to offer students both a functional curriculum and integration with non-disabled peers. These programs can provide appropriate entry into work-study programs, community-based learning opportunities, business apprenticeships, and technical and trade school programs.

Teachers must be sure that students with disabilities can communicate their interests, strengths and limitations to persons in postsecondary and, ultimately, future employment settings. These self-determination skills will empower individuals to seek employment and independent living opportunities on their own. In best practice, encouragement and development of self-determination or self-advocacy skills begins in elementary school. Figure 16.9 provides a list of ideas for promoting self-determination in your students.

The Personal Spotlight, on page 511, tells the story of the life's journey of a young adult with severe learning disabilities and ADHD and the effects that educational exclusion and inclusive practices had on his successful life.

FIGURE 16.9	A Guide to Action: Promoting Students' Self-Determination

A very important part of your inclusive classroom is promoting students' self-determination. To create a classroom that promotes students' self-determination, consider the following points:

- Integrate into the daily schedule activities that encourage students to make choices.
- Be aware of students' preferences.
- Show that you respect students' choices and decisions.
- Include students in planning, implementing, and evaluating instructional activities, and fostering their prosocial behavior.
- Encourage students to take responsibility for their decisions and learning.
- Encourage IEP teams to consider students' self-determination skills.
- Make it easy for students to attend and participate in IEP meetings.
- Teach students to advocate for themselves.
- Create a learning environment that helps students feel good about themselves.
- Encourage students to analyze how their actions contribute to success and failure.
- Give students opportunities to have positive role models, and to participate in service learning and community-based programs.
- Provide students with access to resources that focus on their strength, needs, interests, and experiences.
- Use curricula and teaching materials and activities to foster students' self-determination.
- Encourage all students to assume leadership positions.
- Understand the impact of students' cultural backgrounds on their self-determination.
- Model self-determination for students.

Source: From *Creating Inclusive Classrooms: Effective and Reflective Practices*, p. 273, by S. J. Salend, 2008, Upper Saddle River, NJ: Pearson.

METHODS TO FACILITATE SUCCESS FOR STUDENTS WITH SPECIAL NEEDS IN THE GENERAL EDUCATION CLASSROOM

Students with disabilities traditionally have been placed in general education classrooms for instruction when they were determined to have the requisite academic ability necessary for success. With the advent of the inclusion movement, however, students with disabilities are often placed in such classes for other reasons. For most of these students, success can be engineered by teachers using scientific research-based teaching practices and differentiating or using "contingency strategies" for assisting students who still need assistance. Some students will require the implementation of these adaptations; other students can achieve success when taught to use effective study skills and learning strategies.

Scientific Research-Based Teaching Strategies

The scientific research-based teaching strategies that have been shared throughout this text are critical for students with disabilities to benefit from their educational placement. Even if the IEP goals and general education curricular standards are a perfect match, an ineffective teacher can stop progress. Throughout the implementation of a lesson, an effective teacher is constantly monitoring students to confirm that learning is occurring. When students demonstrate a lack of understanding, a contingency plan must be quickly available to differentiate according to need. Figure 16.10 provides an example of a lesson plan that has been written with the contingency plans included.

Adaptations: Accommodations and Modifications

In secondary classrooms where teachers support the model of differentiation according to need, the adaptations made can be a critical factor in determining the level of success for

PERSONAL SPOTLIGHT

GREAT ATHLETE—CHALLENGED STUDENT

BILL FLOWERS spent his elementary years in Miami in a highly structured, exclusive private school for students with all types of disabilities due to his severe learning disabilities, hyperactivity, impulsivity, and inattention. Bill made progress but it was a lonely existence, commuting daily across town to go to a school none of his neighborhood friends attended. By the time he returned home, they had finished playing and were settling down to dinner and homework. The worst part was that the school had no athletic program and that was the environment in which he excelled. His dad found a community program that would allow Bill to play but again he was the odd man out.

When Bill was in the fifth grade, hurricane Katrina destroyed their home and most of Bill's school; the family decided to move closer to extended family in Alabama. They were appalled to find no private schools for students like Bill; they were even more surprised to find that Bill was welcomed into a general education classroom. He received additional support from a specialist who came into the inclusive classroom. Bill began to be invited to birthday parties and attend sleepovers for the first time. Best of all was the athletic program that allowed him to excel. School was never easy but Bill didn't mind the hard work. In addition to learning support, his teachers provided testing in distraction-reduced settings and with extended time. In high school, he went to tutors for two years to help him "pass math" and prepare for the graduation exam and the ACT. After a long day of school and athletic training, he would shower and head to the tutor. He didn't want the academic challenges to stand in his way.

He practiced football before and after school; his coach talked about his impressive work ethic and he was named Player of the Year for his area, Back of the Year by the Sports Writers Association, and Alabama's Player of the Year by Gatorade. His work paid off and he got a scholarship to play football at Old Miss.

"Some people get academic gifts; my gift is athletics," he said. Bill says college was easier in some ways because of having a note-taker provided as an accommodation. His ADHD made it really hard to listen and take notes; plus, he says his notes looked like "chicken scratch" when he tried to read them later. With the note-taker he could keep his mind on the lecture and learn while the professor talked. As a result, he took most of his tests with the class. College was a real challenge, but Bill was a skilled self-advocate and graduated as planned. The next challenge was employment. Bill didn't know what he wanted to do, but he knew it had to be action-packed—no desk with paperwork for him. He has found his employment niche in medical sales. He is in and out of hospital surgical settings, confidently training doctors to use his product for bone replacement.

When asked about his successes, Bill always gives credit to others; he feels that his disabilities have made him a better person. He uses his setbacks as challenges to conquer, and he wants his story to help others who may not see their disability as a gift and to help those who haven't learned to see the gifts in every person.

---

their students with diverse abilities, interests and needs. The development of the accommodations and modifications should be a collaborative effort, often involving the general and special education teachers as well as the students and parents. The general education teacher typically implements the instructional plan and monitors student achievement, reporting any problems to the special education teacher and the entire IEP team if major adjustments are required. Figure 16.11 provides a checklist that can be used to generate further ideas, to provide documentation of differentiation techniques used, and to evaluate the effectiveness in accommodating individual learning needs.

Adaptations should be designed to offer the least amount of alteration of the regular programming that will still allow the student to benefit from instruction. This approach is fair to nondisabled students and provides the students with disabilities with a realistic sense of their abilities and limitations. If too many adaptations are made, some students may be set up for failure in college or in other academically demanding environments. Students with too many accommodations may also begin to feel that they bring very little to the class; this feeling can further damage an already fragile self-concept. Modifications used in settings or classes designed to prepare an individual for a future job or postsecondary training program should reflect real conditions present in these future environments and realistic adaptations. Table 16.2 provides examples of accommodations that might be needed to differentiate during a lesson and modifications that could be implemented if more significant adaptations are needed.

| FIGURE 16.10 | Differentiating Instruction Through Contingency Plans |

Objective

Given ten word problems involving addition and subtraction, the student will use a calculator to compute the answer with 100 percent accuracy.

Procedures

1. Review previous work, describe today's activity, and emphasize how this skill will be useful to students.
2. Read a sample problem with the class. Determine the correct operation. Turn on the calculator. Show how to enter the first number, the operation sign, the second number, and the equal sign. Identify and record the answer.
3. Repeat with another problem requiring a different operation.
4. Show the class a third problem using a transparency on the overhead projector.
    a. Call on a student to read the problem out loud.
        Contingency: For a student unable to read parts of the problem, read it for him or her; then have the student repeat it.
    b. Determine the correct operation.
        Contingency: Students unable to determine the operation will be provided a list of key words and phrases that provide hints. For example, "How much more?" indicates subtraction.
    c. Turn on the calculator.
        Contingency: Use a red marker to highlight the "on" button for students unable to locate it.
    d. Enter the first digit of the first number.
        Contingency 1: Students unable to determine which number should be entered first will be assisted in setting up the problem on paper first.
        Contingency 2: Students unable to determine which digit of a number should be entered first will be told to enter the digits as they are softly repeated out loud.
    e. Enter the operation sign.
        Contingency: Students unable to locate the operation sign will be referred to a sample problem on the board and asked to match the sign written on the board with the button on the calculator.
    f. Enter the equal sign.
        Contingency: Use a blue marker to highlight the "[=]" button for students unable to locate it.
    g. Record the answer.
5. Repeat with another problem presented to the entire group.
6. Provide a worksheet with ten word problems to those who needed no assistance during the teacher-directed activity.
    Contingency: Continue to work in a small group with those who experienced difficulty.
7. If time permits, allow students who have mastered the skill to go "Christmas shopping" using a catalog from a department store. Tell them they have $200 to spend. They must keep track of their expenses.
    Contingency: Have students previously engaged in small group instruction complete the worksheet containing ten problems. Be available to provide assistance.

Source: From *Instructional Methods for Secondary Students with Learning and Behavior Problems* (4th ed., p. 85), by P. I. Schloss, M. A. Schloss, and C. N. Schloss, 2007. Boston: Allyn & Bacon.

Homework, Grading, and Testing

Homework, grading, and testing stand out as important considerations in students' success within secondary school classrooms. They have become more significant in light of trends toward making academic standards more rigorous and toward accountability in general education classrooms. Higher expectations for student performance in general education classes and the emphasis on national achievement tests affect testing and grading. This section explores these problem areas, focusing on adaptations to facilitate student success.

Homework   Problems in homework often become more pronounced at the secondary level. Given that students typically have four to six teachers, assignments represent a significant hurdle for middle- and high-school students with disabilities. Although the amount of

FIGURE 16.11	**Checklist of Options for Differentiating for Learning Needs**

Student: _____ Teacher: _____ Date(s): _____

[Circle accommodations attempted; mark successful accommodations with plus (+), unsuccessful with minus (−).]

Classroom
Design constructive learning environment.

Preferential seating (specifiy): _____			
Group size:	___1–1 w/teacher	___1–1 w/peer	___Small group	___Large group
Need for movement:	___Little	___Average	___High	
Distraction management:	___Carrels	___Headsets	___Seating	___Other
Noise:	___None	___Quiet	___Moderate	
Lighting:	___Dim	___Average	___Bright	
Temperature:	___Warm	___Average	___Cool	

Other (specify): _____

Schedule
Arrange productive learning schedule.

Peak time:	___Early morning	___Late morning	___Midday	___Afternoon
Lesson length:	___5–10 min.	___15–20 min.	___25–30 min.	___30+ min.
Variation needed:	___Little	___Some	___Average	___Much
Extra time needed:	___Little	___Some	___Average	___Much

Other (specify): _____

Lessons
Use best stimulus/ response format.

	Stimulus Format			***Response Format***	
Visual:	___Observe	___Read	Choose:	___Point	___Mark
Auditory:	___Oral	___Discuss	Tell:	___Restate	___Explain
Touch:	___Hold	___Feel	Write:	___Short answer	___Essay
Model:	___Coach	___Demonstrate	Word process:	___Some	___All
Multisensory:	___Combination		Show:	___Demonstrate	___Make

Other (specify): _____

Materials
Make constructive material adjustments.

___Vary stimulus/response	___Vary directions	___Vary sequence
___Highlight essential content	___Use partial content	___Add steps
___Expand practice	___Add self-checking	___Add supplements
___Segment	___State key concepts in margins	(see below)

Other (specify): _____

Supplements
Provide supplementary aids to facilitate learning.

Instructional Strategies	***Materials***	***Assignments***	***Human Resources***
___Advance organizers	___Adaptive/assistive devise	___Adapted testing	___Co-teacher
___Charted progress	___Audiotapes of text	___Advance assignment	___Cooperative group
___Checklist of steps	___Calculator	___Alternate assignments	___Instructional coach
___Computer activities	___Captioned films	___Extended time	___Interpreter
___Evaluation checklists	___Coded text	___Extra practice	___Peer advocate
___Graphic organizers	___Computer programs	___Outlined tasks	___Peer notetaker
___Modeling	___Games for practice	___Partial outlines	___Peer prompter
___Mnemonic guides	___Highlighted text	___Question guides	___Peer tutor
___Multisensory techniques	___Key term definitions	___Reference access	___Personal attendant
___Organization charts	___Large print texts	___Scripted practice	___Study buddy
___Repeated readings	___Manipulatives	___Segmented tasks	___Volunteer tutor
___Scripted demonstrations	___Math number charts	___Shortened assignments	
___Self-questioning	___Multiple text	___Simplified directions	***Management Strategies***
___Strategy posters	___Parallel text	___Simplified tasks	___Charted performance
___Verbal rehearsal	___Simplified text	___Structured notes	___Checklists
___Video modeling	___Summaries	___Study guides	___Contracts
___Visual imagery	___Video enactments	___Timed practice	___Extra reinforcement
___Other	___Other	___Other	___Other
_____	_____	_____	_____
_____	_____	_____	_____

Source: From *Successful Inclusive Teaching: Proven Ways to Detect and Correct Special Needs* (3rd ed. p. 38), by J. S. Choate, 2002. Boston: Allyn & Bacon.

TABLE 16.2

Curriculum or Instruction Adaptations

STAGE OF INSTRUCTION	ACCOMMODATIONS (EXAMPLES)	MODIFICATIONS (EXAMPLES)
Initial Instruction	• Clear overheads/graphic organizer • Partners repeat or read to each other • Teacher uses signals • Study guide/guided notes • Highlighted text • Teacher position/proximity to particular students	• Different study guide (partially filled out) • Different text • Introduce different but related skill
Guided Practice	• Notated/highlighted/more structured assignment or activity • Teacher/student model • Partners do/check • Partners tutor • Frequent checks by teacher • Alter pace	• Different assignment or activity on same skill or content • Different assignment or activity on related skill or content • Physical guidance by teacher/paraeducator/peer
Independent Practice	• Slower transition from guided practice • More structure	• Do less of same task • Different task • Teach parent/sibling to coach • Do with a partner
Evaluation	• Test under different conditions (more time, different location, test read to student) • Same rubric or standard but different tasks • Portfolio • Mastery standard, but vary time allowed to mastery • Evaluation based on more than curriculum mastery	• Evaluation of different objectives/different outcomes

Source: From *Teaching Content to All: Evidence-Based Inclusive Practices in Middle and Secondary Schools* (p. 315), by B. K. Lenz and D. D. Deshler, 2004. Boston: Allyn & Bacon.

homework assigned provides a challenge, the unique difficulties of students with disabilities are underscored by the types of problems they are likely to have. Just as the characteristics of each exceptionality described in previous chapters can have a negative impact on classroom performance, they create additional challenges as students attempt to complete work without the guidance of a teacher, the modeling of a peer, or the structure of a classroom.

Polloway and colleagues (2005) suggest that although homework can pose a special challenge for students with disabilities and their families, effective intervention techniques have been identified. Teachers and parents can work together to implement these procedures that can increase students' success with homework and ultimately have a positive effect on school achievement. Following is a list of homework practices that are organized as management, assignment, and student considerations, and parent involvement.

Management considerations

- Assess a student's homework skills to identify potential problems.
- Assign homework early in the year and on a regular basis.
- Present clear instructions: State the purpose, give directions, identify the format and materials to be used and an estimate of how long the assignment should take, clarify how the assignment will be graded.
- Use an incentive program. (Figure 16.12 shows a homework pass that can be given for turning in homework. When the specified number is collected, a homework assignment can be skipped.)
- Use assignment notebooks and have parents sign off on work or post assignments on a class web page or through email or texting.

FIGURE 16.12

Example of a homework pass used for reinforcement.

Source: From *Successful Inclusive Teaching* (3rd ed., p. 389), by J. S. Choate, 2000. Boston: Allyn & Bacon.

Classroom Coupon	Expires:

HOMEWORK PASS

Redeem ☐ coupons
for one missed homework assignment

Rules: Void if transferred to any other student. Must be used by the expiration date. Must be used for homework assigned by the teacher who authorized the coupons. May not be reproduced.

Student _____   Teacher _____

Assignment considerations
- Give the purpose of each assignment and establish relevance.
- Select activities appropriate for independent work.
- Use homework adaptations such as shorter assignments that cover the same content, extended due dates, grades based on effort not accuracy or only one component of the assignment, assign group homework.

Student considerations
- Teach study skills such as time management and dictionary skills.
- Consider differentiating homework assignments based on student needs and preferences.
- Help students develop self-management behaviors.

Parental involvement
- Support and reinforce skills learned at school.
- Create environment for homework that occurs at same time daily in a distraction-reduced setting with all needed materials available.
- Provide ongoing encouragement and support.

Grading   The challenges of inclusion of adolescents with disabilities are perhaps most clearly reflected in the area of grading. School systems should develop a diverse committee to study the best practices in grading that support mastery of academic standards and meet legal guidelines to develop a policy for the entire system (Salend & Duhaney, 2002). These guidelines for grading are based on Section 504 and Title II of the ADA, and are the interpretation of Office of Civil Rights (OCR), the agency responsible for supervision of the implementation of these laws. OCR mandates that:

- Grades, honors, class ranking, awards, diplomas, and graduation requirements must be applied equally to *all students*.
- Any modified grading system used must be available to *all students*.
- Any designation used on a report card or transcript to indicate that a student is provided special education services or receives accommodations or a modified curriculum in a general education class is not allowed unless the grades and courses of *all students* are treated in the same manner (Salend, 2008).

When a school system adopts a differentiated grading system, a cover sheet for the report card may be used to document the specific type(s) of differentiation used, but this is only allowed if the cover sheet is attached to the report cards of *all students*. The nearby Differentiated Instruction—Secondary boxed reading provides an example of a report card cover sheet that can be used to indicate the differentiation techniques used in instruction and testing for each individual student.

Generally, each school system will have established policies that govern grading practices; these include:

- The types of grading systems that may be used
- What factors should be considered in determining grades

Differentiating
Secondary Instruction

SAMPLE INSTRUCTIONAL AND TESTING TECHNIQUES REPORT CARD COVER SHEETS

Student's name: _____

Grade: _____

Teacher(s): _____

Instructional Differentiation Techniques

Check all the instructional differentiation techniques used.

- ☐ Word processor/spell checker
- ☐ Note-taking assistance
- ☐ Use of technology (please specify)
- ☐ Learning strategies instruction
- ☐ Specialized seating arrangements
- ☐ Study skills instruction
- ☐ Memory aids and strategies
- ☐ Additional time to complete tasks
- ☐ Manipulatives
- ☐ Electronic textbooks
- ☐ Frequent comprehension checks
- ☐ Daily/weekly planner
- ☐ Redirection
- ☐ Tiered assignments
- ☐ Adapted directions
- ☐ Shorter assignments
- ☐ Scheduling adaptations
- ☐ Frequent reinforcement
- ☐ Modeling
- ☐ Adapted textbooks

- ☐ Visuals to support instruction
- ☐ Adapted materials
- ☐ Adult assistance
- ☐ Peer-mediated instruction
- ☐ Verbal prompts
- ☐ Curriculum overlapping
- ☐ Self-correcting materials
- ☐ Cues to highlight information
- ☐ Adapted homework
- ☐ Calculators
- ☐ Graphic organizers
- ☐ Frequent communication with families
- ☐ Generalization strategies
- ☐ Listening/note-taking guides
- ☐ Frequent feedback
- ☐ Examples/models of correct response formats
- ☐ Prompting
- ☐ Concrete teaching aids
- ☐ Limited distractions
- ☐ Study guides

☐ Other (please specify)_____

Testing Differentiation Techniques

Check all the testing differentiation techniques used.

- ☐ Items omitted
- ☐ Extended time
- ☐ Individual administration
- ☐ Directions/items read
- ☐ Adapted directions
- ☐ Word processor/spell checker
- ☐ Adapted multiple-choice items
- ☐ Calculator
- ☐ Increased space in between items
- ☐ Fewer items
- ☐ Adapted matching items
- ☐ Adapted true-false items
- ☐ Adapted sentence completion items
- ☐ Adapted essay questions

- ☐ Proctor
- ☐ Scribe
- ☐ Separate location
- ☐ Breaks
- ☐ Alternate response mode
- ☐ Administration over several sessions
- ☐ Cues to highlight information
- ☐ Oral test
- ☐ Cooperative group testing
- ☐ Extra credit options
- ☐ Bonus points
- ☐ Writing mechanics waived
- ☐ Use of technology (please specify)

☐ Other (please specify)_____

Source: From *Creating Inclusive Classrooms: Effective and Reflective Practices* (6th ed.) by S. J. Salend (2008) p. 530. Upper Saddle River, NJ: Pearson.

- The degree to which final exams and the evaluation of other activities/products should be considered
- The "cut-off" for passing a class
- The methods for calculating grades, grade-point averages, and rankings in a class (Brookhart, 2004)

Always communicate grading guidelines to parents as well as your students. It is helpful to have a "model" response to a classroom assignment to clearly demonstrate your expectations. Provide progress reviews often so there are no surprises when grades are distributed. Include the students and families in establishing differentiated assignments and grading procedures.

Testing   The inclusion movement has raised concerns regarding how students with special needs will be assessed. Simple adaptations can make the difference between taking a test successfully or poorly. For example, reading a test to a student who is a very poor reader gives the student a chance to display knowledge or skills. If such students have to read the questions themselves, test results will reflect students' poor reading skills and fail to assess knowledge of a particular content area. Teachers can address this situation in the following ways:

- Have another student, teacher, or aide read the test to the student.
- Use technology to scan and read text.
- Give the student additional time to complete the test. The extra time gives the student a chance to read the material first to identify the words and again for better comprehension. (With proper documentation, colleges will often allow time and a half but seldom unlimited time.)
- Reword the test to include only words that are within the student's reading vocabulary.

A full consideration of adaptations in testing, however, extends beyond the consideration of reading ability. Other ways that teachers can make tests more accessible to students is to use the COLA checklist (Figure 16.13), a strategy developed by Rotter (2006) to guide development of written material presented to students. Implementation of these methods for creating instructional materials and tests will benefit all students.

The following examples are additional techniques that can be used to adapt measurement instruments and assessment procedures:

- Administer frequent short tests, rather than a few long tests.
- Divide tests or tasks into smaller, simpler sections or steps.
- Develop practice items or pretest trials using the same response format as the test.
- Consider the appropriateness of the instrument or procedure in terms of age or maturity.
- Give open-book or open-note tests.
- Reduce the number of test items or remove items that require more abstract reasoning or have high levels of difficulty.
- Use different levels of questions for different students.
- Have a student develop a product or packet of materials that show knowledge and understanding of the content of a unit (portfolio assessment).
- Provide alternative projects or assignments.
- Videotape a student performing a task and then play it back to him or her to show skills learned and areas needing improvement.
- Use a panel of students to evaluate one another on task performance.
- Allow students to type answers.
- Allow students to use a computer during testing.
- Allow small groups to work together on a task to be evaluated (such as a project or test).
- Use short written or verbal measures on a daily or weekly basis to provide more feedback on student progress.
- Increase the amount of time allowed to complete the test.
- Alter the types of responses to match a student's strengths (written, oral, short answer, or simple marking).

FIGURE 16.13		**The COLA Checklist**

C	Contrast	There is plenty of white space around important information and answer spaces.
		Color of the text is in clear contrast from background (this includes avoiding the use of pencil or lightly printed dittos).
		Color, underlining, dark borders, and/or highlights are used to point out critical information, such as directions.
		Bold font is used infrequently, for highlighting important information only.
O	Orientation	Important information, such as directions, is in the top-left position.
		All information reads from left to right, top to bottom.
		Material is aligned to the left.
L	Lettering	Material is printed, not handwritten.
		The same clear font is used throughout.
		The font is big enough to read easily at the typical viewing distance.
		The material uses upper- and lowercase letters as they would typically appear in print. (No use of all caps or small caps fonts.)
		Italicized fonts are not used.
A	Artwork	Artword is used only to support information and not to make the paper "pretty."
		The page is not too "busy," and pictures are not distracting.
		Artwork is culturally sensitive

Source: From "Creating Instructional Materials for All Pupils: Try Cola" (p. 281), by K. Rotter, 2006, *Intervention in School and Clinic, 4115,* pp. 273–282.

- Have a student review the course or unit content verbally so that he or she is not limited to test item recall.
- Limit the number of formal tests by using checklists to observe and record learning.
- Assess participation in discussions.
- Give extra credit for correction of mistakes.

Bolt and Thurlow (2004) offer several suggestions for identifying the most appropriate accommodations that will have the greatest impact on the performance of students:

1. Be sure that the accommodation does not compromise the purpose of the test. For example, a math or science test could be read to a student but a test of reading comprehension could not be.
2. Choose the least intrusive options. For example, if a poor reader can function with extra time, he or she should not be given a reader.
3. Let students get used to the accommodation before using it during a "high-stakes assessment."
4. Individuals providing the accommodation should be trained; for example, no prompts or cues should be given unless specified.
5. Monitor the effectiveness of the accommodation. One student was given extended time on a test, but the extra time was during the loud break time of the other 100 students taking the test!

For students to perform successfully on tests, they will need to learn individual test-taking and organizational strategies that are often difficult for students with disabilities. Such strategies are typically subsumed within the area of study skills, discussed in the next section.

Study Skills and Learning Strategies

Teachers' accommodations are insufficient to guarantee that students with special needs will be successful. Students must develop their own skills and strategies to help them overcome, or compensate for, a disability. Understanding how to use study skills will greatly enhance their chances for being successful in future academic, vocational, or social activities. Classroom teachers can help students acquire a repertoire of study skills. Study skills are tools that students can use to assist them with independent learning.

Many students have an innate ability in these areas. For example, some students are good readers, adept at comprehension and able to read fluently; other students find it easy to memorize facts. These students may not need instruction in study skills. For other students, however, study skills represent an "invisible curriculum" that must be taught directly if they are to be successful. For example, the study skill of listening is critical in most educational settings because teachers provide so much information verbally. If students are not able to attend to auditory information, they will miss a great deal of content. Following is a list of ways to help secondary students prepare to study; study; and follow up after studying developed by Lambert and Nowacek (2006):

Preparing to study
- Explain that it is easier to study during the daytime, especially during study halls and time provided in class.
- Assist students in deciding on a routine time and in a distraction-reduced, well-lit area at home for study.
- Help students identify needed materials for study (e.g., study guides, texts, notes, planners, pencils).
- Teach students to develop a study agenda, beginning with hardest items as soon as they are assigned.
- Help students learn to break difficult and long-term assignments into shorter parts with time lines identified that can be checked off as they are completed.
- Remind students to use positive self-talk, reminding themselves that they "can do" instead of "can't do."

Studying in the content areas
- Show students how to prioritize and focus, not jumping from one subject to another without completion.
- Encourage them to study for 50 minutes (using a timer is helpful) and then take a 10-minute break.
- Teach chapter previewing skills, looking first at title, subheads, graphics, and questions to be answered.
- Teach the paraphrasing strategy where the main ideas are developed for each subhead.
- Teach students to use graphic organizers to summarize information and show relationships.
- Teach students to identify what they do not understand and find a solution (e.g. look on web, in reference book, or ask student or teacher).
- Remind them to keep up the positive self-talk ("This is working! I am really making progress.").

Following up after studying
- Help students keep material needed later in organized notebooks or separate folders.
- Have students establish a habit of writing three questions to discuss in class from what they read or studied and putting homework in notebooks and backpacks.
- Encourage students to reflect on what they have learned and relate the new information to what they have already learned.
- Teach students to reward themselves with a favorite activity after working.

Strichart and Mangrum (2010) published a comprehensive workbook for struggling students in grades 6 through 12 that provides activities to teach good study skills including interpreting and creating visual aids, graphic organizers and charts, reading and taking notes from textbooks and in class, and using a variety of sources as references. Figure 16.14

FIGURE 16.14

Stages of note taking.

There are three stages of note taking. The first stage includes things to do before you come to class. The second stage includes things to do during class. The third stage includes things to do after class.

Look at the checklist that follows. It shows the things you should do for each stage of note taking. Place a checkmark ✓ next to each thing you do most or all the time.

Get Ready Stage (First Stage)

_____ I have my note taking materials ready.

_____ I review my notes from the previous class session.

_____ I complete all my reading assignments.

Take Notes Stage (Second Stage)

_____ I listen for signal words and statements that tell me that something is important to write in my notes.

_____ I write using abbreviations and symbols.

_____ I write using the fewest words possible.

_____ I copy information the teacher writes on the chalkboard.

_____ I circle words I write but whose meanings I do not know.

_____ I place a "?" next to anything I write but do not understand.

After Notes Stage (Third Stage)

_____ I ask my teacher or use my textbook and reference books to clarify anything I wrote but did not understand.

_____ I compare my notes with those of other students.

_____ I use the glossary in my textbook or a dictionary to learn the meanings of unknown words.

_____ I rewrite my notes to make them as legible, complete, and accurate as possible.

Source: From *Study Skills for Learning Disabled and Struggling Students Grades 6–12.* (4th ed.) p. 66 by S. S. Strichart & C. T. Mangrum (2010). Upper Saddle River, NJ: Pearson.

contains an overview of the information included to teach the three critical stages in taking notes. Following this introduction, students are taught specific skills such as how to listen for signal words that indicate the important information that should be included in notes, how to use abbreviations, and how to write the fewest words necessary to capture the information.

Closely related to study skills are learning strategies—specific steps to use to guide learning before, during, and after active learning to acquire and use new information and solve problems ("learning to learn"). Learning strategies were cited as "an essential component of high-quality reading instruction" in the No Child Left Behind Act of 2001. Reading comprehension, memory, error monitoring in writing, problem solving in math, and test preparation are just a few of the important skills that can be developed and strengthened through strategy training (Strichart & Mangrum, 2010). A comprehensive source on numerous strategies for learning (and their use) is provided by Lenz and Deshler (2004).

Examples of learning strategies include:

- SCROL (Grant, 1993) is a strategy that helps students learn how to use textbook headings to improve comprehension. There are five steps in the strategy (Scholes, 1998):
  1. *Survey* the heading. Read each heading and subheading and answer the following questions: What do I already know about this topic? What do I expect the author to include in this section?
  2. *Connect* the parts of the reading. How are the headings related to each other? Write down words from the headings that provide connections between them.
  3. *Read* the text. As you read, look for words or phrases that provide important information about the headings. Stop to make sure you understand the major ideas and supporting details at the end of each section. Reread if you don't understand.
  4. *Outline* the major ideas and supporting details in the section. Try to do this without looking back.
  5. *Look back* at the text to check the accuracy of your outline. Correct your outline as needed. (p. 111)

- The COPS strategy (Schumaker, Denton, & Deshler, 1981) is an error-monitoring strategy for writing. The acronym stands for four tasks:
  1. Capitalization
  2. Overall appearance (e.g., neatness, appropriate margins)
  3. Punctuation
  4. Spelling (p. 11)

Research to validate the use of specific strategies within inclusive classrooms has been ongoing for many years and covers a variety of purposes. Although many strategies are used to make content learning more efficient, teachers have been able to develop their own approaches to assist their students in a variety of areas. The range of uses of learning strategies is limited only by one's creativity. Another exciting aspect of instruction in strategies is its potential to benefit students with and without disabilities in inclusive classrooms (Keith & Lenz, 2004).

It is fitting to end this chapter and this text with a final comment regarding positive teacher attitudes. For students to be interested and excited about learning, they need to be taught by teachers who feel the same way. Students also need teachers who respect them, who care about them, and who are fair, consistent, and encourage them to have input into the learning process. Your dedication, motivation, and enthusiasm will be reflected in the response from your students—not every time—but often enough to make the effort worthwhile. Enjoy the journey!

SUMMARY

Secondary Education Curriculum

- Secondary schools offer a variety of curricular options related to postsecondary goals.
- The curricula for students with special needs should facilitate socialization and be responsive to their needs and interests.
- Students with disabilities are required to have a written Individualized Transition Plan (ITP).

Programs for Students with Disabilities in Secondary Schools

- Secondary settings are more challenging for students with special needs.
- The collaborative role for general education teachers is focused on content selection and delivery but must include differentiated techniques for teaching and testing.
- The collaborative role of the special education teacher may include supporting the classroom teacher and providing direct instruction and experience in areas related to transition.

Methods Needed to Facilitate Success for Students in the General Education Classroom

- Scientific research-based teaching strategies must be implemented with accommodations and modifications as needed to meet individual needs.
- Specific challenges for successful inclusion occur in the areas of homework, grading, and testing.
- Acquiring study skills and learning strategies make learning more efficient for all students.

PEARSON myeducationlab

The MyEducationLab for this course can help you solidify your comprehension of Chapter 16 concepts.

- Gauge and further develop your understanding of chapter concepts by taking the quizzes and examining the enrichment materials on the Chapter 16 Study Plan.
- Visit Topic 13, Transition Planning, as well as Topic 12, Content Area Teaching, to:
  - Connect with challenge-based interactive modules, case study units, and podcasts that provide research-validated information about working with students in inclusive settings by visiting the IRIS Center Resources
  - Explore Assignments and Activities, assignable exercises showing concepts in action through video, cases, and student and teacher artifacts
  - Practice and strengthen skills essential to quality teaching through the Building Teaching Skills and Dispositions lessons

Sample IEP for an Elementary Student

INDIVIDUALIZED EDUCATION PROGRAM

STUDENT'S NAME: Betty

DOB 12/15/1996 **SCHOOL YEAR** 2006 - 2007 **GRADE** 4 -

IEP INITIATION/DURATION DATES **FROM** 08/14/06 **TO** 05/26/07

THIS IEP WILL BE IMPLEMENTED DURING THE REGULAR SCHOOL TERM UNLESS NOTED IN EXTENDED SCHOOL YEAR SERVICES.
STUDENT PROFILE

Betty will be entering the fourth grade at Smallville Elementary School in the fall. She will be included in all general education classes with accommodations. At this time she is exhibiting fewer hyperactive behaviors and is able to focus and remain on task with supports during the school day. Betty has been experiencing difficulty in achieving grade level academic content standards in the area of math. Currently, she is working toward third grade standards.

Betty takes great pride in her work. All assigned tasks are generally completed when she is provided with additional time to complete assignments. She also requires additional time to take tests.

Achievement test scores indicate Betty is on grade level in reading and below average in the area of math, particularly in the area of spatial problems. On the *Stanford 10* and the *Alabama Reading & Mathematics Test* (ARMT), Betty solved addition and subtraction problems, including word problems. She was also able to divide whole numbers and make change up to $1.00. She had difficulty completing geometric problems. Betty could not specify locations on a coordinate grid or analyze data. She appears to have difficulty with spatial problems and transferring items from a concrete form to an abstract form. Betty's problems in math affect her ability to comprehend the required content (graphs, angles and spatial problems) at her current grade level.

Her teachers report she gets along well with her peers. She does not initiate responses in class, but will respond upon request.

Betty's parents are very involved in her academic work. They assist with homework and have provided tutoring when needed. Betty is involved in many community and church activities. Betty's parents are concerned with her academic performance and lack of self-esteem.

TAKE NOTE

A narrative of the student's strengths and weaknesses is a better way of describing the student than simply listing test scores.

INDIVIDUALIZED EDUCATION PROGRAM

STUDENT'S NAME: ___Betty_____

SPECIAL INSTRUCTIONAL FACTORS

ITEMS CHECKED "YES" WILL BE ADDRESSED IN THIS IEP: **YES**   **NO**

- Does the student have behavior, which impedes his/her learning or the learning of others?   [ ]   [X]
- Does the student have limited English proficiency?   [ ]   [X]
- Does the student need instruction in Braille and the use of Braille?   [ ]   [X]
- Does the student have communication needs (deaf or hearing impaired only)?   [ ]   [X]
- Does the student need assistive technology devices and/or services?   [ ]   [X]
- Does the student require specially designed P.E.?   [ ]   [X]
- Is the student working toward alternate achievement standards and participating in the Alabama Alternate Assessment?   [ ]   [X]
- Are transition services addressed in this IEP?   [ ]   [X]

TRANSPORTATION AS A RELATED SERVICE

Does the student require transportation as a related service?   [ ] YES   [X] NO
Does the student need accommodations or modifications for transportation?   [ ] YES   [X] NO

If YES, check any transportation accommodations/modifications that are needed.
- [ ]   Bus driver is aware of student's behavioral and/or medical concerns
- [ ]   Wheelchair lift
- [ ]   Restraint system
    Specify: _____

- [ ]   Other
    Specify: _____

NONACADEMIC and EXTRACURRICULAR ACTIVITIES

Will the student have the opportunity to participate in nonacademic/extracurricular activities with his/her nondisabled peers?

- [X]   YES
- [ ]   YES, with supports. Describe: _____
    _____
- [ ]   NO. Explanation must be provided: _____
    _____

METHOD/FREQUENCY FOR REPORTING PROGRESS OF ATTAINING GOALS TO PARENTS

Annual Goal Progress reports will be sent to parents each time report cards are issued every ___9.0___ week(s).

CROSS REFERENCE

Review chapters 6 and 15 to determine specific needs of students with these kinds of learning issues.

TAKE NOTE

Parents must be notified of the progress being made by their children on the same schedule that parents of nondisabled children receive notification.

INDIVIDUALIZED EDUCATION PROGRAM

STUDENT'S NAME: Betty

AREA: Math

PRESENT LEVEL OF ACADEMIC ACHIEVEMENT AND FUNCTIONAL PERFORMANCE:

Betty has not attained all of the third grade content standards in math. She is able to compare (M.3.1.1) and order numbers (M 3.1.2) less than 100, solve addition and subtraction problems and simple word problems (M.3.2). She has difficulty working problems involving spatial relationships and geometric patterns. Betty's lack of knowledge in the areas of spatial and geometric relationships negatively affects achieving grade-level math geometry standards.

MEASURABLE ANNUAL GOAL related to meeting the student's needs:

At the end of 36 weeks, Betty will identify geometric representations for points, lines, perpendicular lines, parallel lines, angles and rays (M.3.8) on weekly classroom tests an average of 9 out of 10 times.

> **TAKE NOTE**
> Annual goals should be directly related to present level of performance.

TYPE(S) OF EVALUATION FOR ANNUAL GOAL:

[X] Curriculum Based Assessment   [X] Teacher/Text Test   [ ] Teacher Observation   [ ] Grades
[ ] Data Collection   [X] State Assessment(s)   [X] Work Samples
[ ] Other: _____
[ ] Other: _____

DATE OF MASTERY: _____

SPECIAL EDUCATION AND RELATED SERVICE(S): (Special Education, Supplementary Aids and Services, Program Modifications, Accommodations Needed for Assessments, Related Services, Assistive Technology, and Support for Personnel.)

Type of Service(s)	Anticipated Frequency of Service(s)	Amount of time	Beginning/ Ending Date	Location of Service(s)
Special Education Special education and general education teachers will plan lessons and activities using the Curriculum Guide: Mathematics.	Weekly	55 min.	08/14/06 to 05/26/07	General Education Classroom
Special education teacher will re-teach lesson in small group.	Daily	20 min.	08/14/06 to 05/26/07	General Education Classroom
Supplementary Aids and Services Betty needs extra time for classroom assignments in mathematics.	Daily	55 min.	08/14/06 to 05/26/07	General and Special Education Classroom
Betty needs a peer helper to assist with classroom activities in mathematics.	Daily	55 min.	08/14/06 to 05/26/07	General Education Classroom
Program Modifications				
Accommodations Needed for Assessments Betty will have extended time on test.	Weekly	55 min.	08/13/06 to 05/26/07	Special Education Classroom
Betty will receive study guides for tests in mathematics.	Weekly	10 min.	08/13/06 to 05/26/07	General Education Classroom
Related Services				
Assistive Technology				
Support for Personnel				

> **TAKE NOTE**
> Specific services that the school will provide to assist the student in achieving goals and objectives must be listed.

INDIVIDUALIZED EDUCATION PROGRAM

STUDENT'S NAME: Betty

GENERAL FACTORS

HAS THE IEP TEAM CONSIDERED::

	YES	NO
• The strengths of the child?	[X]	[ ]
• The concerns of the parents for enhancing the education of the child?	[X]	[ ]
• The results of the initial or most recent evaluations of the child?	[X]	[ ]
• As appropriate, the results of performance on any State or districtwide assessments?	[X]	[ ]
• The academic, developmental, and functional needs of the child?	[X]	[ ]
• The need for extended school year services?	[X]	[ ]

LEAST RESTRICTIVE ENVIRONMENT

Does this student attend the school (or for a preschool-age student, participate in the environment) he/she would attend if non-disabled?   [X] YES   [ ] NO

If no, justify:

Does this student receive all special education services with non-disabled peers?   [ ] YES   [X] NO

If no, justify (justification may not be solely because of needed modifications in the general curriculum):
Betty requires intensive instruction and frequent feedback in mathematics in an environment free of distractions.

[X]   6-21 YEARS OF AGE   **[ ]   3-5 YEARS OF AGE**
(Select one from the drop-down box.)
02-99%-80%of the day inside Gen Ed Environment

Secondary LRE (only if LRE above is Private School-Parent Placed)

TAKE NOTE

The team must consider the least restrictive setting for each student and justify why a lesser restrictive setting is not used.

COPY OF IEP	COPY OF *SPECIAL EDUCATION RIGHTS*
Was a copy of the IEP given to parent at the IEP meeting?	Was a copy of the *Special Education Rights* given to parent
[X] Yes [ ] No	at the IEP meeting? [X] Yes [ ] No
If no, date sent to parent: _____	If no, date sent to parent: _____

Date copy of **amended** IEP provided/sent to parent _____

THE FOLLOWING PEOPLE ATTENDED AND PARTICIPATED IN THE MEETING TO DEVELOP THIS IEP

Position	Signature	Date
Parent	*	4/26/06
Parent	*	4/26/06
LEA Representative	*	4/26/06
Special Education Teacher	*	4/26/06
General Education Teacher	*	4/26/06
Student		
Career/Technical Education Rep		
Other Agency Representative		

INFORMATION FROM PEOPLE NOT IN ATTENDANCE

Position	Name	Date

Sample IEP for a Middle School Student

INDIVIDUALIZED EDUCATION PROGRAM

STUDENT'S NAME: Robert

DOB 03/25/1993   **SCHOOL YEAR** 2006 - 2007   **GRADE** 8 -

IEP INITIATION/DURATION DATES   **FROM** 08/15/06   **TO** 05/14/07

THIS IEP WILL BE IMPLEMENTED DURING THE REGULAR SCHOOL TERM UNLESS NOTED IN EXTENDED SCHOOL YEAR SERVICES.

STUDENT PROFILE

Robert is in the eighth grade at Lincoln Middle School and is in foster care. His foster parents are concerned about Robert's academic and behavioral performance. They are also worried about Robert's lack of appropriate socialization with age-appropriate peers and adults.

Robert has a strong interest in sports and has indicated a desire to play varsity basketball. Currently, he is the trainer for the junior varsity basketball and football teams. A career inventory indicates interests in music and computers.

Robert has moved many times. His birth parents changed locations for various reasons. Since entering school, Robert has lived with four foster families. Records indicate that extreme violence was witnessed while living with his birth parents.

Robert has made significant progress academically although he is functioning below grade level in reading. He will work quietly and intently on a task when he knows exactly what to do and has a high chance of success. He may lose interest after awhile but, if the task is short he will complete it.

Robert is included in all eighth grade general education classes for his core subjects with accommodations. His assessments indicate that he is on eighth grade level in the area of math. He is reading on sixth grade level and reading comprehension is an area of concern. Therefore, he will receive intensive reading instruction in the special education room on a daily basis to close the gaps in reading. Grades for the 2005-2006 school year are poor in all subjects due to behavioral difficulties in the general education classroom. Robert does not complete his class assignments or homework on a consistent basis.

Teachers report that in the general education classroom, Robert continues to make inappropriate gestures that annoy his classmates, speaks very negatively to others, and exhibits impulsive behaviors (i.e. destroying or breaking objects without provocation). He is also noncompliant with reasonable requests and suggestions from adults. At this time, Robert's behavioral and academic difficulties adversely affect his full participation in the general education environment.

A psychiatrist diagnosed Robert with Attention Deficit/Hyperactivity Disorder (ADHD) when he was in the third grade. The school psychologist has reported elevated scales on the Behavior Assessment System for Children-2 (BASC-2) in anxiety and depression. Robert's foster mother reports he receives medication each morning before school to help control his impulsive behaviors. It is clear that supportive behavioral interventions are required to work in conjunction with medication to achieve positive results. Robert will continue to receive mental health counseling focusing on cognitive behavior modification (CBM) for one hour once a week after school. School personnel, the Department of Human Resources and Mental Health will work collaboratively at least once a month to address Robert's academic and behavioral concerns.

TAKE NOTE

A narrative of the student's strengths and weaknesses is a better way of describing the student than simply listing test scores.

INDIVIDUALIZED EDUCATION PROGRAM

STUDENT'S NAME: Robert

SPECIAL INSTRUCTIONAL FACTORS

ITEMS CHECKED "YES" WILL BE ADDRESSED IN THIS IEP:	YES	NO
• Does the student have behavior, which impedes his/her learning or the learning of others?	[x]	[ ]
• Does the student have limited English proficiency?	[ ]	[x]
• Does the student need instruction in Braille and the use of Braille?	[ ]	[x]
• Does the student have communication needs (deaf or hearing impaired only)?	[ ]	[x]
• Does the student need assistive technology devices and/or services?	[ ]	[x]
• Does the student require specially designed P.E.?	[ ]	[x]
• Is the student working toward alternate achievement standards and participating in the Alabama Alternate Assessment?	[ ]	[x]
• Are transition services addressed in this IEP?	[ ]	[x]

CROSS REFERENCE

Review chapters 6 and 16 to determine when transition services must be addressed in IEPs

TRANSPORTATION AS A RELATED SERVICE

Does the student require transportation as a related service?	[ ] YES	[x] NO
Does the student need accommodations or modifications for transportation?	[ ] YES	[x] NO

If YES, check any transportation accommodations/modifications that are needed.

[ ]   Bus driver is aware of student's behavioral and/or medical concerns
[ ]   Wheelchair lift
[ ]   Restraint system
      Specify: _____

[ ]   Other
      Specify: _____

NONACADEMIC and EXTRACURRICULAR ACTIVITIES

Will the student have the opportunity to participate in nonacademic/extracurricular activities with his/her nondisabled peers?

[x]   YES
[ ]   YES, with supports. Describe: _____
      _____

[ ]   NO. Explanation must be provided: _____
      _____

TAKE NOTE

Parents must be notified of the progress being made by their children on the same schedule that parents of nondisabled children receive notification.

METHOD/FREQUENCY FOR REPORTING PROGRESS OF ATTAINING GOALS TO PARENTS

Annual Goal Progress reports will be sent to parents each time report cards are issued every _____9.0_____ week(s).

INDIVIDUALIZED EDUCATION PROGRAM

STUDENT'S NAME: Robert

AREA: Reading

PRESENT LEVEL OF ACADEMIC ACHIEVEMENT AND FUNCTIONAL PERFORMANCE:

Robert can comprehend fifth-grade literary/recreational materials. He uses a wide range of strategies and skills to gain meaning, summarize passages, and draw conclusions to comprehend fifth-grade functional and textual reading materials (R.5.4.3). He cannot interpret literary elements (R.6.2) in sixth-grade material. Robert's difficulty reading text material affects his progress in understanding content and achieving grade-level standards.

MEASURABLE ANNUAL GOAL related to meeting the student's needs:

By the end of the fourth grading period. Robert will be able to define conflict and personification (R.6.2.1) and identify the main idea in 6th grade reading material (R.6.2.2) with 80 percent accuracy.

> **TAKE NOTE**
> Annual goals should be directly related to present level of performance.

TYPE(S) OF EVALUATION FOR ANNUAL GOAL:

[X]   Curriculum Based Assessment   [X]   Teacher/Text Test   [ ]   Teacher Observation   [ ]   Grades
[ ]   Data Collection   [X]   State Assessment(s)   [X]   Work Samples
[ ]   Other: _____
[ ]   Other: _____

DATE OF MASTERY: _____

SPECIAL EDUCATION AND RELATED SERVICE(S): (Special Education, Supplementary Aids and Services, Program Modifications, Accommodations Needed for Assessments, Related Services, Assistive Technology, and Support for Personnel.)

Type of Service(s)	Anticipated Frequency of Service(s)	Amount of time	Beginning/ Ending Date	Location of Service(s)
Special Education The special education teacher will provide intensive reading instruction using a research-based reading program.	Daily	30 min.	08/15/06 to 12/13/06	Special Education Classroom
Supplementary Aids and Services The general education teachers will use the following accommodations in all subjects: provide a seat in front of the classroom; provide notes; and allow more time to complete assignments.	Daily	90 min.	08/15/06 to 05/14/07	General Education Classroom
Program Modifications				
Accommodations Needed for Assessments Tests in assigned curriculum requiring reading may be read by the general or special education teacher allowing extended time for completion.	Weekly	60 min.	08/15/06 to 05/14/07	General Education Classroom
Related Services				
Assistive Technology				
Support for Personnel				

> **TAKE NOTE**
> Specific services that the school will provide to assist the student in achieving goals and objectives must be listed.

INDIVIDUALIZED EDUCATION PROGRAM

STUDENT'S NAME: Robert

AREA: Reading

PRESENT LEVEL OF ACADEMIC ACHIEVEMENT AND FUNCTIONAL PERFORMANCE:

Robert can comprehend fifth-grade literary/recreational materials. He uses a wide range of strategies and skills to gain meaning, summarize passages, and draw conclusions to comprehend fifth-grade functional and textual reading materials (R.5.4.3). He cannot apply reading strategies (R.6.3) to comprehend sixth-grade material. Robert's difficulty reading text material affects his progress in understanding content and achieving grade-level standards.

MEASURABLE ANNUAL GOAL related to meeting the student's needs:

By the end of the fourth grading period. Robert will identify the essential information in 6th grade reading material (R.6.3.4) with 80 percent accuracy.

TYPE(S) OF EVALUATION FOR ANNUAL GOAL:

[ ] Curriculum Based Assessment   [ ] Teacher/Text Test   [X] Teacher Observation   [ ] Grades
[X] Data Collection   [ ] State Assessment(s)   [ ] Work Samples
[ ] Other: _____
[ ] Other: _____

DATE OF MASTERY: _____

SPECIAL EDUCATION AND RELATED SERVICE(S): (Special Education, Supplementary Aids and Services, Program Modifications, Accommodations Needed for Assessments, Related Services, Assistive Technology, and Support for Personnel.)

Type of Service(s)	Anticipated Frequency of Service(s)	Amount of time	Beginning/ Ending Date	Location of Service(s)
Special Education The special education teacher will provide intensive reading instruction using a research-based reading program.	Daily	30 min.	12/14/06 to 02/09/07	Special Education Classroom
Supplementary Aids and Services				
Program Modifications				
Accommodations Needed for Assessments				
Related Services				
Assistive Technology				
Support for Personnel				

TAKE NOTE

Person(s) responsible for addressing goals and objectives should be included in the IEP.

INDIVIDUALIZED EDUCATION PROGRAM

STUDENT'S NAME: Robert

AREA: Reading

PRESENT LEVEL OF ACADEMIC ACHIEVEMENT AND FUNCTIONAL PERFORMANCE:

Robert can comprehend fifth-grade literary/recreational materials. He uses a wide range of strategies and skills to gain meaning, summarize passages, and draw conclusions to comprehend fifth-grade functional and textual reading materials (R.5.4.3). He cannot recognize the use of text elements (R.6.4) in sixth-grade materials. Robert's difficulty reading text material affects his progress in achieving grade-level standards.

MEASURABLE ANNUAL GOAL related to meeting the student's needs:

By the end of the fourth grading period, Robert will identify main idea (R.6.4.1), cause and effect sentences (R.6.4.3), and define persuasive techniques (R.6.4.4) in 6th grade reading material with 80 percent accuracy.

TYPE(S) OF EVALUATION FOR ANNUAL GOAL:

[X] Curriculum Based Assessment   [X] Teacher/Text Test   [ ] Teacher Observation   [ ] Grades
[ ] Data Collection   [X] State Assessment(s)   [X] Work Samples
[ ] Other: _____
[ ] Other: _____

DATE OF MASTERY: _____

SPECIAL EDUCATION AND RELATED SERVICE(S): (Special Education, Supplementary Aids and Services, Program Modifications, Accommodations Needed for Assessments, Related Services, Assistive Technology, and Support for Personnel.)

Type of Service(s)	Anticipated Frequency of Service(s)	Amount of time	Beginning/ Ending Date	Location of Service(s)
Special Education The special education teacher will provide intensive reading instruction using a research-based reading program.	Daily	30 min.	02/10/07 to 05/14/07	Special Education Classroom
Supplementary Aids and Services				
Program Modifications				
Accommodations Needed for Assessments				
Related Services				
Assistive Technology				
Support for Personnel				

CROSS REFERENCE
Refer to Chapter 4 on the IEP process.

INDIVIDUALIZED EDUCATION PROGRAM

STUDENT'S NAME: Robert

AREA: Behavior

PRESENT LEVEL OF ACADEMIC ACHIEVEMENT AND FUNCTIONAL PERFORMANCE:
Teachers report that in the general education classroom, Robert annoys his classmates by making inappropriate gestures, negative comments to others, and destroys or breaks objects for no apparent reason at least twice a week. However, when Robert is participating in athletics, he can control negative outbursts and demonstrates appropriate social skills. Robert's impulsive behavior interferes with completion of assignments and participating in the general education environment.

MEASURABLE ANNUAL GOAL related to meeting the student's needs:
By the end of the fourth grading period. Robert will interact appropriately with age-appropriate peers and adults in a variety of settings 4 out of 5 times a week.

TYPE(S) OF EVALUATION FOR ANNUAL GOAL:
[ ] Curriculum Based Assessment   [ ] Teacher/Text Test   [X] Teacher Observation   [ ] Grades
[X] Data Collection   [ ] State Assessment(s)   [ ] Work Samples
[X] Other: Behavior Charts _____
[ ] Other: _____

DATE OF MASTERY: _____

SPECIAL EDUCATION AND RELATED SERVICE(S): (Special Education, Supplementary Aids and Services, Program Modifications, Accommodations Needed for Assessments, Related Services, Assistive Technology, and Support for Personnel.)

Type of Service(s)	Anticipated Frequency of Service(s)	Amount of time	Beginning/ Ending Date	Location of Service(s)
Special Education The special education teacher will assist Robert with monitoring/charting a self-evaluation system for appropriate behaviors in the classroom	Daily	5 min.	08/15/06 to 05/14/07	General Education Classroom
Supplementary Aids and Services General education teachers in all classes will sign the self-evaluation form if they agree with his ratings of identified behaviors in all subjects.	Daily	5 min.	08/15/06 to 05/14/07	General Education Classroom
Program Modifications				
Accommodations Needed for Assessments				
Related Services The school counselor will provide individual counseling focusing on building self-esteem and social skills.	Weekly	30 min.	08/15/06 to 05/14/07	Counselor's Office
Assistive Technology				
Support for Personnel General education teachers will be trained on the use of the self-evaluation system.	Once	30	08/14/06 to 08/14/06	General Education Classroom

TAKE NOTE
Accommodations and modifications in general education classrooms are common components of IEPs for secondary students

CROSS REFERENCE
Review Chapter 2 for the roles of special education and general education teachers in inclusive settings.

INDIVIDUALIZED EDUCATION PROGRAM

STUDENT'S NAME: Robert

GENERAL FACTORS

HAS THE IEP TEAM CONSIDERED::	YES	NO
• The strengths of the child?	[X]	[ ]
• The concerns of the parents for enhancing the education of the child?	[X]	[ ]
• The results of the initial or most recent evaluations of the child?	[X]	[ ]
• As appropriate, the results of performance on any State or districtwide assessments?	[X]	[ ]
• The academic, developmental, and functional needs of the child?	[X]	[ ]
• The need for extended school year services?	[X]	[ ]

LEAST RESTRICTIVE ENVIRONMENT

Does this student attend the school (or for a preschool-age student, participate in the environment) he/she would attend if non-disabled?   [X] YES [ ] NO
If no, justify:

Does this student receive all special education services with non-disabled peers?   [ ] YES [X] NO
If no, justify (justification may not be solely because of needed modifications in the general curriculum):
Robert needs individual guidance on using appropriate classroom behaviors and intensive reading instruction in an environment with very few distractions.

    [X] **6-21 YEARS OF AGE**   [ ] **3-5 YEARS OF AGE**
(Select one from the drop-down box.)
02-99%-80%of the day inside Gen Ed Environment

Secondary LRE (only if LRE above is Private School-Parent Placed)

> **TAKE NOTE**
> The team must consider the least restrictive setting for each student and justify why a lesser restrictive setting is not used.

COPY OF IEP	COPY OF *SPECIAL EDUCATION RIGHTS*
Was a copy of the IEP given to parent at the IEP meeting? 　[X] Yes　[ ] No If no, date sent to parent: _____	Was a copy of the *Special Education Rights* given to parent at the IEP meeting?　[X] Yes　[ ] No If no, date sent to parent: _____

Date copy of **amended** IEP provided/sent to parent _____

THE FOLLOWING PEOPLE ATTENDED AND PARTICIPATED IN THE MEETING TO DEVELOP THIS IEP

Position	Signature	Date
Parent	*	4/24/06
LEA Representative	*	4/24/06
Special Education Teacher	*	4/24/06
General Education Teacher	*	4/24/06
Student	*	4/24/06
School Counselor		4/24/06
Mental Health Counselor		4/24/06
Family Service Worker		4/24/06

INFORMATION FROM PEOPLE NOT IN ATTENDANCE

Position	Name	Date

Sample IEP for a Secondary School Student

INDIVIDUALIZED EDUCATION PROGRAM

STUDENT'S NAME: Sam

DOB _____05/05/1989_____ SCHOOL YEAR ____2006____ - ____2007____ GRADE ___12___ - _____

IEP INITIATION/DURATION DATES   FROM   08/10/06   TO   05/25/07

THIS IEP WILL BE IMPLEMENTED DURING THE REGULAR SCHOOL TERM UNLESS NOTED IN EXTENDED SCHOOL YEAR SERVICES.

STUDENT PROFILE

Sam is in the 12th grade at Morris High School. He is currently pursuing a regular high school diploma. During 2005-2006, Sam received accommodations and special education support in all of his core academic general education classes. He took and passed 11th grade English, Geometry, Biology, and U.S. History.

Sam is experiencing difficulty in the area of reading comprehension. Scores on achievement tests, curriculum based assessments, and the reading section of the Alabama High School Graduation Exam (AHSGE), indicate a deficit in the area of reading comprehension. Sam passed all sections of the AHSGE except for reading. Sam received reading accommodations for the other sections of the AHSGE. Sam's low level of reading comprehension is impacting his academic performance in all classes. Poor organizational skills also impact Sam's ability to complete and turn in assignments on time. A transition assessment identified organizational skills as a need for improvement. Through a parent interview, Sam's mother expressed concerns about Sam's lack of organizational skills and need for transition assistance.

Sam is a client of Vocational Rehabilitation Services. He received a vocational evaluation in 2005-2006. The Interest Inventory completed as part of the vocational evaluation showed Sam has a high preference for working with computers.

A transition assessment administrated by Sam's special education teacher indicates his greatest needs are in the area of post-secondary education and personal management. Sam attends a Transition Service class one period a day to address academic and transition needs. The career interest/aptitude inventory showed Sam has the ability to pursue a career in or relating to computers. Currently, Sam plans to attend Morris Junior College to pursue a career in computers. Sam will take the college entrance exams and complete the necessary applications for Morris Junior College and/or other junior colleges or technical schools as part of his postsecondary education preparation.

During the 10th grade, Sam obtained a drivers license. He worked at Best Buy during the summer to earn money to pay for a car. Sam continues to work at Best Buy after school.

A Summary of Performance (SOP) will be completed at the end of 12th grade in order to help facilitate Sam's transition to Postsecondary Education and linkage with other agencies.

TAKE NOTE

A narrative of the student's strengths and weaknesses is a better way of describing the student than simply listing test scores.

INDIVIDUALIZED EDUCATION PROGRAM

STUDENT'S NAME: Sam

SPECIAL INSTRUCTIONAL FACTORS

ITEMS CHECKED "YES" WILL BE ADDRESSED IN THIS IEP: YES   NO

- Does the student have behavior, which impedes his/her learning or the learning of others?   [ ]   [X]
- Does the student have limited English proficiency?   [ ]   [X]
- Does the student need instruction in Braille and the use of Braille?   [ ]   [X]
- Does the student have communication needs (deaf or hearing impaired only)?   [ ]   [X]
- Does the student need assistive technology devices and/or services?   [ ]   [X]
- Does the student require specially designed P.E.?   [ ]   [X]
- Is the student working toward alternate achievement standards and participating in the Alabama Alternate Assessment?   [ ]   [X]
- Are transition services addressed in this IEP?   [X]   [ ]

CROSS REFERENCE
Review chapters 6 and 16 to determine when transition services must be addressed in IEPs

TRANSPORTATION AS A RELATED SERVICE

Does the student require transportation as a related service?   [ ] YES [X] NO
Does the student need accommodations or modifications for transportation?   [ ] YES [X] NO

If YES, check any transportation accommodations/modifications that are needed.
- [ ] Bus driver is aware of student's behavioral and/or medical concerns
- [ ] Wheelchair lift
- [ ] Restraint system
  Specify: _____

_____

- [ ] Other
  Specify: _____

_____

NONACADEMIC and EXTRACURRICULAR ACTIVITIES

Will the student have the opportunity to participate in nonacademic/extracurricular activities with his/her nondisabled peers?
[X] YES
[ ] YES, with supports. Describe: _____

_____

[ ] NO. Explanation must be provided: _____

_____

METHOD/FREQUENCY FOR REPORTING PROGRESS OF ATTAINING GOALS TO PARENTS

Annual Goal Progress reports will be sent to parents each time report cards are issued every _____**9.0**_____ week(s).

TAKE NOTE
Parents must be notified of the progress being made by their children on the same schedule that parents of nondisabled children receive notification.

INDIVIDUALIZED EDUCATION PROGRAM

STUDENT'S NAME: Sam

EXIT OPTIONS

[ ] Alabama High School Diploma   [ ] Alabama Occupational Diploma   **Anticipated Date of Exit:**
     with Advanced Academic Endorsement   [ ] Graduation Certificate

[X] Alabama High School Diploma   [ ] Other:

May	2007
Month	Year

PROGRAM CREDIT TO BE EARNED

For each course taken, indicate program credit to be earned.	ENGLISH	MATH	SCIENCE	SOCIAL STUDIES	Transition Service Class	Computer Class	Art Graphic Design	
Alabama High School Diploma with Advanced Academic Endorsement								
Alabama High School Diploma	1	1	1	1	1	1	1	
Alabama Occupational Diploma								
Graduation Certificate								

TRANSITION

(Beginning not later than the first IEP to be in effect when the student is 16 and updated annually thereafter)

Transition Assessments (Check the assessment(s) used to determine the student's measurable transition goals: (*Check all that apply.*)

[X] Student Interview   [ ] Student Survey   [ ] Work Samples   [X] Vocational Assessment

[ ] Interest Inventory   [X] Parent Interview   [ ] Other:

TAKE NOTE

Transition goals must be addressed when students reach the age of 16.

Transition Goals

Postsecondary Education/Employment Goal:
Student will be prepared to participate in postsecondary education/training based on completion of graduation requirements and submission of application for enrollment.

If **Other** is selected, specify:

Community/Independent Living Goal:
Student will be prepared to participate in community activities and live independently based on independent living skill level achieved and identification of community/living options.

If **Other** is selected, specify:

Transition Services   (**Based on this student's strengths, preferences, and interests the following coordinated transition services will be addressed this year.**)

[ ] Vocational Evaluation (VE)   [X] Personal Management (PM)   [ ] Community Participation (CP)

[ ] Employment Development (ED()   [ ] Transportation (T)   [ ] Medical (M)

[X] Postsecondary Education (PE)   [ ] Living Arrangements (LA   [ ] Linkages to Agencies (L)

[ ] Financial Management (FM)   [ ] Advocacy/Guardianship (AG)   [ ] Other: _____

TRANSITION OF RIGHTS

(Beginning not later than the IEP that will be in effect when the student reaches 18 years of age.)

Date student was informed that the rights under the IDEA will transfer to him/her at the age of 19:   05/18/06

INDIVIDUALIZED EDUCATION PROGRAM

STUDENT'S NAME: Sam

AREA: Reading

PRESENT LEVEL OF ACADEMIC ACHIEVEMENT AND FUNCTIONAL PERFORMANCE:
Sam's spoken vocabulary is a relative strength. He averages 6 out of 10 reading comprehension questions correctly on 11th grade classroom assessments. Sam has difficulty using context clues to confirm implied meaning of unfamiliar vocabulary in functional text (R.11.3.2). His difficulty with reading comprehension negatively affects his ability to glean information from written materials.

MEASURABLE ANNUAL GOAL related to meeting the student's needs:
At the end of 36 weeks, Sam will be able to interpret and analyze charts and tables in textual informational and functional materials (R12.2.2) with 90% accuracy on classroom assessments and worksheets within time limits in his assigned curriculum.

TYPE(S) OF EVALUATION FOR ANNUAL GOAL:

[X] Curriculum Based Assessment   [X] Teacher/Text Test   [ ] Teacher Observation   [ ] Grades

[ ] Data Collection   [X] State Assessment(s)   [ ] Work Samples

[ ] Other: _____

[ ] Other: _____

DATE OF MASTERY: _____

SPECIAL EDUCATION AND RELATED SERVICE(S): (Special Education, Supplementary Aids and Services, Program Modifications, Accommodations Needed for Assessments, Related Services, Assistive Technology, and Support for Personnel.)

Type of Service(s)	Anticipated Frequency of Service(s)	Amount of time	Beginning/ Ending Date	Location of Service(s)
Special Education Special education teacher will pre-teach vocabulary words. Special education teacher will re-teach lessons in small group. Special and general education teachers will plan lessons and activities.	1 time per week 2 times per week 1 time per week	20 min. 20 min. 15 min.	08/10/06 to 05/25/07 08/10/06 to 05/25/07 08/10/06 to 05/25/07	Special Education Classroom General Education Classroom General Education Classroom
Supplementary Aids and Services Sam needs extra time for classroom assignments. Read directions and provide peer helper to assist with classroom assignments and activities.	Daily Daily	55 min. 55 min.	08/10/06 to 05/25/07 08/10/06 to 05/25/07	Special Education Classroom General Education Classroom
Program Modifications				
Accommodations Needed for Assessments Sam will have tests read orally and extended time on tests. Sam will receive a study guide for all classroom assessments.	Weekly Weekly	55 min. 55 min.	08/10/06 to 05/25/07 08/10/06 to 05/25/07	Special Education Classroom General Education Classroom
Related Services				
Assistive Technology				
Support for Personnel				

TAKE NOTE
Annual goals should be directly related to present level of performance

TAKE NOTE
Specific services that the school will provide to assist the student in achieving goals and objectives must be listed.

INDIVIDUALIZED EDUCATION PROGRAM

STUDENT'S NAME: Sam

AREA: Organizational Skills

PRESENT LEVEL OF ACADEMIC ACHIEVEMENT AND FUNCTIONAL PERFORMANCE:
Sam is able to keep up with events on his personal calendar. Sam is unable to organize his assignments and class notebook for each academic class. He loses assignments, both classroom and homework. He is unable to complete projects. Sam's difficulty with organization negatively affects his progress in completing assignments and projects to meet grade level standards.

MEASURABLE ANNUAL GOAL related to meeting the student's needs:
At the end of 36 weeks, Sam will implement a system for organizing his assignments and notebooks, as developed and monitored by his special education teacher, for each class 90% of the time.

TYPE(S) OF EVALUATION FOR ANNUAL GOAL:

[ ] Curriculum Based Assessment [ ] Teacher/Text Test [X] Teacher Observation [ ] Grades
[ ] Data Collection [ ] State Assessment(s) [X] Work Samples
[ ] Other: _____
[ ] Other: _____

DATE OF MASTERY: _____

TAKE NOTE

Person(s) responsible for addressing goals and objectives should be included in the IEP.

SPECIAL EDUCATION AND RELATED SERVICE(S): (Special Education, Supplementary Aids and Services, Program Modifications, Accommodations Needed for Assessments, Related Services, Assistive Technology, and Support for Personnel.)

Type of Service(s)	Anticipated Frequency of Service(s)	Amount of time	Beginning/ Ending Date	Location of Service(s)
Special Education Special education teacher will help develop system, check notebooks and calendar. Special education teacher will plan and consult with the general education teacher to ensure that all assignments are in notebook.	Daily Daily	20 min. 20 min.	8/10/06 to 5/25/07 8/10/05 to 5/25/07	Special Education Classroom General Education Classroom
Supplementary Aids and Services Provide copy of notes and list of vocabulary words for all classes.	Daily	20 min.	8/25/06 to 5/25/07	General Education Classroom
Program Modifications				
Accommodations Needed for Assessments				
Related Services				
Assistive Technology				
Support for Personnel				

INDIVIDUALIZED EDUCATION PROGRAM

STUDENT'S NAME: Sam

GENERAL FACTORS

HAS THE IEP TEAM CONSIDERED::

		YES	NO
•	The strengths of the child?	[X]	[ ]
•	The concerns of the parents for enhancing the education of the child?	[X]	[ ]
•	The results of the initial or most recent evaluations of the child?	[X]	[ ]
•	As appropriate, the results of performance on any State or districtwide assessments?	[X]	[ ]
•	The academic, developmental, and functional needs of the child?	[X]	[ ]
•	The need for extended school year services?	[X]	[ ]

LEAST RESTRICTIVE ENVIRONMENT

Does this student attend the school (or for a preschool-age student, participate in the environment) he/she would attend if non-disabled?   **[X]** YES   [ ] NO

If no, justify:

Does this student receive all special education services with non-disabled peers?   [ ] YES   **[X]** NO

If no, justify (justification may not be solely because of needed modifications in the general curriculum):
Due to Sam's inability to read at grade level and organize he will require intensive reading instruction and guidance with developing organizational skills.

[X]   **6-21 YEARS OF AGE**   [ ]   **3-5 YEARS OF AGE**
(Select one from the drop-down box.)
02-99%-80%of the day inside Gen Ed Environment

Secondary LRE (only if LRE above is Private School-Parent Placed)

> **TAKE NOTE**
> The team must consider the least restrictive setting for each student and justify why a lesser restrictive setting is not used.

COPY OF IEP	**COPY OF _SPECIAL EDUCATION RIGHTS_**
Was a copy of the IEP given to parent at the IEP meeting?	Was a copy of the _Special Education Rights_ given to parent
[X] Yes [ ] No	at the IEP meeting? **[X]** Yes [ ] No
If no, date sent to parent:	If no, date sent to parent:

Date copy of **amended** IEP provided/sent to parent

THE FOLLOWING PEOPLE ATTENDED AND PARTICIPATED IN THE MEETING TO DEVELOP THIS IEP

Position	Signature	Date
Parent	*	05/18/06
Parent	*	05/18/06
LEA Representative	*	05/18/06
Special Education Teacher	*	05/18/06
General Education Teacher	*	05/18/06
Student	*	05/18/06
Career/Technical Education Rep	*	05/18/06
Other Agency Representative	*ADRS	05/18/06

INFORMATION FROM PEOPLE NOT IN ATTENDANCE

Position	Name	Date

REFERENCES

Abell, M. M., Bauder, D. K., & Simmons, T. J. (2005). Access to the general curriculum. *Intervention, 41*(2), 76-81.

About.com: Special Education (2010). *Traumatic Brain Injury—TBI.* Available: http://specialed.about.com/od/disabilities/a/tbi,htm.

Abramowicz, H. K., & Richardson, S. A. (1975). Epidemiology of severe mental retardation in children: Community studies. *American Journal of Mental Deficiency, 80*, 18-39.

Acrey, C., Johnstone, C., & Milligan, C. (2005). Using universal design to unlock the potential for academic achievement of at-risk learners. *Teaching Exceptional Children, 38*(2), 22-31.

Adelman, H. S., & Taylor, L. (2002). Building comprehensive, multifaceted, and integrated approaches to address barriers to student learning. *Childhood Education, 78*, 261-269.

Agran, M., Wehmeyer, M., Cavin, M., & Palmer, S. (2010). Promoting active engagement in the general education classroom and access to the general education curriculum for students with cognitive disabilities. *Education and Training in Autism and Developmental Disabilities, 45*, 163-174.

Algozzine, R., Serna, L., & Patton, J. R. (2001). *Childhood behavior disorders: Applied research and educational practices* (2nd ed.). Austin, TX: Pro-Ed.

Allen, K. E. (1992). *The exceptional child: Mainstreaming in early childhood education* (2nd ed.). Albany, NY: Delmar.

American Cancer Society. (2010). *Children and cancer: Information and resources.* Available: www.cancer.org/docroot/CRI_2_6x.

American Civil Liberties Union Freedom Network, (n.d.). Public policy. www.virtualref.com. Retrieved 7/29/10.

American Diabetes Association. (2010). *Diabetes statistics.* Available: www.diabetes.org/diabetes-basics/diabetes-statistics.

American Humane (2004). *Protecting Children, 18*(3).

American Psychiatric Association. (1994). *Diagnostic and statistical manual of mental disorders* (4th ed.). Washington, DC: Author.

American Psychiatric Association. (2000). *Diagnostic and statistical manual of mental disorders (DSM-IV-TR)* (4th ed. rev.). Washington, DC: Author.

American Speech-Language-Hearing Association. (1995, March). Position statement—Facilitated communication. *Journal of Speech, Language, and Hearing Research 37* (Suppl. 14), 12.

American Speech-Language-Hearing Association. (1996, May). Cultural differences in communication and learning styles. Retrieved September 23, 2002 from

http://professional.asha.org/resources/multicultural/reading_2.cfm. Compiled by the Multicultural Issues Board, Rockville, MD: Author.

American Speech-Language-Hearing Association. (1999). Terminology pertinent to fluency and fluency disorders. *Guidelines, 41*, 29-36.

American Speech-Language-Hearing Association. (2002a). *Communication facts: Incidence and prevalence of communication disorders and hearing loss in children (2002 edition).* Retrieved June 29, 2002 from http://professional.asha.org/resources/factsheets/children.cfm.

American Speech-Language-Hearing Association. (2002b). *Roles and responsibilities of speech-language pathologists with respect to reading and writing.* Rockville, MD: Author.

American Speech-Language-Hearing Association. (2008). Incidence and prevalence of communication disorders and hearing loss in children—2008 edition. Rockville, MD: ASHA.

American Speech-Language-Hearing Association Ad Hoc Committee on Service Delivery in the Schools. (1993). Definitions of communication disorders and variations. ASHA, 35(Suppl. 10), 40-41.

Andrews, J. F., & Jordan, D. L. (1998). Multimedia stories. *Teaching Exceptional Children, 30,* 28-34.

Ankeny, E. M., Wilkins, J., & Spain, J. (2009). Mothers' experiences of transition planning for their children with disabilities. *Teaching Exceptional Children, 41*, 28-34.

Archer, A., & Gleason, M. (1995). *Skills for school success.* North Billerica, MA: Curriculum Associates, Inc.—Book 3—1989, 1991, 2002 and Book 4—989, 1991, 2002.

Archer, A., & Gleason, M. (2002). *Skills for school success: Book 5.* North Billerica, MA: Curriculum Associates, Inc.

Archer, A. L., Gleason, M. M., & Vachon, V. L. (2003). Decoding and fluency foundation skills for struggling readers. *Learning Disabilities Quarterly, 26*, 89-101.

Armbruster, B. B., & Anderson, T. H. (1988). On selecting "considerate" content area textbooks. *Remedial and Special Education, 9*, 47-52.

Arroyos-Jurado, E., & Savage, T. A. (2008). Intervention strategies for serving students with traumatic brain injury. *Intervention in School and Clinic, 43*, 252-254.

Aseltine, R. H., & DeMartino, R. (2004). An outcome evaluation of the SOS Suicide Prevention program. *American Journal of Public Health, 94*, 446-451.

Austin, J. F. (1992). Involving noncustodial parents in their student's education. *NASSP Bulletin, 76*, 49-54.

Austin, V. L. (2003). Pharmacological interventions for students with ADD.

Intervention in School and Clinic, 38(5), 289-296.

Autism Society of America. (2008). What causes autism: Medical components of ASD. Retrieved from: http://www.autismsociety.org/site/PageServer?pagename=about_whatcauses.

Aviles de Bradley, A. (2008). Educational rights of children and youth who are homeless. *American Educational History Journal, 35*, 261-277.

Ayvazoglu, N. R., Oh, H., & Kozub, F. MJ. (2006). Explaining physical activity in children with visual impairments: A family systems approach. *Exceptional Children, 72*, 235-248.

Babkie, A. M. (2006). Be proactive in managing classroom behavior. *Intervention in School and Clinic, 41*(3), 184-187.

Babkie, A. M., & Provost, M. C. (2002). Select, write, and use metacognition strategies in the classroom. *Intervention, 37*, 172-175.

Baker, B. M., & Blackwell, P. B. (2004, March-April). Identification and remediation of pediatric fluency and voice disorders. *Journal of Pediatric Health Care, 18* (2), 87-94.

Banks, J. (1992). A comment on "Teacher perceptions of the Regular Education Initiative." *Exceptional Children, 58*, 564.

Barkley, R. A (2006). *Attention deficit hyperactivity disorder: A handbook for diagnosis and treatment* (3rd ed.). New York: Guilford Press.

Barkley, R. A. (2010). *Attention deficit hyperactivity disorder in adults: The latest assessment and treatment strategies.* Sudbury, MA: Jones and Bartlett Publishers.

Barnhill, G. (2011). Teaching academic and functional skills. In E. A. Boutot & B. S. Myles (Eds.), *Autism spectrum disorders: Foundations, characteristics, and effective strategies.* Upper Saddle River, NJ: Pearson Education.

Barnhill, G. P. (2001). What is Asperger Syndrome? *Intervention in School and Clinic, 36*, 259-265.

Barnhill, G. P. (2002). *Right address ... wrong planet: Children with Asperger syndrome becoming adults.* Shawnee, KS: Autism Asperger Publishing.

Barnhill, G. P. (2005). Functional behavioral assessment in schools. *Intervention in School and Clinic, 40*, 131-141.

Barnhill, G. P. (2010). Asperger Syndrome: A guide for parents and educators. In A. Canter, L. Z. Paige, & S. Shaw (Eds.), *Helping children at home and school III: Handouts for families and educators* (pp. S8H6 1-5). Bethesda, MD: The National Association of School Psychologists.

Baron-Cohen, S. (2009, November 10). The short life of a diagnosis. *New York Times.* Retrieved from: http://www.nytimes.com/

2009/11/10/opinion/10baroncohen.html?
8dpc=&_r=1&pagewa.

Barr, R. D., & Parrett, W. H. (1995). *Hope at last for at-risk youth.* Boston: Allyn & Bacon.

Barr, R. D., & Parrett, W. H. (2001). *Hope fulfilled for at-risk and violent youth: K-12 programs that work* (2nd ed.). Boston: Allyn & Bacon.

Barraga, N. C., & Erin, J. N. (1992). *Visual handicaps and learning* (3rd ed.). Austin, TX: Pro-Ed.

Barrish, H. H., Saunders, M., & Wolf, M. M. (1969). Good-behavior game: Effects of individual contingencies for group consequences on disruptive behavior in a classroom. *Journal of Applied Behavior Analysis, 2,* 119-124.

Bateman, B. D., & Linden, M. A. (2007). *Better IEPs: How to develop legally correct and educationally useful programs.* Verona, WI: Attainment.

Bau, A. M. (1999). Providing culturally competent services to visually impaired persons. *Journal of Visual Impairment & Blindness, 93,* 291-297.

Bauman, M. L., & Kemper, T. L. (Eds.). (2005). *The neurobiology of autism* (2nd ed.). Baltimore: Johns Hopkins University Press.

Beirne-Smith, M., Patton, J. R., & Kim, S. H. (2010). *Intellectual disabilities* (8th ed.). Upper Saddle River, NJ: Pearson.

Bender, W. N. (2003). *Relational discipline: Strategies for in-your-face kids.* Boston: Allyn & Bacon.

Bender, W. N. (2008). *Learning disabilities: Characteristics, identification and teaching strategies.* (6th ed.). Boston: Pearson/A&B.

Bergeron, R., Floyd, R. G., & Shands, E. I. (2008). States' eligibility guidelines for mental retardation: An update and consideration of part scores and unreliability of IQs. *Education and Training in Developmental Disabilities, 43,* 123-131.

Berkeley, S., Bender, W. N., Peaster, L. G., & Saunders, L. (2009). Implementation of response to intervention: A snapshot of progress. *Journal of Learning Disabilities, 42*(1), 85-95.

Best, S. J. (2006). Health impairments and infectious diseases. In S. J. Best, K. W. Heller, & J. L. Bigge (Eds.), *Teaching individuals with physical or multiple disabilities* (5th ed., pp. 59-85). Upper Saddle River, NJ: Pearson/Merrill.

Best, S. J. (2006). Physical disabilities. In S. J. Best, K. W. Heller, & J. L. Bigge (Eds.), *Teaching individuals with physical or multiple disabilities* (5th ed., pp. 31-58). Columbus, OH: Pearson/Merrill.

Best, S. J. & Bigge, J. L. (2006). Cerebral palsy. In S. J. Best, K. W. Heller, & J. L. Bigge (Eds.), *Teaching individuals with physical or multiple disabilities* (5th ed., pp. 87-109). Upper Saddle River, NJ: Pearson/Merrill.

Biddulph, G., Hess, P., & Humes, R. (2006). Help a child with learning challenges be successful in the general education classroom. *Intervention in School & Clinic, 41*(5), 315-316.

Biklen, D. (1990). Communication unbound: Autism and praxis. *Harvard Educational Review, 60*(3), 291-314.

Blackbourn, J., Patton, J. R., & Trainor, A. (2003). *Exceptional individuals in focus* (7th ed.). Upper Saddle River, NJ: Pearson.

Blackman, H. P. (1989). Special education placement: Is it what you know or where you live? *Exceptional Children, 55,* 459-462.

Blaunstein, P., & Lyon, R. (2006). *Why kids can't read: Challenging the status quo in education.* Lanham, MD: Rowman & Littlefield.

Boardman, A. G., Arguelles, M., Vaughn, S., Hughes, M., & Klinger, J. (2005). Special education teachers' views of research-based practices. *Journal of Special Education, 39*(3), 168-180.

Bolt, S. E., & Thurlow, M. L. (2004). Five of the most frequently allowed testing accommodations in state policy: Synthesis of research. *Remedial and Special Education, 25,* 141-152.

Bos, C. S., & Vaughn, S. (2002). *Strategies for teaching students with learning and behavior problems* (5th ed.). Boston: Allyn & Bacon.

Bouck, E. C. (2004). Exploring secondary special education for mild mental impairment: A program in search of its place. *Remedial and Special Education, 25,* 367-382.

Bouck, E. C. (2007). Lost in translation?: Educating secondary students with mild mental impairment. *Journal of Disabilities Policies Studies, 18,* 79-87.

Bouck, E. C. Courtad, C. A., Heutsche, A., Okolo, C. M., & Englert, C. S. (2009). The virtual history museum: A universally designed approach to social studies instruction. *Teaching Exceptional Children, 42,* 14-20.

Boutot, E. A. (2007). Fitting in: Tips for promoting acceptance and friendships for students with autism spectrum disorders in inclusive classrooms. *Intervention in School & Clinic, 42*(3), 156-161.

Boutot, E. A., & Bryant, D. P. (2005). Social integration of students with autism in inclusive settings. *Education and Training in Developmental Disabilities, 40,* 14-23.

Bower, E. M. (1969). A brief history of how we have helped emotionally disturbed children and other fairy tales. *Preventing School Failure, 35*(1), 11-16.

Bowman, B. T. (1994). The challenge of diversity. *Phi Delta Kappan, 76,* 218-224.

Bowman-Perrott, L. (2009). ClassWide peer tutoring: An effective strategy for students with emotional and behavioral disorders. *Intervention in School and Clinic, 44,* 259-267.

Brandes, J. A. (2005). Partner with parents. *Intervention in School and Clinic, 41,* 52-54.

Breeding, M., Stone, C., & Riley, K. (n.d.) *LINC: Language in the classroom.* Unpublished manuscript. Abilene, TX: Abilene Independent School District.

Bridgeland, J. M., DiIulio, J. J., & Morison, K. B. (2006). *The silent epidemic: Perspectives on high school dropouts.* Retrieved June 27, 2010 from http://www.civicenterprises.net/pdfs/thesilentepidemic3-06.pdf.

Brobst, J. B., Clopton, J. R., & Hendrick, S. S. (2009). Parenting children with autism spectrum disorders: The couple's relationship. *Focus on Autism and Other Developmental Disabilities, 24,* 38-49.

Brookhart, S. M. (2004). *Grading.* Upper Saddle River, NJ: Pearson.

Broun, L., & Umbarger, G. (2005). *Considerations on the use of medications with people who have autism spectrum disorder.* Position Paper. Division on Developmental Disabilities.

Browder, D. M., Wakeman, S. Y., Flowers, C., Rickelman, R. J., Pugalee, D., & Karvonen, M. (2007). Creating access to the general curriculum with links to grade-level content for students with significant cognitive disabilities: An explication of the concept. *Journal of Special Education, 41*(1), 2-16.

Brown, J., Cohen, P., Johnson, J. G., & Salzinger, S. (1998). A longitudinal analysis of risk factors for child maltreatment: Findings of a 17-year prospective study of officially recorded and self-reported child abuse and neglect. *Child Abuse & Neglect, 22,* 1065-1078.

Brown, M. R. (2007). Educating all students: Creating culturally responsive teachers, classrooms, and schools. *Intervention in Schools & Clinic, 43*(1), 57-62.

Brown, M. R., Higgins, K., & Paulsen, K. (2003). Adolescent alienation: What is it and what can educators do about it? *Intervention in School and Clinic, 39*(1), 3-9.

Brown-Chidsey, R., & Steege, M. W. (2005). *Response to intervention: Principles and strategies for effective practice.* New York: Guildford Press.

Bryan, T., Burstein, K., & Ergul, C. (2004). The social-emotional side of learning disabilities: A science-based presentation of the art. *Learning Disabilities Quarterly, 27*(1), 45-51.

Bryant, B. R., & Bryant, D. P. (2005). Social integration of students with autism in inclusive settings. *Education and Training in Developmental Disabilities, 40*(1), 14-23.

Bryant, B. R., & Bryant, D. P. (2008). Introduction to the special series: Mathematics and learning disabilities. *Learning Disability Quarterly, 31*(1), 3-8.

Bryant, D. P., & Barrera, M. (2009). Changing roles for educators within the framework for response-to-intervention. *Intervention in School and Clinic, 45*(1), 72-79.

Buck, G. H., Bursuck, W. D., Polloway, E. A., Nelson, J., Jayanthi, M., & Whitehouse, F. A. (1996). Homework-related communication problems: Perspectives of special educators. *Journal of Emotional and Behavioral Disorders, 4,* 105-113.

Buck, G. H., Fad, K., Patton, J. R., & Polloway, E. A. (2003). *Pre-referral intervention resource guide.* Austin, TX: Pro-Ed.

Buck, G. H., Williams, K., Patton, J. R. and Polloway, E. A. (Unpublished manuscript.) Lynchburg, Virginia: Lynchburg College.

Buck, G. H., Wilcox-Cook, K., Polloway, E. A., & Smith-Thomas, A. (2002). *Prereferral intervention processes: A survey of practices.* Manuscript submitted for publication.

Burns, M. K., & VanDerHeyden, A. M. (2006). Using response to intervention to assess learning disabilities. *Assessment for Effective Intervention, 32,* 3-5.

Buron, K. D. (2003). *The incredible 5-point scale. Assisting students with autism* spectrum disorders in understanding social interactions and controlling their emotional responses. Shawnee Mission, KS: Autism Asperger Publishing.

Buron, K. D., & Wolfberg, P. (Eds.). (2008). *Learners on the autism spectrum: Preparing highly qualified educators.* Shawnee Mission, KS: Autism Asperger Publishing.

Burstein, N., Sears, S., Wilcoxen, A., Cabello, B., Spagra, M. (2004). Moving toward inclusive practices. *Remedial and Special Education, 25*(2), 104–116.

Bursuck, W. D., & Damer, M. (2007). *Reading instruction for students who are at risk or have disabilities.* Boston: Pearson/Allyn & Bacon.

Bursuck, W. D., Polloway, E. A., Plante, L., Epstein, M. H., Jayanthi, M., & McConeghy, J. (1996). Report card grading and adaptations: A national survey of classroom practices. *Exceptional Children, 62,* 301–318.

Campbell, J. M. (2006). Changing children's attitudes toward autism: A process of persuasive communication. *Journal of Developmental and Physical Disabilities, 18,* 251–272.

Canter, A. Paige. L. Z., Roth, M. D., Romero, L., & Carroll, S. A. (Eds.). *Helping children at home and school III: Handouts for families and educators.* Bethesda, MD: National Association of School Psychologists.

Cantu, N. (1993). OCR clarifies evaluation requirements for ADD. *The Special Educator, 9*(1), 11–12.

Carbone, E. (2001). Arranging the classroom with an eye (and ear) to students with ADHD. *Teaching Exceptional Children, 34,* 72–81.

Carlson, E., Brauen, M., Klein, S., Schroll, K., & Willig, S. (2002). *SPeNSE: Key findings.* Retrieved October 8, 2006 from *http://www.spense.org/Results.html.*

Carltedge, G., & Kourea, L. (2008). Culturally responsive classrooms for culturally diverse students with and at risk for disabilities. *Exceptional Children, 74*(3), 351–371.

Carnahan, C. R., Williamson, P., Clarke, L., & Sorenson, R. (2009). A systematic approach for supporting paraeducators in educational settings. *Teaching Exceptional Children 41,* 34–43.

Carnine, D., Silbert, J., Kameenui, E. J., & Tarver, S. G. (2004). *Direct instruction in reading* (4th ed.). Upper Saddle River, NJ: Merrill/Pearson.

Carr, E. G., Dozier, C. L., Patel, M. R. (2002). Treatment of automatic resistance to extinction. *Research in Developmental Disabilities, 23,* 61–78.

Carr, S. C. (2008). Student and peer evaluation: Feedback for all learners. *Teaching Exceptional Children, 40,* 24–27.

Carroll, D. (2001). Consider paraeducator training roles and responsibilities. *Teaching Exceptional Children, 34,* 60–64.

Carter, N., Prater, M. A., Jackson, A., & Marchant, M. (2009). Educators' perceptions of collaborative planning processes for students with disabilities. *Preventing School Failure, 54,* 60–70.

Cartledge, G., & Kourea, L. (2008). Cultural responsive classrooms for culturally diverse students with and at risk for disabilities. *Exceptional Children, 74,* 351–371.

Castellani, J., Mason, C., & Orkwis, R. (2005). Universal design for learning: A guide for teachers and education professionals. Arlington, VA: Council for Exceptional Children.

Causton-Theoharis, J. N., & Malmgren, K. W. (2005). Increasing peer interactions for students with severe disabilities via paraprofessional training. *Exceptional Children, 71*(4), 431–445.

Causton-Theoharis, J., & Theoharis, G. (2009). Creating inclusive schools for all students. *The School Administrator, 65,* 24–31.

Causton-Theoharis, J. N., Giangreco, M. F., Doyle, M. B., & Vadasy, P. F. (2007). Paraprofessionals—The "sous-chefs" of literacy instruction. *Teaching Exceptional Children, 40,* 56–62.

Cavkaytar, A., & Pollard, E. (2009). Effectiveness of parent and therapist collaboration program (PTCP) for teaching self-care and domestic skills to individuals with autism. *Education and Training in Developmental Disabilities, 44,* 381–395.

Cawley, J. F., Fitzmaurice-Hays, A. M., & Shaw, R. A. (1988). *Mathematics for the mildly handicapped: A guide to curriculum and instruction.* Boston: Allyn & Bacon.

CEC Today (1997). CEC tackles response to intervention. Winter edition.

Centers for Disease Control. (1997). AIDS among children—United States, 1996. *Journal of School Health, 67,* 175–177.

Centers for Disease Control (2007). *Prevalence of diagnosed Tourette syndrome in persons aged 6–17 years—United States, 2007.* Washington, DC: Department of Health and Human Services.

Centers for Disease Control (2009, December, 18). Prevalence of autism spectrum disorders—Autism and developmental disabilities monitoring network, United States, 2006. *Morbidity and Mortality Weekly Report Surveillance Summaries, 56*(SS-10). Retrieved from http://www.cdc.gov/mmwr/preview/mmwrhtml/ss5810a1.htm.

Chalfant, J. C., & Van Dusen Pysh, R. L. (1993). Teacher assistance teams: Implications for the gifted. In C. J. Maker (Ed.), *Critical issues in gifted education:. Programs for the gifted in regular classrooms* (Vol. 3, pp. 32–48). Austin, TX: Pro-Ed.

Chamberlain, S. P. (2003). An interview with Evelyn Green and Perry Green. *Intervention in School and Clinic, 38*(5), 297–0306.

Chamberlain, S. P. (2005). Recognizing and responding to cultural differences in the education of culturally and linguistically diverse learners. *Intervention in School and Clinic, 40*(4), 195–211.

Chamberlain, S. P. (2006). An interview with Don Deshler: Perspectives on teaching students with learning disabilities. *Intervention in School and Clinic, 41*(5), 302–306.

Chamberlain, S. P. (2009). An interview with Diane Bryant and Manuel Barrera: The role of the special educator in Response-to-Intervention. *Intervention in School and Clinic, 45*(1), 72–79.

Childhelp. (n.d.). *National child abuse statistics.* Retrieved 1/1/10 from www.childhelp.org/resources/learning-center/statistics

Chiriboga, D. A., & Catron, L. S. (1991). *Divorce.* New York: University Press.

CHOC Epilepsy Center (n.d.). *Managing children with epilepsy: School nurse guide.* Orange, CA: CHOC.

Choudhury, N., & Benasich, A. A. (2003). A family aggregation study: the influence of family history and other risk factors on language development. *Journal of Speech Language, Hearing Research, 46*(2): 261–272.

Christenson, S. L., Ysseldyke, J. E., & Thurlow, M. L. (1989). Critical instructional factors for students with mild handicaps: An integrative review. *Remedial and Special Education, 10*(5), 21–31.

Christner, B., & Dieker, L. A. (2008). Tourette syndrome: A collaborative approach focused on empowering students, families, and teachers. *Teaching Exceptional Children, 40,* 44–49.

Clark, B. (2002). *Growing up gifted: Developing the potential of children at home and at school* (6th ed.). Upper Saddle River, NJ: Merrill/Pearson.

Clark, B. (2007). *Growing up gifted: Developing the potential of children at home and at school* (7th ed.). Upper Saddle River, NJ: Pearson.

Clark, G. M. (1996). Transition planning assessment for secondary level students with learning disabilities. *Journal of Learning Disabilities, 29,* 79–92.

Clarke, M., & Wilkinson, R. (2008). Interaction between children with cerebral palsy and their peers 2: Understanding initiated VOCA-mediated turns. *Augmentative and Alternative Communication, 24,* 3–15.

Clarkson, W. P. (2003). Beautiful minds. *American School Board Journal, 190*(8), 24–28.

Clary, D. L., & Edwards, S. (1992). Spoken language. In E. A. Polloway, J. R. Patton, J. S. Payne, & R. A. Payne (Eds.), *Strategies for teaching learners with special needs* (4th ed., pp. 185–285). Columbus, OH: Merrill.

Clayton, J., Burdge, M., Denham, A., Kleinert, H. L., & Kearns, J. (2006). A four-step process for accessing the general curriculum for students with significant cognitive disabilities. *Teaching Exceptional Children, 38,* 20–27.

Cline, S., & Schwartz, D. (1999). *Diverse populations of gifted children.* Boston: Allyn & Bacon.

Clinkenbeard, P. R. (1991). Unfair expectations: A pilot study of middle school students' comparisons of gifted and regular classes. *Journal for the Education of the Gifted, 15,* 56–63.

Cohen, J., Reddington, C., Jacobs, D., Meade, R., Picard, D., Singleton, K., Smith, D., Caldwell, M.B., DeMaria, A., & Hsu, Ho-Wen (1997). School realted inssues among HIV infected children. *Pediatrics, 100,* 8–17.

Cohen, L. G., & Spenciner, L. J., (2007). *Assessment of children and youth with special needs.* Boston: Allyn & Bacon.

Colangelo, N., & Davis, G. A. (Eds.). (2003). *Handbook of gifted education* (3rd ed.). Boston: Allyn & Bacon.

Coleman, L. J., & Cross, T. L. (2001). *Being gifted in school: An introduction to developing, guidance, and teaching.* Austin, TX: Pro-Ed.

Coleman, L. J., & Cross, T. L. (2005). *Being gifted in school: An introduction to developing, guidance, and teaching* (2nd ed.). Austin: Pro-Ed.

Coleman, M. C., & Webber, J. (2002). *Emotional and behavioral disorders: Theory and practice* (4th ed.). Boston: Allyn & Bacon.

Committee on Goals 2000 (2000). National Research Council. Washington, DC.

Commonwealth Institute. (2009). *Invest now, save later: The benefits of targeted prekindergarten.* Richmond, VA: Author.

Conner, D. (2006) Stimulants. In R. Barkley (Ed.), *A handbook for diagnosis and treatment* (3rd ed., pp. 658-677). New York: Guilford.

Conroy, E. (1993). Strategies for counseling with parents. *Elementary School Guidance and Counseling, 29,* 60-66.

Conte, R. (1991). Attention disorders. In B. Y. L. Wong (Ed.), *Learning about learning disabilities* (pp. 55-101). New York: Academic Press.

Cook, B. G., Cameron, D. L., & Tankersley, M. (2007). Inclusive teachers' attitudinal ratings of their students with disabilities. *The Journal of Special Education, 40,* 230-238.

Cook, B. G., Tankersley, T. J., Cook, L., & Landrum, M. (2008). Evidence-based practices in special education: Some practical considerations. *Intervention in School and Clinic, 44,* 69-75.

Cook, J. E. (2007, January). *Response to Intervention.* Paper presented at the Alabama State Department of Education Conference in Perdido, AL.

Cooper, H. (1989). *Homework.* White Plains, New York: Longman.

Copeland, S. R., Hughes, C., Carter, E. W., Guth, C., Presley, J. A. Williams, et al. (2004). Increasing access to general education: Perspectives of participants in a high school peer support program. *Remedial and Special Education, 25*(6), 341-351.

Corn, A. L. (2007). On the future of the field of education of students with visual impairments. *Journal of Visual Impairment and Blindness, 95,* 741-744.

Corn, A. L., Hatlen, P. (1995). Developing the national agenda for the education of children and youths with visual impairments. *Re:View, 28,* 5-18.

Council for Exceptional Children. (2005). *Universal design for learning: A guide for teachers and education professionals.* Arlington, VA: Council for Exceptional Children and Merrill/Pearson.

Coutinho, M. J., & Oswald, D. P. (2005). State variation in gender disproportional in special education: Findings and recommendations, *Remedial and Special Education, 26*(1), 7-15.

Coyne, M. D., Zipoli, R. P., & Ruby, M. F. (2006). Beginning reading instruction for students at-risk for reading disabilities. *Intervention, 41*(3) 161-168.

Crane, L. (2002). *Mental retardation: A community integration approach.* Belmont, CA: Thomson Publishing.

Crawford, H. (1998). Classroom acoustics: Creating favorable environments for learning. *ADVANCE for Speech-Language Pathologists & Audiologists, 36,* 25-27.

Crawford, V. (2002). *Embracing the monster: Overcoming the challenges of hidden disabilities.* Baltimore, MD: Brookes.

Cronin, M. E., Patton, J. R., & Wood, J. D. (2007). *Life skills instruction for all students with disabilities* (2nd ed). Austin, Pro-Ed.

Cross, C. (1999). An examination of the literature base on the suicidal behaviors of gifted students. *Roeper Review, 22,* 28-36.

Cross, T. L. (2005). Moving the discussion from patholoty to context: An interview with Laurence J. Coleman. *Roeper Review, 28*(1), p. 5.

Cullinan, D., & Sabornie, E. J. (2004). Characteristics of emotional disturbance in middle and high school students. *Journal of Emotional and Behavioral Disorders, 12*(3), 157-167.

Cummings, C. (1983). *Managing to teach.* Edmonds, WA: Teaching Inc.

Cummings, K. D., Atkins, T., Allison, R., & Cole, C. (2008). Response to intervention: Investigating the new role of special educators. *Teaching Exceptional Children, 40,* 20-31.

Cystic Fibrosis Foundation. (2010). *About Cystic Fibrosis.* Available: www.cff.org/AboutCF/

Dabkowski, D. M. (2004). Encouraging active parent participation in IEP team meetings. *Teaching Exceptional Children, 36,* 34-39.

Dagenais, P. A., Critz-Crosby, P., Fletcher, S. G., & McCutcheon, M. J. (1994). Comparing abilities of children with profound hearing impairments to learn consonants using electropalatography or traditional aural-oral techniques. *Journal of Speech and Hearing Research, 37,* 687-699.

Daly, D. A. (1991, April). *Multi-modal therapy for fluency clients: Strategies that work.* Paper presented at the Spring Convention of the Texas Speech-Language-Hearing Association, Houston, TX.

Danaher, J., Shackelford, J., & Harbin, G. (2004). Revisiting a comparison of eligibility policies for infant/toddler programs and preschool special education programs. *Topics in Early Childhood Special Education, 24*(2), 59-67.

Darrow, A. (2009). Barriers to effective inclusion and strategies to overcome them. *General Music Today, 22,* 29-31.

Davis, C. N., & Harris, T. B. (1992). Teachers' ability to accurately identify disordered voices. *Language, Speech, and Hearing Services in the Schools, 23,* 136-140.

Davis, G. A., & Rimm, S. B. (1998). *Education of the gifted and talented* (4th ed.). Boston: Allyn & Bacon.

Davis, W. E. (1995). Students at risk: Common myths and misconceptions. The *Journal of At-Risk Issues, 2,* 5-10.

Dawson, G., & Osterling, J. (1997). Early intervention in autism. In M. Guralnick (Ed.), *The effectiveness of early intervention* (pp. 307-326). Baltimore: Brookes.

Dawson, G., Rogers, S. J., Smith, M., Munson, J., Winter, J., et al. (2010). Randomized control trial of the Early Denver Start Model: A relationship-based developmental and behavioral intervention for toddlers with autism spectrum disorders: Effects on IQ, adaptive behavior, and autism diagnosis. *Pediatrics, 125,* 1-7.

Deafness.about.com. (2006). Communicating with deaf people. http://deafness.about.com. Retrieved 9/2/2010.

Deci, E. L., Koestner, R., & Ryan, R. M. (1999). A meta-analytic review of experiments examining the effects of extrinsic rewards on intrinsic motivation. *Psychological Bulletin, 125*(6), 627-668.

Deci, E. L., Koestner, R., & Ryan, R. M. (1999). The undermining effect is a reality after all—Extrinsic rewards, task interest, and self-determination: Reply to Eisenberger, Pierce, and Cameron (1999) and Lepper, Henderlong, and Gingras (1999). *Psychological Bulletin, 125*(6), 692-700.

De Fur, S. H. (2002). *Transition planning: A team effort.* Washington, DC: NICHCY.

Del Prete, T. (1996). Asset or albatross? The education and socialization of gifted students. *Gifted Child Today, 19*(2), 24-25, 44-49.

Denning, C. B., Chamberlain, J. A., & Polloway, E. A. (2000). An evaluation of state guidelines for mental retardation: Focus on definition and classification practices. *Education and Training in Mental Retardation and Developmental Disabilities, 35,* 135-144.

Deshler, D. (2005). Adolescents with learning disabilities. *Learning Disabilities Quarterly, 28*(2), 122-123.

Deshler, D. D., & Lenz, B. K. (1989). The strategies instructional approach. *International Journal of Disability, Development, and Education, 36*(3), 203-224.

Deshler, D. D., Ellis, E. S., & Lenz, B. K. (1996). *Teaching adolescents with learning disabilities: Strategies and methods* (2nd ed.). Denver, CO: Love.

Desrochers, J. (1999). Vision problems—How teachers can help. *Young Children, 54,* 36-38.

Devlin, S. D., & Harber, M. M. (2004). Collaboration among parents and professionals with discrete trial training in the treatment for autism. *Education and Training in Developmental Disabilities, 39,* 291-300.

Diagnostic and Statistical Manual of Mental Disorders (2000). Arlington, VA: American Psychiatric Association.

DiPipi-Hoy, C. & Jitendra, A. (2004). A parent-delivered intervention to teach purchasing skills to young adults with disabilities. *Journal of Special Education, 38*(3), 144-157.

Dobbs, F., & Block P. (2004). Assistive technology use and stigma. *Education and Training in Developmental Disabilities, 39*(3), 216-217.

Donne, V., & Zigmond, N. (2008). Engagement during reading instruction for students who are deaf or hard of hearing in public schools. *American Annals of the Deaf, 153,* 294-303.

Dorman, D., Hickson, L., Murdoch, B., & Houston, T. (2009). Longitudinal study of speech perception, speech, and language for children with hearing loss in an auditory-verbal therapy program. *The Volta Review, 109,* 61-85.

Dotinga, R. (2010). Traumatic amputations in children have high costs. *MedlinePlus*. Available: www.nlm.nih.gov/medlineplus.

Dowdy, C. A. (1998). Strengths and limitations inventory: School version. In C. A. Dowdy, J. R. Patton, T. E. C. Smith, & E. A. Polloway (Eds.), *Attention deficit/hyperactivity disorder in the classroom: A practical guide for teachers*. Austin, TX: Pro-Ed.

Downing, J. A. (2002). Individualized behavior contracts. *Intervention, 37*, 164–172.

Downing, J. E., & Chen, D. (2003). Using tactile strategies with students who are blind and have severe disabilities. *Teaching Exceptional Children, 36*, 56–61.

Downing, J. E., & Eichinger, J. (2003). Creating learning opportunities for students with severe disabilities in inclusive classrooms. *Teaching Exceptional Children, 36*, 26–31.

Doyle, W. (1986). Classroom organization and management. In M. C. Wittrock (Ed.), *Handbook of research and teaching* (3rd ed., pp. 392–431). New York: Macmillan.

Doyle, W. (2006). Ecological approaches to classroom management. In C. M. Evertson & C. S. Weinstein (Eds.), *Handbook of classroom management: Research, practice, and contemporary issues.* (97–125). Mahwah, NJ: Lawrence Erlbaum Associates Publishers.

Duhaney, L. M. G., & Salend, S. J. (2000). Parental perceptions of inclusive educational placements. *Remedial and Special Education, 21*, 121–128.

Dunlap, G., & Kern, L. (1997). Behavior analysis and its relevance to special education. In J. L. Paul, M. Churton, H. Roselli-Kostoryz, W. Morse, K. Marfo, C. Lavely, & D. Thomas (Eds.), *Foundations of special education: Basic knowledge informing research and practice in special education* (pp. 270–290). Pacific Grove, CA: Brooks/Cole.

Dunlap, G., Kern, L., & Worcester, J. (2001). ABA and academic instruction. *Focus on Autism and Other Developmental Disabilities, 16*, 129–136.

Dunn, C., Chambers, D., & Rabren, K. (2004). Variables affecting students' decisions to drop out of school. *Remedial and Special Education, 25*(5), 314–323.

Easterbrooks, S. R. (1999). *Adapting regular classrooms for children who are deaf/hard of hearing.* Paper presented at the Council for Exceptional Children Convention, Minneapolis, MN.

Edwards, C. (1996). Educational management of children with hearing loss. In F. N. Martin & J. G. Clark (Eds.), *Hearing care for children* (pp. 303–315). Boston: Allyn & Bacon.

Edyburn, D. L. (2010). Would you recognize universal design for learning if you saw it? Ten propositions for new directions for the second decade of UDL. *Learning Disabilities Quarterly, 33*(1), 33–41.

Egel, A. L. (1989). Finding the right educational program. In M. D. Powers (Ed.), *Children with autism: A parent's guide.* New York: Woodbine House.

Ehlers, V. L., & Ruffin, M. (1990). The Missouri project—Parents as teachers. *Focus on Exceptional Children, 23*(2), 1–14.

Ehrenreich, B. (2001). Prodding the poor to the altar. *Progressive, 65*, 14–16.

Eisenman, L. T. (2007). Self-determination interventions: Building a foundation for school completion. *Remedial and Special Education, 28*(1), 2–8.

Elders, J. (2002). Keynote address. 57th Annual Conference of the Association for Supervision and Curriculum Development, San Antonio, TX.

Elizer, E., & Kauffman, M. (1983). Factors influencing the severity of childhood bereavement reactions. *American Journal of Orthopsychiatry, 53*, 393–415.

Elksnin, L. K., & Elksnin, N. (1998). Teaching social skills to students with learning and behavioral problems. *Intervention in School and Clinic, 33*, 131–140.

Emerick, L. L., & Haynes, W. O. (1986). *Diagnosis and evaluation in speech pathology* (3rd ed.). Upper Saddle River, NJ: Prentice-Hall.

Emery, R. E. (1989). Family violence. *American Psychologist, 44*, 321–327.

Epilepsy Foundation. (2010). *About Epilepsy*. Available: www.epilepsyfoundation.org.

Epilepsy.com. (2007). *Understanding seizures and emergencies.* Available: www.epilepsy.com.

Epstein, M. H. (2004). *BERS-2: Behavioral and Emotional Rating Scale* (2nd ed.). Austin, TX: PRO-ED, Inc.

Epstein, M. H., Kurash, K., & Duchnowski, A. (2005). *Outcomes for children and youth with behavioral and emotional disorders and their families: Programs and evaluation of best practices.* Austin, TX: Pro-Ed.

Epstein, M. H., Nelson, J. R., Trout, A. L., & Mooney, P. (2005). Achievement and ED: Academic status and intervention research in outcomes for children and youth with emotional and behavioral disorders and their families. In M. H. Epstein, M. Kurash, & L. Duchnowski. *Outcomes for children and youth with emotional and behavioral disorders* (2nd ed.). Austin, TX: Pro-Ed.

Epstein, M. H., Polloway, E. A., Bursuck, W., Jayanthi, M., & McConeghy, J. (1996). *Recommendations for effective homework practices.* Manuscript in preparation.

Epstein, M. H., Polloway, E. A., Buck, G. A., Bursuck, W. D., Wissinger, L. M., & Whitehouse, F. (1997). Homework-related communication problems: Perspectives of general education teachers. *Learning Disabilities Research and Practice, 12*, 221–227.

Erickson, J. G. (1992, April). *Communication disorders in multicultural populations.* Paper presented at the Texas Speech–Language–Hearing Association Annual Convention, San Antonio, TX.

Evertson, C. M., & Weinstein, C. S. (Eds.). (2006). *Handbook of classroom management: Research, practice, and contemporary issues.* Mahwah, NJ: Lawrence Erlbaum Associates Publishers.

Evertson, C. M., Emmer, E. T., & Worsham, M. E. (2006). *Classroom management Elementary teachers* (7th ed.). Boston: Allyn & Bacon.

Evertson, C. M., Emmer, E. T., Clements, B. J., Sanford, J. P., & Worsham, M. E. (2006). *Classroom management for elementary teachers* (4th ed.). Upper Saddle River, NJ: Prentice-Hall.

Facts about Tourette Syndrome (2006). Washington, DC: National Institute of Neurological Disorders and Stroke.

Fad, K., Patton, J. R., & Polloway, E. A. (2006). *Behavioral intervention planning: Completing a functional behavioral assessment and developing a behavioral intervention plan* (2nd ed.). Austin, TX: Pro-Ed.

Family First Aid. (n.d.). *Teen pregnancy statistics and teen pregnancy facts.* Retrieved 1/1/10 from www.Familyfirstaid.org/teen-pregnancy.html.

Faraone, S. V., Perlis, R. H., Doyle, A. E., Smoller, J. W., Goralnick, J. J., Holmgren, M. A., Sklar, P. (2005). Molecular genetics of attention-deficit/hyperactivity disorder. *Biol Psychiatry, 57*, 1313–1323.

Favazza, P. C., Phillipsen, L., Kumar, P. (2000). Measuring and promoting acceptance of young children with disabilities. *Exceptional Children, 66*, 491–508.

Feldhusen, H. J. (1993a). Individualized teaching of the gifted in regular classrooms. In C. J. Maker (Ed.), *Critical issues in gifted education: Programs for the gifted in regular classrooms* (Vol. 3, pp. 263–273). Austin, TX: Pro-Ed.

Feldhusen, H. J. (1993b). Synthesis of research on gifted youth. *Educational Leadership, 22*, 6–11.

Fellinger, J., Holzinger, D., Sattel, H., & Laucht, M. (2008). Mental health and quality of life in deaf pupils. *European Child and Adolescent Psychiatry, 15*, 414–423.

Fiore, T. A., Becker, E. A., & Nerro, R. C. (1993). Educational interventions for students with attention deficit disorder. *Exceptional Children, 60*, 163–173.

Fisher, D., Frey, N., & Thousand, J. (2003). What do special educators need to know and be prepared to do for inclusive schooling to work? *Teacher Education and Special Education, 26*(1), 42–50.

Fisher, S. K., & Clark, G. M. (1992). Validating occupational awareness vocabulary words for middle school students with mild disabilities. *Career Development for Exceptional Individuals, 15*, 189–204.

Fisher, S., Clark, G. M., & Patton, J. R. (in press). *Understanding occupational vocabulary.* Austin, TX: Pro-Ed.

Fitzgerald, J. L., & Watkins, M. W. (2006). Parents' rights in special education: The readability of procedural safeguards. *Exceptional Children, 72*, 497–510.

Fleming, J. L., Monda-Amaya, L. E., (2001). Process variables critical for team effectiveness. *Remedial and Special Education, 22*, 158–171.

Fombonne, E. (2005). Epidemiological studies of pervasive developmental disorders. In F. R. Volkmar, R. Paul, A. Klin, & D. Cohen (Eds.), *Handbook of autism and pervasive developmental disorders, Vol 1: Diagnosis, development, neurobiology, and behavior* (pp. 42–69). Hoboken, NJ: John Wiley & Sons.

Forness, S. R. (1999). Stimulant medication revisited: Effective treatment of children with attention deficit disorder. *Journal of Emotional and Behavior Problems, 7*, 230–233.

Forness, S. R., Walker, H. M., & Kavale, K. A. (2003). Psychiatric disorders and treatments: A primer for teachers. *Teaching Exceptional Children, 36* (2), 42-49.

Forum on Child and Family Statistics. (2009). *America's children: Key national indicators of well-being, 2009.* Retrieved 1/1/10 from www.childstats.gov/pubs/index.asp.

Fowler, M. (1992a). *Attention deficit disorder* (NICHY briefing paper). Washington, DC: National Information Center for Children and Youth with Disabilities.

Fowler, M. (1992b). *C.H.A.D.D. educators manual: An in-depth look at attention deficit disorder for an educational perspective.* Fairfax, VA: CASET Associates, Ltd.

Fox, P., & Emerson, E. (2001). Socially valid outcomes of intervention for people with MR and challenging behavior: Views of different stakeholders. *Journal of Positive Behavior Interventions, 3*(3), 183-189.

Frankenberger, W. K. (1984). A survey of state guidelines for the identification of mental retardation. *Mental Retardation, 22,* 17-20.

Frankenberger, W., & Harper, J. (1988). States' definitions and procedures for identifying children with mental retardation: Comparison of 1981-1982 and 1985-1986 guidelines. *Mental Retardation, 26*(3), 133-136.

Freiberg, K. (2005). Non-traditional families and their architectural needs. *Human Factors and Architectural Research Methods: Architecture.*

Friedman, D., & Scaduto, J. J. (1995). Let's do lunch: A business/school partnership that works. *Teaching Exceptional Children, 28,* 22-25.

Friend, M. (1992). *Visionary leadership for today's schools.* Kansas City, KS: Center for Leadership Development.

Friend, M., & Cook, L. (2010). *Interactions: Collaboration skills for school professionals.* Boston: Pearson.

Friend, M.F., & Bursuck, W.D. (2008). *Including students with special needs: A practical guide for classroom teachers* (5th ed.). Boston: Allyn & Bacon.

Fries, K., & Cochran-Smith, M. (2006). Teacher research and classroom management: What questions do teachers ask? In C. M. Everston & C. S. Weinstein (Eds.). *Handbook of classroom management* (48-69). New York: Routledge.

Frost, L., & Bondy, A. (2002). *The Picture Exchange Communication System training manual* (2nd ed.). Newark, DE: Pyramid Educational Products.

Frymier, J., & Gansneder, B. (1989). The Phi Delta Kappa study of students at risk. *Phi Beta Kappan, 71*(2), 142-146.

Fuchs, L. S., & Fuchs, D. (2001). Helping teachers formulate sound test accommodation decisions for students with learning disabilities. *Learning Disability Research and Practice, 16*(3), 174-181.

Fujiura, G.T. (2003). Continuum of intellectual disability: Demographic evidence for the "forgotten generation." *Mental Retardation, 41,* 420-429.

Furner, J. M., Yahya, N., & Duffy, M.A. (2005). Teach mathematics: Strategies to reach all students. *Intervention in School and Clinic, 41*(1), 16-23.

Gagné, F. (1995). From giftedness to talent: A developmental model. *Roeper Review, 18,* 103-112.

Gagnon, E. (2001). *Power cards: Using special interests to motivate children and youth with Asperger Syndrome and autism.* Shawnee Mission, KS: Autism Asperger Publishing.

Gallagher, J. (1997). Least restrictive environment and gifted students. *Peabody Journal of Education, 72,* 153-166.

Garay, S. V. (2003). Listening to the voices of deaf students. *Teaching Exceptional Children, 35,* 56-61.

Garcia, S. B., & Guerra, P. L. (2004). Deconstructing deficit thinking: Working with educators to create more equitable learning environments. *Education and Urban Society, 36*(2), 150-168.

Gardner, H. (1983). *Frames of mind: The theory of multiple intelligences.* New York: Basic Books.

Gardner, H., & Hatch, T. (1989). Multiple intelligences go to school: Educational implications of the theory of multiple intelligences. *Educational Researcher, 18*(8), 4-9.

Gardner, R., Nobel, M. M., Hessler, T., Yawn, C. D., & Heron, T. E. (2007). Tutoring system innovations: Past practice to future prototypes. *Intervention in School and Clinic, 43,* 71-81.

Gargiulo, R. M. (1990). Child abuse and neglect: An overview. In R. L. Goldman & R. M. Gargiulo (Eds.), *Children at risk* (pp. 1-35). Austin, TX: Pro-Ed.

Gargiulo, R. M., & Metcalf, D. (2010). *Teaching in today's inclusive classrooms.* Belmont, CA: Wadsworth.

Gartin, B. C., & Murdick, N. L. (2005). IDEA 2004: The IEP. *Remedial and Special Education, 26*(6), 327-331.

Gay, I. (2003). The teacher makes it more explanable. *Reading Teacher, 56*(8), 812-814.

Gay, Lesbian, and Straight Education Network (GLSEN) (2005). Local School Climate Survey. www.glsen.org. retrieved 8/22/10.

Gersten, R., Jordan, N. C., & Flojo, J. R. (2005). Early identification and intervention for students with math difficulties. *Journal of Learning Disabilities, 38*(4), 293-304.

Getch, Y., Bhukhanwala, F., & Neuharth-Pritchett, S. (2007). Strategies for helping children with diabetes in elementary and middle schools. *Teaching Exceptional Chidlren, 39,* 46-54.

Getty, L.A., & Summy, S. E. (2004). The course of due process. *Teaching Exceptional Children, 36,* 40-43.

Ghere, G., & York-Barr, J. (2007). Paraprofessional turnover and retention in inclusive programs. *Remedial and Special Education, 28,* 21-32.

Giangreco, M. F., Yuan, S., McKenzie, B., Cameron, P., & Fialka, J. (2005). "Be careful what you wish for. . .": Five reasons to be concerned about the assignment of individual paraprofessionals. *Teaching Exceptional Children, 37*(5), 28-34.

Gilliam, J. E., & Miller, L. (2006). *Pragmatic Language Skills Inventory.* Austin: PRO-ED.

Glang, A., Todis, B., Thomas, C. W., Hood, D., Bedell, G., & Cockrell, J. (2008). Return to school following childhood TBI: Who gets services? *NeuroRehabilitation, 23,* 477-486.

Goin, R. P., & Myers, B. J. (2004). Characteristics of infantile autism: Moving toward earlier detection. *Focus on Autism and Other Developmental Disabilities, 19,* 5-12.

Gollnick, D. M., & Chinn, P. C. (2009). Multicultural Education in a Pluralistic Society. Boston. (8th ed.). Allyn & Bacon.

Gomez, C. R., & Baird, S. (2005). Identifying early indicators of autism in self-regulation difficulties. *Focus on Autism and Other Developmental Disabilities, 20,* 106-116.

Gonzalez, V., Brusca-Vega, R., & Yawkey, T. (1997). *Assessment and instruction of culturally diverse students.* Boston: Allyn & Bacon.

Graham, S., Harris, K. R., & MacArthur, C. (2006). Cognitive strategy instruction. In C. MacArthur, S. Graham, & J. Ditgerald, (Eds.). *Handbook for writing research* (pp. 187-207). New York: Guildford.

Grant, J. (1993). Hearing-impaired children from Mexican-American homes. *Volta Review, 95(5),* 212-218.

Gray, C. (1994). *Comic strip conversations.* Arlington, TX: Future Horizons.

Gray, C. (2004). Social Stories™ 10.0: The new defining criteria and guidelines. *Jenison Autism Journal: Creative Ideas in Practice, 15*(4), 2-21.

Green, G. (1996). Early behavioral intervention for autism: What does research tell us? In C. Maurice, G. Green, & S. Luce (Eds.), *Behavioral intervention for young children with autism: A manual for parents and professionals.* Austin, TX: PRO-ED.

Green, G. (2001). Behavior analytic instruction for learners with autism: Advances in stimulus control technology. *Focus on Autism and Other Developmental Disabilities, 16,* 72-85.

Greenspan, S. (1996, October 11). *Everyday intelligence and a new definition of mental retardation.* Presented at Fifth Annual MRDD Conference, Austin, TX.

Greenspan, S. (1997). Emotions and intelligence linked: Early emotional interactions are the source of all cognitive and intellectual development. *Psychiatric News, 32,* 10-11.

Greenspan, S. (2006). Functional concepts in mental retardation: Finding the natural essence of an artificial category. *Exceptionality, 14,* 205-224.

Gregory, R. J. (2004). *Psychological testing: History, principles, and applications* (4th ed.). Boston: Pearson.

Gresham, F. M. (2002). Responsiveness to Intervention. In Bradley, Danielson, & Hallahan (Eds.). Identification of Learning Disabilities: Research to Practice. Mahwah, NJ: Erlbaum.

Griffin, H. C., Williams, S. C., Davis, M. L., & Engleman, M. (2002). Using technology to enhance cues for children with low vision. *Teaching Exceptional Children, 35,* 36-40.

Grinker, R. P. (2007). *Unstrange minds: Remapping the world of autism.* Philadelphia: Basic Books.

Griswold, D. E., Barnhill, G. P., & Myles, B. S. (2002). Asperger's syndrome and academic achievement. *Focus on Autism and Other Developmental Disabilities, 17,* 94-102.

Grossman, H. J. (1983). *Classification in mental retardation.* Washington, DC: American Association on Mental Deficiency.

Guber, P., & Peters, J. (Producers), & Levinson, B. (Director). (1988). *Rainman* [Motion Picture]. United States: Universal Artists.

Guyer B. D. (2002). So you have a learning disability: Do you have what it takes to succeed in college? *LDA Newsbriefs,* May/June, 3-5.

Hagner, D., & Cooney, B. F. (2005). I do that for everybody. *Focus on Autism and Other Developmental Disabilities, 20,* 92-99.

Hall, R. A. (2007). Students who are homeless and the public school system. *The Delta Kappa Gamma Bulletin, 73*(3), 9-12.

Hall, T. (2002). *Differentiated instruction.* Wakefield, MA: National Center on Accessing the General Curriculum.

Hall, T. E., Wolfe, P. S., & Bollig, A. A. (2003). The home-to-school notebook: An effective communication strategy for students with severe disabilities. *Teaching Exceptional Children, 36,* 68-73.

Hallahan, D. P., & Kauffman, J. M. (2003). *Exceptional children: Introduction to special education* (9th ed.). Boston: Allyn & Bacon.

Hallahan, D. P., Kauffman, J. M. & Pullen, P. C. (2009). *Exceptional learners: An introduction to special education* (11th ed.). Upper Saddle River, NJ: Pearson Education.

Hallahan, D. P., Lloyd, J. W., & Stoller, L. (1982). *Improving attention with self-monitoring: A manual for teachers.* Charlottesville, VA: University of Virginia Press.

Hallahan, D. P., Lloyd, J. W., Kauffman, J. M., Weiss, M. P., & Martinez, E. A. (2005). *Learning disabilities: Foundations, characteristics, and effective teaching* (3rd ed.). Boston: Allyn & Bacon.

Haller, A. K., & Montgomery, J. K. (2004). Noise-induced hearing loss in children. *Teaching Exceptional Children, 36,* 22-27.

Halvorsen, A. T., & Neary, T. (2001). *Building inclusive schools: Tools and strategies for success.* Boston: Allyn & Bacon.

Hammerness, P. G. (2009). Biographies of disease: ADHD. Westport, CT: Greenwood Press.

Hammill, D. (2004). What we know about correlates of reading. *Exceptional Children, 70*(4), 453-468.

Hammill, D. D., & Larsen, S. C. (1974). The effectiveness of psycholinguistic training. *Exceptional Children, 41*(1), 5-14.

Hanks, J. A., & Velaski, A. (2003). A summertime collaboration between speech-language pathology and deaf education. *Teaching Exceptional Children, 36,* 58-62.

Hansen, J. B., & Feldhusen, J. F. (1994). Comparison of trained and untrained teachers of gifted students. *Gifted Child Quarterly, 38,* 115-123.

Happe, F., & Frith, U. (2006). The weak coherence account: Detail-focused cognitive style in autism spectrum disorders. *Journal of Autism and Developmental Disorders, 36,* 5-25. doi: 10.1007/s10803-005-0039-0.

Hardmann M. J., Drew, C. J., & Egan, M. W. (1993). *Human exceptionality* (7th ed.). Boston: Houghton-Mifflin.

Harniss, M. K., & Epstein, M. H. (2005) Strength-based assessment in children's mental health. In M. H. Epstein, K. Kurash, & A. J. Duchnowski (Eds.), *Outcomes for children and youth with emotional and behavioral disorders and their families* (2nd ed., pp. 125-141). Austin, TX: Pro-Ed.

Harris, D., & Vanderheiden, G. C. (1980). Augmentative communication techniques. In R. L. Schiefelbusch (Ed.), *Nonspeech language and communication: Analysis and intervention* (pp. 259- 302). Austin, TX: Pro-Ed.

Harris, G. (2010, February 3). Journal retracts 1998 paper linking autism to vaccines. *The New York Times.* Retrieved from: http://nytimes.com/2010/02/03/health/research/03lancet.html?ref=health&pagewanted.

Harrower, J. K., & Dunlap, G. (2001). Including children with autism in general education classrooms: A review of effective strategies. *Behavior Modification, 25,* 762-784.

Hatamizadeh, N., Ghasemi, M., Saeedi, A., & Kazemnejad, A. (2008). Perceived competence and school adjustment of hearing impaired children in mainstream primary school settings. *Child: Care Health and Development, 34,* 789-794.

Healthy People 2000. (1992). Washington, DC: U.S. Government Printing Office.

Hear-It.org. (2010). One in six has hearing loss. http://hear-it.org. retrieved 8/22/10.

Heaton, S., & O'Shea, D. J. (1995). Using mnemonics to make mnemonics. *Teaching Exceptional Children, 28*(1), 34-36.

Heflin, L. J., & Alaimo, D. F. (2007). *Students with autism spectrum disorders: Effective instructional practices.* Upper Saddle River, NJ: Pearson Education.

Heflin, L. J., & Simpson, R. (1998). The interventions for children and youth with autism: Prudent choices in a world of extraordinary claims and promises: Part II. *Focus on Autism and Other Developmental Disabilities, 13,* 212-220.

Hegde, M. N. (2010). *Introduction to communicative disorders* (4th ed.). Austin: PRO-ED.

Heinrich, T. (1999). Sources of stress in mothers of young children with visual impairment. *Journal of Visual Impairment and Blindness, 95,* 623-638.

Heller, K. W., & Fredrick, L. D. (2000). A national perspective of competencies for teachers of individuals with physical and health impairments. *Exceptional Children, 65,* 219-234.

Helping the student with diabetes succeed: A guide for school personnel (2003). Washington, DC: U.S. Department of Health and Human Services.

Hendren, R., & Martin, A. (2005). Pharmacotherapy. In L. J. Baker & L. A. Welkowitz (Eds.), *Asperger's Syndrome. Intervening in schools, clinics, and*

communities (pp. 63-81). Mahwah, NJ: Lawrence Erlbaum Associates.

Henry, K. L. (2007). Who's skipping school: Characteristics of truants in 8th and 10th grade. *Journal of School Health, 77,* 29-35.

Heward, W. L. (1995). *Exceptional children: An introductory survey of special education* (4th ed.). New York: Macmillan.

Heward, W. L. (2009). *Exceptional children: An introduction to special education* (9th ed.). Upper Saddle River, NJ: Merrill/Pearson.

Hiller, J. F. (1990). Setting up a classroom-based language instruction program: One clinician's experience. *Texas Journal of Audiology and Speech Pathology, 16*(2), 12-13.

Hilton, A. (1990). *Parental reactions to having a disabled child.* Paper presented at annual International Conference of the Council for Exceptional Children.

Hines, J. T. (2008). Making collaboration work in inclusive high school classrooms: Recommendations for principals. *Intervention in School and Clinic, 43,* 277-282.

HIV Infosource (2010). New York: NYU Medical Center.

Hobbs, T., & Westling, D. L. (1998). Promoting successful inclusion. *Teaching Exceptional Children, 34,* 10-14.

Holbrook, M. C. (2008). Teaching reading and writing to students with visual impairments: Who is responsible? *Journal of Visual Impairment and Blindness, 96,* 203-206.

Homme, L. (1969). *How to use contingency contracting in the classroom.* Champaign, IL: Research Press.

Hooper, C. R. (2004). Treatment of voice disorders in children. *Language, Speech, and Hearing Services in Schools, 35,* 320-326.

Hoover, J. J., & Patton, J. R. (2004). Differentiating standards-based education for students with diverse needs. *Remedial and Special Education, 25*(2), 74-78.

Hoover, J. J., & Patton, J. R. (2005). Differentiating curriculum and instruction for English-language learners with special needs. *Intervention in School and Clinic, 40*(4), 231-235.

Hoover, J. J., & Patton, J. R. (2006). *Curriculum adaptations for students with learning and behavior problems* (3rd ed.). Austin, TX: Pro-Ed.

Hoover, J. J., & Patton, J. R. (2007). *Teaching study skills to students with learning problems* (2nd ed.). Austin, TX: Pro-Ed.

Hoover, J. J., & Patton, J. R. (2008). The role of special educators in a multitiered instructional system. *Intervention in School and Clinic, 43,* 195-202.

Horner, R. H. (2000). Positive behavior supports. In M. L. Wehmeyer & J. R. Patton (Eds.), *Mental retardation in the 21st century* (pp. 181-196). Austin, TX: Pro-Ed.

Horrocks, J. L., White, G., & Roberts, L. (2008). Principals' attitudes regarding inclusion of children with autism in Pennsylvania public schools. *Journal on Autism and Developmental Disorders, 38,* 1462-1473.

Hostetler, S. G., Schwartz, L., Shields, B. J., Xiang, H., & Smith, G. A. (2005). Characteristics of pediatric traumatic amputations treated in hospital emergency departments: United States, 1990-2002. *Pediatrics, 116*, 667-674.

Houwen, S., Visscher, C., Lemmink, K.A.P. M., & Hartman, E. (2009). Motor skill performance of children and adolescents with visual impairments: A review. *Exceptional Children, 75*, 464-492.

Hughes, C., Copeland, S. R., Guth, C., Rung, L. L., Hwang, B., Kleeb, G., et al. (2001). General education students' perspectives on their involvement in a high school peer buddy program. *Education and Training in Mental Retardation and Developmental Disabilities, 36*, 343-355.

Hulett, K. E. (2009). *Legal aspects of special education*. Upper Saddle River, NJ: Merrill.

Hume, K., Bellini, L., & Pratt, R. (2005). The usage and perceived outcomes of early intervention and early childhood programs for young children with autism. *Topics in Early Childhood Education, 25*(4), 195-207.

Hunt, P., Doering, K., & Hirose-Hatae, A. (2001). Across-program collaboration to support students with and without disabilities in general education classrooms. *Journal of the Association for Persons with Severe Handicaps, 26*, 240-256.

Hutton, A. M., & Caron, S. L. (2005). Experiences of families with children with autism in rural New England. *Focus on Autism and Other Developmental Disabilities, 20*, 180-189.

Huurre, T.M., Komulainen, E. J., & Aro, H.M. (1999). Social support and self-esteem among adolescents with visual impairments. *Journal of Visual Impairment and Blindness, 93*, 26-38.

Hyatt, K. J. (2007). The new IDEA: Changes, concerns, and questions. *Intervention in School and Clinic, 42*(3), 131-136.

IDEA (2004). Individuals with Disabilities Education Act. Washington, DC: U.S. Government Printing Office.

Idol, L. (2006). Toward inclusion of special education students in general education: A program evaluation of eight schools. *Remedial and Special Education, 27*(2), 77-94.

Immunization Safety Review Committee of the Institute of Medicine (2004). *Immunization Safety review: Vaccines and autism*. Washington, DC: The National Academies Press. Retrieved from: http://books.nap.edu/openbook.php?record_id=10997&page=R1.

Individuals with Disabilities Education Act. (2004). Washington DC: Government Printing Office.

Iovannone, R., Dunlap, G., Huber, H., & Kincaid, D. (2003). Effective educational practices for students with autism spectrum disorders. *Focus on Autism and Other Developmental Disabilities, 18*, 150-165.

Jakobson, A., & Kikas, E. (2007). Cognitive functioning in children with and without attention-deficit/hyperactive disorder with and without comorbid learning disabilities. *Journal of Learning Disabilities, 40*(3), 194-202.

Jaquish, C., & Stella, M.A. (1986). Helping special students move from elementary to secondary school. *Counterpoint, 7*(1), 1.

Johnson, E., & Arnold, N. (2004). Validating an alternative assessment. *Remedial and Special Education, 25*(5), 266-275.

Johnson, G., & Jefferson-Aker, C. R. (2001). HIV/AIDS prevention: Effective instructional strategies for adolescents with mild mental retardation. *Teaching Exceptional Children, 33*, 28-32.

Johnson, R. (n.d.). How many gay people are there? Retrieved 1/1/10 from About.com (http://gaylife.About.com/od/comingout/a/population.htm).

Jones, V. (2006). How do teachers learn to be effective classroom managers? In C. M. Everston & C. S. Weinstein (Eds.), *Handbook of classroom management: Research, practice, and contemporary issues* (887-907). Mahwah, NJ: Lawrence Erlbaum Associates Publishers.

Jones, V. F., & Jones, L. S. (2007). *Comprehensive classroom management* (8th ed.). Boston: Allyn & Bacon.

Kaderavek, J. N., & Pakulski, L. A. (2002). Minimal hearing loss is not minimal. *Teaching Exceptional Children, 34*, 14-18.

Kalachnik, J. E., Leventhal, B. L., James, D. H., Sovner, R., Kastner, T.A., Walsh, K., et al. (1998). Guidelines for the use of psychotropic medication. In S. Reiss & M. G. Aman (Eds.), *Psychotropic medications and developmental disabilities: The international consensus handbook* (pp. 45-72). Columbus: The Ohio State University Press.

Kamradt, B., Gilbertson, S.A., & Lynn N. (2005). Wraparound Milwaukee. In M. Epstein, J. Kurash, & L. Duchnowski (Eds.), *Outcomes for children and youth with emotional and behavioral disorders.* (pp. 307-328) Austin, TX: Pro-Ed.

Kaplan, P. S. (1996). *Pathways for exceptional children: School, home, and culture.* St. Paul, MN: West.

Kaplan, P. S. (1999). *Pathways for exceptional children: School, home, and culture.* St. Paul, MN: West.

Katsiyannis, A., & Maag, J.W. (2001). Manifestation determination as a golden fleece. *Exceptional Children, 68*, 89-96.

Katsiyannis, A., Yell, M. L., & Bradley, R. (2001). Reflections on the 25th anniversary of the Individuals with Disabilities Education Act. *Remedial and Special Education, 22*, 324-334.

Kauffman, J. M, & Landrum, T. J. (2009a). *Characteristics of emotional and behavioral disorders of children and youth* (9th ed.). Upper Saddle River, NJ: Merrill.

Kauffman, J. M, & Landrum, T. J. (2009b). Politics, civil rights, and disproportional identification of students with emotional and behavioral disorders. *Exceptionality, 17*, 177-188.

Kauffman, J. M., Mostert, M. P., Trent, S. C., & Hallahan, D. P. (2002). Managing classroom behavior: *A reflective case-based approach* (3rd ed.). Boston: Allyn & Bacon.

Kavale, K.A. (2001a). Decision making in special education: The function of meta-analysis. *Exceptionality, 9*, 245-268.

Kavale, K.A., (2001b). *Discovering models in the identification of learning disabilities.* Executive summary. Washington, DC: LD Summit.

Kavale, K.A., & Forness, S. R. (2000). History, rhetoric, and reality: Analysis of the inclusion debate. *Remedial and Special Educaiton, 21*, 279-296.

Kavale, K.A., & Mostert, M. P. (2004). Social skills interventions for individuals with learning disabilities. *Learning Disabilities Quarterly, 27*(1), 31-43.

Keith, B., & Lenz, B. (2004). Creating school-wide conditions for high quality learning strategies classroom. *Intervention, 41*(5), 261-268.

Keller, C. L., Bucholz, J., & Brady, M. P. (2007). Yes, I Can! Empowering paraprofessionals to teach learning strategies. *Teaching Exceptional Children 39*(3), 18-23.

Kellough, R. D., & Kellough, N. D. (2008). *Teaching young adolescents: Methods and resources for middle grades teaching.* Upper Saddle River, NJ: Pearson/Merrill.

Kelly, S. M. (2009). Use of assistive technology by students with visual impairments: Findings from a national survey. *Journal of Visual Impairment and Blindness, 97*, 470-480.

Keogh, B.K. (2000). Risk, families, and schools. *Focus on Exceptional Children, 33*, 1-10.

Kerr, M. M., & Nelson, C. M. (2010). *Strategies for addressing behavior problems in the classroom* (6th ed.). Upper Saddle River, NJ: Pearson.

Kerrin, R. G. (1996). Collaboration: Working with the speech-language pathologist. *Intervention in School and Clinic, 32*(1), 56-59.

Keyser-Marcus, L., Briel, L., Sherron-Targett, P., Yasuda, S., Johnson, S., & Wehman, P. (2002). Enhancing the schooling of students with traumatic brain injury. *Teaching Exceptional Children, 34*, 62-67.

King-Sears, M. E., & Bradley, D. F. (1995). Classwide peer tutoring. *Preventing School Failure, 40*(1), 27-31.

Kirk, S.A. (1962). *Educating exceptional children.* Boston: Houghton Mifflin.

Kirk, S.A., Gallagher, J. J., & Anastasiow, A. (2000). *Educating exceptional children* (8th ed.). Boston: Houghton Mifflin.

Kirsten, I. (1981). *The Oakland picture dictionary.* Wauconda, IL: Don Johnston.

Kitano, M.K. (1993). Intellectual abilities and psychological intensities in young children: Implications of the gifted. *Roeper Review, 13*, 5-11.

Klassen, R. M. (2010). Confidence to manage learning: The self-efficacy for self-regulated learning of early adolescents with learning disabilities, *Learning Disability Quarterly, 33*, 19-30.

Kluwin, T. N. (1996). Getting hearing and deaf students to write to each other through dialogue journals. *Teaching Exceptional Children, 28*, 50-53.

Kogan, M. D., Blumberg, S. J., Schieve, L.A., Boyle, C.A., Perrin, J. M., Ghandour, R. M., & van Dyck, P. C. (2009). Prevalence of parent-reported diagnosis of autism spectrum disorder among children in the US, 2007. *Pediatrics, 124*(5), 1395-1403. doi: 10.1542/peds.2009-1522.

Kohn A. (1993). Rewards versus learning: A response to Paul Chance. *Phi Delta Kappan, 74*(10), 783-787.

Kohn, A. (1993). *Punished by rewards: The trouble with gold stars, incentive plans, A's, praise, and other bribes.* Boston, MA: Houghton, Mifflin and Company.

Kohn, A. (1996a). *Beyond discipline: From compliance to community.* Washington, DC: Association for Supervision and Curriculum Development.

Kohn, A. (1996b). What to look for in the classroom. *Educational Leadership, 54,* 54-55.

Konrad, M. (2008). Involve students in the IEP process. *Intervention in Schools & Clinic, 43*(4), 236-239.

Kortering, L. J. (2009). School completion issues in special education. *Exceptionality, 17,* 1-4.

Kortering, L. J., & Christenson, S. (2009). Engaging students in school and learning: The real deal for school completion. *Exceptionality, 17,* 5-15.

Kroeger, S. D., & Kouche, B. (2006). Using peer-assisted learning strategies to increase response to intervention in inclusive middle math settings. *Teaching Exceptional Children, 38*(5), 6-13.

Kruczek, T., & Vitanza, S. (1999). Treatment effects with an adolescent abuse survivor's group. *Child Abuse & Neglect, 23,* 477-485.

Kubler-Ross, E. (1969). *On death and dying.* New York: Macmillan.

Kurtis, S. A., Matthews, C. E., & Smallwood, T. (2009). (Dis)Solving the differences: A physical science lesson using universal design. *Intervention in School and Clinic, 44,* 151-159.

LaCoste-Caputo, J. (2009). Teacher gives refugee students a chance. Retrieved on 4.22.09 from http://www.printhis.clickability.com/ pt/cpt?action=cpt&title=Teacher+... ssionate_teacher_gives_refugee_students_ a_chance.html&partnerID+345999.

Lahey, M. (1988). *Language disorders and language development.* New York: Macmillan.

Lake, J. F., & Billingsley, B. S. (2000). An analysis of factors that contribute to parent-school conflict in special education. *Remedial and Special Education, 21,* 240-250.

Lamar-Dukes, P., & Dukes, C. (2005). Consider the roles and responsibilities of the inclusion support teacher. *Intervention, 41*(1), 55-59.

Lambert, M. A., & Nowacek, J. (2006). Help high school students improve their study skills. *Intervention in School and Clinic, 41*(4), 241-243.

Landrum, T. J., & Kauffman, J. M. (2006). Behavioral approaches to classroom management. In C. M. Evertson & C. S. Weinstein (Eds.). *Handbook of classroom management* (131-165). New York: Cambridge University Press.

Landrum, T. J., Tankersley, M., & Kauffman, J. M. (2006). What is special about special education for students with emotional or behavioral disorders? In B. G. Cook & B. R. Schirmer (Eds.), *What is special about special education?* (pp. 12-25). Austin, TX: Pro-Ed.

Lane, K. L., Wehby, J. H., Robertson, E. J., & Rogers, L. A. (2007). How do different types of high school students respond to schoolwide positive behavior support

programs? Characteristics and responsiveness of teacher-identified students. *Journal of Emotional & Behavioral Disorders, 15*(1), 3-20.

Lang, L. (1998). Allergy linked to common ear infection. *ADVANCE for Speech-Language Pathologists and Audiologists, 36,* 8-9.

LDOnline. (2010). www.ldonline.org.

Lee, S. H., Palmer, S. B., Turnbull, A. P., & Wehmeyer, M. L. (2006). A model for parent-teacher collaboration to promote self-determination in young children with disabilities. *Teaching Exceptional Children, 38,* 36-41.

Lee, S., Wehmeyer, M. L., Soukup, J. H., & Palmer, S. B. (2010). Impact of curriculum modification on access to the general education curriculum for students with disabilities. *Exceptional Children, 76,* 213-233.

Lenz, B. K., Deshler, D. D., & Kissam, B. R. (2004). *Teaching content to all: Evidence-based inclusive practices in middle and secondary schools.* Boston: Allyn & Bacon.

Levin, B. B. (2003). *Case studies of teacher development: An in-depth look at how thinking about pedagogy develops over time.* Mahwah, NJ: Lawrence Erlbaum Associates Publishers.

Lewis, A. C. (1992). Ready to learn? *Education Digest, 57,* 61-63.

Lewis, S., & McKenzie, A. R. (2009). Knowledge and skills for teachers of students with visual impairment supervising the work of paraeducators. *Journal of Visual Impairment and Blindness, 97,* 481-494.

Li, A. (2004). Classroom strategies for improving and enhancing visual skills in students with disabilities. *Teaching Exceptional Children, 36,* 38-42.

Li, A. (2009) Identification and intervention for students who are visually impaired and who have autism spectrum disorders. *Teaching Exceptional Children, 41,* 22-31.

Lisnov, L., Harding, C. G., Safer, L. A., & Kavanagh, J. (1998). Adolescents' perceptions of substance abuse prevention strategies. *Adolescence, 33,* 301-312.

Little, M. (2008). Research to practice: RTI and SLD: Connections and considerations. *Learning Disability Quarterly,* Fall, 5-8.

Livingston, J. N., & Nahimana, C. (2006). Problem child or problem context: An ecological approach to young black males. *Reclaiming Children and Youth, 14,* 209-214.

Lloyd, J. W., & Hallahan, D. F. (2005). Going forward: How the field of learning disabilities has and will contribute to education. *Learning Disability Quarterly, 28*(2), 133-138.

Lloyd, J. W., Forness, S. R., & Kavale, K. A. (1998). Some methods are more effective than others. *Intervention in School & Clinic, 33*(4), 195-200.

Lloyd, J. W., Landrum, T., & Hallahan, D. P. (1991). Self-monitoring applications for classroom intervention. In G. Stoner, M. R. Shinn, & H. M. Walker (Eds.), *Interventions for achievement and behavior problems* (pp. 201-213). Washington, DC: NASP.

Loder, R. T. (2004). Demographics of traumatic amputations in children. *Journal of Bone and Joint Surgery.*

Loehr, J. (2002). *Read the picture stories for articulation* (2nd ed.). Austin, TX: Pro-Ed.

Lohrmann, S., & Bambara, L. (2006). Elementary education teachers' beliefs about essential supports needed to successfully include students with developmental disabilities who engage in challenging behaviors. *Research and Practice for Persons with Severe Disabilities, 31,* 157-173.

Lovaas, O. I. (1987). Behavioral treatment and normal educational and intellectual functioning in young autistic children. *Journal of Consulting and Clinical Psychology, 55*(1), 3-9.

Lovitt, T. C., & Horton, S. V. (1991). Adapting textbooks for mildly handicapped adolescents. In G. Stoner, M. R. Shinn, & H. M. Walker (Eds.). *Interventions for achievement and behavior problems* (439-472). Silver Spring, MD: National Association of School Psychologists.

Luckasson, R., Borthwick-Duffy, S., Buntinx, W. H. E., Coulter, D. L., Craig, E. M., Reeve, A., Schalock, R. L., Snell, M. E., Spitalnik, D. M., & Spreat, S. (2002). *Mental retardation: Definition, classification, and systems of supports.* Washington, DC: American Association on Mental Retardation.

Luckasson, R., Coulter, D., Polloway, E. A., Reis, S., Schalock, R., Snell, et al. (1992). *Mental retardation: Definition, classification, and systems of supports.* Washington, DC: American Association on Mental Retardation.

Luckner, J. (1994). Developing independent and responsible behaviors in students who are deaf or hard of hearing. *Teaching Exceptional Children, 26,* 13-17.

Luckner, J. (1999). An example of two coteaching classrooms. *American Annals of the Deaf, 44,* 24-34.

Luckner, J. L., & Bowen, S. (2006). Assessment practices of professionals serving students who are deaf or hard of hearing: An initial investigation. *American Annals of the Deaf, 151,* 410-419.

Ludlow, B. L., Keramidas, C. G., & Landers, E. J. (2007). Project STARS: Using desktop conferencing to prepare autism specialists at a distance. *Rural Special Education Quarterly, 26*(4), 27-35.

Lyon, R. (2010). Information retrieved from website: ReidLyon.com. June, 2010.

Maag, J. W., & Katsiyannis, A. (1998). Challenges facing successful transition for youths with E/BD. *Behavioral Disorders, 23*(4), 209-221.

Mackie, E. (1996). *Oral-motor activities for school aged-children.* Austin, TX: Pro-Ed.

MacMillan, D. L. (2007, December). *Mental retardation over five decades: Lessons we might have learned.* Presentation at the Next Generation of Research in Intellectual Disabilities: Charting the Course (A Special Olympics working conference). Miami, FL.

MacMillan, D. L., Siperstein, G. N., & Leffert, J. S. (2006). Children with mild mental retardation: A challenge for classification practices—revised. In H. N. Switzky, & S. Greenspan (Eds.). *What is mental retardation? Ideas for an evolving disability in the 21st century* (pp. 197-220). Washington, DC: AAMR.

Madaus, J. (2006). Employment outcomes of university graduates with Learning Disabilities. *Learning Disabilities Quarterly, 29,* 19-30.

Madaus, J. W., & Shaw, S. F. (2004). Section 504: Differences in the regulations for secondary and postsecondary education. *Intervention in School and Clinic, 40*(2), 81-87.

Madaus, J. W., Ruban, L. M., Foley, T. E., & McGuire, J. M. (2003). *Learning Disabilities Quarterly, 26,* 159-169.

Maheady, L., Harper, G. F., & Mallette, B. (2001). Peer-mediated instruction and interventions and students with mild disabilities. *Remedial and Special Education, 22,* 4-14.

Maheady, L., Harper, G., & Mallette, B. (2003). Preparing preservice teachers to implement class wide peer tutoring. *Teacher Education and Special Education, 27*(4), 408-418.

Maker, C. J. (1993). Gifted students in the regular education classroom: What practices are defensible and feasible? In C. J. Maker (Ed.), *Critical issues in gifted education: Programs for the gifted in regular classrooms* (Vol. 3, pp. 413-436). Austin, TX: Pro-Ed.

Malott, R. W., Whaley, D. L., & Malott, M. E. (1997). *Elementary principles of behavior* (3rd ed.). Upper Saddle River, NJ: Prentice-Hall.

Managing Asthma in the School Environment (2005). Washington, DC: U.S. Department of Health and Human Services.

Margolis, H., & McCabe, P. P. (2006). Improving self-efficacy and motivation: What to do, what to say. *Intervention in School & Clinic, 41*(4), 218-227.

Marland, S. P. (1972). *Career education: A proposal for reform.* New York: McGraw-Hill.

Marschark, D., & Muyskens, P., (2002). Problem-solving model for decision making with high incidence disabilities. *Learning Disabilities Research and Practice, 18,* 187-200.

Marzano, R. J. (2003). *Classroom management that works.* Alexandria, VA: ASCD.

Mastropieri, M. A., & Scruggs, T. E. (1994). *Effective instruction for special education* (2nd ed.). Austin, TX: Pro-Ed.

Mastropieri, M. A., & Scruggs, T. E. (1997). Best practices in promoting reading comprehension in students with learning disabilities: 1976 to 1996. *Remedial and Special Education, 18,* 197-218.

Mastropieri, M. A., & Scruggs, T. E. (2001). Promoting inclusion in secondary classrooms. *Learning Disability Quarterly, 24,* 265-274.

Mastropieri, M. A., Scruggs, T. E., & Graetz, J. E. (2003). Reading comprehension instruction for secondary students: Challenges for struggling students and teachers. *Learning Disabilities Quarterly, 26*(2), 103-116.

Mastropieri, M. A., Scruggs, T. E., Graetz, J., Norland, J., Gardizi, W., & McDuffie, K. (2005). Case studies in co-teaching in the content areas: Successes, failures, and challenges. *Intervention in School & Clinic 40*(5), 260-270.

Mathes, P., & Torgesen, J. (1998, November). *Early reading basics: Strategies for teaching reading to primary-grade students who are at risk for reading and learning disabilities.* Paper presented at the Annual Council for Learning Disabilities Conference, Albuquerque, NM.

Mayer, C. (2009). Issues in second language literacy education with learners who are deaf. *International Journal of Bilingual Education and Bilingualism, 12,* 325-334.

McAfee, J. (2002). *Navigating the social world: A curriculum for individuals with Asperger's syndrome, high functioning autism and related disorders.* Arlington, TX: Future Horizons.

McCarney, S. B. (2006). *Pre-referral intervention manual: The most common learning and behavior problems encountered in the educational environment* (3rd ed.). Columbia, MO: Hawthorne Educational Services.

McConaughy, S. H., & Wadsworth, M. E. (2000). Life history reports of young adults previously referred for mental health services. *Journal of Emotional and Behavioral Disorders, 8,* 202-215.

McConnell, K., Patton, J. R., & Polloway, E. A. (2006). *Behavioral intervention planning (BIP-III)* (3rd ed.). Austin, TX: Pro-Ed.

McConnell, M. E., Hilvitz, P. B., & Cox, C. J. (1998). Functional assessment: A systematic process for assessment and intervention in general and special education classrooms. *Intervention in School and Clinic, 34,* 10-20.

McDonnell, J. J., Hardman, M. L., & McDonnell, A. P. (2005). *An introduction to persons with moderate and severe disabilities.* Boston: Allyn & Bacon.

McDougall, D. (1998). Research on self-management techniques used by students with disabilities in general education settings: A descriptive review. *Remedial and Special Education, 19,* 310-320.

McEwan, E. K. (2006). *How to survive and thrive in the first three weeks of school.* Thousand Oaks, CA: Corwin Press.

McGinty, A. S., & Justice, L. M. (2006). Classroom-based versus pullout speech-language intervention: A review of the experimental evidence. *EBP Briefs, 1*(1), 1-25.

McGrail, L. (1998). Modifying regular classroom curricula for high-ability students. *Gifted Child Today, 21,* 36-39.

McGrew, K., & Evans, J. (2004). Expectations for students with cognitive disabilities: Is the cup half empty or half full? Can the cup flow over? (Synthesis Report 54). Minneapolis, MN: University of Minnesota, National Center on Educational Outcomes.

McKamey, E. S. (1991). Storytelling for children with learning disabilities: A first-hand account. *Teaching Exceptional Children, 23,* 46-48.

McKeever, P. (1983). Siblings of chronically ill children: A Literature review with implications for research and practice. *American Journal of Orthopsychiatry, 53,* 209-217.

McKenna, K. (2007). Confronting the autism epidemic: New expectations for children with autism means a new role for public schools. *Harvard Newsletter, 23*(5), 1-3, 6.

McLaughlin-Cheng, E. (1998). The Asperger syndrome and autism: A literature review and meta-analysis. *Focus on Autism and Other Developmental Disabilities, 13,* 234-245.

McLeskey, J., Henry, D., & Hidges, D. (1998). Inclusion: Where is it happening? *Teaching Exceptional Children, 31*(2), 4-10.

McLeskey, J., Rosenberg, M. S., & Westling, D. L. (2010). *Inclusion: Effective practices for all students.* Boston: Pearson.

McLeskey, J., Rosenberg, M. S., & Westling, D. L. (2010). Inclusion: Effective practices for all students. Upper Saddle River, N.J.: Pearson.

McMaster, K. N., & Fuchs, D. (2002). Effects of cooperative learning on the academic achievement of students with learning disabilities. *Learning Disabilities Research and Practice, 17,* 107-117.

McMaster, K. L., Kung, S., Han, I., & Cao, M. (2008). Peer-assisted learning strategies: A "tier 1" approach to promoting English learners' response to intervention. *Exceptional Children, 74,* 194-214.

McNamara, B. E. (2007). *Learning disabilities: Bridging the gap between research and classroom practice.* Upper Saddle River, NJ: Pearson.

McNaughton, D., Rackensperger, T., Benedk-Wood, E., Krezman, C., Williams, M. B., & Light, J. (2008). "A child needs to be given a chance to succeed": Parents of individuals who use AAC describe the benefits and challenges of learning AAC technologies. *Augmentative and Alternative Communication, 24,* 43-55.

McNeill, J. H., & Fowler, S. A. (1996). Using story reading to encourage children's conversations. *Teaching Exceptional Children, 28*(2), 43-47.

McPartland, J. M., & Slavin, R. E. (1990). *Policy persepctives increasing achievement of at-risk students.* Washington: DC: U.S. Department of Education.

McReynolds, L. (1990). Functional articulation disorders. In G. H. Shames & E. H. Wiig (Eds.), *Human communication disorders: An introduction* (2nd ed.) (pp. 139-182). Columbus, OH: Merrill.

Meadan, H., & Monda-Amaya, L. (2008). Collaboration to promote social competence for students with mild disabilities in the general classroom: A structure for providing social support. *Intervention in School and Clinic, 43,* 158-167.

MedicineNet.com (2010). *Asthma.* www .medicinenet.com/asthma. Retrieved 10/9/10.

Mentoring Programs for at-Risk Youth (pp. 5-6) by National Dropout Prevention.

Mercer, C. D., & Pullen, P. C. (2009). *Students with learning disabilities* (6th ed.). Upper Saddle River, NJ: Pearson.

Meyer, D. (2001). Meeting the unique concerns of brothers and sisters of children with special needs. *Insight, 51,* 28-32.

Mihalas, S., Morse, W. C., Allsopp, D. H., & McHatton, P. A. (2009). Cultivating caring relationships between teachers and secondary students with emotional and behavioral disorders: Implications for research and practice. *Remedial and Special Education, 30*, 108-125.

Miller, P. (2009). Learning with a missing sense: What can we learn from the interaction of a deaf child with a turtle? *American Annals of the Deaf, 154*, 71-82.

Miller, R. J. (1995). Preparing for adult life: Teaching students their rights and responsibilities. *CEC Today, 1*(7), 12.

Miller, S. P. (2002). *Validated practices for teaching students with diverse needs.* Boston: Allyn & Bacon.

MMWR. (Dec. 25, 2009). QuickStats: Percentage of preterm births—United States and selected European countries, 2004. *MMWR Weekly, 58*(50), 1418.

Moore, J. L., & Ford, D. Y. (2005). Under-achievement among gifted students of color: Implications for educators. *Theory into Practice, 44*, 167-177.

Moores, D. (2001). *Educating the deaf: Psychology, principles, and practices* (6th ed.). Upper Saddle River, NJ: Merrill.

Moores, D. F. (2007). *Educating the deaf: Psychology, principles, and practices.* Boston: Houghton-Mifflin.

Moores, D. F. (2008). Inclusion, itinerant teachers, and the pull-out model. *American Annals of the Deaf, 153*, 273-274.

Moores, D. F. (2009a). Demographics and sample bias estimates of the deaf and hard of hearing school age population. *American Annals of the Deaf, 154*, 261-262.

Moores, D. F. (2009b). Residential schools for the deaf and academic placement past, present, and future. *American Annals of the Deaf, 154*, 3-4.

Morgan, S. R. (1994a). *At-risk youth in crises: A team approach in the schools* (2nd ed.). Austin, TX: Pro-Ed.

Morgan, S. (1994b). *Children in crisis: A team approach in the schools* (2nd ed.). Austin, TX: Pro-Ed.

Moriarity, D. (1967). *The loss of loved ones.* Springfield, IL. Charles C Thomas.

Morocco, C. C., Aguilar, C. M., Clay, K., Brigham, N., & Zigmond, N. (2006). Good high schools for students with disabilities: Introduction to the special issue. *Learning Disabilities Research & Practice, 21*, 135-145.

Morris, S. (2002). Promoting social skills among students with nonverbal learning disabilities. *Teaching Exceptional Children, 34*, 66-70.

Morrison, G. S. (1997). *Teaching in America.* Boston: Allyn & Bacon.

Mueller, T. G. (2009). IEP facilitation: A promising approach to resolving conflicts between families and schools. *Teaching Exceptional Children, 41*, 60-65.

Munger, R., & Morse, W. C. (1992). When divorce rocks a child's world. *The Educational Forum, 43*, 100-103.

Munk, D. D., & Bursuck, W. D. (2001). Preliminary findings on personalized grading plans for middle school students with learning disabilities. *Exceptional Children, 67*, 211-234.

Munk, D. D., & Bursuck, W. D. (2004). "Personalized grading plans: A systematic approach to making the grades of included students more accurate and meaningful." *Focus on Exceptional Children, 36*, 1-12.

Murawski, W. W., & Dieker, L. (2008). 50 ways to keep your co-teacher. *Teaching Exceptional Children, 40*, 40-46.

Murawski, W. W., & Hughes, C. E. (2009). Response to intervention, collaboration, and coteaching: A logical combination for successful systemic change. *Preventing School Failure, 53*, 277.

Murdick, N. L., Gartin, B. C., & Crabtree, T. (2007). *Special education law.* Upper Saddle River, NJ: Merrill.

Murray, C. (2003). Risk factors, protective factors, vulnerability, and resilience: A framework for understanding and supporting the adult transitions of youth with high-incidence disabilities. *Remedial and Special Education, 24*, 16-26.

Murray, C., & Greenberg, M. T. (2006). Examining the importance of social relationships and social contexts in the lives of children with high incidence disabilities. *Journal of Special Education, 39*(4), 220-233.

Murray, C., & Naranjo, J. (2008). Poor, black, LD, and graduating. *Remedial and Special Education, 29*(3), 145-160.

Muscular Dystrophy Association (2005). *A teacher's guide to neuromuscular disease.* Washington, DC: MDA.

Myles, B. S., & Simpson, R. L. (1998). Aggression and violence by school-age children and youth: Under the aggression cycle and prevention/intervention strategies. *Intervention in School and Clinic, 33*, 259-264.

Myles, B. S., & Simpson, R. L. (2002). Asperger syndrome: An overview of characteristics. *Focus on Autism and Other Developmental Disabilities, 17*, 132-137.

Myles, B. S., Cook, K. T., Miller, N. E., Rinner, L., & Robbins, L. A. (2000). *Asperger syndrome and sensory issues: Practical solutions for making sense of the world.* Shawnee Mission, KS: Autism Asperger Publishing.

Myles, B. S., Hilgenfeld, T. D., Barnhill, G. P., Griswold, D. E., Hagiwara, T., & Simpson, R. L. (2002). Analysis of reading skills in individuals with Asperger syndrome. *Focus on Autism and Other Developmental Disabilities, 17*, 44-47.

Nagel, L., McDougall, D., & Granby, C. (1996). Students' self-reported substance use by grade level and gender. *Journal of Drug Education, 26*, 49-56.

Naremore, R. C. (1980). Language disorders in children. In T. J. Hixon, L. D. Shriberg, & J. H. Saxman (Eds.), *Introduction to communication disorders* (pp. 111-132). Upper Saddle River, NJ: Prentice-Hall.

National Association for the Gifted (2006). *Legislative Update.* p. 1.

National Autism Center. (2009a). *Evidence-based practice and autism in the schools: A guide to providing appropriate interventions to students with autism spectrum disorders.* Randolph, MA: Author.

National Autism Center. (2009b). *Findings and conclusions of the National Standards Project.* Randolph, MA: Author.

National Autism Center. (2009c). *National standards report.* Randolph, MA: Author.

National Cancer Institute (2010). *Childhood Cancers.* Washington, DC: U.S. National Institutes of Health. www.cancer.gov retrieved 8/20/2010.

National Center for Education Statistics. (1989). *Digest of educational statistics, 1989.* Washington, DC: U.S. Department of Education, Office of Research and Improvement.

National Center for Education Statistics (2009). *Digest of Educational Statistics.* Washington, DC: U.S. Department of Education.

National Center for Educational Statistics (2010). *National forum on educational statistics.* Washington, DC: Author.

National Center for Homeless Education (2005). *Common signs of homelessness.* www.serve.org/nche_web/warning.php. Retrieved 9/19/2010.

National Center for Special Education Research. (2007, April). *Facts from NLTS2: Secondary school experiences for students with autism.* Retrieved from: http://ies.ed .gov/ncser/pubs/20073005/index.asp.

National Centers for Disease Control (2009). Prevalence of autism spectrum disorders— Autism and developmental disabilities monitoring network.

National Childhood Cancer Foundation (2003). *Types of childhood cancer.* Washington, DC: Author. www.curesearc.org retrieved 9/5/2010.

National Coalition for the Homeless (2006). *A Dream Denied.* Washington, DC: Author.

National Coalition for the Homeless. (2009). *Homeless families with children.* Retrieved 1/1/10 from www.nationalhomeless.org/ factsheets/families.html.

National Heart, Lung, and Blood Institute. (1998). How asthma friendly is your school? *Journal of School Health, 68*, 167-168.

National Institute of Neurological Disorders and Stroke (2010). *NINDS Tourette syndrome information page.* Bethesda, MD: Author. www.ninds.nih.gov/disorders/ tourette retrieved 7/27/2010.

National Institute on Drug Abuse (2006). *Science of drug abuse.* Washington, DC: Author.

National Institutes of Health. (2000). Consensus and development conference statement: Diagnosis and treatment of attention-deficit/hyperactivity disorder. *Journal of the American Academy of Child and Adolescent Psychiatry, 39*(2), 182-193.

National Institutes of Health. (2010). *Medline plus: Asthma in children.* Available: www.nlm.nih.gov/medlineplus/ asthmainchildren.html.

National Joint Committee on Learning Disabilities. (2005 June). Responsiveness to intervention and learning disabilities: A report prepared by the National Joint Committee on Learning Disabilities. *Learning Disabilities Quarterly, 28*, 249-260.

National Joint Committee on Learning Disabilities. (2006). Learning disabilities in young children: Identification and intervention. *Learning Disability Quarterly, 30*, 63-72.

National Law Center on Homelessness and Poverty. (1990). *Shut out: Denial of education to homeless children.* Washington, DC: Author.

National Law Center on Homelessness and Poverty (2004). *Homelessness in the United States and the human right to housing.* Washington, DC: Author.

National Reading Panel (NRP). (2000). *Teaching children to read: A report from the National Reading Panel.* Washington, DC: U.S. Government Printing Office.

National Research Council. (2001). *Educating children with autism.* Washington DC: National Academy Press.

National study on inclusion: Overview and summary report. (1995). National Center on Educational Restructuring Inclusion, 1–8.

National Youth Gang Center, 1999). *National gang survey.* Washington, DC: Author.

Nelson, J. A. P., Caldarella, P., Young, K. R., & Webb, N. (2008). Using peer praise notes to increase the social involvement of withdrawn adolescents. *Teaching Exceptional Children, 41,* 6–11.

Nelson, J. R., Benner, G. J., & Cheney, D. (2005). An investigation of the language skills of students with emotional disturbance served in public schools. *Journal of Special Education, 39*(2), 97–105.

Nelson, J. R., Benner, G. J., Neill, S., & Stage, S. A. (2006). Interrelationships among language skills, externalizing behavior, and academic fluency and their impact on the academic skills of students with ED. *Journal of Emotional and Behavioral Disorders, 14*(4), 209.

Nelson, J. R., Hurley, K. D., Synhorst, L., Epstein, M. H., Stage, S., & Buckley, J. (2009). The child outcomes of a behavior model. *Exceptional Children, 76*(1), 7–30.

Nelson, K. C., & Prindle, N. (1992). Gifted teacher competencies: Ratings by rural principals and teachers. *Journal of the Education of the Gifted, 15,* 357–369.

Nelson, L. G. L., Summers, J. A., & Turnbull, A. P. (2004). Boundaries in family-professional relationships. *Remedial and Special Education, 25,* 153–165.

Newman, L., Wagner, M., Cameto, R., & Knokey, A. (2009). *The post-high school outcomes of youth with disabilities up to 4 years after high school. A report from the National Longitudinal Transition Study-2 (NLTS2)* (NCSER 2009-3017). Washington, DC: U. S. Government Printing Office.

Nieto, S. (2004). Black, white, and us: The meaning of Brown v. Board of Education for Latinos. *Multicultural Perspectives, 6*(4), 22–25.

Niles, M. D., & Peck. L. R. (2008). How poverty and segregation impact child development: Evidence from the Chicago longitudinal study. *Journal of Poverty, 12,* 306–332.

No Child Left Behind Act. 34 CFR Part 200 (2001).

Norwich, B. (2008). What future for special schools and inclusion? Conceptual and professional perspectives. *British Journal of Special Education, 35*(3), 136–143.

Nowacek, E. J., & McShane, E. (1993). Spoken language. In E. A. Polloway & J. R. Patton (Eds.), *Strategies for teaching learners with special needs* (5th ed., pp. 183–205). Columbus, OH: Merrill.

O'Leary (2006). New and improved transition services–Individuals with Disabilities Education Improvement Act of 2004, *LDA Newsbriefs, 41*(1), 1–5.

Olson, J. L., & Platt, J. M. (1996). *Teaching children and adolescents with special needs* (2nd ed). Upper Saddle River, NJ: Merrill.

Orr, A. C., & Hammig, S. B. (2009, Summer). Inclusive postsecondary strategies for teaching students with learning disabilities: A review of the literature. *Learning Disability Quarterly, (32),* 181–196.

Ortiz, A. A. (2002). Prevention of school failure and early identification. In A. J. Artiles & A. A. Ortiz (Eds.), *English language learners with special needs.* Washington, DC: Center for Applied Linguistics.

Oswald, D. P., Coutinho, M. J., Best, A. M., & Singh, N. N. (1999). Ethnic representation in special education: The influence of school-related economic and demographic values. *The Journal of Special Education, 32,* 194–206.

Overton, T. (2009). *Assessing learners with special needs: An applied approach.* Upper Saddle River, NJ: Pearson.

Oyer, H. J., Crowe, B., & Haas, W. H. (1987). *Speech, language, and hearing disorders: A guide for the teacher.* Boston: Little, Brown.

Ozonoff, S., & Schetter, P. L. (2007). Executive dysfunction in autism spectrum disorders: From research to practice. In L. Meltzer (Ed.), *Executive dysfunction in education: From theory to practice* (pp. 133–160). New York: Guilford Press.

Painter, D. D. (2009). Providing differentiated learning experiences through multigenre projects. *Intervention in School and Clinic, 44*(5), 288–293.

Pane, J. F., McCaffrey, D. F., Kalra, N., & Zhou, A. J. (2008). Effects of students' displacement in Louisiana during the first academic year after hurricanes of 2005. *Journal of Education for Students Placed at Risk, 13,* 168–211.

Parish, S. L., Rose, R. A., & Andrews, M. E. (2010). TANF's impact on low-income mothers raising children with disabilities. *Exceptional Children, 76,* 234–253.

Parke, B. N. (1989). *Gifted students in regular classrooms.* Boston: Allyn & Bacon.

Parker, A. T., & Pogrund, R. L. (2009). A review of research on the literacy of students with visual impairments and additional disabilities. *Journal of Visual Impairment and Blindness, 97,* 635–648.

Patton, J. R. (1994). Practical recommendations for using homework with students with learning disabilities. *Journal of Learning Disabilities, 27,* 570–578.

Patton, J. R., & Cronin, M. E. (1993). *Life skills instruction for all students with disabilities.* Austin, TX: Pro-Ed.

Patton, J. R., & Dunn, C. R. (1998). *Transition from school to adult life for students with special needs: Basic concepts and recommended practices.* Austin, TX: Pro-Ed.

Patton, J. R., & Keyes, D. (2006). Death penalty issues following *Atkins. Exceptionality, 14,* 237–255.

Patton, J. R., & Keyes, D. W. (in press). Death penalty issues. *Exceptionality.*

Patton, J. R., Cronin, M. E., & Wood, J. D. (1999). *Infusing real-life topics into extracurriculuar activities.* Austin, TX: Pro-Ed.

Patton, J. R., Jayanthi, M., & Polloway, E. A. (2001). Home-school collaboration about homework. *Reading and Writing Quarterly, 17,* 230–236.

Patton, J. R., Polloway, E. A., & Smith, T. E. C. (2000). Educating students with mild mental retardation. In M. L. Wehmeyer & J. R. Patton (Eds.), *Mental retardation in the 21st century.* Austin, TX: Pro-Ed.

Patton, J. R., Polloway, E. A., Smith, T. E. C., Edgar, E., Clark, G. M., & Lee, S. (1996). Individuals with mild mental retardation: Postsecondary outcomes and implications for educational policy. *Education and Training in Mental Retardation and Developmental Disabilities, 31,* 77–85.

Patton, J. R., Cronin, M., Polloway, E. A., Hutchison, D. R., & Robinson, G. A. (1989). Curricular considerations: A life skills orientation in best practices. In G. A. Robinson, Patton, J. R., Polloway, E. A., & Sargent, L. (Eds). *Mild Mental Retardation.* Reston, VA: Division on Autism and Developmental Disabilities.

Peck, A., & Scarpati, S. (2004). Techniques for program support. *Teaching Exceptional Children, 39*(1), 4.

Peebles-Wilkins, W. (2006). Evidence-based suicide prevention. *Children & Schools, 28,* 195–196.

Pemberton, J. B., Rademacher, J. A., Tyler-Wood, T., & Careijo, M. V. (2006). Aligning assessments with state curricular standards. *Intervention, 41*(5), 283–289.

Peters, S. J. (2007). "Education for All?" A historical analysis of international inclusive education policy and individuals with disabilities. *Journal of Disability Policy Studies, 18,* 98–108.

Peterson, J. M., & Hittie, M. M. (2010). *Inclusive teaching: The journey towards effective schools for all learners* (2nd ed.). Boston: Pearson.

Pfiffner, L., & Barkley, R. (1991). Educational placement and classroom management. In R. Barkley (Ed.), *Attention deficit hyperactivity disorder: A handbook for diagnosis and treatment* (pp. 498–539). New York: Guilford Press.

Phelps-Terasaki, D., & Phelps-Gunn, T. (2007). *Test of Pragmatic Language* (2nd ed.). Austin: PRO-ED.

Pierangelo, R., & Giuliani, G. (2006). *Learning disabilities: A practical approach to foundations, assessment, diagnosis, and teaching.* Boston: Allyn & Bacon.

Pierce, C. (1994). Importance of classroom climate for at-risk learners. *Journal of Educational Research, 88,* 37–44.

Plummer, D. L. (1995). Serving the needs of gifted children from a multicultural perspective. In J. L. Genshaft, M. Bireley, & C. L. Hollinger (Eds.), *Serving gifted and talented students: A resource for school personnel* (pp. 285–300). Austin, TX: Pro-Ed.

Policy Perspectives Increasing Achievement of Students Who Are At-Risk at Each Grade Level, by J. M. McPartland and R. E. Slavin, 1990. Washington, DC: U.S. Department of Education.

Polloway, E. A. (2005). Perspectives on mild mental retardation: The status of a category of exceptionality. In J. J. Hoover (Ed.). *Current issues in special education: Meeting diverse needs in the twenty-first century* (pp. 36-46). Boulder, CO: BUENO Center for Multicultural Education, University of Colorado.

Polloway, E. A. (2006). Mild mental retardation: A concept in search of clarity, a population in search of appropriate education and supports, a profession in search of advocacy. *Exceptionality, 14*, 183-189.

Polloway, E. A., & Lubin, J. (2010). *Feebleminded.* In Encyclopedia of American Disability History. S. Burch & P. K. Longmore (Eds.). Orange, CA: Disability History Association.

Polloway, E. A., & Patton, J.R. (2005). Strategies for teaching learners with special needs. (8th ed.). Upper Saddle River, NJ: Pearson.

Polloway, E. A., & Smith, J. D. (1983). Mild mental retardation: Population, programs, and perspectives. *Exceptional Children, 50*, 149-159.

Polloway, E. A., Bursuck, W. D., & Epstein, M. H. (2001). Homework for students with learning disabilities: The challenge of home-school communication. *Reading and Writing Quarterly, 17*, 181-187.

Polloway, E. A., Bursuck, W., Jayanthi, M., Epstein, M., & Nelson, J. (1996). Treatment acceptability: Determining appropriate interventions within inclusive classrooms. *Intervention in School and Clinic, 31*, 133-144.

Polloway, E. A., Epstein, M. H., Bursuck, W. D., Jayanthi, M., & Cumblad, C. (1994). Homework practices of general education teachers. *Journal of Learning Disabilities, 27*, 500-509.

Polloway, E. A., Epstein, M. H., & Bursuck, W. D. (2002). Homework for students with learning disabilities. *Reading and Writing Quarterly, 17*, 181-187.

Polloway, E. A., Lubin, J., Smith, J. D., & Patton, J. R. (2010). Mild intellectual disabilities: Legacies and trends in concepts and educational practices. *Education and Training in Developmental Disabilitie,. 45*, 54-68.

Polloway, E. A., Miller, L., & Smith, T. E. C. (2003). *Language instruction for students with disabilities* (3rd ed.). Denver, CO: Love.

Polloway, E. A., Miller, L., & Smith, T.E.C. (2011). *Language instruction for students with disabilities* (4th ed.). Denver: Love Publishing.

Polloway, E. A., Patton, J. R., & Nelson, M. (2010). Intellectual disabilities. In D. P. Hallahan, J. M., Kauffman, & P. Pullen (Eds.), *Handbook of special education.* New York: Routledge.

Polloway, E. A., Patton, J. R., & Serna, L. (2008). *Strategies for teaching learners with special needs* (9th ed.). Upper Saddle River, NJ: Merrill/Pearson.

Polloway, E. A., Patton, J. R., Smith, J. D., & Roderique, T. W. (1992). Issues in program design for elementary students with mild retardation: Emphasis on curriculum development. *Education and Training in Mental Retardation, 27*, 142-150.

Polloway, E. A., Smith, J. D., & Antoine, K. (2010). Biological aspects and the promise of prevention. In M. E. Beirne-Smith, et al. (Eds.), *Intellectual disabilities* (8th ed.). Upper Saddle River, NJ: Pearson.

Polloway, E. A., Patton, J. R., Smith, J. D., Antoine, K., & Lubin, J. (2009). State guidelines for intellectual disabilities: A re-visitation of previous analyses in light of changes in the field. *Education and Training in Developmental Disabilities, 44*, 14-24.

Polloway, E. A., Smith, J. D., Patton, J. R., & Smith, T. E. C. (1996). Historic changes in mental retardation and developmental disabilities. *Education and Training in Mental Retardation and Developmental Disabilities, 31*, 3-2.

Prasse, D.P. (2006). Legal supports for problem-solving systems. *Remedial and Special Education, 27*, 7-14.

Prater, M.A. (2003). She will succeed! Strategies for success in inclusive classrooms. *Teaching exceptional children, 35*(5), 58-64.

Prater, M.A., & Dyches, T.T. (2008). Books that portray characters with disabilities. *Teaching Exceptional Children, 40*, 32-39.

Prater, M.A., Dyches, T.T., & Johnstun, M. (2006). Teaching students about learning disabilities through children's literature. *Intervention in School & Clinic, 42*(1), 14-24.

Prater, M.A., Joy, R., Chilman, B., Temple, J., & Miller, S. R. (1991). Self-monitoring of on-task behavior by adolescents with learning disabilities. *Learning Disability Quarterly, 14*, 164-177.

President's Committee for People with Intellectual Disabilities. (2007). *Holding truths to be self-evident: Affirming the value of people with intellectual disabilities.* Washington, DC: Author.

Prestia, K. (2003). Tourette's syndrome: Characteristics and interventions. *Intervention in School and Clinic, 39*, 67-71.

Public Law 94-142 (1975). *Federal Register, 42*, 42474-42518.

Public Law 101-476 (1990). *Federal Register, 54*, 35210-35271.

Pugach, M. C., & Warger, C. L. (2001). Curriculum matters. *Remedial and Special Education, 22*, 194-196.

Pugh, S. (1999). Working with families of individual students. *Gifted Children Today, 22*, 26-31.

Puzzanchera, C. (April 2009). Juvenile arrests 2007. *Juvenile Justice Bulletin.* Retrieved 1/1/10 from www.ojp.usdoj.gov.

Quay, H., & Peterson, D. (1987). *Revised behavior problem checklist.* Coral Gables, FL: University of Miami.

Quilty, K. M. (2007). Teaching paraprofessionals how to write and implement social stories for students with autism spectrum disorders. *Remedial and Special Education, 28*, 182-189.

Quinn, M. M., Kavale, K. A., Mathur, S. R., Rutherford, R. B., Jr., & Forness, S. R. (1999). A meta-analysis of social skill interventions for students with emotional and behavioral disorders. *Journal of Emotional and Behavioral Disorders, 7*, 54-64.

Quintero, N., & McIntyre, L. L. (2010). Sibling adjustment and maternal well-being: An examination of families with and without a child with autism spectrum disorder. *Focus on Autism and Other Developmental Disabilities, 25*, 37-46.

Ramos-Ford, V., & Gardner, H. (1997). Giftedness from a multiple intelligences perspective. In N. Colangelo & G.A. Davis (Eds.), *Handbook of gifted education* (2nd ed., pp. 54-66). Boston: Allyn & Bacon.

Raskind, M. H., Goldberg, R. J., Higgins, E. L., & Herman, K. L. (2002). Teaching life success to students with learning disabilities: Lessons learned from a 20-year study. *Intervention in Schools and Clinic, 37*(4), 201-208.

Reeve, R. E. (1990). ADHD: Facts and fallacies. *Intervention in School and Clinic, 26*, 71-78.

Reid, R., & Nelson, J. R. (2002). The utility, acceptability, and practicality of functional behavioral assessment for students with high-incidence problem behaviors. *Remedial and Special Education, 23*, 15-23.

Reid, R., Gonzalez, J. E., Nordness, P. D., Trout, A., & Epstein, M. H. (2004). A meta-analysis of the academic status of students with Emotional/Behavioral disturbance. *Journal of Special Education, 38*(3), 130-143.

Reis, S. M., & Schack, G. D. (1993). Differentiating products for the gifted and talented: The encouragement of independent learning. In C. J. Maker (Ed.), *Critical issues in gifted education: Programs for the gifted in regular classrooms* (Vol. 3, pp. 161-186). Austin, TX: Pro-Ed.

Renzulli, J. S. (1979). *What makes giftedness: A reexamination of the definition of the gifted and talented.* Ventura, CA: Ventura County Superintendent of Schools Office.

Renzulli, J. S., Reis, S. M., & Smith, L. M. (1981). *The revolving door identification model.* Wethersfield, CT: Creative Learning Press.

Renzulli, J.S., & Reis, S.M. (1991). The reform movement and the quiet crisis in gifted education. *Gifted Child Quarterly, 35*, 26-36.

Reutebuch, C. K. (2008). Succeed with a response-to-intervention model. *Intervention in School and Clinic, 44*, 126-128.

Riley, T. (1999). The role of advocacy: Creating change for gifted children throughout the world. *Gifted Child Today, 22*, 44-47.

Roach, V. (1995). Supporting inclusion: Beyond the rhetoric. *Phi Delta Kappan, 77*, 295-299.

Robin, S. S., & Johnson, E. O. (1996). Attitude and peer cross pressure: Adolescent drug and alcohol use. *Journal of Drug Education, 26*, 69-99.

Robinson, T., & Rapport, M.J. (1999). Providing special education in the juvenile justice system. *Remedial and Special Education, 20*, 19-27.

Roentgen, U. R., Gelderblom, G. J., Soede, M., & de Witte, L. P. (2008). Inventory of electronic mobility aids for persons with visual impairments: A literature review. *Journal of Visual Impairment and Blindness, 96*, 702-724.

Rogers, S. J., & Dawson, G. (2010). *Early Start Denver Model for young children with autism: Promoting language, learning, and engagement.* New York: Guilford Press.

Roman, C., Baker-Nobles, L., Dutton, G. N., Luiselli, T. E., Flener, B. S., Jan, J. E., Lantzy, A., Matsuba, C., Mayer, D. L., Newcomb, S., & Nielsen, A. S. (2010). Statement on cortical visual impairment. *Journal of Visual Impairment and Blindness,* 69-72.

Rooney, K. (1993). *Attention deficit hyperactivity disorder: A videotape program.* Richmond, VA: State Department of Education.

Roseberry-McKibbin, C., & Brice, A. (2002). Choice of language instruction: One or two? *Teaching Exceptional Children, 33,* 10-16.

Rosenberg, M. S., O'Shea, L., & O'Shea, D. J. (1991). *Student teacher to master teacher: A handbook for preservice and beginning teachers of students with mild and moderate handicaps.* New York: Macmillan.

Rosenberg, M. S., Wilson, R., Maheady, L., & Sindelar, P. (1992). *Educating students with behavior disorders.* Boston: Allyn & Bacon.

Rosselli, H. (1993). Process differentiation for gifted learners in the regular classroom: Teaching to everyone's needs. In C. J. Maker (Ed.), *Critical issues in gifted education: Programs for the gifted in regular classrooms* (Vol. 3, pp. 139-155). Austin, TX: Pro-Ed.

Rothstein, A. (2006). Students as coaches. *Education Week, 25,* 31-32.

Rothstein, R. (2009). Equalizing opportunity: Dramatic differences in children's home life and health mean that schools can't do it alone. *American Educator, 33*(2), 4-7, 45-47.

Rotter, K. (2006). Creating instructional materials for all pupils: Try COLA. *Intervention in School and Clinic, 41*(5), 273-282.

Rourke, B. P. (2005). Neuropsychology of LD: Past and present. *Learning Disabilities Quarterly, 28*(2), 111-114.

Ruble, L. A., & Dalrymple, M. J. (2002). COMPASS: A parent–teacher collaboration model for students with autism. *Focus on Autism and Other Developmental Disabilities, 17,* 76-83.

Rueda, R., Monzo, L., Shapiro, J., Gomez, J., & Blacher, J. (2005). Cultural models of transition: Latina mothers of young adults with developmental disabilities. *Exceptional Children, 71,* 401-414.

Runswick-Cole, K. (2008). Between a rock and a hard place: Parents' attitudes to the inclusion of children with special needs in mainstream and special schools. *British Journal of Special Education, 35,* 173-180.

Ryan, J. B., Reid, R., & Epstein, M. H. (2004). Peer-mediated intervention studies on academic achievement for students with EBD. *Remedial & Special Education, 25*(6), 330-341.

Rylance, B. J. (1998). Predictors of post-high school employment for youth identified as severely emotionally disturbed. *The Journal of Special Education, 32,* 184-192.

Ryser, G., & McConnell, K. (2003). *Scales for diagnosing attention deficit/hyperactivity disorder.* Austin, TX: Pro-Ed.

Sabornie, E. J., & deBettencourt, L. U. (2009). *Teaching students with mild and high-incidence disabilities at the secondary level* (3rd ed.). Upper Saddle River, NJ: Pearson.

Sabornie, E. J., Cullinan, D., Osborne, S. S., & Brock, L. B. (2005). Intellectual, academic, and behavioral functioning of students with high-incidence disabilities: A cross-categorical meta-analysis. *Exceptional Children, 72*(1), 47-63.

Sacks, S. Z., Wolffe, K. E., & Tierney, D. (1998). Lifestyles of students with visual impairments: Preliminary studies of social networks. *Exceptional Children, 98,* 463-478.

Safe & Smart (1998). Washington, DC: U.S. Department of Education.

Safran, J. S. (2002). A practical guide to research on Asperger's syndrome. *Intervention in School and Clinic, 37,* 283-293.

Salend, S. J. (1990) Recxport card models that support communication and differentiation of instruction. *Teaching Exceptional Children, 37*(4), 23-28.

Salend, S. J. (2001). *Creating inclusive classrooms: Effective and reflective practices* (4th ed.). Upper Saddle River, NJ: Merrill/Pearson.

Salend, S. J. (2008). *Creating inclusive classrooms: Effective and reflective practices* (6th ed.). Upper Saddle River, NJ: Merrill/Pearson.

Salend, S. J. (2008). Determining appropriate testing accommodations. *Teaching Exceptional Children, 40*(4), 14-22.

Salend, S., & Duhaney, L. G. (2002). Grading students in inclusive settings. *Teaching Exceptional Children, 34,* 13-14.

Salend, S. J., & Rohena, E. (2003). Students with attention deficit disorders: An overview. *Intervention in School and Clinic, 38*(5), 259-266.

Salend, S. J., & Salinas, A. G. (2003). Language differences or learning difficulties: The work of the multidisciplinary team. *Teaching Exceptional Children, 35*(4), 36-43.

Salvia, J., & Ysseldyke, J. E. (2010). *Asessment in special and inclusive education* (10th ed.). Boston: Houghton-Mifflin.

Sander, E. K. (1972). When are speech sounds learned? *Journal of Speech and Hearing Disorders, 37,* 62.

Sandieson, R. (1998). A survey on terminology that refers to people with mental retardation/developmental disabilities. *Education and Training in Mental Retardation and Developmental Disabilities, 33,* 290-295.

Santangelo, T. (2009). Collaborative problem solving effectively implemented, but not sustained: A case for aligning the sun, the moon, and the stars. *Exceptional Children, 75,* 185-209.

Santangelo, T., Harris, K. R., & Graham, S. (2008). Using self-regulated strategy development to support students who have "trubol giting thangs into werds." *Remedial and Special Education, 29*(2), 78-89.

Santrock, J. W., & Warshak, R. A. (1979). Father custody and social development in boys and girls. *Journal of Social Issues, 35,* 112-125.

Sargent, L. R. (1991). *Social skills for school and community.* Reston, VA: CEC-MR.

Scanlon, D., & Melland, D. F. (2002). Academic and participant profiles of school-age dropouts with and without disabilities. *Exceptional Children, 68,* 239-258.

Schall, C. (2002). A consumer's guide to monitoring medication for individuals with ASD. *Focus on Autism and Other Developmental Disabilities, 17,* 228-235.

Schalock, R. L., Borthwick-Duffy, S. A., Bradley, V. J., Buntinx, W. H. E., Coulter, D. L., Craig, E. M., Gomez, S. C., Lachapelle, Y., Luckasson, R., Reeve, A., Shogren, K. A, Snell, M. E., Spreat, S., Tasse, M. J., Thompson, J. R., Verdugo-Alonso, M. A., Wehmeyer, M. L., & Yeager, M. H. (2010). *Intellectual disability: Definition, classification, and systems of supports.* Washington, DC: American Association on Intellectual and Developmental Disabilities.

Schalock, R., Luckasson, R. A., Shogren, K. A., Borthwick-Duffy, S., Bradley, V., Buntinx, W. H. E., Coulter, D. L., Craig, E. M., Gomez, S. C., Lachapelle, Y., Luckasson, R., Reeve, A., Shogren, K. A., Snell, M. E., Spreat, S., Tasse, M. J., Thompson, J. R., Verdugo-Alonso, M. A., Wehmeyer, M. L., & Yeager, M. H. (2007). The renaming of mental retardation: Understanding the change to the term intellectual disability. *Intellectual and Developmental Disabilities, 45,* 116-124.

Scheffler, R., Hinshaw, S., Modrek, S., & Levine, P. (2007). The global market for DHD medications. *Health Affairs, 26*(2), 450-457.

Scheuerman, B., & Webber, J. (2002). *Autism: Teaching does make a difference.* Belmont, CA: Wadsworth.

Schiever, S. W. (1993). Differentiating the learning environment for gifted students. In C. J. Maker (Ed.), *Critical issues in gifted education: Programs for the gifted in regular classrooms* (Vol. 3, pp. 201-214). Austin, TX: Pro-Ed.

Schloss, P., Schloss, A., & Shloss, C. N. (2007). *Instructional methods for secondary students with learning and behavior problems.* Boston: Allyn & Bacon.

Scholes, C. (1998). General science: A diagnostic teaching unit. *Intervention, 34*(2), 107-114.

Schraer-Joiner, L., & Pause-Weber, M. (2009). Strategies for working with children with cochlear implants. *Music Educators Journal, 96,* 37-42.

Schuck, S. E. B., & Crinella, F. M. (2005). Why children with ADHD do not have low IQs, *Journal of Learning Disabilities, 38*(3), 262-280.

Schulz, J. B., & Carpenter, C. D. (1995). *Mainstreaming exceptional students: A guide for classroom teachers.* Boston: Allyn & Bacon.

Schumaker, J. B., Denton, P. H., & Deshler, D. D. (1984). *The paraphrasing strategy.* Lawrence: University of Kansas.

Schumm, J. S., & Strickler, K. (1991). Guidelines for adapting content area textbooks: Keeping teachers and students content.

Intervention in School and Clinic, 27(2), 79–84.

Schumm, J. S., Vaughn, S., & Leavell (1994). Getting ready for inclusion. *Learning Disabilities Research and Practice, 10*(3), 169–179.

Scott, B. J., Vitale, M. R., & Masten, W. G. (1998). Implementing instructional adaptations for students with disabilities in inclusive classrooms: A literature review. *Remedial and Special Education, 19,* 106–119.

Scott, T. M., & Nelson, M. C. (1998). Confusion and failure in facilitating generalized social responding in the school setting: Sometimes 2 + 2 = 5. *Behavioral Disorders, 23,* 264–275.

Scruggs, T. E. & Mastropieri, M. A. (2000). The effectiveness of mnemonic instruction for students with learning and behavior problems: An update and research synthesis. *Journal of Behavioral Education, 10,* 163–173.

Scruggs, T. E., Mastropieri, M. A., & McDuffie, K. A. (2007). Co-teaching in inclusive classrooms: A metasynthesis of qualitative research. *Exceptional Children, 73,* 392–416.

Sebald, A., & Luckner, J. (2007). Successful partnerships with families of children who are deaf. *Teaching Exceptional Children, 39,* 54–59.

Seeley, K. (1995). Classwide peer tutoring. Unpublished manuscript, Lynchburg College, VA.

Sevcik, R. A., & Romski, M. (2000). *AAC: More than three decades of growth and development.* Washington, DC: American Speech–Language–Hearing Association.

Sexton, D., Snyder, P., Wolfe, B., Lobman, M., Stricklin, S., & Akers, P. (1996). Early intervention inservice training strategies: Perceptions and suggestions from the field. *Exceptional Children, 62,* 485–496.

Shane, H. C., & Sauer, M. (1986). *Augmentative and alternative communication.* Austin, TX: Pro-Ed.

Shaner, M. Y. (1991). Talented teachers for talented students. *G/C/T, 22,* 14–15.

Shanker, A. (1994–1995). Educating students in special programs. *Educational Leadership, 52,* 43–47.

Shapiro, E. S., & Clemens, N. H. (2009). A conceptual model for evaluating systems effects of response to intervention. *Assessment for Effective Intervention, 35,* 3–16.

Shapiro, E. S., & Cole, C. L. (1994). *Behavior change in the classroom: Self-management interventions.* New York: Guilford Press.

Shapiro, E. S., DuPaul, G. J., & Bradley-Klug, K. L. (1998). Self-management as a strategy to improve the classroom behavior of adolescents with ADHD. *Journal of Learning Disabilities, 31,* 545–555.

Sharpe, W. (2008). *The ABCs of school success: Tips, checklists, strategies for equipping your child.* Grand Rapids, MI: Revel.

Shepherd, T. L. (2010). *Working with students with emotional and behavior disorders.* Upper Saddle River, NJ: Merrill.

Shogren, K. A., Bradley, V. J., Gomez, S. C., Yeager M. H., Schalock, R. L., & Borthwick-Duffy, S. (2009). Public policy and the enhancement

of desired outcomes for persons with intellectual disability. *Intellectual and Developmental Disabilities, 47,* 307–319.

Shotten, L., Simpson, J., & Smith, M. (2007). The experience of appraisal, coping, and adaptive psychosocial adjustment following traumatic brain injury: A qualitative investigation. *Brain Injury, 21,* 857–869.

Sileo, J. M., & van Garderen, D. (2010). Creating optimal opportunities to learn mathematics. *Teaching Exceptional Children, 42,* 14–21.

Sileo, N. M. (2005). Design HIV/AIDS prevention education: What are the roles and responsibilities of classroom teachers? *Intervention in School and Clinic, 40,* 177–181.

Sileo, T. W., Sileo, A. P., & Prater, M. A. (1996). Parent and professional partnerships in special education: Multicultural considerations. *Intervention in School & Clinic, 31,* 145–153.

Silverman, A. B., Reinherz, H. Z., & Giaconia, R. M. (1996). The long-term sequelae of child and adolescent abuse: A longitudinal community study. *Child Abuse and Neglect, 20,* 709–723.

Silverman, F. H., & Miller, L. (2006). *Introduction to communication sciences and disorders.* Austin: PRO-ED.

Silverstein, A., Silverstein, B., & Nunn, L. (2008). *The ADHD update: Understanding attention-deficit/hyperactivity disorder.* Berkeley Heights, NJ: Enslow Publishers, Inc.

Simmons, D., Fuchs, D., Hodge, J., & Mathes, P. (1994). Importance of instructional complexity and role reciprocity to classwide peer tutoring. *Learning Disabilities Research and Practice, 9,* 203–212.

Simpson, R. (1998). Behavior modification for children and adolescents with exceptionalities. *Intervention in School and Clinic, 33,* 219–226.

Simpson, R. (2001). ABA and students with autism spectrum disorders. *Focus on Autism and Developmental Disabilities, 16,* 68–71.

Simpson, R. L. (2004). Finding effective intervention and personnel preparation practices for students with autism spectrum disorders. *Exceptional Children, 70,* 135–144.

Simpson, R. L., LaCava, P. G., & Graner, P. S. (2004). The no child left behind act: Challenges and implications for educators. *Intervention in School and Clinic, 40*(2), 67–76.

Siperstein, G. N., Parker, R. C., Bardon, J. N., & Widman, K. F. (2007). A national study of youth attitudes toward the inclusion of students with intellectual disabilities. *Exceptional Children, 73,* 435–455.

Skiba, R. J., Simmons, A. D., Ritter, S., Gibb, A. G., Rausch, M. K., Cuadrado, J., & Chung, C. (2008). Achieving equity in special education: History, status, and current challenges. *Exceptional Children, 74,* 264–288.

Skoto, B. G., Koppebnhaver, D. A., & Erickson, K. A. (2004). Parent reading behaviors and communication outcomes in girls with Rett syndrome. *Exceptional Children, 70,* 145–166.

Slavin, R. E. (1997). *Educational psychology: Theory into practice.* (2nd ed.) Boston: Allyn & Bacon.

Smith, C. R. (2004). *Learning Disabilities: The interaction of students and their environments.* Boston: Allyn & Bacon.

Smith, D. D., & Rivera, D. P. (1995). Discipline in special education and general education settings. *Focus on Exceptional Children, 27*(5), 1–14.

Smith, J. D. (2006). Speaking of mild mental retardation: It's no box of chocolates, or is it? *Exceptionality, 14,* 191–204.

Smith, P. (2007). Have we made any progress? Including students with intellectual disabilities in regular education classrooms. *Intellectual and Developmental Disabilities, 45,* 297–309.

Smith, R. (2004). *Conscious classroom management.* San Rafael, CA: Conscious Teaching Publications.

Smith, R. M., Salend, S. J., & Ryan, S. (2001). Watch your language. *Teaching Exceptional Children, 33,* 18–24.

Smith, T. (2001). Discrete trial training in the treatment of autism. *Focus on Autism and Other Developmental Disabilities, 16,* 86–92.

Smith, T. E. C. (2002). Section 504: Basic requirements for schools. *Intervention in School and Clinic, 37,* 2–6.

Smith, T. E. C. (2005). IDEA 2004: Another round in the reauthorization process. *Remedial and Special Education, 26,* 314–319.

Smith, T. E. C., & Dowdy, C. A. (1998). Educating young children with disabilities using responsible inclusion. *Child Education, 74*(5), 317–320.

Smith, T. E. C., & Patton, J. R. (2007). *Section 504 and public schools* (2nd ed.). Austin, TX: Pro-Ed.

Smith, T. E. C., Finn, D. M., & Dowdy, C. A. (1993). *Teaching students with mild disabilities.* Ft. Worth, TX: Harcourt Brace Jovanovich.

Smith, T. E. C., Price, B. J., & Marsh, G. E. (1986). *Mildly handicapped children and adults.* St. Paul, MN: West.

Smith, T. J., & Adams G. (2006). The effects of comorbidity AD/HD and learning disabilities on parent-reported behavioral and academic outcomes in children. *Learning Disabilities Quarterly, 29*(2), 17–21.

Smith, T., Groen, A. D., & Wynn, J. W. (2000). Randomized trial of intensive early intervention for children with pervasive developmental disorder. *American Journal on Mental Retardation, 102,* 238–249.

Smith, T., Polloway, E. A., Patton, J. R., & Beyer, J. F. (2008). Individuals with intellectual and developmental disabilities in the criminal justice system and implications for transition planning. *Education and Training in Developmental Disabilities, 43*(4), 10.

Smith, T., Polloway, E. A., Smith, J. D., & Patton, J. R. (2007). Self-determination for persons with developmental disabilities: Ethical considerations for teachers. *Education and Training in Developmental Disabilities, 42,* 144–151.

Smith, T. E. C., Gartin, B., Murdick, N., & Hilton, A. (2006). *Families and children with special needs.* Upper Saddle River, NJ: Pearson.

Smith, T.E.C., Polloway, E.A., Patton, J., & Dowdy, C. (2007). *Teaching students with special needs in inclusive settings.* Boston: Allyn & Bacon.

Smutny, J. F., Walker, S.Y., & Meckstroth, E.A. (1997). *Teaching young gifted children in the regular classroom: Identifying, nurturing, and challenging ages 4-9.* Minneapolis, MN: Free Spirit.

Snell, M. E., & Brown, F. (2006). *Instruction of students with severe disabilities.* (6th ed.). Upper Saddle River, NJ: Pearson/Merrill.

Snell, M. E., Luckasson, R., Butinx, W. H., Coulter, D. L., Craig, M., Gomez, S. C., Reeves, G., Schalock, R. L., Shogren, K.A., Spreat, S., Tasse, M., Thompson, J. R., Vergug, M.A., Wehmeyer, M. L., & Yeager, M. H. (2009). The characteristics and needs of people with intellectual disabilities who have higher IQs. *Intellectual and Developmental Disabilities, 47*, 220-233.

Snell, M. E., Spreat, S., Tasse, M. J., Thompson, J. R., Verdugo-Alonso, M.A., Wehmeyer, M. L., & Yeager, M. H. (2010). *Intellectual disability: Definition, classification, and systems of supports.* Washington, DC: American Association on Intellectual and Developmental Disabilities.

Solomon, C. R., & Serres, F. (1999). Effects of parental verbal aggression on children's self-esteem and school marks. *Child Abuse & Neglect, 23*, 339-351.

Sousa, D. (2006). *How the brain learns* (3rd ed.). Thousand Oaks, CA: Corwin Press.

Southern, W.T., & Jones, E. D. (1991). Academic acceleration: Background and issues. In W.T. Southern & E. D. Jones (Eds.), *Academic acceleration of gifted children* (pp. 1-17). New York: Teachers College Press.

Spina Bifida Association (2006). Spina bifida fact sheet. www.spinabifidaassociation.org retrieved 7/27/2010.

Spina Bifida Association. (2010). What is spina bifida? Available: www.spinabifidaassociation.org.

Spinath, F. M., Harlaar, N., Ronald, A., & Plomin, R. (2004). Substantial genetic influence on mild mental impairment in early childhood. *American Journal on Mental Retardation, 109*, 34-43.

Spinelli, C.G. (2004). Dealing with cancer in the classroom. *Teaching Exceptional Children, 36*, 14-21.

Sprague, J., Cook, C.R., Browning-Wright, D., & Sadler, C. (2008). *Response to intervention for behavior: Integrating academic and behavior supports.* Palm Beach: LRP Publications.

SRI International. (2005). *Facts from NLTS2: High school completion by youth with disabilities.* Menlo Park, CA: Author.

Stafford, A. M. (2005). Choice making: A strategy for students with severe disabilities. *Teaching Exceptional Children, 37*, 12-16.

Stahmer, Collins & Palinkas. (2005). *Focus on Autism and Other Developmental Disabilities.*

Steere, D. E., Rose, E., & Cavaiuolo (2007). *Growing up: Transition to adult life for students with disabilities.* Boston: Allyn & Bacon.

Steere, M. L., & Cavaoulo, S. D. (2002). Local school boards under review: Their role and effectiveness in relation to students

academic achievement. *Review of Educational Research, 72(4)*, 229-278.

Sternberg, R. J. (1991). Understanding adult intelligence. *Adult Learning, 2*, 8-11.

Steuernagel, T. (2005). Increases in identified cases of autism spectrum disorders. Policy Implications. *Journal of Disability Policy Studies, 16*, 138-146.

Stevenson, J., & Willott, J. (2007). The aspiration and access to higher education of teenage refugees in the UK. *Compare, 37*, 671-687.

Stewart, D.A., & Kluwin, T. N. (2001). *Teaching deaf and hard of hearing students.* Boston: Allyn & Bacon.

Stivers, J. (2008). Strengthen your coteaching relationship. *Intervention in School and Clinic, 44*, 121-125.

Stivers, J., Francis-Cropper, L., & Straus, M. (2008). Educating families about inclusive education: A month-by-month guide for teachers of inclusive classes. *Intervention in School and Clinic, 44*, 10-17.

Stodden, R.A. (2002). Division completes name change. *MRDD Express, 12*(3), 8.

Strand, S., & Lindsay, G. (2009). Evidence of ethnic disproportionality in special education in an English population. *The Journal of Special Education, 43*, 174-190.

Strangman, N., Hall, T., & Meyer, A. (nd). *Graphic organizers and implications for universal design for learning* (Cooperative Agreement No. H324H990004). National Center on Accessing the General Curriculum: US Department of Education/Office of Special Education Programs.

Strichart, S. S., & Mangrum, C. T. (2010). *Study skills for learning disabled and struggling students grades 6-12.* (4th ed.). Upper Saddle River, NJ: Merrill.

Strong, K., & Sandoval, J. (1999). Mainstreaming children with a neuromuscular disease: A map of concerns. *Exceptional Children, 65*(3), 353-366.

Stuart, S. K., & Rinaldi, C. (2009). A collaborative planning framework for teachers implementing tiered instruction. *Teaching Exceptional Children, 42*, 52-57.

Study Guides and Strategies, (2009). www.studygs.net. Retrieved 8/11/2010.

Sugai, G., & Horner, R. H. (2008). What we know and need to know about preventing problem behavior in schools. *Exceptionality, 16*, 67-87.

Sulzer-Azaroff, B., Hoffman, A. O., Horton, C. B., Bondy, A., & Frost, L. (2009). The Picture Exchange Communication System (PECS): What do the data say? *Focus on Autism and Other Developmental Disabilities, 24*, 89-103. doi: 10.1177/1088357609332743.

Summers, J.A., Hoffman, L., Marquis, J., Turnbull, K.A., Poston, D., & Nelson, L.L. (2005). Measuring the quality of family-professional partnerships in special education services. *Exceptional Children, 72*, 65-81.

Swain, K. D., Friehe, M. M., & Harrington, J. M. (2004). Teaching listening strategies in the inclusive classroom. *Intervention in School and Clinic, 40*(1), 48-54.

Tankersley, M. (1995). A group-oriented management program: A review of research on the good behavior game and implications for teachers. *Preventing School Failure, 40*, 19-28.

Tannenbaum, A. J. (1997). The meaning and making of giftedness. In N. Colangelo & G.A. Davis (Eds.), *Handbook of gifted education* (2nd ed.). Boston: Allyn & Bacon.

Tannock, M.T. (2009). Tangible and intangible elements of collaborative teaching. *Intervention in School and Clinic, 44*, 173-178.

Tavzel, C. S., & Staff of LinguiSystems. (1987). *Blooming recipes.* East Moline, IL: LinguiSystems.

Taylor, R.L. (2009). *Assessment of exceptional students* (8th ed.). Upper Saddle River, NJ: Pearson.

Tennant, C., Bebbington, P. R., & Hurry, J. (1980). Parental death in childhood and risk of adult depressive disorders: A review. *Pyschological Medicine, 10*, 289-299.

Terman, L. M., & Oden, M. H. (1959). *Genetic studies of genius (Vol. 5): The gifted group at mid-life.* Stanford, CA: Stanford University Press.

The National Center for Education Statistics (2009). *Condition on education.* Washington, DC: Author.

Thomas, P. J., & Carmack, F. F. (1993). Language: The foundation of learning. In J. S. Choate (Ed.), *Successful mainstreaming: Proven ways to detect and correct special needs* (pp. 148-173). Boston: Allyn & Bacon.

Thompson, A.E., & Kaplan, C.A. (1999). Emotionally abused children presenting to child psychiatry clinics. *Child Abuse & Neglect, 23*, 191-196.

Thompson, J. R., Bradley, V. J., Buntinx, W. H. E., Schalock, R. L. Shogren, K.A., Snell, M. E., Wehmeyer, M. L., Borthwick-Duffy, S., Coulter, D., Craig, E. M., Gomez, S. C., Lachapelle, Y., Luckasson, R.A., Reeve, A., Preat, S., Tasse, M. J., Verdugo, M.A., & Yeager, M. H. (2009). Conceptualization and the support needs of people with intellectual disability. *Intellectual and Developmental Disabilities, 47*, 135-146.

Tirosh, E., & Canby, J. (1993). Autism with hyperlexia: A distinct syndrome? *American Journal on Mental Retardation, 98*, 84-92.

Tomlinson, C. (2005). Grading and differentiation: Paradox or good practice? *Theory into Practice, 44*(3), 262-269.

Tomlinson, C.A. (1999). *The differentiated classroom: Responding to the needs of all learners.* Alexandria, VA: Association for Supervision and Curriculum Development.

Tomlinson, C.A. (2005). *How to differentiate instruction in mixed-ability classrooms* (2nd ed.) Upper Saddle River, NJ: Pearson.

Tomlinson, C.A. (2005). *The differentiated classroom: Responding to the needs of all learners.* Upper Saddle River, NJ: Pearson.

Tomlinson, C.A., & Eidson, C. C. (2003). *Differentiate in practice: A resource guide for differentiating curriculum.* Alexandria, VA: Association for Supervision and Curriculum Development.

Tomlinson, C.A. (1997). Challenging expectations: Case studies of high-potential, culturally diverse young children. *Gifted Child Quarterly, 41*, 5-18.

Tomlinson-Keasey, C., & Little, T. D. (1990). Predicting educational attainment, occupational achievement, intellectual skill, and personal adjustment among gifted men and women. *Journal of Educational Psychology, 82*, 442-455.

Tools for Schools (1998). *School reform models supported by the national institute on the education of at-risk students*. Washington, DC: National Institute on the Education of At Risk Students.

Tooms, R. E. (2010). *Acquired amputations in children. Digital Resource Foundation for the Orthotics and Prosthetics Community*. Available: www.oandplibrary.org/alp.chap32-01.asp.

Torgesen, C.W., Miner, C.A., & Shen, H. (2004). Developing student competence in self-directed IEPs. *Intervention in School and Clinic, 39*, 162-167.

Trad, P.V. (1999). Assessing the patterns that prevent teenage pregnancy. *Adolescence, 34*, 221-238.

Truscott, S. D., Cohen, C. E., & Sams, D. P. (2005). The curriculum states of pre-referral intervention teams. *Remedial and Special Education, 26*(3), 130-140.

Tryon, P. A., Mayes, S. D., Rhodes, R. L., & Waldo, M. (2006). Can Asperger's disorder be differentiated from autism using DSM-IV criteria? *Focus on Autism and Other Developmental Disabilities, 21*, 2-6.

Tsal, Y., Shalev, & Mevorach, C. (2005). The diversity of attention deficits in ADHD: The prevalence of four cognitive factors in ADHD versus controls. *Journal of Learning Disabilities, 38*(2), 142-157.

Turnbull, H. R. (2005). Individuals with disabilities education act reauthorization: Accountability and personal responsibility. *Remedial & Special Education, 26*(6), 320-326.

Turnbull, H. R., & Turnbull, A. P. (2000). *Free appropriate public education* (6th ed.). Denver, CO: Love.

Turnbull, R., & Turnbull, A. (2001). *Families, professionals, exceptionalities: A special partnership*. Upper Saddle River, NJ: Merrill.

Turnbull, R., Turnbull, A., & Wehmeyer, M. (2010). *Exceptional lives: Special education in today's schools*. Upper Saddle River, NJ: Merrill/Pearson.

Turnbull, A., Zuna, N., Hong, J.Y., Hu, X., Kyzar, K., Obremski, S., Summers, J.A., Turnbull, R., & Stowe, M. (2010). Knowledge-to-action guides: Preparing families to be partners in making educational decisions. *Teaching Exceptional Children, 42*, 42-53.

Tyron, P., Mayes, S. D., Rhodes, R. L., & Waldo, M. (2006). Can Asperger's disorder be differentiated from autism using DSM-IV criteria? *Focus on Autism and Other Developmental Disabilities, 21*(1), 2-6.

Uhing, B. M., Mooney, P., & Ryser, G. R. (2005). Differences in strength assessment scores for youth with and without emotional disturbance. *Journal of Emotional and Behavioral Disorders, 13*(3), 181-187.

Umbarger, G. T. (2007). State of evidence regarding complementary and alternative medical treatments for autism spectrum disorders. *Education and Training in Developmental Disabilities, 42*, 437-447.

U.S. Census Bureau (2006). Poverty rates by age: 1959-2002. Current Population Survey, 1960-2003. Washington, DC: Author.

U.S. Census Bureau (2008). Statistical abstract. Washington, DC: Author.

U.S. Department of Education. (1991, September 16). *Memorandum: Clarification of policy to address the needs of children with attention deficit disorders within general and/or special education*. Washington, DC: Author.

U. S. Department of Education. (1999). *The condition of education, 1998*. Washington, DC: Author.

U.S. Department of Education. (2002). *23rd annual report to Congress on the implementation of the Individuals with Disabilities Education Act*. Washington, DC: Author.

U.S. Department of Education. (2003). *24th annual report to Congress on the implementation of the Individuals with Disabilities Education Act*. Washington, DC: Author.

U.S. Department of Education (2003). *Managing asthma: A guide for schools*. Washington DC.

U.S. Department of Education. (2005). *24th annual report to Congress on the implementation of the Individuals with Disabilities Education Act*. Washington, DC: Author.

U.S. Department of Education. (2006). *25th annual report to Congress on the implementation of the Individuals with Disabilities Education Act*. Washington, DC: Author.

U.S. Department of Education. (2007). *26th annual report to Congress on the implementation of the Individuals with Disabilities Education Act*. Washington, DC: Author.

U.S. Department of Education (2008). National Center for Educational Statistics. Washington, DC: Author.

U.S. Department of Education (2008). *27th annual report to Congress on the implementation of the Individuals with Disabilities Education Act*. Washington, DC: Author.

U.S. Department of Education (2009). National Center for Educational Statistics. Washington, DC: Author

U.S. Department of Education, National Center for Education Statistics. (2009). *Digest of Education Statistics, 2008* (NCES 2009-020), Table 50.

U.S. Department of Education. (2009). *28th annual report to Congress on the implementation of the Individuals with Disabilities Education Act*. Washington, DC: Author.

U.S. Department of Education. (2009). *29th annual report to Congress on the implementation of the individuals with disabilities education act*. Washington, DC: Author.

U.S. Department of Education, Office of Special Education and Rehabilitative Services, Office of Special Education Programs. (2005). *26th Annual Report to Congress on the Implementation of the Individuals with Disabilities Education Act (Vol. 1)*.

U.S. Department of Health and Human Services. (2003) *Helping the student with diabetes succeed: A guide for school personnel*. Washington, DC: Author.

U.S. Department of Health and Human Services (2006). March 2006. *National Survey on Drug Use and Health: National Findings*. U.S. Department of Health and Human Services.

U.S. Department of Housing and Urban Development. (n.d.). *Federal definition of homeless*. Retrieved 1/1/10 from http://portal.hud.gov/portal/HUD/topics/homelessness/definition.

U.S. Department of State. (n.d.). *Bureau of population, refugees, and migration*. Retrieved 1/1/10 from http://www.state.gov/g/prm.

U.S. Office of Education. (1977). Assistance to states for education of handicapped children: Procedures for evaluating specific learning disabilities. *Federal Register, 42*, 65082-65085.

Van Eerdewegh, M. M., Bieri, M. D., Parrilla, R. H., & Clayton, P. J. (1982). The bereaved child. *British Journal of Psychiatry, 140*, 23-29.

van Garderen, D., & Whittaker, C., (2006). Planning different multicultural instruction in secondary classes. *Teaching Exceptional Children, 44*, 12-15.

Van Haren, B., & Fiedler, C. R. (2008). Support and empower families of children with disabilities. *Intervention in School and Clinic, 43*, 231-235.

Van Karnebeek, C., Scheper, F., Abeling, N., Alders, M., Barth, P., Hoover, J., & Hennekam, R. (2005). Etiology of intellectual and developmental disabilities in children referred to a tertiary care center: A prospective study. *American Journal on Mental Retardation, 110*, 253-267.

VanTassel-Baska, J. (1981). Appropriate education for gifted learners. *Educational Leadership, 47*, 13-15.

VanTassel-Baska, J. (1989). Appropriate curriculum for gifted learners. *Educational Leadership, 47*, 13-15.

VanTassel-Baska, J. (1997). Excellence as a standard for all education. *Roeper Review, 20*, 9-13.

VanTassel-Baska, J., & Stambaugh, T. (2005). Challenges and possibilities for serving gifted learners in the regular classroom. *Theory into Practice, 44*, 211-217.

VanTassel-Baska, J., Patton, J., & Prillaman, D. (1989). Disadvantaged gifted learners at-risk for educational attention. *Focus on Exceptional Children, 22*(3), 1-16.

Vaughn, C., & Long, W. (1999). Surrender to win: How adolescent drug and alcohol users change their lives. *Adolescence, 34*, 9-22.

Vaughn, S., Bos, C., & Schuum, J. (2007). *Teaching students who are exceptional, diverse, and at-risk in the general education classroom* (4th ed.) Boston: Pearson.

Vaughn, S., Gersten, R., & Chard, D. J. (2000). The underlying message in learning disabilities intervention research: Findings from research synthesis. *Exceptional Children, 67*, 99-114.

Vermaes, I. P. R. (2008). Parents' personality and parenting stress in families of children with spina bifida. *Child: Care, Health, and Development, 34*, 665-674.

Vesely, P. J., & Gryder, N. L. (2009). Word of the day improves and redirects student attention while supporting vocabulary development. *Intervention in School and Clinic, 44,* 282-287.

Villa, R. A., Thousand, J. U. S., & Nevin, A. I. (2008). *A guide to co-teaching: Practical tips for facilitating student learning* (2nd ed.). Thousand Oaks, CA: Corwin Press.

Vogeltanz, N. D., Wilsnack, S. C., Harris, T. R., Wilsnack, R. W., Wonderlich, S. A., & Kristjanson, A. F. (1999). Prevalence and risk factors for childhood sexual abuse in women: National survey findings. *Child Abuse & Neglect, 23,* 579-592.

Volkmar, F. R. (May 5, 2004). Fred Volkmar on Asperger's syndrome. National Public Radio. http://www.npr.org/templates/story.php?storyId[equals]1872620.

Volkmar, F. R. (2005). *Handbook on autism* (3rd ed.). New York: Wiley.

Volkmar, F. R., & Klin, A. (2005). Issues in classification of autism and related conditions. In F. R. Volkmar, R. Paul, A. Klin, & D. Cohen (Eds.), *Handbook of autism and pervasive developmental disorders, Vol 1: Diagnosis, development, neurobiology, and behavior* (pp. 5-41). Hoboken, NJ: John Wiley & Sons.

Voltz, D., Brazil, N., & Ford, A. (2001). What matters most in inclusive education. *Intervention in School and Clinic, 37,* 23-30.

Waber, D. P. (2010). *Rethinking learning disabilities: Understanding children who struggle in school.* New York: The Guildford Press.

Wadsworth, D. E., & Knight, D. (1999). Endorsement of family issues in curriculum offerings of teacher training programs nationwide. *Education, 120,* 315-326.

Wagner, M. C. (2010). Rediscovering dyslexia: New approaches for identification and classification. In Reid, G., Fawcett, A., Manis, F., & Siegel, L. (Eds.), *The handbook of dyslexia.* Sage Publications.

Wagner, M., & Davis, M. A. (2006). How are we preparing students with emotional disturbances for the transition to young adulthood? findings from the national longitudinal transition study—2. *Journal of Emotional & Behavioral Disorders, 14*(2), 86-98.

Wagner, M., Kutash, K., Duchnowski, A. J., Epstein, M. H., & Sumi, W. C. (2005). The children and youth we serve: A national picture of the characteristics of students with emotional disturbances receiving special education. *Journal of Emotional & Behavioral Disorders, 13*(2), 79-96.

Wagner, M., Newman, L., Cameto, R., Garza, N., & Levine, P. (2005). *After high school: A first look at the post-school experiences of youth with disabilities: A report from the National Longitudinal Transition Study-2 (NTLS-2).* Menlo Park, CA: SRI International.

Walberg, H. J. (1991). Does homework help? *School Community Journal, 1*(1), 13-15.

Walker, A. R., Uphold, N. M., Richter, S., & Test, D. W. (2010). Review of the literature on community-based instruction across grade levels. *Education and Training in Autism and Developmental Disabilities, 45,* 242-266.

Walker, B. (1993, January). *Multicultural issues in education: An introduction.* Paper presented at Cypress–Fairbanks Independent School District In-Service, Cypress, TX.

Walker, H., Golly, A., McLane, J. Z., & Kimmich, M., (2005). The Oregon first step to success report. *Journal of Emotional and Behavior Disorders, 13,* 160-173.

Walker, J. E., & Shea, T. M. (1995). *Behavior management: A practical approach for educators* (6th ed.). Upper Saddle River, NJ: Merrill.

Walker, J. E., Shea, T. M., & Bauer, A. M. (2006). *Behavior management: A practical approach for educators* (9th ed.). Upper Saddle, NJ: Pearson.

Wallis, C. (2009a). New studies see higher rate of autism: Is the jump real? *New York Times.* Retrieved from: http://www.time.com/time/health/article/0,8599,1927824,00.html.

Wallis, C. (2009b). A powerful identity, a vanishing diagnosis. *New York Times.* Retrieved from: http://www.nytimes.com/2009/11/03/health/03asperger.html?_r=2&pagewanted=print.

Walther-Thomas, C., Korinek, L., McLaughlin, V. L., & Williams, B. T. (2000). *Collaboration for inclusive education.* Boston: Allyn & Bacon.

Wanat, C. L. (1992). Meeting the needs of single-parent children: School and parent views differ. *NASSP Bulletin, 76,* 43-48.

Warren, D. H. (1994). *Blindness and children: An individual differences approach.* New York: Cambridge University Press.

Wasburn-Moses, L. (2005). Roles and responsibilities of secondary special education teachers in an age of reform. *Remedial and Special Education, 26*(3), 1512-158.

Wayman, K., Lynch, E., & Hanson, M. (1990). Home-based early childhood services: Cultural sensitivity in a family systems approach. *Topics in Early Childhood Special Education, 10*(4), 65-66.

Webber, J. (1997). Responsible inclusion: Key components for success. In P. Zionts (Ed.), *Effective inclusion of students with behavior and learning problems.* Austin, TX: Pro-Ed.

Webber, J., & Scheuermann, B. (2008). *Educating students with autism: A quick start manual.* Austin, TX: PRO-ED.

WebMD. (2009). *Epilepsy.* www.webmd.com/epilepsy/default.htm.

Wehby, J. H., Symons, F. J., Canale, J. A., & Go, F. J. (1998). Teaching practices in classrooms for students with emotional and behavioral disorders: Discrepancies between recommendations and observations. *Behavioral Disorders, 24,* 51-56.

Wehmeyer, M. (1993). Self-determination as an educational outcome. *Impact, 6*(4), 16-17, 26.

Wehmeyer, M. L. (2006). Universal design for learning, access to the general education curriculum, and students with mild mental retardation. *Exceptionality, 14,* 225-235.

Wehmeyer, M. L., & Yaeger, M. H. (2010). *Intellectual disability: Definition, classification, and systems of supports.* Washington, DC: American Association on Intellectual and Developmental Disabilities.

Weinbender, M. L. M., & Rossignol, A. M. (1996). Lifestyle and risk of premature sexual activity in a high school population of Seventh-Day Adventists: Valuegenesis 1989. *Adolescence, 31,* 265-275.

Weiner, H. M. (2003). Effective inclusion. *Teaching Exceptional Children, 35*(6), 12-18.

Wenz-Gross, M., & Siperstein, G. N. (1998). Students with learning problems at risk in middle school: Stress, social support, and adjustment. *Exceptional Children, 65,* 91-100.

Werts, M. G., Lambert, M., & Carpenter, E. (2009). What special education directors say about RTI. *Learning Disability Quarterly, 32,* 245-254.

Werts, M. G., Harris, S., Tillery, C. Y., & Roark, R. (2004). What parents tell us about paraeducators. *Remedial and Special Education, 25,* 232-239.

West, G. K. (1986). *Parenting without guilt.* Springfield, IL: Thomas.

West, G. K. (1994, Nov. 10). Discipline that works: Part 1. *The News and Daily Advance,* 3-4.

West, G. K. (2002). *Parent education programs and benefits for parents of children with disabilities.* Unpublished manuscript, Lynchburg College, Lynchburg, VA.

Westling, D. L., & Fox, L. (2009). *Teaching students with severe disabilities* (4th ed.). Upper Saddle River, NJ: Pearson.

Westling, D. L., & Koorland, M. A. (1988). *The special educator's handbook.* Boston: Allyn & Bacon.

Westling, D. L., Cooper-Duffy, K., Prohn, K., Ray, M., & Herzog, M. J. (2005). Building a teacher support program. *Teaching Exceptional Children, 37*(5), 8-13.

Westling, D. L., Herzog, M. J., Cooper-Duffy, K., Prohn, K., & Ray, M. (2006). The teacher support program: A proposed resource for the special education profession and an initial validation. *Remedial & Special Education, 27*(3), 136-147.

Weyandt, L. L. (2001). *An ADHD primer.* Boston: Allyn & Bacon.

Whitby, P. J. S., & Mancil, G. R. (2009). Academic achievement profiles of children with high functioning autism and Asperger syndrome: A review of the literature. *Education and Treatment in Developmental Disabilities, 44,* 551-560.

White, C. C., Lakin, K. C., Bruininks, R. H., & Li, X. (1991). *Persons with mental retardation and related conditions in state-operated residential facilities: Year ending June 30, 1989, with longitudinal trends from 1950 to 1989.* Minneapolis, MN: University of Minnesota, Institute on Community Integration.

Wiggins, K., & Damore, S. (2006). "Survivors" or "friends"? A framework for assessing effective collaboration. *Teaching Exceptional Children, 38*(5), 49-56.

Wiig, E. H., & Semel, E. (1984). *Language assessment and intervention for the learning disabled* (2nd ed.). Columbus, OH: Merrill.

Wilczynski, S. (2009). Evidence-based practice and autism spectrum disorders. The National Standards Project. *Communiqué, 38*(5), 1, 24–25.

Wild, T. A., & Trundle, K. C. (2010). Conceptual understandings of seasonal change by middle school students with visual impairments. *Journal of Visual Impairment and Blindness, 98,* 107–116.

Wilde, L. D., Koegel, L. K., & Koegel, R. L. (1992). *Increasing success in school through priming: A training manual.* Santa Barbara, CA: University of California.

Williams, C. B., & Finnegan, M. (2003). From myth to reality: Sound information for teachers about students who are deaf. *Teaching Exceptional Children, 35,* 40–45.

Williams, K. (1995). Understanding the student with Asperger syndrome: Guidelines for teachers. *Focus on Autistic Behavior, 10,* 9–16.

Williamson, P., McLeskey, J., Hoppey, D., & Rentz, T. (2006). Educating students with mental retardation in general education classrooms. *Exceptional Children, 72,* 347–361.

Wilson, G. L. (2008). Be an active co-teacher. *Intervention in School and Clinic, 43,* 240–243.

Windle, M., & Mason, W. A. (2004). General and specific predictors of behavioral and emotional problems among adolescents. *Journal of Emotional and Behavioral Disorders, 12*(1), 49.

Winebrenner, S. (2000). Gifted students need an education, too. *Educational Leadership, 58,* 52–57.

Wing, L. (1981). Asperger's syndrome: A clinical account. *Psychological Medicine, 11,* 115–129.

Wing, L. (1996). *The autistic spectrum: A guide for parents and professionals.* London: Constable.

Witt, J. C., & Elliott, S. N. (1985). Acceptability of classroom management strategies. In T. R. Kratochwill (Ed.), *Advances in school psychology* (Vol. 4, pp. 251–288). Hillsdale, NJ: Erlbaum.

Wolfe, P. S. (1997). Deaf-blindness. In P. Wehman (Ed.), *Exceptional individuals* (pp. 357–381). Austin, TX: Pro-Ed.

Wolfe, P. S., & Hall, T. E. (2003). Making inclusion a reality for students with severe disabilities. *Teaching Exceptional Children, 35,* 56–61.

Wong, E. Y. H., Chou, S. L., Lamoureux, E. L., & Keeffe, J. E. (2008). Personal costs of visual impairment by different eye diseases and severity of visual loss. *Ophthalmic Epidemiology, 15,* 339–344.

Wood, D. K., & Frank, A. R. (2000). Using memory-enhancing strategies to learn multiplication facts. *Teaching Exceptional Children, 32,* 78–82.

Wood, J. M., Chaparro, A., Anstey, K. J., Hsing, Y. E., Johnsson, A. K., Morse, A. L., & Wainwright, S. E. (2009). Impact of simulated visual impairment on the cognitive test performance of young adults. *British Journal of Psychology, 100,* 593–602.

Worcester, J. A., Nesman, T. M., Mendez, L. M. R., & Keller, H. R. (2008). Giving voice to parents of young children with challenging behavior. *Exceptional Children, 74,* 509–525.

Yamaguchi, B. J., Strawser, S., & Higgins, K. (1997). Children who are homeless: Implications for educators. *Intervention in School and Clinic, 33,* 90–98.

Yell, M. L. (2006). *The law and special education.* Upper Saddle River, NJ: Pearson.

Yell, M. L., Drasgow, E., & Lowery, K. A. (2006). NCLB and students with autism spectrum disorder. *Journal of Autism and Other Developmental Disabilities, 20*(3), 130–139.

Yell, M. L., Katsiyannis, A., & Shiner, J. G. (2006). The No Child Left Behind Act, adequate yearly progress, and students with disabilities. *Teaching Exceptional Children, 38*(4), 32–39.

Yell, M. L., Katsiyannis, A., Ryan, J. B., McDuffie, K. A., & Mattocks, L. (2008). Ensure compliance with the Individuals with Disabilities Education Improvement Act of 2004. *Intervention in School and Clinic, 44,* 45–51.

Young, G., & Gerber, P. J. (1998). Learning disabilities and poverty: Moving toward a new understanding of learning disabilities as a public health and economic risk issue. *Learning Disabilities, 9,* 1–6.

Young, M. E., Kersten, L., & Werch, T. (1996). Evaluation of patient-child drug education program. *Journal of Drug Education, 26,* 57–68.

Yssel, N., Engelbrecht, P., Oswald, M. O., Eloff, I., & Swart, E. (2007). Views on inclusion: A comparative study of parents' perceptions in South Africa and the United States. *Remedial and Special Education, 28,* 356–365.

Zager, D., & Shamow, N. (Ed.). (2005). Teaching students with autism spectrum disorders. In D. Zager (Ed.), *Autism spectrum disorders: Identification, education, and treatment* (3rd ed., pp. 295–326). Mahwah, NJ: Lawrence Erlbaum.

Zentall, S. (2006). *ADHD and education: Foundations, characteristics, methods, and collaboration.* Upper Saddle River, NJ: Merrill/Pearson.

Zhang, D. (2001b). Self-determination and inclusion: Are students with mild mental retardation more self-determined in regular classrooms? *Education and Training in Mental Retardation and Developmental Disabilities, 36*(4), 357–362.

Ziegler, J. C., et al. (2005, September 27). Deficits in speech perception predict language learning impairment. *Proceedings of the National Academy of Sciences of the United States of America, 102*(3a): 14110–14115.

Zimmerman, W. (2006). *The American male: General characteristics of male health and educational trends.* Unpublished manuscript, Lynchburg College, Lynchburg VA.

Zirkel, P. A. (2009). What does the law say? *Teaching Exceptional Children, 41*(5), 73–75.

Zurkowski, J. K., Kelly, P. S., & Griswold, D. E. (1998). Discipline and IDEA 1997: Instituting a new balance. *Intervention in School and Clinic, 34,* 3–9.

Zwaigenbaum, L., Bryson, S., Roberts, W., Brian, J., & Szatmari, P. (2005). Behavioral manifestations of autism in the first year of life. *International Journal of Developmental Neuroscience, 23,* 143–152.

NAME INDEX

Note: Page number followed by a *b* indicates boxed text, *f* indicates figures, and *t* indicates tables.

SUBJECT INDEX

Note: Page number followed by a *b* indicates boxed text, *f* indicates figures, and *t* indicates tables.